D1239050

DATE DUE

| | | | |
|---|---|---|---|
| | | | |
| | | | |
| | | | |
| | | | |
| | | | |
| | | | |
| | | | |
| | | | |
| | | | |
| | | | |
| | | | |
| | | | |
| | | | |

GAYLORD                                    PRINTED IN U.S.A.

**To Renew Books**
**PHONE (510) 258-2233**

# PERSONALITY AND PSYCHOPATHOLOGY:
## Building a Clinical Science

# PERSONALITY AND PSYCHOPATHOLOGY:
## Building a Clinical Science
*Selected Papers of Theodore Millon*

**A WILEY-INTERSCIENCE PUBLICATION**

**JOHN WILEY & SONS, INC.**

New York  •  Chichester  •  Brisbane  •  Toronto  •  Singapore

*Library of Congress Cataloging-in-Publication Data:*

Millon, Theodore.
    Personality and psychopathology : building a clinical science :
    selected papers of Theodore Millon / Theodore Millon.
        p.      cm.
    Includes index.
    ISBN 0-471-11685-8 (cloth)
    1. Personality disorders.   2. Personality assessment.   I. Title.
    [DNLM:   1. Personality Disorders—collected works.
    2. Psychopathology—collected works.     WM 190 M656p   1996]
    RC554.M545   1996
    616.85′8—dc20

                                                    95-10576


Printed in the United States of America

10 9 8 7 6 5 4 3 2 1

To my four bright, loving, and joyful grandchildren,

**ALYSSA, KATHERINE, MOLLY, and ELIZABETH,**

May your futures always be enlightening and enriching.

# Preface and Acknowledgments

The papers reprinted in this volume are primarily theoretical and methodological (rather than empirical), selected to highlight my argument favoring a logical and deductive basis both for grounding and guiding the practice of psychological assessment and psychological therapy. The papers have not been organized chronologically owing to the fact that many of my ideas on the subject grew in a less than planful or optimal sequence. Epistemological progressions are not orderly affairs. No less than the desultory lives of our patients, they unfold at times in a most unanticipated, if not random fashion. To create a measure of order and logic, I have selected and arranged these papers to fit a schema that has served increasingly to inform my thinking. This book's progression advances from what I judge to be the foundation of a fourfold structure for all clinical sciences, that of a system of explanatory propositions, namely *theory,* to that of a classification of its constituents and constructs, that is, its *taxonomy,* to *instrumentation,* or its objectifying and quantifying empirical tools, and finally to that of *intervention,* the strategic goals and tactical modalities employed in providing therapy. It is the coordination of these four components that comprises and generates a systematic clinical science; it also provides the overarching framework for these selected essays.

I am most grateful to the editors and publishers for whom these papers were originally written and for their permission to make them available for reprinting in this book.

Paper 1 is a slightly abbreviated version of Chapter 1, originally published in *Toward a New Personology: An Evolutionary Model,* 1990, reprinted with permission by the copyright holder, John Wiley & Sons, Inc. Paper 2 is an abridged version of Chapter 19, originally published in *Personality Disorders and the Five-Factor Model of Personality,* 1993, reprinted with permission by the copyright holder, The American Psychological Association Press. Paper 3 is an abridged version of Chapter 2, originally published in *Modern Psychopathology,* 1969, reprinted with permission by the copyright holder, Theodore Millon. Paper 4 is an abbreviated version of Chapter 46, originally published in *Theories of Personality and Psychopathology,* 1983, reprinted with permission by the copyright holder, Harcourt Brace. Paper 5 is an abridged version of Chapter 30, originally published in *Contemporary Directions in Psychopathology: Toward the DSM-IV,* 1986, reprinted with permission by the copyright holder, Guilford Press. Paper 6 is an abbreviated version of Chapter 21, originally published in *The Diversity of Normality,* 1991, reprinted with permission by the copyright holder, Basic Books/Harper Collins. Paper 7 is a complete version of an article, originally published in the *Journal of Abnormal Psychology, 100,* 245–261, 1991, reprinted with permission by the copyright holder, The American Psychological Association. Paper 8 is an abridged version of Chapter 21, originally published in *Personality and the Behavior Disorders,* 1984, reprinted with permission by the copyright holder, John Wiley & Sons, Inc. Paper 9 is a complete version of an article, originally published in the *Journal of Personality Disorders, 1,* 354–372, 1987, reprinted with permission by the copyright holder, Guilford Press. Paper 10 is an abridged version of Chapter 21, originally published in the *Handbook of Depression,* 1987, reprinted with permission by the copyright holder, Guilford Press. Paper 11 is an abbreviated version of an article, originally published in the *Journal of Personality Assessment, 48,* 450–466, 1984, reprinted with permission by the copyright holder, L. Erlbaum Publishers. Paper 12 is an abridged version of Chapter 4, originally published in *Research Methods in Psychopathology,* 1972, reprinted with permission by the copyright holder, John Wiley & Sons, Inc. Paper 13 is an abbreviated version of Chapter 2, originally published in the *Millon Clinical Multiaxial Inventory—II Manual,* 1987, reprinted with permission by the copyright holder, Theodore Millon. Paper 14 is an abridged version of Chapter 2, originally published in the *Millon Index of Personality Styles,* 1994, reprinted with permission by the copyright holder, Theodore Millon. Paper 15 is an abridged version of Chapter 15, originally published in *Modern Psychopathology,* 1969, reprinted with permission by the copyright holder, Theodore Millon. Paper 16 is a complete version of an article, originally published in *Psychotherapy, 25,* 209–219, 1988, reprinted with permission by the copyright holder, Division 29, APA. Paper 17 is a complete version of an article, originally published in the *Journal of Psychotherapy Integration, 3,* 331–352, 1993, reprinted with permission by the copyright holder, Plenum Press.

Throughout my career, I have been challenged by numerous opportunities to present my thoughts to a large and eager readership with different interests, diverse needs, and divergent levels of expertise. In many cases, I chose not to re-write de novo ideas that were already well formulated; instead, I have rewoven themes and texts from earlier works into new manuscripts according to their special purposes and diverse audiences. Juxtaposed as they appear in these selected papers, however, these reweavings will at times be somewhat repetitive. Nevertheless, I have decided to leave the text of these documents intact to maintain the integrity of their original form, to demonstrate elements of continuity and change in my thinking, and to provide a basis for those who may wish to trace the evolution of my ideas through the varied contexts and periods in which they were presented.

THEODORE MILLON

*May 1995*

# Contents

# PART I

# *INTRODUCTION*

# Connecting Personology to Other Scientific Realms of Nature

It is necessary to go beyond current conceptual boundaries, more specifically to explore carefully reasoned, as well as "intuitive" hypotheses that draw their principles, if not their substance, from more established "adjacent" sciences. Not only may such steps bear new conceptual fruits, but they may provide a foundation that can undergird and guide our own discipline's explorations. Much of personology, no less psychology as a whole, remains adrift, divorced from broader spheres of scientific knowledge, isolated from firmly grounded, if not universal principles, leading one to continue building the patchwork quilt of concepts and data domains that characterize the field. Preoccupied with but a small part of the larger puzzle, or fearing accusations of reductionism, many fail thereby to draw on the rich possibilities to be found in other realms of scholarly pursuit. With few exceptions, cohering concepts that would connect this subject to those of its sister sciences have not been developed.

We seem trapped in (obsessed with?) horizontal refinements. A search for integrative schemas and cohesive constructs that link its seekers closely to relevant observations and laws developed in more advanced fields is needed. The goal—albeit a rather "grandiose" one—is to refashion the patchwork quilt into a well-tailored and aesthetic tapestry that interweaves the diverse forms in which nature expresses itself.

And what better sphere is there within the psychological sciences to undertake such syntheses than with the subject matter of personology. Persons are the only organically integrated system in the psychological domain, evolved through the millennia and inherently created from birth as natural entities, rather than culture-bound and experience-derived gestalts. The intrinsic cohesion of persons is not merely a rhetorical construction, but an authentic substantive unity. Personologic features may often be dissonant, and may be partitioned conceptually for pragmatic or scientific purposes. but they are segments of an inseparable biopsychosocial entity.

To take this view is not to argue that different spheres of scientific inquiry should be equated, nor is it to seek a single, overarching conceptual system encompassing biology, psychology and sociology (Millon, 1983). Arguing in favor of establishing explicit links between these domains calls neither for a reductionistic philosophy, a belief in substantive identicality, or efforts to so fashion them by formal logic. Rather, one should aspire to their substantive concordance, empirical consistency, conceptual interfacing, convergent dialogues, and mutual enlightenment.

Integrative consonance such as described is not an aspiration limited to ostensibly diverse sciences, but is a worthy goal within the domains of each science. Particularly relevant in this regard are efforts that seek to coordinate the often separate realms that comprise a clinical science, namely: its theories, the classification system it has formulated, the diagnostic tools it employs, and the therapeutic techniques it implements. Rather than developing independently and being left to stand as autonomous and largely unconnected functions, a truly mature clinical science will embody explicit: (1) *theories,* that is, explanatory and heuristic conceptual schemas that are consistent with established knowledge in both its own and related sciences, and from which reasonably accurate propositions concerning pathological conditions can be both deduced and understood, enabling thereby the development of a formal (2) *nosology,* that is, a taxonomic classification of disorders that has been derived logically from *the theory,* and is arranged to provide a cohesive organization within which its major categories can readily be grouped and differentiated, permitting thereby the development of coordinated (3) *instruments,* that is, tools that are empirically grounded and sufficiently sensitive quantitatively to enable the theory's propositions and hypotheses to be adequately investigated and evaluated, and the categories comprising its nosology to be readily identified (diagnosed) and measured (dimensionalized), specifying therefrom target areas for (4) *interventions,* that is, strategies and techniques of therapy, designed in accord with the theory and oriented to modify problematic clinical characteristics consonant with professional standards and social responsibilities.

The following papers are sequenced to follow the four elements that comprise a coordinated clinical science. Primary attention will be given in the first section to that of theory. The substantive principles to be presented draw heavily in both their inspiration and content from contemporary thought in physics and evolutionary biology.

A few words should be said at the outset concerning the undergirding framework used to structure the personology model. Bipolar or dimensional schemas are almost universally present in the literature; the earliest may be traced to ancient Eastern religions, most notably the Chinese *I Ching* texts and the Hebrews' *Kabala.* More modern, though equally speculative bipolar systems have been proposed by keen and broadly informed observers, such as Sigmund Freud and Carl Jung, or by empirically well-grounded and dimensionally oriented methodologists, such as Raymond Cattell and Hans Eysenck. Each of their proposals fascinate either by virtue of their intriguing portrayals or by the compelling power of their "data" or logic. For me, however, all failed in their quest for the ultimate character of human nature in that their conceptions float, so to speak, above the foundations built by contemporary physical and biological sciences. Formulas of a psychological nature must not only coordinate with, but be anchored firmly to observations derived specifically from modern principles of physical and biological evolution. It is on these underpinnings of knowledge that the polarity model presented in the following chapters has been grounded, and from which a deeper and clearer understanding may be obtained concerning the nature of both normal and pathological functioning.

Nevertheless, what follows remains conjectural, if not overly extended in its speculative reach. In essence, it seeks to explicate the structure and styles of personality with reference to deficient, imbalanced, or conflicted modes of ecologic adaptation and reproductive strategy. Some readers will judge these conjectures persuasive; a few will consider them "interesting," but essentially unconfirmable; still others will find little of merit in them. Whatever one's appraisal, the theoretical model that follows may best be approached in the spirit in which it was formulated—an effort to bring together observations from different domains of science in the hope that principles derived in adjacent fields can lead to a clearer understanding of their neighbors.

All natural sciences have organizing principles that not only create order but also provide the basis for generating hypotheses and stimulating new knowledge. A good theory not only summarizes and incorporates extant knowledge, but is heuristic, that is, has "systematic import," as Hempel has phrased it, in that it originates and develops new observations and new methods.

It is unfortunate that the number of theories that have been advanced to "explain" personality and its disorders is directly proportional to the internecine squabbling found in the literature. Paroxysms of "scientific virtue" and pieties of "methodological purity" rarely are exclaimed by theorists themselves, but by their less creative disciples. As I previously commented (Millon, 1969):

Theories arise typically from the perceptive observation and imaginative speculation of a creative scientist. This innovator is usually quite aware of the limits and deficiencies of his "invention" and is disposed in the early stages of his speculation to modify it as he develops new observations and insights. Unfortunately, after its utility has been proven in a modest and limited way, the theory frequently acquires a specious stature. Having clarified certain ambiguities and survived initial criticisms, it begins to accumulate a coterie of disciples. These less creative thinkers tend to accept the theory wholeheartedly and espouse its superior explanatory powers and terminology throughout the scientific market place. They hold to its propositions tenaciously and defend it blindly and unequivocally against opposition. In time it becomes a rigid and sacred dogma and, as a result, authority replaces the test of utility and empirical validity. Intelligent men become religious disciples; their theory is a doctrine of "truth," not a guide to the unknown. (p. 41)

Ostensibly toward the end of pragmatic sobriety, those of an antitheory bias have sought to persuade the profession of the failings of premature formalization, warning that one cannot arrive at the desired future by lifting science by its own bootstraps. To them, there is no way to traverse the road other sciences have traveled without paying the dues of an arduous program of empirical research. Formalized axiomatics, they say, must await the accumulation of "hard" evidence that is simply not yet in. Shortcutting the route with ill-timed systematics will lead down primrose paths, preoccupying attentions as one wends fruitlessly through endless detours, each of which could be averted by holding fast to an empiricist philosophy and methodology.

No one argues against the view that theories that float, so to speak, on their own, unconcerned with the empirical domain should be seen as the fatuous achievements they are and the travesty they make of the virtues of a truly coherent conceptual system. Formal theory should not be "pushed" far beyond the data, and its derivations should be linked at all points to established observations. However, a theoretical framework can be a compelling instrument for coordinating and giving consonance to complex and diverse observations—if its concepts are linked to relevant facts in the empirical world. By probing "beneath" surface impressions to inner structures and processes, previously isolated facts and difficult to fathom data may yield new relationships and expose clearer meanings. Paul Meehl has noted (1978) that theoretical systems comprise related assertions, shared terms, and coordinated propositions that provide fertile grounds for deducing and deriving new empirical and clinical observations. Scientific progress occurs, then, when observations and concepts elaborate and refine previous work. However, this progression does not advance by "brute empiricism" alone, that is, by merely piling up more descriptive and more experimental data. What is elaborated and refined in theory is understanding, an ability to see relations more plainly, to conceptualize categories more accurately, and to create greater overall coherence in a subject, that is, to integrate its elements in a more logical, consistent, and intelligible fashion.

A problem arises when introducing theory into the study of personality and its disorders. Given an intuitive ability to "sense" the correctness of a psychological insight or speculation, theoretical efforts that impose structure or formalize these insights into a scientific system will be perceived not only as cumbersome and intrusive, but alien as well. This discomfiture and resistance does not arise in fields such as particle physics, where everyday observations are not readily available and where innovative insights are few and far between. In such subject domains, scientists are not only quite comfortable, but also turn readily to deductive theory as a means of helping them explicate and coordinate knowledge. It is paradoxical, but true and unfortunate, that personologists learn their subject quite well merely by observing the ordinary events of life. As a consequence of this ease, personologists appear to shy from and hesitate placing trust in the "obscure and complicating," yet often fertile and systematizing powers inherent in formal theory, especially theories that are new or that differ from those learned in their student days.

Adding to these hesitations is the fact that the formal structure of most personality theories is haphazard and unsystematic; concepts often are vague, and procedures by which empirical consequences may be derived are tenuous. Instead of presenting an orderly arrangement of concepts and propositions by which hypotheses may be clearly derived, most theorists present a loosely formulated pastiche of opinions, analogies, and speculations. Brilliant as many of these speculations may be, they often leave the reader dazzled rather than illuminated. Ambiguous principles in structurally weak theories make it impossible to derive systematic and logical hypotheses; this results in conflicting derivations and circular reasoning. Many theories in both personality and psychopathology have generated brilliant deductions and insights, but few of these ideas can be attributed to their structure, the clarity of their central principles, the precision of their concepts, or their formal procedures for hypothesis derivation. It is here, of course, where the concepts and laws of adjacent sciences may come into play, providing models of structure and derivation, as well as substantive theories and data that may undergird and parallel the principles and observations of one's own field.

Despite the shortcomings in historic and contemporary theoretical schemas, systematizing principles and abstract concepts can "facilitate a deeper seeing, a more penetrating vision that goes beyond superficial appearances to the order underlying them" (Bowers, 1977). For example, pre-Darwinian taxonomists such as Linnaeus limited themselves to "apparent" similarities and differences among animals as a means of constructing their categories. Darwin was not "seduced" by appearances. Rather, he sought to understand the principles by which overt features came about. His classifications were based not only on descriptive qualities, but on explanatory ones . . . .

It is in both the spirit and substance of Darwin's "explanatory principles" that the reader should approach the proposals that follow. The principles employed are essentially the same as those which Darwin developed in seeking to explicate the origins of species. However, they are listed to derive—not the origins of species—but the structure and style of each of the personality disorders that are described in the *DSM-III-R* on the basis of clinical observation alone. Aspects of these formulations have been published in earlier books (Millon, 1969/1985, 1981, 1986), but they are anchored explicitly to evolutionary and ecological theory for the first time in this work. Identified in earlier writings as a biosocial learning model for personality and psychopathology, the theory has sought to generate the recognized categories of personality disorder through formal processes of deduction. A similar deductive process will be presented here. . . .

To propose that fruitful ideas may be derived by applying evolutionary principles to the development and functions of personologic traits has a long, if yet unfulfilled, tradition. Spencer (1870) and Huxley (1870) offered suggestions of this nature shortly after Darwin's seminal Origins was published. The school of "functionalism," popular in psychology in the early part of this century, likewise drew its impetus from evolutionary concepts as it sought to articulate a basis for individual difference typologies (McDougall, 1908).

In more recent times, we have seen the emergence of sociobiology, a new "science" that explores the interface between human social functioning and evolutionary biology (Wilson, 1975, 1978). Contemporary formulations by psychologists have likewise proposed the potentials and analyzed the problems involved in cohering evolutionary notions, individual differences. and personality traits (A. Buss, 1987; D. Buss, 1984). The common goal among these proposals is not only the desire to apply analogous principles across diverse scientific realms, but also to reduce the enormous range of trait concepts and typologies that have proliferated through history. This goal might be achieved by exploring the power of evolutionary theory to simplify and order previously disparate personologic features. For example, all organisms seek to avoid injury, find nourishment, and reproduce their kind if they are to survive and maintain their populations. Each species displays commonalities in its adaptive or survival style. Within each species, however, there are differences in style and differences in the success with which its various members adapt to the diverse and changing environments they face. In these simplest of terms, personality would be conceived as representing the more-or-less distinctive style of adaptive functioning that an organism of a particular species exhibits as it relates to its typical range of environments. "Disorders" of personality, so formulated, would represent particular styles of maladaptive functioning that can be traced to deficiencies, imbalances, or conflicts in a species' capacity to relate to the environments it faces.

Before elaborating where these "disorders" arise within the human species, a few more words must be said concerning analogies between evolution and ecology on the one hand, and personality, on the other.

During its life history an organism develops an assemblage of traits that contribute to its individual survival and reproductive success, the two essential components of "fitness" formulated by Darwin. Such assemblages, termed "complex adaptations"

and "strategies" in the literature of evolutionary ecology, are close biological equivalents to what psychologists have conceptualized as personality styles and structures. In biology, explanations of a life history strategy of adaptations refer primarily to biogenic variations among constituent traits, their overall covariance structure, and the nature and ratio of favorable to unfavorable ecologic resources that have been available for purposes of extending longevity and optimizing reproduction. Such explanations are not appreciably different from those used to account for the development of personality styles or functions.

Bypassing the usual complications of analogies, a relevant and intriguing parallel may be drawn between the phylogenic evolution of a species' genetic composition and the ontogenic development of an individual organism's adaptive strategies (i.e., its "personality style"). At any point in time, a species will possess a limited set of genes that serve as trait potentials. Over succeeding generations the frequency distribution of these genes will likely change in their relative proportions depending on how well the traits they undergird contribute to the species' "fittedness" within its varying ecological habitats. In a similar fashion, individual organisms begin life with a limited subset of their species' genes and the trait potentials they subserve. Over time the *salience* of these trait potentials—not the proportion of the genes themselves—will become differentially prominent as the organism interacts with its environments. It "learns" from these experiences which of its traits "fit" best, that is, most optimally suited to its ecosystem. In phylogenesis, then, actual gene frequencies change during the generation-to-generation adaptive process, whereas in ontogenesis it is the *salience* or prominence of gene-based traits that changes as adaptive learning takes place. Parallel evolutionary processes occur, one within the life of a species, the other within the life of an organism. What is seen in the individual organism is a shaping of latent potentials into adaptive and manifest styles of perceiving, feeling, thinking and acting; these distinctive ways of adaptation, engendered by the interaction of biologic endowment and social experience, comprise the elements of what is termed personality styles. It is a formative process in a single lifetime that parallels gene redistributions among species during their evolutionary history.

Two factors beyond the intrinsic genetic trait potentials of advanced social organisms have a special significance in affecting their survival and replicability. First, other members of the species play a critical part in providing postnatal nurturing and complex role models. Second, and no less relevant, is the high level of diversity and unpredictability of their ecological habitats. This requires numerous, multifaceted, and flexible response alternatives, either preprogrammed genetically or acquired subsequently through early learning. Humans are notable for unusual adaptive pliancy, acquiring a wide repertoire of "styles" or alternate modes of functioning for dealing both with predictable and novel environmental circumstances. Unfortunately, the malleability of early potentials for diverse learnings diminishes as maturation progresses. As a consequence, adaptive styles acquired in childhood, and usually suitable for comparable later environments, become increasingly immutable, resisting modification and relearning. Problems arise in new ecologic settings when these deeply ingrained behavior patterns persist, despite their lessened appropriateness; simply stated, what was learned and was once adaptive, may no longer "fit." Perhaps more important than environmental diversity, then, is the divergence between the circumstances of original learning and those of later life, a schism that has become more problematic as humans have progressed from stable and traditional to fluid and inconstant modern societies.

From the viewpoint of survival logic, it is both efficient and adaptive either to preprogram or to train the young of a species with traits that fit the ecologic habitats of their parents. This "wisdom" rests on the usually safe assumption that consistency, if not identicality will characterize the ecologic conditions of both parents and their offspring. Evolution is spurred when this continuity assumption fails to hold, that is, when formerly stable environments undergo significant change. Radical shifts of this character could result in the extinction of a species. It is more typical, however, for environments to be altered gradually, resulting in modest, yet inexorable redistributions of a species' gene frequencies. Genes which subserve competencies that prove suited to the new conditions become proportionately more common; ultimately, the features they engender come to typify either a new variant of, or a successor to the earlier species.

All animal species intervene in and modify their habitats in routine and repetitive ways. Contemporary humans are unique in evolutionary history, however, in that both the physical and social environment has been altered in precipitous and unpredictable ways; these interventions appear to have set in motion consequences not unlike the equilibrium "punctuations" theorized by modern paleontologists (Eldredge & Gould, 1972). This is best illustrated in the origins of our recent borderline personality "epidemic" (Millon, 1987):

Central to our recent culture have been the increased pace of social change and the growing pervasiveness of ambiguous and discordant customs to which children are expected to subscribe. Under the cumulative impact of rapid industrialization, immigration, urbanization, mobility, technology, and mass communication, there has been a steady erosion of traditional values and standards. Instead of a simple and coherent body of practices and beliefs, children find themselves confronted with constantly shifting styles and increasingly questioned norms whose durability is uncertain and precarious. . . . Few times in history have so many children faced the tasks of life without the aid of accepted and durable traditions. Not only does the strain of making choices among discordant standards and goals beset them at every turn, but these competing beliefs and divergent demands prevent them from developing either internal stability or external consistency. (p. 363)

As recorded earlier, Murray has said that, "life is a continuous procession of explorations . . . learnings and relearnings" (1959). Yet, among species such as humans, early adaptive potentials and pliancies may fail to crystallize owing to the fluidities and inconsistencies of the environment, leading to the persistence of "immature and unstable styles" that fail to achieve coherence and effectiveness. Few can remain as flexible and functional as was Murray through his 100 years, less three.

Lest the reader assume that those seeking to wed the sciences of evolution and ecology find themselves fully welcome in their respective fraternities, there are those who assert that "despite pious hopes and intellectual convictions, [these two disciplines] have so far been without issue" (Lewontin, 1979). This judgment is now both dated and overly severe, but numerous conceptual and methodological impediments do face those who wish to bring these fields of biologic inquiry into fruitful synthesis—no less employing them to construe the styles and disorders of personality. Despite such concerns, recent developments bridging ecological and evolutionary theory are well underway, and hence do offer some justification for extending their principles to human styles of adaptation.

To provide a conceptual background from these sciences, and to furnish a rough model concerning the styles of personality disorder, four domains or spheres in which evolutionary and ecological principles are demonstrated are labeled as *Existence, Adaptation, Replication,* and *Abstraction.* The *first* relates to the serendipitous transformation of random or less organized states into those possessing distinct structures of greater organization; the *second* refers to homeostatic processes employed to sustain survival in open ecosystems; the *third* pertains to reproductive styles that maximize the diversification and selection of ecologically effective attributes; and the *fourth* concerns the emergence of competencies that foster anticipatory planning and reasoned decision making.

# REFERENCES

Bowers, K. S. (1977). There's more to Iago than meets the eye: A clinical account of personal consistency. In D. Magnusson and N. S. Endler, eds., *Personality at the Crossroads.* Hillsdale, NJ: Erlbaum.

Buss, A. H. (1987). Personality: Primitive heritage and human distinctiveness. In J. Aronoff, A. I. Rabin, and R. A. Zucker, eds., *The Emergence of Personality.* New York: Springer.

Buss, D. M. (1984). Evolutionary biology and personality psychology. *American Psychologist, 39,* 1135–1147.

Eldredge, N., and Gould, S. (1972). Punctuated equilibria: An alternative to phyletic gradualism. In T. Schopf, ed., *Models in Paleobiology.* San Francisco: Freeman.

Huxley, T. H. (1870). Mr. Darwin's critics. *Contemporary Review, 18,* 443–476

Lewontin, R. C. (1979). Sociobiology as an adaptationist program. *Behavioral Science, 24,* 5–14.

McDougall, W. (1908). *Introduction to social psychiatry.* New York: Scribners.

Meehl, P. (1978). Theoretical risks and tabular asterisks: Sir Karl, Sir Ronald, and the slow progress of soft psychology. *Journal of Consulting and Clinical Psychology, 46,* 806–834.

Millon, T. (1969). *Modern psychopathology.* Philadelphia: Saunders (reprinted, 1985. Prospect Heights, IL: Waveland Press).

Millon, T. (1981). *Disorders of personality: DSM-III, Axis II.* New York: Wiley-Interscience.

Millon, T. (1983). The DSM-III: An insider's perspective. *American Psychologist, 38,* 804–814.

Millon, T. (1986). A theoretical derivation of pathological personalities. In T. Millon and G. Klerman, eds., *Contemporary Directions in Psychopathology.* New York: Guilford.

Millon, T. (1987). On the genesis and prevalence of the borderline personality disorder: A social learning thesis. *Journal of Personality Disorders, 1,* 354–372.

Murray, H. A. (1959). Preparations for the scaffold of a comprehensive system. In S. Koch, ed., *Psychology: A Study of a Science* (Vol. 3). New York: McGraw-Hill.

Spencer, H. (1870). The principles of psychology. London: Williams and Norgate.

Wilson, E. O. (1975). *Sociobiology: The new synthesis.* Cambridge: Harvard University Press.

Wilson, E. O. (1978). *On human nature.* Cambridge: Harvard University Press.

# Personality Disorders: Conceptual Distinctions and Classification Issues

Most of the empirical discoveries and theoretical constructs that have occupied the attention of psychologists and psychiatrists have suffered the fate that General Douglas MacArthur thought unique to old generals, that is, they never die, they just fade away. As Meehl (1978) put it some years ago:

There is a period of enthusiasm about a new theory, a period of attempted application to several fact domains, a period of disillusionment as the negative data come in, a growing bafflement about inconsistent and unreplicable empirical results, multiple resorts to ad hoc excuses, and then finally people just sort of lose interest in the thing and pursue other endeavors. (p. 807)

Theories, constructs, and findings of such fortune are legion, a sad comment on the "scientific" status of our subject, no less our naive eagerness to follow one evanescent or insubstantial fad after another. Although most conceptual pursuits in the other psychologies have come and gone, justly or otherwise (as others have remained immutably entrenched despite impressive rebuttals or incompatible evidence), there are encouraging signs that cumulative knowledge and a refining process may be under way in the study of personality.

Especially promising is the observation that the essential elements that give substance to personality—the fact that people exhibit distinctive and abiding characteristics—have survived through the ages, albeit under diverse rubrics and labels. This durability attests, at the very least, either to

personality's intuitive consonance with authentic observation, its intrinsic, if naive, human interest, or to its decided and convincing utility. The apparent viability of the concept, as well as its invulnerability in academic circles, is all the more noteworthy when one considers the number of spirited, if misguided, efforts in recent years to undo it. This achievement is even more impressive when one considers the number of recently popular constructs that have faded to a status more consonant with their trivial character or have, under the weight of their scientific inefficacy, succumbed to scholarly weariness or boredom. By contrast, personality and its disorders appear not only to have weathered mettlesome assaults, as witnessed by the position reversals of its most ardent critics (e.g., Mischel, 1973, 1979), but also appear to be undergoing a wide-ranging renaissance in both clinical and scientific circles. This resurgence may be worth elaborating briefly because it signifies the coalescence of powerful, if disparate, trends.

First, from a rather mundane and practical viewpoint, most mental health practitioners use their professional skills today in outpatient rather than inpatient settings. Their "clients" are no longer the severely disturbed "state hospital" psychotics but ambulatory individuals seen in private offices or community clinics; these clients are beset with personal stressors, social inadequacies, or interpersonal conflict, which are typically reported in symptoms such as anxiety, depression, or alcoholism but which signify the outcroppings of long-standing patterns of maladaptive behaving, feeling, thinking, and relating: in other words, their "personality style."

Second, a few words should be said concerning the special role of the recent third and the revised editions of the *Diagnostic and Statistical Manual of Mental Disorders* (DSM-III and DSM-III-R, respectively; American Psychiatric Association, 1980, 1987) in giving prominence to the personality disorders. With this official system, personality not only gained a place of consequence among syndromal categories but became central to its multiaxial schema. The logic for assigning personality its own axis is more than a matter of differentiating syndromes of a more acute and dramatic form from those that may be overlooked by virtue of their long-standing and prosaic character. More relevant to this partitioning decision was the assertion that personality can serve usefully as a substrate of affective, cognitive, and behavioral dispositions from which clinicians can better grasp the "meaning" of their patients' more transient or florid disorders. In the recent DSMs, then, personality disorders have not only attained a nosological status of prominence in their own right, but they have also been assigned a contextual role that makes them fundamental to the understanding of other psychopathologies.

Third, there has been a marked shift in the focus of psychological therapies from that of "surface" symptoms to that of "underlying" personality functions (Beck & Freeman, 1990). This reorientation reflects an intriguing evolution that has been shared among diverse theories since the mid-part of this century. Auchincloss and Michels (1983) describe this progression in an illuminating review of the analytical concept of "character." They wrote, "Today it is generally accepted that character disorders, not neurotic symptoms, are the primary indication for analysis. . . . Psychoanalysis (as a technique) and character analysis have become synonymous" (p. 2). Recent contributions of ego, self, and object-relations

theorists have extended the awareness of the highly varied consequences of early psychic difficulties. Today, character structure is seen not only as a system of defensive operations but as a complex organization of structures that are the focus of therapeutic attention and intervention. Similar shifts in emphasis are also evident in the recent writings of cognitive behavioral and interpersonal therapeutic theorists.

It is not only the changing patient population of clinical practice or the recently evolved role given character in both therapeutic theory and the DSM that signifies the growing prominence of the construct. In the realms of "hard science," that of quantitative assessment and psychometrics, psychologists and psychiatrists alike have turned their skills toward the reliable identification and valid measurement of the new "disorders" of personality. This focus may be seen most clearly in the content of recently developed clinical instruments. These assessment tools contrast in scope and intent with both the historically important projective techniques, such as the Rorschach, and well-established, nondynamic objective inventories such as the Minnesota Multiphasic Personality Inventory (Hathaway & McKinley, 1967). Newly minted are a group of impressively constructed clinical interview schedules, such as the diagnostic interview to assess patients for borderline personality disorder (Gunderson, Kolb, & Austin, 1981), which seek to build a composite picture of a single, comprehensive entity, in this case the "borderline personality," or the broadly based self-report inventory, the Millon Clinical Multiaxial Inventory (Millon, 1977, 1987), with its psychometrically validated series of scales designed to identify and describe the dynamics of all 13 DSM-III-R and fourth edition DSM (DSM-IV; American Psychiatric Association, in press) Axis II disorders. As this book attests, an effort is now underway to bridge the traditional focus of psychologists on personality traits and factors with the renewed scientific examination of personality disorders. It is a rapprochement that I very much favor (Millon, 1990), viewing the present volume as an important step in fostering this long overdue reconciliation of methods and perspectives. Although I am not as convinced as are the editors of this book that their specific approach is the most fruitful one available, I have no doubt that it will spark fresh ideas and insights to guide ongoing empirical studies and theoretical analyses.

This paper is divided into two sections: The first part addresses matters that are related to defining the constructs of personality and personality disorders themselves, and the second part examines issues that are related to alternate conceptions of how the different personality disorders may best be classified.

## CONCEPTUAL DISTINCTIONS

Opinions differ concerning how best to define personality, normal or otherwise. There is general agreement, however, that personality is an inferred abstraction, a concept or a construct, rather than a tangible phenomenon with material existence. Problems inevitably arise, however, when professionals reify these conceptual constructs into substantive entities. To paraphrase Kendell (1975), "familiarity leads us to forget their origins in human imagination." The disorders of personality should certainly not be construed as palpable "diseases." They are man-made constructions that have been invented to facilitate scientific understanding and professional communication.

### WHAT SHOULD THE CONSTRUCTS OF PERSONALITY AND PERSONALITY DISORDER REPRESENT?

Personality may be conceived as the psychological equivalent of the human body's biological system of structures and functions. The body as a whole comprises a well organized yet open system of relatively stable structures that interconnect functionally as they process a wide range of both internal and external events in a coherent and efficient manner. The diversity of functions carried out by the body is awesome in its complexity and efficacy, as is the internal organization of structures that are impressively elaborate in their intricacy and articulation. The distinctive configuration of structures and functions that have evolved ensures that the system as a whole remains both viable and stable. This is achieved by processes that maintain internal cohesion and by actions that use, control, or adapt to external forces. A biological disorder arises when one or several of the following occurs: (a) the balance and synchrony among internal components go awry; (b) a particular structure is traumatized or deteriorates, with the result that it repetitively or persistently malfunctions or (c) foreign entities such as bacteria or viruses intrude themselves, either overwhelming or insidiously undermining the system's integrity.

The construct of personality may be conceived as a psychic system of structures and functions that parallels that of the body. It is not a potpourri of unrelated traits and miscellaneous behaviors but a tightly knit organization of stable structures (e.g., internalized memories and self-images) and coordinated functions (e.g., unconscious mechanisms and cognitive processes). Given continuity in one's constitutional equipment and a narrow band of experiences for learning behavioral alternatives, this psychic system develops an integrated pattern of characteristics and inclinations that are deeply etched, cannot be easily eradicated, and pervade every facet of the life experience. This system is the sum and substance of what the construct of personality would "mean." Mirroring the body's organization, the psychic system is a distinctive configuration of interlocking perceptions, feelings, thoughts, and behaviors that provides a template and disposition for maintaining psychic viability and stability. From this perspective, personality disorders would be best conceived as stemming from failures in the system's dynamic pattern of adaptive competencies. Just as physical ill health is never a simple matter of an intrusive alien virus but reflects also deficiencies in the body's capacity to cope with particular physical environments, so too is psychological ill health not merely a product of psychic stress alone but represents deficiencies in the personality system's capacity to cope with particular psychosocial environments.

Implied in the preceding paragraph is the assertion that adequate clinical analyses of both physical and mental disorders require data beyond those that inhere in the individual alone. In the biological realm, it must encompass knowledge of relevant features of the physical environment; in the psychological domain, it calls for an awareness of the character of the psychosocial environment. Kendell (1975) points to the reciprocal nature of this person-environment field in the following example:

A characteristic which is a disadvantage in one environment may be beneficial in another. The sickle cell trait is a deviation from the norm which in most environments produces a slight but definite biological disadvantage. In an environment in which malaria is endemic, however, it is positively beneficial. . . . This is a particularly serious matter where mental illness is concerned because here the environment, and especially its social aspects, is often of paramount importance. Qualities like recklessness and aggressiveness, for example, may lead a man to be regarded as a psychopath in one environment and to be admired in another. (p. 15)

For the greater part of the history of psychodiagnostics, attention has focused on the patient's internal characteristics alone. When one moves to an ecological perspective (Millon, 1990), external social and interpersonal dynamics are given equal status. As noted in Kendell's illustration, it may be clinically impossible to disentangle these elements when appraising the clinical consequences of an internal characteristic, for example, whether the sickle cell trait is advantageous or disadvantageous. For diagnostic purposes, internal and external factors are inextricably linked elements. Intrapsychic structures and dispositions are essential, but they will prove functional or dysfunctional depending on their efficacy in specific interpersonal, familial, or social contexts.

The rationale for broadening the notion of a disorder to include the interplay of both internal and external systems is especially appropriate when evaluating personality pathology. Not only does personality express itself in everyday, routine interactions within group and familial settings, but the ordinary characteristics that compose the patient's personality will elicit reactions that feed back to shape the future course of whatever impairments the person may already have. Thus, the behaviors, mechanisms, and self-attitudes that individuals exhibit with others will evoke reciprocal responses that influence whether their problems will improve, stabilize, or intensify. It is not only how experiences are processed intrapsychically, therefore, but also how social and familial dynamics unfold that will determine whether the patient functions in an adaptive or maladaptive manner.

Historically, personality disorders have been in a tangential position among psychopathological syndromes, never having achieved a significant measure of recognition in the literature of either abnormal psychology or clinical psychiatry. Until recently, they have been categorized in the official nomenclature with a melange of other, miscellaneous, and essentially secondary syndromes. The advent of DSM-III changed this status radically. With the DSM-III multiaxial format, which was a significant breakthrough in its own right (Williams, 1985a, 1985b), personality pathologies comprise, by themselves, one of only two required "mental disorder" axes. Henceforth, diagnoses assess not only the patient's current symptom picture, via Axis-I, but in addition, those pervasive features that characterize the enduring personality pattern, as recorded on Axis-II. In effect, the revised multiaxial format requires that symptom states no longer be diagnoses as clinical entities isolated from the broader context of the patient's lifelong style of relating, coping, behaving, thinking, and feeling—that is, his or her personality.

This conception of personality breaks the long entrenched habit of conceiving syndromes of psychopathology as one or another variant of a disease, that is, some "foreign" entity or lesion that intrudes insidiously within the person to undermine his or her socalled normal functions. The archaic notion that all mental disorders represent external intrusions or internal disease processes is an offshoot of prescientific ideas such as demons or spirits that ostensibly "possess" or cast spells on the person. The role of infectious agents and anatomical lesions in physical medicine reawakened this archaic view. Of course, personality researchers no longer believe in demons, but many still hold the conception of some alien or malevolent force invading or unsettling the patient's otherwise healthy status.

Such naive notions carry little weight among modern-day medical and behavioral scientists. Given the increasing awareness of the complex nature of both health and disease, modern scientists recognize that most physical disorders result from a dynamic and changing interplay between individuals' capacities to cope and the environment within which they live. It is the patients' overall constitutional makeup—their vitality, stamina, and immune system—that serves as substrate that inclines them to resist or succumb to potentially troublesome environmental forces. Psychopathological disorders should be conceived as reflecting the same interactive pattern. Here, however, it is not the immunological defenses or enzymatic capacities but the patient's personality pattern—that is, coping skills and adaptive flexibilities—that determines whether the person will master or succumb to his or her psychosocial environment. Just as physical ill health is likely to be less a matter of some alien virus than a dysfunction in the body's capacity to deal with infectious agents, so too is psychological ill health likely to be less a product of some intrusive psychic strain than a dysfunction in the personality's capacity to cope with life's difficulties. Viewed this way, the structure and characteristics of personality become the foundation for the individual's capacity to function in a mentally healthy or ill way.

## DIFFERENTIATING NORMAL FROM DISORDERED PERSONALITIES

No sharp line divides normal from pathological behavior; they are relative concepts representing arbitrary points on a continuum or gradient. Not only is personality so complex that certain areas of psychological functioning operate normally while others do not, but environmental circumstances change such that behaviors and strategies that prove adaptive at one time fail to do so at another. Moreover, features differentiating normal from abnormal functioning must be extracted from a complex of signs that not only wax and wane but often develop in an insidious and unpredictable manner.

Pathology results from the same forces that are involved in the development of normal functioning, important differences in the character, timing, and intensity of these influences will lead some individuals to acquire pathological structures and functions, whereas others develop adaptive ones. When an individual displays an ability to cope with the environment in a flexible manner, and when his or her typical perceptions and behaviors foster increments in personal satisfaction, then the person may be said to possess a normal or healthy personality. Conversely, when average or everyday responsibilities are responded to inflexibly or defectively, or when the individual's perceptions and behaviors result in increments of personal discomfort or curtail opportunities to learn and to grow, then we may speak of a pathological or maladaptive pattern.

Numerous attempts have been made to develop definitive criteria for distinguishing psychological normality from abnormality. Some of these criteria focus on features that characterize the so-called normal, or ideal, state of mental health (e.g., Offer & Sabshin, 1974); others have sought to specify theoretically grounded criteria for concepts such as normality or abnormality; (see Millon, 1991b). The most common criterion used is a statistical one in which normality is determined by those behaviors that are found most frequently in a social group; and pathology or abnormality, by features that are uncommon in that population. Among diverse criteria used to signify normality are a capacity to function autonomously and competently, a tendency to adjust to one's environment effectively and efficiently, a subjective sense of contentment and satisfaction, and the ability to self-actualize or to fulfill one's potentials. Psychopathology would be noted by deficits among the preceding.

## DIFFERENTIATING PERSONALITY DISORDERS FROM OTHER PSYCHOPATHOLOGIES

Although the term disorder is used as a label for all of the major syndromes of the official nosology, current classification systems can go awry if their categories encompass too wide a range of clinical conditions. There is a need to subdivide the subject of psychopathology along useful points of distinction. As discussed in Millon (1987, 1990), a logical framework for a taxonomy of mental disorders would be one based on several theoretically grounded dimensions and bipolarities that lend themselves to quantitative distinctions. At the simplest level, they would be differentiated by the degree to which manifest pathological processes fall on a continuum from "circumscribed" (focal) to "pervasive" (systemic) and on a continuum from "transient" (acute) to "enduring" (chronic). It is largely on the basis of these two simple distinctions that differentiations may be made among

personality disorders, clinical syndromes, and adjustment reactions.

## DIFFERENTIATING PERSONALITY DISORDERS, CLINICAL SYNDROMES, AND ADJUSTMENT REACTIONS

Reflecting the two polarities of circumscribed—pervasive and transient—enduring is the extent to which observed pathologies can be attributed to ingrained traits or internal characteristics versus recent stressors or external precipitants. As previously discussed, pathology always reflects a person-environment interaction. Nevertheless, it is useful to distinguish types of pathology in terms of the extent to which their determinants derive from personological versus situational forces, an issue that evoked considerable debate in the field of personality research during the past two decades.

Personality disorders (Axis-II) are best conceived as those conditions that are "activated" primarily by internally embedded structures and pervasive ways of functioning. At the opposite end of this person-situation or internal-external continuum are the adjustment reactions, which are best construed as specific pathological responses attributable largely to circumscribed environmental precipitants. Between these polar extremes lie what have been termed clinical syndromes (Axis-I), that is, categories of psychopathology that are anchored more or less equally and simultaneously to internal personal attributes and external situational events. Exhibited as intensifications of a patient's characteristic style of functioning or as disruptions in his or her underlying psychic make-up, clinical syndromes are conceived as responses to situations for which the individual's personality structure is notably vulnerable.

Viewed from a different perspective, the attributes that compose personality have an inner momentum and autonomy; they are expressed with minimal inducement or external provocation. In contrast, the responses that compose adjustment reactions are conceived as stimulus-specific. They not only operate independently from the individual's personality but are elicited by events that are apt to be judged consensually as "objectively" troublesome. Clinical syndromes are similar to adjustment reactions (both compose Axis-I of the DSM) in that they are prompted also by external events, but their close connection to inner personality traits results in the intrusion of memories and affects that complicate what might otherwise be a simple response to the environment. Hence, these syndromes often fail to "make objective sense," often appearing irrational and strangely complicated. To the knowledgeable clinician, however, these syndromes signify the presence of an unusual vulnerability on the part of the patient; in effect, a seemingly neutral stimulus has reactivated a painful hidden memory or emotion. Viewed in this manner, clinical syndromes arise in individuals who are encumbered with notably adverse biological dysfunctions or early experiences.

Unfortunately, the rather neat conceptual distinctions that I have just made are not readily observed in the "real" world of clinical conditions. Interaction and overlap will almost always blur the boundaries that have been drawn given that psychopathologies are rarely qualitatively distinct "disease entities."

## INTERRELATIONSHIPS AMONG PERSONALITY DISORDERS AND CLINICAL SYNDROMES

The view that mental disorders are composed of distinct entities reflects the personality research field's level of scientific development rather than the intrinsic nature of psychopathological phenomena. Hempel (1961), for example, noted that in their early stages all sciences tend to order their variables into separate or discrete classes. As progress occurs, advanced methods of analysis become available to enable scientists to deal with the interplay of elements comprising their field and, thereby, specify

how formerly unconnected characteristics overlap and interrelate. It would appear, then, that as personological and psychopathological sciences progress, syndromes are likely to be conceived less as discrete independent entities but more as converging and reciprocal entities that exhibit both interconnected and distinct features (Grove & Tellegen, 1991).

A step toward the twin goals of differentiation and coordination was taken in DSM-III, in which the two major axes are separate yet interrelated. Axis I consists of the clinical syndromes—those symptom states that wax and wane in their severity over time and that display themselves as the more acute and dramatic forms of psychopathology. On Axis II are found the personality disorders, which represent the more enduring and pervasive characteristics that often underlie, and provide a context for understanding, the more florid and transient Axis I symptomatologies. Each axis is recorded separately, yet they are conceived as representing interrelated clinical features. In its multiaxial construction, DSM-III sought to encourage clinicians to explore relationships among diagnostic categories. It was hoped that clinical syndromes would no longer be seen as standing on their own as discrete entities; rather, they would be viewed as precursors, extensions, or substrates for one another. More specifically, the clinical syndromes would be understood, at least in part, to be disruptions of functioning among the personality disorders, springing forth, so to speak, to dominate the clinical picture under stressful or otherwise vulnerable circumstances. Envisioned in this fashion, clinical syndromes are not distinct diagnostic entities but are interrelated with complex personality characteristics.

How are these two elements of clinical psychopathology likely to be related (Docherty, Feister, & Shea, 1986)? Of the numerous explanations offered to account for these relationships, the most widely held possibility is that personality is etiological, that is, that personality disorders precede the onset of the clinical syndrome and therefore establish a vulnerability to symptom formation (Klerman, 1973). This viewpoint, which is most heavily supported by psychoanalytic theorists, emphasizes the developmental history and early family environment as factors that shape individuals and predispose them to the clinical states of anxiety, worthlessness, or dejection (McCranie, 1971).

A related explanation of the connection between the two axes is that certain personalities may repeatedly create stressful life circumstances that precipitate development of clinical episodes (Akiskal, Khani, & Scott-Strauss, 1979). Illustrative of this are borderline personalities with their erratic lifestyle and propensity toward tumultuous relationships and self-destructive behaviors.

In a related hypothesis, characterological features may render an individual vulnerable to certain psychosocial stressors. The growing body of research on stress events, anxiety, and depression reflects the mounting interest in this theory. Studies have shown that depressions are frequently preceded by stressful events that are often associated with separation or loss (Paykel, Myers, & Dienelt, 1970). Because not all people who experience stress become anxious or depressed, it is felt that a genetic predisposition and/or life history factors (e.g., personality style, effectiveness of coping mechanisms, or available supports) may predispose certain individuals toward a clinical outcome (Becker, 1977). The dependent individual, for example, tends to be quite susceptible to feelings of anxiety and depression under the conditions of interpersonal loss, abandonment, or rejection.

Another explanatory approach suggests that many personality disorders may actually represent subclinical manifestations of major clinical syndromes (Akiskal, Hirschfeld, & Yerevanian, 1983; Akiskal et al., 1979). From this perspective, lifelong affective traits or "affective personalities" (e.g., the cyclothymic personality) may represent gradual stages of transition to full syndromic affective episodes (e.g., manic-depressive illness).

Similarly, the schizotypal personality disorder may be a dilute form of schizophrenia, and the avoidant personality disorder may be a chronic and pervasive variant of clinical anxiety or social phobia.

It has also been argued that rather than increasing vulnerability to a clinical state such as depression, personality may exert a pathoplastic effect, that is, it colors and molds the particular expression of the clinical symptoms (Paykel, Klerman, & Prusoff, 1976). Depending on the premorbid personality, symptoms such as hopelessness, anxiety, or self-deprecation may serve a variety of goals. In this hypothesis, the secondary gains of certain clinical states may elicit nurturance from others, excuse the avoidance of unwanted responsibilities, rationalize poor performance, or safely permit the expression of anger toward others. Partly determined by the gains received, clinical syndromes may take the form of dramatic gestures, irritable negativism, passive loneliness, or philosophical intellectualization.

Docherty et al. (1986) offered another possible basis for the comorbidity of certain Axis I and Axis 11 disorders, one they termed the coeffect thesis. As they state it:

This model proposes that the personality disorder and the syndrome disorder are separate psychobiological structures. However, it is proposed that they both arise from a common cause or third factor, a single disease process that generates both entities. In this model, neither the personality disorder nor the syndrome disorder is causative of the other. They are simply correlates. Each is caused by a common third variable. For example, a particular form of child-raising experience may give rise to dependent personality and also, independently, to vulnerability to depressive episodes. (p. 317)

Not to be overlooked in these patterns of relationship is the evidence that personality characteristics may influence a clinically disturbed individual's response to both psychopharmacological and psychotherapeutic treatment (Akiskal et al., 1980; Chamey, Nelson, & Quinlan, 1981).

## CLASSIFICATION ISSUES

Whatever data are included to provide the substantive body of a classification, personological or otherwise, decisions must be made concerning the framework into which the nosology will be cast, the rules that will govern the classes into which the clinical attributes and defining features will be placed, and the compositional properties that will characterize these attributes and features (Millon, 1991a). These issues deal with the overall architecture of the nosology, regardless of whether it is organized horizontally, vertically, or circularly, regardless of whether all or only a limited and fixed subset of features should be required for class membership; regardless of whether its constituents should be conceived as categories or dimensions; and regardless of whether they should be based on manifest observables or latent features, as well as a host of other differentiating characteristics from which one may choose. A few of the more significant of these elements and the choices to be made among them are discussed in this section, a task of no simple proportions because there is nothing logically self-evident, nor is there a traditional format or contemporary consensus to guide selections among these alternatives (Grove & Tellegen, 1991; Gunderson, Links, & Reich, 1991; Livesley, 1991).

Because reliable and useful classifications were developed long before the advent of modern scientific thought and methods acquired by intelligent observation and common sense alone, what special values are derived by applying the complicated and rigorous procedures required in developing explicit criteria, categorical homogeneity, and diagnostic efficiency? Is rigor, clarity, precision, and experimentation more than a compulsive and picayunish concern for details, more than the pursuit for the honorific title of "science"? Are the labors of differentiating clinical attributes or exploring categorical cutting scores in a systematic fashion worth the time and effort involved?

There is little question in this "age of science" that the answer would be yes. But why? What are the distinguishing virtues of precision in one's terminology, the specification of observable conceptual referents, and the analysis of covariant attribute clusters? What sets these procedures apart from everyday methods of categorizing knowledge? Most relevant, is conceptual definition and classification possible in the domain of personological disorders? Can these most fundamental of scientific activities be achieved in a subject that is inherently inexact and of only modest levels of intrinsic order, that is, a subject in which even the very slightest variations in context or antecedent conditions—often of a minor or random character—produce highly divergent consequences (Bandura, 1982)? Because this "looseness" within the network of variables in psychic pathology is unavoidable, are there any grounds for believing that such endeavors could prove more than illusory? Persuasive answers to these questions that are of a more philosophical nature must be bypassed in this all-too-concise chapter; those who wish to pursue this line of analysis would gain much by reading, among others, Pap (1953), Hempel (1965), and Meehl (1978). In the following section I discuss, albeit briefly, a more tangible and psychologically based rationale for believing that formal classification in personality pathology may prove to be at least a moderately fruitful venture.

### CAN PERSONALITY DISORDERS BE CLASSIFIED?

There is a clear logic to classifying "syndromes" in medical disorders. Bodily changes wrought by infectious diseases and structural deteriorations repeatedly display themselves in a reasonably uniform pattern of signs and symptoms that "make sense" in terms of how anatomic structures and physiological processes are altered and then dysfunction. Moreover, these biological changes provide a foundation not only for identifying the etiology and pathogenesis of these disorders but also for anticipating their course and prognosis. Logic and fact together enable one to construct a rationale to explain why most medical syndromes express themselves in the signs and symptoms they do, as well as the sequences through which they unfold.

Can the same be said for personological and psychopathological classifications? Is there logic, or perhaps evidence, for believing that certain forms of clinical expression (e.g., behaviors, cognitions, affects, mechanisms) cluster together as do medical syndromes; that is, not only covary frequently but make sense as a coherently organized and reasonably distinctive group of characteristics? Are there theoretical and empirical justifications for believing that the varied features of personality display a configurational unity and expressive consistency over time? Will the careful study of individuals reveal congruency among attributes such as overt behavior, intrapsychic functioning, and biophysical disposition? Is this coherence and stability of psychological functioning a valid phenomenon, that is, not merely imposed on observed data by virtue of clinical expectation or theoretical bias?

There are reasons to believe that the answer to each of the preceding questions is yes. Stated briefly and simply, the observations of covariant patterns of signs, symptoms, and traits may be traced to the fact that people possess relatively enduring biophysical dispositions, which give a consistent coloration to their experience, and that the range of experiences to which people are exposed throughout their lives is both limited and repetitive (Millon, 1969, 1981). Given the limiting and shaping character of these biogenic and psychogenic factors, it should not be surprising that individuals develop clusters of prepotent and deeply ingrained behaviors, cognitions, and affects that clearly distinguish them from others of dissimilar backgrounds. Moreover, once a number of the components of a particular personality pattern are identified,

knowledgeable clinicians can trace the presence of other, unobserved but frequently correlated features comprising that pattern.

If one accepts the assumption that most people do display a pattern of internally consistent characteristics, then one is led next to the question of whether groups of patients evidence commonality in the patterns that they display. The notion of clinical categories rests on the assumption that there are a limited number of such shared covariances, for example, regular groups of diagnostic signs and symptoms that can confidently be used to distinguish certain classes of patients. (It should be noted that because patients can profitably be classified into categories does not negate the fact that patients, so classified, display considerable differences as well, differences that are routinely observed with medical diseases.)

Another question that must be addressed concerning the nature of personological categories may be phrased best as follows: Why does the possession of characteristic A increase the probability, appreciably beyond chance, of also possessing characteristics B, C, and so on? Put in a less abstract way, why do particular behaviors, attitudes, mechanisms, and so on, covary in repetitive and recognizable ways rather than exhibit themselves in a more-or-less haphazard fashion? Put in an even more concrete way, why do behavioral defensiveness, interpersonal provocativeness, cognitive suspicion, affective irascibility, and excessive use of the projection mechanism co-occur in the same individual rather than be uncorrelated and randomly distributed among different individuals?

The "answers" are, first, that temperament and early experience simultaneously effect the development and nature of several emerging psychological structures and functions; that is, a wide range of behaviors, attitudes, affects, and mechanisms can be traced to the same origins, which thereby leads to their frequently observed covariance. Second, once an individual possesses these initial characteristics, they set in motion a series of derivative life experiences that shape the acquisition of new psychological attributes that are causally related to the characteristics that preceded them in the sequential chain. Common origins and successive linkages increase the probability that certain psychological characteristics will frequently be found to pair with specific others, which thereby results in repetitively observed symptom or trait clusters. Illustrations of these reciprocal covariances and serially unfolding concatenations among longitudinal influences (e.g., etiology) and concurrent attributes (e.g., signs, traits) may be found in Millon (1969, 1981, 1990).

Although grievances itemizing the inadequacies of both current and historical systems of classification have been voiced for years, as are suggestions that endeavors to refine these efforts are fussy and misdirected, if not futile and senseless pretensions that should be abandoned, the presence of such systems is both unavoidable—owing to humankind's linguistic and attribution habits—as well as inevitable—owing to humankind's need to differentiate and record, at the very least, the most obvious of dissimilarities among the psychologically impaired. Given the fact that one or another set of classes is inevitable, or as Kaplan (1964, p. 279) once phrased it, "it is impossible to wear clothing of no style at all," it would appear both sensible and fitting that one should know the explicit basis upon which such distinctions are to be made, rather than have them occur helter-skelter in nonpublic and nonverifiable ways. Furthermore, if personality pathology is to evolve into a true science, then its diverse phenomena must be subject to formal identification, differentiation, and quantification procedures. Acts such as diagnosis and assessment presuppose the existence of discernable phenomena that can be recognized and measured. Logic necessitates, therefore, that psychopathological states and processes be distinguished from one another, being thereby classified or grouped

in some manner before they can be subjected to identification and quantification

Whatever data are included to provide the substantive body of a classification system, decisions must be made concerning the structural framework into which the groupings will be fit, the rules that will govern the clinical attributes and defining features selected, and the compositional properties that will characterize these attributes. These issues deal with the overall architecture of the classification, regardless of whether its constituents should be conceived as categories or dimensions, as well as a host of other differentiating characteristics from which one may choose. A number of the more significant of these structural elements, and the choices to be made among them, have been discussed in this section, a task of no simple proportions because there is nothing logically self-evident, nor is there a traditional format or contemporary consensus to guide selections among these alternatives (for a fuller discussion of this topic see Millon, 1987; Frances & Widiger, 1986).

## CATEGORICAL TYPES, DIMENSIONAL TRAITS, AND PROTOTYPAL MODELS

Important differences separate medical from psychological traditions in their approach to classifying their primary subject domains. Psychology's substantive realms have been approached with considerable success by using methods of dimensional analysis and quantitative differentiation (e.g., intelligence measures, aptitude levels, trait magnitudes, etc.). By contrast, medicine has made its greatest progress by increasing its accuracy in identifying and categorizing discrete disease entities. The issue separating these two historical approaches as it relates to the subject domain of personality disorders may best be examined by posing the following: Should personality pathology be conceived and organized as a series of dimensional traits that combine to form a unique profile for each individual, or should certain central characteristics be selected to exemplify and categorize personality types found commonly in clinical populations?

The view that personality pathology might best be conceived as dimensional traits has only recently begun to be taken as a serious alternative to the more classic categorical approach. Certain trait dimensions have been proposed in the past as relevant to these disorders (e.g., dominance-submission, extroversion-introversion, and rigidity-flexibility), but these have not been translated into the full range of personality syndromes. Some traits have been formulated such that one extreme of a dimension differs significantly from the other in terms of their clinical implications; an example would be emotional stability versus emotional vulnerability. Other traits are psychologically curvilinear such that both extremes have negative implications; an example of this would be found in an activity dimension such as listlessness versus restlessness.

There are several advantages to dimensional models that should be noted. Most important is that they combine several clinical features or personality traits into a single profile. By their comprehensiveness, little information of potential significance is lost, nor is any single trait given special attention, such as when only one distinctive characteristic is brought to the foreground in a categorical typology. Furthermore, a trait profile permits the inclusion of unusual or atypical cases; in topologies, odd, infrequent, or "mixed" conditions often are excluded because they do not fit the prescribed categories. Given the diversity and idiosyncratic character of many clinical personalities, a dimensional system encourages the representation of individuality and uniqueness rather than "forcing" patients into categories for which they are ill-suited. Another advantage of a dimensional format is that the strength of traits is gauged quantitatively, and therefore, each characteristic extends into the normal range; as a consequence, normality and abnormality are merely arranged as points on a continuum

rather than as distinct and separable phenomena.

Despite their seeming advantages, dimensional systems have not taken strong root in the formal diagnosis of personality pathology. Numerous complications and limitations have been noted in the literature, and these are briefly noted.

First is the fact that there is little agreement among dimensional theorists concerning the number of traits necessary to represent personality. Historically, for example, Menninger (1963) contended that a single dimension would suffice; Eysenck (1960) asserted that three are needed; whereas Cattell (1965) claimed to have identified as many as 33 and believes there are many more. However, recent models, most notably the five-factor model (FFM; Costa & McCrae, 1990; Goldberg, 1990; Norman, 1963), have begun to achieve a modest level of consensus. The problem here is that theorists may "invent" dimensions that are in accord with their expectations rather than "discovering" them as if they were intrinsic to nature, merely awaiting scientific detection. The number of traits or factors required to assess personality may not be determined by the ability of research to disclose some inherent truth but rather by predilections for conceiving studies and organizing the data they generate (Kline & Barrett, 1983; Millon, 1990).

Second, describing personality with more than a few trait or factor dimensions may produce complex profiles or intricate configurations that require algebraic or otherwise resourceful representation. There is nothing intrinsically wrong with such quantitative and original schemata, but they may pose considerable difficulty in comprehension, as well as require inventive syntheses among clinicians. Not only are most mental health workers hesitant about working with multivariate statistics or innovative configurations, but the consequent feeling that one is lost in one's own professional discipline is not likely to make such schemata attractive, much less practical for everyday use. Apart from matters of convenience and comfort, innovative representations are likely themselves to be grouped into categories before their commonalities and differences can be communicated. In effect, once a population has been identified as possessing a similar profile or dimensional pattern, it will likely become a category. Thus, although the original format may have been a factorial or dimensional pattern, it will likely become a category, and those who are grouped within a particular category will invariably be spoken of as a "type."

Categorical models have been the preferred schema for representing both clinical syndromes and personality disorders. It should be noted, however, that most contemporary categories neither imply nor are constructed to be all-or-none typologies. Although categorical models single out and give prominence to certain features of behavior, they do not overlook the other features but merely assign them lesser significance. It is this process of assigning centrality or relative dominance to particular characteristics that distinguishes a schema of categories from one composed of trait dimensions. Conceived in this manner, a type simply becomes a superordinate category that subsumes and integrates psychologically covariant traits that, in turn, represent a set of correlated habits that, in their turn, stand for a response displayed in a variety of situations. When this superordinate type is found with some frequency in clinical populations, there is reason to conclude that it may be useful as a concept that gives coherence to seemingly diverse symptoms.

Among the advantages of categorical typologies is their ease of use by clinicians who must make relatively rapid diagnoses with large numbers of patients whom they see briefly. Although clinical attention in these cases is drawn to only the most salient features of the patient, a broad range of traits that have not been directly observed are strongly suggested. It is this capacity to suggest characteristics beyond those immediately observed that adds special value to an established system of types. For example, if one assumes that an individual is diagnosed as a histrionic personality following the observation that his or her behaviors were seductive and dramatic, then, although the database is limited, there is reason to believe that this individual is also likely to be characterized as stimulus-seeking, needful of attention, interpersonally-capricious, emotionally labile, and so on. In effect, assignment to a particular type or category often proves useful by alerting the clinician to a range of unobserved but frequently correlated behaviors. This process of extending the scope of associated characteristics contrasts with the tendency of dimensional schemata to fractionate personality into separate and uncoordinated traits. Typologies restore and recompose the unity of personality by integrating seemingly diverse elements into a single coordinated syndrome. Moreover, the availability of well-established syndromes provides standard references for clinicians who would otherwise be faced with repeated analyses and de novo personality constructions.

There are, of course, objections to the use of categorical typologies in personality. They contribute to the fallacious belief that psychopathological syndromes are discrete entities, even medical diseases, when, in fact, they are merely concepts that help focus and coordinate observations. Furthermore, categories often fail to identify and include important aspects of behavior because they reflect a decision to narrow the list of characteristics that are considered primary. Of course, the discarding of information is not limited to categories; dimensional schemata also choose certain traits or factors to the exclusion of others. The problem, however, is that categorical types tend to give primacy to only a single characteristic. Another criticism is that the number and diversity of types are far less than the individual differences observed in clinical work. Not only are there problems in assigning many patients to the limited categories available, but clinicians often claim that the more they know a patient, the greater the difficulty they have in fitting him or her into a single category. A final criticism reflects the diversity of competing systems available; numerous classifications have been formulated in the past century, and one may question whether any system is worth using if there is so little consensus among categorists themselves. Is it possible to conclude from this review that categorical or dimensional schemata are potentially the more useful for personality classifications? An illuminating answer may have been provided by Cattell, who wrote:

The description by attributes [traits] and the description by types must . . . be considered face and obverse of the same descriptive system. Any object whatever can be defined either by listing measurements for it on a set of [trait] attributes or by sequestering it to a particular named [type] category. (1970, p. 40)

In effect, Cattell concluded that the issue of choosing between dimensional traits and categorical types is both naive and specious because they are two sides of the same coin. The essential distinction to be made between these models is that of comprehensiveness. Types are higher order syntheses of lower order dimensional traits; they encompass a wider scope of generality. For certain purposes it may be useful to narrow attention to specific traits; in other circumstances a more inclusive level of integration may be appropriate (Grove & Tellegen, 1991).

There is another, more recent, solution to the question of how the data of personality pathology might best be organized. The construct "prototype" has a long history, but only recently has it been introduced as a potentially useful option for classifying psychopathology. As presently formulated it appears to meld several attributes of both categorical and dimensional schemata. It may prove especially apt as personality researchers seek to develop a format for representing both the composite of diverse elements that comprise personality (the dimensional aspect) as well as the features that distinguish personality from other forms of

psychopathology, namely, its durability and pervasiveness (the categorical aspect).

Cantor, Smith, French, and Mezzich (1980) noted that the "classical" approach to diagnosis depends on the identification of singly necessary or jointly sufficient features. By contrast, the prototypal view merely requires that sets be composed of correlated features. As a result of this conceptual openness:

prototypes permit extensive heterogeneity of category instances. Thus, one instance may contain most of the correlated features of the prototype and another may contain hardly any at all. . . . Prototypes make sense out of variations in typicality, where typical instances are simply those that share many correlated features with the category prototype . . . . The higher the overlap, the faster, more accurately, and more confidently the instance can be classified. An immediate consequence of this prototype-matching process is that typical instances will be categorized more efficiently than atypical ones, because typical instances have greater featural overlap with their prototypes . . . . To the degree that the prototypes for two categories have many common features and few distinctive ones, the categorizer may have difficulty distinguishing between members of these categories . . . . There is one more factor that must be considered in a prototype-matching process. This factor reflects the degree of richness of a category prototype (as measured by the total number of its features) as well as the distinctiveness of the prototype (as measured by the number of its features that are not shared by rival categories). (pp. 184–185)

It is evident that the prototype approach shares many of the attributes associated with the dimensional approach, notably the diversity of the correlated traits and symptoms involved and, hence, the heterogeneity found among similarly diagnosed patients. Albeit implicitly, the prototype model guided the thinking of several DSM Task Force members who formulated both the rules and diagnostic criteria of the manual, for example, the opportunity to select only a subset of the criteria that composed a category, the presence of "mixed" syndromes, and even the encouragement of multiple diagnoses. Cantor et al. (1980) observed that these DSM changes:

help to emphasize, rather than obscure, the probabilistic nature of diagnostic categorizations. On the basis of the new manual, clinicians can now be trained to expect heterogeneity among patients and to recognize the probabilistic nature of diagnostic categorization. Also, utilization of confidence typicality ratings in diagnosis can be encouraged, and diagnoses can be made on the basis of degree of fit between the patient's clusters of symptoms and the prototypes for various different categories. (p. 192)

Diverging from a single, overarching attribute that characterizes a categorical typology, the prototype concept appears well suited to represent the pervasive and durable features that distinguish personality disorders from the frequently transient and narrowly circumscribed expressive sphere of the clinical syndromes.

The fact that some diagnostic classes in contemporary nosologies (e.g., DSM-III, *International Classification of Diseases—9th Revision* [World Health Organization, 1991]) are composed essentially of a single clinical feature (e.g., depression), whereas others encompass several mixed features (e.g., histrionic personality), has not only confounded discussions of categoricality versus dimensionality but has contributed a share of confusion to theory, research, and practice, as well.

Skinner (1986) has elaborated several "hybrid models" in an effort to integrate elements of a number of divergent schemata. In what he termed the class-quantitative approach, efforts are made to synthesize quantitative dimensions and discrete categories. Likewise, Livesley (1986a, 1986b) has formulated a schema to bridge both conceptual models.

I previously described an endeavor of a similar nature (Millon, 1984, 1986, 1990). Termed the *prototypal* domain model, this schema mixes categorical and dimensional elements in a personological classification.

As in the official DSM schema, several criteria are specified for each disorder, but these criteria encompass a large set of clinical domains (e.g., mood/temperament, cognitive style). It is the diagnostic criterion that is conceived to be prototypal, not the personality as a whole. Each specific domain is given a prototypal standard for each personality. To illustrate: If the clinical attribute "interpersonal conduct" was deemed of diagnostic value in assessing personality disorders, then a specific prototypal criterion would be identified to represent the characteristic or distinctive manner in which each personality disorder ostensibly conducts its interpersonal life.

By composing a classification schema that includes all relevant clinical domains (e.g., self-image, expressive acts, interpersonal conduct, cognitive style) and that specifies a prototypal feature for every domain for each of the personality disorders, the proposed format would then be fully comprehensive in its clinical scope and possess directly comparable prototypal features for its parallel diagnostic categories. A schema of this nature would furnish both detailed substance and clinical symmetry to its taxonomy.

To enrich this schema's qualitative categories (the several prototypal features comprising the clinical range seen in each domain) with quantitative discriminations (numerical intensity ratings), clinicians would not only identify which prototypal features (e.g., distraught, hostile, labile) in a clinical domain (e.g., mood/temperament) best characterizes a patient, but they would record a rating or number (e.g., from 1 to 10) to represent the degree of prominence or pervasiveness of the chosen feature(s). Clinicians would be encouraged in such a prototypal schema to record and quantify more than one feature per clinical domain (e.g., if suitable, to note both "distraught" and "labile" moods, should their observations lead them to infer the presence of two prototypal characteristics in that domain).

The prototypal domain model illustrates that categorical (qualitative distinction) and dimensional (quantitative distinction) approaches need not be framed in opposition, much less be considered mutually exclusive. Assessments can be formulated to (a) recognize qualitative (categorical) distinctions in what prototypal features best characterize a patient, which thereby permits the multiple listing of several such features, and (b) differentiate these features quantitatively (dimensionally) so as to represent their relative degrees of clinical prominence or pervasiveness. The prototypal domain approach includes the specification and use of categorical attributes in the form of distinct prototypal characteristics, yet this approach allows for a result that permits the diversity and heterogeneity of a dimensional schema.

## MANIFEST AND LATENT TAXA

The major classes of nosological systems are called taxa (singular: taxon); they may be differentiated in a number of ways. What may be labeled as manifest taxa involve classes that are based on observable or phenotypic commonalities (e.g., overt behaviors). *Latent taxa* pertain to groupings formed on the basis of abstract mathematical derivations (factor or cluster analysis) or the propositional deductions of a theory, each of which ostensibly represents the presence of genotypic commonalities (e.g., etiologic origins or trait similarities).

The polar distinction between manifest taxa, at the one end, and latent taxa, at the other, represents in part a broader epistemological dichotomy that exists between those who prefer to use data derived from observational contexts versus those who prefer to draw their ideas from more theoretical or mathematically deduced sources. A parallel distinction was first drawn by Aristotle when he sought to contrast the understanding of disease with reference to knowledge of latent principles—which ostensibly deals with all instances of a disease, however

diverse, versus direct observational knowledge, which deals presumably only with specific and individual instances. To Aristotle, knowledge that is based on direct experience alone represented a more primitive type of knowledge than that informed by mathematics or conceptual theory which could, through the application of principles, explain not only why a particular disease occurs but illuminate commonalities among seemingly diverse ailments. This same theme was raised in the writings of the distinguished 19th century neurologist, Hughlings Jackson. For example, Jackson drew a distinction between two kinds of disease classifications: The first, termed *theoretical,* was designed to advance the state of knowledge; the second, termed *clinical,* was organized for routine or daily practice. Both were seen as necessary, but Jackson asserted that with each elucidation of a contemporary disease there would be an accretion of theory, which would result in the ultimate supplanting of "mere" clinical knowledge.

### Manifest Clinical Taxa

For the greater part of history (Zilboorg & Henry, 1941; Menninger, 1963), psychiatric taxonomies were formed on the basis of clinical observation, that is, the witnessing of repetitive patterns of behavior and emotion among a small number of carefully studied mental patients. Etiologic hypotheses were generated to give meaning to these patterns of covariance (e.g., Hippocrates anchored differences in observed temperament to his humoral theory, and Kraepelin distinguished two major categories of severe pathology—dementia praecox and manic-depressive disease—in terms of their ostensive divergent prognostic course). The elements comprising these theoretic notions were post hoc, however; they were imposed after the fact on prior observational data, rather than serving as a generative source for taxonomic categories. The most recent example of a clinical taxonomy—one tied explicitly to phenomenological observation and constructed by intention to both atheoretical and nonquantitative elements is, of course, the DSM-III. Spitzer, chairperson of the DSM Task Force, stated in DSM-III (American Psychiatric Association, 1980) that "clinicians can agree on the identification of mental disorders on the basis of their clinical manifestations without agreeing on how the disturbances came about" (p. 7).

Albeit implicitly, DSM-III is a product of speculation regarding latent causes or structures. Nevertheless, a major goal of the DSM Task Force was to eschew theoretic notions, while adhering to as strict an observational philosophy as possible. In doing so, only those attributes that could be readily seen or consensually validated were to be permitted as diagnostic criteria. Numerous derelictions from this epistemology are notable, nevertheless, especially among the personality disorders, for which trait ascriptions call for inferences beyond direct sensory inspection.

Not all who seek to render taxa on the basis of observational clinical data insist on keeping latent inferences to a minimum (Tversky, 1977); and by no means do those who draw their philosophical inspiration from a manifest mindset restrict themselves to the mere specification of surface similarities (Medin, Altom, Edelson, & Freko, 1982). It is not only those who use mathematical procedures and who formulate theoretically generated nosologies who "succumb" to the explanatory power and heuristic value of pathogenic or structural inferences. Feinstein (1977), a distinguished internist, provides an apt illustration of how one person's "factual" observations may be another's latent inference. As Feinstein put it:

In choosing an anchor or focus for taxonomy, we can engage in two distinctly different types of nosologic reasoning. The first is to form names, designations or denominations for the observed evidence, and to confine ourselves exclusively to what has actually been observed. The second is to draw inferences from the observed evidence arriving at inferential titles representing entities that have not actually been observed. For example, if a patient says "I have substantial chest pain, provoked by exertion, and relieved by rest," I, as an internist, perform a denomination if I

designate this observed entity as angina pectoris. If I call it coronary artery disease, however, I perform an inference, because I have not actually observed coronary artery disease. If a radiologist looking at a coronary arteriogram or a pathologist cutting open the coronary vasculature uses the diagnosis coronary artery disease, the decision is a denomination. If the radiologist or pathologist decides that the coronary disease was caused by cigarette smoking or by a high fat diet, the etiologic diagnosis is an inference unless simultaneous evidence exists that the patient did indeed smoke or use a high fat diet. (p. 192)

In large measure, clinically based taxa gain their importance and prominence by virtue of consensus and authority. Cumulative experience and habit are crystallized and subsequently confirmed by official bodies such as the various DSM committees (Millon, 1986). Specified criteria are denoted and articulated; these criteria then acquire definitional, if not stipulative, powers—at least in the eyes of those who come to accept the selected manifest clinical attributes as infallible taxonomic indicators.

## Latent Mathematical Taxa

Inasmuch as manifest clinical taxa stem from the observations and inferences of diagnosticians, they comprise, in circular fashion, the very qualities that clinicians are likely to see and deduce. Classes so constructed will not only direct future clinicians to focus on and mirror these same taxa in their patients, but they may lead future nosologists away from potentially more useful constructs with which to fathom less obvious patterns of attribute covariation. As noted earlier, it is toward the end of penetrating beneath the sensory domain to more latent commonalities that taxonomists have turned to either numerical methods or to theoretical principles. It is the former that will be examined in this section.

Andreasen and Grove (1982) summarized the advantages of what they variously term empirical or numerical methods of computing patient similarities as follows:

First, the empirical method gives an opportunity for the observed characteristics of the subjects to determine the classification and perhaps to lead to a classification that the clinician was unable to perceive using clinical judgment alone. Second, the empirical method allows a great deal of information on the subjects to enter into the genesis of the classifications; human beings can keep in mind only a relatively small number of details concerning a case at any given time, but the empirical approach can process very large sets of measurements. Third, empirical or numerical approaches can combine cases in more subtle ways than can clinicians; combinations of features too complex to grasp intuitively may yield better classifications than simple combinations. (p. 45)

There has been a rapid proliferation of new and powerful mathematical techniques for both analyzing and synthesizing vast bodies of clinical data. This expansion has been accelerated by the ready availability of inexpensive computer hardware and software programs. Unfortunately, such mushrooming has progressed more rapidly than its fruits can be digested. As a consequence, to quote Kendell (1975), who commented early in this technological development, "most clinicians . . . have tended to oscillate uneasily between two equally unsatisfactory postures of ignoring investigations based on these techniques, or accepting their confident conclusions at face value" (p. 106).

There are numerous purposes to which this growing and diverse body of quantitative methods can be put, of which only a small number are relevant to the goal of aiding in taxonomic construction. Other statistical techniques relate to the validation of existent nosologies (e.g., discriminant analyses) rather than to their creation. Among those used to facilitate taxonomic development, some focus on clinical attributes as their basic units, whereas patients themselves are the point of attention of others. For example, factor analysis condenses sets of clinical attributes and organizes them into syndromic taxa. Cluster analysis, by contrast, is most suitable for sorting the characteristics of patients on the basis of

their similarities into personological taxa. A brief review of the former technique is appropriate in this chapter; other mathematical procedures that may usefully be used in taxonomic construction and evaluation, such as latent class, log-linear, and discriminant analysis, as well as multivariate analysis of variance, may be examined in a number of relevant texts.

Factorial techniques represent relationships among attributes (signs, symptoms) and have their primary value in identifying core dimensions. Although subsequent research suggests the contrary, early reviewers concluded that their statistical properties render them unsuitable to the task of uncovering personal similarities or to optimally classify individuals (Torgerson, 1968; Zubin, 1968).

The notion that the presence of covarying symptoms might signify underlying disease entities can be traced to the 17th-century writings of Thomas Syndenham. In connecting this notion to factor analytic techniques, Blashfield (1984) commented:

Sydenham, who promoted the concept of syndrome . . . argued that a careful observer of patients could note that certain sets of symptoms tended to co-occur. If these co-occurring sets of symptoms were seen repeatedly across a number of patients, this observance would suggest that the syndrome may represent more than a chance collection of symptoms, instead, the consistent appearance of a syndrome would suggest a disease with a common etiology and a common treatment. Factor analysis . . . can be thought of as a statistical tool used to isolate syndromes of co-occurring symptoms. . . . In addition, factor analysis provides a statistical estimate of the "underlying factor" that explains the association among a collection of related symptoms. (pp. 169–170)

The designation *factor analysis* is a generic term encompassing a variety of numerical procedures that serve to achieve different goals, the details of which are not relevant to this chapter. In essence, it seeks to reveal the underlying structure of its attributes by identifying factors that account for the covariation of the attributes. Toward this end, linear combinations of the attributes are sequentially chosen to cumulate as much variance as possible. Factors that are derived in this manner are often "rotated" after their initial mathematical solution to increase their psychological meaning.

Despite the ostensively productive lines of investigation that factorial techniques have demonstrated (a book such as this is clear evidence for its utility), several problems continue to be raised concerning its applicability as an instrument of classification construction. Thus, early in the application of factorial techniques, Kendell (1975) reported that skepticism in the field remains high:

largely because of the variety of different factor solutions that can be obtained from a single set of data and the lack of any satisfactory objective criterion for preferring one of these to the others. The number of factors obtained and their loadings are often affected considerably by relatively small changes in the size or composition of the subject sample, or in the range of test employed. (p. 108)

Furthermore, Sprock and Blashfield (1984) concluded that:

deciding when to stop the process of selecting the number of factors, rotating the solutions, and interpreting the factors are all highly subjective and at the discretion of the user. Therefore, many distrust the results. (p. 108)

In addition to these methodological caveats, a number of conceptual forewarnings must be kept in mind regarding the structural implications of a factorial approach. As is known among those involved in the development of psychometric instruments (Loevinger, 1957; Millon, 1977, 1986), a reasonable degree of "fidelity" should exist between the pattern of relationships among the scales of a test and its structural model of psychopathology. For the same reasons, taxa should conform in their pattern of relationships to their taxonomy's structural conception (Smith & Medin,

1981). For example, assume that a model of psychopathology posits its taxa as both monothetic and independent, that is, each containing exclusive and uncorrelated attributes. If that is how psychopathology has been conceived, then a factorial structure would fit it handsomely: The attributes comprising each taxa would not only intercorrelate positively, but they correlate negatively with all of the other taxa comprising the nosology. Factors would exhibit fidelity to such a psychopathological model.

However, and despite the popularity of factor analysis with many a distinguished psychometrician, the psychological composition of factorial structures is far from universally accepted. Not only do few psychopathological entities give evidence of factorial "purity" or attribute independence, but factorial solutions tend to be antithetical to the predominant polythetic structure and overlapping relationships that exist among clinical conditions. Neither personological nor syndromic taxa consist of entirely homogeneous and discrete clinical attributes. Rather, taxa are composed of diffuse and complex characteristics that share many attributes in common, factorially derived or otherwise.

Nevertheless, the existence of this book demonstrates the growing literature and impressive findings that support one such model, the FFM (Costa & McCrae, 1990; Digman, 1990; Goldberg, 1990; McCrae & Costa, 1985; Norman, 1963). Costa and McCrae have provided strong evidence for the power of the "Big Five" as a latent mathematical framework for unraveling diverse and more complex structures of numerous other personality instruments. In their recent writings they have extended the applicability of these five factors as descriptive underpinnings for the DSM-III personality disorders. It is this view that comprises both the intent and substance of the present book. This is not the chapter or setting for such purposes, but it should be noted in passing that other equally astute and productive investigators have registered a measure of dissent from both the sufficiency of scope of the FFM or its adequacy as a latent explicator of the personality disorders (Grove & Tellegen, 1991; Livesley, 1991; Tellegen & Waller, 1987; Waller & Ben-Porath, 1987). Beyond these skeptics of the fruitfulness of the FFM are those who question the wisdom of using latent mathematical methods at all. In his usual perspicacious manner, Kendell's comment of more than a decade ago (1975), upon reviewing the preceding 20-year period, may be judged by some as no less apt today as then:

Looking back on the various studies published in the last twenty years it is clear that many investigators, clinicians and statisticians, have had a naive, almost Baconian, attitude to the statistical techniques they were employing, putting in all data at their disposal on the assumption that the computer would sort out the relevant from the irrelevant and expose the underlying principles and regularities, and assuming all that was required of them was to collect the data assiduously beforehand. Moreover, any statistician worth his salt is likely to be able, by judicious choice of patients and items, and of factoring or clustering procedures, to produce more or less what he wants to. (p. 118)

To summarize, factorial methods of taxonomic construction may rest on a model that does not automatically accord with the combinations and covariations that characterize the intrinsic structure of pathology. Despite these caveats, factor analytic methods may yet prove helpful as a tool to identify and clarify certain of the more central attributes that comprise these complex taxa. The task of combining factor attributes into patterns and configurations that correspond to the personality disorders is one that transcends the powers of mathematical technique. To achieve this task one must still depend on clinical "artistry" or the deductive powers of a theory-based model, which is another approach to uncovering latent principles for constructing a nosology, and one that is addressed in the following section.

## Latent Theoretical Approaches

The biases of statisticians in shaping data are likely to be implicit or arcane, whereas those of taxonomic theorists are explicit and straightforward. For the most part, the concepts and orientations of theorists are stated as plainly as their subject permits, although the propositions and deductions they derive therefrom rarely are as empirically clear as one might wish.

Nevertheless, distinguished philosophers such as Hempel (1965) and Quine (1977) considered that mature sciences must progress from an observationally based stage to one that is characterized by abstract concepts, or theoretical systemizations. It is the judgment of these philosophers that classification alone does not make a true scientific taxonomy and that overt similarity among attributes does not necessarily comprise a scientific category (Smith & Medin, 1981). The card catalog of the library or an accountant's ledger sheet, for example, are well-organized classifications but can hardly be viewed as a taxonomy or a science.

The characteristic that distinguishes *latent theoretical* taxonomy from latent mathematical taxonomy is its success in grouping its elements according to logically consonant explanatory propositions. These propositions are formed when certain attributes that have been isolated or categorized have been shown or have been hypothesized to be dynamically or causally related to other attributes or categories. The latent taxa comprising a theoretical nosology are not, therefore, mere collections of overtly similar factors or categories but are linked or unified into a pattern of known or presumed relationships among them. This theoretically grounded configuration of relationships would be the foundation and essence of a heuristic taxonomy.

Certain benefits can be derived from systematizing data in a theoretical fashion that are not readily available either from clinical or numerical procedures (Wright & Murphy, 1984). Given the countless ways of observing and analyzing a set of data, a system of explanatory propositions becomes a useful guide to clinicians as they sort through and seek to comprehend the stream of amorphous signs and chaotic symptoms they normally encounter. Rather than shifting from one aspect of behavior, thought, or emotion to another, according to momentary and uncertain impressions of importance, theoretically guided clinicians may be led to pursue in a logical and perhaps more penetrating manner only those aspects that are likely to be related and to experience thereby a sense of meaningful order (Dougherty, 1978). In addition to furnishing this guidance, a theoretically anchored taxonomy provides diagnosticians with a consistent set of hypotheses concerning clinical relationships that they may not have observed before. It enlarges the sensitivity and scope of knowledge of observers by alerting them to previously unnoticed relationships among attributes and then guides these new observations into a theoretically coherent body of knowledge.

Before concluding this chapter, I ask: What is it that distinguishes a theoretically grounded taxonomy from one that provides a mere explanatory summary of known observations and inferences?

Simply stated, the answer lies in its power to generate observations and relationships other than those used to construct it. This generative power is what Hempel (1965) termed the "systematic import" of a scientific classification. In contrasting what are familiarly known as "natural" (theoretically guided, deductively based) and "artificial" (conceptually barren, similarity-based) classifications, Hempel wrote (1965):

Distinctions between "natural" and "artificial" classifications may well be explicated as referring to the difference between classifications that are scientifically fruitful and those that are not; in a classification of the former kind, those characteristics of the elements that serve as criteria of membership in a given class are associated, universally or with high probability, with

more or less extensive clusters of other characteristics. (p. 116)

Classification of this sort should be viewed as somehow having objective existence in nature, as carving nature at the "joints" in contradistinction of "artificial" classifications, in which the defining characteristics have few explanatory or predictive connections with other traits. In the course of scientific development, classifications defined by reference to manifest, observable characteristics will tend to give way to systems based on theoretical concepts. (p. 148)

DSM-III and DSM-III-R were developed intentionally and explicitly to be atheoretical. This stance was taken not from an antipathy to theory per se but rather to maximize acceptance of the document by clinicians of diverse viewpoints. Extolling the tenets in the DSM of one or another theoretical school would, it was believed, alienate those holding dissimilar perspectives and thereby disincline them from adopting and using the manual.

It is unfortunate that the number of theories that have been advanced to "explain" personality and psychopathology is directly proportional to the squabbling found in the literature. Paroxysms of "scientific virtue" and pieties of "methodological purity" rarely are exclaimed by theorists themselves but are by their less creative disciples. As I have previously commented (Millon, 1969):

Theories arise typically from the perceptive observation and imaginative speculation of creative scientists. This innovator is usually quite aware of the limits and deficiencies of his "invention" and is disposed in the early stages of his speculation to modify it as he develops new observations and insights. Unfortunately, after its utility has been proven in a modest and limited way, the theory frequently acquires a specious stature. Having clarified certain ambiguities and survived initial criticisms, it begins to accumulate a coterie of disciples. These less creative thinkers tend to accept the theory wholeheartedly and espouse its superior explanatory powers and terminology throughout the scientific market place. They hold to its propositions tenaciously and defend it blindly and unequivocally against opposition. In time it becomes a rigid and sacred dogma and, as a result, authority replaces the test of utility and empirical validity. Intelligent men become religious disciples; their theory is a doctrine of "truth," not a guide to the unknown. (p. 41)

Ostensibly toward the end of pragmatic sobriety, those of an antitheory bias have sought to persuade the profession of the failings of premature formalization, warning that one cannot arrive at the future yearned for by lifting the science of psychology by its own bootstraps. To these individuals, there is no way to traverse the road other sciences have traveled without paying the dues of an arduous program of empirical research. Formalized axiomatics, they say, must await the accumulation of "hard" evidence that is simply not yet in. Shortcutting the route with ill-timed theoretical systematics, such as a latent taxonomy, will lead the profession down primrose paths, preoccupying its attentions as it winds fruitlessly through endless detours, each of which could be averted by holding fast to an empirical philosophy or a clinical methodology.

No one argues against the view that theories that float, so to speak, on their own, unconcerned with the empirical domain or clinical knowledge, should be seen as the fatuous achievements they are, and the travesty that these theories may make of the virtues of a truly coherent nosological system should not be overlooked. Formal theory should not be "pushed" far beyond the data, and its derivations should be linked at all points to established clinical observations. Given the vast scope of personalities as well as the extent of knowledge still to be gathered, nosological theories are best kept limited today in both their focus and their specificity. As I have stated previously (Millon, 1987), structurally weak theories make it impossible to derive systematic and logical nosologies; this results in conflicting derivations and circular reasoning. Most nosological theories of psychopathology have generated brilliant deductions and insights, but few of these ideas can be attributed to

their structure, the precision of their concepts, or their formal procedures for hypothesis derivation.

Nevertheless, impressive theoretical concepts with taxonomic implications continue to be generated by contemporary thinkers in the field of personality disorders; a forthcoming book composed of chapters authored by a group of such theorists attests to the maturity of this model of taxonomic construction (Clarkin, in press).

In conclusion, and despite the shortcomings of historical concepts of personality pathology, latent mathematics models and latent theories may "facilitate a deeper seeing, a more penetrating vision that goes beyond superficial appearances to the order underlying them" (Bowers, 1977).

## REFERENCES

Akiskal, H.S., Hirschfeld, R., & Yerevanian, B. (1983). The relationship of personality to affective disorders. *Archives of General Psychiatry, 40,* 801–810.

Akiskal, H. S., Khani, M. K., & Scott-Strauss, A. (1979). Cyclothymic temperamental disorders. *Psychiatric Clinics of North America, 2,* 527, 554.

Akiskal, H. S., Rosenthal, T. L., Paykal, R. F., Lemmi, H., Rosenthal, R. H., & Scott-Strauss, A. (1980). Characterological depressions: Clinical and sleep EEG findings separating "subaffective dysthymias" from "character-spectrum disorders." *Archives of General Psychiatry, 37,* 777–783.

American Psychiatric Association. (1980). *Diagnostic and statistical manual of mental disorders* (3rd ed.). Washington, DC: Author.

American Psychiatric Association. (1987). *Diagnostic and statistical manual of mental disorders* (3rd ed., rev.). Washington, DC: Author.

American Psychiatric Association. (in press). *Diagnostic and statistical manual of mental disorders* (4th ed.). Washington, DC: Author.

Andreasen, N., & Grove, W. (1982). The classification of depression: A comparison of traditional and mathematically derived approaches. *American Journal of Psychiatry, 139,* 45–52.

Auchincloss, E. L., & Michels, R. (1983). Psycho-analytic theory of character. In J. P. Frosch (Ed.), *Current perspectives in personality disorders* (pp. 3–19). Washington, DC: American Psychiatric Press.

Bandura, A. (1982). The psychology of chance encounters and life paths. *American Psychologist, 37,* 747–755.

Beck, A. T., & Freeman, A. (1990). *Cognitive therapy of personality disorders.* New York: Guilford Press.

Becker, J. (1977). *Affective disorders.* New York: General Leaming Press.

Blashfield, R. K. (1984). *The classification of psychopathology.* New York: Plenum.

Bowers, K. S. (1977). There's more to Iago than meets the eye. In D. Magnusson & N. S. Endler (Eds.), *Personality at the crossroads* (pp. 112–131). Hillsdale, NJ: Erlbaum.

Cantor, N., Smith, E. E., French, R. D., & Mezzich, J. (1980). Psychiatric diagnosis as prototype categorization. *Journal of Abnormal Psychology, 89,* 181–193.

Cattell, R. B. (1965). *The scientific analysis of personality.* Chicago: Aldine.

Cattell, R. B. (1970). The integration of functional and psychometric requirements in a quantitative and computerized diagnostic system. In A. R. Mahrer (Ed.), *New approaches to personality classification* (pp. 9–52). New York: Columbia University Press.

Chamey, D. S., Nelson, J. C., & Quinlan, D. M. (1981). Personality traits and disorder in depression, *American Journal of Psychiatry, 138,* 1601–1604.

Clarkin, J. (in press). *Major personality disorder theorists.* New York: Guilford.

Costa, P. T., Jr., & McCrae, R. R. (1990). Personality disorders and the five-factor model of personality. *Journal of Personality Disorders, 4,* 362–371.

Digman, J. M. (1990). Personality structure: Emergence of the five-factor model. *Annual Review of Psychology, 41,* 417–440.

Docherty, J. P., Feister, S. J., & Shea, T. (1986). Syndrome diagnosis and personality disorder. In A. Frances & R. E. Hale (Eds.), *American Psychiatric Association Annual Conceptual Distinctions and Classification Issues Review* (Vol. 5, pp. 315–355). Washington, DC: American Psychiatric Association.

Dougherty, J. W. D. (1978). Salience and relativity in Classification. *American Ethnologist, 5,* 66–80.

Eysenck, H. J. (1960). *The structure of human personality.* London: Routledge & Kegan Paul.

Feinstein, A. R. (1977). A critical overview of diagnosis in psychiatry. In V. M. Rakoff, H. C. Stancer, & H. B. Kedward (Eds.), *Psychiatric diagnosis* (pp. 189–206). New York: Brunner/Mazel.

Frances, A., & Widiger, T. (1986). The classification of personality disorders: An overview of problems and solutions. In A. Frances & R. E. Hale (Eds.), *American Psychiatry on Annual Review* (Vol. 5, pp. 240–257). Washington, DC: American Psychiatric Association.

Goldberg, L. R. (1990). An alternative "definition of personality": The B factor structure. *Journal of Personality and Social Psychology, 59,* 1216–1229.

Grove, W. M., & Tellegen, A. (1991). Problems in the classification of personality disorders. *Journal of Personality Disorders, 5,* 31–41.

Gunderson, J. G., Kolb, J. E., & Austin, V. (1981). The diagnostic interview for borderline patients. *American Journal of Psychiatry, 138,* 896–903.

Gunderson, J. G., Links, P. S., & Reich, J. H. (1991). Competing models of personality disorders. *Journal of Personality Disorders, 5,* 60–68.

Hathaway, S. R., & McKinley, J. C. (1967). *Minnesota Multiphasic Personality Inventory Manual.* New York: Psychological Corporation.

Hempel, C. G. (1961). Introduction to problems of taxonomy. In J. Zubin (Ed.), *Field studies in the mental disorders* (pp. 3–22). New York: Grune & Stratton.

Hempel, C. G. (1965). *Aspects of scientific explanation.* New York: Free Press.

Kaplan, A. (1964). The conduct of inquiry. San Francisco: Chandler.

Kendell, R. E. (1975). *The role of diagnosis in psychiatry.* Oxford, UK: Blackwell Scientific.

Klerman, G. L. (1973). The relationship between personality and clinical depressions: Overcoming the obstacles to verifying psychodynamic theories. *International Journal of Psychiatry, 11,* 227–233.

Kline, P., & Barrett, P. (1983). The factors in personality disorders: Ideal types, prototypes, or dimensions? *Journal of Personality Disorders, 5,* 52–59.

Livesley, W. J. (1986a). Theoretical and empirical issues in the selection of criteria to diagnose personality disorders. *Journal of Personality Disorders, 1,* 88–94,

Livesley, W. J. (1986b). Trait and behavior prototypes of personality disorder. *American Journal of Psychiatry, 43,* 1018–1022.

Livesley, W. J. (1991). Classifying personality disorders: Ideal types, prototypes or dimensions. *Journal of Personality Disorders, 5,* 52–69.

Loevinger, J. (1957). Objective tests as measurements of psychological theory. *Psychological Reports, 3,* 635–694.

McCrae, R. R., & Costa, P. T., Jr. (1985). Updating Norman's "adequate taxonomy": Intelligence and personality dimensions in natural language and in questionnaires. *Journal of Personality and Social Psychology, 49,* 710–721.

McCranie, E. J. (1971). Depression, anxiety and hostility. *Psychiatric Quarterly, 45,* 117–133.

Medin, D. L., Altom, M. W., Edelson, S. M., & Freko, D. (1982). Correlated symptoms and simulated medical classification. *Journal of Experimental Psychology: Learning and Memory and Cognition, 8,* 37–50.

Meehl, P. (1978). Theoretical risks and tabular asterisks: Sir Karl, Sir Ronald, and the slow program of soft psychology. *Journal of Consulting and Clinical Psychology, 46,* 806–834.

Menninger, K. (1963). *The vital balance.* New York: Viking.

Millon, T. (1969). *Modern psychopathology: A biosocial approach to maladaptive learning and functioning.* Philadelphia: W. B. Saunders.

Millon, T. (1977). *Millon Clinical Multiaxial Inventory manual.* Minneapolis, MN: National Computer Systems.

Millon, T. (1981). *Disorders of personality: DSM-III: Axis II.* New York: John Wiley & Sons.

Millon, T. (1984). On the renaissance of personality assessment and personality theory. *Journal of Personality Assessment, 48,* 450–466.

Millon, T. (1986). Personality prototypes and their diagnostic criteria. In T. Millon & G. L. Klerman (Eds.), *Contemporary directions in psychopathology: Towards the DSM-IV* (pp. 671–712). New York: Guilford.

Millon, T. (1987). On the nature of taxonomy in psychopathology. In C. Last & M. Hersen (Eds.), *Issues in diagnostic research* (pp. 3–83). New York: Plenum.

Millon, T. (1990). *Toward a new personology: An evolutionary model.* New York: John Wiley & Sons.

Millon, T. (1991a). Classification in psychopathology: Rationale, alternatives, standards. *Journal of Abnormal Psychology, 100,* 245–261.

Millon, T. (1991b). Normality: What can we learn from evolutionary theory. In D. Offer & M. Sabshin (Eds.), *The diversity of normal behavior* (pp. 356–404). New York: Basic Books.

Mischel, W. (1973). On the empirical dilemmas of psychodynamic approaches: Issues and alternatives. *Journal of Abnormal Psychology, 82,* 335–344.

Mischel, W. (1979). On the interface of cognition and personality. *American Psychologist, 34,* 740–754.

Norman, W. T. (1963). Toward an adequate taxonomy of personality attributes: Replicated factor structure in peer nomination personality attributes. *Journal of Abnormal and Social Psychology, 66,* 574–583.

Offer, D., & Sabshin, M. (1974). Normality: Theoretical and clinical concepts of mental health (rev. ed.). New York: Basic Books.

Pap, A. (1953). Reduction-sentences and open concepts. *Methods, 5,* 3–30.

Paykel, E. S., Klerman, G. L., & Prusoff, B. A. (1976). Personality and symptom pattern in depression. *British Journal of Psychiatry, 129,* 327–334.

Paykel, E. S., Myers, J. K., & Dienelt, M. N. (1970). Life events and depression. *Archives of General Psychiatry, 221,* 753–760.

Quine, W. V. O. (1977). Natural kinds. In S. P. Schwartz (Ed.), *Naming, necessity and natural groups* (pp. 22–39). Ithaca, NY: Cornell University Press.

Skinner, H. (1986). Construct validation approach to psychiatric classification. In

T. Millon & G. L. Klerman (Eds.), *Contemporary directions in psychopathology: Towards the DSM-IV*. New York: Guilford.

Smith, E. E., & Medin, D. L. (1981). *Categories and concepts*. Cambridge, MA: Harvard University Press.

Sprock, L., & Blashfield, R. K. (1984). Classification and nosology. In M. Hersen, A. Kazdin, & A. Bellack (Eds.), *The clinical psychology handbook*. Elmsford, NY: Pergamon Press.

Tellegen, A., & Waller, N. G. (1987, August). *Reexamining basic dimension natural language trait descriptions*. Paper presented at the 95th annual meeting of the American Psychological Association, New York.

Torgerson, W. T. (1968). Multidimensional representation of similarity structures. In M. M. Katz, J. O. Cole, & W. E. Barton (Eds.), *Classification in psychiatry and psychopathology*, (pp. 212–220). Washington, DC: Public Health Service Publications.

Tversky, A. (1977). Features of similarity. *Psychological Review, 84*, 327–352.

Waller, N. G., & Ben-Porath, Y. S. (1987). Is it time for clinical psychology to embrace the five-factor model of personality? *American Psychologist, 42*, 887–889,

Williams, J. B. W. (1985a). The multiaxial system of the DSM-III: Where did it come from and where should it go? Its origins and critiques. *Archives of General Psychiatry, 42*, 175–180.

Williams, J. B. W. (1985b). The multiaxial system of the DSM-III: Where did it come from and where should it go? Empirical studies, innovations, and recommendations. *Archives of General Psychiatry, 42*, 181–186.

World Health Organization. (1991). International classification of diseases (Vols. 1–3; 9th ed. rev.). Geneva, Switzerland: Author.

Wright, J. C., & Murphy, G. L. (1984). The utility of theories in intuitive statistics: The robustness of theory-based judgments. *Journal of Experimental Psychology: General, 113*, 301–322.

Zilboorg, G., & Henry, G. W. (1941). *A history of medical psychology*. New York: Norton.

Zubin, J. (1968). Biometric assessment of mental patients. In M. M. Katz, J. O. Cole, & W. E. Barton (Eds.), *Classification of psychiatry and psychopathology* (pp. 353–357). Washington, DC: Public Health Service Publications.

# PART II

# *THEORY*

# Contemporary Theoretical Models

Nature does not meet our need for a tidy and well-ordered universe. The complexity and intricacy of the natural world make it difficult not only to establish clear-cut relationships among phenomena but to find simple ways in which these phenomena can be classified or grouped. In our desire to discover the essential order of nature we are forced to select only a few of the infinite number of elements which could be chosen; in this selection we narrow our choice only to those aspects of nature which we believe best enable us to answer the questions we pose. The elements we have chosen may be labeled, transformed and reassembled in a variety of ways. But we must keep in mind that these labels and transformations are not "realities." The definitions, concepts and theories scientists create are only optional tools to guide their observation and interpretation of the natural world; it is necessary to recognize, therefore, that different concepts and theories may coexist as alternative approaches to the same basic problem. . . .

Let us look at the question: What is psychopathology? Clearly, mental disorders are expressed in a variety of ways; it is a complex *phenomenon* which can be approached at different levels and can be viewed from many angles. On a behavioral level, for example, disorders could be conceived as a complicated pattern of responses to environmental stress. Phenomenologically, they could be seen as expressions of personal discomfort and anguish. Approached from a physiological viewpoint, they could he interpreted as sequences of complex neural and chemical activity. And intrapsychically, they could be organized into unconscious processes that defend against anxiety and conflict.

Given these diverse possibilities, we can readily understand why psychopathology may be approached and defined in terms of any of several levels we may wish to focus upon, and any of a variety of functions or processes we may wish to explain. Beyond this, each level or angle of approach lends itself to a number of specific theories and concepts, the usefulness of which must be gauged by their ability to solve the particular problems and purposes for which they were created. That the subject matter of psychopathology is inherently diverse and complex is precisely the reason why we must not narrow our choice of approach to one level or one theory. Each has a legitimate and potentially fruitful contribution to make to our study.

In this present chapter, we will discuss first the goals, structure and orientation of scientific systems in general, and with this background in mind, analyze the different theoretical approaches to psychopathology which are currently in use.

## GOALS OF SCIENTIFIC SYSTEMS

Man acquired reliable and useful knowledge about his environment long before the advent of modern scientific thought. Information, skill and instrumentation were achieved without "science" and its methods of symbolic abstraction, research and analysis. If useful knowledge could be acquired by intelligent observation and common sense alone, what special values are derived by applying the complicated and rigorous procedures of the scientific method? Is rigor, clarity, precision and experimentation more than a compulsive and picayunish concern for details, more than the pursuit for the honorific title of "science"? Are the labors of coordinating knowledge and exploring unknown factors in a systematic fashion worth the time and effort involved? There is little question in our "age of science" that the answer would be yes! But why? What are the distinguishing virtues of scientific systems? What sets them apart from the everyday common sense methods of acquiring knowledge? It is these questions to which we must turn next.

Since the number of ways we can observe, describe and organize the natural world is infinite, the terms and concepts we create to represent these activities are often confusing and obscure. For example, different words are used to describe the same behavior, and the same word is used for different behaviors. Some terms are narrow in focus, others are broad and many are difficult to define. Because of the variety of events that can be considered and the lack of precision in language, useful information gets scattered in hodgepodge fashion across the whole landscape of a scientific topic, and communication gets bogged down in terminological obscurities and semantic controversies.

One of the goals of scientific systems is to avoid this morass of confusion. Not all phenomena related to a subject are attended to at once. Certain elements are selected from the vast range of possibilities because they seem relevant to the solution of specific and important problems. To create a degree of consistency among scientists interested in a problem these elements are grouped or classified according to their similarities and differences and given specific labels which describe or define them. This process of classification is indispensable for systematizing observation and knowledge. But it is only a first step.

Classification of knowledge alone does not make a scientific system. The card catalog of a library or an accountant's ledger sheets are well organized classifications but hardly to be viewed as a system of science. The characteristic which distinguishes a scientific classification system from others is its attempt to group elements according to established or hypothesized explanatory propositions. These propositions are formed when certain properties which have been isolated and classified have been shown or have been hypothesized to be related to other classified properties or groupings. The groupings of a scientific system, therefore, are not mere collections of miscellaneous or random information, but a linked or unified pattern of known or presumed relationships. This pattern of relationships is the foundation of a scientific system.

Certain benefits derive from systematizing knowledge in this fashion. Given the countless ways of observing and analyzing a set of complex events, a system of explanatory propositions becomes a useful guide to the observer. Rather than shifting from one aspect of behavior to another, according to momentary impressions of importance, he is led to pursue in a logical and consistent manner only those aspects which are likely to be related.

In addition, a scientific system enables the perceptive scientist to generate hypotheses about relationships that have not been observed before. It enlarges the scope of knowledge by alerting the observer to possible new relationships among phenomena, and then ties these new observations into a coherent body of knowledge. Thus, from a small number of basic explanatory propositions, a scientific system develops broad applicability and subsumes a wide range of phenomena.

This generality or comprehensiveness leads to another important advantage. Because of the scope of the system, different observers are given an opportunity to check or verify the validity of its explanatory propositions. Thus, hasty generalizations, erroneous speculations and personal biases are readily exposed by systematic scrutiny. This exposure assures that propositions are supported *by shared* evidence and that the range of their validity is clearly delimited.

Bringing these points together then, we can see that a scientific system attempts to coordinate and seek relationships among a general but clearly delimited class of phenomena. The means by which a scientific system accomplishes these ends will be our next topic of discussion.

# STRUCTURE AND ORIENTATION OF SCIENTIFIC THEORIES

Scientific endeavor consists of two types of activities. The *first* is the informal and systematic observation of empirical events and objects. The *second* involves the creation of abstract linguistic or mathematical symbols invented by the theorist to represent relationships among observable events, or relationships which he believes exist but have not been observed. This second, or symbolic and theoretical activity of science, will be our focus in this chapter.

As noted earlier, scientific systems consist of explanatory propositions which create order or render intelligible otherwise unrelated phenomena. There are two kinds of propositions in a scientific system, empirical laws and theories. An *empirical law* is a statement representing a universally established relationship observed among a group of empirical phenomena. A *theory,* in contrast, is composed of invented abstractions in the form of models, concepts, rules and hypotheses which function as provisional exploratory tools to aid the scientist in his search for empirical laws. Theories are subject to frequent change; empirical laws are durable.

Before we can discuss intelligently current theories of psychopathology we must examine the structural form into which theories are cast.

## Formal Structure of Theories

Four major components of theory may be distinguished for our purposes: (1) an abstract *model* which serves as an analog or a visualizable pattern representing the overall structure of the theory; (2) a *conceptual terminology* by which various classes of phenomena relevant to the theory are symbolized or labeled; (3) a set of *correspondence rules* which coordinate relationships among the theoretical terms in accordance with the model; and (4) *hypotheses* which specify the manner in which these relationships may be tested in the empirical world.

## Models

A model is an analogy which exploits certain aspects of a familiar or easily visualized system to guide the understanding of a less familiar or difficult subject. For example, theorists have utilized an electronic computer model to describe the processes and structure of psychopathology. Thus, human beings are likened to computers in that both receive complex information from the environment, integrate this information through devious circuits with prior information and emit relatively uncomplicated responses. More commonly, psychopathology has been organized in accordance with a biological disease model. In this format, psychopathology is conceived as if it stemmed from the intrusion of a foreign agent upon normal biological functioning; as in most physical ailments, symptoms are considered to be the organism's reaction to the intrusion.

Few theorists expect the models they adopt to represent accurately all of the features of psychopathology. Rather, the model is used merely as a way to visualize psychopathology "as if it worked like this."

Models pose a number of risks to the theorist. Certain features of a model which may have proved useful in its original setting are often assumed mistakenly to be appropriate elsewhere. Should such a model be adopted, the theorist will waste his time constructing erroneous hypotheses and pursuing unprofitable research. The adoption of the disease model in psychiatry, for example, has been viewed by many psychologists to have led to years of fruitless biochemical research. Similarly, the intrapsychic conflict model underlying psychoanalytic theory has been seen to have delayed the development of more effective psychotherapies. Unfortunately, there are no simple ways to tell beforehand whether a given model will prove to be fruitful or misguided. What should be kept clear in one's thinking is that the model adopted for a theory should not be confused with the theory itself.

## Conceptual Terminology

The elements of a theory are represented by a set of concepts, that is, a language by which members of a scientific group communicate about a subject. Concepts may be seen as serving two functions. *First,* they possess a value in that they facilitate the *manipulation of theoretical ideas.* Concepts are systematically linked to other concepts; it is through the interplay of these concepts that meaningful ideas are formulated and deductive statements are made in the form of propositions and hypotheses. *Second,* most concepts possess an *empirical significance,* that is, they are linked in some explicit way to the observable world; although some concepts may represent processes or events which are not observable, they may be defined or anchored to observables. It is this translatability into the empirical domain that allows the theoretician to test his propositions in the world of "reality."

Ideally, all concepts of a scientific theory should be empirically anchored, that is, correspond to properties in the observable world. This would minimize confusion regarding the objects and events to which a term applies. Moreover, concepts should be more precise than words used in ordinary language; although everyday conversational language has relevance to significant events in the real world, it gives rise to ambiguity and confusion because of the varied uses to which conventional words are often put. Scientific concepts should be defined "precisely" in order to assure that their meaning is clear and specific.

Empirical precision, in the fullest sense of the term, can be achieved only if every concept in a theory is defined by a single observable phenomenon, that is, a different concept or label would be used for every difference that can be observed in the empirical world. This ideal simply is not feasible for reasons which will become apparent shortly. Psychological concepts do differ, however, in the degree to which they satisfy this criterion. A discussion of three types of concepts—operational definitions, intervening variables and hypothetical constructs—will be of value in noting these distinctions and their consequences.

### Operational Definitions

Certain concepts are defined literally by observable events and possess no meaning other than these events; they have been termed *operational definitions.* To paraphrase Bridgman (1927), the founder of "operationism," an operational definition is a concept that is defined by the procedure employed to measure the particular empirical event it represents; thus, the meaning of a concept is synonymous with how man measures it, not with what he says about it. For example, the concept "learning" would involve nothing more than the set of operations by which it is measured. There would be a different concept for learning when it is measured by the number of errors a child makes on a task than when measured by the speed with which he completes the same task. The advantage of operational definitions is obvious; concepts are unambiguous, and propositions utilizing these concepts are translatable directly into the empirical phenomena they represent.

Useful as operational definitions may be, they present several problems. Theoretical concepts should be generalizable, that is, they should enable the theorist to include a variety of observations with his concept. Operational definitions are restrictive; they preclude predictions to new situations that are even slightly different from the original situation.

Certainly, one of the primary goals of a theory is to integrate diverse observations with a minimum number of concepts; a strict operational approach would flood us with an infinite number of concepts and clutter thinking with irrelevant distinctions. The major value of operational definitions is cautionary; it alerts the theorist to the importance of conceptual precision and empirical relevance.

### Intervening Variables

Certain concepts cannot be measured by currently available techniques (e.g., the earth's core and biochemical processes in memory). Also, internal or organismic processes which connect observable phenomena may not themselves be observable and must be inferred or invented until such time as they can be observed. These unobservables, often referred to as mediating structures or processes, are necessary in all phases of theory construction. Two types of concepts, intervening variables and hypothetical constructs, deal with these mediating factors; their similarities and differences are worthy of note.

*An intervening variable* is a concept which represents a guess regarding an unobserved mediating process which may account for an observed event. Although they signify an unknown mediating process, intervening variables are defined by and entirely reducible to empirical events. For example, the concept "habit," formulated as an intervening variable, may be defined empirically by the number of trials an individual was given to learn a task, or by the demonstrated speed with which he performs it. Although the term "habit" implies a residue of experience within the individual, which cannot be observed, its existence is inferred from a *variety of observables,* e.g., the number of opportunities to learn a task or the skill of performance.

There is a similarity between intervening variables and operational definitions in that both are defined by or anchored to empirical phenomena. But they differ in two important respects. First, a *variety* of empirical phenomena may be used to define an intervening variable; in this respect it is less precise than an operational definition. Second, although both intervening variables and operational definitions are anchored to observables, intervening variables always *imply* the existence of a mediating process whereas operational concepts need not.

### Hypothetical Constructs

The difference between an intervening variable and a hypothetical construct is largely a matter of degree. *Hypothetical constructs* are admittedly speculative concepts which are formulated without explicit reference to observable phenomena. Their freedom from specific empirical referents distinguishes them from intervening variables. Because they are not defined or anchored to observable events, their use in theory often is questioned. Clarity gets muddled and deductions often are tautological when psychological data are "explained" in terms of a series of hypothetical constructs. For example, statements such as "the mechanisms of the ego are blocked in the anal-character when libidinous energies are dammed up by super-ego introjections," are, at best, puzzling. Postulating connections between one set of hypothetical constructs and another leads to facile but often meaningless "explanations." Such use results in imprecise formulations which are difficult to decipher because we cannot specify observables by which they can be anchored or evaluated.

Vagueness and surplus-meaning are both the weakness and strength of the hypothetical construct. A theory is a human artifact; not every concept of a theory should be linked to empirical events since the purpose of a theory is to extend the range of our knowledge. Moreover, unrealistic standards of empirical anchorage in the early stages of theory construction may discourage the kind of imaginative speculation necessary to decipher elusive and obscure phenomena. Vague and risky as hypothetical constructs may be, they often are necessary tools in the development of a productive theory.

## Correspondence Rules

Even if all the terms of a theory were empirically anchored and precise, something further would have to be added to indicate how these terms are combined and related to one another. Without a set of rules by which its concepts are integrated, a theory lacks internal coherence and its function as a tool for explaining and predicting empirical events is hampered markedly. Many labels have been coined for this linkage or correspondence system; it has often been referred to as the *syntax* of a theory because of its similarity to the rules of grammar.

These rules serve as deductive procedures by which theoretical concepts are arranged or combined to provide new inferences or insights about empirical relations. They give a theory a coherent system of interlocking channels through which diverse facts may be related and derived. For example, the calculational rules of mathematics are frequently used in science as inferential principles which guide the manipulation of concepts and their subsequent derivation into empirical hypotheses. When formulated logically and explicitly, correspondence rules provide tremendous power for systematizing experience and generating research hypotheses.

## Hypotheses

Correspondence rules in psychopathological theories are usually loose and imprecise, if formulated at all. As a consequence, hypotheses, that is, provisional explanations which are stated as predictions about empirical relationships, are rarely derived rigorously from the correspondence rules of a theory. In most undeveloped sciences, hypotheses are formulated as a result of perceptive observations and intuitive hunches.

Whether hypotheses are rigorously derived or intuitively conjectured, it is important that their final form be translatable into empirical terms. We must recall that the ultimate goal of a theory is the development of empirical laws. Such laws develop not only through ingenious speculation or derivation, but also by factual *confirmation*. Unless a hypothesis can be translated into a specific empirical test, its validity cannot be confirmed.

Our discussion has presented a condensation of relatively conventional notions about the structure of theory as formulated by logicians and philosophers of science. Most students may be unacquainted with these terms and may have found them difficult to grasp or see in perspective. . . . Although the serious student would do well to obtain a thorough grounding in these fundamental elements of theory, a sophisticated understanding is not essential to follow the major ideas presented later in the chapter. What should be clear, however, is that a theory is not "reality," that it is not an inevitable or predetermined representation of the objective world. Theories are merely optional instruments utilized in the early stages of knowledge. They serve to organize experience in a logical manner, and function as explanatory propositions by which experiences may be analyzed or inferences about them drawn. Their ultimate goal is the establishment of new empirical laws.

Theories arise typically from the perceptive observation and imaginative speculation of a creative scientist. This innovator is usually quite aware of the limits, finds deficiencies of his "invention" and is disposed in the early stages of his speculation to modify it as he develops new observations and insights. Unfortunately, after its utility has been proven in a modest and limited way, the theory frequently acquires a specious stature. Having clarified certain ambiguities and survived initial criticisms, it begins to accumulate a coterie of disciples. These less creative thinkers tend to accept the theory wholeheartedly and espouse its superior explanatory powers and terminology throughout the scientific market place. They hold to its propositions tenaciously and defend it blindly and unequivocally against opposition. In time it becomes a rigid and sacred dogma and, as a result, authority replaces the test of utility and empirical validity. Intelligent men become religious disciples; their theory is a doctrine of "truth," not a guide to the unknown.

Should we avoid theories knowing their frequent fate? The answer, of course, is no! Man will interpret his experience either through implicit or formal theories regardless of the dangers and assumptions involved. Rather than dismissing theories as inevitable "religious doctrines," we should formulate criteria by which we can evaluate their genuine utility.

## ORIENTATION OF THEORIES

The previous section dealt with the formal structure of theory, its models, concepts and derivation procedures which serve as its framework or organization. But theories differ not only in these formal attributes. All are designed to guide the discovery of empirical laws, but each has a bias or orientation as to what kinds of laws should be sought, what methods should be used to discover these laws and what kinds of empirical phenomena should be observed. Theorists engage in intense debates as to which of several alternative approaches is best; unfortunately, the poor student wastes needless hours in trying to decide which "side" is correct. It is important for the student to recognize at the outset that there is no "correct" choice; no rules exist in nature to tell us which laws are best or most important.

To complicate matters, the orientations of most theories are not explicit. As a result, the student is presented with a fantastic array of overlapping data and concepts which appears disconnected and contradictory and leaves him dazzled and confused. Without differences in orientation clearly in mind, the student is like the young Talmudic scholar who, after immersing himself for weeks in ancient manuscripts, rose suddenly one morning, danced joyously in the streets and shouted, "I have found the most wonderful answer; somebody please tell me the question!"

To make sense and give order to the data of his science, the student must know what kinds of laws each theory seeks to find. Only then can he construct meaning and coherence in his studies. With the goals of each theory clearly before him, he may separate them according to the laws they wish to find and compare them intelligently as to their success in answering the questions they pose in common. It should be obvious that theories seeking biochemical laws cannot be compared to theories seeking behavioral laws. And theories seeking causal sequences between past and present events should not be compared to theories seeking correlation among present events, and so on.

The student might ask at this point why different kinds of theories are needed. Cannot one theory encompass all that need be known in psychopathology? For the time being, at least, the answer must be no. At this stage of our knowledge, theories must serve as instruments to answer particular rather than universal questions. The clinician in the consulting room needs a different kind of theory to facilitate his understanding of verbal therapeutic interaction than does the psychopharmacologist, who seeks to discover the effects of biochemical properties.

A major source of confusion for Students stems from their difficulty in recognizing the existence within psychopathology of different levels of scientific observation and conceptualization. No such difficulties seem to exist with regard to drawing distinctions between broad fields such as physics and chemistry or biology and sociology. Students experience problems when they are faced with distinctions *within* each of these wider disciplines; they fail to recognize that scientists refine their focus and concentrate selectively on increasingly narrow bands of data, each of which gives rise to highly delimited concepts and theories. Thus, some physicists concern themselves with elementary particles, whereas others study gravitational fields; similarly, some chemists focus on the bonding of simple molecules, whereas others investigate complex biochemical processes.

Scientists approach "nature" from different vantage points, selecting just those elements of this awesomely complex phenomenon which they believe will best enable them to answer the questions they pose. Not only do chemists focus on different facets of nature than do physicists, but *within* each of these two disciplines, scientists further subdivide the field of study. In effect, then, each of these subdivisions of a science deals with *a different* class of empirical data. Psychopathology is no different than physics or chemistry in this regard. It, too, can be studied from many vantage points. It can be observed and conceptualized in legitimately different ways by behaviorists, phenomenologists, psychodynamicists and biochemists.

It is important to recognize, further, that no single level of observation or conceptualization *alone* is sufficient to encompass all of the complex and multidimensional features of a field such as psychopathology. The processes and structures which comprise the field may be described in terms of conditioned habits, or reaction formations, or cognitive expectancies, or neurochemical dysfunctions. These different levels of data and conceptualization cannot, and should not, be arranged in a hierarchy, with one level viewed as primary, or reducible to another; nor can they be compared in terms of some "objective truth value." Alternative levels or approaches merely are different; they observe and conceptualize different types of data, and lead, therefore, to different theories and different empirical laws. Despite fruitless debates to the contrary, there is no intrinsic conflict between theories and laws which deal with different data; they are complementary, and *not* contradictory approaches to the subject. No one expects the propositions of a physicist to be the same as those of a chemist; nor should we expect those of a behaviorist to be the same as those of a phenomenologist.

What we wish to stress then, is that theories are best differentiated according to the kinds of data they elect to study and conceptualize. These choices are purely pragmatic,

and questions of comparative utility or validity should be asked only of theories which deal with the same kinds of data. Data are the basic ingredients for concepts and for the theories which coordinate these concepts. Irrelevant controversies and confusions are avoided if the conceptual level, or the kinds of data to which they refer, are specified clearly. Where this is done properly, the student and researcher can determine whether two concepts are comparable, whether the same conceptual level refers to different data, whether different theories apply to the same data and so on.

There are many ways in which the subject matter of psychopathology can be differentiated according to "data levels." L'Abate (1964) has proposed levels of integration, interpretation and functioning and development, while Ford and Urban (1963) have organized them in terms of degree of accessibility, order of abstraction and hierarchical structure.

What classification scheme of levels will serve our purpose best? The four major historical traditions presented in chapter I suggest a particularly useful basis for us to follow, and one which corresponds closely to the four theoretical orientations in psychopathology today. These contemporary orientations reflect not only relatively distinct historical traditions but, perhaps more importantly, differ also in the kinds of data they elect to conceptualize. For example, followers in the tradition of psychiatric medicine focus upon the *biophysical* substrate of pathology; those within the psychodynamic tradition of psychiatry conceptualize *unconscious intrapsychic* processes; theorists within the clinical-personology tradition tend to be concerned with *conscious phenomenologic* experience; and those in the academic-experimental tradition attend primarily to overt *behavioral data.* These four levels—biophysical, intrapsychic, phenomenological and behavioral—reflect, therefore, both different sources of data and the four major theoretical orientations in psychopathology.

In the following sections we will specify these four levels of theoretical analysis in greater detail. This will provide us with a picture of which data a theory has judged significant to its purposes and which it has deemphasized. By arranging contemporary theories according to level of data observation and conceptualization we will be able to understand better the variety of definitions of psychopathology which have been developed. From this basis also, we should have a sound foundation for comparing the varied concepts and explanatory propositions which have been formulated regarding the etiologic development and therapeutic modification of psychopathology.

The sciences, as we know them, are largely the result of an evolutionary process of haphazard variation in natural selection. The variation is continually being produced by the uncoordinated efforts of innumerable individual investigators, the selection by communication of results and critical appraisal by peers or posterity. An inevitable characteristic of this process is that whenever one surveys the state of any particular field of science one finds it, from the standpoint of organization and elegance, nothing less than a sorry mess. Numerous locally grounded theories, entirely distinct neither from one another nor from the noisy background, vie for attention. Disciplines form along irrational lines and persevere long after interdisciplinary boundaries, originally useful guidelines, have hardened into blockades (Estes, 1965).

It is comforting to know that the discouraging state of affairs described in the above quote is not peculiar to psychopathology. It was inevitable that so broad a subject as psychopathology would produce a scattering of diverse viewpoints. Complex problems lend themselves to many approaches, and divisions of labor in so varied a field become not only a matter of choice but also one of necessity.

The historical evolution of these diverging approaches was described in chapter 1; fortunately, diversification has resulted in a broad spectrum of knowledge about pathological phenomena. But these random evolutions have marked disadvantages as well. Scientists who are preoccupied with only a small segment of the field often have little knowledge of the work of others. Intent on a narrow approach to the subject, they lose sight of perspective, and their respective contributions are scattered and disconnected. What is needed today is a synthesis in which divergent elements of knowledge are brought together to be seen as parts of an integrated whole. Until a psychological Newton or Einstein comes along, however, the student must do the next best thing: develop an attitude by which the various branches and levels of psychopathology are viewed as an interrelated, if not an integrated unit. He must learn the language and orientation of each of the major approaches as if they were all part of an indivisible piece. Until such time as a bridge is created to coordinate each theory and level of approach to the others, no one theory or approach should be viewed as all-embracing, or accepted to the exclusion of the others. A multiplicity of viewpoints must prevail.

An earlier review of the substantive orientations of theories of psychopathology led us to classify them into four levels. These levels were felt to be useful since they corresponded well with historical traditions, contemporary professional orientations and, perhaps most important, with the major types of data which theorists observe and conceptualize. These levels were labeled (1) biophysical, (2) intrapsychic, (3) phenomenological and (4) behavioral. Useful as this division may be, it incorporates many divergent subgroupings: for example, the biophysical category will include theorists whose interests focus more narrowly on either genetics, biochemistry or physiology. Nevertheless, each level is, more or less, distinct from the others by virtue of its attention to a reasonably delimited class of data, a common scientific vocabulary and a central or guiding doctrine.

Any discussion of psychopathological theory should bring us to the question of defining psychopathology. It should be obvious from the foregoing that no single definition is possible. Psychopathology will be defined in terms of the theory one employs. An idiographically oriented theorist who emphasizes the importance of phenomenological experience will include uniqueness and self-discomfort in his definition of psychopathology; a biochemical theorist will formulate his definition in terms of biochemical dysfunctions, and so on. In brief, once a particular level and theory has been adopted, the definition of psychopathology follows logically and inevitably. Clearly, no single definition conveys the wide range of observations and orientations with which psychopathology may be explored.

Unfortunately, the observations and concepts and propositions of the various theoretical approaches to psychopathology have not been collected within one cover. At present, no single journal covers all aspects of psychopathology either, nor is there a permanent professional organization which cuts across disciplinary lines on a regular basis. To fill this void is a monumental task and far beyond the scope of this chapter. At best, we can attempt to provide a brief panoramic view of these approaches and, hopefully, convey certain essential features which they incorporate. . . .

## BIOPHYSICAL THEORIES

Theories at this level assume that biophysical factors such as anatomy and biochemistry are the primary determinants of psychopathology. Ample evidence from medical science exists to justify this assumption. In the present section we will examine the orientation of theorists who hold this view. In addition, we will detail several of the more prominent theories and discuss the basic model they utilize to guide their formulations.

The first question we must ask is: what is the basis of psychopathology according to biophysical theorists? Though by no means

mutually exclusive, the theorists have proposed two answers.

One group contends that most pathology can be traced to man's natural biological variability; accordingly, they attempt to relate these variations to measures of personality functioning and psychopathology. Scientists who follow this line of thinking may be considered to be quantitatively oriented since (1) they assume that men differ along the statistical "normal curve," and (2) they seek to discover correlations between biophysical variability and the presence of mental disorder. Roger Williams, the distinguished biochemist, has argued the case for investigating these natural biological variations as follows (1960):

Consider the fact (I do consider it a fact and not a theory) that every individual person is endowed with a distinctive gastrointestinal tract, a distinctive nervous system, and a morphologically distinctive brain; furthermore that the differences involved in this distinctiveness are never trifling and often are enormous. Can it be that this fact is inconsequential in relation to the problem of personality differences?

I am willing to take the position that this fact is of the *utmost* importance. The material in the area of anatomy alone is sufficient to convince anyone who comes upon the problem with an open mind that here is an obvious frontier which should yield many insights. Those who have accepted the Freudian idea that personality disorders arise from infantile conditioning will surely be led to see that, *in addition,* the distinctive bodily equipment of each individual infant is potentially important.

At the risk of being naive, it appears that the whole story we have been unfolding hangs together. Individual infants are endowed with far-reaching anatomical distinctiveness. The same distinctiveness carries over into the sensory and biochemical realms, and into their individual psychologies.

The disease model, as adopted from medicine and used by many biophysical theorists as an analogy for psychopathology, possesses two main features. Symptoms, according to this model, are merely surface reflections of either (1) an underlying biological defect or (2) the compensatory or adaptive reaction to that defect.

The first feature of the model is illustrated in physical medicine by infections, genetic errors, obstructions, inflammations or other insults to normal functioning which display themselves overtly as fevers, fatigue, headaches and so on. Significant progress was made in physical medicine when it shifted its focus from these surface symptoms to the underlying pathology. Those who accept this model assume that an underlying biophysical defect ultimately will be found for the "superficial" symptoms of mental disorders, that is, for the maladaptive behavior and poor interpersonal relations of mental patients.

The second feature of the medical disease model, that symptoms represent compensatory adaptations to the basic impairment, derives from the work of the French biologist, Claude Bernard, in the nineteenth century. Of particular interest was his observation that adaptive reactions often are more destructive to the organism than the basic defect itself; adaptive efforts, intended as temporary and reparative, often became continuous and destructive. For example, microorganisms infecting the lung elicit physiological reactions which counter the invasion. Unfortunately, the magnitude of the reaction often is excessive and protracted, leading to lung congestion, pneumonia and death.

Biophysical theorists adopting the disease model are inclined to use only the first feature of the model. To them the only difference between psychological and biological disorders is that the former, affecting the central nervous system, manifested itself in mental symptoms, whereas the latter, affecting other organ systems, manifests itself in physical symptoms. The parallel they see between biological and psychological disorders has led to serious objections, which may be summarized as follows: adherents of the disease model (1) attribute psychopathology to biological defects whose existence is questionable, (2) exclude the role of psychological

and interpersonal factors in psychopathology and (3) overlook the second feature of the disease model, that dealing with the individual's compensatory reaction to stress or impairment. Let us elaborate these criticisms briefly.

1. Regarding the first point, Szasz (1960) questions the wisdom of pursuing the "myth" of neuroanatomical defects and biochemical dysfunctions. To him, the belief that tangible biological phenomena are the cause of mental disorders is a myth, that is, a false verbal analogy founded on an acceptance of the medical disease model. If Szasz's criticism is taken to mean that not all forms of psychopathology can be attributed to biological causes, it certainly is correct. But this criticism is largely an attack upon a straw man, for no biophysical theorist takes such an extreme position. Biophysical theorists do not deny the role of psychological factors; they merely state that *certain* types of psychopathology can be attributed primarily to biophysical impairments, and that even these are shaped to some extent by the unique environmental experiences of the individual.

2. The second criticism of the disease model, that psychopathology should be viewed as a problem of living (Adams, 1964), also seems irrelevant. Psychopathology can be viewed as a "problem of living" and as a physical disease. These are merely different levels of analysis, not incompatible frames of reference. For example, a deaf person may respond in a maladaptive fashion to social life because of his anatomical impairment. Which facet of his overall problem we wish to focus upon depends on the purposes of our investigation—we can stress either his interpersonal difficulties or his biophysical impairment. The failure to recognize that psychopathology likewise can be approached at different levels of analysis will lead only to fruitless controversies.

3. The third criticism leveled at those who have adopted the disease model states that they have overlooked the feature of the model which deals with the organism's adaptive response to his impairment. This criticism perhaps is more justified than the others, but may be unfair given the limited state of biophysical knowledge. Biophysical theorists contend that they must first discover the existence of underlying defects before they can study the manner in which individuals adapt to them. Other theorists, however, feel that little will be gained from a detailed knowledge of biophysical impairments alone. According to their view, it is the adaptive reaction of the individual which is the most significant part of the disease model. The failure of certain biophysical theorists to utilize both aspects of the disease model does not justify condemnation, however. A model, if we will recall, is merely a tool, a heuristic device to stimulate theoretical ideas and empirical research. One may utilize one aspect of a model and overlook others. Certainly, accepting a model in toto does not assure us of its usefulness. Which aspect of the disease model will prove most fruitful will be answered not by debate, but by research. In any event, the adaptation aspect of the disease model has not been intentionally overlooked; it serves as the foundation for the complex and varied intrapsychic theories to which our attention turns next.

## INTRAPSYCHIC THEORIES

Biophysical theories usually are limited in scope and are anchored closely to observable and measurable data. In contrast, theories dealing with intrapsychic processes are organized often into comprehensive systems which lack a firm anchor to the empirical world. They rely heavily on inference and speculation and, as a result, are influenced in large measure by the models that theorists

use as their guide. It is for this reason that we must outline the basic model adopted by intrapsychic theorists at the beginning of our discussion. Afterward, we will examine the typical sources they have used to obtain their data and the types of concepts they have devised to represent them. Lastly, we will outline the major theories in use today.

The traditional medical disease model, as applied to the study of psychopathology, contains two assumptions about pathological symptoms. The first assumption, which is given primary importance in biophysical theories, states that symptoms reflect the existence of a biological defect. The second assumption, generally overlooked by biophysical theorists, states that symptoms represent compensatory or defensive adaptations to a basic impairment. This second assumption is emphasized by intrapsychic theorists.

Intrapsychic theorists substitute psychological factors for biological diseases in their model, that is, they supplant biological diseases with concepts of psychic trauma or conflict, and supplant the notion of biological defensive reactions with the concept of psychic adaptive compensations. In the same manner as we possess biological stabilizers to correct upsetting defects, we possess adaptive psychological mechanisms by which anxieties and conflicts may be counteracted. And just as defensive biological reactions occasionally prove more destructive than the original assault, so too do psychological mechanisms prove maladaptive.

Anxiety is the primary psychological "defect" resulting in maladaptive reactions. When the individual's basic security is threatened, he invokes intricate defensive maneuvers to deny or distort his awareness of the threat he faces. The intensity of this anxiety will determine, to a great degree, whether the defensive reaction will prove adaptive or maladaptive.

Intrapsychic theorists stress the importance of early childhood anxieties since these experiences may dispose the individual to a lifelong pattern of pathological adaptation. Childhood anxieties establish deeply ingrained defensive systems which may lead the individual to react to new situations as if they were duplicates of what occurred in childhood. These anticipatory defenses persist throughout life and result in progressive or chronic disorders.

Intrapsychic theorists may differ in which experiences they view to be crucial to the production of anxiety, but all agree that psychopathology arises as a result of efforts to relieve anxiety and that these efforts often progress into more serious difficulties.

An illustration of this sequence of maladaptation may be useful at this point. If a youngster avoids his peers as a means of forestalling anticipated rejection, he will prevent himself from engaging in activities that might teach him how to enhance his acceptance by them. Furthermore, withdrawal will deprive him of certain future needs he may have, such as companionship, sexual gratification and love. If, instead of withdrawal, he reacts to his peers with hostility and rage, he will evoke counter-aggression and thereby intensify his rejection. As a circular pattern of maladaptation continues, he may become isolated from others entirely and develop highly idiosyncratic patterns of thought which will alienate him only further from society. As a result, he will lose touch with the world of reality and become preoccupied only with his own thoughts and feelings. As his isolation increases, he may be unable to avoid feelings of emptiness and confusion. A sense of futility may emerge and his defensive efforts may collapse, leading him to sink into a state of utter desolation and disorganization.

Intrapsychic theorists hold that childhood experiences of anxiety are the primary cause of pathology; although adult experiences are ceded some importance, their significance is shaped or colored by past influences. Thus, these theorists stress continuity in development, believing that adult personality is related in a determinant way to early experiences.

Three classes of experience have been noted as conducive to pathological development: (1) the extent to which basic needs are frustrated, (2) the conflicts to which the child is exposed and (3) the attitudes and settings in which experiences are learned. A brief discussion of each of these factors will be useful.

1. When we think of how profoundly helpless an infant is in meeting his own survival needs, we can appreciate his dependence upon parental support and nourishment. The security the child feels is tied directly to the manner and extent to which his parents supply his needs. A vital link exists, therefore, between parental attitudes and behaviors, and the security and comfort of the child.

   This link is especially crucial during the earliest years of life when the child is completely at the mercy of parental whims and desires. For example, the child's persistent demand for nutrition may evoke parental balking, withdrawal or harshness. Harsh weaning may be experienced as a sign of parental rejection, ridicule and hostility, and may undermine the youngster's self-confidence and security. He may handle the anxieties this experience creates only by distorting or denying what he has experienced.

2. Difficulties may arise because the child's reasoning processes are undeveloped. He may be unable to grasp and separate conflicting attitudes conveyed by his parents. For example, he may have been admonished, on several occasions, to be kind and considerate to his friends; at other times he may have been urged to be aggressive and competitive. Unclear as to which circumstances call for one or the other of these incompatible responses, he finds himself confused and anxious. As a solution, he may decide that it is best to be indifferent and to disengage himself from others. As another example, a child may have been taught that sexual feelings are degrading and sinful. As a consequence, he may be unable to experience adult sexual satisfaction without feeling conflict and anxiety.

3. The manner and setting in which attitudes and feelings are taught often are more important than what is taught. If ridicule, intimidation and punishment are employed to inculcate attitudes and behaviors, the child will learn not only to submit to his parents' desires, but to fear and hate his parents. Any method of adverse training adds anxiety and conflict to what is learned. As a result, the child will respond with a variety of maladaptive reactions such as anger, ambivalence, guilt and fear at the same time as he learns "to behave."

The emphasis given to early childhood experience by intrapsychic theorists represents their contention that disorders of adulthood are a direct product of the continued and insidious operation of past events. To them, knowledge of the past provides information indispensable to understanding adult difficulties. To the question, "what is the basis of adult disorders?" they would answer: "the anxieties of childhood and the progressive sequence of defensive maneuvers which were devised to protect against a recurrence of these feelings."

Intrapsychic theorists contend that these two determinants of adult behavior, childhood anxieties and defensive maneuvers, are ·unconscious, that is, cannot be brought to awareness except under unusual conditions. It is the search for these unconscious processes which is the distinguishing feature of the intrapsychic approach. The obscure and elusive phenomena of the unconscious are the data which they uncover and use for their concepts. These data consist first, of repressed childhood anxieties that persist within the individual and attach themselves insidiously to ongoing experiences, and second, of unconscious adaptive processes which protect the individual against the resurgence of these anxieties. The *intrapsychic* label we have attached to these theorists reflects, therefore, their common focus on these two elements of the unconscious.

How is the unconscious manifested? Essentially, through indirect methods. Since the unconscious cannot be seen by direct means, it must be inferred.

Unconscious processes are revealed most often when we let down our guard, as in "slips of the tongue," or when we put aside the controls of wakeful activity, as in sleep, or when we relinquish our contact with reality, as in serious mental disorders.

Unconscious data may be obtained also in specially designed clinical settings. The technique of *free association,* where the patient is asked to relax his usual controls and to verbalize every passing thought or emotion, often elicits unconscious processes which are not evident in daily life. The seemingly unrelated fragments of free association—memories, hopes and casual commentaries turn out to be neither random nor irrelevant, but display a pattern of repetitive themes. These themes are interpreted as evidence for the existence of unconscious forces which underlie and direct conscious behavior. *Dream interpretation* is another clinical method of uncovering unconscious processes. In sleep, without the controls of reality and responsibility, unconscious processes display themselves freely in symbolic dream imagery. The method of *projective tests* is another clinically created procedure for inferring the unconscious. Here, ambiguous stimuli are presented to the subject and he is forced to draw upon his own inner resources in order to make a response. Idiosyncratic responses result and unconscious processes often are displayed.

Questions have been raised as to whether or not scientific concepts can be founded on unconscious data. Intrapsychic theories have been criticized as unscientific mixtures of metaphorical analogies, speculative notions and hypothetical constructs because their data are anchored so tenuously to the observable world.

Added to this rather harsh judgment is the equally critical view that the methods of collecting unconscious data are both unreliable and imprecise. How can concepts of the unobservable unconscious be empirically anchored? Can one accept what the patient says without having it corroborated by external evidence? Is the patient an unbiased judge, or is he motivated to agree with his all-knowing therapist? Are free associations really free, or do patients produce what their therapists implicitly suggest?

These and many other questions have been raised about the subjective and methodologically uncontrolled procedures used for the development of intrapsychic theories. Without tools such as tape recorded therapeutic interviews, corroborative data from relatives and experimentally controlled longitudinal studies, the probability of objectifying the concepts and propositions of intrapsychic theories is highly unlikely. To critics, the ingenious speculations of intrapsychic theorists are, at best, a starting point, a preliminary set of propositions which *must* be articulated into clearly specifiable behaviors which can be confirmed or disproved.

Despite these criticisms, many of which are equally applicable to other theoretical approaches, intrapsychic processes are a necessary part of the study of man's pathological functioning. Although these processes are difficult to formulate according to the tenets of scientific objectivity, their existence cannot be denied or overlooked. Efforts to unravel them will fall prey inevitably to theoretical obscurity and methodological difficulty, yet the search is mandatory.

## PHENOMENOLOGICAL THEORIES

Intrapsychic and phenomenological approaches are similar in many respects. Both gather their data in naturalistic settings, deriving their concepts from clinical observation rather than from experimental laboratory research. Both recognize that their concepts and hypotheses are crude approximations of complex processes, but they contend that less rigorous notions are appropriate in the early stages of a science; thus, methodological

quantification and conceptual precision are not devalued, but deemphasized since they are viewed to be premature, given our current state of knowledge.

The major distinction between intrapsychic and phenomenological schools of thought lies in their respective emphasis upon unconscious versus conscious processes. Intrapsychic theorists believe that the most important aspects of functioning are those factors which a person cannot or will not say about himself. In contrast, phenomenologists believe that the person's introspective reports, taken at their face value, are most significant.

Phenomenologists stress that the individual reacts to the world only in terms of his unique perception of it. No matter how transformed or unconsciously distorted it may be, it is the person's way of perceiving events which determines his behavior. Concepts and propositions must be formulated, therefore, not in terms of objective realities or unconscious processes, *but* in accordance with how events actually are perceived by the individual; concepts must not disassemble these subjective experiences into depersonalized or abstract categories.

The phenomenon of consciousness is one of the most controversial topics in both psychological and philosophical literature, and there are some knotty questions which have been raised about the methods by which conscious data may be obtained. No one doubts that self-awareness exists; but how can phenomenological reality as experienced by another person be categorized, measured or even sensed?

At best, observers must adopt an empathic attitude, a sensing in one's self of what another may be experiencing. But this method is justly suspect, fraught with the distortions and insensitivities of the observer. To obviate this difficulty, phenomenologists assume that the verbal statements of the individual accurately reflect *its* phenomenal reality. Any datum which represents the individual's portrayal of his experience is grist, therefore, for the phenomenologist's mill.

Serious criticisms have been raised against this introspective method. Are there not deliberate omissions and inaccuracies in verbal reports? How can a scientific theory be founded on subjective reports, reports whose meaning will vary from person to person? Do not patients repress and deny the most crucial elements of their experiences? And, if significant events are hidden or forgotten, of what value are the remaining data? Worse yet, how can deceptive reports be accepted at their face value as the data for a scientific theory?

Several counter-arguments have been offered in defense of phenomenological methods. The limitations of self-reports are granted. However, phenomenologists contend that an individual's verbal reports reveal the most important influences upon his behavior. Is it not simple efficiency to ask a person directly what is disturbing him and how this disturbance came to pass? Is his report more prone to error than an observer's speculations gathered from the odds and ends of a case history study? Is it less reliable than deductions which are drawn from dreams and free associations? The fact that some verbal recollections and feelings are misleading is no reason to dismiss them as useless; they summarize events in terms closest to the individual's experience of them, and often embody knowledge that is not otherwise available.

These pro and con arguments miss the point. Phenomenological reports are an important source of data. But they are only one of many sources. There should be no argument between proponents of one method versus another. Each method reflects an arbitrary decision as to which source of data will weigh more in the construction of a theory. Theories using different types of data are complementary frames of reference for investigating the problems of personality and psychopathology. The task for the future is not choosing alternatives between these sources of data, but in establishing a connection between them.

# BEHAVIORAL THEORIES

Recent behavior theories of pathology have used concepts generated originally in experimental learning research. They are not simple translations of psychoanalytic concepts into behavior terminology, as were earlier theories of behavior pathology, but are based on the ostensible "empirical" laws of learning. Theorists using these concepts lay claim to the virtues of science since their heritage lies with the objective studies of systematic learning research and not with the dubious methods of clinical speculation.

That learning concepts are helpful in understanding pathology cannot be denied, but behavior theorists take a stronger position. They state that pathology is learned behavior that develops according to the same laws as those governing the development of normal behavior. Disturbed behavior differs from normal behavior only in magnitude, frequency and social adaptiveness. Were these behaviors more adaptive, or less frequent and extreme, they would possess no other distinguishing features.

The use of learning concepts to explain behavior pathology is based on the assumption that laws demonstrated in simple laboratory settings may be generalized to more complex behavior. Accordingly, psychopathology is considered a complicated pattern of learned maladaptive responses, and nothing else; all patterns of response—normal or abnormal can be derived from a few basic laws of learning.

Although several concepts have been considered central to the process of learning (e.g., imitation and thinking), most writers in the behaviorist tradition place primary emphasis on the role of *conditioning*. Conditioning has been demonstrated repeatedly in well-controlled laboratory research, but the ingredients involved in establishing a conditioned response are still subject to considerable theoretical controversy.

Two different theories of conditioning are currently in vogue. The simpler theory, known variously as *contiguity* or association, states that any response will become attached to any stimulus as long as the two are associated, usually in temporal sequence. No additional factor need be postulated to account for learning according to theorists of this persuasion. Somewhat more complicated is *reinforcement* theory, which states that the bond between a stimulus and a response is established only if the two are associated in conjunction with the reduction of some need or drive, such as hunger, thirst or anxiety. To both groups of theorists, the strength of the S-R bonds depends on the continued operation of their respective principle of conditioning. Complex learnings, such as those acquired through processes of imitation and thinking, can be understood as more intricate or higher level combinations of basic contiguity or reinforcement principles.

In contiguity theory, if a different stimulus is paired with the response, or in reinforcement theory, if need-reduction fails to occur, the original S-R bond will be weakened and eventually *extinguished.* Both groups of theorists note further that Stimuli which are similar to the stimulus in the original S-R bond can evoke the response of the bond. This concept, known as *generalization,* accounts for the observation that individuals transfer old responses to new situations, and do so to the extent of similarity between the old and the new situations.

The following quote illustrates the basic learning model (Eysenck, 1959):

How, then, does modern learning theory look upon neurosis? In the first place, it would claim that neurotic symptoms are learned patterns of behavior which for some reason or other are inadaptive. . . .

The point . . . on which the theory here advocated breaks decisively with psychoanalytic thought of any description is on this. Freudian theory regards neurotic symptoms as adaptive mechanisms which are evidence of repression; they are "the visible upshot of unconscious causes." Learning theory does not postulate any such "unconscious causes," but regards neurotic

symptoms as simple learned habits; there is no neurosis underlying the symptom, but merely the symptom itself. *(Get rid of the symptom and you have eliminated the neurosis.)*

Pathology is defined by most behavior theorists either as socially maladaptive or socially deficient behavior. In contrast to most theorists of other schools, where psychopathology is associated exclusively with the presence of undesirable feelings or irrational actions, behaviorists place equal stress on "absent behaviors," that is, indications that the patient has failed to learn social skills and attitudes for effective functioning in his cultural group. Their position differs clearly from biophysical theorists, who define mental illness as physical disease or dysfunction; it differs also from intrapsychic theorists, who consider pathology defined best in terms of unconscious processes; and it differs from the phenomenologists, whose definition is based on subjective feelings of discomfort. Ullmann and Krasner state the behaviorist's position in the following (1965):

the designation of a behavior as pathological or not, is dependent upon the individual's society. Specifically, while there are no single behaviors that would be said to be adaptive in all cultures, there are in all cultures definite expectations or roles for functioning adults in terms of familial and social responsibility. The person whose behavior is maladaptive does not fully live up to the expectations for one in his role, does not respond to all the stimuli actually present, and does not obtain the typical or maximum forms of reinforcement available to one of his status. . . . Behavior that one culture might consider unadaptive, be it that of the shaman or the paranoid, is adaptive in another culture. . . . Maladaptive behavior is behavior that is considered inappropriate by those key people in a person's life.

Several objections have been raised against culturally relativistic and socially adaptive definitions of pathology, such as formulated in the above quote. For example, certain classic types of psychiatric disorder appear in all cultures. How can one account for this uniformity without postulating some universal underlying disease? To this question behaviorists reply that classic textbook cases are figments of a theorist's imagination; moreover, uniformity in diagnostic classification is a psychiatric fiction as evidenced by the fact that classification is highly unreliable, and most nosological systems are constantly revised and rarely hold up under research analysis. What ever regularities are found to exist can be accounted for, according to behaviorists, by similarities in cultural patterns of conditioning. For example, once an individual is identified as ill, he is exposed to a uniform set of conditions which shape his behavior (e.g., restriction of privileges, threats of "shock" therapy, decreases in social relationships, hospital atmospheres and so on). Regularities observed among these patients are a product, therefore, of common learning experiences, not common "diseases."

These theorists borrow their concepts from experimental learning research; as such, one would expect their work to be subject to little scientific faulting. The failure to live up to this expectation demonstrates the difficulty of transferring concepts from one field to another. Borrowing concepts from another field may be no more than a specious ennoblement of one's efforts, a cloak of falsely appropriated prestige which duly impresses the naive. One might ask, for example, whether the laboratory-based concepts borrowed from the prestigious field of learning are genuinely useful in psychopathology, or whether they are merely bandied about in an allegorical and superficial manner. Scientific sounding terminology may be no more than a set of flimsy analogies, offering no new explanatory powers or insights; old wine in new bottles is still old wine.

There is reason to suspect, further, that the "basic" laws of learning are not so basic after all; much dissent exists among learning theorists as to which concepts and laws are "basic." Examination of the literature on learning exposes marked disagreements on even the simplest of conditioning processes. Can "laws" of learning be applied to highly complex clinical processes when the existence of these laws in simple situations is a matter of dispute?

Another criticism of behavior theories in psychopathology is their failure to formulate concepts dealing with the development of disorders. What little they say on this matter is usually a rewording of intrapsychic theories. Where they do strike out on their own, as do the Skinnerians, they appear preoccupied with how behavior is learned, and not with when and what is learned. The Skinnerian focus on the process rather than the content of learning has added an important dimension to the study of psychopathology. But without reference to the kinds of experience which lead to pathological learning, the theory creates a sterile and artificial man, an empty creature who behaves according to vacant and abstract principles. By reducing the reality of experience to abstract stimuli and responses, psychopathology becomes a barren pattern of mechanical reactions. Sentimental and "unscientific" as these objections may appear, they bring home the point that an explanation of "real" behavior requires more than a set of abstract principles. Though these principles may be "basic," they remain static until the content and meaning of experience fills them out.

## REFERENCES

Adams, H. B. Mental illness or interpersonal behavior. *Amer. Psychol., 19,* 191–196, 1964.

Altschule, M. *Bodily Physiology in Mental and Emotional Disorders.* New York: Grune and Stratton, 1953.

Bandura, A. Psychotherapy as a learning process. *Psychol. Bull., 58,* 143–159, 1961.

Bandura, A. A social learning interpretation of psychological dysfunctions. In London, P., and Rosenhan, D. (eds.), *Foundations of Abnormal Psychology.* New York: Holt, Rinehart and Winston, 1968.

Bandura, A., and Walters, R.H. *Social Learning and Personality Development.* New York: Holt, Rinehart and Winston, 1963.

Beck, S. J. The science of personality: Nomothetic or idiographic? *Psychol. Rev., 60,* 353–359, 1953.

Bindra, D. Experimental psychology and the problem of behavior disorders. *Canad. J.. Psychol., 13,* 135–150, 1959.

Binswanger, L. Existential analysis and psychotherapy. *Psychoanal. and psychoanal. Rev., 45,* 79–83, 1958.

Bleuler, E. The physiogenic and psychogenic in schizophrenia. *Amer. J. Psychiat., 87,* 203–2119, 1930.

Boss, M. *The Psychology of Dreams.* New York: Philosophical Library, 1958.

Campbell, J. D. *Manic-Depressive Disease.* Philadelphia: Lippincott, 1953.

Cattefl, R. B. *The Scientific Analysis of Personality.* Baltimore: Penguin Books, 1965.

Cronbach, L. J. The two disciplines of scientific psychology. *Amer. Psychol., 12,* 671–684, 1957.

Dallenbach, K. The place of theory in science. *Psychol. Rev., 60,* 33–44, 1953.

Delgado, J. M. R. Emotions. In Vernon, J. (ed.), *Introduction to Psychology: A Self-Selection Textbook.* Dubuque, Iowa: W. C. Brown, 1966.

Delgado, J. M. R., Roberts, W. W., and Miller, N. Learning motivated by electrical stimulation of subcortical structures in the monkey brain. *J. Comp. Physiol. Psychol., 49,* 373–380, 1954.

Dollard, J., and Miller, N. *Personality and Psychotherapy.* New York: McGraw-Hill, 1950.

Erikson, E. *Childhood and Society.* New York: Norton, 1950.

Erikson, E. Identity and the life cycle. In Klein, G. S. (ed.), *Psychological Issues.* New York: International University Press, 1959.

Estes, W. K. From chipmunks to bulldozers to what? *Contemp. Psychol., 10,* 196–199, 1965.

Eysenck, H. J. The science of personality: Nomothetic! *Psychol. Rev., 61,* 339–342, 1954.

Eysenck, H. J. (ed.) *Behavior Therapy and the Neuroses.* London: Pergamon Press, 1959.

Eysenck, H. J., and Raabman, S. *Causes and Cures of Neurosis.* London: Routledge and Kegan Paul, 1965.

Fairbairn, W. R. D. *Psychoanalytic Studies of the Personality.* London: Tavistock, 1952.

Festinger, L. *A Theory of Cognitive Dissonance.* Evanston, IL: Row, Peterson, 1957.

Fish, F. A neurophysiological theory of schizophrenia. *J. Ment. Sci., 109,* 828–838, 1961.

Ford, D., and Urban, H. *Systems of Psychotherapy.* New York: John Wiley & Sons, 1963.

Fromin, E. *Man for Himself.* New York: Rinehart, 1947.

Gellhorn, E. *Physiological Foundations of Neurology and Psychiatry.* Minneapolis: University of Minnesota Press, 1953.

Hartmann, H. *Ego Psychology and the Problem of Adaptation.* New York: International University Press, 1958.

Heath, R. G. Schizophrenia: Biochemical and physiologic aberrations. *Int'l. J. Neuropsychiat., 2,* 597–610, 1966.

Heath, R. G. (ed.) *Studies in Schizophrenia.* Cambridge: Harvard University Press, 1954.

Hebb, D. O. Alice in Wonderland, or psychology among the biological sciences. In Harlow, H., and Woolsey, C. (eds.), *Biological and Biochemical Bases of Behavior.* Madison: University of Wisconsin Press, 1958a.

Hebb, D. O. The motivating effects of exteroceptive stimulation. *Amer. Psychol., 13,* 109–113, 1958b.

Heilbrunn, G. Psychoanalysis, yesterday, today and tomorrow. *A.M.A. Arch. Gen. Psychiat., 4,* 321–330. 1961.

Hoagland, H. Metabolic and physiologic disturbances in the psychoses. In *Biology of Mental Health and Disease.* New York: Hoeber, 1952.

Hoffer, A., and Osmond, H. The adrenochrome model and schizophrenia. *J. Nerv. Ment. Dis., 128,* 18–35, 1959.

Hoskins, R. G. *The Biology of Schizophrenia.* New York: Norton, 1946.

Katkovsky, W. Social-learning theory and maladjustment. In Gorlow, L., and Katkovsky, W. (eds.), *Readings in the Psychology of Adjustment.* Second edition. New York: McGraw-Hill, 1968.

L'Abate, L. *Principles of Clinical Psychology.* New York: Grune and Stratton, 1964.

Maslow, A. *Toward a Psychology of Being.* Princeton: Van Nostrand, 1962.

May, R., Angel, E., and Ellenberger, H. F. (eds.) *Existence: A New Dimension in Psychiatry and Psychology.* New York: Basic Books, 1958.

Mowrer, O. H. Learning theory and behavior therapy. In Wolman, B. (ed.), *Handbook of Clinical Psychology.* New York: McGraw-Hill, 1965.

Olds, J. Pleasure centers of the brain. *Sci. Amer., 195,* 104–116, 1956.

Olds, J. Hypothalamic substrates of reward. *Physiol. Rev., 42,* 554–604, 1962.

Osmond, H., and Smythies, J. Schizophrenia: A new approach. *J. Ment. Sci., 98,* 309–315, 1952.

Rapaport, D. The theory of ego autonomy: A generalization. *Bull. Menninger Clin., 22,* 13–35, 1958.

Rapaport, D. The structure of psychoanalytic theory: A systematizing attempt. In Koch, S. (ed.), *Psychology: A Study of a Science,* Vol. 3. New York: McGraw-Hill, 1959.

Rashkis, H. A. The organization factor as an explanatory principle in functional psychosis. *A.M.A. Arch. Neurol. Psychiat., 80,* 513–519, 1958.

Riesman, D. *The Lonely Crowd.* New Haven: Yale, 1950.

Rogers, C. A theory of therapy, personality, and interpersonal relationships, as developed, in client-centered framework. In Koch, S. *Psychology: A Study of a Science.* New York: McGraw-Hill, 1959.

Rosenzweig, N. A mechanism in schizophrenia. *A.M.A. Arch. Neurol. Psychiat., 1955.*

Rotter, J. B. *Social Learning and Clinical Psychology.* Englewood Cliffs: Prentice-Hall, 1954.

Rotter, J. B. Generalized expectancies for into versus external control of reinforcements. *Psychol. Monogr., 80,* 1–28, 1966.

Rubin, L. S. Patterns of adrenergic-cholinergic balance in the functional psychoses. *Psyc. Rev., 69,* 501–519, 1962.

Shlien, J., (ed.) *Research in Psychotherapy,* Vol. 3. Washington, DC: American Psychological Association, 1968.

Singer, R. D. Organization as a unifying concept in schizophrenia. *A.M.A. Arch. Gen. Psy.,* 61–74, 1960.

Skinner, B. F. What is psychotic behavior? In *Theory and Treatment of the Psychoses.* St. Louis: Washington University Press, 1956.

Skinner, B. F. *Cumulative Record.* New York: Appleton-Century-Crofts, 1959.

Spitz, R. A. *The First Year of Life.* New York: International University Press, 1965.

Szasz, T. The myth of mental illness. *Amer. Psychol., 15,* 113–118, 1960.

Ullmann, L., and Krasner, L. (eds.) *Case Behavior Modification.* New York: Holt, Rinehart and Winston, 1965.

Williams, R. J. *The biological approach to the study of personality.* Berkeley Conference on Personality Development, 1960.

Woolley, D. W. *The Biochemical Bases of Psychoses.* New York: John Wiley & Sons, 1962.

Woolley, D. W., and Shaw, E. A biochemical pharmacological suggestion about certain mental disorders. *Sci., 119,* 587–588, 1954.

Wolpe, J. *Psychotherapy by Reciprocal Inhibition.* Stanford: Stanford University Press, 1958.

# PAPER 4

# *An Integrative Theory of Personality and Psychopathology*

There are those who contend that the major traditions of psychology and psychiatry have, for too long now, been doctrinaire in their assumptions. These critics claim that theories which focus their attention on only one level of data cannot help but generate formulations that are limited by their narrow preconceptions; moreover, their findings must, inevitably, be incompatible with the simple fact that psychological processes are multidetermined and multidimensional in expression. In rebuttal, those who endorse a single-level approach assert that theories which seek to encompass this totality will sink in a sea of data that can be neither charted conceptually nor navigated methodologically. Clearly, those who undertake to propose "integrative theories" are faced with the formidable task, not only of exposing the inadequacies of single-level theories, but of providing a convincing alternative that is both comprehensive and systematic. It is for the reader to judge whether integrative theorists possess the intellectual skills and analytic powers necessary, not only to penetrate the vast labyrinths of man's mind and behavior, but to chart these intricate pathways in a manner that is both conceptually clear and methodologically testable.

As the title of this paper suggests, an attempt will be made to formulate a schema that is neither doctrinaire nor loosely eclectic in its approach; rather, the theory presented is intended to be both broad in scope and sufficiently systematic in its application of principles to enable the major varieties of psychopathology to be derived logically and coherently. In the following the major themes of the manuscript are presented in condensed form.

## BIOSOCIAL DEVELOPMENT

A. For pedagogical purposes, it is often necessary to separate biogenic from psychogenic factors as influences in personality development; this bifurcation does not exist in reality. Biological and experiential determinants combine and interact in a reciprocal interplay throughout life. This sequence of biogenic-psychogenic interaction evolves through a never-ending spiral; each step in the interplay builds upon prior interactions and creates, in turn, new potentialities for future reactivity and experience. *Etiology in psychopathology may be viewed, then, as a developmental process in which intraorganismic and environmental forces display not only a reciprocity and circularity of influence but an orderly and sequential continuity throughout the life of the individual.*

The circular feedback and serially unfolding character of the developmental process defy simplification, and must constantly be kept in mind when analyzing the etiological background of personality. There are few unidirectional effects in development; it is a multideterminant transaction in which a unique pattern of biogenic potentials and a distinctive constellation of psychogenic influences mold each other in a reciprocal and successively more intricate fashion.

B. Each individual is endowed at conception with a unique set of chromosomes that shapes the course of his physical maturation and psychological development. The physical and psychological characteristics of children are in large measure similar to their parents because they possess many of the same genetic units. Children are genetically disposed to be similar to their parents not only physically but also in stamina, energy, emotional sensitivity, and intelligence.

Each infant displays a distinctive pattern of behaviors from the first moments after birth. These characteristics are attributed usually to the infant's "nature," that is, his constitutional makeup, since it is displayed prior to the effects of postnatal influences.

It is erroneous to assume that children of the same chronological age are comparable with respect to the level and character of their biological capacities. Not only does each infant start life with a distinctive pattern of neurological, physiochemical, and sensory equipment, but he progresses at his own maturational rate toward some ultimate but unknown level of potential. Thus, above and beyond initial differences and their not insignificant consequences are differences in the rate with which the typical sequence of maturation unfolds. Furthermore, different regions in the complex nervous system within a single child may mature at different rates. To top it all, the potential or ultimate level of development of each of these neurological capacities will vary widely, not only among children but within each child.

C. The maturation of the biological substrate for psychological capacities is anchored initially to genetic processes, but its development is substantially dependent on environmental stimulation. The concept of *stimulus nutriment* may be introduced to represent the belief that the quantity of environmental experience activates chemical processes requisite to the maturation of neural collaterals. Stimulus impoverishment may lead to irrevocable deficiencies in neural development and their associated psychological functions, stimulus enrichment may prove

equally deleterious by producing pathological over developments or imbalances among these functions.

D. The notion of sensitive developmental periods may be proposed to convey the belief that stimuli produce different effects at different ages, that is, there are limited time periods during maturation when particular stimuli have pronounced effects which they do not have either before or after these periods. It may be suggested, further, that these peak periods occur at points in maturation when the potential is greatest for growth and expansion of neural collaterals and other psychologically relevant structures.

Three neuropsychological stages of development, representing peak periods in neurological maturation, may be proposed. Each developmental stage reflects transactions between constitutional and experiential influences which combine to set a foundation for subsequent stages; if the interactions at one stage are deficient or distorted, all subsequent stages will be affected since they rest on a defective base.

1. The first stage, termed *sensory-attachment* in the theory, predominates from birth to approximately 18 months of age. This period is characterized by a rapid maturation of neurological substrates for sensory processes, and by the infant's attachment and dependency on others.

2. The second stage, referred to as *sensorimotor-autonomy*, begins roughly at 12 months and extends in its peak development through the sixth year. It is characterized by a rapid differentiation of motor capacities which coordinate with established sensory functions; this coalescence enables the young child to locomote, manipulate, and verbalize in increasingly skillful ways.

3. The third stage, called the period of *intracortical-initiative*, is primary from about the fourth year through adolescence. There is a rapid growth potential among the higher cortical centers during this stage, enabling the child to reflect, plan, and act

independent of parental supervision. Integrations developed during earlier phases of this period undergo substantial reorganization as a product of the biological and social effects of puberty.

E. Maladaptive consequences can arise as a result of either stimulus impoverishment or stimulus enrichment at each of the three stages.

1. From experimental animal research and naturalistic studies with human infants, it appears that marked stimulus impoverishment during the sensory-attachment period will produce deficiencies in sensory capacities and a marked diminution of interpersonal sensitivity and behavior. There is little evidence available with regard to the effects of stimulus enrichment during this stage; it may be proposed, however, that excessive stimulation results in hypersensitivities, stimulus seeking behaviors, and abnormal interpersonal dependencies.

2. Deprived of adequate stimulation during the sensorimotor stage, the child will be deficient in skills for behavioral autonomy, will display a lack of exploratory and competitive activity, and be characterized by timidity and submissiveness. In contrast, excessive enrichment and indulgence of sensorimotor capacities may result in uncontrolled self-expression, narcissism, and social irresponsibility.

3. Among the consequences of understimulation during the intracortical initiative stage is an identity diffusion, an inability to fashion an integrated and consistent purpose for one's existence, and an inefficiency in channeling and directing one's energies, capacities, and impulses. Excessive stimulation, in the form of over-training and over-guidance, results in the loss of several functions, notably spontaneity, flexibility, and creativity.

F. There has been little systematic attention to the child's own contribution to the course of his development. Environmental theorists of psychopathology have viewed disorders to be the result of detrimental experiences that the individual has had no part of producing himself. This is a gross simplification. Each infant possesses a biologically based pattern of reaction sensitivities and behavioral dispositions which shape the nature of his experiences and may contribute directly to the creation of environmental difficulties.

*The biological dispositions of the maturing child are important because they strengthen the probability that certain kinds of behavior will be learned.*

Highly active and responsive children relate to and learn about their environment quickly. Their liveliness, zest, and power may lead them to a high measure of personal gratification. Conversely, their energy and exploratory behavior may result in excess frustration if they over-aspire or run into insuperable barriers; unable to gratify their activity needs effectively, they may grope and strike out in erratic and maladaptive ways.

Adaptive learning in constitutionally passive children also is shaped by their biological equipment. Ill-disposed to deal with their environment assertively and little inclined to discharge their tensions physically, they may learn to avoid conflicts and step aside when difficulties arise. They are less likely to develop guilt feelings about misbehavior than active youngsters who more frequently get into trouble, receive more punishment, and are therefore inclined to develop aggressive feelings toward others. But in their passivity, these youngsters may deprive themselves of rewarding experiences and relationships; they may feel "left out of things" and become dependent on others to fight their battles and to protect them from experiences they are ill-equipped to handle on their own.

It appears clear from studies of early patterns of reactivity that *constitutional tendencies evoke counterreactions from others which accentuate these initial dispositions.* The child's biological endowment shapes not only his behavior but that of his parents as well.

If the child's primary disposition is cheerful and adaptable and has made his care easy, the mother will tend quickly to display a positive reciprocal attitude, conversely, if the child is tense and wound up, or if his care is difficult and time consuming, the mother will react with dismay, fatigue, or hostility. Through his own behavioral disposition then, the child elicits a series of parental behaviors which reinforce his initial pattern.

Unfortunately, the reciprocal interplay of primary patterns and parental reactions has not been sufficiently explored. It may prove to be one of the most fruitful spheres of research concerning the etiology of psychopathology and merits the serious attention of investigators. The *biosocial-learning approach* presented in this paper stems largely from the thesis that the child's constitutional pattern shapes and interacts with his social reinforcement experiences.

G. The fact that early experiences are likely to contribute a disproportionate share to learned behavior is attributable in part to the fact that their effects are difficult to extinguish. This resistance to extinction stems largely from the fact that learning in early life is presymbolic, random, and highly generalized.

Additional factors which contribute to the persistence and continuity of early learnings are social factors such as the repetitive nature of experience, the tendency for interpersonal relations to be reciprocally reinforcing, and the perseverance of early character stereotypes.

Beyond these are a number of self-perpetuating processes which derive from the individual's own actions. Among them are protective efforts which constrict the person's awareness and experience, the tendency to perceptually and cognitively distort events in line with expectancies, the inappropriate generalization to new events of old behavior patterns, and the repetitive compulsion to create conditions which parallel the past.

Children learn complicated sequences of attitudes, reactions, and expectancies in response to the experiences to which they were exposed.

Initially, these responses are specific to the particular events which prompted them; they are piecemeal, scattered, and changeable. Over the course of time, however, through learning what responses are successful in obtaining rewards and avoiding punishments, the child begins to crystallize a stable pattern of instrumental behaviors for handling the events of everyday life. These coping and adaptive strategies come to characterize his way of relating to others, and comprise one of the most important facets of what we may term his personality pattern.

## ON THE NATURE OF PERSONALITY PATTERNS

As noted above, in the first years of life children engage in a wide variety of spontaneous behaviors. Although they display certain characteristics consonant with their innate or constitutional dispositions, their way of reacting to others and coping with their environment tends, at first, to be capricious and unpredictable; flexibility and changeability characterize their moods, attitudes, and behaviors. This seemingly random behavior serves an exploratory function; each child is "trying out" and testing during this period alternative modes for coping with his environment. As time progresses, the child learns which techniques "work," that is, which of these varied behaviors enable him to achieve his desires and avoid discomforts. Endowed with a distinctive pattern of capacities, energies, and temperaments, which serve as base, he learns specific preferences among activities and goals and, perhaps of greater importance, learns that certain types of behaviors and strategies are especially successful for him in obtaining these goals. In his interaction with parents, siblings, and peers, he learns to discriminate which goals are permissible, which are rewarded, and which are not.

Throughout these years, then, a shaping process has taken place in which the range of initially diverse behaviors becomes narrowed, selective and, finally, crystallized into particular preferred modes of seeking and achieving. In time, these behaviors persist and become accentuated; not only are they highly resistant to extinction but they are reinforced by the restrictions and repetitions of a limited social environment, and are perpetuated and intensified by the child's own perceptions, needs, and actions. Thus, given a continuity in basic biological equipment, and a narrow band of experiences for learning behavioral alternatives, the child develops a distinctive pattern of characteristics that are deeply etched, cannot be eradicated easily, and pervade every facet of his functioning. In short, these characteristics *are* the essence and sum of his personality, his automatic way of perceiving, feeling, thinking, and behaving.

When we speak of a personality pattern, then, we are referring to those intrinsic and pervasive modes of functioning which emerge from the entire matrix of the individual's developmental history, and which now characterize his perceptions and ways of dealing with his environment. We have chosen the term *pattern* for two reasons: first, to focus on the fact that these behaviors and attitudes derive from the constant and pervasive interaction of both biological dispositions and learned experience; and second, to denote the fact that these personality characteristics are not just a potpourri of unrelated behavior tendencies, but a tightly knit organization of needs, attitudes, and behaviors. People may start out in life with random and diverse reactions, but the repetitive sequence of reinforcing experiences to which they are exposed gradually narrows their repertoire to certain habitual strategies, perceptions, and behaviors which become prepotent, and

come to characterize their distinctive way of relating to the world. . . .

## INTERPERSONAL COPING STRATEGIES

A. This section turns to a formulation that employs a set of theoretical concepts for deducing and coordinating personality syndromes. The full scope of this schema has been published by the author in earlier texts. Identified as a *biosocial-learning theory,* it attempts to generate the established and recognized personality categories through formal deduction and to show their covariation with other mental disorders.

In reviewing the many theories that have been formulated through the centuries, a reader cannot help but be impressed by both the number and diversity of concepts and types proposed. In fact, one might well be inclined to ask, first, where the catalog of possibilities will end and, second, whether these different frameworks overlap sufficiently to enable the identification of common trends or themes. In response to this second question, we find that theorists, going back to the turn of this century, began to propose a threefold group of dimensions that were used time and again as the raw materials for personality construction. Thus, Freud's "three polarities that govern all of mental life" were "discovered" by theorists both earlier and later than he . . . The three dimensions of *active-passive, subject-object,* and *pleasure-pain* were identified either in part or in all their components by (numerous theorists) . . . For example, the subject-object distinction parallels Jung's introversive-extroversive dichotomy; active-passive is the same polarity utilized by Adler and is traceable directly to a major distinction drawn by Aristotle. Clearly, then, a review of the basic ingredients selected for building personality typologies since the turn of the century uncovers an unusual consensus. It is these very three dimensions that were "discovered" once more by the author.

B. When theorists speak of the *active-passive* dimension they usually mean that the vast range of behaviors engaged in by a person may be fundamentally grouped in terms of whether the individual takes the initiative in shaping surrounding events or whether behavior is largely reactive to those events. The distinction of *pleasure-pain* recognizes that motivations are ultimately aimed in one of two directions, toward events which are attractive or positively reinforcing versus away from those which are aversive or negatively reinforcing. Similarly, the distinction of subject-object, or *self-other,* recognizes that among all objects and things in our environment there are two that stand out above all others in their power to affect us: our own selves and others. Using this threefold framework as a foundation, the author derived a series of personality "coping strategies" that correspond in close detail to each of the "official" personality disorders in the DSM-III.

Coping strategies may be viewed as complex forms of instrumental behavior, that is, ways of achieving positive reinforcements and avoiding negative reinforcements. These strategies reflect what kinds of reinforcements individuals have learned to seek or avoid (pleasure-pain), where individuals look to obtain them (self-others), and how individuals have learned to behave in order to elicit or escape them (active-passive). Eight basic coping patterns and three severe variants were derived by combining the *nature* (positive or pleasure versus negative or pain), the *source* (self versus others), and the *instrumental behaviors* (active versus passive) engaged in to achieve various reinforcements. Describing pathological strategies of behavior in reinforcement terms merely casts them in a somewhat different language than that utilized in the past.

C. A major distinction derived from the theoretical model is that people may be differentiated in terms of whether their primary *source of reinforcement* is within themselves or within others. This distinction corresponds to the dependent and independent patterns.

*Dependent* personalities have learned that feeling good, secure, confident, and so on, that is, those feelings associated with pleasure or the avoidance of pain—are best provided by *others*. Behaviorally, these personalities display a strong need for external support and attention; should they be deprived of affection and nurturance they will experience marked discomfort, if not sadness and anxiety.

*Independent* personality patterns, in contrast, are characterized by a reliance on the *self*. These individuals have learned that they obtain maximum pleasure and minimum pain if they depend on themselves rather than others. In both dependent and independent patterns, individuals demonstrate a distinct preference as to whether to turn to others or to themselves to gain security and comfort.

Such clear-cut commitments are not made by all personalities. Some, those whom we speak of as *ambivalent,* remain unsure as to which way to turn; that is, they are in conflict regarding whether to depend on themselves for reinforcement or on others. Some of these patients vacillate between turning to others in an agreeable conformity one time, and turning to themselves in efforts at independence, the next. Other ambivalent personalities display overt dependence and compliance; beneath these outwardly conforming behaviors, however, are strong desires to assert independent and often hostile feelings and impulses.

Finally, certain patients are characterized by their diminished ability to experience both pain and pleasure; they have neither a normal need for pleasure nor a normal need to avoid punishment. Another group of patients are also distinguished by a diminished ability to feel pleasurable reinforcers, but they are notably sensitive to pain; life is experienced as possessing few gratifications but much anguish. Both groups share a deficit capacity to sense pleasurable reinforcers, although one is hyperreactive to pain. We describe both of these as *detached* patterns; unable to experience rewards from themselves or from others, they drift increasingly into socially isolated and self-alienated behaviors.

D. Another theory-derived distinction reflects the fact that we instrumentally elicit the reinforcements we seek in essentially one of two ways: *actively* or *passively.*

Descriptively, those who are typically *active* tend to be characterized by their alertness, vigilance, persistence, decisiveness, and ambitiousness in a goal-directed behavior. They plan strategies, scan alternatives, manipulate events, and circumvent obstacles, all to the end of eliciting pleasures and rewards, or avoiding the distress of punishment, rejection, and anxiety. Although their goals may differ from time to time, they initiate events and are enterprising and energetically intent on controlling the circumstances of their environment.

By contrast, *passive* personalities engage in few overtly manipulative strategies to gain their ends. They often display a seeming inertness, a lack of ambition and persistence, an acquiescence, and a resigned attitude in which they initiate little to shape events and wait for the circumstances of their environment to take their course.

E. Using these polarities as a basis, the author derived a classification that combined in a four-by-two matrix the dependent, independent, ambivalent, and detached styles with the activity-passivity dimension. This produced eight basic types, with three severe variants, for a total of 11 theory-derived personality patterns. Despite their close correspondence to the official DSM-III personality disorders, these coping patterns are conceived as heuristic, and not as reified diagnostic entities. In the following paragraphs the eight milder pathological patterns are described first, followed by the three more severe variants. The labels assigned by the author and the DSM-III are noted in parentheses.

1. The *passive-dependent* coping strategy (Millon Submissive personality; DSM-III Dependent disorder) is characterized by a search for relationships in which one can lean upon others for affection, security, and leadership. This personality's lack of both initiative and autonomy is often a consequence of parental overprotection. As a function of these early experiences, these individuals have simply learned the comforts of assuming a passive role in interpersonal relations, accepting whatever kindness and support they may find, and willingly submitting to the wishes of others in order to maintain their affection.

2. The *active-dependent* coping strategy (Millon Gregarious personality; DSM-III Histrionic disorder) shows an insatiable and indiscriminate search for stimulation and affection. This personality's sociable and capricious behaviors give the appearance of considerable independence of others, but beneath this guise lies a fear of autonomy and an intense need for signs of social approval and attention. Affection must be replenished constantly and must be obtained from every source of interpersonal contact.

3. The *passive-independent* coping strategy (Millon Narcissistic personality; DSM-III Narcissistic disorder) is noted by an egotistic self-involvement. As a function of early experience these persons have learned to overvalue their self-worth; their confidence in their superiority may, however, be based on false premises. Nevertheless, they assume that others will recognize their specialness, maintain an air of arrogant self-assurance, and, without much thought or even conscious intent, benignly exploit others to their own advantage.

4. The *active-independent* coping strategy (Millon Aggressive personality; DSM-III Antisocial disorder) reflects a learned mistrust of others and a desire for autonomy and retribution for what are felt as past injustices. There is an indiscriminate striving for power and a disposition to be rejecting of others; these actions are seen as justified because people are

unreliable and duplicitous. Autonomy and hostility are claimed to be the only means to head off deceit and betrayal.

5. The *passive-ambivalent* coping strategy (Millon Conforming personality; DSM-III Compulsive disorder) is based on a conflict between hostility toward others and a fear of social disapproval. These persons resolve their ambivalence not only by suppressing resentment but by overconforming and over-complying, at least on the surface. Lurking behind this front of propriety and restraint, however, are anger and intense oppositional feelings that, on occasion, break through their controls.

6. The *active-ambivalent* coping strategy (Millon Negativistic personality; DSM-III Passive-aggressive disorder) represents an inability to resolve conflicts similar to those of the passive-ambivalent; however, this ambivalence remains close to consciousness and intrudes into everyday life. These individuals get themselves into endless wrangles and disappointments as they vacillate between deference and conformity, at one time, and aggressive negativism, the next. Their behavior displays an erratic pattern of explosive anger or stubbornness intermingled with moments of guilt and shame.

7. The *passive-detached* coping strategy (Millon Asocial personality; DSM-III Schizoid disorder) is characterized by social impassivity. Affectionate needs and emotional feelings are minimal, and the individual functions as a passive observer detached from the rewards and affections, as well as from the demands, of human relationships.

8. The *active-detached* coping strategy (Millon Avoidant personality; DSM-III Avoidant disorder) represents a fear and mistrust of others. These individuals maintain a constant vigil lest their impulses and longing for affection result in a repetition of the pain and anguish they have experienced with others previously. Only by active withdrawal can they protect themselves. Despite desires to relate, they have learned that it is best to deny these feelings and keep an interpersonal distance.

Three additional personality coping strategies are identified at a moderately dysfunctional level of pathology. They are differentiated from the first eight by several criteria, notably deficits in social competence and periodic (but reversible) psychotic episodes. Less integrated and effective in coping than their milder personality counterparts, they appear especially vulnerable to the strains of everyday life. Their major features and similarities to DSM-III personality disorders are briefly summarized.

9. The author's *cycloid personality* corresponds to the DSM-III "borderline personality disorder" and represents a moderately dysfunctional dependent or ambivalent orientation. These personalities experience intense endogenous moods, with recurring periods of dejection and apathy interspersed with spells of anger, anxiety, or euphoria. Many reveal recurring self-mutilating and suicidal thoughts, appear preoccupied with securing affection, have difficulty maintaining a clear sense of identity, and display a cognitive-affective ambivalence evident in simultaneous feelings of rage, love, and guilt toward others.

10. The *paranoid* personality is described in a similar fashion by both the author and the DSM-III. It represents a dysfunctional independent coping strategy. Here are seen a vigilant mistrust of others and an edgy defensiveness against anticipated criticism and deception. There is an abrasive irritability and a tendency to precipitate exasperation and anger in others. Expressed often is a fear of losing independence, leading this personality to vigorously resist external influence and control.

11. The DSM-III schizotypal disorder and the author's *schizoid* personality both display a constellation of behaviors that reflect a poorly integrated or dysfunctional detached personality pattern. These persons prefer isolation with minimal personal attachments and obligations. Behavioral eccentricities are notable, and the individual is often perceived by others as strange or different. Depending on whether the pattern is passive or active, there will be either an anxious wariness and hypersensitivity, or an emotional flattening and deficiency of affect.

## ON THE SEVERITY OF THE PERSONALITY DISORDERS

In presenting the syndromes of personality, we sequenced them in terms of their level of severity. However, a question must be asked: How are severity levels gauged; that is, what criteria are employed to determine whether one personality disorder is typically more severe than another?

Two classification systems in current use pay special attention to criteria differentiating personality disorders along the dimension of severity, those of Kernberg and of the author.

Direct comparison is not feasible since the character types presented by Kernberg do not correspond to the DSM-III personality disorders. Nevertheless, it will be useful to put aside DSM-III comparability and consider the conceptual distinctions that differentiate Kernberg's views from those of the author.

The major distinction between Kernberg and the author is not found in the clinical signs they include to gauge severity but rather in the ones they choose to emphasize. For Kernberg, primary attention is given to the internal structural characteristics of the personality, whereas for the author the *external* social system and interpersonal dynamics are given a status equal that of internal organization.

Kernberg focuses on "nonspecific manifestations of ego weakness," as illustrated in shifts toward primary process thinking, defensive operations characterized as "splitting," increasingly primitive idealizations, and early forms of projection and omnipotence. Though differences do exist, both Kernberg and the author identify the following similar features: loss of impulse control, disturbed psychological cohesion, rigid versus diffused ego functions, adaptive inflexibility, ambivalent or conflict-ridden defenses, blurrings of self and nonself, and so on. My own view goes beyond these, however, by stressing a systems perspective that interprets the internal structure as being functional or dysfunctional depending on its efficacy and stability within the context of interpersonal, familial, and other social dynamics. Thus, I speak additionally of such severity criteria as deficits in social competence, checkered personal relationships, digressions from early aspirations, and repetitive interpersonal quandaries and disappointments. From this view severity is conceived as a person-field interaction that includes not only intrapsychic dynamics but interpersonal dynamics as well. Although Kernberg stresses the importance of internalized object relations, the author assigns them a major role by equating both "internalized" past and contemporary "real" social relationships. In this way, the boundaries of both structure and dynamics are expanded such that internal structural features are placed within a context or system of external social dynamics.

A positive consequence of broadening the criteria of severity is that personality pathology need no longer be traced exclusively to intrapsychic origins in conflict and defense. By enlarging our vista so as to include interpersonal efficacy within a social context, our reference base for conceptualizing disordered personality has been expanded. A shift from the view that all pathogenic sources derive from internal conflicts is consistent with Fenichel's notion of "sublimation" character types and reinforces the ego analysts' assertion of conflict-free spheres of development and learning. No longer restricted by the limiting intrapsychic outlook, personality disorders can now be conceived best as any behavior pattern that is consistently inappropriate, maladaptive, or deficient in the social and familial system within which the individual operates. And, in accord with this broader systems perspective, several personality syndromes described by the author and formulated for the DSM-III are recognized as having developed "conflict-free"—that is, they are products of inadequate or misguided learning; others, of course, are conceived more traditionally as primarily "reactive"—that is, they are consequences of conflict resolutions. For example, some dependent personalities unfold in large measure as a result of simple parental overprotection and insufficiently learned autonomous behaviors, and not from instinctual conflicts and regressive adaptations.

The logic for broadening the criteria of severity to include the interplay of both individual and social systems seems especially appropriate when considering personality syndromes. Not only do personality traits express themselves primarily within group and familial environments, but the patient's style of communication, interpersonal competency and social skill will, in great measure, elicit reactions that feed back to shape the future course of whatever impairments the person may already have. Thus, the behavior and attitudes that individuals exhibit with others will evoke reciprocal reactions that influence whether their problems will improve, stabilize or intensify. Internal organization or structure is significant, of course, but the character or style of relating interpersonally may have as much to do with whether the sequence of social dynamics will prove rewarding or destructive. It is not only the structural ego capacity, therefore, but also the particular features of social and familial behavior that will dispose the patient to relate to others in a manner that will prove increasingly adaptive or maladaptive.

B. Utilizing a systems perspective that includes the interplay of both internal and external dynamics groups the eleven personality disorders of the DSM-III into three broad categories.

1. The first includes the dependent, histrionic, narcissistic, and antisocial personality disorders. These four personality patterns are *either* dependent or independent in their style of interpersonal functioning. Their intrapsychic structures enable them to conceive of themselves and to deal with others in a relatively coherent, "nonsplit," or nonconflictful manner—that is, in a reasonably consistent and focused rather than a diffused or divided way. Moreover, because the needs and traits that underlie their coping style dispose them to seek out others and to relate socially, they are able either to adapt to or to control their interpersonal environment so as to be sustained and nourished emotionally, and thereby maintain their psychic cohesion.

2. The *second* group, that viewed at a mid-level of personality severity, includes the compulsive, passive-aggressive, schizoid, and avoidant personality disorders. These represent a lower level of functioning than the first group for several reasons. In the two ambivalent types, the compulsive and passive-aggressive personalities, there is a split within both their interpersonal and their intrapsychic orientations; they are unable to find a coherent or consistent direction to focus either their personal relationships or their defensive operations. They are in conflict, split between assuming an independent or dependent stance; hence, they often undo or reverse their social behaviors and frequently feel internally divided. The second pair of this foursome, the two detached types, labeled the schizoid and avoidant personalities in the DSM-III, are judged at a mid-level of severity because they are characteristically isolated or estranged from external support systems. As a consequence, they

are likely to have few subliminatory channels and fewer still interpersonal sources
of nurturance and stability, the lack of
which will dispose them to increasingly
autistic preoccupations and regressions.

3. The third set, reflecting still lower levels
   of personality functioning, includes the
   DSM-III borderline, paranoid, and schizotypal disorders. All three are socially "in-
   competent," difficult to relate to, and
   often isolated, hostile, or confused; hence,
   they are not likely to elicit the interpersonal support that could bolster their flag-
   ging defenses and orient them to a more
   effective and satisfying life-style. Moreover, a clear breakdown in the cohesion of
   personality organization is seen in both
   schizotypal and borderline disorders. The
   converse is evident in the paranoid, where
   there is an overly rigid and narrow focus
   to the personality structure. In the former
   pair there has been a dissolution or diffusion of ego capacities; in the latter,
   the paranoid pattern, there is an inelastic-
   ity and constriction of personality, giving
   rise to a fragility and inadaptability of
   functions.

# A Theoretical Derivation of Pathological Personalities

Scholars often find it useful to step back from their intense and close involvement in their subject, disengage themselves from its current themes and assumptions, and reflect on a series of philosophically naive yet fundamental questions, such as:

What is essential to the subject?

What distinguishes it from others?

What are the questions for which I should find answers?

What observations and concepts have given the field its legitimacy as a science ?

Do these data and ideas limit or distort my thinking?

Can the empirical elements of the subject be identified in a more efficient and reliable manner than previously?

Can its central notions be defined more relevantly or articulated more insightfully than heretofore?

Might I formulate relationships among its elements in a more productive and coherent way than has been done in the past?

The content of this paper reflects efforts to answer questions such as these. It also provides the rationale for a theory, as well as the clinical prototypes generated by that theory. The subject matter to which the theory applies—personality disorders—encompasses the several, relatively distinct ways in which individuals persistently and pervasively function in an interpersonally and intrapsychically pathogenic manner. Before presenting the theory and its derivations, it may be useful to briefly note a number of issues relevant to the concept of personality itself as well as its disorders.

## GENERAL ISSUES

The vast majority of empirical discoveries and theoretical constructs that have occupied the attention of psychologists and psychiatrists have suffered the fate that General Douglas MacArthur thought unique to old generals, that is, they never die, they just fade away. As Meehl (1978) has put it:

There is a period of enthusiasm about a new theory, a period of attempted application to several fact domains, a period of disillusionment as the negative data come in, a growing bafflement about inconsistent and unreplicable empirical results, multiple resort to ad hoc excuses, and then finally people just sort of lose interest in the thing and pursue other endeavors. (p. 807)

Theories, constructs, and findings of such fortune are legion, a sad comment on the "scientific" status of our subject, no less our naive eagerness to follow one evanescent or insubstantial fad after another. Although most conceptual pursuits in the softer psychologies have come and gone, justly or otherwise (as others have remained immutably entrenched despite impressive rebuttals or incompatible evidence), there are encouraging signs that cumulative knowledge and a refining process may be underway in the study of personality.

Especially promising is the observation that the essential elements that give substance to personality—the fact that people exhibit distinctive and abiding characteristics—have survived through the ages, albeit under diverse rubrics and labels. This durability attests, at the very least, either to personality's intuitive consonance with authentic observation, its intrinsic, if naive human interest, or its decided and convincing utility. The apparent viability of the concept as well as its invulnerability in academic circles is all the more noteworthy when one considers the number of spirited, if misguided, efforts in recent years to undo it. This achievement is even more impressive when one considers the number of recently popular constructs that have faded to a status more consonant with their trivial character, or have, under the weight of their scientific inefficacy, succumbed to scholarly weariness or boredom. By contrast, personality and its disorders appear not only to have weathered mettlesome assaults, witness the position reversals of its most ardent critics (e.g., Mischel, 1973, 1979) but appear to be undergoing a wide-ranging renaissance in both professional and scientific circles. This resurgence may be worth elaborating briefly, for it signifies the coalescence of powerful, if disparate trends.

First, from a rather mundane and practical viewpoint, most mental health practitioners employ their professional skills today in outpatient rather than inpatient settings. Their "clients" are no longer the severely disturbed "State Hospital" psychotic, but ambulatory individuals seen in private offices or community clinics, beset with personal stressors, social inadequacies, or interpersonal conflicts, typically reported in symptoms such as anxiety, depression, or alcoholism, but which signify the outcroppings of longstanding patterns of maladaptive behaving, feeling, thinking, and relating: in other words, their "personality style."

Second, there has been a marked shift in the focus of dynamic therapies from that of "surface" neurotic symptoms to that of "underlying" personality functions. This reorientation reflects the intriguing evolution of psychoanalytic theory since the turn of the century. Auchincloss and Michels (1983) describe this progression in an illuminating review of the psychoanalytic concept of "character." They write, "Today it is generally accepted that character disorders, not neurotic symptoms, are the primary indication for analysis. . . . Psychoanalysis (as a technique) and character analysis have become synonymous" (p. 2).

As character theory progressed from the ideas of Abraham on libidinal development to those of Reich on defensive armor, personality (character) changed from being a developmentally phase-specific cluster of symptoms to a system of intrapsychic resistances that blocked the treatment of these symptoms. Recent contributions of ego, self, and object-relations theorists have extended our awareness of the highly varied consequences of early psychic deprivations. Today, character structure is seen not only as a system of defensive operations, but a complex organization of structures that are the focus of therapeutic attention and intervention.

It is not only the changing patient population of clinical practice or the recently evolved role given "character" and "personality organization" in analytic theory that signifies the growing prominence of the construct. In the realms of "hard science," that of quantitative clinical assessment and psychometrics, psychologists and psychiatrists alike have turned their skills toward the reliable identification and valid measurement, not of "traits" of personality, a well-worn subject of diminished scientific merit, but of the new "disorders" of personality (Reich, 1984). This change in focus may be seen most clearly in the content of recently developed clinical instruments. These assessment tools contrast in scope and intent with both the historically important projective techniques, such as the Rorschach, and the well established, if nondynamic objective inventories, such as the Minnesota Multiphasic Personality Inventory (MMPI). Newly minted are a group of impressively constructed clinical interview schedules, such as the DIB (Gunderson, Kolb, & Austin, 1981), which seek to build a composite picture of a single, comprehensive entity, in this case the "borderline personality," or the broadly based self-report inventory, the MCMI (Millon, 1983a), with its psychometrically validated series of scales designed to identify and describe the dynamics of all 11 DSM-III, Axis-II disorders.

A few words should be said concerning the special role of the DSM-III (American Psychiatric Association, 1980) in giving prominence to the personality disorders. With the advent of this official system, personality not only gained a place of consequence among syndromal categories, but became central to its multiaxial schema. The logic for assigning personality its own axis is more than a matter of differentiating syndromes of a more acute and dramatic form from those that may be overlooked by virtue of their longstanding and prosaic character, a position assumed by Kendell (1983). More relevant to this partitioning decision was the assertion that personality can serve usefully as a dynamic substrate of affective, cognitive, and behavioral dispositions from which clinicians can better grasp the "meaning" of their patients' more transient or florid disorders. In the DSM-III, then, personality disorders have not only attained a nosological status of prominence in their own right, but they have been assigned a contextual role that makes them fundamental to the understanding of other psychopathologies.

## PERSONALITY AS A SYSTEM

Opinions differ concerning how best to define personality. There is general agreement, however, that it is an inferred abstraction rather than a tangible phenomenon with material existence. Problems

inevitably arise, however, when professionals reify these conceptual constructs into substantive entities. To paraphrase Kendell (1975), "familiarity leads us to forget their origins in human imagination." Certainly, personality should not be construed as a palpable "disease." It is a man-made construction invented to facilitate scientific understanding and professional communication. Should constructs fail in these aims, they should be recast or discarded. Unfortunately, most are likely to fade slowly, as do old generals, receding ever deeper into the dustbins of history.

What should the construct "personality" represent?

It may best be conceived as the psychological equivalent of the body's biological system of structures and functions. To elaborate: Our body as a whole comprises a well-organized, yet open system of relatively stable structures that interconnect functionally as they process a wide range of both internal and external events in a coherent and efficient manner. The diversity of functions carried out by the body is awesome in its complexity and efficacy, as is the internal organization of structures impressively elaborate in its intricacy and articulation. The distinctive configuration of structures and functions that have evolved ensures that the system as a whole remains both viable and stable. This is achieved by processes that maintain internal cohesion and by actions that utilize, control, or adapt to external forces. A biological disorder arises when one or several of the following occurs: The balance and synchrony among internal components go awry; a particular structure is traumatized or deteriorates, with the result that it repetitively or persistently malfunctions; foreign entities such as bacteria or viruses intrude themselves, either overwhelming or insidiously undermining the system's integrity.

The construct "personality" represents a psychic system of structures and functions which parallel those of the body. It is not a potpourri of unrelated traits and miscellaneous behaviors, but a tightly knit organization of stable structures (e.g., internalized memories and self-images) and coordinated functions (e.g., unconscious mechanisms and cognitive processes). Given continuity in one's constitutional equipment and a narrow band of experiences for learning behavioral alternatives, this "system" develops an integrated pattern of characteristics and inclinations that are deeply etched, cannot be easily eradicated, and pervade every facet of life experience. The system is the sum and substance of what is meant by personality. Mirroring the body's organization, it is a distinctive configuration of interlocking perceptions, feelings, thoughts, and behaviors that provide a template and disposition for maintaining psychic viability and stability. From this perspective, mental disorders are best conceived as stemming from failures in the personality system's dynamic pattern of adaptive competencies, just as physical ill health is never a simple matter of an intrusive alien virus, but reflects also deficiencies in the body's capacity to cope with particular physical environments, so too is psychological ill health not merely a product of psychic stress alone, but represents deficiencies in the personality system's capacity to cope with particular psychosocial environments.

Implied in the preceding paragraph is the assertion that adequate clinical analyses of both physical and mental disorders require data beyond those which inhere in the individual alone. In the biological realm, it must encompass knowledge of relevant features of the physical environment; in the psychological domain, it calls for an awareness of the character of the psychological environment. Kendell points to the reciprocal nature of this person-environment field in the following illustration (1975):

A characteristic which is a disadvantage in one environment may be beneficial in another. The sickle cell trait is a deviation from the norm which in most environments produces a slight but definite biological disadvantage. In an environment in which malaria is endemic, however, it is positively beneficial. . . . This is a particularly serious matter where mental illness is concerned because here the environment, and especially its social aspects, is often of paramount importance. Qualities like recklessness and aggressiveness, for example, may lead a man to be regarded as a psychopath in one environment and to be admired in another. (p. 15)

For the greater part of our psychodiagnostic history, attention has focused on the patient's internal characteristics alone. When one moves to a systems perspective, external social and interpersonal dynamics are given equal status. As noted in Kendell's illustration, it may be clinically impossible to disentangle these elements when appraising the clinical consequences of an internal characteristic, for example, whether the sickle cell trait is advantageous or disadvantageous. For diagnostic purposes, internal and external factors are inextricably linked elements. Intrapsychic structures and dispositions are essential, but they will prove functional or dysfunctional depending on their efficacy in specific interpersonal, familial, or social contexts. (It should be noted parenthetically that to assert that internal and external factors are interdependent and reciprocal is not to say that they contribute equal shares to the variance or prevalence of a particular pathology.)

The rationale for broadening the notion of a "disorder" to include the interplay of both internal and external systems is especially appropriate when evaluating personality syndromes. Not only does personality express itself in everyday, routine interactions within group and familial settings, but the ordinary characteristics that comprise the patient's personality will elicit reactions that feed back to shape the future course of whatever impairments the person may already have. Thus, the behaviors, mechanisms, and self-attitudes that individuals exhibit with others will evoke reciprocal responses that influence whether their problems will improve, stabilize, or intensify. It is not only how experiences are processed intrapsychically, therefore, but also how social and familial dynamics unfold that will determine whether the patient functions in an adaptive or maladaptive manner. . . .

## SYSTEMS VERSUS DISORDERS AND REACTIONS

The use of quotes around the term "disorder" reflects a recognition that nosological classifications can go awry if their categories encompass too wide a range of clinical conditions; there is need to subdivide the subject of psychopathology along critical points of distinction. As discussed in Millon (in press), the ideal framework for a taxonomy of mental disorders should be based on dimensions such as space and time. Translated into nosological terms, space means the degree to which the manifestation of a pathological process falls on a continuum from "circumscribed" (focal) to "pervasive" (systemic). Time represents the duration of the psychopathology, that is, where it falls on a continuum from "transient" (acute) to "enduring" (chronic). It is largely on these grounds that an attempt is made here to differentiate among personality systems, symptom disorders, and behavior reactions (Millon, 1969).

In addition to the two dimensions of circumscribed—pervasive and transient—enduring, the primary basis for distinguishing the concepts of system, disorder, and reaction is the extent to which the observed pathology can be attributed to ingrained or internal characteristics versus external psychosocial stressors or precipitants. We recognize, as previously discussed, that pathology always reflects a person-environment interaction. Nevertheless, it will be useful to distinguish types of pathology in terms of the extent to which their determinants derive from personological versus situational or less equally and simultaneously to internal personal attributes and external situational events. Exhibited as intensifications of a patient's characteristic style of functioning or as disruptions in his or her underlying

psychic structures, symptom disorders are conceived as reactions to situations for which the individual's personality system is notably vulnerable.

Viewed from a different perspective, the structural and functional attributes that comprise personality have an inner momentum and autonomy; they are expressed with minimal inducement or external provocation. In contrast, the responses comprising behavior reactions are conceived as stimulus specific. They not only operate independent of the individual's personality, but are elicited by events that are apt to be judged consensually as "objectively" troublesome. Symptom disorders are similar to behavior reactions in that they are prompted also by external events, but their close connection to inner personality dynamics results in the intrusion of memories and affects that complicate what might otherwise be a simple reaction to the environment. Hence, they often fail to "make objective sense," appearing irrational and strangely complicated. To the knowledgeable clinician, however, a disorder signifies the presence of an unusual vulnerability on the part of the patient; in effect, a seemingly neutral stimulus has reactivated a painful hidden memory or emotion. Viewed in this manner, symptom disorders arise in individuals who are encumbered with notably adverse past experiences. The upsurge of deeply rooted feelings presses to the surface, overrides present realities, and becomes the prime stimulus to which the individual responds. It is this flooding into the present of the reactivated past that gives symptom disorders much of their symbolic, bizarre, and hidden meaning.

In contrast to symptom disorders, behavior reactions are simple and straightforward. They do not "pass through" a chain of complicated internal structures and circuitous functional transformations before emerging in manifest form. Uncontaminated by the intrusion of distant memories and intrapsychic processes, behavior reactions tend to be rational and understandable in terms of precipitating stimuli. Isolated from past emotions and defensive manipulations, they are expressed in an uncomplicated and consistent fashion, unlike symptom disorders, whose features are highly fluid, wax and wane, and take different forms at different times.

The terminology and categories of the DSM-III have not been differentiated in accord with the preceding discussion; the label "disorder" is applied to all pathological syndromes, including those termed "personality disorders." There may be good reason to reflect further on these distinctions as we plan the DSM-IV.

It will suffice for the present to translate these distinctions into DSM-III terms. Axis-II, personality (trait or disorder), represents a system of deeply ingrained structures and broadly exhibited functions that persist and endure over extended periods and have come to characterize the individual's distinctive manner of relating to his environmental system. Both symptom disorders and behavior reactions closely correspond to the categories comprising the clinical syndromes of Axis-I. And with reference to the preceding section, we might consider Axis-IV, psychosocial stressors, to be a somewhat foreshortened representation of the environmental (social and familial) system. Framed in this schema, symptom disorders (Axis-I) may best be conceived of as the upshot of a dynamic interaction between Axis-II (personality) and Axis-IV (stressors). . . .

## PERSONALITY PROTOTYPES

This paper will address the issue of whether the construct "prototype" itself can usefully be conceived as paralleling the medical concept of "syndrome." In so doing, we must ask whether "psychological" syndromes, either in fact or logic, exist in the same sense as do biological syndromes. Prior to providing a rationale for the reality of psychological syndromes, especially as they apply to personality pathology, we will outline the manner in which the concept of prototypes,

borrowed from cognitive psychology and recently introduced as a formulation for construing and categorizing mental disorders, can be adopted meaningfully as the psychological equivalent of medical syndromes; if it proves apt in this regard, DSM-IV might properly retitle its Axis II section to read "Personality Prototypes."

## SYNDROMES, TYPES, AND PROTOTYPES

To refresh our memories and make our definitions more explicit, the medical terms "signs" and "symptoms" represent either objectively recorded or subjectively reported changes in state or function that often arise in conjunction with known pathological processes; these changes not only serve to alert the diagnostician that a pathological process may be under way, but often help identify both its location and character.

The concept "syndrome" represents the clustering of a set of signs or symptoms that frequently co-occur or covary. Not all of the signs and symptoms of a disease are likely to be immediately observed, but the presence of a subset of a syndromic pattern often suggests that other features that typify it might be uncovered upon closer examination. This searching and diagnostically confirming procedure is described well by Dahlstrom (1972):

Some pattern of complaints, clinical findings, and signs is tentatively identified. Study of individuals manifesting this syndromic pattern proceeds retrospectively in an effort to identify both antecedent conditions and precipitating events (etiology), concurrently in an effort to identify additional signs or symptoms that may be part of the syndrome and possibly enhance differential diagnostic accuracy (nosology or diagnostics), and prospectively to plot the subsequent course of the disorder (prognosis) or evaluate the impact of various ameliorative interventions (therapeusis). The aims of these investigations are of course to develop some formulation of the nature of the disorder and to be able to prevent future manifestations in the afflicted individual and in others (prophylaxis) or at least ameliorate the condition when it does appear. (p. 8)

By convention, syndromes do not identify a person, but define a disorder; that is, they represent pathological processes that affect particular and limited structures or functions of the individual, but are neither synonymous nor coterminous with the individual as a whole. As a result of their restricted nature, several syndromes may coexist in the same person. Not only do they occupy less "space," so to speak, than does the entire individual, but syndromes are usually time-limited, that is, both impermanent and possessing a circumscribed temporal course. Variations in quantitative severity from person to person and from time to time within a single person also characterize syndromes. Not only is there a waxing and waning in the salience of its component signs and symptoms, but only a few of its typical indices are likely to be manifest at any one time. Owing both to its changeability and partial expression, definitive assignments of a syndrome often require the presence of certain necessary or joint criteria. Rarely, however, are the signs and symptoms comprising these criteria syndromically exclusive, that is, never found in other syndromes.

Whereas the term syndrome represents a cluster or set of covarying symptoms, the term "type" designates a group of individuals who exhibit in common a single, preeminent characteristic that distinguishes them from other individuals. Among other points of differentiation, types usually are conceived as holistic, that is, to represent or synthesize the individual's total psychological functioning. Further, the singular feature that sets the concept of type apart from other similar concepts is that its referents are usually assumed to be both durable and pervasive, that is, stable over time and consistent across situations. The qualities of holism, stability, and consistency have made the notion of "types" especially attractive to theorists as a framework for categorizing personalities.

The construct "prototype" has a long history, but only recently has it been introduced as a potentially useful option for classifying psychopathology. As presently formulated it appears to meld several attributes of both syndrome and type. It may prove especially apt as we seek to develop a schema for representing both the composite of diverse elements that comprise personality (the syndrome aspect) as well as the features that distinguish personality from other forms of psychopathology, namely, holism, durability, and pervasiveness (the type aspect).

How has the concept of prototype been defined?

Horowitz, Post, French, Wallis, and Siegelman (1981) describe the construct succinctly:

A prototype consists of the most common features or properties of members of a category and thus describes a theoretical ideal or standard against which real people can be evaluated. All of the prototype's properties are assumed to characterize at least some members of the category, but no one property is necessary or sufficient for membership in the category. Therefore, it is possible that no actual person would match the theoretical prototype perfectly. Instead, different people would approximate it to different degrees. The more closely a person approximates the ideal, the more the person typifies the concept. (p. 575)

Mischel (1984) characterizes the prototypal approach as useful in recognizing the:

. . . especially "fuzzy" nature of natural categories along the lines articulated by Wittgenstein. Category knowledge about persons and situations is represented by a loose set of features that are correlated, but only imperfectly, with membership in that category. The approach implies that categorization decisions (e.g., about who is a prototypic extrovert or used car salesman type) will be probabilistic and that the members of a category will vary in degree of membership. There will be many ambiguous borderline cases that yield overlapping, fuzzy boundaries between the categories. To study such fuzzy sets, one seeks the clearest and best exemplars (the most prototypic members), omitting the less prototypic, borderline instances. The prototype approach both to persons and to situations lends itself readily to the construction of orderly taxonomies containing categories at different levels of abstraction or inclusiveness. (p. 356)

Cantor, Smith, French, and Mezzich (1980) note that the "classical" approach to diagnosis depends on the identification of singly necessary or jointly sufficient features. By contrast, the prototypal view merely requires that sets be comprised of correlated features. As a result of this conceptual openness:

. . . prototypes permit extensive heterogeneity of category instances. Thus, one instance may contain most of the correlated features of the prototype and another may contain hardly any at all . . . prototypes make *sense* out of variations in typicality, where typical instances are simply those that share many correlated features with the category prototype. . . . The higher the overlap, the faster, more accurately, and more competently the instance can be classified. An immediate consequence of this prototype matching process is that typical instances will be categorized more efficiently than atypical ones, because typical instances have greater featural overlap with their prototypes. . . . To the degree that the prototypes for two categories have many common features and few distinctive ones, the categorizer may have difficulty distinguishing between members of these categories. . . . There is one more factor that must be considered in a prototype-matching process. This factor reflects the degree of richness of a category prototype (as measured by the total number of its features) as well as the distinctiveness of the prototype (as measured by the number of its features that are not shared by rival categories). (pp. 184–185)

It is evident that the prototype approach shares many of the attributes associated with the syndrome concept, notably the diversity of choices among its correlated signs and symptoms, and hence the heterogeneity found among similarly diagnosed patients. Albeit implicitly, the prototype model guided the thinking of several DSM-III Task Force members who formulated both the rules and diagnostic criteria of the manual, for example, the opportunity to select only a subset of the criteria that composed a category, the presence of "mixed" syndromes, even the encouragement of multiple diagnoses. Cantor et al. (1980) record that these DSM-III changes:

. . . help to emphasize, rather than obscure, the probabilistic nature of diagnostic categorizations. On the basis of the new manual, clinicians can now be trained to expect heterogeneity among patients and to recognize the probabilistic nature of diagnostic categorizations. Also, utilization of confidence/typicality ratings in diagnosis can be encouraged, and diagnoses can be made on the basis of degree of fit between the patient's cluster of symptoms and the prototypes for various different categories. (p. 192)

Although diverging from the single, overarching attribute that characterizes a typology (e.g., extroversion or introversion) the prototype concept is well-suited to represent the "typical," pervasive, durable, and holistic features that distinguish personality categories from the more symptomatic, less wide-spread, frequently transient, and narrowly circumscribed clinical syndromes.

## DEVELOPMENT OF PERSONALITY PROTOTYPES

There is a logic to the syndrome concept in medical disorders. Bodily changes wrought by infectious diseases and structural deteriorations repeatedly display themselves in a reasonably uniform pattern of signs and symptoms that "makes sense" in terms of how anatomic structures and physiological processes are altered and dysfunction. Moreover, these biological changes provide a foundation for identifying the etiology of these disorders as well as for recognizing their pathogenesis, course, and prognosis. Logic and fact together enable us to construct a rationale to explain why most medical syndromes express themselves in the signs and symptoms they do.

Can the same be said for psychological syndromes, specifically "personality prototypes"? Is there a logic, perhaps even evidence, for believing that certain signs and symptoms (e.g., behaviors, cognitions, affects, mechanisms) cluster together as do medical syndromes, that is, not only covary frequently, but make sense as a coherently organized and reasonably distinctive group of clinical characteristics? Are there theoretical and empirical justifications for believing that the varied features of personality display a configurational unity and expressive consistency over time? Will the careful study of individuals reveal congruency among attributes such as overt behavior, intrapsychic functioning, and biophysical disposition? Is this coherence and stability of psychological functioning a valid phenomenon, that is, not merely imposed upon observed data by virtue of clinical expectation or theoretical bias?

We contend that the answer to each of the preceding questions is yes. Stated simply, the observation of prototypic personality patterns by clinicians may be connected to the fact that people possess relatively enduring biophysical dispositions which give a consistent coloration to their experiences, and that the range of experiences to which people are exposed throughout their lives is both limited and repetitive (Millon, 1969, 1981). Given the limiting and shaping character of biological and psychological factors, it should not be surprising that individuals develop clusters of prepotent and deeply ingrained behaviors, cognitions, and affects that clearly distinguish them from others of dissimilar backgrounds. Once several of the components of a particular cluster are identified, knowledgeable observers should be able to infer the likely presence of other, unobserved, but frequently correlated features comprising that cluster.

If we accept the assumption that most people do display a cluster of internally consistent characteristics, we are led next to the question of whether groups of patients

evidence commonality in the clusters they display. The concepts of clinical syndrome and personality prototype rest on the assumption that there are a limited number of such shared clusters, that is, diagnostic signs and symptoms, pathogenic or not, which can confidently be used to distinguish certain groups or classes of patients. The fact that patients can profitably be classified into such syndromes or prototypes does not, of course, negate the fact that patients, so categorized, display considerable differences as well, a fact observed, of course, with medical diseases quite routinely. The philosopher, Grunbaum (1952), illustrates this point in the following:

Every individual is unique by virtue of being a distinctive assemblage of characteristics not precisely duplicated in any other individual. Nevertheless, it is quite conceivable that the following . . . might hold. If a male child having specifiable characteristics is subjected to maternal hostility and has a strong paternal attachment at a certain stage of his development, he will develop paranoia during adult life. If this . . . holds, then children who are subjected to the stipulated conditions in fact become paranoiacs, however much they may have differed in other respects in childhood and whatever their other differences may be once they are already insane. (p. 672)

What are the "specifiable characteristics" and what are the life experiences that give rise to clusters of clinical behavior that comprise identifiable syndromes or prototypes? If we review our literature in psychopathology, we will see that much of it addresses this specific question. Although this chapter is not the place to review so vast a body of theory, knowledge, and speculation, a few paragraphs indicating how personality prototype clusters are acquired may be useful.

The question to be addressed may best be phrased as follows: Why does the possession of characteristic A increase the probability, appreciably beyond chance, of also possessing characteristics B, C, and so on? Less abstractly, why do particular behaviors, attitudes, mechanisms, and so on covary in repetitive and recognizable ways rather than exhibit themselves in a more or less haphazard fashion? And, even more concretely, why do each of the following: behavioral defensiveness, interpersonal provocativeness, cognitive suspicion, affective irascibility, and excessive use of the projection mechanism, co-occur in the same individual rather than be uncorrelated and randomly distributed among different individuals?

The "answers," to be elaborated shortly, are, first, that temperament and early experience simultaneously affect the development and nature of several emerging psychological structures and functions; that is, a wide range of behaviors, attitudes, affects, and mechanisms can be traced to the same origins, leading thereby to their frequently observed covariance. Second, once an individual possesses these initial characteristics, they will, in turn, set in motion a series of derivative life experiences that will shape the acquisition of new psychological attributes causally related to the characteristics that preceded them in the sequential chain. . . .

## CLINICAL ATTRIBUTES

Individuals differ in the degree to which their behaviors are enduring and pervasive. Moreover, each individual displays this durability and pervasiveness only in certain of his or her characteristics; that is, each of us possesses a limited number of attributes that are resistant to changing times and situational influences, whereas other of our attributes are readily modified. Furthermore, it should be noted that the features which exhibit this consistency and stability in one person may not be the same features exhibited by others. These core qualities of persistence and extensiveness appear only in characteristics that have become crucial in maintaining the individual's structural balance and functional style, for example, passive-dependent, active-detached. To illustrate: The "interpersonal" attribute of significance for some is being

agreeable, never differing or having conflict; for another, it may be interpersonally critical to keep one's distance from people so as to avoid rejection or the feeling of being humiliated; for a third, the influential interpersonal characteristic may be that of asserting one's will and dominating others.

Each personality prototype should comprise a small and distinct group of primary attributes that persist over time and exhibit a high degree of consistency across situations (Mischel, 1984). These enduring (stable) and pervasive (consistent) characteristics are what we search for when we "diagnose" personality.

In the following paragraphs, we will identify a number of the major attributes of personality that possess clinical significance. More specifically, we will outline a set of structural and functional characteristics that not only will aid us in differentiating among the pathological personalities, but will provide us with diagnostic criteria for identifying each personality prototype.

Many of the signs, symptoms, and characteristics that patients exhibit can usefully be categorized and dimensionalized for purposes of clinical analysis. One set of distinctions, that differentiating diagnostic features in accord with biophysical, intrapsychic, phenomenological, and behavioral data levels, reflects the focus of the four classical and doctrinaire approaches that characterize the study of psychopathology, namely, the biological, the psychoanalytic, the cognitive, and the behavioral (Millon, 1983b).

Valuable though it may be to organize a schema which represents these historic models, it may be more useful to put them aside in favor of an arrangement that represents the personality system in a manner similar to that of the body system, that is, dividing its components into *structural* and *functional* attributes. The biological subjects of anatomy and physiology, respectively, investigate embedded and essentially permanent structures, which serve as mechanisms for action, and functions, which regulate internal changes and external transactions.

Dividing the characteristics of the psychological world into structural and functional realms is by no means a novel notion. Psychoanalytic theory has dealt since its inception with topographic constructs such as conscious, preconscious, and unconscious, and later with structural concepts such as id, ego, and superego; likewise, a host of "quasi-stationary" functional processes, such as the so-called ego apparatuses, notably motility, attention, perception, and cognition, have been posited and studied (Gill, 1963; Rapaport, 1959).

There are several benefits to differentiating the more-or-less stable and organized clinical attributes (structures) from those that represent processing and modulating features (functions). For the present, it will suffice simply to define the terms "function" and "structure" as they apply to clinical matters; we may then proceed to identify those attributes that are most relevant to personality diagnosis.

## FUNCTIONAL ATTRIBUTES

Functional characteristics represent dynamic processes that transpire within the intrapsychic world and between the individual and his psychosocial environment. For definitional purposes, we might say that functional clinical attributes represent "expressive modes of regulatory action," that is, behaviors, cognitions, perceptions, affect, and mechanisms which manage, adjust, transform, coordinate, balance, discharge, and control the give and take of inner and outer life.

Not only are there several modes of regulatory action (e.g., behavioral, cognitive, affective), but there are numerous variations in the way each of these functional modalities are manifested or expressed (e.g., affectively flat, affectively hostile, affectively labile). Every individual employs every modality in the course of his life, but individuals differ with respect to the modalities they enact most frequently and, even more so, diverge in which of the expressive variations of these functions they typically manifest. As Bowers

has put it (1977): "The way a person performs a common behavior is sometimes quite revealing. One person ordinarily eats and makes love fastidiously; another person is given to gluttony in both circumstances. The more idiosyncratically expressive a common behavior is . . . (the more it is) attributable to a relatively stable personality and behavioral organizations" (p. 75).

Particular modalities and expressive variations characterize certain personalities best, but even the most distinctive of personalities will display several variations of a modality. Dissimilar individuals differ in which modality variations they express most often, but these differences are largely a matter of *quantitative frequency* (dimensionality) and not *qualitative distinctness* (categorality).

Four functional clinical attributes relevant to personality will be briefly described. Thirteen expressive variations, one associated with each personality prototype.

1. **Behavioral Presentation.** These relate to the observables of physical and verbal behavior, usually recorded by noting what the patient does and how he does it. Through inference, observations of overt behavior enable us to deduce either what the patient unknowingly reveals about him or herself or, often conversely, what he or she wishes us to think or to know about him or her. The range and character of behavioral functions are not only wide and diverse, but they convey both distinctive and worthwhile clinical information, from communicating a sense of personal incompetence to exhibiting general defensiveness to demonstrating a disciplined self-control, and so on.

2. **Interpersonal Conduct.** A patient's style of relating to others may be captured in a number of ways, such as the manner in which his or her actions impact on others, intended or otherwise, the attitudes that underlie, prompt, and give shape to these actions, the methods by which he or she engages others to meet his or her needs, or

his or her way of coping with social tensions and conflicts. Extrapolating from these observations, the clinician may construct an image of how the patient functions in relation to others, be it antagonistically, respectfully, aversively, secretively, and so on.

3. **Cognitive Style.** How the patient perceives events, focuses his or her attention, processes information, organizes thoughts, and communicates his or her reactions and ideas to others are among the most useful indices to the clinician of the patient's distinctive way of functioning. By synthesizing these signs and symptoms, it may be possible to identify indications of what may be termed an impoverished style, or distracted thinking, or cognitive flightiness, or constricted thought, and so on.

4. **Unconscious Mechanism.** Although "mechanisms" of self-protection, need gratification, and conflict resolution are consciously recognized at times, those that remain unconscious and thereby avoid reflective appraisal often begin a sequence of events that intensifies the very problems they were intended to circumvent. Mechanisms usually represent internal processes and, hence, are more difficult to discern and describe than processes anchored closer to the observable world. Despite the methodological problems they present, the task of identifying which mechanisms are chosen (e.g., rationalization, displacement, reaction-formation) and the extent to which they are employed is central to a comprehensive personality assessment.

## STRUCTURAL ATTRIBUTES

These attributes represent a deeply embedded and relatively enduring template of imprinted memories, attitudes, needs, fears, conflicts, and so on, which guide the experience and transform the nature of ongoing life events. Psychic structures have an orienting and preemptive effect in that they alter the character of action and the impact of subsequent experiences in line with preformed inclinations and expectancies. By selectively lowering thresholds for transactions that are consonant with either constitutional proclivities or early learnings, future events are often experienced as variations of the past. The following describes both the character and persistence of these structural residues of early experience (Millon, 1969).

Significant experiences of early life may never recur again, but their effects remain and leave their mark. Physiologically, we may say they have etched a neurochemical change; psychologically, they are registered as memories, a permanent trace and an embedded internal stimulus. In contrast to the fleeting stimuli of the external world, these memory traces become part and parcel of every stimulus complex which activates behavior. Once registered, the effects of the past are indelible, incessant and inescapable. They now are intrinsic elements of the individual's makeup; they latch on and intrude into the current events of life, coloring, transforming and distorting the passing scene. Although the residuals of subsequent experiences may override them, becoming more dominant internal stimuli, the presence of earlier memory traces remains in one form or another. In every thought and action, the individual cannot help but carry these remnants into the present. Every current behavior is a perpetuation, then, of the past, a continuation and intrusion of these inner stimulus traces.

The residuals of the past do more than passively contribute their share to the present. By temporal precedence, if nothing else, they guide, shape or distort the character of current events. Not only are they ever present, then, but they operate insidiously to transform new stimulus experiences in line with past (p. 200).

For purposes of definition, structural attributes might be described as "cognitive-affective substrates and action dispositions of a quasi-permanent nature." Possessing a network of interconnecting pathways, these structures contain the internalized residues of the past in the form of memories and affects that are associated intrapsychically with conceptions of self and others.

Four structural attributes relevant to personality will be briefly described.

1. **Self-Image.** As the inner world of symbols is mastered through development, the "swirl" of events that buffet the young child gives way to a growing sense of order and continuity. One major configuration emerges to impose a measure of sameness upon an otherwise fluid environment, the perception of self-as-object, a distinct, ever-present, and identifiable "I" or "me." Self-identity provides a stable anchor to serve as a guidepost and to give continuity to changing experience. Most persons have an implicit sense of who they are, but differ greatly in the clarity and accuracy of their self-introspections. Few can articulate the psychic elements that comprise this image, such as stating knowingly whether they view themselves as primarily alienated, or inept, or complacent, or conscientious, and so on.

2. **Internalized Content.** As noted previously, significant experiences from the past leave an inner imprint, a structural residue composed of memories, attitudes, and affects that serve as a substrate of dispositions for perceiving and reacting to life's ongoing events. Analogous to the various organ systems of which the body is composed, both the character and substance of these internalized representations of the past can be differentiated and analyzed for clinical purposes. Variations in the nature and content of this inner world can be associated with one or another personality and lead us to employ descriptive terms to represent them, such as shallow, vexatious, undifferentiated, concealed, and irreconcilable.

3. **Intrapsychic Organization.** The overall architecture that serves as a framework for an individual's psychic interior may display weakness in its structural cohesion, exhibit deficient coordination among its components, and possess few mechanisms to maintain balance and harmony, regulate internal conflicts, or mediate external pressures. The concept of intrapsychic organization refers to the structural strength, interior congruity, and functional efficacy of the personality system. "Organization" is a concept akin to and employed in conjunction with current psychoanalytic notions such as borderline and psychotic levels, but this usage tends to be limited, relating essentially to quantitative degrees of integrative pathology, not to variations either in integrative character or configuration. "Stylistic" variants of this structural attribute will be associated with each of the 13 personality prototypes; their distinctive organizational qualities will be represented with descriptors such as "inchoate," "disjoined," and "compartmentalized."

4. **Expressive Mood.** Few observables are more relevant to clinical analysis than the predominant character of an individual's affect and the intensity and frequency with which he or she expresses it. The "meaning" of extreme emotions is easy to decode. This is not so with the more subtle moods and feelings that insidiously and repetitively pervade the patient's ongoing relationships and experiences. Not only are the expressive features of mood conveyed by terms such as distraught, labile, fickle, or hostile communicated via self-report, but they are revealed as well, albeit indirectly, in the patient's level of activity, speech quality, and physical appearance.

## DIAGNOSTIC CRITERIA

The purpose of this section is to make more explicit and tangible, to operationalize, so to speak, the concepts that have been presented ... Although true operational definitions call for the specification of precise methods of quantifying theoretical constructs, these will not be addressed here; readers interested in "operational" psychometric techniques relevant to the personality concepts presented here might find it of value to read the manual for the Millon Clinical Multiaxial Inventory (Millon, 1983a), a self-report inventory anchored both to the author's theory and to the syndromes of DSM-III.

Termed "operational criteria" in the early stages of DSM-III development, the outline of specified signs and symptoms comprising the basis of assigning each of the manual's syndromes was subsequently and more properly retitled "diagnostic criteria." . . .

## COMPARABILITY OF CRITERIA

It seems reasonable to assume that greater clarity in clinical communications as well as greater research reliability will follow the systematic use of diagnostic criteria. However, as noted previously . . . "Most of the criteria (in the DSM-III) lack empirical support. Some are inadequately explicit or, conversely, are overly concrete in their operational referents. Many are redundant both within and with other diagnostic classes. Others are insufficiently comprehensive in syndromal scope or display a lack of parallelism and symmetry among corresponding categories" (Millon, 1987, p. 53).

Part of the difficulty in specifying more definitive or explicit criteria lies in the intrinsic nature of psychopathology itself, or as Meehl (1978) has put it, "from the organism's real compositional nature and structure and the causal texture of its environment." Nevertheless, diagnostic criteria for personality prototypes will enable us to be, to quote Meehl again, "quasi-exact about the inherently inexact." And to quote again (Millon, 1987, p. 53), "Syndromes of the DSM-III are conceptual prototypes, and not tangible entities. . . . Given that these syndromes are, in the main, only theoretical constructs, it will more than suffice for both clinical and research purposes to employ what has been devised a standardized, reliable, and internally coherent mosaic of criterion descriptors."

Despite the inherent limitations that are built into syndromic and prototypic categories, several shortcomings among the DSM-III diagnostic criteria should and can be remedied . . . Difficulties arise in part from a lack of comparability among diagnostic criteria: for example some categories require all defining features to be present (e.g., dependent personality), whereas others allow choice among the criteria (e.g., borderline personality). According to Frances and Widiger (1986, p. 395), Axis II is "inconsistent in the extent to which the members of each category are assumed to be homogeneous with respect to the definitional features." The authors indicate that this heterogeneity in diagnostic requirements will bear directly on the efficiency and utility of each definitional feature as well as possibly compromise the validity of the covariates that ostensibly comprise each syndrome.

Heterogeneous requirements are especially problematic in classically structured syndromes, that is, those requiring singly necessary or jointly sufficient diagnostic criteria. Prototypic categories, by contrast, are composed intentionally in a heterogeneous manner, that is, they accept the legitimacy of syndromic diversity and overlap. Nevertheless, there still is need to reduce the "fuzziness" between boundaries so as to eliminate excessive numbers of unclassifiable and borderline cases. One step toward the goal of sharpening diagnostic discriminations is to spell out a distinctive criterion for every diagnostically relevant clinical attribute aligned with every prototypal category. For example, if the attribute "interpersonal conduct" is deemed of clinical value in assessing personality, then singular diagnostic criteria should be specified to represent an entire characteristic or distinctive manner in which *each* personality "conducts its interpersonal life."

By composing a taxonomic schema that includes all relevant clinical attributes (e.g., behavior, affect, cognitive), and specifies a defining feature on every attribute for each of the 13 personalities, the proposed prototypal model would both be fully comprehensive in its clinical scope and possess parallel and directly comparable criteria among all Axis II categories. A format of this nature will not only furnish logic and symmetry to the DSM taxonomy, but will enable investigators to be systematic in determining the relative diagnostic efficacy of presumed prototypal covariates. Moreover, clinicians would be able to appraise both typical and unusual syndromal patterns as well as establish the coherence, if not the "validity" of both recently developed and classically established diagnostic entities. These goals are being carried out in a current nationwide study by the author and his colleagues in which some 100 participating clinicians are assessing the personality attributes of approximately 1,000 patients. The investigation has set out to obtain data not only on each of the preceding matters, but also to determine the conditional probabilities of various hypothesized criteria combinations, to calculate "specificity" and "selectivity" measures employing independent clinical and psychometric criterion gauges, to attempt to specify the optimum number of criteria for assigning each personality diagnosis, and so on.

## QUALITATIVE AND QUANTITATIVE NATURE OF CRITERIA

In the study to which we have just referred, clinical judges are asked not only to identify which criterion (e.g., distraught, hostile, labile) of an attribute (e.g., expressive mood) best characterizes a particular patient, but to record a number (from 1 to 10) to represent the degree of prominence or pervasiveness of that attribute's criterion. Moreover, judges are encouraged, where appropriate, to record and quantify more than one criterion per clinical attribute (e.g., if suitable, to note both "distraught" mood and "labile" mood).

The purpose of this procedure is to affirm the view that categorical (qualitative distinction) and dimensional (quantitative distinction) models of classification need not be framed in opposition, no less be considered mutually exclusive (Millon, 1981; Widiger & Kelso, 1983). Assessments can be formulated, first, to recognize qualitative (categorical) distinctions in *what* behavior best characterizes a patient, permitting the multiple listing of several such behaviors, and, second, to differentiate these behaviors quantitatively (dimensionally) so as to represent their relative degrees of clinical prominence or pervasiveness. For example, on the "interpersonal conduct" attribute, patient A may be appraised as deserving quantitative ratings of 10 on the "aversive" criterion, 6 on the "ambivalent" criterion, and 4 on the "secretive" criterion. Patient B may be assigned a rating of 9 on the "ambivalent" criterion, 7 on "aversive," and 2 on "paradoxical." Both patients are characterized by the "aversive" and "ambivalent" criteria, but to differing extents; they are not only distinguishable quantitatively (dimensionally) on two of the same qualitative or categorical criteria, but differ as well on qualitative grounds, one has exhibited "secretive," the other "paradoxical" interpersonal conduct.

Cumulative "scores" across multiple clinical attributes obtained via such assessment procedures will result in personality configurations composed of mixed diagnostic assignments. These diagnostic profiles are highly informative and can be especially useful, for example, in identifying which attribute should serve as the initial focus of therapy, for example, deciding to address that criterion of interpersonal conduct that may benefit by "group or family techniques, or pinpointing a feature of mood expression that may be especially responsive to "psychopharmacologic treatment," or discerning the character and level of intrapsychic organization that may be conducive to psychodynamically oriented therapy," and so on.

## REFERENCES

American Psychiatric Association. (1980). *Diagnostic and statistical manual of mental disorders*. Washington, DC: Author.

Auchincloss, E. L., & Michels, R. (1983). Psycho-analytic theory of character. In J. P. Frosch (Ed.), *Current perspectives on personality disorders*. Washington, DC: American Psychiatric Press.

Bandura, A. (1977). Self-efficacy: Toward a unifying theory of behavior change. *Psychological Review, 84,* 191–215.

Blatt, S. J., & Shichman, S. (1983). Two primary configurations of psychopathology. *Psychoanalysis and Contemporary Thought, 6,* 187–254.

Bowers, K. S. (1977). There's more to Iago than meets the eye: A clinical account of personal consistency. In D. Magnusson & N. S. Endler (Eds.), *Personality at the crossroads*. Hillsdale, NJ: Erlbaum.

Brenner, C. (1959). The masochistic character: Genesis and treatment. *Journal of the American Psychoanalytic Association, 7,* 197–226.

Buss, A. H., & Plomin, R. (1975). *A temperament theory of personality development*. New York: Wiley.

Cantor, N., Smith, E. E., French, R. D., & Mezzich, J. (1980). Psychiatric diagnoses as prototype categorization. *Journal of Abnormal Psychology, 89,* 181–193.

Dahlström, W. G. (1972). *Personality systematics and the problem of types*. Morristown, NJ: General Learning Press.

Escalona, S., & Heider, G. (1959). *Prediction and outcome*. New York: Basic Books.

Fairbairn, W. R. D. (1954). *An object relations theory of personality*. New York: Basic Books.

Fiske, D. W., & Maddi, S. R. (Eds.). (1961). *Functions of varied experience*. Homewood, IL: Dorsey Press.

Fowles, D. C. (1980). The three arousal model: Implications of Gray's two-factor learning theory for heart rate, electrodermal activity, and psychopathy. *Psychophysiology, 17,* 87–104.

Fowles, D. C. (1983). Motivational effects on heart rate and electrodermal activity: Implications for research on personality and psychopathology. *Journal of Research in Personality, 17,* 48–71.

Freud, A. (1965). *Normality and pathology of childhood: Assessments of development*. New York: International Universities Press.

Freud, S. (1925). On narcissism: An introduction. In J. Strachey (Ed. and Trans.), *Collected papers* (Vol. 4). London: Hogarth Press. (Original work published 1914)

Freud, S. (1925). The instincts and their vicissitudes. In J. Strachey (Ed. and Trans.), *Collected papers* (Vol. 4). London: Hogarth Press. (Original work published 1915)

Gedo, J. (1979). *Beyond interpretation: Toward a revised theory for psychoanalysis*. New York: International Universities Press.

Gill, M. M. (1963). *Topography and systems in psychoanalytic theory*. New York: International Universities Press.

Goldberg, A. (Ed.). (1978). *The psychology of the self—A casebook*. New York: International Universities Press.

Gray, J. A. (1972). Learning theory, the conceptual nervous system and personality. In V. D. Nebylitsyn & J. A. Gray (Eds.), *Biological bases of individual behavior*. New York: Academic Press.

Gray, J. A. (1975). *Elements of a two-process theory of learning*. New York: Academic Press.

Gray, J. A. (1982). *The neuropsychology of anxiety*. New York: Oxford University Press.

Grünbaum, A. (1952). Causality and the science of human behavior. *American Scientist, 4,* 665–676.

Gunderson, J. G., Kolb, J. E., & Austin, V. (1981). The diagnostic interview for borderline patients. *American Journal of Psychiatry, 138,* 896–903.

Horowitz, L. M., Post, D. L., French, R. D., Wallis, K. D., & Sieglman, E. Y. (1981). The prototype as a construct in abnormal psychology. 2. Classifying disagreement in psychiatric judgment. *Journal of Abnormal Psychology, 90,* 575–585.

Jacobson, E. (1964). *The self and the object world*. New York: International Universities Press.

Kendell, R. E. (1975). *The role of diagnosis in psychology*. Oxford: Blackwell Scientific Publications.

Kendell, R. E. (1983). DSM-III: A major advance in psychiatric nosology. In R. Spitzer, J. B. W. Williams, & A. E. Skodol (Eds.), *International perspectives on DSM-III*. Washington, DC: American Psychiatric Press.

Kernberg, O. (1975). *Borderline conditions and pathological narcissism.* New York: Jason Aronson.

Klein, M. (1952). *Developments in psychoanalysis.* London: Hogarth.

Kohut, H. (1971). *The analysis of the self.* New York: International Universities Press.

Loewenstein, R. (1957). A contribution to the psychoanalytic theory of masochism. *Journal of the American Psychoanalytic Association, 5,* 197–234.

Mahler, M. S., Pine, F., & Bergman, A. (1975). *The psychological birth of the human infant.* New York: Basic Books.

Meehl, P. E. (1978). Theoretical risks and tabular asterisks: Sir Karl, Sir Ronald, and the slow progress of soft psychology. *Journal of Consulting and Clinical Psychology, 46,* 806–834.

Menaker, E. (1953). Masochism—A defense reaction of the ego. *Psychoanalytic Quarterly, 22,* 205–220.

Millon, T. (1969). *Modern psychopathology: A biosocial approach to maladaptive learning and functioning.* Philadelphia, PA: Saunders.

Millon, T. (1981). *Disorders of personality: DSM-III, Axis II.* New York: Wiley.

Millon, T. (1983a). *Millon clinical multiaxial inventory, manual* (3rd ed.). Minneapolis, MN: National Computer Systems.

Millon, T. (Ed.). (1983b). *Theories of personality and psychopathology* (3rd ed.). New York: Holt, Rinehart & Winston.

Millon, T. (1987). On taxonomic models in psychopathology. In C. G. Last & M. Hersen (Eds), *Issues in diagnostic research.* New York: Plenum Press.

Mischel, W. (1973). Toward a cognitive social reconceptualization of personality. *Psychological Review, 80,* 252–283.

Mischel, W. (1979). On the interface of cognition and personality. *American Psychologist, 34,* 740–754.

Mischel, W. (1984). Convergences and challenges in the search for consistency. *American Psychologist, 39,* 351–364.

Murphy, G. (1947). *Personality: A biosocial approach to origins and functions.* New York: Harper.

Murphy, L. B., & Moriarty, A. E. (1976). *Vulnerability, coping and growth.* New Haven, CT: Yale University Press.

Rapaport, D. (1959). The structure of psychoanalytic theory: A systematizing attempt. In S. Koch (Ed.), *Psychology: A study of a science* (Vol. 3). New York: McGraw-Hill.

Reich, J. (1984, May). Instruments measuring Axis II of DSM-III: A review. In *DSM-III—A continuing review.* Symposium presented at the meeting of the American Psychiatric Association, Los Angeles.

Thomas, A., & Chess, S. (1977). *Temperament and development.* New York: Brunner/Mazel.

Widiger, T., & Kelso, K. (1983). Psychodiagnosis of Axis II. *Clinical Psychology Review, 3,* 491–510.

# PAPER 6

# *Criteria of Normality: What Can We Learn from Evolutionary Theory?*

Important "scientific" advances were introduced in the third edition of the American Psychiatric Association's *Diagnostic and Statistical Manual of Mental Disorders* (DSM-III). Among them was the specification of relatively explicit "diagnostic criteria" for each disorder. Rather than a discursive description, each category was composed of a set of clearly articulated behavior and biographic characteristics. Henceforth, a specified number of these criteria were required for a patient to be assigned a diagnostic label. Despite minor controversies concerning the theoretical and empirical adequacy of the DSM's criteria, there is considerable agreement regarding their ultimate utility (Millon, 1987). This utility should be achieved as well, I believe, if we specify criteria for the "normality" construct. Accordingly, I present a set of "criteria" that reflect the evolutionary polarities described earlier in the chapter. Some limitations and caveats are in order before we proceed. Owing to the multiple perspectives that can legitimately be brought to bear in defining "normality" (Offer & Sabshin, 1966), as well as the many values, functions, and goals the construct may serve, there is little likelihood that any set of criteria would be satisfactory to all. That multiple criteria are needed should be self-evident, although the specifics of which they are composed will remain controversial. Given my belief in the applicability of evolutionary principles to all spheres of nature's expression, I have sought to anchor my criteria as closely as possible to these "universal" principles in the realm of human functioning—that is, in those transactions that relate to existential survival (pain-pleasure), ecological adaptation (passive-active), and species replication (others-self).

A balance among normals must be struck between the two extremes that comprise each polarity; a measure of integration among the three basic polarities themselves is also an index of normality. However, normality does not require precise equidistance between polar extremes. Positions of balance will vary as a function of the overall configuration both within and among polarities, which, in their turn, will depend on the wider ecosystems within which individuals operate. In other words, and as is well recognized, there is no one form or expression of normality. Various polarity positions, and the traits and behaviors they underlie, will permit diverse "styles of normality," just as marked deficits and imbalances among the polarities may manifest themselves in diverse "styles of abnormality" (Millon, 1990).

Given the numerous and diverse ecological milieus that humans face in our complex modern environment, there is reason to expect that most "normals" will display multiple adaptive styles, sometimes more active, sometimes less so, occasionally focused on self, occasionally on others, at times oriented to pleasure, at times oriented to the avoidance of pain. Despite the presence of relatively enduring and characteristic styles, adaptive flexibility typifies most normal individuals; that is, they are able to shift from one position on a polar continuum to another as the circumstances of life change.

89

Let us turn next to the six polarity-based criteria for normality. They are grouped, two each, under the three polarity headings of existence, adaptation, and replication. Each criterion is stated alongside its evolutionary polarity. Elaborated within each section are the data or theory supportive of the criterion—that is, findings, for example, of an ostensive biological substrate for the criterion, formulations by "normality/health" theorists, as well as clinical illustrations that demonstrate some of the pathologic consequences following from failures to meet the criterion.

## EXISTENCE

An interweaving and shifting balance between the two extremes that comprise the pain-pleasure bipolarity typifies normality. Both of the following criteria should be met in varying degrees as life circumstances require. In essence, a synchronous and coordinated personal style would have developed to answer the question of whether the person should focus on experiencing only the pleasures of life versus concentrating his or her efforts on avoiding its pains.

### LIFE PRESERVATION: AVOIDING DANGER AND THREAT

One might assume that a criterion based on the avoidance of psychic or physical pain would be sufficiently self-evident not to require specification. As is well known, debates have arisen in the literature as to whether mental health/normality reflects the absence of mental disorder, being merely the reverse side of the mental illness or abnormality coin. That there is a relationship between health and disease cannot be questioned; the two are intimately connected, conceptually and physically. On the other hand, to define health solely as the absence of disorder will not suffice. As a single criterion among several, however, features of behavior and experience that

signify both the lack of (for example, anxiety, depression) and an aversion to (for example, threats to safety and security) pain in its many and diverse forms provide a necessary foundation upon which other, more positively constructed criteria may rest. Substantively, positive normality must comprise elements beyond mere nonnormality or abnormality. And despite the complexities and inconsistencies of personality, from a definitional point of view normality does preclude nonnormality.

Turning to the evolutionary aspect of pain avoidance, that pertaining to a distancing from life-threatening circumstances, psychic and otherwise, we find an early historical reference in the writings of Herbert Spencer, a supportive contemporary of Darwin. In 1870 Spencer averred:

Pains are the correlative of actions injurious to the organism, while pleasures are the correlatives of actions conducive to its welfare.

Those races of beings only can have survived in which, on the average, agreeable or desired feelings went along with activities conducive to the maintenance of life, while disagreeable and habitually avoided feelings went along with activities directly or indirectly destructive of life.

Every animal habitually persists in each act which gives pleasure, so long as it does so, and desists from each act which gives pain. . . . It is manifest that in proportion as this guidance approaches completeness, the life will be long; and that the life will be short in proportion as it falls short of completeness.

We accept the inevitable corollary from the general doctrine of Evolution, that pleasures are the incentives to life-supporting acts and pains the deterrents from life-destroying acts (pp. 279–284). More recently Freedman and Roe (1958) wrote:

We . . . hypothesize that psychological warning and warding-off mechanisms, if properly studied, might provide a kind of psychological evolutionary systematics. Exposure to pain, anxiety, or danger is likely to be followed by efforts to avoid a repetition of the noxious stimulus situation with which the experience is associated.

Obviously an animal with a more highly developed system for anticipating and avoiding the threatening circumstance is more efficiently equipped for adaptation and survival. Such unpleasant situations may arise either from within, in its simplest form as tissue deprivation, or from without, by the infliction of pain or injury. Man's psychological superstructure may be viewed, in part, as a system of highly developed warning mechanisms. (p. 458)

As for the biologic substrate of "pain" signals, Gray (1975) suggests two systems, both of which alert the organism to possible dangers in the environment. Those mediating the behavioral effects of unconditioned (instinctive?) aversive events are termed the fight/flight system (FFS). This system elicits defensive aggression and escape and is subserved, according to Gray's pharmacologic inferences, by the amgydala, the ventromedial hypothalamus, and the central gray of the midbrain; neurochemically, evidence suggests a difficult-to-unravel interaction among aminobutyric acids (for example, gamma-ammobutyric acid), serotonin, and endogenous opiates (for example, endorphins). The second major source of sensitivity and action in response to "pain" signals is referred to by Gray as the behavioral inhibition system (BIS), consisting of the interplay of the septal-hippocampal system, its cholinergic projections and monoamine transmissions to the hypothalamus, and then on to the cingulate and prefrontal cortex. Activated by signals of punishment or nonreward, the BIS suppresses associated behaviors, refocuses the organism's attention, and redirects activity toward alternate stimuli.

"Harm avoidance" is a concept proposed recently by Cloninger (1986, 1987). As he conceives the construct, it is a heritable tendency to respond intensely to signals of aversive stimuli (pain) and to learn to inhibit behaviors that might lead to punishment and frustrative nonreward. Those high on this dimension are characterized as cautious, apprehensive, and inhibited; those low on this valence would likely be confident, optimistic, and carefree. Cloninger

subscribes essentially to Gray's behavioral inhibition system concept in explicating this polarity, as well as the neuroanatomic and neurochemical hypotheses Gray proposed as the substrates for its "pain-avoidant" mechanisms.

Let us shift from biologic/evolutionary concepts to proposals of a similar cast offered by thinkers of a distinctly psychological turn of mind. Notable here are the contributions of Maslow (1968, 1970), particularly his hierarchic listing of "needs." Best known are the five fundamental needs that lead to self-actualization, the first two of which relate to our evolutionary criterion of life preservation. Included in the first group are the "physiologic" needs such as air, water, food, and sleep, qualities of the ecosystem essential for survival. Next, and equally necessary to avoid danger and threat, are what Maslow terms the *safety needs,* including the freedom from jeopardy, the security of physical protection and psychic stability, as well as the presence of social order and interpersonal predictability.

That pathological consequences can ensue from the failure to attend to the realities that portend danger is obvious; the lack of air, water, and food are not issues of great concern in civilized societies today, although these are matters of considerable import to environmentalists of the future and to contemporary poverty-stricken nations.

It may be of interest next to record some of the psychic pathologies of personality that can be traced to aberrations in meeting this first criterion of normality. For example, among those termed avoidant personalities (Millon 1981), we see an excessive preoccupation with threats to one's psychic security, an expectation of and hyperalertness to the signs of potential rejection that leads these persons to disengage from everyday relationships and pleasures. At the other extreme of the criterion we see a risk-taking attitude, a proclivity to chance hazards and to endanger one's life and liberty, a behavioral pattern characteristic of those we label antisocial personalities. Here there is little of the caution and prudence expected in the normality criterion of avoiding danger and threat; rather, we observe its opposite, a rash willingness to put one's safety in jeopardy, to play with fire and throw caution to the wind. Another pathological style illustrative of a failure to fulfill this evolutionary criterion is seen among those variously designated as masochistic and self-defeating personalities. Rather than avoid circumstances that may prove painful and self-endangering, these nonnormal personality styles set in motion situations in which they will come to suffer physically and/or psychically. Either by virtue of habit or guilt absolution, these individuals induce rather than avoid pain for themselves.

## LIFE ENHANCEMENT: SEEKING REWARDING EXPERIENCES

At the other end of the "existence polarity" are attitudes and behaviors designed to foster and enrich life, to generate joy, pleasure, contentment, fulfillment, and thereby strengthen the capacity of the individual to remain vital and competent physically and psychically. This criterion asserts that existence/survival calls for more than life preservation alone; beyond pain avoidance is pleasure enhancement.

This criterion asks us to go at least one step further than Freud's parallel notion that life's motivation is chiefly that of "reducing tensions" (that is, avoiding/minimizing pain), maintaining thereby a steady state, if you will, a homeostatic balance and inner stability. In accord with my view of evolution's polarities, I would assert that normal humans are driven also by the desire to enrich their lives, to seek invigorating sensations and challenges, to venture and explore, all to the end of magnifying if not escalating the probabilities of both individual viability and species replicability.

Regarding the key instrumental role of "the pleasures," Spencer (1870) put it well more than a century ago: "pleasures are the correlatives of actions conducive to [organismic] welfare . . . the incentives to life-supporting acts" (pp. 279, 284). The view that there exists an organismic striving to expand one's inherent potentialities (as well as those of one's kin and species) has been implicit in the literature for ages. That "the pleasures" may be both sign and vehicle for this realization was recorded even in the ancient writings of the Talmud, where it states: "everyone will have to justify himself in the life hereafter for every failure to enjoy a legitimately offered pleasure in this world" (Jahoda, 1958, p. 45).

As far as contemporary psychobiological theorists are concerned, brief mention will be made again of the contributions of Gray (1975, 1981) and Cloninger (1986, 1987). Gray's neurobiologic model centers heavily on activation and inhibition (active-passive polarities) as well as on signals of reward and punishment (pleasure-pain polarity). Basing his deductions primarily on pharmacologic investigations of animal behavior, Gray has proposed the existence of several interrelated and neuroanatomically grounded response systems that activate various positive and negative affects. He refers to what he terms the behavioral activation system (BAS) as an "approach system" that is subserved by the reward center uncovered originally by Olds and Milner (1954). Ostensibly mediated at brain stem and cerebellar levels, it is likely to include dopaminergic projections across various strata and is defined as responding to conditioned rewarding and safety stimuli by facilitating behaviors that maximize their future recurrence (Gray, 1975). There are intricacies in the manner with which the BAS is linked to external stimuli and its anatomic substrates, but Gray currently views it as a system that subserves signals of reward, punishment relief, and pleasure.

Cloninger (1986, 1987) has generated a theoretical model composed of three dimensions, which he terms "reward dependence," "harm avoidance" to which I referred previously, and "novelty seeking." Proposing that each is a heritable personality disposition, he relates them explicitly to specific monoaminergic pathways; for example, high reward dependence is connected to low noradrenergic activity, harm avoidance to high serotonergic activity, and high novelty seeking to low dopaminergic activity. Cloninger's reward dependence dimension reflects highs and lows on the positive-gratifying-pleasure valence, whereas the harm avoidance dimension represents highs and lows on the negative-pain-displeasure valence. Reward dependence is hypothesized to be a heritable neurobiological tendency to respond to signals of reward (pleasure), particularly verbal signals of social approval, sentiment, and succor, as well as to resist events that might extinguish behaviors previously associated with these rewards. Cloninger portrays those high on reward dependence to be sociable, sympathetic, and pleasant; in contrast, those low on this polarity are characterized as detached, cool, and practical. Describing the undergirding substrate for the reward/pleasure valence as the behavior maintenance system (BMS), Cloninger speculates that its prime neuromodulator is likely to be norepinephrine, with its major ascending pathways arising in the pons, projecting onward to hypothalamic and limbic structures, and then branching upward to the neocortex.

Turning again to pure psychological formulations, both Rogers (1963) and Maslow (1968) have proposed concepts akin to my criterion of enhancing pleasure. In his notion of "openness to experience," Rogers asserts that the fully functioning person has no aspect of his or her nature closed off. Such individuals are not only receptive to the experiences that life offers but are able also to use them in expanding all of life's emotions, as well as being open to all forms of personal expression. Along a similar vein, Maslow speaks of the ability to maintain a freshness to experience, to keep up one's capacity to appreciate relationships and events. No matter how often events or persons are encountered, one is neither sated nor bored but is disposed to view them with an ongoing sense of "awe and wonder."

Perhaps less dramatic than the conceptions of either Rogers and Maslow, I believe that this openness and freshness to life's transactions is an instrumental means for extending life, for strengthening one's competencies and options, and for maximizing the viability and replicability of one's species. More mundane and pragmatic in orientation than their views, this conception seems both more substantive theoretically and more consonant a rationale for explicating the role the pleasures play in undergirding "reward experience" and "openness to experience."

As before, a note or two should be recorded on the pathological consequences of a failure to meet a criterion. These are seen most clearly in the personality disorders labeled schizoid and avoidant. In the former there is a marked hedonic deficiency, stemming either from an inherent deficit in affective substrates or the failure of stimulative experience to develop either or both attachment behaviors or affective capacity (Millon, 1981). Among those designated avoidant personalities, constitutional sensitivities or abusive life experiences have led to an intense attentional sensitivity to psychic pain and a consequent distrust in either the genuineness or durability of the "pleasures," such that these individuals can no longer permit themselves to experience them. Both of these personalities tend to be withdrawn and isolated, joyless and grim, neither seeking nor sharing in the rewards of life.

## ADAPTATION

As with the pair of criteria representing the aims of existence, a balance should be achieved between the two criteria comprising modes of adaptation, those related to ecological accommodation and ecologic modification, or what I have termed the passive-active polarity. Normality calls for a synchronous and coordinated personal style that weaves a balanced answer to the question of whether one should accept what the fates have brought forth or take the initiative in altering the circumstances of one's life.

## ECOLOGICAL ACCOMMODATION: ABIDING HOSPITABLE REALITIES

On first reflection, it would seem to be less than optimal to submit meekly to what life presents, to "adjust" obligingly to one's destiny. As described earlier, however, the evolution of plants is essentially grounded (no pun intended) in environmental accommodation, in an adaptive acquiescence to the ecosystem. Crucial to this adaptive course, however, is the capacity of these surroundings to provide the nourishment and protection requisite to the thriving of a species.

Could the same be true for the human species? Are there not circumstances of life that provide significant and assured levels of sustenance and safekeeping (both psychic and physical?) And, if that were the case, would not the acquisition of an accommodating attitude and passive life-style be a logical consequence? The answer, it would seem, is yes. If one's upbringing has been substantially secure and nurturant, would it not be "not normal" to flee or overturn it?

We know that circumstances, other than in infancy and early childhood, rarely persist throughout life. Autonomy and independence is almost inevitable as a stage of maturation, ultimately requiring the adoption of "adult" responsibilities that call for a measure of initiative, decision making, and action. Nevertheless, to the extent that the events of life have been and continue to be caring and giving, is it not perhaps wisest, from an evolutionary perspective, to accept this good fortune and "let matters be"? This accommodating or passive life philosophy has worked extremely well in sustaining and fostering those complex organisms that comprise the plant kingdom. Hence passivity, the yielding to environmental forces, may be in itself not only unproblematic but, where events and circumstances provide the "pleasures" of life and protect against their "pains," positively

adaptive and constructive. Accepting rather than overturning a hospitable reality seems a sound course; or as it is said, "If it ain't broke, don't fix it."

Is passivity part of the repertoire of the human species, does it serve useful functions, and where and how is it exhibited? A few words in response to these questions may demonstrate that passivity is not mere inactivity but a stance or process that achieves useful gains.

For example, universal among mammalian species are two basic modes of learning, the respondent or conditioned type and the operant or instrumental type. The former is essentially a *passive* process, the simple pairing of an innate or reflexive response to a stimulus that previously did not elicit that response. In like passive fashion, environmental elements that occur either simultaneously or in close temporal order become connected to each other in the organism's repertoire of learning, such that if one of these elements recurs in the future, the expectation is that the others will follow or be elicited. The organisms do not have to do anything active to achieve these learnings; inborn reflexive responses and/or environmental events are merely associated by contiguity.

Operant or instrumental learnings, in contrast, represent the outcome of an active process on the part of the organism, one that requires an effort and execution on its part that has the effect of altering the environment. Whereas respondent conditioning occurs as a result of the passive observation of a conjoining of events, operant conditioning occurs only as a result of an active modification by the organism of its surroundings, a performance usually followed by a positive reinforcer (pleasure) or the successful avoidance of a negative one (pain). Unconditioned reflexes, such as a leg jerk in reaction to a knee tap, will become a passively acquired conditioned respondent if a bell is regularly sounded prior to the tap, as will the shrinking reflex of an eye pupil passively become conditioned to that bell if it regularly preceded exposure to a shining light.

The passive-active polarity is central to formulations of psychoanalytic theory. Prior to the impressively burgeoning literature on "self" and "object relations" theory of the past two decades, the passive-active antithesis had a major role in both classical, "instinct" and post-World War II "ego" schools of analytic thought. The contemporary focus on "self" and "object" is considered in discussions of the third polarity, that of self-other. However, we should not overlook the once key and now less popular constructs of both instinct theory and ego theory. It may be worth noting, as well as of special interest to the evolutionary model presented in this chapter, that the beginnings of psychoanalytic metapsychology were oriented initially to instinctual derivatives (where pleasure and pain were given prominence), and then progressed subsequently to the apparatuses of the ego (Hartmann, 1939; Rapaport, 1953/1967)—where passivity and activity were centrally involved.

The model of activity, as Rapaport puts it, is a dual one; first, the ego is strong enough to defend against or control the intensity of the id's drive tensions or, second, through the competence and energy of its apparatuses, the ego is successful in uncovering or creating in reality the object of the id's instinctual drives. Rapaport conceives the model of passivity also to be a dual one; first, either the ego gradually modulates or indirectly discharges the instinctual energies of the id or, second, lacking an adequately controlling apparatus, the ego is rendered powerless and subject thereby to instinctual forces. Translating these formulations into evolutionary terms, effective actions by the ego will successfully manage the internal forces of the id, whereas passivity will result either in accommodations or exposure to the internal demands of the id.

Turning to contemporary theorists more directly concerned with normality and health, the humanistic psychologist Maslow (1970) states that "self-actualized" individuals accept their nature as it is, despite personal weaknesses and imperfections. Comfortable with themselves and the world around them, they do not seek to change "the water because it is wet, or the rocks because they are hard" (p. 153). They have learned to accept the natural order of things. Passively accepting nature, they need not hide behind false masks or transform others to fit "distorted needs." Accepting themselves without shame or apology, they are equally at peace with the shortcomings of those with whom they live and relate.

Where do we find clinical nonnormality that reflects failures to meet the accommodating/abiding criterion?

One example of an inability to leave things as they are is seen in what the DSM-III terms the histrionic personality disorder. These individuals achieve their goals of maximizing protection, nurturance, and reproductive success by engaging busily in a series of manipulative, seductive, gregarious, and attention-getting maneuvers. Their persistent and unrelenting manipulation of events is designed to maximize the receipt of attention and favors as well as to avoid social disinterest and disapproval. They show an insatiable if not indiscriminate search for stimulation and approval. Their clever and often artful social behaviors may give the appearance of an inner confidence and self-assurance; but beneath this guise lies a fear that a failure on their part to ensure the receipt of attention will, in short order, result in indifference or rejection, and hence their desperate need for reassurance and repeated signs of approval. Tribute and affection must constantly be replenished and are sought from every interpersonal source. As they are quickly bored and sated, they keep stirring up things, becoming enthusiastic about one activity and then another. There is a restless stimulus-seeking quality in which they cannot leave well enough alone.

At the other end of the polarity are personality disorders that exhibit an excess of passivity, failing thereby to give direction to their own lives. Several Axis II disorders demonstrate this passive style, although their passivity derives from and is expressed in appreciably different ways.

Schizoid personalities, for example, are passive owing to their relative incapacity to experience pleasure and pain; without the rewards these emotional valences normally activate, they are devoid of the drive to acquire rewards, leading them to become apathetically passive observers of the ongoing scene. Dependents typically are average on the pleasure/pain polarity, yet they are usually as passive as schizoids. Strongly oriented to others, they are notably weak with regard to "self." Passivity for them stems from deficits in self-confidence and competence, leading to deficits in initiative and autonomous skills as well as a tendency to wait passively while others assume leadership and guide them. Passivity among obsessive-compulsive personalities stems from their fear of acting independently, owing to intrapsychic resolutions they have made to quell hidden thoughts and emotions generated by their intense self-other ambivalence. Dreading the possibility of making mistakes or engaging in disapproved behaviors, they became indecisive, immobilized, restrained, and passive. High on pain and low on both pleasure and self, self-defeating personalities operate on the assumption that they dare not expect nor deserve to have life go their way; giving up any efforts to achieve a life that accords with their "true" desires, they passively submit to others' wishes, acquiescently accepting their fate. Finally, narcissists, especially high on self and low on others, benignly assume that "good things" will come their way with little or no effort on their part; this passive exploitation of others is a consequence of the unexplored confidence that underlies their self-centered presumptions.

## ECOLOGIC MODIFICATION: MASTERING ONE'S ENVIRONMENT

The active end of the bipolarity signifies the taking of initiative in altering and shaping life's events. As stated previously, such persons are best characterized by their alertness, vigilance, liveliness, vigor, and forcefulness, their stimulus-seeking energy and drive. Some plan strategies and scan alternatives to circumvent obstacles or avoid the distress of punishment, rejection, and anxiety. Others are impulsive, precipitate, excitable, rash, and hasty, seeking to elicit pleasures and rewards. Although specific goals vary and change from time to time, actively aroused individuals intrude on passing events and energetically and busily modify the circumstances of their environment.

Neurobiological research has proven to be highly supportive of the activity or arousal construct ever since Papez (1937), Moruzzi and Magoun (1949), and MacLean (1949, 1952) assigned what were to be termed the reticular and limbic systems' both energizing and expressive roles in the central nervous system.

First among historic figures to pursue this theme was Ivan Pavlov. In speaking of the basic properties of the nervous system, Pavlov referred to the strength of the processes of *excitation and inhibition,* the equilibrium between their respective strengths, and the mobility of these processes. Although Pavlov's theoretical formulations (1927) dealt with what Donald Hebb (1955) termed a "conceptual nervous system," his experiments and those of his students led to innumerable direct investigations of brain activity. Central to Pavlov's thesis was the distinction between strong and weak types of nervous system.

Closely aligned to Pavlovian theory, Gray (1964) has asserted that those with weak nervous systems are easily aroused, nonsensation-seeking introverts who prefer to experience low stimulation rather than high levels. Conversely, those with strong nervous systems would arouse slowly, be likely to be sensation-seeking extroverts who find low stimulation levels boring and high levels both exciting and pleasant.

Akin also to the active modality are the recent views of Cloninger (1986, 1987). To him, novelty-seeking is a heritable tendency toward excitement in response to novel stimuli or cues for reward (pleasure) or punishment relief (pain) that leads to exploratory activity. Consonant with its correspondence to the activity polarity, individuals who are assumed to be high in novelty-seeking are characterized as impulsive, excitable, and quickly distracted or bored. Conversely, those at the passive polarity or the low end of the novelty-seeking dimension are portrayed as reflective, stoic, slow-tempered, orderly, and only slowly engaged in new interests.

Turning from ostensive biologic substrates to speculative psychological constructs, de Charms (1968) has proposed that "Man's primary motivational propensity is to be effective in producing changes in his environment" (p. 269). A similar view has been conveyed by White (1959) in his concept of effectance, an intrinsic motive, as he views it, that activates persons to impose their desires upon environments. De Charms elaborates his theme with reference to man as "Origin" and as "Pawn," constructs akin to the active polarity, on the one hand, and to the passive polarity, on the other. He states this distinction as follows:

That man is the origin of his behavior means that he is constantly struggling against being confined and constrained by external forces, against being moved like a pawn into situations not of his own choosing. . . . An Origin is a person who perceives his behavior as determined by his own choosing; a Pawn is a person who perceives his behavior as determined by external forces beyond his control. . . . An Origin has strong feelings of personal causation, a feeling that the locus for causation of effects in his environment lies within himself. The feedback that reinforces this feeling comes from changes in his environment that are attributable to personal behavior. This is the crux of personal causation, and it is a powerful motivational force directing future behavior. (1968, pp. 273–274)

Allport (1955) had argued earlier that history records many individuals who were not content with an existence that offered them little variety, a lack of psychic tension, and minimal challenge. Allport considers it normal to be "pulled forward" by a vision of the future that awakened within persons their drive to alter the course of their lives. He suggests that people possess a need to "invent" motives and purposes that would consume their inner energies. In a similar vein, Fromm (1955) proposed a need on the part of man to rise above the roles of passive creatures in an accidental if not random world. To him, humans are driven to transcend the state of merely having been created; instead, humans seek to become the creators, the active shapers of their own destiny. Rising above the passive and accidental nature of existence, humans generate their own purposes and thereby provide themselves with a true basis of freedom.

## REPLICATION

As before, I consider both of the following criteria necessary to the definition and determination of normality. I see no necessary antithesis between the two. Humans can be both self-actualizing and other-encouraging, although most persons are likely to lean toward one or the other side. A balance that coordinates the two provides a satisfactory answer to the question of whether one should be devoted to the support and welfare of others or fashion one's life in accord with one's own needs and desires.

### REPRODUCTIVE NURTURANCE: CONSTRUCTIVELY LOVING OTHERS

As described earlier, recombinant replication achieved by sexual mating entails a balanced though asymmetric parental investment in both the genesis and nurturance of offspring. By virtue of her small number of eggs and extended pregnancy, the female strategy for replicative success among most mammals is characterized by the intensive care and protection of a limited number of offspring. Oriented to reproductive nurturance rather than reproductive propagation, most adult females, at least until recent decades in Western society, bred close to the limit of their capacity, attaining a reproductive ceiling of approximately twenty viable births. By contrast, not only are males free of the unproductive pregnancy interlude for mating, but they may substantially increase their reproductive output by engaging in repetitive matings with as many available females as possible.

The other versus self antithesis follows from additional aspects of evolution's asymmetric replication strategy. Not only must the female be oriented to and vigilant in identifying the needs of and dangers that may face each of her few off spring, but it is reproductively advantageous for her to be sensitive to and discriminating in her assessment of potential mates. A "bad" mating—one that issues a defective or weak offspring—has graver consequences for the female than for the male. Not only will such an event appreciably reduce her limited reproductive possibilities and cause her to forego a better mate for a period of time, but she may exhaust much of her nurturing and protective energies in attempting to revitalize an inviable or infertile offspring. By contrast, if a male indulges in a "bad" mating, all he has lost are some quickly replaceable sperm, a loss that does little to diminish his future reproductive potentials and activities.

Before we turn to other indices and views of the self-other polarity, let us be mindful that these conceptually derived extremes do not evince themselves in sharp and distinct gender differences. Such proclivities are matters of degree, not absolutes, owing not only to the consequences of recombinant "shuffling" and gene "crossing over" but to the influential effects of cultural values and social learning. Consequently, most "normal" individuals exhibit intermediate characteristics on this as well as on the other two polarity sets.

The reasoning behind different replication strategies derives from the concept of inclusive fitness, the logic of which we owe to the theoretical biologist W. D. Hamilton (1964). The concept's rationale is well articulated in the following quote (Daly & Wilson, 1978):

Suppose a particular gene somehow disposes its bearers to help their siblings. Any child of a parent that has this gene has a one-half of probability of carrying that same gene by virtue of common descent from the same parent bearer. . . . From the gene's point of view, it is as useful to help a brother or sister as it is to help the child.

When we assess the fitness of a . . . bit of behavior, we must consider more than the reproductive consequences for the individual animal. We must also consider whether the reproductive prospects of any kin are in any way altered. *Inclusive fitness is a sum of the consequences for one's own reproduction, plus the consequences for the reproduction of kin multiplied by the degree of relatedness of those kin.*

An animal's behavior can therefore be said to serve a strategy whose goal is the maximization of inclusive fitness. (pp. 30–31; italics added)

Mutual support and encouragement represents efforts leading to reciprocal fitness, a behavioral pattern consonant with Darwin's fundamental notions. Altruism, however, is a form of behavior in which there is denial of self for the benefit of others, a behavioral pattern acknowledged by Darwin himself as seemingly inconsistent with his theory (1871, p. 130). A simple extrapolation from natural selection suggests that those disposed to engage in self-sacrifice would ultimately leave fewer and fewer descendants; as a consequence, organisms motivated by "self-benefiting" genes would prevail over those motivated by "other-benefiting" genes, a result leading to the eventual extinction of genes oriented to the welfare of others. The distinguished sociobiologist Wilson, states the problem directly: "How then does altruism persist?" (1978, p. 153). An entomologist of note, Wilson had no hesitation in claiming that altruism not only persists but is of paramount significance in the lives of social insects. In accord with his sociobiologic thesis, he illustrates the presence of altruism in animals as diverse as birds, deer, porpoises, and chimpanzees, which share food and provide mutual defense—for example, to protect the colony's hives bees enact behaviors that lead invariably to their death.

Two underlying mechanisms have been proposed to account for cooperative behaviors such as altruism. One derives from the concept of inclusive fitness, briefly described in preceding paragraphs; Wilson (1978) terms this form of cooperative behavior "hard-core" altruism, by which he means that the act is "unilaterally directed" for the benefit of others and that the bestower neither expects nor expresses a desire for a comparable return. Following the line of reasoning originally formulated by Hamilton (1964), J. P. Rushton (1984), a controversial Canadian researcher who has carried out illuminating r/K studies of human behavior, explicates this mechanism as follows:

Individuals behave so as to maximize their inclusive fitness rather than only their individual fitness; they maximize the production of successful off spring by both themselves and their relatives. . . . Social ants, for example, are one of the most altruistic species so far discovered. The self-sacrificing, sterile worker and soldier ants . . . share 75% of their genes with their sisters and so by devoting their entire existence to the needs of others . . . they help to propagate their own genes. (p. 6)

The second rationale proposed as the mechanism underlying other oriented and cooperative behaviors Wilson terms "soft-core" altruism to represent his belief that the bestower's actions are ultimately self-serving. The original line of reasoning here stems from Trivers's (1971) notion of reciprocity, a thesis suggesting that genetically based dispositions to cooperative behavior can be explained without requiring the assumption of kinship relatedness. All that is necessary is that the performance of cooperative acts be mutual, that is, result in concurrent or subsequent behaviors that are comparably beneficial in terms of enhancing the original bestower's survivability and/or reproductive fertility.

Wilson's conclusion that the self-other dimension is a bedrock of evolutionary theory is worth quoting:

In order to understand this idea more clearly, return with me for a moment to the basic theory of evolution. Imagine a spectrum of self-serving behavior. At one extreme only the individual is meant to benefit, then the nuclear family, next the extended family (including cousins, grandparents, and others who might play a role in kin selection), then the band, the tribe, chiefdoms, and finally, at the other extreme, the highest sociopolitical units. (1978, p. 158)

Intriguing data and ideas have been proposed by several researchers seeking to identify specific substrates that may relate to the other-oriented polarities. In what has been termed the affiliation/attachment drive, Everly (1988), for example, provides evidence favoring an anatomic role for the cingulate gyrus. Referring to the work of Henry and Stephens (1977), MacLean (1985), and Steklis and Kling (1985), Everly concludes that the ablation of the cingulate eliminates both affiliative and grooming behaviors. The proximal physiology of this drive has been hypothesized as including serotonergic, noradrenergic, and opiod neurotransmission systems (Everly, 1988; Redmond, Maas, & Kling, 1971). MacLean (1985) has argued that the affiliative drive may be phylogenically coded in the limbic system and may undergird the "concept of family" in primates. The drive toward other-oriented behaviors, such as attachment, nurturing, affection, reliability, and collaborative play, has been referred to as the "cement of society" by Henry and Stevens (1977).

Let us move now to the realm of psychological and social proposals. Dorothy Conrad (1952) specified a straightforward list of constructive behaviors that manifest "reproductive nurturance" in the interpersonal sphere. She records them as follows:

*Has positive affective relationship:* The person who is able to relate affectively to even one person demonstrates that he is potentially able to relate to other persons and to society.
*Promotes another's welfare:* Affective relationships make it possible for the person to

enlarge his world and to act for the benefit of another, even though that person may profit only remotely.

*Works with another for mutual benefit:* The person is largely formed through social interaction. Perhaps he is most completely a person when he participates in a mutually beneficial relationship. (pp. 456–457)

More eloquent proposals of a similar character have been formulated by the noted psychologists Maslow, Allport, and Fromm.

According to Maslow (1970), once humans' basic safety and security needs are met, they next turn to satisfy the belonging and love needs. Here we establish intimate and caring relationships with significant others in which it is just as important to give love as it is to receive it. Noting the difficulty in satisfying these needs in our unstable and changing modern world, Maslow sees the basis here for the immense popularity of communes and family therapy. These settings are ways to escape the isolation and loneliness that result from our failures to achieve love and belonging.

One of Allport's (1961) criteria of the "mature" personality, which he terms a warm relating of self to others, refers to the capability of displaying intimacy and love for a parent, child, spouse, or close friend. Here the person manifests an authentic oneness with the other and a deep concern for his or her welfare. Beyond one's intimate family and friends, there is an extension of warmth in the mature person to humankind at large, an understanding of the human condition and a kinship with all peoples.

To Fromm (1968), humans are aware of the growing loss of their ties with nature as well as with each other, feeling increasingly separate and alone. Fromm believes humans must pursue new ties with others to replace those that have been lost or can no longer be depended on. To counter the loss of communion with nature, he feels that health requires that we fulfill our need by a brotherliness with mankind, a sense of involvement, concern, and relatedness with the world. And

with those with whom ties have been maintained or reestablished, humans must fulfill their other-oriented needs by being vitally concerned with their well-being as well as fostering their growth and productivity.

In a lovely coda to a paper on the role of evolutionary and human behavior, Freedman and Roe (1958) wrote:

Since his Neolithic days, in spite of his murders and wars, his robberies and rapes, man has become a man-binding and a time-binding creature. He has maintained the biological continuity of his family and the social continuity of aggregates of families. He has related his own life experiences with the social traditions of those who have preceded him, and has anticipated those of his progeny. He has accumulated and transmitted his acquired goods and values through his family and through his organizations. He has become bound to other men by feelings of identity and by shared emotions, by what clinicians call empathy. His sexual nature may yet lead him to widening ambits of human affection, his acquisitive propensities to an optimum balance of work and leisure, and his aggressive drives to heightened social efficiency through attacks on perils common to all men. (p. 457)

The pathological consequences of a failure to embrace the polarity criterion of "others" are seen most clearly in the personality disorders termed antisocial and narcissistic. Both personalities exhibit an imbalance in their replication strategy; in this case, however, there is a primary reliance on self rather than others. They have learned that reproductive success as well as maximum pleasure and minimum pain is achieved by turning exclusively to themselves. The tendency to focus on self follows two major lines of development.

In the narcissistic personality, development reflects the acquisition of a self-image of superior worth, learned largely in response to admiring and doting parents. Providing self-rewards is highly gratifying if one values oneself or possesses either a "real" or inflated sense of self-worth. Displaying manifest confidence, arrogance, and an exploitative egocentricity in social contexts, this self-orientation has been termed the passive-independent style in the theory, as the individual "already" has all that is important—him- or herself.

Narcissistic individuals are noted for their egotistic self-involvement, experiencing primary pleasure simply by passively being or attending to themselves. Early experience has taught them to overvalue their self-worth; this confidence and superiority may be founded on false premises, however; that is, it may be unsustainable by real or mature achievements. Nevertheless, they blithely assume that others will recognize their specialness. Hence they maintain an air of arrogant self-assurance and, without much thought or even conscious intent, benignly exploit others to their own advantage. Although the tributes of others are both welcome and encouraged, their air of snobbish and pretentious superiority requires little confirmation either through genuine accomplishment or social approval. Their sublime confidence that things will work out well provides them with little incentive to engage in the reciprocal give and take of social life.

Those whom the theory characterizes as exhibiting the active-independent orientation resemble the outlook, temperament, and socially unacceptable behaviors of the DSM-III-R Antisocial personality disorder. They act to counter the expectation of pain at the hand of others; this is done by actively engaging in duplicitous or illegal behaviors in which they seek to exploit others for self-gain. Skeptical regarding the motives of others, they desire autonomy and wish revenge for what are felt as past injustices. Many are irresponsible and impulsive, actions they see as justified because they judge others to be unreliable and disloyal. Insensitivity and ruthlessness with others are the primary means they have learned to head off abuse and victimization.

In contrast to the narcissistic personality, this second pattern of self-orientation develops as a form of protection and counteraction. These types turn to themselves first to avoid the depredation they anticipate and second to compensate by furnishing self-generated rewards in their stead. Learning that they cannot depend on others, these personalities counterbalance this loss not only by trusting themselves alone but by actively seeking retribution for what they see as past humiliations. Turning to self and seeking actively to gain strength, power, and revenge, they act irresponsibly, exploiting and usurping what others possess as sweet reprisal. Their security is never fully "assured," even when they have aggrandized themselves beyond their lesser origins.

In both narcissistic and antisocial persons we see nonnormality arising from an inability to experience a constructive love for others. For the one, there is an excessive self-centeredness, and for the other, there is the acquisition of a compensatory destructiveness driven by social retribution and self-aggrandizement.

## REPRODUCTIVE PROPAGATION: ACTUALIZING SELF POTENTIALS

The converse of reproductive nurturance is *not* reproductive propagation but rather the lack of reproductive nurturance. Thus, to fail to love others constructively does not assure the actualization of one's potentials. Both may and should exist in normal/healthy individuals.

Although the dimension of self-other is arranged to highlight its polar extremes, it should be evident that many, if not most, behaviors are employed to achieve the goals of both self and kin reproduction. Both ends are often simultaneously achieved; at other times one may predominate. The behaviors comprising these strategies are "driven," so to speak, by a blend of activation and affect, that is, combinations arising from intermediary positions reflecting both the life enhancement and life preservation polarity of pleasure-pain, interwoven with similar intermediary positions on the ecologic accommodation and ecologic modification polarity of activity-passivity. Phrasing "replication" in terms of the abstruse and metaphorical constructs does not obscure it, I hope, but rather sets this third polarity on the deeper foundations of existence and adaptation, foundations composed of the first two polarities previously described.

Here I provide a few words on certain ostensive biologic substrates associated with a self-orientation, outline the views of several contemporary psychologists and psychiatrists who have assigned the criterion of self-actualization a central role in their formulations, and note an example or two of how the failure to meet this criterion can often result in specific pathologies of personality.

At the self-oriented pole, Everly (1988) proposes an autonomy/aggression substrate that manifests itself in a strong need for control and domination as well as in hierarchic status striving. According to MacLean (1986), it appears that the amygdaloid complex may play a key role in driving organisms into self-oriented behaviors. Early studies of animals with ablated amygdalas showed a notable increase in their docility (Kluver & Bucy, 1939), as have nonhuman primates exhibited significant decreases in social hierarchy status (Pribram, 1962). Although the evidence remains somewhat equivocal, norepinephrine and dopamine seem to be the prime neurotransmitters of this drive; the testosterone hormone appears similarly implicated (Feldman & Quenzar, 1984).

Regarding psychological constructs that parallel the notion of self-actualization, their earliest equivalent was in the writings of Spinoza (1677/1986), who viewed development as that of becoming what one was intended to be, nothing other than that, no matter how exalted the alternative might appear to be.

Carl Jung's (1961) concept of individuation shares important features with that of actualization in that any deterrent to becoming the individual one may have become would be detrimental to life. Any imposed "collective standard is a serious check to individuality," injurious to the vitality of the person, a form of "artificial stunting."

Perhaps it was my own early mentor, Kurt Goldstein (1939, 1940), who first coined the concept under review with the self-actualization designation. As he phrased it, "There is only one motive by which human activity is set going: the tendency to actualize oneself" (1939, p. 196). The early views of Jung and Goldstein have been enriched by later theorists, notably Fromm, Perls, Rogers, and Maslow. Focusing on what he terms the sense of identity, Fromm (1955) spoke of the need to establish oneself as a unique individual, a state that places the person apart from others. Further—and it is here where Fromm makes a distinct self-oriented commitment—the extent to which this sense of identity emerges depends on how successful the person is in breaking "incestuous ties" to one's family or clan. Persons with well-developed feelings of identity experience being in control of their lives rather than being controlled by the lives of others.

Perls (1969) enlarged on this theme by contrasting self-regulation versus external regulation. Normal/healthy persons do their own regulating, with no external interference, be it the needs and demands of others or the strictures of a social code. What we must actualize is the "true inner self," not an image we have of what our ideal selves should be. That is the "curse of the ideal." To Perls, each must be what he or she "really is."

Following the views of his forerunners, Maslow (1970) stated that self-actualization is the "supreme development" and use of all our abilities, ultimately becoming what we have the potential to become. Noting that self-actualists often require detachment and solitude, Maslow asserted that such persons are strongly self-centered and self-directed, make up their own mind and reach their own decisions, without the need to gain social approval.

In like manner, Rogers (1963) posited a single, overreaching motive for the normal/healthy person-maintaining, actualizing, and enhancing one's potential. The goal is not that of maintaining a homeostatic balance or a high degree of ease and comfort, but rather to move forward in becoming what is intrinsic to self and to enhance further that which one has already become. Believing that humans have an innate urge to create, Rogers stated that the most creative product of all is one's own self.

Where do we see failures in the achievement of self-actualization, a giving up of self to gain the approbation of others? Two personality disorders can be drawn upon to illustrate forms of self-denial.

Those with dependent personalities have learned that feeling good, secure, confident, and so on—that is, those feelings associated with pleasure or the avoidance of pain—is provided almost exclusively in their relationships with others. Behaviorally, these persons display a strong need for external support and attention; should they be deprived of affection and nurturance, they will experience marked discomfort, if not sadness and anxiety. Any number of early experiences may set the stage for this other-oriented imbalance. Dependent individuals often include those who have been exposed to an overprotective training regimen and who thereby fail to acquire competencies for autonomy and initiative; experiencing peer failures and low self-esteem leads them to forego attempts at self-assertion and self-gratification. They learn early that they themselves do not readily achieve rewarding experiences; the experiences are secured better by leaning on others. They learn not only to turn to others as their source of nurturance and security but to wait passively for others to take the initiative in providing safety and sustenance. Clinically, most are characterized as searching for relationships in which others will reliably furnish affection, protection, and leadership. Lacking both initiative and autonomy, they assume a dependent role in interpersonal relations, accepting what kindness and support they may find and willingly submitting to the wishes of others in order to maintain nurturance and security.

A less benign but equally problematic centering on the wishes of others and the denial of self is seen in the obsessive-compulsive personality. These persons display a picture of distinct other-directedness, a consistency in social compliance and interpersonal respect. Their histories usually indicate having been subjected to constraint and discipline when they transgressed parental strictures and expectations. Beneath the conforming other-oriented veneer they exhibit are intense desires to rebel and assert their own self-oriented feelings and impulses. They are trapped in an ambivalence; to avoid intimidation and punishment they have learned to deny the validity of their own wishes and emotions and, in their stead, have adopted as "true" the values and precepts set forth by others. The disparity they sense between their own urges and the behaviors they must display to avoid condemnation often leads to omnipresent physical tensions and rigid psychological controls.

I hope that readers who have reached this final paragraph have not developed a hardening of the spirit of inquiry, a loss of those imaginative outreachings that open one to fresh albeit conjectural theses. Perhaps this speculative essay will prove to have a modicum of practical and theoretical value. Surely I, and not Darwin, should be faulted if his contributions have unjustly been extended to the subject of normatology.

## REFERENCES

Allport, G. 1955. *Becoming—Basic considerations for a psychology of personality.* New Haven: Yale University Press.

Allport, G. 1961. *Pattern and growth in personality.* New York: Holt, Rinehart & Winston.

American Psychiatric Association. 1980. *Diagnostic and statistical manual of mental disorders,* 3rd ed. Washington, DC: American Psychiatric Association.

Barash, D. P. 1982. *Sociobiology and behavior,* 2nd ed. New York: Elsevier.

Bertalanffy, L. von 1945. *Problems of life.* New York: John Wiley & Sons.

Bowers, K. S. 1977. There's more to Iago than meets the eye: A clinical account of personal consistency. In *personality at the crossroads,* ed. D. Magnusson and N. S. Endler, pp. 63–81. Hillsdale, NJ: Lawrence Erlbaum.

Buss, A. H., 1984. *Temperament, early developing personality traits.* Hillsdale, NJ: Lawrence Erlbaum.

Buss, A. H., and Plomin, R. 1975. *A temperament theory of personality development.* New York: John Wiley & Sons.

Buss, D. M. 1984. Evolutionary biology and personality psychology. *American Psychologist, 39,* 1135–1147.

Cloninger, C. R. 1986. A unified biosocial theory of personality and its role in the development of anxiety states. *Psychiatric Developments, 3,* 167–226.

Cloninger, C. R. 1987. A systematic method for clinical description and classification of personality variants. *Archives of General Psychiatry, 44,* 573–588.

Cole, L. C. 1954. The population consequences of life history phenomena. *Quarterly Review of Biology 29,* 103–137.

Conrad, D. C. 1952. Toward a more productive concept of mental health. *Mental Hygiene 36,* 456–466.

Daly, M., and Wilson, M. 1978. *Sex, evolution and behavior.* Boston: Grant Press.

Darwin, C. R. 1871. *The descent of man and selection in relation to sex.* London: Murray.

de Charms, R. 1968. *Personal causation: The internal affective determinants of behavior.* New York: Academic Press.

Everly, G. 1988. *The biological basis of personality: The contribution of paleo-cortical anatomy and physiology.* Paper presented at the First International Congress on Disorders of Personality, Copenhagen, Denmark, August.

Feldman, R., and Quenzar, L. 1984. *Fundamentals of neuropharmacology.* Sunderland, MA: Sinauer.

Freedman, L. Z., and Roe, A. 1958. Evolution and human behavior. In *Behavior and evolution,* ed. A. Roe and G. Simpson, pp. 455–479. New Haven: Yale University Press.

Freud, S. 1895. Project for a scientific psychology. In *Standard edition* (Vol. 1). London: Hogarth Press.

Freud, S. [1915] 1925. The instincts and their vicissitudes. In *The collected papers of Sigmund Freud* ed. E. Jones, (Vol. 4.) London: Hogarth Press.

Freud, S. 1940. *An outline of psychoanalysis.* New York: Live Tight.

Fromm, E. 1955. *The sane society.* New York: Holt, Rinehart & Winston.

Fromm, E. 1968. *The revolution of hope: Toward a humanized technology.* New York: Harper & Row.

Gilligan, C. 1982. *In a different voice.* Cambridge, MA: Harvard University Press.

Gleick, J. 1987. *Chaos: Making a new science.* New York: Viking.

Goldstein, K. 1939. *The organism.* New York: American Book.

Goldstein, K. 1940. *Human nature in the light of psychopathology.* Cambridge, MA: Harvard University Press.

Gray, J. A., ed. 1964. *Pavlov's typology.* New York: Pergamon.

Gray, J. A. 1973. Causal theories of personality and how to test them. In *Multivariate analysis and psychological theory,* ed. J. R. Royce. New York: Academic Press.

Gray, J. A. 1975. *Elements of a two-process theory of learning.* New York: Academic Press.

Gray, J. A. 1981. A critique of Eysenck's theory of personality. In *A Model for personality,* ed. H. J. Eysenck. New York: Springer-Verlag.

Gribbin, J. 1986. *In search of the big bang.* Toronto: Bantam.

Hamilton, W. D. 1964. The genetical evolution of social behavior: I and II. *Journal of Theoretical Biology, 7,* 1–52.

Hartmann, H. 1939. *Ego psychology and the problem of adaptation.* New York: International Universities Press.

Hebb, D. O. 1955. Drives and the C.N.S. (conceptual nervous system). *Psychological Review, 62,* 243–254.

Hempel, C. G. 1965. *Aspects of scientific explanation.* New York: Free Press.

Henry, J. P., and Stephens, P. 1977. *Stress, health, and the social environment,* New York: Springer-Verlag.

Huxley, T. H. 1870. Mr. Darwin's critics. *Contemporary Review, 18,* 443–476.

Jahoda, M. 1958. *Current concepts of positive mental health.* New York: Basic Books.

Jung, C. G. 1961. *Memories, dreams, reflections.* New York: Vintage Books.

Kluver, H., and Bucy, P. 1939. Preliminary analysis of functions of the temporal lobes in monkeys. *Archives of Neurology and Psychiatry, 42,* 979–1000.

Lewin, K. 1936. *Principles of topological psychology.* New York: McGraw-Hill.

Lotka, A. J. 1924. *Elements of mathematical biology.* New York: Dover.

MacLean, P. 1949. Psychosomatic disease and the "visceral brain." *Psychosomatic Medicine, 11,* 338–353.

MacLean, P. 1952. Some psychiatric implications of physiologic studies on front temporal portions of the limbic system. *Electroencephalography and Clinical Neurophysiology, 4,* 407–418.

MacLean, P. 1985. Brain evolution relating to family, play, and the separation call. *Archives of General Psychiatry, 42,* 405–417.

MacLean, P. 1986. Culminating developments in the evolution of the limbic system. In *The Limbic System,* ed. B. Doane and K. Livingston. New York: Raven Press.

Mandelbrot, B. 1977. *The fractal geometry of nature.* New York: Freeman.

Mandell, A. J., and Salk, J. 1984. Developmental fusion of intuition and reason: A metabiological onogeny. In *Normality and the life cycle,* ed. D. Offer and M. Sabshin, pp. 302–314. New York: Basic Books.

Maslow, A. H. 1968. *Toward a psychology of being,* 2nd ed. New York: Van Nostrand.

Maslow, A. H. 1970. *Motivation and personality,* 2nd ed. New York: Harper & Row.

Mayr, E. 1964. The evolution of living systems. *Proceedings of the National Academy of Science, 51,* 934–941.

Millon, T. 1969. *Modern psychopathology.* Philadelphia: Saunders (Reprinted 1985. Prospect Heights, IL: Waveland Press).

Millon, T. 1981. *Disorders of personality: DSM-III, Axis II.* New York: Wiley-Interscience.

Millon, T. 1986. Personality prototypes and their diagnostic criteria. In *Contemporary directions in psychopathology,* ed. T. Millon and G. L. Klerman, pp. 671–712. New York: Guilford Press.

Millon, T. 1987. On the nature of taxonomy in psychopathology. In *Issues in diagnostic research,* (pp. 3–87). New York: Plenum Press.

Millon, T. 1990. *Toward a new personology: An evolutionary Model.* New York: Wiley-Interscience.

Moruzzi, G., and Magoun, H. 1949. Brain stem reticular formation and activation of the EEG. *Electroencephalography and Clinical Neurophysiology, 1,* 45–73.

Offer, D., and Sabshin, M. 1966. *Normality.* New York: Basic Books.

Offer, D., and Sabshin, M., eds. 1984. *Normality and the life cycle.* New York: Basic Books.

Olds, J., and Milner, P. 1954. Positive reinforcement produced by the electrical stimulation of septal region and other regions of rat brain. *Journal of Comparative and Physiological Psychology, 47,* 419–427.

Papez, J. 1937. A proposed mechanism of emotion. *Archives of Neurology and Psychiatry, 38,* 725–743.

Pavlov, I. 1927. *Conditioned reflexes.* Oxford: Oxford University Press.

Perls, F. 1969. *Gestalt therapy verbatim.* Lafayette, CA: Real People Press.

Pribram, K. 1962. Interrelations of psychology and the neurological disciplines. In *Psychology: A study of a science,* ed. S. Koch, pp. 119–157. New York: McGraw-Hill.

Prigogine, I. 1972. Thermodynamics of evolution. *Physics Today, 25,* 23–28, 38–44.

Prigogine, I. 1976. Order through fluctuation: Self-organization and social system." In *Evolution and consciousness,* ed. E. Jantsch and C. Waddington. Reading, MA: Addison-Wesley.

Quine, W. V. O. 1961. *From a logical point of view,* 2nd ed. New York: Harper & Row.

Quine, W. V. O. 1977. Natural kinds. In *Naming, necessity and natural groups,* ed. S. P. Schwartz. Ithaca: Cornell University Press.

Rapaport, D. 1953. Some metapsychological considerations concerning activity and passivity. In *The collected papers of David Rapaport* (1967), ed. M. M. Gill, pp. 530–568. New York: Basic Books.

Redmond, D., Maas, J., and Kling, A. 1971. Social behavior of monkeys selectively depleted of monoamines. *Science, 174,* 428–431.

Rogers, C. R. 1963. Toward a science of the person. *Journal of Humanistic Psychology, 3,* 79–92.

Rushton, J. P. 1984. Sociobiology: Toward a theory of individual and group differences in personality and social behavior. In *Annals of theoretical psychology,* (Vol. 2), ed. J. R. Royce and L. P. Moos, pp. 1–48. New York: Plenum Press.

Rushton, J. P. 1985. Differential K Theory: The sociobiology of individual and group differences. *Personality and Individual Differences, 6,* 441–452.

Russell, J. A. 1980. A circumplex model of affect. *Journal of Personality and Social Psychology, 39,* 1161–1178.

Schrodinger, E. 1944. *What is life?* Cambridge: Cambridge University Press.

Skinner, B. F. 1938. *The behavior of organisms: An experimental analysis.* New York: Appleton.

Skinner, B. F. 1953. *Science and human behavior.* New York: Macmillan.

Smith, E. E., and Medin, D. L. 1981. *Categories and concepts.* Cambridge, MA: Harvard University Press.

Spencer, H. 1870. *The principles of psychology.* London: Williams and Norgate.

Spinoza, B. de. 1677/1986. *Ethics: On the correction of understanding.* London: Dent.

Steklis, H., and Kling, A. 1985. Neurobiology of affiliation in primates. In *The psychobiology of attachment and separation,* ed. M. Reite and T. Fields. Orlando, FL: Academic Press.

Tellegen, A. 1985. Structure of mood and personality and their relevance to assessing anxiety, with an emphasis on self-report. In *Anxiety and the anxiety disorders,* ed. A. H. Tuma and J. Maser, pp. 681–706. Hillsdale, NJ: Lawrence Erlbaum.

Thom, R. 1972. *Structural stability and morphogenesis.* Reading, MA: Benjamin.

Trivers, R. L. 1971. The evolution of reciprocal altruism. *Quarterly review of biology, 46,* 35–57.

Trivers, R. L. 1974. Parental investment and sexual selection. In *Sexual selection and the descent of man 1871–1971,* ed. B. Campbell. Chicago: Aldine.

Tryon, E. 1973. Vacuum genesis. *Nature, 246,* 396–401.

White, R. W. 1959. Motivation reconsidered: The concept of competence. *Psychological Review, 66,* 297–323.

Wilson, E. O. 1975. *Sociobiology: The new synthesis.* Cambridge, MA: Harvard University Press.

Wilson, E. O. 1978. *On human nature.* Cambridge, MA: Harvard University Press.

# PART III

# *TAXONOMY*

# Classification in Psychopathology: Rationale, Alternatives, and Standards

*The elements that constitute a scientific taxonomy are outlined and presented with reference to the structure of psychopathologic categorization and diagnosis. The terminology, logic, and conceptual issues associated with clinical classification are discussed. Alternatives for the selection of substantive clinical attributes, the overall structural format into which categories are organized, and construction procedures used in developing a psychopathologic taxonomy are elaborated, as are a number of criteria for evaluating the taxonomy's utility and efficacy.*

The metatheoretical logic and scientific study of classification are of recent origin and have been given their most important impetus in several major works, notably those by Simpson (1961) and by Sokal and Sneath (1963). Both volumes were oriented to the application of quantitative methods in biological taxonomies by setting forth explicit principles and procedures to achieve scientific goals, such as interjudge reliability and external validity. Of no less importance was a seminal article by Hempel (1961) in which he specifically addressed psychopathologists; with unerring logic, it served not only to raise conceptual considerations involved in developing productive taxonomies but to alert clinicians to the key role that theoretical clarity and empirical synthesis must play. Before these splendid and influential contributions, psychopathologic classification reflected belief systems that were based on impressionistic clinical similarities; most were not grounded in quantifiable data, used unrepresentative populations, and were devoid of a cohering theory.

Psychopathology is an outgrowth of both psychology and medicine. As such, efforts to construct a taxonomy must contend with the goals, concepts, and complications inherent in both disciplines (e.g., context moderators, definitional ambiguities, overlapping symptomatologies, criterion unreliabilities, multidimensional attributes, population heterogeneities, instrument deficits, and ethical constraints).

The current state of psychopathologic nosology and diagnosis resembles that of medicine a century ago. Concepts remain overwhelmingly descriptive. To illustrate, the third edition of the *Diagnostic and Statistical Manual of Mental Disorders* (DSM-III; American Psychiatric Association, 1980) was not only formulated to be atheoretical but addressed itself exclusively to observable phenomena. It is not that inferences and theory have failed in the past to provide useful knowledge but that segments of the mental health profession have not been convinced of their scientific utility, at least not sufficiently to use this knowledge for a nosology. On the other hand, despite the fact that much observation and experimentation have been done, the significance of their products lacks an adequate consensus. Thus, we remain unsure today whether to conceive *depression* as a taxon (category) or an attribute (symptom), whether to view it as a dimension or as a set of discrete types, or whether to conceive it as a neuroendocrinological disease or as an existential problem of life. Although debates on these issues often degenerate into semantic arguments and theoretic hairsplitting, it is naive to assume that metaphysical verbiage and philosophical word quibbling are all that is involved. Nevertheless, the language we use, and the assumptions it reflects, are very much a part of our scientific disagreements.

In this article, I hope to illustrate at least one point, namely, that philosophical issues and scientific modes of analysis must be considered in formulating a psychopathologic taxonomy. Arguably, the following considerations will not in themselves reveal clear resolutions to all nosological quandaries. More likely their role will be to unsettle prevailing habits and thereby to force us to progress, if for no other reason than because our cherished beliefs and assumptions have been challenged. I begin this excursion with some quasi-philosophical considerations.

## ON CLASSIFYING NATURE

More than 20 years ago (Millon, 1969/1987), I voiced my chagrin that nature was not made to suit one's need for a tidy and well-ordered universe. The complexity and intricacy of the natural world make it difficult not only to establish clear-cut relations among phenomena but to find simple ways in which these phenomena can be classified or grouped. In the desire to discover the essential order of nature, one is concerned with only a few of the infinite number of elements that may be chosen, and one's choices are narrowed only to those aspects of nature that may best answer the questions that are posed. The elements we choose are labeled, transformed, and reassembled in a variety of ways, but such products are not realities. The concepts and categories that scientists construct are only optional tools to guide the observation and interpretation of the natural world; different concepts and categories may be formulated as alternatives to understanding the same subject of inquiry (Schwartz, 1991). The subject domains into which the natural world is

subdivided differ in the degree to which their phenomena are inherently differentiated and organized. Some are by nature more articulated and quantifiable than others. To illustrate, the laws of physics, in its most recondite spheres, relate to highly probabilistic processes, but the features of the everyday physical world are highly ordered and predictable. Theories in this latter realm (e.g., mechanics and electricity) serve largely to uncover the lawful relations that do in fact exist in nature; it was the task of turn-of-the-century physicists to fashion a network of constructs that faithfully mirrored the phenomena they studied. By contrast, probabilistic realms of physics (e.g., short-lived elementary particles) or systems of recent evolutionary development (e.g., human interactions) are inherently weakly organized and lack articulated or invariant connections among their constituent elements (Millon, 1990). In knowledge domains that relate to the less ordered spheres of nature (the softer sciences), classifiers and theorists find it necessary to impose a somewhat arbitrary measure of systematization; in so doing, they construct a measure of clarity and coherence not fully consonant with the naturally unsettled and indeterminate character of their subject. Rather than equivocate or succumb to the futility of it all, noble or pretentious efforts are made to arrange and categorize these inexact and probabilistic elements so that they simulate a degree of precision and order that transcends any that they intrinsically possess. In fields such as economics and psychopathology, classifications are, in considerable measure, splendid fictions, compelling notions, or austere formulas devised to give coherence to their inherently imprecise subjects.

Given the semi-arbitrary nature of this task, one can readily understand why psychopathologic states and processes may be classified in terms of any of several data levels (e.g., behavioral, intrapsychic, or phenomenological) or in terms of any of a variety of attributes (e.g., interpersonal conduct, mood or affect, or self-image). Beyond this, each data level lends itself to a number of specific concepts and categories, the usefulness of which must be gauged by their ability to solve the particular problems for which they were created. That the subject matter of psychopathology is inherently diverse and imprecise is a major reason why one must hesitate to narrow the clinical data that constitute a classification to one level or to one approach. Each source and orientation has a legitimate and potentially fruitful contribution to make. No classification in psychopathology today is an inevitable representation of the real world. Rather, current classifications, for example, the forthcoming DSM-IV and the 10th edition of the *International Classification of Disease and Related Health Problems* (ICD-10; World Health Organization, 1990), are, at best, interim tools for advancing knowledge and facilitating clinical goals (Sartorius, 1990). They serve to orient our scientific work and function as an organizing scheme to give order to our clinical experiences.

## CLASSIFICATORY TERMINOLOGY

As I noted earlier in this article, formal methods of differentiating and denoting psychopathological phenomena are of only recent origin. As a consequence, the terminology of this field may not be familiar, even to the mature and professional reader. Also, because of the field's recent development and its formation within the biological sciences, the meaning of several key concepts may remain unclear, which can result in inconsistent usage and diverse connotations. To reduce these ambiguities and enable the reader to become more familiar with the rationale of this emerging area of study, it may be useful to record the more or less conventional meanings of several frequent terms as well as introduce new variants of old designations.

First, the term *classification* itself may be broadly defined as a procedure for constructing groups or categories and for assigning entities (disorders or persons) to these categories on the basis of their shared attributes or relations. The product of this procedure consists of a nonarbitrary set of categories called a *classification system.* The process of assigning previously unallocated entities to their appropriate categories is termed *identification;* in clinical settings, where entities comprise patterns of clinical attributes or the patients who possess the attributes, identification is referred to as *diagnosis.*

The term *taxonomy* is usually applied to scientific classification systems; it refers to the sorting and arranging of entities of scientific interest into natural categories on the basis of key features they share or of concepts they illustrate in common. The term is used also to represent the metatheory and systematic study of the classification process itself (Simpson, 1961); in this context, it encompasses the logic, principles, and methods of constructing categorical systems, as well as. the rules by which identifications are made. The adjective *taxonomic* is used to refer to matters that pertain specifically to taxonomies. In clinical domains the word *nosology* relates to a taxonomy of pathological phenomena (e.g., diseases or disorders); *nomenclature* pertains to the names or labels used to designate the categories of taxonomy, be it nosological or otherwise.

A major category of a taxonomic (nosologic) system is termed *a taxon;* taxa may be differentiated in a number of different ways. What I label as *manifest taxa* comprise categories that are based on observable or phenotypic commonalities (e.g., overt behaviors). *Latent taxa* pertain to categories formed on the basis of abstract mathematical derivations or the propositional deductions of a theory, each of which ostensibly represents the presence of genotypic commonalities (e.g., etiologic origins or intrapsychic similarities). In psychopathology the subject domains of taxa may be differentiated into three sets. *Syndromal taxa* pertain to a group of clinical signs and symptoms (diseases or disorders) that represent but a partial segment, albeit an important one, of a persons total psychological makeup. I use the term *personological taxa* to represent a pattern of clinically relevant traits (personality disorders) that have a person's overall psychological makeup as their focus. Of more recent origin are *situational taxa,* categories that encompass relevant sources of environmental influence (psychosocial stressors).

The adjective *taxonic* refers to matters that pertain to taxa. Taxa may encompass elements of broader or lesser scope and abstraction. In a stepwise and ever-widening hierarchy of taxonic tiers, there may be broadly encompassing categories that subsume taxa of lesser range; for example, the overarching taxon personality disorders is a category of higher rank that embraces and includes more particular personality types, such as borderline and narcissistic, each of which is a taxon in its own right.

A number of overlapping concepts relate to the composition of nosologic taxa, notably *clinical attributes, defining features,* and *diagnostic criteria.* The first pertains to a broad class of clinically relevant characteristics of either current psychological functioning (signs, symptoms, or traits) or longitudinal relevance (etiology, course, prognosis, or treatment response). Each attribute is usually differentiated into specific subclasses to represent distinctive psychological properties of clinical import (e.g., separating traits into those of interpersonal conduct, cognitive style, and expressive mood). To refine matters further, several variants of each subclass of clinical attributes may be specified to help differentiate among a group of comparable nosologic taxa. For example, the trait subclass of interpersonal conduct may be subdivided into a series of specific indicators that not only identify but typify and help to discriminate each personality disorder from the others. These exemplifying and distinctive qualities are referred to as a taxon's defining features. To illustrate, antisocial personalities may be characterized by the defining feature of irresponsible interpersonal conduct, dependent persons may be identified by their submissive conduct, compulsive persons may typically be respectful interpersonally, narcissists may be notably exploitive, and so

on. A particular set of to-be-included and to-be-excluded defining features, arranged in accord with specific rules (e.g., monothetic or polythetic), is termed the *diagnostic criteria* of the taxon.

Rules for how many and which defining features must be present to make a diagnosis may be either monothetic or polythetic. In the former case, to produce what has been referred to as *classical* taxonomies (Cantor & Mischel, 1979; Rosch, 1978), all of the defining features that constitute a taxon must be in evidence for a diagnosis to be given, which results in entirely homogeneous taxa. Polythetic rules are typically used in what are known as *prototypal* taxonomies and require that only a subset of possible or ideal diagnostic features be exhibited; being more open than classical taxa, prototypal ones permit heterogeneity through membership diversity. Monothetic rules are fixed and invariant, whereas polythetic rules may be either inflexible or flexible; in the latter case, changing combinations of defining features may suffice in different circumstances to fulfill a taxon's diagnostic criteria.

## RATIONALE

Reliable and useful classifications were developed long before the advent of modern scientific thought and methods. Information and instrumentation were achieved without science per se or its symbolic abstractions and techniques of research. If useful classifications can be acquired by observation and common sense alone, what special values are derived by applying the complicated and rigorous procedures required in developing explicit criteria, taxonic homogeneity, and diagnostic efficiency? Are clarity, precision, and experimentation more than compulsive and picayune concerns for detail, more than the pursuit for the honorific title of science? Are the labors of differentiating attributes or establishing optimal cutting scores worth the time and effort involved?

There is no doubt in this age of science that the answer is yes. But why? What are the distinguishing virtues of precision in one's terminology, the specification of observable referents, the analysis of covariant attribute clusters? What sets these procedures apart from ordinary ways of categorizing knowledge?

## LOGIC OF CLASSIFICATION

The number of ways one can observe, describe, and organize the natural world is infinite. As a consequence, the terms and concepts one creates to represent these activities are often confusing and obscure. Different words are used to describe the same behavior, and the same word is used for different behaviors. Some terms are narrow in focus, others are broad, and some are difficult to define. Because of the diversity of events to which one can attend or the lack of precision in the language we use, different processes are confused and similar events get scattered hodgepodge across a scientific landscape; as a consequence, communication gets bogged down in terminological obscurities and semantic controversies (Schwartz, 1991).

One of the purposes of formalizing the phenomena that constitute a scientific subject is to avoid this morass of confusion. Not all phenomena related to the subject need be attended to at once. Certain elements may be selected from the vast range of possibilities because they seem relevant to the solution of a specific question, and to create a degree of reliability among those interested in a subject, its elements are defined as precisely as possible and classified according to their core similarities and differences (Dougherty, 1978; Tversky, 1977). In a subject like psychopathology, these categories are given specific labels that serve to represent them. This process of definition and classification is indispensable for systematizing scientific observation and knowledge.

Is conceptual definition and differential classification possible in psychopathology?

Can these most fundamental of scientific activities be achieved in a subject that is inherently inexact and of only modest levels of intrinsic order, one in which even the very slightest variations in context or antecedent conditions—often of a minor or random character—produce highly divergent outcomes (Bandura, 1982)? Because this looseness within the network of variables in psychopathology is unavoidable, are there grounds for believing that such endeavors can prove more than illusory? Persuasive answers of a more philosophical nature must be bypassed in this article; those who wish to pursue this theme would gain much by reading, among others, Pap (1953), Hempel (1965), and Meehl (1978). I do touch, albeit briefly, on a more tangible and psychologically based rationale for believing that formal classification in psychopathology may prove at least moderately fruitful.

There is a sound logic to classifying syndromes in medical disorders. Bodily changes wrought by infectious diseases and structural deteriorations repeatedly display themselves in a moderately uniform pattern of signs and symptoms that make sense in terms of how anatomic structures and physiological processes are altered and dysfunction. Moreover, these biological changes provide a foundation not only for identifying the pathogenesis of these disorders but also for anticipating their course and prognosis. Logic and fact together enable one to construct a rationale as to why most medical syndromes express themselves in the signs and symptoms they do, as well as the sequences through which they unfold.

Can the same logic be applied to psychopathological classifications? Is there a clear rationale, perhaps even evidence, for believing that certain forms of clinical expression (e.g., behaviors, cognitions, affects, and mechanisms) cluster together as do medical syndromes, that is, not only covary but make sense as a coherently organized and reasonably distinctive group of characteristics? Are there theoretical and empirical justifications for assuming that the varied features of personality display a configurational unity and expressive consistency over time? Does the careful study of persons reveal congruency among such diverse attributes as overt behavior, intrapsychic functioning, and biophysical disposition? Is this coherence and stability of psychological functioning a valid phenomenon, that is, not merely imposed on observed data by virtue of clinical expectation or theoretical bias?

There is a rationale, albeit not a perfect one, to believe that the answer to each of the preceding questions is yes. Stated briefly and simply, the observation of covariant patterns of signs, symptoms, and traits may be traced to the fact that persons possess rather enduring biophysical dispositions that give a consistent coloration to their experience and that the range of experiences to which they are exposed throughout their lives is both limited and repetitive (Millon, 1981). Given the limiting and shaping character of these biogenic and psychogenic influences, it is not surprising that persons develop clusters of prepotent and deeply ingrained behaviors, cognitions, and affects that clearly distinguish them from others of dissimilar backgrounds. Furthermore, once a number of the components of a known clinical pattern are identified, knowledgeable clinicians are able to deduce the presence of other, unobserved but frequently correlated features that constitute that pattern.

If one accepts the view that most persons display a pattern of internally consistent characteristics, one is led next to the question of whether groups of patients evidence commonality in the patterns they display. The notion of clinical categories rests on the assumption that there are a limited number of such shared covariances, for example, regular groups of diagnostic signs and symptoms that can confidently be used to distinguish certain classes of patients. (It must be noted that because patients can profitably be classified into categories does not negate the fact patients so classified display considerable differences as well,

differences that are routinely observed with medical diseases.)

Another question about the nature of clinical categories that must be addressed may be phrased as follows: Why does the possession of characteristic A increase the probability, appreciably beyond chance, of also possessing characteristics B, C, and so on? Less abstractly, why do particular behaviors, attitudes, mechanisms, and so on, covary in repetitive ways rather than exhibit themselves in a more or less haphazard fashion? Even more concretely, why do behavioral defensiveness, interpersonal provocativeness, cognitive suspicion, affective irascibility, and excessive use of the projection mechanism co-occur in the same person rather than be uncorrelated and randomly distributed among patients?

First, temperament and early experience simultaneously effect the development and nature of several emerging psychological structures and functions: That is, a wide range of behaviors, attitudes, affects, and mechanisms can be traced to the same origins, which therefore leads to their frequently observed covariance. Second, once a person possesses these initial characteristics, they set in motion a series of derivative life experiences that shape the acquisition of new psychological attributes causally related to the characteristics that preceded them in the sequential chain. Given particular common origins and their consequent successive linkages increases the probability that certain psychological characteristics will combine with specific others characteristics and thereby result in repetitively observed symptom clusters, or what are termed *clinical syndromes*. Illustrations of these reciprocal covariances and serially unfolding concatenations among longitudinal influences (e.g., etiology) and concurrent attributes (e.g., signs or traits) may be found in most abnormal and psychiatric texts.

Although grievances over the inadequacies of both our current and historic classification systems have been voiced for years, as have been suggestions that endeavors to refine these efforts are fussy and misdirected, if not futile and senseless pretensions that ought to be abandoned, the presence of categorical systems is both unavoidable—because of humankind's linguistic and attributional habits—as well as inevitable—because of the need to differentiate and to record the most obvious of dissimilarities among the psychologically impaired. Given that one or another set of categories is inevitable, or as Kaplan (1964) once phrased it, "it is impossible to wear clothing of no style at all" (p. 279), it is both sensible and fitting that the explicit basis on which such distinctions are to be made is known, rather than have them occur helter-skelter in nonpublic and nonverifiable ways. Moreover, if psychopathology is to evolve into a true science, its diverse phenomena must be subject to formal identification, differentiation, and quantification. Diagnosis and assessment presuppose the existence of discernible phenomena that can be recognized and measured. Logic necessitates, therefore, that psychopathologic states and processes be distinguished from one another and be thereby categorizable to some degree before they can be subjected to identification and quantification.

## CONCEPTUAL ISSUES

What exactly is a clinical attribute? That is, what is it that constitutes a taxon, and on what grounds shall we decide that it exists? To pose this question is not mere sophistry. For example, a serious issue demanding the attention of responsible philosophers, psychiatrists, and psychologists (Medin, Altom, Edelson, & Freko, 1982; Smith & Medin, 1981) is the very nature of the construct *disease entity*. Noting the complexities inherent in conceiving so universal a concept as disease, Kendell (1975) wrote that:

Contemporary writers still make frequent reference to "disease entities" . . . almost invariably without defining their meaning. Like "disease"

itself, "entity" has become one of those dangerous terms which is in general use without ever being defined, those who use it fondly assuming that they and everyone else knows its meaning. (p. 65)

Feinstein (1977) noted the circular nature of many definitions in the following illustration:

The complex situation we have been contemplating can be greatly simplified if only we are allowed a bit of circular reasoning. At the root of the difficulty is the problem of deciding what is a diagnosis. We can dispose of that difficulty by defining a diagnosis as the name for a disease. We are now left with defining disease, which we can call a state of abnormal health. Abnormal health is readily defined as a departure from normal health. And then, completing the circle, normal health can be defined as the absence of disease. (p. 189)

As Feinstein goes onto say, *disease* is an abstract and multifaceted concept that remains so even if one prefers to represent it with other terms such as ailment, sickness, illness, or disorder.

Those who have more than a tangential interest in the nature of psychopathologic classification cannot help but be apprehensive over the profound problems that arise in merely defining its constituents, no less in their specification, criteria, and measurement.

I now survey the extent to which constructs such as *taxa* and *attribute* have tangible empirical referents. The basic issue is whether these concepts are anchored to observable or to inferred phenomena.

The constituents of a nosological classification are represented by a set of terms or labels, that is, a language by which members of a clinical group communicate about a subject. These terms serve two functions. First, they facilitate the manipulation of ideas. Clinical or theoretical concepts are systematically (if implicitly) linked; it is through their interplay that meaningful clinical ideas are formulated and deductive scientific statements are proposed. Second, most concepts possess an empirical significance; that is, they are linked in some way to the observable world. Although some may represent processes or events that are not apparent, they can be defined by or anchored with reference to the explicit and tangible. It is this translatability into the empirical domain that allows nosologists to test their schema in the clinical world.

Ideally, all of the concepts that constitute a nosology ought to be empirically anchored, that is, correspond to observable properties in clinical practice; this minimizes confusion about the attributes of which a taxon is composed (Schwartz, 1991). Furthermore, nosologic labels must be more precise and clinically descriptive than the words of ordinary language; although everyday language has relevance to significant real world events, it gives rise to ambiguity and confusion because of the varied uses to which conventional words are often put. Taxonic concepts must be defined as precisely and with as much clinical relevance as possible in order to assure that their meaning is clear and pertinent.

Empirical precision can be achieved only if every defining feature that distinguishes a taxon is anchored to a single and observable phenomenon; that is, a different datum will be used for every difference that can be observed in the clinical world. This goal is simply not feasible, nor is it desirable for reasons to be noted shortly. Classificatory terms do differ, however, in the extent to which they achieve empirical precision. There are points along a gradation from conceptual specificity to conceptual openness that may be identified; it may aid readers to recognize certain features that distinguish among both attributes and taxa.

Some concepts are defined literally by the procedures that measure observable events and possess no meaning other than the results obtained in this manner. They reflect what Bridgman (1927) termed *operational definitions*. The meaning of an operationally defined concept becomes synonymous with how

we measure it, not with what we say about it. Its scientific advantage is obvious: Taxa and the attributes of which they are composed are unambiguous, and diagnostic identifications associated with these taxons are translatable directly into the clinical attributes they represent.

Useful as these definitions may be, they present several problems (Schwartz & Wiggins, 1986; Spitzer, 1990). Diagnostic terms must be generalizable; that is, they ought to enable the clinician to include a variety of measures and observations as gauges of a taxon. Operational definitions are too restrictive. They preclude extensions to new situations that are even slightly different from the original defining condition. One of the primary goals of a classification is to integrate diverse observations with a minimum number of terms. A strict operational approach floods clinicians with an infinite number of attributes and taxa and clutters thinking with largely irrelevant distinctions.

Intrapsychic processes and dispositional traits are nebulous and concealed, hidden from the observable world, and hence, only to be inferred. These unobservable mediating structures and processes are not merely useful but may be necessary elements in constructing an effective psychopathologic nosology. Because of their abstract and hypothetical character, these indeterminate constructs are known in philosophy as *open concepts* (Pap, 1953). Some are defined by, and largely reducible to, a set of diverse empirical events. For example, the concept projection may be gauged by observing persons ascribe their own traits to others, by the presence of certain scores on a psychological test, by a history of litigious actions, and so on. Although the term projection implies a concealed intrapsychic process within a person that cannot itself be observed, its existence may be inferred from a variety of observables.

Many open and fully speculative concepts are formulated with minimal or no explicit reference. Their failure to be anchored to the realm of observables has led some to question their suitability in scientific contexts. No doubt, clarity gets muddled, and deductions are often tautological when a diagnosis is explained in terms of a series of such constructs. For example, statements such as "in the borderline the mechanisms of the ego become diffused when libidinous energies overwhelm superego introjections" are, at best, puzzling. Postulating connections between one set of open concepts and another may lead to facile but often confusing clinical statements, as any periodic reader of contemporary psychoanalytic literature can attest. Such use results in formulations that are difficult to decipher because one cannot specify observables by which the formulations can be anchored or evaluated.

Open concepts usually assume their meaning with reference to a theoretical network of variables and constructs within which they are embedded. The significance they derive thereby accounts both for their weaknesses and strengths as components of taxonomy (Spitzer, 1990).

Because classification is a human artifact, not every one of its terms needs to be linked to observable events, especially if its purpose is to extend the generalizability of knowledge (Dougherty, 1978). Unrealistic standards of empirical anchorage, particularly in the early stages of taxonomic construction, often discourage the kind of imaginative speculation necessary to decode and to integrate elusive phenomena. Vague and risky as open concepts may be, they prove among the most useful tools available in developing a productive classification.

# ALTERNATIVES

What data from the stream of ongoing clinical events and processes ought to be selected to serve as the basic units of taxa? Must we restrict ourselves only to observables, or will inferred processes be permitted? Ought the data to comprise behaviors only, or will self-reports or physiological signs be admissible? What of past history or of socioeconomic or situational factors? Is everything grist for the taxonic mill? Must the attributes of diagnostically comparable syndromes be uniform, that is, consist of the same class of data, or will biological indexes be included only in some, cognitive processes only in others, and so on? What structural framework shall we use to organize the components of the taxonomy, and what rules will govern the taxa into which its defining features will be placed? Shall its overall architecture be horizontal, vertical, or circular in format, and shall its constituents comprise categories or dimensions? Shall we construct or select its elements on the basis of formal statistical techniques of analysis, such as numerically derived clusters, or shall we turn to theory and choose an element on the basis of logically deduced constructs? Such questions as these, and the issues and alternatives they raise, are central to the taxonomic enterprise, considerations of a formal character that have only recently been examined in constructing psychopathologic nosologies.

## SUBSTANTIVE ATTRIBUTES

Psychopathology has been studied from many vantage points and observed and conceptualized in legitimately different ways by behaviorists, phenomenologists, psychodynamicists, and biochemists. No point of observation or conceptualization encompasses all of the complex and multidimensional features of psychopathology clinical processes and events have been described in terms of conditioned habits, reaction formations, cognitive expectancies, or neurochemical dysfunctions. These domains cannot be arranged in a hierarchy, with one level viewed as reducible to another (Millon, 1990). Neither can they be compared in terms of some objective truth value. Alternative substantive domains merely are different; they facilitate the observation and conceptualization of different clinical attributes and lead, therefore, to different taxa. The point is that taxa may be differentially composed in accord with the kinds of clinical data (e.g., etiology, symptoms, and treatment response) they comprise as their basic constituents. Choices often are pragmatic, and questions of comparative utility cannot be determined a priori. However, irrelevant controversies and needless confusions can be avoided if the class of attributes from which taxa are composed has been specified clearly. When done properly, clinicians and researchers can determine whether two taxonomies are comparable, whether the same diagnostic label refers to different clinical phenomena, whether different taxa encompass the same attributes, and so on. As Panzetta (1974) stated:

As one begins to consider the variety of starting-off points then we quickly appreciate that the first step in the nosologic process is inherently arbitrary. I would insist that we begin by acknowledging that the arbitrary focus is not, per se, a deficiency but rather a reality which flows naturally from the tremendous complexity of human behavior. It is useless to try to develop the "correct" initial focus. There is no correct focus, only several alternatives. (p. 155)

Sneath and Sokal (1973) recorded the wide array of attributes available in every discipline that can be potentially useful in forming a taxonomy. The task is that of identifying which are likely to be most relevant and optimally productive. The history of psychopathology provides guidelines that may prove fruitful, for example, the well-established and important distinction between longitudinal and concurrent attributes. The former represents the progression of various clinical phenomena across time and circumstance, and the latter addresses the diverse ways in which these phenomena manifest themselves contemporaneously and simultaneously across a number of expressive dimensions.

## LONGITUDINAL ATTRIBUTES

Data that concern causal factors as clinical attributes for taxa would be extremely useful, if only such knowledge were available. Unfortunately, etiologic data are scanty and unreliable. Moreover, they are likely to remain so

because of the obscure, complex, and interactive nature of influences that shape psychopathologic phenomena. In great measure, etiologic attributes are conjectures that rest on tenuous empirical grounds; most reflect schools of thought that posit their favorite hypotheses. These speculations are best construed as questions that deserve empirical testing on the basis of taxa formed by less elusive data.

Among the few etiologic schemata that lend themselves to taxonomic goals is Zubin's (1968) differentiation of six categories: social-cultural (ecological), developmental, learning, genetic, internal environment, and neurophysiological. Systematic and orderly though models such as Zubins may be, they do not fully address issues associated with alternate levels of analysis, nor do they trace the intricate and varied causal chains that unfold ultimately into a clinical state.

Beyond the issue of identifying which of several levels of an interactive causal system may be selected as etiological attributes, there are questions of a more philosophical and methodological nature concerning what exactly is meant by etiology and in what precise way it may be gauged. Meehl (1972) addressed this matter succinctly:

A metatheoretical taxonomy of causal factors and a metataxonomy of causal relations (such as "necessary but not sufficient condition," "interaction effects," "threshold effects," and the like) are badly needed. In medicine, we recognize several broad etiologic classes such as deficiency diseases, autoimmunity diseases, disease due to microorganisms, hereditary-degenerative diseases, developmental anomalies, diseases due to trauma. . . . The concept "specific etiology" . . . appears to have half a dozen distinguishable and equally defensible meanings (e.g., sine qua non, critical threshold, uniformly most powerful factor) that might be useful under various circumstances. (p. 22)

The yearning among taxonomists for a neat package of etiologic attributes simply cannot be reconciled with the complex philosophical and methodological issues and the difficult to disentangle networks of both subtle and random influences that shape our mental disorders. It also makes understandable the decision of the DSM-III Task Force to set etiological and course variables aside as clinical grist for its taxonic mills.

Turning from the antecedent to the consequent side of the clinical course, logic argues that the nature of a mental disorder must be at least partially revealed by its response to treatment. The data available on this matter, however, provide little that goes beyond broad generalizations. This contrasts with medicine at large, in which a variety of interventions are specific to particular disorders. Notable in medicine are a variety of challenge or stressor tasks that serve to identify patient vulnerabilities (e.g., introducing allergens to uncover susceptibilities or to elicit reaction sensitivities). Considerations of ethics and human sensibilities preclude adopting parallel strategies in psychopathology even where intent is clearly beneficial, as in psychological treatment interventions, the problems encountered in discerning and differentiating optimal clinical attributes are many, for example, the inevitability of spontaneous remissions and unanticipated life events. Even if we could partial out the effects of these confounding events, could we identify the ingredients that account for beneficial reactions in a heterogeneous patient population? Furthermore, what conclusions can be drawn about a therapy whose efficacy is wide-ranging, that is, demonstrable among disorders whose origins and expression are highly diverse? Complicating matters further is the fact that every technique of therapy claims high efficacy across a wide band of sundry diagnostic classes. One then concludes that treatment response, as with etiology, may prove ultimately to be a useful taxonic attribute; for the present, however, reliable data are not in hand.

## CONCURRENT ATTRIBUTES

Given the problematic nature of longitudinal attributes, what remains to constitute psychopathologic taxa are coexistent attributes of a contemporaneous nature, notably objective signs, on the one hand, and subjectively reported symptoms, on the other. To these two classical indicators of disorder may be added the essentially inferred attributes of personality traits. Information about these clinical features may be derived from four conceptually and methodologically distinct data sources, namely, the biophysical, intrapsychic, phenomenological, and behavioral.

### Signs

These data comprise more or less objectively recorded changes in state or function that indicate both the presence and character of clinically relevant processes or events. Two sources provide the main body of clinical signs: biophysical markers and behavioral acts.

As for the first data set, biophysical markers, there are few anatomical, biochemical, and neurophysiological gauges among the standard diagnostic taxa, despite their tangible, objective, and quantitative nature. This failure is not only surprising but disconcerting, given the vast number of psychopathologic studies over the years that have hypothesized and investigated potential biophysical markers obtained from a multitude of measures, such as urine or blood analysis, diverse muscle appraisals, skin gauges, cardiac assessments, eye movements, metabolic indexes, electroencephalograph rhythms, and so on.

That so few of these biophysical measures have aided the definition of clinical attributes can be traced to a number of factors. Most cannot be arranged into clearly discriminable categories, and with few exceptions, normative distributions on relevant clinical populations are either unavailable or inconsistent. For many, reliability measures are lacking or indicate high levels of variability over time and across settings. To complicate interpretive efforts, low intercorrelations are typically found among measures that ostensibly represent the same basic functions. Moreover, the expense of technical equipment is high, and the availability of needed expertise is often so scarce as to make many of these procedures out of reach for all but well funded research investigators.

As for explicit behavioral acts, the second of the major objective indexes, it has been the methodological goal of behavioral purists to avoid drawing inferences about internal or subjective processes. Hence, they seek to use techniques that ostensibly bypass explicit dependence on subjective symptomatic data. As promising as overt behavior may be as a source for clinical attributes, numerous concerns about its utility have been registered, not the least of which is its unpredictability, that is, its high variability across setting and time (e.g., the recording of verbal behaviors fails to generate reliable normative data across diverse circumstances). This is in contrast with data produced by well-constructed rating instruments. Most of these are reasonably reliable, succeed in discriminating among relevant patient groups, and possess adequate normative data for differential or comparative purposes.

Rather commonplace behaviors of potential diagnostic significance have recently come under systematic scrutiny and analysis. Of promise is the work of Buss and Craik (1983, 1987) and of Livesley (1985, 1991). Attempting to provide a descriptive (i.e., nonexplanatory) basis for diagnostically relevant features, these investigators have developed lists of familiar acts observed in the course of everyday life that may typify certain clinical characteristics. Despite these promising advances, behavioral methods are long on neat measures of a rather trivial character, with tangential or limited substantive significance in the realm of psychopathologic taxonomy (Block, 1989).

### Symptoms

In contrast to clinical signs, symptoms are subjective in nature, represented by reports from patients of their conscious recollections and recorded experiences (e.g., moods, feelings, perceptions, memories, attitudes, and

so on). Together with clinical signs, symptoms focus on phenomenological processes and events that relate directly to diagnostic matters. It is here where the psychopathologist has an advantage over the physicist or the biologist, for neither can ask the objects of their study to reflect on their experience, no less to communicate it in articulate or meaningful ways. As Strauss (1986) framed it:

To some extent, the field has been discouraged by previous claims and promises regarding the understanding of subjective experiences such as these. Although the claims were often overstated, and the assessment of these processes is complex, neither reason is adequate for avoiding a major attempt to develop creative ways for looking at the role of such subjective experiences in the course of psychopathology and their relevance to diagnosis. (p. 362)

Contributing to the utility of symptomatic data is their ease of evocation. Moreover, structured assessments, such as interview schedules and self-report inventories, minimize potential sources of distortion. Nevertheless, these methods are subject to difficulties that can invalidate data (e.g., one cannot assume that subjects will interpret questions in the same way, that they possess sufficient self-knowledge to respond informatively, or that they may not be faking or dissembling).

Although the substantive content of phenomenological symptoms are elusive and often unreliable and are fraught with philosophical and methodological complexities, taxonomists cannot afford the luxury of bypassing them—symptoms lie at the very heart of all psychopathologic inquiries. The events they portray are real and represent facets of experience far richer in scope and diversity than concrete observables.

### Traits

In contrast to signs, which represent objective biologic measures or behavioral acts, and symptoms, which are phenomenologically reported recollections and experiences, traits characterize inferred psychological habits and stable dispositions of broad generality and diverse expression. This long-established psychological construct has been used in two ways: First, it encompasses various characteristic habits, moods, and attitudes, and second, through inference it identifies dispositions to act, feel, and think in certain ways. Traits can be considered to be both more and less than signs and symptoms. For example, several traits can coalesce to form the expression of a single behavioral sign. Conversely, several different specific symptoms may be the upshot of a single trait. Furthermore, each trait may express itself in diverse signs and symptoms. Clearly, there is no one-to-one correspondence between traits and signs or symptoms.

Traits often are inferred rather than observed, generalized rather than specific, and dispositional rather than consequential. They are assumed to be enduring and pervasive. However, only certain traits of a person display this durability and pervasiveness; that is, only some of them prove to be resistant to the influences of changing times and circumstances. Other forms of behavior, attitude, and emotion are presumably more transient and malleable. It is noteworthy that traits that exhibit consistency and stability in one person may not be the same as those in others. These qualities are most prominent among characteristics that are central to maintaining a persons overall psychological balance and style of functioning. To illustrate, the interpersonal conduct trait of significance for some is that of being agreeable, never differing or having conflict; for others it may be interpersonally important to maintain one's distance from others so as to avoid rejection or being humiliated; for a third group the influential interpersonal trait may be that of asserting one's will and dominating others.

The sources used to identify clinical traits are highly diverse, from methods designed to uncover intrapsychic processes, such as free association, dream analysis, hypnosis, and projective techniques, to such phenomenological methods as structured interviews and self-report inventories, and to behavioral methods of observation and rating, be they systematic or otherwise.

It is no understatement to say that the rich vein of clinical attributes uncovered by dispositional and intrapsychic traits has been a boon to clinical theory, but a source of perplexity and despair to taxonomists. More than any other domain, dispositional data and methods produce information that is fraught with complexities and obscurities that can bewilder the most sophisticated of classifiers. Part of the difficulty stems from the fact that the identification of hidden traits is highly inferential. Because the dispositional structure and processes that make up traits can be only partially observed and take different manifest forms in different contexts, it is difficult to identify them reliably and, hence, to assign them a standard place in a taxonomy. Matters are made more difficult by the absence of intrapsychic normative and base rate data, as well as by the lack of strong validations support.

## STRUCTURAL FORMAT

Whatever features are chosen to provide the substantive body of a taxonomy, decisions must be made about the structural framework into which the taxonomy will be cast, the rules that will govern the taxa into which its clinical attributes and defining features will be placed, and the compositional properties that will characterize these attributes and features. These are problems of the essential architecture of the taxonomy whether it should be organized horizontally, vertically, or circularly, whether all or only a limited and fixed subset of features are required for taxonic membership, whether its constituents are conceived as categories or dimensions—as well as a host of other differentiating characteristics from which one may choose. I discuss several modern structural designs, and the options available among them, a task of no simple proportions given that there is nothing logically self-evident nor is there a traditional format or contemporary consensus to guide selections among these alternatives.

## TAXONOMIC STRUCTURE

Ought the various attributes that comprise the substantive data of psychopathology be listed more or less randomly or be ordered into a series of logical or functional groups that attempt to mirror the inherent nature of psychopathology? The obvious answer is the latter.

Several frameworks for structuring psychopathology have been formulated in recent years, and they are not mutually exclusive. From a design viewpoint, they can be described as having vertical, horizontal, or circular structures. The vertical, referred to as the *hierarchical* framework, organizes the various taxa of psychopathology (e.g., depressive disorder or schizophrenic disorder) in a series of echelons in which lower tiers are subsumed as subsets of those assigned higher ranks. The second, or *horizontal* framework, is known as the multiaxial schema; it orders different classes of attributes (e.g., symptoms or etiologies) in a series of aligned or parallel categories. The DSM-III and its revision (DSM-III-R; American Psychiatric Association, 1987) encompass both hierarchical and multiaxial structural forms, albeit with modest logic and success. The circular framework is referred to as the *circumplical* model. It has not received official recognition, although it has gained considerable currency among theorists oriented toward the role of interpersonal attributes.

### Hierarchical Models

These are typically arranged in the form of taxonic decision trees. Once a particular branch, that is, a higher order diagnosis, has been chosen, subsequent taxonic choices are limited to the several twigs that constitute that branches subdivisions. To illustrate, once it has been decided with DSM-III-R criteria

that a patient is exhibiting a mood disorder, the clinician may further differentiate the disturbance as either a bipolar disorder or a depressive disorder. If the choice was bipolar, the clinician may move further down the hierarchy to select among bipolar, mixed, bipolar manic, bipolar, depressed, or cyclothymia.

A consequence of so carefully fashioned a sequential chain of categories is that successive taxa in the classification invariably are more specific and convey more precisely differentiated information than those that precede them. This increasing distinctness and exactitude, necessary ingredients in a successful hierarchical schema, assures that each successive category possesses authentic clinical features not found in categories previously listed.

Sequential patterns of the decision-tree type would be a remarkable achievement for any hierarchical nosology, if they were naturally or logically justified (Millon, 1983). Not only is there no inherent structure to psychopathology that permits so rigorous an arrangement, but the various DSMs, for instance, impose only a modest degree of sequential rigor on the taxonomic organization. The problems of pursuing a hierarchical method for differential diagnosis are compounded by the fact that the DSM not only permits but encourages multiple diagnoses, a problem aggravated further by the manual's standard multiaxial framework. Not only does the hierarchical goal of orderly and successive diagnostic choice points run hard against the structural character of DSM taxa, but its formalism and sequential requirements are undermined repeatedly by the multidiagnostic aims and intrinsic multiaxial schema of the DSM.

### Multiaxial Models

This format, the second of the overarching structural models, encounters few of the logical difficulties and assumptions found in hierarchical systems. The formal adoption of the multiaxial schema in the DSM-III and in the ICD-10 approaches a paradigm shift (Millon, 1983). It reflects a distinct turn from the traditional infectious disease model in which the clinicians job is to disentangle distracting symptoms and to clear away confounding situational problems so as to pinpoint the underlying or true pathophysiologic state. By contrast, the multiaxial model (Essen-Moller & Wohlfahrt, 1947; Mezzich, 1979; Williams, 1985a, 1985b) not only recognizes that distracting and confounding circumstances are aspects worthy of attention but encourages recording them on their own representative axis as part of an interactive complex. The multiaxial structure aligns many of the potentially relevant factors that can illuminate the nature of a clinical condition and provides a means of registering their distinguishing attributes. In contrast to the more traditional hierarchical model, in which a single class of attributes (signs or etiologies) is differentiated, the multiaxial format permits multiple classes of data (again, signs and etiologies) and thereby encourages diagnostic formulations that comprise several facets of information relevant to clinical decision making.

The very comprehensiveness of the multiaxial model can prove to be its undoing. Such systems provide a more thorough picture than do schemata of unitary axes, but they are, as a consequence, more complicated and demanding to implement and require a wider band of data and a greater clarity and diversity of judgments than clinicians are accustomed to performing. They often impose a procedural complexity on an otherwise expedient process. From a pragmatic view a fully comprehensive multiaxial assessment may be an unnecessary encumbrance in routine diagnostic work, impractical for everyday decision making, and abhorrent to clinicians accustomed to the diagnostic habit of intuitive synthesis.

### Circumplical Models

These models have been used in the arrangement of both taxa and attributes. In neither case have they been recognized in formal psychopathologic taxonomies but, rather, have gained their primary use as a structural tool for ordering interpersonal traits (Benjamin, 1974, 1986; Lorr, 1966), most notably in conjunction with personality processes and disorders (Kiesler, 1983; Leary, 1957; Pincus & Wiggins, 1990; Plutchik & Platman, 1977; Sim & Romney, 1990; Strack, Lorr, & Campbell, 1990).

Circumplical models are structured so as to locate similar taxa in adjoining or nearby segments of a circle; taxa located diametrically on the circle are considered psychologically antithetical. Plutchik and Conte (1985) provided evidence that emotions, traits of personality, and personality disorders line up in parallel ways on a circumplex, which suggests that this structure can arrange diverse concepts into a common framework and lead thereby to the identification of relations that may otherwise not be recognized. As interesting as this formulation may be for organizing conceptual categories, the circumplex appears at present to be essentially an academic tool of theoretic rather than clinical value, despite indications that promise the latter as well.

## TAXONIC STRUCTURE

Taxonic units in psychopathology may be monothetic or polythetic in structure. All of the attributes that constitute a monothetic taxon must be in evidence for a diagnosis to be correctly made. In polythetic taxa various and different optional subsets of the full attribute list can suffice to justify a diagnosis.

### Classical versus Prototypal Taxa

Classical taxa comprise categories made up of discrete entities that are homogeneous with respect to their defining features, that is, arranged in a restrictive, monothetic format (Cantor & Mischel, 1979; Rosch, 1978). Failures to identify all of the attributes of a taxon result from obscuring and confounding conditions or from deficits in observational technology and skill.

Frances and Widiger (1986) characterized the major features and difficulties with classical taxa as follows:

The classical model of categorization conceives of disorders as qualitative, discrete entities and assumes that the defining features are singly necessary and jointly sufficient, that the boundaries between categories are distinct, and that members are homogeneous with respect to the defining features. . . . Although the classical model works well for abstract categories (e.g., "square"), it fails to do justice to the complexity of naturally occurring taxonomic problems. All squares share the features of having four equal sides joined at right angles . . . [but] actual objects, plants, animals, and persons, however, often fail to share a set of singly necessary and jointly sufficient features. . . . If a classical typology is an inappropriate model for classification of objects, birds, and plants, it is clearly inappropriate for psychiatric diagnosis. (p. 392)

Horowitz, Post, French, Wallis, and Siegelman (1981) described the contrasting prototypal construct succinctly:

A Prototype consists of the most common features or properties of members of a category and thus describes a theoretical ideal or standard against which real people can be evaluated. All of the Prototype's properties are assumed to characterize at least some members of the category, but no one property is necessary or sufficient for membership in the category. Therefore, it is possible that no actual person would match the theoretical prototype perfectly. Instead different people would approximate it to different degrees. The more closely a person approximates the ideal, the more the person typifies the concept. (p. 575)

The Prototypal structure assumes a measure of taxonic heterogeneity and, hence, is likely to require a polythetic format. Its open and permissive taxonic structure is more consonant with the natural fuzziness of conceptual boundaries (Cantor & Genero, 1986; Osherson & Smith, 1981; Schwartz, Wiggins, & Norko, 1989; Wittgenstein, 1953), as well as the inherent inexactness of natural reality

(Meehl, 1978; Millon, 1969/1987, 1990). Referring to the classical approach, Widiger and Frances (1985a, 1985b) have written that once patients are placed in the same taxon, there is a tendency to exaggerate their similarities, ignore their differences, and focus on the stereotypic features that distinguish the category, all at the expense of bypassing disconfirming traits and downplaying idiosyncratic behaviors. By contrast, they stated that polythetically constructed taxa limit stereotyping, permit diagnostic flexibility, and encourage within-groups variability. On the other hand, no pathognomic signs will be present, persons similarly diagnosed will vary in their degree of prototypicality, and defining features will differ in their diagnostic efficiency.

## Categorical versus Dimensional Taxa

My discussion of structural alternatives has progressed from options between three taxonomic configurations (hierarchical vs. multiaxial vs. circumplical) to a selection between two taxonic structures (classical vs. prototypal). I continue this progression toward increasing specifics, addressing the choices that need to be made with concern for the compositional character of taxa and attributes. Here, the issue is raised as to whether taxa and their attributes ought to be conceived qualitatively (categorically) or quantitatively (dimensionally).

For monothetic (classical) taxa, authors have asked whether clinical syndromes (e.g., dysthymia) ought to be conceived as qualitatively discrete categories or whether they ought to be conceived on a quantitative dimension of severity (Frances, 1982). The issue among those who arrange polythetic rules (usually prototypal) is whether different combinations of defining features can be conceived as forming quantitative variations of the same qualitative category. This latter approach focuses not on taxa themselves but on their clinical attributes and defining features. For this issue each attribute is conceived as a quantifiable dimension along such lines as salience or severity. What is categorized is not the taxon, but the several variants of a clinical attribute (e.g., if interpersonal conduct is a relevant attribute for diagnosing personality disorder taxa, then choices may be made first among the several interpersonal defining feature options, such as aversive, seductive, or secretive). Second, once the interpersonal options have been chosen (qualitative categorization), each may be given a score to represent their degree of salience or severity (quantitative dimensionalization).

The first of the two approaches to the issue is related to categorical versus dimensional taxa. The issue applies especially to clinical attributes, for which the trend toward prototypal models and polythetic definitions is more central. The taxonic issue may be stated in the form of a question. Ought taxa be conceived and organized as a series of dimensions that combine to form distinctive profiles for each person, or ought certain characteristics found commonly in clinical populations be selected to exemplify and classify taxa (Livesley, 1991)?

Dimensional conceptions emphasize quantitative gradations among persons rather than qualitative, discrete, all-or-none class distinctions. To illustrate, Kendell (1968) proposed that a single dimension may suffice to represent the continuum he found between neurotic and psychotic depressions. By contrast, and consistent with the clear boundaries between taxa expected with a categorical schema, Paykel (1971) found minimal overlapping among four classes, those of psychotic, anxious, hostile, and young depressed persons.

Several advantages to dimensional models may be noted. First, they combine several clinical attributes (or their defining features) in a single configuration. This comprehensiveness results in a limited loss of information, and no single attribute is given special significance, as is the case when only one distinctive characteristic is brought to the forefront. Dimensional profiles facilitate the assignment of unusual or atypical cases. In categorical formats odd or mixed conditions are often excluded because they fail to fit the prescribed criteria. Given the idiosyncratic character of many clinical conditions, a dimensional system permits representation and assignment of interesting and unique cases without forcing them into procrustean categories for which they are ill-suited. A major advantage of the dimensional model is that the strength of its constituent features is gauged quantitatively, wherein each characteristic extends into the normal range. As a consequence, normality and abnormality are construed as points on a continuum rather than as distinct and separable phenomena.

Despite these advantages, dimensional taxa have not fared well in psychiatric classifications (Gunderson, Links, & Reich, 1991). Numerous complications have been noted in the literature; for example, there is little agreement among theorists as to the number of dimensions necessary to represent psychopathological phenomena. Menninger (1963) contended that a single dimension suffices, Eysenck (1960) asserted that three are needed, whereas Cattell (1965) claimed to have identified as many as 33 and believed there to be many more. In fact, theorists appear to invent dimensions in accord with their expectations, rather than to discover them as if they were intrinsic to nature, merely awaiting scientific detection. The number of dimensions required to assess psychopathologic phenomena appear to be determined not by the ability of research to disclose some inherent truth but rather by researchers' predilections for conceiving their investigations and interpreting the findings.

Categorical models are the traditional form used to represent clinical conditions. There are a number of reasons for this preference. First, most taxa neither imply nor are constructed to be all-or-none categories. Certain features are given prominence, yet others are not overlooked, but rather, they are merely assigned lesser significance.

The success of categorical taxa may be traced to the ease with which clinicians can use them in making rapid diagnoses with numerous briefly seen patients. Although clinical attention is drawn to only the most salient patient attributes, other less conspicuous characteristics are often observed, suggested, or inferred. The quality of intimating characteristics beyond the immediately observed contributes to the value of established categorical taxa. This power of extending its scope to associated attributes contrasts the categorical approach with the tendency of dimensional schemata to segment, if not fractionate, persons and disorders into separate components. Categories restore the unity of patient's pathology by integrating seemingly diverse elements into a single, coordinated configuration. Well-established categorical taxa often provide a standard of reference for clinicians who are otherwise faced with reconstructions or de novo diagnostic creations (Gunderson et al., 1991).

There are objections to the use of categorical taxa. For example, they contribute to the fallacious belief that psychopathological processes constitute discrete entities, even medical diseases, when in fact they are merely concepts that help focus and coordinate our observations. Moreover, categories often fail to identify or include significant aspects of behavior because of the decision to narrow their list to a set of predetermined characteristics. This discarding of information is not limited to categories; dimensional schemata also select certain attributes to the exclusion of others. The problem, however, is that certain categorical schemata give primacy only to one or two attributes. A related criticism is that both the number and diversity of categories in most taxonomies are far less than the clinically significant individual differences observed in everyday practice. Not only are there problems in assigning many patients to the limited categories available, but clinicians often claim that the more they know patients, the greater the difficulty they have in fitting them into a category.

Issues of categoricality versus dimensionality are more properly the province of attributes than of taxa. For example, the Axis I syndrome (taxon) depressive disorders really represents a clinical attribute; the distinction between its two major subcategories, major depression and dysthymia, may essentially be a matter of quantitative severity and, hence, reflect dimensionality. Furthermore, the distinction between bipolar disorders and depressive disorders may be best conceived as variations in two clinical attributes, not taxa; the former (which encompasses the latter) reflects the operation of two mood attributes, mania and depression, each of which may vary as a single dimension, although both may be found in certain persons (bipolar), whereas only one may be exhibited in others (depression). The fact that some taxa are composed essentially of a single clinical attribute, whereas others encompass several distinct attributes, has not only confounded discussions of categoricality versus dimensionality but has contributed a share of confusion to theory, research, and practice as well.

To restore aspects of the problem, Skinner (1986) elaborated several hybrid models that integrate elements of these ostensibly divergent schemas. In what Skinner termed the *class-quantitative approach,* efforts are made to synthesize quantitative dimensions and discrete categories. An endeavor of this nature was described in a couple of my articles (Millon, 1984, 1986). To integrate a mixed categorical-dimensional model for personologic taxa, it was proposed that essential to this integration was the specification of a distinctive defining feature for each clinical attribute of each personality disorder. If the clinical attribute expressive mood is deemed of diagnostic value in assessing personality disorders, then a specific defining feature will be identified to represent the distinctive manner in which each personality disorder manifests its emotional feelings. To further enrich the qualitative categories (the several defining features that compose the clinical range of each attribute) with quantitative discriminations (numerical intensity ratings), clinicians will not only identify which features (e.g., distraught, hostile, labile) of a clinical attribute (e.g., expressive mood) best characterize a patient but also record a number (e.g., 1–10) to represent the degree of prominence or pervasiveness of the chosen defining features. Clinicians will be encouraged in such a prototypal schema to record and quantify more than one defining feature per clinical attribute (e.g., if suitable, to note both distraught and labile moods, if their observations and inferences so incline them). Such a procedure as this illustrates that categorical (qualitative distinction) and dimensional (quantitative distinction) taxonic models need not be framed in opposition or no less be considered mutually exclusive.

## CONSTRUCTION METHODS

How have psychiatric taxonomies come into being? In the main, traditional classifications have been the product of a slowly evolving accretion of clinical experience (Menninger, 1963), which has been fostered and formalized periodically by the systematizing efforts of respected clinician-scholars such as Kraepelin (1899). It may be expected that empirical data or theoretical advances on matters of causality or structure will serve as a primary heuristic impetus, but such has not been the case. With but a few, brief exceptions (e.g., the short-lived DSM-I and DSM-II [American Psychiatric Association, 1952, 1968] psychoanalytic explication of neurotic disorders, which was subsequently expunged as an organizing construct in the DSM-III), theory-generated or research-grounded taxonomies have fared rather poorly. A more recent spur to developing classifications has originated in a series of quantitative methods known as *cluster analyses* (Sneath & Sokal, 1973). Time will tell whether these mathematical tools will generate taxa of sufficient conse-

quence to gain acceptance in the clinical world. Describing taxonomic advances in the biological sciences, Sokal (1974) wrote:

In classification, theory has frequently followed methodology and has been an attempt to formalize and justify the classificatory activity of workers in various sciences. In other instances, classificatory systems have been set up on a priori logical or philosophical grounds and the methodology tailored subsequently to fit the principles. Both approaches have their advantages and drawbacks; modern work tends to reflect an interactive phase in which first one and then the other approach is used, but in which neither principles nor methodology necessarily dominate. (p. 115)

Taxonomic methods in psychopathology are much less advanced than those in the biological sciences, but they are approaching the threshold at which some of the same controversies that occurred in their biological forerunners are likely to arise. Although each of the alternative construction methods to be discussed shortly may prove fruitful, psychiatric taxonomists are already engaged in debates as to which is best. It is important to recognize that there is no correct choice, and no rules can be found in nature to confirm which are best or likely to be profitable. To make sense and give order to the taxonomies they use, clinicians must know what approach to construction was followed and what attributes constituted their data base. With the techniques and building blocks of these methods clearly in mind, clinicians may assess them intelligently and judge their relevance to the questions they pose.

A few words must be said about the similarities between methods of taxonomic formation and procedures for developing psychometric tools. Skinner (1981, 1986) has drawn on the logic outlined by Loevinger (1957) for sequentially validating diagnostic tests and applies it creatively to the composition of taxonomies. The mutually reinforcing strength achieved by a combination of Loevinger's three validation strategies may be kept in mind as I elaborate each of the three construction options. In Loevinger's seminal article, she recommended progress from the theoretical to the statistical (internal) to the clinical (external), a sequence especially suitable to the validation of diagnostic tests, and one which both Jackson (1971) and Millon (1977) followed in fashioning their psychometric inventories. I will reverse this sequence to accord with the historical order in which taxonomies have and are likely to continue to be composed.

## CLINICALLY BASED DISORDERS

Until recently psychiatric taxonomies were formed solely on the basis of clinical observation, the witnessing of repetitive patterns of behavior and emotion among a small number of carefully studied mental patients. Hypotheses were generated to give meaning to these patterns of covariance (e.g., Hippocrates anchored differences in observed temperament to his humoral theory, and Kraepelin distinguished two major categories of severe pathology, dementia praecox and manic-depressive disease, in terms of their ostensive divergent prognostic course). The elements of these theoretic notions were post hoc, however, imposed after the fact, rather than serving as a generative source for taxonomic categories. The most recent example of a clinical taxonomy, tied explicitly to phenomenal observation and constructed to be both atheoretical and nonquantitative is, of course, the DSM. Spitzer, chairperson of the DSM-III Task Force, stated in the DSM-III (American Psychiatric Association, 1980) that "clinicians can agree on the identification of mental disorders on the basis of their clinical manifestations without agreeing on how the disturbances came about" (p. 7).

Despite assertions to the contrary, recent DSMs are a product of implicit causal or etiologic speculation. Nevertheless, the Task Force sought to eschew theoretic or pathogenic notions, adhering to as strict an empiricist philosophy as possible. Only those attributes that can be readily observed or consensually validated were to be permitted as diagnostic criteria. Numerous derelictions from this epistemology were notable, however, especially among the Personality disorders, whose trait ascriptions call for inferences beyond direct sensory inspection.

By no means do all who draw their philosophical inspiration from an empiricist mind-set restrict themselves to the mere specification of surface similarities (Medin et al., 1982). It is not only those who formulate theoretically generated nosologies who succumb to the explanatory power and heuristic value of pathogenic, dynamic, and structural inferences. Feinstein (1977), a distinguished internist, provided an intriguing illustration of how one man's factual observations may be another's inference.

In choosing an anchor or focus for taxonomy, we can engage in two distinctly different types of nosologic reasoning. The first is to form names, designations, or denominations for the observed evidence and to confine ourselves exclusively to what has actually been observed. The second is to draw inferences from the observed evidence, arriving at inferential titles representing entities that have not actually been observed. For example, if a patient says, "I have substantial chest pain, provoked by exertion, and relieved by rest," I, as an internist, perform a denomination if I designate this observed entity as angina pectoris. If I call it coronary artery disease, however, I perform an inference, since I have not actually observed coronary artery disease. If a radiologist looking at a coronary arteriogram or a pathologist cutting open the coronary vasculature uses the diagnosis coronary artery disease, the decision is a denomination. If the radiologist or pathologist decides that the coronary disease was caused by cigarette smoking or by a high fat diet, the etiologic diagnosis is an inference unless simultaneous evidence exists that the patient did indeed smoke or use a high fat diet. (p. 192)

In great part, clinically based taxa gain their import and prominence by virtue of consensus and authority. Cumulative experience and tradition are crystallized and subsequently confirmed by official bodies. Specified criteria are denoted and articulated, and they acquire definitional, if not stipulative powers, at least among those who come to accept the attributes selected as infallible taxonic indicators.

## NUMERICALLY DERIVED CLUSTERS

Clinically based categories stem from the observations and inferences of diagnosticians; as such, they comprise, in circular fashion, the very qualities that clinicians are likely to see and deduce. Categories constructed in this manner will not only direct future clinicians to mirror these same taxa in their patients but may lead future nosologists away from potentially more useful schemes with which to fathom less obvious patterns of attribute covariation. Toward the end of penetrating beneath the sensory domain to more latent commonalities, taxonomists have been led to turn either to numerical methods or to theoretical principles.

Andreasen and Grove (1982) enumerated the advantages of what they termed *empirical* and *numerical* methods for computing patient similarities:

First, the empirical method gives an opportunity for the observed characteristics of the subjects to determine the classification and perhaps to lead to a classification that the clinician was unable to perceive using clinical judgment alone. Second, the empirical method allows a great deal of information on the subjects to enter into the genesis of the classifications; human beings can keep in mind only a relatively small number of details concerning a case at any given time, but the empirical approach can process very large sets of measurements. Third, empirical or numerical approaches can combine cases in more subtle ways than can clinicians; combinations of features too complex to grasp intuitively may yield better classifications than simple combinations. (p. 45)

There has been a rapid proliferation of powerful mathematical techniques both for analyzing and synthesizing vast bodies of clinical data. This expansion has been accelerated by the availability of inexpensive computer hardware and software programs. Unfortunately, this mushrooming has progressed more rapidly than its fruits can be digested. As Kendell (1975) said, early in this development, "most clinicians . . . have tended to oscillate uneasily between two equally unsatisfactory postures of ignoring investigations based on these techniques, or accepting their confident conclusions at face value" (p. 106).

This growing and diverse body of quantitative methods can be put to many uses, of which only a small number are relevant to the goal of taxonomic construction. Some statistical techniques relate to the validation of existent nosologies (e.g., discriminant analyses) rather than to their creation. Among those used for taxonomic development, some focus on clinical attributes as their basic units, whereas patients themselves are the point of attention for others (Grove & Tellegen, 1991). For example, factor analysis condenses initially diverse sets of clinical attributes and organizes them into potential syndromic taxa. Cluster analysis, by contrast, is most suitable for sorting patient similarities into personologic taxa. Reviews of these two numerical techniques, as well as other mathematical procedures for taxonomic construction and evaluation, such as latent class, log-linear, discriminant analysis, and multivariate analysis of variance, may be examined in a number of useful publications (Blashfield, 1984; Grove & Andreasen, 1986; Hartigan, 1975; Kendell, 1975).

Although cluster algorithms have begun to mirror broad diagnostic classes, these slender advances do not answer the question of whether cluster analysis produces categories that resemble the natural structure of psychopathology any better than those of our more traditional or clinically based nosologies, nor is there any evidence that they provide more accurate predictions of such nonstructural concerns as prognosis and treatment response.

Several authors have summarized the current state of affairs as well as have addressed the problems that are likely to persist in the use of numerical construction procedures.

Clinicians have at best given only a lukewarm reception to such classifications. They have been skeptical about the value of clustering methods to identify "naturally" occurring subgroups. Furthermore, the classifications generated by these methods have not seemed particularly meaningful or relevant to everyday clinical practice. (Skinner & Blashfield, 1982, p. 727)

Kendell's (1975) comment of more than a decade ago, on reviewing the preceding 20-year period, is, rather sadly, no less apt today than it was then.

Looking back on the various studies published in the last twenty years it is clear that many investigators, clinicians and statisticians, have had a naive, almost Baconian, attitude to the statistical techniques they were employing, putting in all the data at their disposal on the assumption that the computer would sort out the relevant from the irrelevant and expose the underlying principles and regularities, and assuming all that was required of them was to collect the data assiduously beforehand. (p. 118)

## THEORETICALLY DEDUCED CONSTRUCTS

In the early stages of knowledge, the categories of a classification rely invariably on observed similarities among phenomena (Tversky, 1977). As knowledge advances, overt similarities are discovered to be an insufficient, if not false basis for cohering categories and imbuing them with scientific meaning (Smith & Medin, 1981). As Hempel (1965) and Quine (1977) have pointed out, it is theory that provides the glue that holds a classification together and gives it both its scientific and its clinical

relevance. In Hempel's (1965) discussion of classificatory concepts, he wrote that:

the development of a scientific discipline may often be said to proceed from an initial "natural history" stage . . . to subsequent more and more "theoretical" stages. . . . The vocabulary required in the early stages of this development will be largely observational. . . . The shift toward theoretical systematization is marked by the introduction of new, "theoretical" terms . . . more or less removed from the level of directly observable things and events.

These terms have a distinct meaning and function only in the context of a corresponding theory. (pp. 139–140)

As Hempel (1965) stated, mature sciences progress from an observationally based stage to one that is characterized by abstract concepts and theoretical systemizations. It is the judgment of contemporary philosophers of science that classification alone does not make a scientific taxonomy and that similarity among attributes does not necessarily constitute a scientific category (Smith & Medin, 1981). The characteristic that distinguishes a latent scientific classification is its success in grouping its elements according to theoretically consonant explanatory propositions. These propositions are formed when certain attributes that have been categorized have been shown or have been hypothesized to be logically or causally related to other attributes or categories. The latent taxa that undergird a scientific nosology are not, therefore, mere collections of overtly similar attributes or categories but a linked or unified pattern of known or presumed relations among them. This theoretically grounded pattern of relations provides the foundation of a scientific taxonomy.

Several benefits derive from systematizing clinical data in a theoretical fashion that are not readily available either from clinical or numerical procedures (Wright & Murphy, 1984). Given the countless ways of observing and analyzing a set of data, a system of explanatory propositions becomes a useful guide to clinicians as they seek to comprehend the stream of amorphous signs and chaotic symptoms they normally encounter. Rather than shift from one aspect of behavior, thought, or emotion to another, according to momentary impressions of importance, theoretically guided clinicians may be led to pursue in a logical and perhaps more penetrating manner only those aspects that are likely to be related (Dougherty, 1978). In addition to furnishing this guidance, a theoretically anchored taxonomy may enable diagnosticians to generate insights into clinical relations they may not have grasped before. Furthermore, it ought to enlarge the sensitivity and scope of knowledge of observers by alerting them to previously unseen relations among attributes and then to guide these new observations into a coherent body of knowledge.

Taxonomic theories need be neither fully comprehensive nor extensively supported to inspire and guide the early phases of taxonomic development. Meehl (1972) addressed these points with relevance to his concept of the schizoid taxon.

I would not require that a genuinely integrated theory explain everything about schizophrenia, a preposterous demand, which we do not customarily make of any theory in the biological or social sciences. At this stage of our knowledge, it is probably bad strategy to spend time theorizing about small effects, low correlations, minor discrepancies between studies and the like.

Being a neo-Popperian in the philosophy of science, I am myself quite comfortable engaging in speculative formulations completely unsubstantiated by data. To "justify" concocting a theory, all one needs is a problem, plus a notion (I use a weak word advisedly) of how one might test one's theory (subject it to the danger of refutation). (p. 11)

The reader may be taken aback by Meehl's seemingly tolerant views and conclude that theory can lead to scientific irresponsibility, one that justifies the taking of a rigorous atheoretical stance. As I imply previously, however, the belief that one can take positions that are free of theoretical bias is naive,

if not nonsensical (Heelan, 1977; Hempel, 1965; Kukla, 1989; Leahey, 1980; Weimer, 1979). Those who claim to have eschewed theory are likely to have (unknowingly) subscribed to a position that gives primacy to such experience-near data as overt behaviors and biological signs, as opposed to experience-distant data that require a greater measure of inference. The positivist (empiricist) position may once have held sway in philosophy, as it still does in some psychiatric and psychological quarters (Schwartz & Wiggins, 1986), but it is difficult, as Meehl (1978) noted, "to name a single logician or a philosopher (or historian) of science who today defends strict operationism in the sense that some psychologists claim to believe in it" (p. 815).

What distinguishes a true theoretically based taxonomy from one that merely provides an explanatory summary of known observations and inferences?

Essentially, the answer lies in its power to generate new attributes, relations, or taxa, that is, ones other than those used to construct it. This generative power is what Hempel (1961) termed the "systematic import" (p. 6) of a scientific classification. In contrasting what are familiarly known as *natural* (theoretically guided and based in deduction) and *artificial* (conceptually barren and based in similarity) classifications, Hempel (1965) wrote:

Distinctions between "natural" and "artificial" classifications may well be explicated as referring to the difference between classifications that are scientifically fruitful and those that are not; in a classification of the former kind, those characteristics of the elements which serve as criteria of membership in a given class are associated, universally or with high probability, with more or less extensive clusters of other characteristics.

Classification of this sort should be viewed as somehow having objective existence in nature, as "carving nature at the joints" in contradistinction of "artificial" classification, in which the defining characteristics have few explanatory or predictive connection with other traits.

In the course of scientific development, classifications defined by reference to manifest, observable characteristics will tend to give way to systems based on theoretical concepts. (pp. 146–148 )

# STANDARDS

Feinstein (1977) commented that classification systems "can be a product of sheer speculation or arbitrary caprice" (p. 196). Hence, once a taxonomy has been constructed, be it comprehensive or circumscribed, it behooves clinicians and scientists to examine it as a unit, that is, to evaluate its constituent taxa as well as the specific attributes and defining features that constitute each taxon. To ensure a minimum of "sheer speculation and . . . caprice," taxonomic developers must keep in mind several principles or standards that may optimize both the validity and utility of their creations. Such guidelines may prove especially useful in the formulation and construction phases of a taxonomy and serve to orient developers in ways that may enhance their system's ultimate efficacy.

I now note a few of the principles or standards that may guide both the construction and evaluation of taxonomic taxa and attributes. More extensive discussion of these and other standards may be found in Sneath and Sokal (1973) and in Millon (1987). For pedagogic purposes I make a distinction between standards most applicable to the diagnostic attributes that constitute taxa and those more relevant to the structure of the taxonomy.

## OPTIMAL ATTRIBUTE STANDARDS

What are some of the properties of clinical attributes that enable them to serve as a secure base for diagnostic criteria? A few are worth noting.

### Feature Comparability

One method of refining diagnostic comparisons is to spell out a series of defining features for every relevant clinical attribute associated with a set of parallel diagnostic taxa. For example, as I note earlier, if the clinical attribute interpersonal conduct is deemed of diagnostic value in identifying and differentiating personality disorder taxa, then a distinctive description must be written to represent the characteristic or singular manner in which persons with each personality disorder conducts their interpersonal life. A format of this nature furnishes symmetry among the taxa that constitute a taxonomy and enables investigators to systematically compare each taxon's diagnostic validity (e.g., sensitivity and specificity) as well as the relative diagnostic efficiency (e.g., positive and negative predictive power) for each relevant attribute (e.g., their interpersonal conduct).

### Empirical Reference

As I mention previously, attributes that depend on higher order inferences contribute to diagnostic unreliability. When feasible, the features that comprise diagnostic criteria ought to be assigned properties in the observable world. Problems arise when one seeks to represent intrinsically unobservable processes (e.g., defense mechanisms) or when one attempts to balance the desire for generality or openness among attributes with the standard of empirical precision. Can attributes be empirically anchored, and thereby the ambiguity in language be minimized, while the attributes are simultaneously freed to encompass wide-ranging phenomena, including those that reflect interior processes?

### Quantitative Range

Clinical features usually express themselves as a matter of degree rather than simple presence or absence (e.g., severity of depression and level of anxiety). It is useful, therefore, if the clinical attributes that comprise taxa permit the registration of a wide range of intensity or frequency differences. This psychometric property of quantitative gradation is one of the notable strengths of psychological tests, but it is not limited to them.

## Optimal Structural Standards

Unless a taxonomy is easy to understand and use, it is quite unlikely to gain adherents in the clinical world, no matter how well formulated and scientifically sound it may otherwise be.

### Clinical Relevance

Some historic taxonomies were shrouded in a cloak of words and dense concepts. The structure of others was so opaque that assumptions were concealed, principles difficult to extract, and consistent connections to the clinical world impossible to establish. In short, the structure and language of the taxonomy and its taxa were formulated more complexly and obscurely than necessary.

Relevance and simplicity suggest that a taxonomy depend on a minimum number of assumptions, concepts, and categories. Alone, these standards neither eliminate taxonomic opaqueness nor validate the clinical utility of a taxonomy's derivations. They merely suggest that excess and misguided baggage be eliminated so that the features of clinical relevance in the system be seen more clearly.

### Representative Scope

If a taxonomy is too narrow in its range of applicability, failing to encompass disorders for which clinicians have diagnostic responsibility, then its level of utility and acceptance will be markedly diminished. Ideally, the number of taxa and attributes that a taxonomy subsumes ought not to be limited. However, it is wise to recognize that a disparity will exist between the potential range of a taxonomy's applicability and its actual range of empirical support.

### Concurrent Robustness

A question arises as to whether taxonic groupings retain their membership composition under new conditions and with attributes other than those used to construct them initially. For example, monothetic (homogeneous) taxa based on a single source of data (e.g., test scores), on one type of attribute (e.g., interpersonal conduct), or on one class of patients (e.g., inpatients) may fail to cross-generalize, that is, to remain stable, distinct, and uniform when based on parallel, yet unidentical sources of data (e.g., structured interviews), attributes (e.g., cognitive style), or populations (e.g., outpatients).

## CLOSING COMMENTS

Although this article is long, it is but a brief sketch of a burgeoning field. Perhaps this introduction will tempt the reader, who has tested its waters ever so lightly, to plunge more deeply into the subject. At present, there are no unequivocal answers to the many questions posed in psychopathologic taxonomy, be they the matters of selecting attributes, choosing structures, or opting for one construction method or another.

In my critical remarks I have not meant to imply that the philosophies and techniques of classification today are irrelevant or that the theoretical or diagnostic underpinnings of contemporary practice are valueless. Rather, I wish to encourage current taxonomic conceptualizers to step back and reflect more deeply on established assumptions and formulations. On the one hand, taxonomies in psychopathology must not reduce the richness of the natural clinical world into a playing field for competing and abstruse speculations, nor must it become a passive receptacle shaped by the dehumanized and arcane methods of mathematical analysis. Protected from convention, vogue, presumption, or cabalism, taxonomic psychopathology will become neither dogmatic, trivial, or formalistic nor devoid of a substantive life of its own. Prevailing frameworks must continue to be challenged, and imaginative alternatives encouraged.

# REFERENCES

American Psychiatric Association. (1952). *Diagnostic and statistical manual of mental disorders* (1st ed.). Washington, DC: Author.

American Psychiatric Association. (1968). *Diagnostic and statistical manual of mental disorders* (2nd ed.). Washington, DC: Author.

American Psychiatric Association. (1980). *Diagnostic and statistical manual of mental disorders* (3rd ed.). Washington, DC: Author.

American Psychiatric Association. (1987). *Diagnostic and statistical manual of mental disorders* (Rev. 3rd ed.). Washington, DC: Author.

Andreasen, N., & Grove, W. (1982). The classification of depression: A comparison of traditional and mathematically derived approaches. *American Journal of Psychiatry, 139*, 45–52.

Bandura, A. (1982). The psychology of chance encounters and life paths. *American Psychologist, 37*, 747–755.

Benjamin, L. S. (1974). Structural analysis of social behavior. *Psychological Review, 81*, 392–425.

Benjamin, L. S. (1986). Adding social and intrapsychic descriptors to Axis I of DSM-III. In T. Millon & G. L. Klerman (Eds.), *Contemporary directions in psychopathology. Towards the DSM-IV* (pp. 599–637). New York: Guilford Press.

Blashfield, R. K. (1984). *The classification of psychopathology.* New York: Plenum Press.

Block, J. (1989). Critique of the act frequency approach to personality. *Journal of Personality and Social Psychology, 56*, 234–245.

Bridgman, P. W. (1927). *The logic of modern physics.* New York: Macmillan.

Buss, D. M., & Craik, K. H. (1983). The act frequency approach to personality. *Psychological Review, 90*, 105–126.

Buss, D. M., & Craik, K. H. (1987). Act criteria for the diagnosis of personality disorders. *Journal of Personality Disorders, 1*, 73–81.

Cantor, N., & Genero, N. (1986). Psychiatric diagnosis and natural categorization: A close analogy. In T. Millon & G. L. Klerman (Eds.), *Contemporary directions in psychopathology. Towards the DSM-IV* (pp. 233–256). New York: Guilford Press.

Cantor, N., & Mischel, W. (1979). Prototypes in person perception. In L. Berkowitz (Ed.), *Advances in experimental social psychology* (Vol. 12). New York: Academic Press.

Cattell, R. B. (1965). *The scientific analysis of personality.* Chicago: Aldine.

Dougherty, J. W. D. (1978). Salience and relatively in classification. *American Ethnologist, 5*, 66–80.

Essen-Moller, E., & Wohlfahrt, S. (1947). Suggestions for the amendment of the official Swedish classification of mental disorders. *Acta Psychiatrica Scandinavica, 47(Suppl.),* 551–555.

Eysenck, H. J. (1960). *The structure of human personality.* London: Routledge & Kegan Paul.

Feinstein, A. R. (1977). A critical overview of diagnosis in psychiatry. In V. M. Rakoff, H. C. Stancer, & H. B. Kedward (Eds.), *Psychiatric diagnosis* (pp. 189–206). New York: Brunner/Mazel.

Frances, A. (1982). Categorical and dimensional systems of personality diagnosis: A comparison. *Comprehensive Psychiatry, 23*, 516–527.

Frances, A., & Widiger, T. A. (1986). Methodological issues in personality disorder diagnosis. In T. Millon & G. L. Klerman (Eds.), *Contemporary directions in psychopathology. Towards the DSM-IV* (pp. 381–400). New York: Guilford Press.

Grove, W. M., & Andreasen, N. C. (1986). Multivariate statistical analysis in psychopathology. In T. Millon & G. L. Klerman (Eds.), *Contemporary directions in psychopathology. Towards the DSM-IV* (pp. 347–362). New York: Guilford Press.

Grove, W. M., & Tellegen, A. (1991). Problems in the classification of personality disorders. *Journal of Personality Disorders, 5*, 31–41.

Gunderson, J. G., Links, P. S., & Reich, J. H. (1991). Competing models of personality disorders. *Journal of Personality Disorders, 5*, 60–68.

Hartigan, J. A. (1975). *Clustering algorithms.* New York: Wiley.

Heelan, P. A. (1977). The nature of clinical science. *Journal of Medicine and Philosophy, 2*, 20–32.

Hempel, C. G. (1961). Introduction to problems of taxonomy. In J. Zubin (Ed.), *Field studies in the mental disorders* (pp. 3–22). New York: Grune & Stratton.

Hempel, C. G. (1965). *Aspects of scientific explanation.* New York: Free Press.

Horowitz, L. M., Post, D. L., French, R. de S., Wallis, K. D., & Siegelman, E. Y. (1981). The prototype as a construct in abnormal psychology: 2. Clarifying disagreement in psychiatric judgments. *Journal of Abnormal Psychology, 90,* 575–585.

Jackson, D. W. (1971). The dynamics of structured personality tests. *Psychological Review, 78,* 229–248.

Kaplan, A. (1964). *The conduct of inquiry.* San Francisco: Chandler.

Kendell, R. E. (1968). *The classification of depressive illness.* London: Oxford University Press.

Kendell, R. E. (1975). *The role of diagnosis in psychiatry.* Oxford, United Kingdom: Blackwell.

Kiesler, D. J. (1983). The 1982 Interpersonal Circle: A taxonomy for complementarity in human transactions. *Psychological Review, 90,* 185–214.

Kraepelin, E. (1899). *Psychiatric: Ein lerhrbuch* (6th ed.). Leipzig: Barth.

Kukla, A. (1989). Nonempirical issues in psychology. *American Psychologist, 44,* 785–794.

Leahey, T. (1980). The myth of operationism. *Journal of Mind and Behavior, 1,* 127–143.

Leary, T. (1957). *Interpersonal diagnosis and personality.* New York: Ronald Press.

Livesley, W. J. (1985). The classification of personality disorder: 1. The choice of category concept. *Canadian Journal of Psychiatry, 30,* 353–358.

Livesley, W. J. (1991). Classifying personality disorders: Ideal types, prototypes or dimensions. *Journal of Personality Disorders, 5,* 55–59.

Loevinger, J. (1957). Objective tests as measurements of psychological theory. *Psychological Reports, 3,* 635–694.

Lorr, M. (1966). *Explorations in typing and psychotics.* New York: Pergamon Press.

Medin, D. L., Altom, M. W., Edelson, S. M., & Freko, D. (1982). Correlated symptoms and simulated medical classification. *Journal of Experimental Psychology: Learning, Memory, and Cognition, 8,* 37–50.

Meehl, P. E. (1972). Specific genetic etiology, psychodynamics, and therapeutic nihilism. *International Journal of Mental Health, 1,* 1027.

Meehl, P. E. (1978). Theoretical risks and tabular asterisks: Sir Karl, Sir Ronald, and the slow progress of soft psychology. *Journal of Consulting and Clinical Psychology, 46,* 806–834.

Menninger, K. (1963). *The vital balance.* New York: Viking.

Mezzich, J. E. (1979). Patterns and issues in the multiaxial psychiatric diagnosis. *Psychological Medicine, 9,* 125–137.

Millon, T. (1977). *Millon Clinical Multiaxial Inventory manual.* Minneapolis, MN: National Computer Systems.

Millon, T. (1981). *Disorders of personality. DSM-III, Axis II.* New York: Wiley.

Millon, T. (1983). The DSM-III. An insider's perspective. *American Psychologist, 38,* 804–814.

Millon, T. (1984). On the renaissance of personality assessment and personality theory. *Journal of Personality Assessment, 48,* 450–466.

Millon, T. (1986). Personality prototypes and their diagnostic criteria. In T. Millon & G. L. Klerman (Eds.), *Contemporary directions in psychopathology: Towards the DSM-IV* (pp. 671–712). New York: Guilford Press.

Millon, T. (1987). *Modern psychopathology: A biosocial approach to maladaptive learning and functioning.* Prospect Heights, IL: Waveland Press. (Original work published 1969, Philadelphia: Saunders.)

Millon, T. (1987). On the nature of taxonomy in psychopathology. In C. G. Last & M. Hersen (Eds), *Issues in diagnostic research* (pp. 3–85). New York: Plenum Press.

Millon, T. (1990). *Toward a new personology. An evolutionary model.* New York: Wiley Interscience.

Osherson, D. N., & Smith, E. E. (1981). On the adequacy of prototype theory as a theory of concepts. *Cognition, 9,* 35–58.

Panzetta, A. E. (1974). Towards a scientific psychiatric nosology: Conceptual and pragmatic issues. *Archives of General Psychiatry, 30,* 154–161.

Pap, A. (1953). Reduction-sentences and open concepts. *Methods, 5,* 3–30.

Paykel, E. S. (1971). Classification of depressed patients: A cluster analysis derived grouping. *British Journal of Psychiatry, 118,* 275–288.

Pincus, A. L., & Wiggins, J. S. (1990). Interpersonal problems and conceptions of personality disorders. *Journal of Personality Disorders, 4,* 342–352.

Plutchik, R., & Conte, H. R. (1985). Quantitative assessment of personality disorders. In J. O. Cavenar (Ed.), *Psychiatry* (Vol. 1). Philadelphia: Lippincott.

Plutchik, R., & Platman, S. R. (1977). Personality connotations of psychiatric diagnoses: Implications for a similarity model. *Journal of Nervous and Mental Diseases, 165,* 418–422.

Quine, W. V. O. (1977). Natural kinds. In S. P. Schwartz (Ed.), *Naming, necessity and natural groups.* Ithaca, NY. Cornell University Press.

Rosch, E. (1978). Principles of categorization. In E. Rosch & D. B. Lloyds (Eds.), *Cognition and categorization.* Hillsdale, NJ: Erlbaum.

Sartorius, N. (1990). Sources and traditions of psychiatric classification: Introduction. In N. Sartorius, A. Jablensky, D. A. Regier, J. D. Burke, Jr., & R. M. A. Hirschfeld (Eds.), *Sources and traditions of classification in psychiatry* (pp. 1–6). Bern, Switzerland: Hogrefe & Huber.

Schwartz, M. A. (1991). The nature and classification of the personality disorders: A reexamination of basic premises. *Journal of Personality Disorders, 5,* 25–30.

Schwartz, M. A., & Wiggins, O. P. (1986). Logical empiricism and psychiatric classification. *Comprehensive Psychiatry, 27,* 101–114.

Schwartz, M. A., Wiggins, O. P., & Norko, M. A. (1989). Prototypes, ideal types, and personality disorders: The return of classical psychiatry. *Journal of Personality Disorders, 3,* 1–9.

Sim, J. P., & Romney, D. M. (1990). The relationship between a circumplex model of interpersonal behaviors and personality disorders. *Journal of Personality Disorders, 4,* 329–341.

Simpson, G. G. (1961). *Principles of animal taxonomy.* New York: Columbia University Press.

Skinner, H. A. (1981). Toward the integration of classification theory and methods. *Journal of Abnormal Psychology, 90,* 68–87.

Skinner, H. (1986). Construct validation approach to psychiatric classification. In T. Millon & G. L. Klerman (Eds.), *Contemporary directions in psychopathology: Towards the DSM-IV* (pp. 307–329). New York: Guilford Press.

Skinner, H., & Blashfield, R. (1982). Increasing the impact of cluster analysis research: The case of psychiatric classification. *Journal of Consulting and Clinical Psychology, 50,* 727–735.

Smith, E. E., & Medin, D. L. (1981). *Categories and concepts.* Cambridge, MA: Harvard University Press.

Sneath, P. H. A., & Sokal, R. R. (1973). *Numerical taxonomy.* San Francisco: Freeman.

Sokal, R. R. (1974). Classification: Purposes, principles, progress, prospects. *Science, 185,* 1115–1123.

Sokal, R. R., & Sneath, P. H. A. (1963). *Principles of numerical taxonomy.* San Francisco: Freeman.

Spitzer, M. (1990). Why philosophy? In M. Spitzer & B. A. Maher (Eds.), *Philosophy and psychopathology.* New York: Springer-Verlag.

Strack, S., Lorr, M., & Campbell, L. (1990). An evaluation of Millon's circular model of personality disorders. *Journal of Personality Disorders, 4,* 353–362.

Strauss, J. S. (1986). Psychiatric diagnoses: A reconsideration based on longitudinal processes. In T. Millon & G. L. Klerman (Eds.), *Contemporary directions in psychopathology: Towards the DSM-IV* (pp. 257–264). New York: Guilford Press.

Tversky, A. (1977). Features of similarity. *Psychological Review, 84,* 327–352.

Weimer, W. (1979). *Notes on the methodology of scientific research.* Hillsdale, NJ: Erlbaum.

Widiger, T. A., & Frances, A. (1985a). Axis II personality disorders: Diagnostic and treatment issues. *Hospital and Community Psychiatry, 36,* 619–627.

Widiger, T. A., & Frances, A. (1985b). The DSM-III personality disorders: Perspectives from psychology. *Archives of General Psychiatry, 42,* 615–623.

Williams, J. B. W. (1985a). The multiaxial system of DSM-III. Where did it come from and where should it go?: Its origins and critiques. *Archives of General Psychiatry, 42,* 175–180.

Williams, J. B. W. (1985b). The multiaxial system of DSM-III. Where did it come from and where should it go? II. Empirical studies, innovations, and recommendations. *Archives of General Psychiatry, 42,* 181–186.

Wittgenstein, L. (1953). *Philosophical investigations.* Oxford, United Kingdom: Blackwell.

World Health Organization. (1990). *International classification of diseases and related health problems* (10th ed.). Geneva: Author.

Wright, J. C., & Murphy, G. L. (1984). The utility of theories in intuitive statistics: The robustness of theory-based judgments. *Journal of Experimental Psychology: General, 113,* 301–322.

Zubin, J. (1968). Biometric assessment of mental patients. In M. M. Katz, J. O. Cole, & W. E. Barton (Eds.), *Classification of psychiatry and psychopathology* (pp. 353–376). Washington, DC: Public Health Service Publications.

# The DSM-III: Some Historical and Substantive Reflections

This paper must be introduced with an admission of responsibility: I participated as a member of the American Psychiatric Association Committee charged with the task of revising the official classification system, the DSM-III (APA, 1980). As a reflection of my role on the Task Force, this paper cannot help but be biased, although, as a consequence, it does provide an "insider's" glimpse of the group whose "product" guides the present "state of the field."

The wide range of themes and topics the Task Force encompassed in its deliberations makes it difficult not only to be comprehensive in coverage but also to furnish a coherently organized or highly focused presentation. Foregoing such goals, I will instead concentrate on those features I judge as representing the DSM-III's most signal conceptual and substantive advances. Worthy of record also are clarifications of public controversies that arose during the committee's tenure, as well as several myths that were widely promulgated concerning the operation, no less the motivation, of the Task Force. Shortcomings in the DSM-III, of which many are noteworthy, will be recorded, as will suggestions for nosological alternatives and refinements.

## ORIGINS AND GOALS OF THE DSM-III

### THE TASK FORCE

Implicit in the charge to the Task Force on Nomenclature and Statistics was the expectancy that it would revamp the DSM in a manner consonant with current empirical knowledge, theory, and practice. Also implicit was the assumption that the product would be viewed by allied mental health professions as having been cognizant of their diverse interests and orientations.

To meet this mandate, Robert Spitzer, M.D., was selected to serve as Task Force chairman in May 1974. He asked five psychiatrists, two psychologists, and one psychometrician to join him that September to serve as the core group of appointees. In addition to Spitzer, the initial assemblage consisted of Nancy Andreasen, M.D., Ph.D., Jean Endicott, Ph.D., Donald F. Klein, M.D., Morton Kramer, Sc.D., Theodore Millon, Ph.D., Henry Pinsker, M.D., George Saslow, M.D., Ph.D., and Robert Woodruff, M.D. Most were well-recognized contributors to the research and theoretical literature; as a committee, they formed an unusual alliance, possessing a significant array of professional interests combined with a substantial diversity in theoretical orientations. New members were added in later years to further broaden the Task Force's perspectives and expertise, but the original nucleus worked intensely and productively as a single, unified committee for over a year, meeting frequently, debating issues vigorously, and establishing a firm foundation and structural framework for both the form and the function of the DSM-III. Important modifications continued to evolve, of course, but the basic conceptual schema and its distinctive innovative features were set well in place by the end of the first full year of deliberation, for example, the use of operational criteria, the multiaxial format that separated clinical (Axis I) from personality (Axis II) disorders, the systematic and comprehensive description of disorders, and the plan to implement extensive and formal field trials.

Having laid the groundwork for the structure and having selected the features that would set the DSM-III apart from earlier nomenclature systems, the Task Force took its major role to be that of a steering committee to guide and evaluate the ongoing work of the 14 substantive advisory committees it appointed. Although it is often valid to apply that well-worn chestnut "A camel is a horse designed by a committee," the final product of the Task Force is a much more coherent package than would be expected given the awesome number and heterogeneity of its decision-making committees.

Unquestionably, the DSM-III lacks the tight-knit integration that only a single synthesis could have brought to it. Despite the diversity of its advisers, the DSM-III retained the deeply etched template stamped onto it by the small, original Task Force group, each member of which continued in his or her role as project overseer and advisory committee participant.

What proved especially gratifying, as well as fruitful in achieving a strongly shared consensus, was the open and equalitarian spirit that prevailed in the Task Force's early deliberations. Not that there was a paucity of vigorous disagreement or that impassioned polemics were invariably resolved, but these divergences and spirited controversies did not result in group discord, traditional academic schisms, or professional power struggles; for example, the psychologists on the Task force not only had full voting rights—when votes were necessary—but also provided perhaps more than their share of ideas, disputations, and formal text drafts.

In addition to the framework they constructed to give shape and structure to the DSM-III, Task Force members shared a number of implicit values, as well as explicit goals, that guided their review of the text and criteria drafts submitted by the advisory committees. They recognized that no ideal classification was possible in clinical psychopathology—that all nosological systems would be imperfect and, regardless of what advances were made in knowledge and theory, that the substantive and professional character of mental health would be simply too multidimensional in structure and too multivariate in function ever to lend itself to a single, fully satisfactory system. It was acknowledged also that a consensus was never likely to be found among either psychiatrists or psychologists as to how a classification might be best organized (e.g., dimensions, categories, observables), no less what it should contain (e.g., etiology, prognosis, structure, severity).

In light of the foregoing, the Task Force agreed to take an explicitly nondoctrinaire approach, evident not only by avoiding the introduction of particular theoretical biases concerning the nature and etiology of mental disorders but also by actively expunging them wherever they were found in the DSM-II, actions which evoked the ire of several deeply mortified professional organizations. The Task Force was equally committed to the goal of syndromic inclusiveness. The intent here was to embrace as many conditions as are commonly seen by practicing clinicians, thereby maximizing the opportunity of future investigators to evaluate the character of each condition as a valid syndromic entity. Choosing the inclusive, rather than the exclusive, route was a position that stirred considerable dismay in a variety of quarters but for highly divergent reasons. The initial requirement for a potentially new category was that its diagnostic criteria be outlined with specificity and relative distinctness from other syndromes. The ultimate inclusion test was whether the condition had been utilized with reasonable frequency, as well as whether it drew positive comments concerning its clarity from a significant number of clinicians participating in the field trials.

In addition to the principles enunciated above, the Task Force was guided by the following considerations in its DSM-III plans: Expand the classification to maximize its utility for outpatient populations; differentiate levels of severity and course within syndromes; maintain compatibility, where feasible, with the ICD-9; rely on empirical data to establish the diagnostic criteria; and be receptive to the concerns and critiques submitted by interested professional and patient representatives.

## PROGRESS REVIEWS

Having drawn the basic architectural design and many of the DSM-III's initial syndromic drafts, Task Force representatives spoke formally for the first time about their work at a special session during the annual meeting of the American Psychiatric Association in May 1975. Following this inaugural appearance, the Task Force turned the manual's elaboration and refinement phases over to 14 advisory committees, several of which contributed substantively to both the conception and writing of those drafts for which they were responsible. Additional consultants were invited periodically to contribute in areas of their expertise. The Task Force continued as a body to evaluate successive drafts submitted by the substantive area committees, appraising them with reference to the goals, rationale, and standards they had set earlier for the manuscript.

The classification model and syndromic criteria of the DSM-III were extensively and critically appraised at a major conference held in St. Louis in June 1976. Entitled "DSM-III in Mid-Stream," it drew both the critiques and commendations of over 100 invited participants with backgrounds relevant to both the nosological and major diagnostic categories of the projected document. Serving as representatives of allied mental health organizations, only a handful of these "midstream" evaluators had a part in the development of the 1976 draft manual. The conference proved of considerable value in that it

served to highlight several deficiencies and ambiguities, as well as to provide reinforcement for the Task Force's commitments to both the multiaxial schema and the specification of what was subsequently termed the "diagnostic," rather than the "operational," criteria.

As a follow-up to the midstream conference, a formal invitation was extended to a number of interested professional mental health societies, encouraging them to establish liaison committees to the Task Force. Among those which formed such groups were The Academy of Psychiatry and the Law, the American Academy of Child Psychiatry, the American Academy of Psychoanalysis, the American Association of Chairmen of Departments of Psychiatry, the American College Health Association, the American Orthopsychiatric Association, the American Psychoanalytic Association, and the American Psychological Association. Each liaison group received major drafts of the DSM-III and was invited both to relay its concerns and to provide suitable recommendations. Most liaison committees chose an essentially pro forma role, offering little commentary or feedback to the Task Force. By contrast, impassioned controversies were stirred among both the American Psychoanalytic Association and the American Psychological Association. These disputations fostered new and troublesome misconceptions and extended dialogues and written interchanges, all of which ultimately brought forth reasoned and balanced solutions; more will be said concerning the issues surrounding these disputes in a later section.

In April 1977, a comprehensive volume encompassing detailed diagnostic descriptions and criteria drafts of the DSM-III's major syndromic categories was printed for general distribution and critical review. Although preliminary field testing had already begun in December 1976, the timing of this comprehensive printed draft was designed to coincide with the beginning of a series of formal national field trials in the fall of 1977 under the aegis of the Task Force and the sponsorship of NIMH. As with other documents possessing long-term implications, it was wisely decided by the Task Force that the proposed manual be fully evaluated several times *during,* rather than following, its development. This would not only keep subsequent problems to a minimum but also increase the likelihood that the final version would prove maximally acceptable to clinicians and researchers *prior* to official adoption.

The two-year NIMH-sponsored project, conducted from September 1977 to September 1979 included several sequential drafts of the DSM-III; it not only solicited evaluations based on case history studies but also requested specific judgments concerning the more innovative aspects of the manual, as well as recommendations on a number of knotty diagnostic problems. The responses of more than 800 clinicians, from both private settings and over 200 public facilities, were obtained based on data from some 12,000 patients. Noteworthy were the findings of a formal questionnaire which indicated that clinicians of widely diverse theoretical views appraised the penultimate DSM-III draft in a highly and uniformly positive fashion.

Despite efforts to maintain reasonable levels of compatibility with the ICD-9, the Task Force saw its primary duty to be substantive and innovative. For this, and other reasons—notably the rather widespread dissatisfaction of several nonpsychiatric medical specialties with the ICD-9—significant disparities continue to exist between the two taxonomies and nomenclatures. To accommodate the areas of dissatisfaction, a so-called clinical modification of the standard ICD, termed the ICD-9-CM, was developed in 1978 for primary use in the United States. The major difference between the two ICDs is the addition of a fifth-digit code to the indexing system of the ICD-9-CM; for both psychiatric and other medical specialties the added digit not only permits greater diagnostic latitude but also enables the introduction of more refined discriminations and qualifiers. Most relevantly, the ICD-9-CM can now encompass the entire range of syndromic categories that comprise the DSM-III. The converse is not true, however; that is, although all the codes in the standard ICD are included in the ICD-9-CM, many of the standard ICD diagnoses have not been incorporated in the DSM-III.

Its work essentially completed, the Task Force submitted its final DSM-III document to the Council on Research and Development at the American Psychiatric Association's annual meeting in May 1979. Here it was approved and forwarded to the organization's board of trustees, where it was formally endorsed as the officially authorized document to be scheduled for publication and implementation as the *Diagnostic and Statistical Manual of Mental Disorders,* 3rd edition, in 1980.

## SOME CONTROVERSIES AND MYTHS

At almost the moment the DSM-III's first draft reached the public eye, a rash of criticisms—from mild to fevered—spread upon the scene at professional symposia (Dreger, Note 1; Lorr, Note 2; Millon, Note 3; Salzinger, Note 5; Willems, Note 6) and in a wide variety of periodicals (Garmezy, 1978; McLemore & Benjamin, 1979; McReynolds, 1979; Schacht & Nathan, 1977; Zubin, 1978). Most troublesome was the fact that so inchoate a glimpse of what "might" be forthcoming—and how one might, in turn, be affected thereby—led so many otherwise cautious and reasonable judges to leap to premature conclusions that proved far from the final mark. "Philosophical" and "conceptual" positions were ascribed to the Task Force as if the committee were composed of clones that rubber-stamped some higher authority, rather than being a highly diverse and outspoken collection of independently minded professionals with clearly disparate views.

Troublesome also were the questionable, if not malicious, motives attributed to the committee. The Task Force was attacked as the spokesperson for an "imperialistic" assault by psychiatry designed to gain hegemony over the mental health service marketplace; its partially visible efforts were seen not merely as unsuitable for scientific progress, or for the viability of one or another professional discipline, but were conceived by some as leading inevitably to the undoing of patients themselves, particularly children. Others used the occasion to criticize the document for having expanded its predecessors tenfold, encompassing ostensible "problems of living" that do not qualify as mental disorders. Still others lamented the deletion of favorite syndromes, so sorely missed as to lead them to pursue all avenues that might undo approval of the manuscript by the board of trustees of the American Psychiatric Association unless their cherished concepts were reinstated in the manual. That the taxonomy and nomenclature of the forthcoming DSM-III signified to some a dismaying reaffirmation of the medical model was, somewhat perversely, counterbalanced by the vehement denunciation of others that it had abandoned that very model. Many of these skirmishes and reprehensions were the mere ravings of a misinformed or misguided readership. Others represented issues of genuine substance that transcended the usual professional bickering and theoretical hairsplitting.

Reviewing the critiques from the vantage point of having been an active Task Force participant, I was reminded repeatedly of the Rashomon tale—except that none of the dissenters were even at the scene. Although perhaps blinded by the very fact of being present, I did manage, however, to retain my "outsider" identity as a psychologist working in psychiatry's vineyards. More aptly, I felt like a historian who was witness to the drafting of a preliminary sketch for a future nonfiction study and, before either the details or the ending was worked out, stumbled across a series of critical reviews, not of the completed book but of a novelized movie adaptation that was based tangentially on the early outlines. Little of what I heard or read corresponded to either the process of the DSM-III's evolution or the product that finally emerged.

Lest the reader think otherwise, let me assure you that I am no apologist for the DSM-III's shortcomings; nor do I have especially fond illusions concerning the altruism or the power and economic interests of the psychiatric profession. I have a long agenda of unfinished work for the DSM-IV (Millon & Klerman, in press). Neither do I dismiss the troubling struggles that currently exist between the professions of psychiatry and psychology. But I do believe that it would be a grievous error to place upon the substantive character of the DSM-III whatever legitimate misgivings one may have about the nature of this disquieting professional rivalry. However wrongheaded or deficient the manual may be, it is, in fact, an outgrowth of scholarly debate and empirical test and not of any real or imagined ventures of psychiatric imperialism. This is not the chapter for elaboration, but I can assert confidently, and contrary to the beliefs of many of my psychological colleagues, first, that the changes wrought in the DSM-III are more consonant with the rigorous empiricism that characterizes psychology rather than psychiatry—witness the requirement of adherence to specified and explicit diagnostic *criteria*—and, second, that the DSM-III subscribes to the contextual orientation which increasingly typifies psychological thought—witness the fact that diagnosis must set the presenting clinical syndrome (Axis I) within the framework of a longitudinal pattern of enduring personality traits (Axis II), as well as within a broad, cross-sectional context of situational or psychosocial precipitants (Axis IV).

It will be useful to turn next to a brief exposition of several of the more memorable public controversies that were stirred during the Task Force's five year tenure; the facts should help discredit some myths.

## CONTROVERSIES WITH PSYCHOLOGY: "MENTAL DISORDERS ARE A SUBSET OF MEDICAL DISORDERS"

Few issues evoked so strong a professional outcry as the belief that the statement "Mental disorders are a subset of medical disorders" would be promulgated as an official pronouncement in the DSM-III. How did this misguided phrase gain its coinage?

At a May 1975 meeting of the then small and close-knit Task Force, the issue was raised as to whether the forthcoming DSM should contain a definition of "mental disorders." It seemed a reasonable thesis at the time, and members of the Task Force were invited to draft proposals accordingly, as well as to distribute them to other committee participants prior to a scheduled fall meeting. Only one member of the Task Force was courageous (or foolish?) enough to take it upon himself to write a full-fledged essay on the rationale of what he believed would be an acceptable definition. Despite its commendable scholarly nature, this draft proved overly abstruse and theoretical, lacking both the specificity and the concreteness with which the main DSM text was to be characterized. Professor Spitzer was notably disquieted, despairing that the committee might subscribe by default to this solitary proposal; hence, he requested that an opportunity be given to him and Prof. Jean Endicott, another Task Force appointee and long-time research colleague, to draft an alternate statement and definition. The proposal they prepared shortly thereafter included the statement "Mental disorders are a subset of medical disorders." It was publicly presented for the first time in a paper at the May 1976 American Psychiatric Association meeting, having been discussed only cursorily and assuredly not given official status or coinage as a formal statement by the Task Force, a point explicitly acknowledged *subsequently* by Spitzer and Endicott. Nevertheless, many, having either heard or read it

shortly thereafter (Spitzer, Sheehy, & Endicott, 1977), assumed incorrectly that Spitzer and Endicott's was the official voice of the Task Force. (Parenthetically, as should be well known by now, when the statement was put forward for formal committee vote, it was rejected as a counterproductive concept.)

Despite numerous memoranda from Spitzer and Endicott restating that their's was a *personal* and not a Task Force viewpoint, as well as an explicit disclaimer in the literature to the effect that the phrase should not be construed as meaning that mental disorders were the exclusive province of the psychiatric profession or that this one discipline was the sole possessor of the skills requisite for their amelioration (Spitzer et al., 1977), a storm of both official and unofficial protest from psychologists ensued following its publication. Several of the articles published at the time reflected either the frightened voices or the provocative trumpeting of self-servers whose concerns were the protection of psychology's vested commercial interests; others were more reasoned and scholarly critiques that illuminated the remaining deficits of what their authors saw as an anachronistic medical taxonomy and nomenclature. In the end, the uproar proved to be a tempest in a teapot. At no time would the Task Force have jeopardized acceptance of the substantive advances it had wrought in the DSM-III by including a statement so obviously provocative to one of the major mental health professions. Perhaps one or two Task Force members might have seen the fight as worth making, but it would have been a pyrrhic victory, at best. Fortunately, when the concept was put to the test of a Task Force vote in February 1978, it was soundly, and wisely, defeated.

A related issue of no small import was the accusation that the DSM-III conceived every syndrome as intrinsically organic, thereby reflecting a "power play" by psychiatry to preempt the mental health field. In response to this concern, a distinguished former president of the American Psychological Association (Albee, 1977) wrote, "To attribute marital conflict or delinquency . . . to a biological defect, to biochemical, nutritional, neurological, or other organic conditions . . . is to sell our psychological birthright for short term gain." That this assertion was notably in error can be seen by the text the Task Force approved in April 1979 for insertion in its glossary as the definition of mental disorder. (Regrettably, this statement was subsequently modified at the editorial level *without* Task Force approval; substitute wording was inadvertently and unfortunately introduced.)

No precise definition is available that unambiguously defines the boundaries of this concept. (This is also true of such concepts as physical disorder or mental or physical health.) However, in the DSM-III each of the mental disorders is conceptualized as a clinically significant behavioral or psychological syndrome or pattern of an individual that is associated, by and large, with either a painful symptom (distress) or impairment in one or more important areas of functioning (disability).

Note should be made here of the phrase "each of the mental disorders is conceptualized as a clinically significant behavioral or psychological syndrome."

## CONTROVERSIES WITH PSYCHOANALYSIS: "NEUROSIS: REAL OR ARTIFACT"

Troubles brewed within psychiatry's house, as well. Some background history may be useful here.

The chairman of the Task Force responsible for the DSM-II recorded in his foreword to the 1968 manual that his committee sought to eschew terms and taxonomic principles which might convey a doctrinaire position concerning either the character or the etiology of syndromes in which definitive knowledge concerning such matters was lacking in fact. He recognized that by leaving issue of this nature unspecified or ambiguous, his committee would be inviting readers to attribute to such issues whatever meanings and interpretations they found congenial to their theoretical or clinical

biases; he averred, however, that such construals would be wholly unjustified. In great measure, the DSM-II Task Force did achieve its goal of disclaiming pretensions to knowledge they lacked except in the case of syndromes inspired and interpreted in accord with psychoanalytic concepts of etiology and dynamics, for example, neurosis psychophysiologic disorders. Here, the committee's aspirations wavered badly having submitted early in their consultations to the entreaties of a powerful analytic lobby.

Such deference and acquiescence, it was believed, would never prove the case with the DSM-III. Convinced that it would avoid the pitfalls of etiologic speculation, and desiring to maintain an explicitly empirical orientation, the new Task Force set its sights clearly toward the goal of expunging principles that signified the favoring of one notion of psychogenesis over another. So adamant position may have appeared unduly rigid and may, in fact, have been an unwise if not incomprehensible, decision to some. But doubts such as these did not faze the committee after observing the theoretic polemics its own members displayed in their early dialogues. An empirically grounded manual that would alienate the smallest number of clinicians possible would be a more realistic and desirable goal, it was concluded, than the potentially more laudable, if less probable outcome of achieving interpretive consensus.

The Task Force could hardly have anticipated the storm of protest that arose when it resolved to do away with the label "neurosis" and, perhaps more significantly, its synthesizing rationale in psychoanalytic theory. As a unifying theme for explicating and coordinating diverse syndromes, the neurotic concept had outlived its usefulness both as a nomenclature designation and as classificatory principle. Not only was the term misbegotten and anachronistic, having evolved through a long and checkered history of misguided reinterpretations, but the exclusiveness of the analytic interpretive model could no longer be sustained in light of equally plausible explanatory and empirically demonstrable alternatives; for example, a "snake phobia" may stem from repressed conflicts in which residual anxieties are symbolically displaced; it may also reflect directly conditioned or generalized avoidant learning; also possible are constitutionally low biological thresholds for a highly prevalent "instinctive" response. The furor and threats that ensued deserve public censure for they were no mere idle posturings. A review of the agonizing events that followed will be instructive in that they illuminate the awesome power of unremitting "political" pressure designed to thwart a courageous and scientific effort to undo questionable tenets and conceptual presumptions that are unsupportable by usual empirical or clinical criteria.

As is well known, by late 1978 the public media picked up the neurosis story, taking what appears as some delight in exposing what should have been a dispassionate professional debate. Having been thrust into front-page notoriety, the psychoanalytic campaign to dissuade the Task Force from its appointed rounds delivered its first official broadside: Desist or we will develop our own nosology and terminology. This was responded to with suggestions that the Task Force could appoint a committee to draft a special DSM-III appendix for clinicians oriented to a psychodynamic viewpoint in which the official nomenclature would be explicated in terms more suitable to their theory. This proposal gained some adherents within the Task Force but charmed few in official psychoanalytic quarters. The stakes rose sharply as psychoanalytic groups sought to bring pressure on official psychiatric bodies. By the spring of 1979, the Task Force received a letter signifying considerable success on their part; it stated:

At the meeting of the Area III Council (of the American Psychiatric Association) on March 10, 1979, the following motion was passed:
MOVED: Area III is opposed to the elimination of "neurosis" as a diagnostic term in DSM-III.

In subsequent discussion it was determined that Area III would move at the assembly meeting in the Spring to not approve the adoption of DSM-III unless it included this diagnostic category.

Indications were that assembly representatives from all areas would coalesce and bring down the wrath of the analytic community by blocking acceptance of the DSM-III at the annual American Psychiatric Association board meeting that May. This was no mundane crusade. Hence, to avoid what was anticipated to be a brutal and potentially destructive confrontation, the Task Force proposed that the issue be cleverly finessed by separating the concept "neurotic disorder" from that of "neurotic process." Neurotic "disorder," signifying mere descriptive properties, could then be introduced as a formal DSM-III designation without necessarily connoting the operation of a neurotic "process," that is, a sequence in which intrapsychic conflicts are resolved unconsciously via various defense mechanisms, as well as being expressed symbolically in symptomatic form. An approved statement recording this distinction and its ostensive rationale was recommended for insertion in the introduction to the DSM-III; hence an additional brief note in the summary chart of the DSM-III reads:

"In order to facilitate the identification of the categories that in DSM-II were grouped together in a class of the neuroses, the DSM-III terms are included separately in parentheses after the corresponding categories."

Not all factions of the Task Force shared or were heartened by this last-minute solution. One refractory member expressed his ire and contempt for the compromise, as well as what he judged to be the Task Force's dereliction of duty, thus:

The political pressure to reinsert the term "neurosis" into the DSM-III stems from those who . . . are not objecting to the absence of the term . . . because American nosology would be deprived of a useful descriptive term: they wish it reinserted because they wish a covert affirmation of their psychogenic hypotheses. The attempts to supposedly clarify the issue by redefining the term "neurotic disorder" as a purely descriptive term is really an attempt to obfuscate the real impact of its reintroduction.

I think the role of the Task Force should be to act as an advisory group of nosological experts. We should make our recommendations to the APA. If the APA, in its wisdom, sees fit to reject any or all of our recommendations, that is its business. We have done our job and they have done their job.

To respond to this sort of unscientific and illogical, but psychologically understandable, pressure . . . is unworthy of scientists who are attempting to advance our field via clarification and reliable definition.

## CONTROVERSIES OVER LANGUAGE: THE CONCEPT OF DISORDERS

Carlo de Sanctis, a contemporary Italian child psychiatrist, recounted his thoughts while observing a group of adolescent girls learning to water ski. They would start their run, he noted, with their legs together tightly; as they moved forward their skis would gradually drift further apart, until the young ladies would inevitably descend into the water ever so gracefully on their youthfully firm and attractively spaced buttocks. Commenting on his observation, de Sanctis said, "I went to medical school before the terminological reforms of the Geneva Anatomical Convention. What are now known as the adductors of the thighs were then known as *the protectator virginitatis*" (cited in Lemkau, 1969).

Lemkau (1969) notes that a major fault of nosological systems, which subsequent editions invariably seek to correct, is that of having imparted more than a mere designation in the names it assigned its subject matter. As noted in the charming vignette just sketched, the task of constructing a suitable terminology proves problematic even in so "tangible" a subject as physical anatomy. How much more susceptible are conceptual syndromes, such as in psychopathology, to the vagaries

and errors of superfluous connotation? For this reason, the mission of devising a nomenclature devoid of misguided and value free implications was judged one of no small proportion to the DSM-III Task Force. Its members applied a toothcomb of fine grading to winnow out all possible misconceptions and solecisms that might contaminate or misdirect the course of future clinical and research endeavors.

A linguistic principle employed by the Task Force was that labels not only be interpretable and modernized but consist, where possible, of everyday language, that is, be composed of familiar English words which convey simply and directly the behaviors they seek to represent. This seemingly modest, if not virtuous, goal evoked greater resistance than anyone could have anticipated. For example, the term "catatonia" was defended vigorously and remains fixed in the nomenclature, although I venture that less than 1% of the DSM-III readership are aware of either its origins or its translation. Fortunately, and by contrast, "hebephrenia" was successfully deleted, replaced by the commonplace descriptive word "disorganized." Similarly, the label "histrionic" was chosen to supplant "hysteria" as an Axis II personality designation, as was "somatoform," selected to supersede it as an Axis I clinical syndrome. New terms such as "avoidant" and "narcissistic" were likewise adopted not only to personify the most salient feature to characterize their respective syndromes but also by virtue of being familiar words, readily understood in everyday parlance.

Akin to the foregoing, the standard syntax and language conventions employed in the DSM-III were framed such that designated labels would be construed to define the syndrome and not the person who exhibits it. Thus people are never referred to in the DSM-III as "schizophrenics" but as persons who portray a "schizophrenic disorder." Also worthy of note in this regard is the eradication of the medical term "patient" and the sweeping substitution of words such as *person* or *individual*.

Lest the reader be led to believe the Task Force was invariably successful in holding to its principles, or in otherwise failing to regress from its "noble" aspirations, any brief skimming of the DSM-III nomenclature should disabuse the reader of such thoughts. Numerous derelictions can be readily exposed, for example, the choice of the obscure term "dysthymia" as the appellation for recurrent or mild depressions, or of "factitious" for simulated disorders. Transgressions such as these were of minor import when compared to a concerted effort to rescind an earlier and signal-linguistic decision to apply the label "disorder" consistently to all syndromes. As one of its guiding principles, the committee chose this term for all conditions lacking an empirically demonstrable etiology. The principle reflected the Task Force's decision to eschew all insupportable theoretical or pathogenic implications. In addition, the Task Force sought to highlight the inherent diversity that characterizes most syndromes by phrasing the term in its plural form; for example, the new nomenclature lists the label as "schizophrenic disorders." Despite the firm commitment it made to this principle, the Task Force began to drift off course, to which I responded with some alarm, in a memo dated July 16, 1978, as follows:

This memo is in response to the letter of July 10 suggesting a series of modifications in labeling the affective disorders. What prompts me is not any strong pro or con reaction to the substantive suggestions, but rather to a reported "decision" that was tucked away in the memo to the effect that, henceforth, the label "schizophrenia" will replace that of "schizophrenic disorders," thereby undoing a Task Force decision that was agreed upon in late 1974.

I very much agree with the point that "we are obliged to coin terms that are simple as well as descriptive," and toward that end will support such suggestions as substituting "major depression" for "major depressive disorder," and those pertaining to deletions of the term "chronic" where it is redundant or noncontrasting. My concern, however, is that simplicity and symmetry not become overriding principles that may conflict and undo other goals such as clarity and accuracy.

As some of you may recall, I argued strongly at an early Task Force meeting in St. Louis that we adopt the term "disorders" as a modifier for *each major* syndrome category. This was, in part, a response to the problems that arose as a consequence of etiological theses that were implied in both DSM-I and DSM-II, most prominently illustrated with the schizophrenic syndrome. To recall, the label "schizophrenic reaction" was employed in DSM-I and, in DSM-II, the label was "simplified" to "schizophrenia." The objections raised were that the former implied a syndrome elicited "in response to a situational stressor," whereas the latter implied the identification of a homogeneous "disease entity," a focal ailment within the patient akin to such medical disorders as tuberculosis or measles. Both of these etiological theses, though conveyed subtly and indirectly by their promulgators, proved to be misleading and empirically insupportable. Today, we believe that there are a variety of schizophrenic disorders, a spectrum, if you will; that is, a heterogeneous syndrome, etiologically biogenic in some cases, psychogenic in others, and most likely interactive in the majority.

Without belaboring the academics of the issue, I would like to ask the Task Force to review the principles that guide such decisions as when to use the "disorders" term and when not. For me, when a label is a commonplace and clearly *descriptive English term,* with no etiological implications or undertones, such as "depression," the modifier "disorder" or "disorders" may occasionally be dropped. However, where the key term in the label suggests properties beyond mere description, such as implying the identification of a homogeneous entity (e.g., schizophrenia, cyclothymia, and dysthymia), then I contend that by leaving them stand we are doing a disservice to the profession and undermining our own explicit commitment to "steer clear" of introducing dynamics or suggesting causalities in what is essentially a descriptive text.

I hate to convey my objections so strongly, particularly since I am probably the most disposed of the Task Force members to the attractions of symmetry and parallelism. However, the cost in creating misleading implications seems too great for the ostensible gains of simplicity and balance.

As evident in the final DSM-III text, the Task Force's early plan to uniformly apply the label "disorders" did remain firm.

## CONTROVERSIES OVER HOMOSEXUALITY: SCIENCE OR POLITICS?

Late in the tenure of the DSM-II, the board of trustees of the American Psychiatric Association reevaluated the well-established diagnostic category of "homosexuality" and substituted in its stead a classification termed "sexual orientation disturbance." This new label reflected a compromise among opposing factions of the profession concerning whether homosexual behavior per se was or was not a valid mental disorder. The descriptive text of the revised DSM-II syndrome stated that the condition applies to "individuals whose sexual interests are directed primarily toward people of the same sex and who are either disturbed by, in conflict with, or wish to change their sexual orientation." This reconciliation between contrary, and often implacably held, views was judged successful by the vast majority of practitioners, essentially those who were not beholden to any of the more radical positions.

Despite the recency and apparent satisfactory character of the DSM-II reassessment, the place of homosexuality was questioned again upon news of a forthcoming DSM-III, much to the dismay of those Task Force members who recalled the intense, uncompromising, and often bitter debates which preceded the final DSM-II accommodation. The Task Force's Advisory Committee on Psychosexual Disorders was asked to carry the brunt of what proved to be a new and even more trying imbroglio. Several designations evolved during the committee's desultory journey to fashion a synthesis among contending viewpoints, among them: homodysphilia, dyshomophilia, homosexual conflict disorder, amorous relationship disorder (this latter proposal represented an effort to record sexual role conflicts experienced by heterosexual, as well as homosexual,

individuals), and finally, ego-dystonic homosexuality.

As implied in the preceding paragraph, an argument advanced in favor of dismissing the ego-dystonic concept was the assertion that it was illogical to classify homosexual discontent if one were not to categorize similarly troubled heterosexuals. Also argued, with no small merit, was the observation that depressed feelings prompted by an inability to function heterosexually are no different from depressed feelings arising from other sources, which are routinely assigned the diagnostic rubric of depression. Further compounding the issue is the fact that most homosexuals experience no discomfort as a consequence of their sexual proclivities; why identify the very few, then, and select them as the basis for a special diagnostic classification? Moreover, when homosexuals do feel dismay, it often reflects society's role expectations and discriminations rather than an intrinsic dissatisfaction of sexual preference. Needless to say, these contentions were challenged by clinicians who were no less convinced of the correctness of their beliefs; they noted evidence such as the nonnormative character of these behaviors, the presumptive pathological upbringing of homosexual patients, the ostensive constitutional defect that subserves the "disease," and so on.

After numerous text revisions, an avalanche of letters from distinguished professionals and public spokespersons, as well as the inability to achieve full consensus, the final responsibility for attaining a resolution was passed up from the advisory committee to the Task Force itself. Here, the recommendations of the majority faction of the advisory committee were appraised against several broad principles and criteria, including the consequences of one or another decision for both the public at large and the various professions of mental health. Since no ideal solution was possible, it was decided, in effect, to let the individual himself or herself, and not the Task Force or the practitioner, establish whether there is or is not a disorder. Thus the person involved must state that he or she desires to achieve heterosexual relationships and views his or her homosexual impulses to be both unwanted and distressing. Given the inchoate, yet entangled, web of social values and scientific facts surrounding homosexual behavior, the only consensus that seemed both just and sensible would be one fashioned by the person who experienced the phenomenon. It was on that note that the Task Force put aside one of its more vexing, yet intriguing, assignments.

## CONCEPTUAL ADVANCES AND FAILURES

Perhaps the only realistic and significant question to be posed in appraising a new taxonomy and nomenclature is not whether they mirror the state of the science perfectly, or whether they provide answers to all possible questions professionals within the discipline may ask, but whether they are advances over preceding nosological systems and whether they will be employed with greater clinical accuracy and facility by future practitioners and researchers. The text turns next to these latter questions.

That the DSM-III has been responded to well is evident in both formal questionnaire replies and in the rather startling number of copies that have been sold to date, a figure that is best grasped by the fact that more orders were received in the first six months following its publication than for both previous DSM editions combined, including their 30-plus reprintings.

### COMPREHENSIVE AND SYSTEMATIC DESCRIPTION

It is almost inevitable that more detail will be incorporated in a later form of a nosology than in earlier versions. Hence, though far from a comprehensive textbook, failing to encompass matters of theory, etiology, and treatment, the DSM-III is nevertheless substantially more extensive and thorough than both of its predecessors. Being exhaustive and inclusionary, however, required that information on each syndrome be ordered in a reasonably standardized and systematic format. The organizational sequence that was adopted proceeds with the following information: essential (necessary) features: associated (frequent) features; and, where reasonably reliable data are available, age of onset, course, impairment, complications, predisposing factors, sex ratio, familial pattern, and differential diagnosis. Both the scope and organizational structure given the descriptive text signifies an important advance in the DSM-III, for the schema not only provides a logical guide for clinicians seeking information but also establishes a coherent framework within which the data of future studies can be systematically introduced.

### DIAGNOSTIC CRITERIA

The comprehensive and systematic character of the DSM-III is of maximal utility to the clinician. The spelling out of diagnostic criteria is also beneficial to the practitioner in that it serves to highlight the specific inclusion and exclusion components that comprise the elements of a diagnostic decision. It is this very precision in articulating specific and uniform rules of definition, originally and significantly termed "operational" criteria, that makes the DSM-III so serviceable and potentially fruitful also as a research tool. Not only do the criteria delineate the components that will enable reasonably homogeneous group assignments, but their application as a standard national (and, it is hoped, international) gauge will ensure at least a modicum of reliability and comparability among studies undertaken at diverse research settings. To illustrate, the "borderline" pattern will no longer be characterized one way at Massachusetts General Hospital, another at the Menninger Clinic, a third at Michael Reese Hospital, and a fourth at Langley Porter Institute; each setting would likely uncover distinctive, yet discrepant, syndromic properties in the past since each selected its study population using dissimilar diagnostic criteria. Although the painfully slow progress of verifiable empirical knowledge in mental health cannot be attributed solely to the paucity of replicable research, the joint use of uniform DSM-III criteria should help stem the tide of insubstantial, unreliable, or, at best, minimally generalizable data that has come to characterize publications in the field.

It is reasonable to assume that greater reliability and research comparability will flow from the use of standardized diagnostic criteria, but it should be recorded that these criteria offer no more than promise and an aspiration at this time. Some interjudge-reliability data have been obtained in the DSM-III field trials, and these are encouraging, especially when compared to prior studies utilizing earlier classifications. Nevertheless, most of the criteria lack empirical support. Some are inadequately explicit or, conversely, are overly concrete in their operational referents. Many are redundant both within and with other diagnostic classes. Others are insufficiently comprehensive in syndromic scope or display a lack of parallelism and symmetry among corresponding categories.

At best, then, the diagnostic criteria of the DSM-III represent a significant *conceptual step* toward a future goal when clinical characteristics of appropriate specificity and breadth will provide both reliable and valid indices for identifying the major syndromic prototypes. Although this chapter neither has the space nor is the setting within which to elaborate the theme, it should be said that the categorical syndromes of the DSM-III are conceptual prototypes and not tangible entities. Hence it would be not only specious but also paralogical to aspire to develop sophisticated discriminations such as criterion "weights." Given that these syndromes are, in the main, only theoretical constructs, it will more than suffice for both clinical and research purposes to employ what has been devised—a standardized, reliable, and

internally coherent mosaic of criterion descriptors. To the extent that the DSM-III has provided this foundation of clinical prototypes, it can fairly be judged to have made an advance worthy of commendation.

## DIAGNOSTIC DECISION TREES

It is partly a consequence of the prototypical nature of psychopathological constructs that certain kinds of "scientific" effort, such as developing criterion weights, are intrinsically illusory. Among other "silk purse" endeavors explored by members of the Task Force was the "decision tree" method for facilitating differential diagnosis. Although the ostensive purpose of the decision tree appendix in the manual is to aid clinicians in understanding the organizational and hierarchical order of the classification schema, it was, at heart, a method to optimize the ruling in and ruling out of alternate diagnostic possibilities by a series of decision-point choices. Not only is the sequence of this branching procedure painstakingly formalized and, hence, cumbersome to pursue, but it rests on a number of philosophical and pragmatic assumptions that are either counterfactual or untenable.

First, the DSM-III decision tree method presumes the presence of a hierarchical ordering of categories in which diagnostic classes listed earlier in the nosology comprises symptoms that may be found in later classes but in which the reverse is not true. A prime consequence of so carefully fashioned a sequential chain of categories would be the fact that successive syndromes in the classification invariably are more specific and convey more precisely differentiated information than those which precede them. This increasing distinctness and exactitude, necessary ingredients in a successful decision tree or branching procedure, assures that each successive category possesses authentic clinical features not found in categories previously listed. A serial pattern of this nature would be a remarkable nosological achievement for the DSM-III, were it so in fact. Not only is there no inherent structure to psychopathology that permits so rigorous an arrangement, but the DSM-III *imposes* only a modest degree of sequential rigor on its classificatory organization. For this, and other reasons to be enumerated shortly, the decision tree concept has proved not to be one of the Task Force's more notable achievements.

Second, differential diagnosis assumes that psychopathological phenomena adhere to the classical model of discriminable "disease entities." However, the compositional structure of DSM-III diagnostic criteria derives from a prototypical model (Cantor, Smith, French, & Mezzich, 1980), that is, one which allows for syndromic heterogeneity, recognizes the inevitable covariation of diverse symptoms within single categories, and acknowledges that no one symptom or even pattern of symptoms is either necessary or sufficient to define the category. The problems of pursuing a method designed for purposes of differential diagnosis is compounded further by the fact that the DSM-III not only permits but also encourages multiple diagnoses, a problem aggravated further by the manual's standard multiaxial framework. Thus not only does the decision tree goal of definitive diagnosis run hard against the prototypical character of DSM-III syndromes, but its formalism and sequential requirements would be undermined repeatedly by the multidiagnostic aims and intrinsic multiaxial schema of the DSM-III.

Third, the process of articulating clinical data in so formal and demanding a manner as required by the decision tree sequence *may not* be faulted as specious by some, but it does impose a procedural complexity upon an otherwise facile and expedient process. From a pragmatic view, then, it is likely to be considered an unnecessary encumbrance for routine diagnostic tasks, quite impractical for everyday decision making, and, perhaps most relevantly, abhorrent to clinicians accustomed to the diagnostic habit of "intuitive" synthesis. Should the method guarantee significantly greater diagnostic accuracy in the future, prove useful for deepening

clinical understanding, or aid in the selection of efficacious treatment modalities, then it might gain a sufficient following to override the inertia of traditional practice. Failing in these regards, as seems inevitable, it is likely to remain, as it has, a novel and essentially academic concept.

## Multiaxial Format

The formal adoption of the multiaxial schema in the DSM-III signifies a reformulation of the task of psychodiagnosis that approaches the magnitude described by Kuhn (1962) as a paradigm shift. It represents a distinct turn from the traditional medical disease model where the clinician's job is to disentangle and clear away "distracting" symptoms and signs so as to pinpoint the underlying or "true" pathophysiologic state. By contrast, the multiaxial assessment model (Essen-Moller & Wohlfahrt, 1947; Mezzich, 1979; Rutter, Shaffer, & Shepherd, 1975; Stengel, 1959; Strauss, 1975) not only recognizes that "distracting" symptoms and signs are aspects worthy of attention but records each of them on its own representative axis as part of an interactive complex of elements that, only in their entirety, *are* the pathologic state.

A brief review of the various classes of information that comprise the DSM-III multiaxial system may be useful as I proceed to comment on its strengths and weaknesses. Well known by now is the fact that the classification consists of five axes, the first three of which are required as the bases for an official diagnosis.

*Axis I* constitutes the more-or-less traditional mental disorders, those relatively circumscribed or distinct symptom states, labeled "clinical syndromes" in the DSM-III, which are often transient or florid in character. Also indexed on Axis I are a number of special categories, including those conditions which are not attributable to a mental disorder but have nevertheless become the prime focus of the clinician's attention or treatment efforts.

*Axis II* is composed of two segments, one for children and the other for adults. The child section encompasses a variety of relatively specific, albeit questionable, developmental disorders, such as maturational delays in language or speech articulation. Conceptually more significant is the innovative segregation of the personality disorders in the adult section into a separate axis, thus isolating them from the clinical syndromes which comprise the other axis. This bifurcation ensures that the more enduring and often more prosaic styles of personality functioning are not overlooked when attention is given the frequently more urgent and behaviorally dramatic clinical syndromes. It also takes cognizance of the fact that the lifelong coping styles and emotional vulnerabilities that comprise personality can provide a context within which the more salient and usually transient clinical states are likely to arise and be understood. Although the DSM text notes that individuals may have disorders on both axes, the Task Force was more purposeful in recommending that both axes be routinely recorded wherever justified. Toward the end it encouraged the formal notation of all relevant personality "traits" on Axis II, even when a distinctive personality "disorder" was not in evidence.

*Axis III* provides for the recording of physical disorders which may be potentially important or relevant to the understanding or management of the patient. Separating health disorders into mental (Axis I and Axis II) and physical (Axis III), though of questionable philosophical merit, acknowledges a tradition in which disturbances with primary behavioral or psychosocial manifestations are kept conceptually distinct from those with manifestations that are primarily somatic or physical. The justification for including a physical disorder axis in a taxonomy designed for mental disorders merely recognizes that information of this nature may (1) offer suggestive etiological leads (e.g., soft neurological signs), (2) identify physical ailments that may stem in part from the impact of psychological factors (e.g., ulcerative colitis), and (3) note facts that should be considered in planning therapeutic regimens (e.g., coronary artery disease).

*Axis IV* consists of judgments concerning the presence and severity of "psychosocial stressors." The official recognition that psychosocial environments play a role in the development and exacerbation of mental disorders, though patently obvious, is nevertheless an achievement of great import. Not only does it acknowledge the empirical fact that disturbances which arise in response to stressors have better prognoses than those which do not, but more impressively, it signifies in an officially recorded fashion the realization that psychosocial factors establish a context within which disorders not only unfold but are sustained and exacerbated. Psychosocial information is to be coded in two ways. First, a numerical rating is given to represent the "objectively judged" severity of all concurrent stressors that are impacting upon the individual, independent of his or her vulnerability or capacity to cope with them. Second, the specific natures of the stressors themselves are to be briefly described; the suggested categories include family issues, interpersonal problems, and occupational difficulties.

The presence in the DSM-III of *Axis V,* the "highest level of adaptive functioning" in the past year, reveals another signal achievement, the resolve that individuals who are seen clinically at the time of their greatest distress not be diagnosed and potentially "stigmatized" as if their present behaviors were fixed and constant. Not only does the recognition of the individual's recent level of adaptive functioning serve as a useful prognostic index, but it furnishes a longitudinal context within which to appraise a person's current functioning. Moreover, it addresses the "positive" attributes and strengths of the individual, so often overlooked in the clinician's understandable preoccupation with "negative" attitudes and troublesome behaviors.

Much to the chagrin of a number of Task Force members, both Axis IV and Axis V were made optional, ostensibly to avoid possible breaches of confidentiality in social and personal realms that were judged nonessential to the treatment enterprise. Though vigorously denounced at a Task Force meeting, the decision was upheld on the advice of a psychiatric committee on insurance and confidentiality.

The inclusion in DSM-III of Axis II (personality), Axis IV (psychosocial stressors), and Axis V (highest adaptive functioning), even though not required at times, augers well for a radical reconception of psychopathologic diagnosis. Henceforth, the official classification directs the clinician to address not the "disease entity" but an entire panorama of contextual dimensions, notably the person's overall style of psychological functioning, the qualities of his or her current situational environment, and his or her strengths and potentials for constructive and healthy coping.

It should be noted that the absence of axes beyond the five listed in the DSM-III was not due to a failure to acknowledge them. Dimensions such as "course" and "severity" were debated extensively in Task Force discussions. In both cases it was concluded that they lack universal applicability and, hence, should be coded selectively in syndromic categories where they would provide useful information. Unfortunately, the number of coded digits available for purposes such as these proved to be appreciably less than originally anticipated. Hence, "severity," though originally scheduled for use in several diagnostic classes, failed to survive in any category. The fate of "course" as an informational code was only slightly less sullied; it survived as a recorded datum in a few syndromic categories, notably as the fifth-digit code in both schizophrenic and substance-use groups.

Considerable attention was also given to two other, potentially quite useful, informational axes, those of "etiology" and "treatment response." Although insufficient time

was available for an empirical field trial, or even a systematic review, the notion of devising an etiologic axis that would permit clinicians to formulate their thoughts on both the origins and development of a disorder was an appealing one to several Task Force members. The model proposed for review would enable the diagnostician to select and rank order from a diverse list of known or hypothesized causal agents, such as genetic factors, interpersonal relations, situational stressors, intrapsychic conflicts, and so on. Not only would a list of this nature furnish useful data concerning what clinicians conceive to be the primary elements of etiology in diverse disorders, but it would provide a basis for understanding what relationships exist between causal formulations and those of treatment choice. The data generated by an axis such as this might, of course, say more about the biases of clinicians than about the attributes of patients. Etiology failed to take hold as a viable axis because the Task Force judged our current state of knowledge to be flawed and skimpy, at best. More time for systematic analysis and field testing was required than was available to piece together a reasonably coherent and informed schema.

A different fate, though one that also failed to achieve formal stature, lay in store for propositions favoring the inclusion of axes for either "treatment choice" or "treatment response." At the very first meetings of the Task Force it was concluded that a system which indexed both treatment regimen and treatment effect would, were systematic data gathered over time, provide exceptionally valuable information connecting diagnosis and therapy. With the exception of psychopharmacologic agents, however, the state of the general therapeutic art was judged both too inchoate and too complex to have its component parts disentangled in a meaningfully discriminable fashion. A consequence of this judgment was a decision to invite a wide range of treatment-based professional organizations to systematize their knowledge and technology in a manner relevant to diagnoses and to collect their work in a volume officially entitled *DSM-III and Treatment Planning*. This venture was known in Task Force memos as "Project Flower," the latter designation signifying our adherence to Chairman Mao's philosophical dictum, "Let all flowers bloom." In accord with this precept, the Task Force encouraged clinicians of divergent therapeutic orientations to formulate a rationale and methodology for treating the heterogeneous syndromes comprising the DSM-III. Invited to contribute chapters were the American Psychoanalytic Association, the American Academy of Psychoanalysis, the Association for the Advancement of Behavior Therapy, the Society for Biological Psychiatry, the American Group Therapy Association, and the American Association of Marriage and Family Therapists; the perspectives of the American Psychological Association and the American Academy of Child Psychiatry were to be represented by members of these associations who participated in the several treatment-based groups. Several months passed before draft chapters were received by the Task Force. Unfortunately, most of these chapters exposed the narrow and highly routinized technologies that each school of treatment conceived as optimal for highly dissimilar syndromes. The Task Force simply could not put its stamp of approval on such self-serving documents.

Additional proposals for this, that, or another axis were recommended to the Task Force, many of which were well-reasoned treatises. Perhaps at some point in the distant future, when substantive fact and coherent theory are more characteristic of the field than they are today, several of these suggestions may be usefully incorporated into later DSM versions. Until that time, as one Task Force member wrote in response to his concerns regarding "axis proliferation":

It is not the purpose of the DSM-III to allow everybody with their own idiosyncratic beliefs a set of categories that they can refer to since such a list would be indefinitely long. . . . Let us assure everybody that we are in favor of free speech and the creative use of everyone's background and mentality. Therefore, if they wish to make annotations . . . concerning etiology . . . or coping styles, they are free to do so. They can write anything on their charts that they please. That's their privilege.

And so the Task Force closed its book on multiaxial dimensions—until the DSM-IV.

## SUBSTANTIVE ADVANCES AND FAILURES

Many of the changes in the DSM-III have been described in earlier sections. In addition to modifications in nomenclature, taxonomy, and the multiaxial format, there are changes in the definition and rationale of particular disorders that justify brief synopses, especially as to how they differ from comparable DSM-II classifications. Given the more detailed discussions that will be presented in later chapters, this section will comment only briefly on some points of contrast. It will follow the sequential order of the DSM-III for these purposes.

### DISORDERS USUALLY FIRST EVIDENT IN INFANCY, CHILDHOOD, OR ADOLESCENCE

Problems associated with constructing an adequate classification of childhood disorders often stem from the nature of childhood itself. Neither childhood nor adolescence is stable in the sense that adulthood is. Disorders that evolve during these early periods are subject to the processes of maturation such that their clinical pictures must, perforce, change significantly with age. Moreover, disorders among children tend to be more undifferentiated and, hence, more difficult to organize as coherent syndromes. Compounding these complications further is the fact that children are more malleable and, therefore, more vulnerable to transitional life events than are adults; rarely do they exhibit the more consistent and ingrained styles of behavior observed in more mature persons.

Whether the DSM-III succeeded in overcoming the proliferation and variability among disorders that are typical of childhood by adding numerous new categories cannot be ascertained at this time. On the one hand, an increase in the number of categories does provide for more refined and subtle discriminations than existed heretofore; on the other, the specification of more varieties may impose a forced stability on phenomena that are inherently transient and highly changeable in their character. The fact that there are four times as many categories in the DSM-III childhood section as were in the DSM-II may prove either progressive or regressive; it is hoped, of course, that the greater degree of specification signifies an increase in clinical knowledge.

Considerable consternation has been voiced concerning the broad sphere of childhood behaviors that have been encompassed as "mental disorders" within the nomenclature. Whether the extension to new realms of functioning is an overreaching and unjustified step on the part of the Task Force or whether it signifies a valid effort to specify and differentiate among important childhood disorders is a matter of empirical test and not of polemic debate. The DSM-III does include a number of V codes, for example (childhood or adolescent antisocial behavior, academic problem), that recognize a range of ordinary childhood problems which mimic pathological behaviors and maturational delays but do not signify a mental disorder in accord with the DSM-III diagnostic criteria. Clinicians who have serious diagnostic doubts or hasten to avoid the potential stigmatizing effects of a formal diagnosis should not hesitate to represent their assessment with an appropriate V code. The presence of this "escape hatch" was not designed, however, to eschew a sphere of clinical responsibility. On the other hand, differentiation and inclusion among diagnostic classes must be based on conceptual clarity and clinical utility and not on a cavalier cognitive restructuring of the diagnostic taxonomy. Whether the systematic reorganization and differentiation of the DSM-III childhood

and adolescent disorders proves consonant with the best of clinical aspiration remains to be seen (Quay, Note 4).

## SCHIZOPHRENIC DISORDERS

Whether justified or not, the classification of "schizophrenic disorders" remain the most fully developed and elaborated syndrome in the DSM-III. However, and despite the vast number of research, clinical, and theoretical papers published about it in the preceding decade, the concept of schizophrenic disorder has been more narrowly focused and defined than in the DSM-II. Among major criteria is an extended six-month period comprising symptomatology the magnitude of psychotic delusions, hallucinations, as well as other thought disturbances. Its onset must precede the age of 45 and have signified deterioration from a previous level of functioning. The criteria selected are more consonant with the views of Schneider (1976) than those of Kraepelin and are based largely on research indicating a significant prevalence among family members. The consequent greater homogeneity of the clinical population should enable "true" schizophrenics to be differentiated from those whose behaviors merely appear similar to schizophrenia. Whether such discriminations will hold up empirically and whether they will have significance either prognostically or therapeutically remains a matter for the future to determine.

Noteworthy is the introduction of two terms representing syndromes with comparable symptomatology but of briefer duration: "schizophreniform," label for syndromes enduring for greater than a two-week period but less than six months, and "brief reactive psychoses," a phrase designating those evidencing parallel symptomatology but lasting less than two weeks. A fourth and fifth coding digit may be utilized to assist in the further differentiation of eight syndromic subtypes or length and periodicity of course.

Whether the more sharply defined and narrowed boundaries of the DSM-I conception will prove fitting and fruitful is a matter of debate. The highly detailed and differentiated spelling out of characteristics suggests that the syndrome is more complexly variegated than it often proves clinically to be. Does this reflect the vast literature on the subject more than the diversity and richness of the population itself? The diagnostic criteria articulate quite a range behaviors, including delusions, thought broadcasting, bizarre thinking, and auditory hallucinations—a most colorful mosaic, yet one in which a significant and perhaps universally observed characteristic, that of "blunted affect," is among a wide-ranging group of symptoms subsumed within a single criterion number. It is hoped that future research will assist us in more accurately separating the primary symptoms of the disorder from those which are more "interesting" but less frequent or clinically salient.

## AFFECTIVE DISORDERS

The "affective disorders" in DSM-II were defined by the presence of a psychotic level of severity. By contrast, the DSM-III section includes all affective disorders, those of moderate and marked severity, those possessing either one or both of the manic and depressive components, and those which are unremitting and those which are more periodic. Two major factors determine the subdivisions of the affective disorder category: The first identifies those syndromes that are both episodic and of psychotic severity; the second comprises those tending toward chronicity and of moderate severity. Each of the preceding groups is divided into two subsets. The first contains those syndromes noted by the exclusive presence of depression; the second includes those in which both depressive and manic episodes occur. We end up, therefore, with four major syndromes in the affective disorder classification. Those which are of a severe and episodic nature and, further, exhibit depression exclusively, are labeled the "major depressions." Those similarly severe and episodic, but which evidence both depressive and manic periods, are referred to as "bipolar disorders." Moving to the second pair of this quartet, those syndromes displaying chronicity, moderate levels of severity, and depressive symptomatology exclusively are labeled "dysthymic disorders"; similar, moderately severe and chronic patterns, but with mixed or varying depressive and manic symptomatology, are referred to as "cyclothymic disorders." The severe and episodic pair are subsumed under the designation of "major affective disorders," whereas those of moderate severity and chronic duration are listed under the "specific affective disorders."

## ANXIETY DISORDERS

Various milder syndromes that previously were classed together have now been separated, following the elimination of the concept of neurosis as a unifying and overarching theme. Thus the "anxiety disorders" now include only those syndromes in which anxiety is either directly felt or displayed behaviorally. Excluded are a wide range of disorders that had previously been listed under the neuroses, owing to the belief that anxiety was present unconsciously but transformed into substitute symptoms via the operation of various defense mechanisms. The major syndromes within the anxiety category now include the "phobic disorders" which, in turn, subsume "agoraphobia," "social phobia," and "simple phobia"; these three presumably differ in their clinical picture, age of onset, and response to treatment. Next among the anxiety disorders is a classification entitled "anxiety states," which subsumes three subcategories: "panic disorder," "generalized anxiety," and "obsessive-compulsive disorders"; the logic that unified this grouping escaped the grasp of both myself and several of my Task Force colleagues. The third subgroup of the anxiety disorders is termed "post-traumatic stress disorder"; these are differentiated further into an acute type and a chronic or delayed variety.

## SOMATOFORM DISORDERS

This new title seeks to avoid the traditional term and concept of "hysteria." It represents a mental disorder in which symptoms suggestive of a physical disorder not only fail to produce palpable organic findings but often are a variance with known physiological mechanisms and anatomic structures. Included in these disorders are the "conversions," "hypochondriasis," and a new listing, the "psychogenic pain disorders." Another new label, "somatization disorder," has been introduced to represent individuals who have exhibited recurrent, multiple somatic difficulties over several years for which medical attention has been sought repeatedly despite a continuing failure to uncover an organic basis.

## ADJUSTMENT DISORDER

The "adjustment disorder" listing replaces the DSM-II category entitled "transient situational disturbances." Among its prime diagnostic criteria is the presence of an identifiable psychosocial stressor within a three-month period prior to the manifestation of the condition. Also characteristic of those exhibiting this disorder is the expectation that they will remit to their premorbid state after the stressor subsides. The adjustment classification is not to be utilized in cases where the response to the stressor is of so-called psychotic proportions. In a significant change from the DSM-II format, adjustment disorders are no longer categorized in terms of the individual's stage of life but, rather, in line with the predominant symptomatology exhibited, for example, with depressed mood, with mixed emotional features, and so on.

## PSYCHOLOGICAL FACTORS AFFECTING PHYSICAL CONDITION

The terminology used to represent these syndromes was modified following the Task Force's decision to disavow an exclusive adherence to a psychoanalytic interpretation of psychosomatic disorders. Moreover, numerous physical states, not previously encompassed within the traditional realm of psychosomatic disorders, give evidence of having been substantially influenced by psychological factors. The new DSM-III listings now permit the recording of these psychological influences in a much wider range of physical disorders than heretofore without necessarily connoting a primary role for psychodynamic processes. The procedure for diagnosing these syndromes requires coding the physical ailment on Axis III; all that is recorded on Axis I is the code number for this category.

## V CODES

Before proceeding to the personality disorder classifications, brief mention must be made of the V-code category, which represents "conditions not attributable to a mental disorder that are a focus of attention or treatment." Among the V-code social maladjustments that are often under the care of mental health professionals are "marital problems," "life circumstance problems," "occupational problems," "parent-child problems," "academic problems," as well as a variety of "antisocial behaviors" that do not signify the presence of a mental disorder.

## PERSONALITY DISORDERS

The most important fact concerning the DSM-III personality disorders is their partition from the main body of clinical syndromes and their placement in a separate axis. Clinicians in the past were often faced with the task of deciding whether a patient was best diagnosed as possessing a personality or a symptom syndrome; that choice is no longer necessary. Henceforth, clinicians may record not only the current clinical picture but also those characteristics which typify the individual's behaviors over extended periods, both prior to and concurrent with the present complaint. The new multiaxial format enables practitioners to place the clinical syndromes of Axis I within the context of the individual's lifelong and pervasive style of functioning, recorded as Axis II.

The personality disorders of DSM-III have been grouped, somewhat arbitrarily, into three clusters, the first characterized by odd or eccentric behaviors, the second by dramatic, emotional, or erratic behaviors, and the third by the notable presence of anxiety or fear. These clusters were devised by staff associates working with the Task Force chairman but were never affirmed by the committee as a whole to be either a relevant or a useful way to categorize the personality disorders. In fact, I wrote the following as part of a more extensive memorandum to my Task Force colleagues in 1978 in response to having seen the suggested clustering format for the first time:

I cannot understand the importance of those dimensions that led us to cluster personality disorders in the manner described. Any number of different dimensions could have been selected to group the eleven personality disorders in any of an almost infinite arrangement of sets or combinations. Why the specific one suggested in the text was selected out of these is not clear to me. Does it have some prognostic significance, some etiological import, logic in terms of a deductive theoretical model?

My own preference would be either to drop the new grouping entirely and list them alphabetically or to group them in terms of their known prevalence or potential severity. The likely severity of pathology, such as the probability to which these syndromes succumb to severe versus mild disorders, strikes me as a useful distinction if we are to make any one at all among these disorders.

There are two classification systems that are in current use which pay special attention to criteria for differentiating personality disorders along the dimension of severity, those of Kernberg (1967, 1970) and Millon (1969, 1981). The major distinction between Kernberg and Millon is not found in the clinical signs they include to gauge severity but, rather, in the ones they choose to emphasize. For Kernberg, primary attention is given to the *internal* structural characteristics of the personality, whereas for Millon the *external* social system and interpersonal dynamics are given a status equal to that of internal organization. A rationale for utilizing both intrapsychic and external dynamics as a basis for determining severity was outlined by Millon in the following:

The logic for broadening the criteria of severity to include the interplay of both individual and social systems seems especially appropriate when considering personality syndromes. Not only do personality traits express themselves primarily within group and familial environments, but the patient's style of communication, interpersonal competency, and social skill will, in great measure, elicit reactions that feed back to shape the future course of whatever impairments the person may already have. Thus, the behavior and attitudes that individuals exhibit with others will evoke reciprocal reactions that influence whether their problems will improve, stabilize or intensify. Internal organization or structure is significant, of course, but the character or style of relating interpersonally may have as much to do with whether the sequence of social dynamics will prove rewarding or destructive. It is not only the structural ego capacity, therefore, but also the particular features of social and familial behavior that will dispose the patient to relate to others in a manner that will prove increasingly adaptive or maladaptive. (1981, p. 651)

Utilizing this mixed intrapsychic and interpersonal system perspective led Millon to group the 11 personality disorders of the DSM-III into three broad categories. The first includes the dependent, histrionic, narcissistic, and antisocial personality disorders. The second group, that viewed at a moderate level of severity, numbers the compulsive, passive-aggressive, schizoid, and avoidant personality. The third set, reflecting still less competent levels of functioning, comprises the borderline, paranoid, and schizotypal disorders. An extended discussion of the rationale and clinical characteristics of these three levels of personality pathology are fully presented in Millon (1981).

Brief note should be made of a number of DSM-II personality disorders that are no longer part of the DSM-III group. Among them are the "asthenic" and the "inadequate" personalities, both of which were discarded owing to the infrequency with which they were utilized. The "cyclothymic" personality was transferred to the affective disorders classification, a decision that raised some controversy among Task Force members. Similarly, the "explosive" personality disorder was transferred from the personality classification to that of the "impulsive disorders" in light of its highly circumscribed and intermittent nature.

Among the new DSM-III categories are the "avoidant," "dependent," and "narcissistic" personalities. The initial drafts for the entire personality disorder section were written by the author in his role as a Task Force appointee. In these texts considerable attention was given to the contrast between the avoidant and the schizoid disorders. The avoidant's detachment is based upon a strong desire for social acceptance combined with a fear of rejection. In the schizoid the prime characteristic is a passively detached style of interpersonal behavior owing to a presumed intrinsic deficit in the capacity for affective and social gratification.

The dependent personality disorder parallels earlier DSM-I descriptions and represents diminished self-confidence combined with a search for security providing relationships. The narcissistic personality draft was not written within the framework of currently popular psychoanalytic authors, notably Kohut (1971) and Kernberg (1975) but, rather, derived from a social learning developmental model (Millon, 1969). The new "schizotypal" and "borderline" personality types were likewise written from a perspective at variance from traditional psychiatric roots. The schizotypal personality was conceived largely as an advanced or more severely dysfunctional variant of the schizoid and avoidant personalities and is characterized by intense social detachment and ec-

centric behaviors. To a parallel degree, the borderline personality was formulated to be a disintegrated dependent, histrionic, and passive-aggressive mix in which the individual's personal cohesion and interpersonal competence has insidiously deteriorated. Among the more controversial topics at Task Force meetings were discussions pertaining to the concept of an "antisocial" personality disorder. The diagnostic criteria selected for this syndrome are more properly suited for what may be termed the "criminal personality"; despite serious objections from many quarters, the criteria were retained with only modest alterations. The historical forerunners of the antisocial personality can be traced back some two to three centuries and provide an illuminating and fascinating tale of the role of medical misconceptions and cultural biases (Millon, 1981).

## TOWARD THE DSM-IV

Now that the DSM-III has been formally published and has become the standard nosology, it will soon assume a life of its own, utilized and interpreted in diverse ways by clinicians and researchers of all theoretical schools to suit whatever special purposes and orientations they may have. The rationale that led to the original concepts and terminology formulated by the Task Force will now play but a small part, as DSM-III users will increasingly transform the instrument to fit their own purposes. Few will be satisfied with every aspect of the manual, and it is sufficiently broad in scope to permit almost any clinician, theoretician, or researcher to wish to modify one or another segment because of his or her dissatisfactions. It is hoped that empirical research, theoretical evaluation, and constructive proposals will lead to a better DSM by the end of the decade (Millon & Klerman, in press).

Although it is clear that the Task Force's efforts to compromise diverse clinical and research perspectives contributed to its failure to produce a thoroughly unified manual, it is nevertheless desirable, in my view, that an even broader base of perspectives be brought to bear in the construction of the DSM-IV. For example, although several psychologists played active roles in the formulation of the DSM-III, the American Psychological Association and the National Association of Social Workers should be included as part of the official planning group for the next version. Had the Task Force included a more substantial representation of clinical psychologists and clinical social workers, several of the more knotty problems that arose would undoubtedly have been resolved more expeditiously. More important, their perspectives regarding the conceptual character and clinical relevance of the manual would have made the product both more scientific and more professionally useful. The following statement of Zigler and Phillips (1961), made in summarizing their review of the status of the field some twenty years ago, is still applicable today: "At this stage of our investigation, the system employed should be open and expanding. . . . Systems of classification must be treated as tools for further discovery, not bases for polemic disputation."

With this viewpoint as an introduction, let us proceed to suggestions concerning features which, if added to those already instituted in the DSM-III, will increase the clarity and utility of the DSM-IV.

## CONCEPTUALIZING SYNDROMES AS PROTOTYPES

There is need to explicitly recognize the intrinsic heterogeneity of the syndromes comprising the DSM-III and thereby formalize the paradigm shift that has occurred from a "disease entity" to a "prototypical" diagnostic model. The Task Force moved implicitly in the direction of what Cronbach and Meehl (1955) have termed "bandwidth fidelity," in which a balance is struck between conceptual breadth and measurement

of identification precision. Cantor et al. address this issue as follows:

> The recent revisions in the standard diagnostic manual have brought the system even closer to the prototype view than before. Diagnostic criteria are now presented as prototypes—larger sets of correlated features rather than selected defining ones: guidelines for diagnosis also emphasize the potential heterogeneity of the symptoms of like-diagnosed patients. Moreover, a potential for overlap in clinical features across different diagnostic categories is underscored. . . . They help to emphasize, rather than obscure, the probabilistic nature of diagnostic categorizations.
>
> The recent changes . . . represent a shift in beliefs similar to ones occurring in other domains, away from the classical view of categorization systems and toward the prototype view. (1980, pp. 191–192)

## EMPLOYING A COHERENT AND QUANTIFIABLE THEORY

The DSM-III classification was not only derived intentionally in an atheoretical manner, but no coherent theoretical system was seriously explored to provide a consistent framework for coordinating the various syndromes (Millon, 1969, 1981). Such a conceptual schema would be helpful, even if the established nosology was reliably anchored to empirical research, which it is not. If all the principal clinical syndromes or personality disorders could be logically derived from a systematic theoretical foundation, this would greatly facilitate an understanding of psychopathology, organize this knowledge in an orderly and consistent fashion, and connect the data it provides to other realms of psychological theory and research, where they could then be subjected to empirical verification or falsification (Hempel, 1952; Popper, 1972). In this manner, psychopathology might advance much in the way as has physics. In describing the features that have given physics much of its success as a scientific discipline, Meehl notes, "The physicist's scientific power comes from two . . . sources, namely, the immense deductive fertility of the formalism and the accuracy of the measuring instruments" (1978, p. 825).

In line with the preceding, Skinner (1981) has proposed the development of classification frameworks based on theories supplemented by parallel "operational measures." Using as a guide the principles and methods of "construct validation," originally developed in the field of psychometrics, Skinner evaluates a number of clinical theory constructs that possess supporting quantifying instruments as possible bases for a new classification schema. Notable among those that fit the construct validation model he espouses is the "schizoid taxon concept" proposed by Meehl (1979), the "interpersonal system" devised by Benjamin (1979), and the "biosocial personality theory" of psychopathology formulated by Millon (1969, 1981).

## SPECIFYING RELATIONSHIPS AMONG SYNDROMES

Although the DSM-III provides a multiaxial schema in which relationships that exist among clinical categories can be noted, each syndrome is still organized as if it were a discrete entity of clustered clinical signs independent and distinct from other syndromes. A framework that would spell out the inevitable overlap that occurs among diagnostic groups would enable the clinician to immediately identify the intrinsic covariations that do exist among clinical disorders. Especially valuable would be the illumination of relationships between personality vulnerabilities and coping styles, on the one hand, and specific clinical symptom disorders, on the other. What is likely to be needed to achieve this end is more than a format that merely organizes the fragmented nature of the current nosology, but one, as noted previously, that is based on theoretical principles which furnish the logic and point out the bases for commonalities and interconnections observed in the clinical world.

## COMPARABILITY AND PARALLELISM AMONG SYNDROMES

Although it may be difficult to identify and "carve those joints" which meaningfully divide the raw behaviors and traits that comprise clinical symptoms, we should, at the very least, utilize similar units and intervals throughout the diagnostic criteria of the DSM. Inconsistencies in the clinical phenomena that embody the diagnostic criteria will only result in a lack of comparability and parallelism among clinical assessments. Certain commonalities must be routinely addressed to ensure that the different syndromes can be compared and differentiated. Although, for example, the dimensions that can be included to assess personality disorders may range across a very wide domain of clinical phenomena, it would make good scientific and practical sense if certain specific realms were consistently addressed, for example, affective response, style of cognitive functioning, pattern of interpersonal behaviors, self-concept, and so on.

## CONSTRUCTION OF A SITUATIONAL TAXONOMY

It is an exceptional achievement that the DSM-III instituted even its rudimentary taxonomy of psychosocial stressors. This should be seen, however, only as a beginning, a preparatory step for future DSMs to recognize more fully that behaviors and settings interact in lawful, interdependent systems and, most relevantly, that people do behave differently in different settings (Barker, 1966; Endler & Magnusson, 1976; Millon, 1975; Moos, 1972; Willems, Note b). Serious thought must be given to formulate a taxonomic schema that will provide a systematic framework for sampling clinically relevant psychosocial situations, both stressful and commonplace. As I noted in an earlier paper:

A rose may be a rose, but it is a different rose if it is presented to your wife in a birthday bouquet than if seen in passing as one among many in a garden. . . . Behavioral signs cannot be abstracted from their psychological and situational context without leading to false equivalencies. . . . Hallucination 1 is simply not the same as hallucination 2 if they are a part of different behavioral and situational configurations. It is precisely this patterned and multivariate cluster of behaviors, set within a comparably delineated situational context, that can best serve as a framework for developing new syndrome groupings. (1975, p. 461)

## PROVIDING AN INTERPERSONAL ORIENTATION

Numerous writers have suggested that the interpersonal dimension provides a particularly useful conceptual foundation for developing a diagnostic schema (Leary & Coffey, 1955; McLemore & Benjamin, 1979; Millon, 1969, 1981; Wiggins, 1982). Similarly, other authors have indicated that interpersonal behaviors are of particular significance from the viewpoint of providing a useful prognostic index, contributing to understanding therapeutic interactions and exposing significant aspects of etiology. Now that greater attention is being directed toward the personality disorders in the DSM-III, the logic for strengthening the interpersonal dimension is further enhanced. This can best be illustrated by the fact that the interpersonal "style" an individual employs to achieve goals and to resolve conflicts with others invariably evokes counteractions that will directly influence whether his or her problems stabilize, improve, or lead to further distress and decompensation. It is with these considerations in mind that the next task force might do well to ensure that interpersonal aspects of behavior are further highlighted in the specification of future diagnostic criteria.

## NEED TO INCORPORATE RESEARCH DATA

It has been argued (McReynolds, 1979), and not without justification, that in most fields of scientific inquiry the advent of new concepts and categories reflects the emergence of new observations and insights. Such would

be the case in psychopathology if there were fundamental technological advances or discoveries that led to an increased understanding and capacity to describe new clinical disorders and syndromes. Unfortunately, what few advances have taken place in either theory or methodology cannot account for the tremendous proliferation of new or refined DSM-III categories. With some notable exceptions, for example, changes in the criteria for schizophrenia and the addition of theoretically derived personality syndromes, most DSM-III syndromes adhere closely to those formulated by Kraepelin, Freud, and their followers some three-quarters of a century ago. Substantial empirical and theoretical advances have certainly taken place in recent decades, but few of these have influenced the overall framework and syndromic particulars of the DSM. For example, the careful studies of Lorr (1966; Lorr, Klett, & McNair, 1963) suggest numerous modifications that would increase both the distinctness and homogeneity of the more severe disorders, but these have played almost no role in rethinking the major syndromic groups. Most encouraging, however, is the introduction of diagnostic criteria and the realignment of categories into several data axes. These steps make the DSM-III a significantly more researchable instrument, one that both facilitates and is much more open to empirical evaluation than its predecessors. Hence the Task Force failed to construct an instrument that reflected previous research, but it has developed one that encourages more precise and comparable studies in the future. It is hoped that future task forces will avail themselves of the research data that will be generated as a consequence of the heuristic framework provided by the DSM-III.

## INCLUSION OF ETIOLOGICAL CONSIDERATIONS

Classification based on etiology is well established in most fields of medicine and would be a notable achievement in psychopathology. However, this aspiration faces many difficulties given the complex network of subtle and almost random influences that give rise and shape to the mental disorders. The fact that the Task Force bypassed etiological variables so as to minimize dispute and to facilitate acceptance of the DSM-III by clinicians of diverse orientations is no reason to abandon the search. The DSM-III criteria will facilitate etiological as well as other research endeavors, and the data these bring forth should be considered in the reconstruction of syndrome categories. There is no intrinsic reason why etiological variables cannot play as important a role in psychopathologic classification as do descriptive and inferred clinical properties. Along similar lines, there is need to include, where feasible, the continuity displayed in behavior through life and, more relevantly and specifically, the developmental progression that often exists between the individual's premorbid personality style and subsequent clinical disorder.

## INCORPORATION OF THERAPEUTIC IMPLICATIONS

It is unfortunate that classifications based on clinical description alone will often group patients who, upon more careful evaluation, react to life situations, including their response to treatment, in substantially different manners. Hence, given its centrality to the clinical enterprise, classification categories should be designed to embody whatever data are accessible concerning the therapeutic efforts of various treatment modalities. With the minor exception of the psychopharmacologic agents, the DSM-III offers very little that is concrete in this regard, owing in great measure, of course, to the scanty evidence at hand for such purposes. Here, as noted previously, the empirically oriented framework and criteria of the DSM-III should facilitate future, systematic research of this nature. It is hoped that studies which deal with both the prediction of therapeutic response and the matching of treatment to diagnosis will become increasingly available for consideration in classifying DSM-IV-diagnostic syndromes.

## CONCLUDING COMMENTS

Reflecting on his labors while serving as chairman of the Task Force for the DSM-II, Gruenberg (1969) noted that the instability of mental health diagnostic schemas over the centuries led him to wonder whether the excitement concerning the appropriateness of one or another classification might not actually reflect a deep need on the part of its contributors to obscure their lack of knowledge. Engaging in fruitless but easily belabored debates over new terms and clever categories may be a simple displacement of effort in which one pretends that "correct" labels and taxonomies are themselves the knowledge gaps that exist. Having participated over an intense five-year period as a member of the DSM-III committee, I am considerably more charitable about the purposes and success with which this Task Force met its responsibilities. I have no illusions, however, that we completed the task. On the other hand, I am convinced that the DSM-III represents not only a significant step forward in and of itself but that it also provides a solid foundation for further progress.

## REFERENCES

Albee, G. W. Letter to the editor. *APA Monitor,* 1977, *89* (11)9, 1–2.

American Psychiatric Association. *Diagnostic and Statistical Manual of Mental Disorders (DSM-III).* Washington, DC: Author, 1980.

Barker, R. *The stream of behavior.* New York: Appleton-Century-Crofts, 1966.

Cantor, N., Smith, E. E., French, R., & Mezzich, J. Psychiatric diagnoses as prototype categorization. *Journal of Abnormal Psychology,* 1980, *89,* 181–193.

Cronbach, L. J., & Meehl, P. E. Construct validity in psychological tests. *Psychological Bulletin,* 1955, *529,* 281–302.

Endler, N. S., & Magnusson, D. Toward an interactional psychology of personality. *Psychological Bulletin*, 1976, *93*, 956–974.

Essen-Moller, E., & Wohfahrt, S. Suggestions for the amendment of the official Swedish classification of mental disorders. *Acta Psychiatrica Scandinavica, Supplementum*, 1947, No. 47, 551–555.

Garmezy, N. Never mind the psychologists: Is it good for children? *Clinical Psychologist*, 1978, *31*(3/4)9, 1–6.

Gruenberg, E. M. How can the new diagnostic manual help? *International Journal of Psychiatry*, 1969, *7*, 368–374.

Hempel, C. G. *Fundamentals of concept formation in empirical science.* Chicago: University of Chicago Press, 1952.

Kernberg, O. F. Borderline personality organization. *Journal of the American Psychoanalytic Association*, 1967, *15*, 641–685.

Kernberg, O. F. A psychoanalytic classification of character pathology. *Journal of the American Psychoanalytic Association*, 1970, *18*, 800–822.

Kohut, H. *The analysis of self.* New York: International Universities Press, 1971.

Kuhn, T. S. *The structure of scientific revolutions.* Chicago: University of Chicago Press, 1962.

Leary, T., & Coffey, H. S. Interpersonal diagnoses: Some problems of methodology and validation. *Journal of Abnormal and Social Psychology*, 1955, *50*, 110–124.

Lemkau, P. V. The anatomy of a group of illnesses and states. *International Journal of Psychiatry*, 1969, *79*, 412–413.

Lorr, M. *Explorations in typing psychotics.* Oxford: Pergamon, 1966.

Lorr, M., Klett, C. J., & McNair, D. M. *Syndromes of psychosis.* New York: Macmillan, 1963.

McLemore, C. W., & Benjamin, L. S. Whatever happened to interpersonal diagnosis? A psychological alternative to DSM-III. *American Psychologist*, 1979, *34*, 17–34.

McReynolds, W. T. DSM-III and the future of applied social science. *Professional Psychology*, 1979, *10*, 123–132.

Meehl, P. E. Theoretical risks and tabular risks: Sir Karl, Sir Ronald, and the slow progress of soft psychology. *Journal of Consulting and Clinical Psychology*, 1978, *469*, 806–834.

Meehl, P. E. A funny thing happened to us on the way to the latent entities. *Journal of Personality Assessment*, 1979, *439*, 364–380.

Mezzich, J. Patterns and issues in multiaxial psychiatric diagnosis. *Psychological Medicine*, 1979, *99*, 125–137.

Millon, T. *Modern psychopathology: A biosocial approach to maladaptive learning and functioning.* Philadelphia: Saunders, 1969.

Millon, T. Reflections on Rosenhan's "On being sane or insane places." *Journal of Abnormal Psychology*, 1975, *84*, 456–461.

Millon, T. *Disorders of personality. DSM-III, Axis II.* New York: Wiley, 1981.

Millon, T., & Klerman, G. *1. Contemporary diagnosis in psychopathology: Towards the DSM-IV.* New York: Guilford, in press.

Moos, R. Assessment of the psychosocial environments of community-oriented psychiatric treatment programs. *Journal of Abnormal Psychology*, 1972, *799*, 9–18.

Popper, K. R. *The logic of scientific discovery.* London: Hutchinson, 1972.

Rutter, M., Shaffer, D., & Shepherd, M. *A multiaxial classification of child psychiatric disorders.* Geneva: World Health Organization, 1975.

Schacht, T., & Nathan, P. E. But is it good for the psychologists? Appraisal and status of DSM-III. *American Psychologist*, 1977, *32*, 1017–1025.

Schneider, K. *Klinische Psychopathblogie.* Stuttgart: Thieme, 1976.

Skinner, H. A. Toward the integration of classification theory and methods. *Journal of Abnormal Psychology*, 1981, *90*, 68–87.

Spitzer, R. L., Sheehy, M., & Endicott, J. DSM-III: Guiding principles. In V. M. Rakoff, H. C. Stancer, & H. B. Kedward (Eds.), *Psychiatric diagnosis.* New York: Brunner/Mazel, 1977.

Stengel, E. Classification of mental disorders. *Bulletin of the World Health Organization*, 1959, *219*, 601–663.

Strauss, J. S. A comprehensive approach to psychiatric diagnosis. *American Journal of Psychiatry*, 1975, *132*, 1193–1197.

Wiggins, J. S. Circumplex models of interpersonal behavior in clinical psychology. In P. C. Kendall & J. N. Butcher (Eds.), *Handbook of research methods in clinical psychology*. New York: Wiley, 1982.

World Health Organization. *Manual of the international statistical classification of diseases, injuries and causes of death* (9th rev.). Geneva: Author, 1977.

Zigler, E., & Phillips, L. Psychiatric diagnoses and symptomatology. *Journal of Abnormal and Social Psychology,* 1961, *639,* 69–75.

Zubin, J. But is it good for science? *Clinical Psychologist,* 1978, *31*(2), 1–7.

# On the Genesis and Prevalence of the Borderline Personality Disorder: A Social Learning Thesis

Despite exegetic brilliance, I am concerned that the Talmudic habit of intricate and abstruse argument, most notably within the analytic community, has drawn us into recondite intellectual territories, leading us to overlook the impact of more obvious and palpable social forces generative of the borderline personality disorder (BPD). Though less labyrinthine and tortuous, the data base for biologic conjectures favoring constitutional origins is nonetheless equivocal, if not controvertible. Unfortunately, the riveting effects of the internecine struggles between and within competing analytic and biologic theories keep us fixated on obscure and largely unfalsifiable etiologic hypotheses, precluding thereby serious consideration of notions that may possess superior logic and validity. It is toward this latter goal that the present commentary is addressed.

By no means is the role of constitution or early experience dismissed. Nevertheless, the logical and evidential base for currently popular hypotheses is briefly examined and left wanting. Supplementary proposals that favor the deductive and probative primacy of social learning factors are posited. They point to a wide array of influences that either set in place or further embed those deficits in psychic cohesion that lie at the heart of the disorder. Specifically, the view is advanced that our contemporary epidemic of BPD can best be attributed to two broad sociocultural trends that have come to characterize much of Western life this past quarter century, namely the emergence of social customs that exacerbate rather

than remediate early, errant parent-child relationships and, second, the diminished power of formerly reparative institutions to compensate for these ancient and ubiquitous relationship problems.

To raise questions about either the validity or adequacy of one or another theoretical model is not to take issue with all aspects of its formulations; much of what has been proposed concerning the nature and origins of the BPD has both substantive merit and heuristic value. One may offer a compelling, if not persuasive, alternative and yet be entirely sympathetic to the major tenets of that which has been critically examined. Such is the case in what follows; the alternative proposed is more in the nature of an addendum than a supplantation. Hence, we will begin our essay with reference to views shared rather than disputed.

Before noting themes in common, a few additional words of précis should be said about the faddistic character of the borderline construct. It is, in my judgment, overly diagnosed, having become a wastebasket for many patients who demonstrate that protean constellation of multiple symptoms that characterize the syndrome. Exhibiting almost all of the clinical attributes known to descriptive psychopathology, borderline conditions lend themselves to a simplistic, if not perverse form of diagnostic logic; that is, patients who display a potpourri of clinical indices, especially where symptomatic relationships are unclear or seem inconsistent, must perforce be borderlines.

Having stated my dismay over contemporary diagnostic fashions and fallibilities, let me record my firm belief in both the clinical existence and the significantly increased incidence of borderline conditions these past two to three decades (Simonsen & Mellergard, in press). Voguish or not, I believe the emergence of these disorders is a "real" phenomenon, albeit, in my view, not for the reasons advanced by contending analytic and biologic theories.

## SPHERES OF SUBSTANTIVE AGREEMENT

Overdiagnosed and elusive as the syndrome has been—approached from innumerable and diverse analytic perspectives (e.g., Eriksonian, Kernbergian, Mahlerian, Kohutian), as well as clothed in an assortment of novel conceptual terms (identity diffusion, self-object representations, projective identification)—there remain, nevertheless, certain shared observations that demonstrate the continued clinical astuteness and heuristic fertility of the analytic mindset. Whatever doubts one may have with respect to either the logical or methodological merit of conjectures posed by our modern cadre of third-generation analytic thinkers (Eagle, 1984), they deserve more than passing commendation, not only for their willingness to break from earlier and perhaps anachronistic etiologic notions, but for their perspicacity in discerning and portraying the key features of a new and major clinical entity. Similarly, contemporary biogenic theorists (e.g., Klein, Akiskal) are to be congratulated for the care with which they have adduced empirical data favoring their views.

Overlooking for the present seemingly intractable conflicts between and within analytic, biologic, and social learning schools of thought (Millon, 1987a), let me note what I believe to be the key borderline features that contemporary theorists of each orientation appear to judge salient and valid.

There is reasonable consensus that a pervasive instability and ambivalence intrudes constantly into the stream of the borderline's everyday life, resulting in fluctuating attitudes, erratic or uncontrolled emotions, and a general capriciousness and undependability. Impulsive, unpredictable, and often explosive, it is difficult for others to be comfortable in their presence. Both relatives and acquaintances feel "on edge," waiting for these patients to display a sullen and hurt look or become obstinate and nasty. In being unpredictably contrary, manipulative, and volatile, borderlines often elicit rejection rather than the support they seek. Displaying marked shifts in mood, they may exhibit extended periods of dejection and apathy interspersed with spells of anger, anxiety, or excitement.

Dejection, depression, and self-destructive acts are common. Their anguish and despair is genuine, but it also is a means of expressing hostility, a covert instrumentality to frustrate and retaliate. Angered by the failure of others to be nurturant, borderlines employ moods and threats as vehicles to "get back," to "teach them a lesson." By exaggerating their plight and by moping about, borderlines avoid responsibilities and place added burdens on others, causing their families not only to care for them, but to suffer and feel guilt while doing so. In the same way, cold and stubborn silence may function as an instrument of punitive blackmail, a way of threatening others that further trouble is in the offing. Easily nettled, offended by trifles, borderlines are readily provoked into being sullen and contrary. They are impatient and irritable, unless things go their way.

Cognitively capricious, borderlines may exhibit rapidly changing and often antithetical thoughts concerning themselves and others, as well as the odds and ends of passing events. They voice dismay about the sorry state of their life, their sadness, their resentments, their "nervousness." Many feel discontent, cheated, and unappreciated, their efforts have been for naught; they have been misunderstood and are disillusioned. The obstructiveness, pessimism, and immaturity which others attribute to them are only a reflection, they feel, of their "sensitivity" and the inconsiderateness that others have shown. But here again, ambivalence intrudes; perhaps, they say, it is their own unworthiness, their own failures, and their own "bad temper" which is the cause of their misery and the pain they bring to others.

The affective and interpersonal instability of borderlines may be traced in great measure to their defective psychic structures, their failure to develop internal cohesion and hierarchic priorities. Both a source and a consequence of this lack of inner harmony is the borderlines' uncertain sense of self, the confusions they experience of either an immature, nebulous, or wavering sense of identity. Hence, the deeper structural undergirding for intrapsychic regulation and interpersonal processing provides an inadequate scaffolding for both psychic continuity and self-integration. Segmented and fragmented, subjected to the flux of their own contradictory attitudes and enigmatic actions, their very sense of being remains precarious. Their erratic and conflicting inclinations continue as both cause and effect, generating new experiences that feed back and reinforce an already diminished sense of wholeness. . . .

## SUPPLEMENTARY SOCIAL LEARNING THESIS

Although the logic of biogenic conjectures justifies critical examination, the following comments will be limited to the philosophic and empirical grounding of psychoanalytic theories, owing to their far greater currency among contemporary clinicians.

The premise that early experience plays a central role in shaping personality attributes is one shared by both analytic and social learning theorists. To say the preceding, however, is not to agree as to which specific factors during these developing years are critical in generating particular attributes, nor is it to agree that known formative influences are either necessary or sufficient. Analytic theorists almost invariably direct their etiologic attentions to the realm of early childhood experience. Unfortunately, they differ vigorously among themselves (e.g.. Kernberg, Kohut, Mahler/Masterson, Erikson) as to which aspects of nascent life are crucial to development.

A few words of a more-or-less philosophic nature are in order concerning the concept of "etiology" itself; as in other matters that call for an incisive explication of the nature of psychopathologic constructs, the reader is directed to the writings of Meehl (1972, 1977). In these essays it is made abundantly clear that the concept of etiology itself is a "fuzzy notion," one that not only requires the careful separation of constituent empirical elements, but one that calls for differentiating its diverse conceptual meanings, ranging from "strong" influences that are both causally necessary and/or sufficient, through progressively "weaker" levels of specificity, in which causal factors exert consistent, though quantitatively marginal differences to those which are merely coincidental or situationally circumstantial. . . .

The preceding critique of the epistemic and probative foundations of our discipline's theoretic assertions may seem unduly severe, perhaps even discourteous to analytic colleagues whose views have been singled out for critical note. Despite appearances, however, I consider myself a loyal, if peripheral "follower," one not only sympathetic to both historic and contemporary psychoanalytic formulations, but one whose own views have been informed by and continue to rest on the foundations they provide. Thus, despite retaining aspects of my earlier conceptions of the "borderline" levels of personality pathology (Millon, 1969, 1981), I have restructured ideas in significant ways this past decade owing to the thoughtful contributions of numerous contemporary analytic writers.

What follows is not intended, therefore, to supplant the core notions proposed by present-day analytic theorists concerning the experiential background of the BPD, despite their own divergences and the unfalsifiability of their propositions—but should be seen as an addendum, a proposal that contends that societal customs which served in the past to repair disturbances in early parent-child relations have declined in their efficacy, and have been "replaced" over the past two to three decades with customs that exacerbate these difficulties, contributing thereby to what I would term our contemporary BPD "epidemic."

The central questions guiding this commentary are, first, what are the primary sources of influence that give rise to symptoms that distinguish the BPD, namely an inability to maintain psychic cohesion in realms of affect, self-image, and interpersonal relationships; and second, which of these sources has had its impact heightened over the past two to three decades, accounting thereby for the rapid and marked increase in the incidence of the disorder?

The first question will not be elaborated, other than to note the observation that well-reasoned yet contending formulations have been posited by constitutional, analytic, and social learning theorists; and, despite important divergencies, there is a modest consensus that biogenic, psychogenic, and sociogenic factors each contribute in relevant ways.

It is the second question which calls for explication: it relates to which of these three etiologic factors, each productive of the borderlines' diffuse or segmented personality structure—constitutional disposition, problematic early nurturing, or contemporary social changes—has shown a substantial shift in recent decades; is it some unidentified yet fundamental alteration in the intrinsic biological makeup of current-day youngsters; is it some significant and specifiable change in the character with which contemporary mothers nurture their infants and rear their toddlers; or is it traceable to fundamental and rapid changes in Western culture that have generated divisive and discordant life experiences, while reducing the availability of psychically cohering and reparative social customs and institutions?

Despite the fact that tangible evidence favoring one or another of these possibilities is not accessible in the conventional sense of empirical "proof," it is our contention that the third "choice" is probatively more sustainable and inferentially more plausible. Toward these ends, two sociocultural trends generative of the segmented psychic structures that typify the BPD will be elucidated. Although they are interwoven substantively and chronologically, these trends are separated for conceptual and pedagogic purposes. One adds to the severity of psychic dissonance; it appears to have been on the upgrade. The other has taken a distinct downturn, and its loss also contributes to diminished psychic cohesion.

## INCREASE IN DIVISIVE AND DIFFUSING SOCIAL CUSTOMS

We are immersed deeply both in our time and culture, obscuring thereby our ability to discern many profound changes that may be underway in our society's institutions, changes often generative of unforeseen psychic and social consequences, Tom Wicker, the distinguished columnist for the *New York Times,* portrays sequential effects such as these in the following graphic quote (1987):

When a solar-powered water pump was provided for a well in India, the village headman took it over and sold the water, until stopped. The new liquid abundance attracted hordes of unwanted nomads. Village boys who had drawn water in buckets had nothing to do and some became criminals. The gap between rich and poor widened, since the poor had no land to benefit from irrigation. Finally, village women broke the pump, so they could gather again around the well that had been the center of their social lives.

Not all forms of contemporary change can so readily be reversed. "Progress" wrought by modern-day education and technology is too powerful to be turned aside or nullified, no less reversed, despite "conservative" efforts to revoke or undo their inexorable effects.

Klerman (1987), reviewing the increased prevalence of depressive disorders among the young today, contends that an as yet unidentified cohort effect, which he terms "Agent Blue," may be operative. Inclined to ascribe this pathologic drift to Easterlin and Crimmin's (1985) thesis that the baby boom has created a deterioration in economic possibilities among contemporary youth. Klerman notes that this group was raised in relative affluence and is physically the most healthy population in history; nevertheless, they paradoxically are suffering an epidemic of mental disorders.

Whether or not one assigns our increased incidence in youthful affective disorders to the waxing and waning of population parameters, it is both intuitively and observationally self-evident that sweeping cultural changes can affect innumerable social practices, including those of an immediate and personal nature, such as patterns of child nurturing and rearing, marital affiliation, family cohesion, leisure style, entertainment content, and so on. We will turn next to contemporary changes such as these, narrowing our focus to those cultural transitions conducive to the formation of psychic diffusion and division.

### Mirrored Social Discordance

It would not be too speculative to assert that the organization, coherence, and stability of a culture's institutions are in great measure reflected in the psychic structure and cohesion of its members. In a manner analogous to the DNA double helix, in which each paired strand unwinds and selects environmental nutrients to duplicate its jettisoned partner, so too does each culture fashion its constituent members to fit an extant template. In societies whose customs and institutions are fixed and definitive, the psychic composition of its citizenry will likewise be structured; and where a society's values and practices are fluid and inconsistent, so too

will its residents evolve deficits in psychic solidity and stability.

This latter, more amorphous, cultural state, so characteristic of our modern times, is clearly mirrored in the interpersonal vacillations and affective instabilities that typify the BPD. Central to our recent culture have been the increased pace of social change and the growing pervasiveness of ambiguous and discordant customs to which children are expected to subscribe. Under the cumulative impact of rapid industrialization, immigration, urbanization, mobility, technology, and mass communication, there has been a steady erosion of traditional values and standards. Instead of a simple and coherent body of practices and beliefs, children find themselves confronted with constantly shifting styles and increasingly questioned norms whose durability is uncertain and precarious.

No longer do youngsters find the certainties and absolutes which guided earlier generations. The complexity and diversity of everyday experience play havoc with simple "archaic" beliefs, and render them useless as instruments to deal with contemporary realities. Lacking a coherent view of life, maturing youngsters find themselves groping and bewildered, swinging from one set of principles and models to another, unable to find stability either in their relationships or in the flux of events. Few times in history have so many children faced the tasks of life without the aid of accepted and durable traditions. Not only does the strain of making choices among discordant standards and goals beset them at every turn, but these competing beliefs and divergent demands prevent them from developing either internal stability or external consistency. And no less problematic in generating such disjoined psychic structures is the escalation of emotionally capricious and interpersonally discordant role models.

### Schismatic Family Structures

Although transformations in family patterns and relationships have evolved fairly continuously over the past century, the speed and nature of transitions since the Second World War have been so radical as to break the smooth line of earlier trends. Hence, today the typical child no longer has a clear sense of either the character or the purpose of his father's work activities, much less a detailed image of the concrete actions that comprise that work. Beyond the little there is of the father's daily routines to model oneself after, mothers of young children have shifted their activities increasingly outside the home, seeking career fulfillments or needing dual incomes to sustain family aspirations. Not only are everyday adult activities no longer available for direct observation and modeling, but traditional gender roles, once distinct and valued, have become blurred and questionable. Today, there is little that is rewarded and esteemed by the larger society that takes place for children to see and emulate. What "real" and "important" people do cannot be learned from parents who return from a day's work too preoccupied or too exhausted to share their esoteric activities. Lost, then, are the crystallizing and focusing effects of identifiable and stable role models which give structure and direction to maturing psychic processes. This loss contributes significantly to the maintenance of the undifferentiated and diffuse personality organization so characteristic of many borderlines.

With the growing dissolution of the traditional family structure there has been a marked increase in parental separation, divorce, and remarriage. Children subject to persistent parental bickering and family restructuring not only are exposed to changing and destructive models for imitative learning but develop the internal schisms that typify borderline behaviors. The stability of life, so necessary for the acquisition of a consistent pattern of feeling and thinking, is shattered when erratic conditions or marked controversy prevail. There may be an ever-present apprehension that a parent will be totally lost through divorce; dissension may lead to the

undermining of one parent by the other, and a nasty and cruel competition for the loyalty and affections of children may ensue. Constantly dragged into the arena of parental schisms, the child not only loses a sense of security and stability, but is subjected to paradoxical behaviors and contradictory role models. Raised in such settings a child not only suffers the constant threat of family dissolution but, in addition, is often forced to serve as a mediator to moderate conflicts between the parents. Forced to switch sides and divide loyalties, the child cannot be "an individual," but must internalize opposing attitudes and emotions to satisfy antagonistic parental desires and expectations. The different roles the child must assume to placate the parents are markedly divergent: as long as the parents remain at odds, the child persists with behaviors, thoughts, and emotions that are intrinsically irreconcilable.

For many children divorce not only undermines the sense that one can count on things to endure, but it often dislodges formerly secure and crucial internalizations within one's psychic self, upsetting the fusions and integrations that evolved among once incorporated parental models and standards. Alienated from parental attachments, as well as often disillusioned and cynical, these internalized structures may now be totally jettisoned. Moreover, the confidence that one can depend in the future on a previously internalized belief or precept may now be seriously undermined. Devoid of stabilizing internalizations, such youngsters may come to prefer the attractions of momentary and passing encounters of high salience and affective power. Unable to gauge what to expect from their environment, how can they be sure that things that are true today will be there tomorrow? Have they not experienced capriciousness when things appeared stable? Unlike children who can predict their fate, good, bad, or indifferent—such youngsters are unable to fathom what the future will bring. At any moment, and for no apparent reason, they may receive the kindness and support they crave; equally possible, and for equally unfathomable reasons, they may be the recipient of hostility and rejection. Having no way of determining which course of action will bring security and stability, such youngsters vacillate, feeling hostility, guilt, compliance, assertion, and so on, shifting erratically and impulsively from one tentative action to another. Unable to predict whether one's parents will be critical or affectionate, they must be ready for hostility when most might expect commendation, assume humiliation when most would anticipate reward. Eternally "on-edges" emotions build up, raw to the touch, ready to react impulsively and unpredictably at the slightest provocation.

### Capricious TV Models

Other "advances" in contemporary society have stamped deep and distinct impressions as well, ones equally effectively loaded, erratic, and contradictory. The rapidly moving, emotionally intense, and interpersonally capricious character of TV role models, displayed in swiftly progressing half-hour vignettes that encompass a lifetime, add to the impact of disparate, highly charged, and largely inimical value standards and behavior models. What is incorporated is not only a multiplicity of selves, but an assemblage of unintegrated and discordant roles, displayed indecisively and fit-fully, especially among those youngsters bereft of secure moorings and internal gyroscopes. The striking images created by our modem-day flickering parental surrogate have replaced all other sources of cultural guidance for many; hence, by age 18, the typical American child will have spent more time watching TV than in going to school or relating directly to his parents.

TV may be nothing but simple pablum for those with comfortably internalized models of real human relationships, but for those who possess a world of diffuse values and standards, or one in which parental precepts and norms have been discarded, the impact of these "substitute" prototypes is especially powerful, even idealized and romanticized. And what these TV characters and story plots present to vulnerable youngsters are the stuff of which successful half-hour "life stories" must be composed to capture the attention and hold the fascination of their audiences—violence, danger, agonizing dilemmas, and unpredictability, each expressed and resolved in an hour or less—precisely those features of social behavior and emotionality that come to characterize the affective and interpersonal instabilities of the borderline.

### Mind-Blurring Drugs

To add to this disorienting and cacophonous melange are aggravations consequent to drug and alcohol involvements. Although youth is a natural period for exploratory behaviors of which many are both socially adaptive and developmentally constructive, much of what is explored entails high risks with severe adverse consequences in both the short and long run. Viewed, however, from the perspective of youngsters who see little in life that has proven secure or desirable, the risks of these all too-accessible substances are experienced neither as intimidating nor perilous. While they may be considered by many to be casual and recreational, their psychic effects are quite hazardous, especially among the already vulnerable. Thus, for the borderline-prone, the impact of these substances will only further diminish the clarity and focus of their feeble internalized structures, as well as dissolving whatever purposefulness and aspirations they may have possessed to guide them toward potentially reparative actions. Together, these mind-blurring effects add fresh weight to already established psychic diffusions.

## DECREASE IN REPARATIVE AND COHERING SOCIAL CUSTOMS

As noted previously, the task of attaining integration is not an easy one in a world of changing events and practices. What is best?

What is right? How shall I handle this or think about that? Questions such as these plague the growing child at every turn. On top of these everyday perplexities, how can children subjected additionally to parental hostility or indifference acquire guidelines for a well-integrated and socially approved system of beliefs and actions? From what source can a consistent, valued, and effective set of internalized feelings, attitudes, and relationships be consolidated?

The fabric of traditional and organized societies not only comprises standards designed to educate and inculcate the young, but it also provides "insurance," if you will, backups to compensate and repair system defects and failures. Extended families, church leaders, schoolteachers, and neighbors provide nurturance and role models by which children experiencing troubling parental relationships can find a means of support and affection, enabling them thereby to be receptive to society's established body of norms and values. Youngsters subjected to any of the diffusing and divisive forces described previously must find one or another of these culturally sanctioned sources of surrogate modeling and sustenance to give structure and direction to their emerging capacities and impulses. Without such bolstering, maturing potentials are likely to become diffuse and scattered. Without admired and stable roles to emulate, such youngsters are left to their own devices to master the complexities of their varied and changing worlds, to control the intense aggressive and sexual urges which well up within them, to channel their fantasies, and to pursue the goals to which they may aspire. Many become victims of their own growth, unable to discipline their impulses or find acceptable means for expressing their desires. Scattered and unguided, they are unable to fashion a clear sense of personal identity, a consistent direction for feelings and attitudes, a coherent purpose to existence. They become "other-directed" persons who vacillate at every turn, overly responsive to fleeting stimuli, shifting from one erratic course to another.

Ultimately, without the restitutive and remedial power of beneficent parental surrogates, they fail to establish internalized values to anchor themselves and to guide their future.

This aimless floundering and disaffiliated stagnation may be traced in part to the loss in contemporary society of meliorative and reparative customs and institutions that once "made sure" that those who had been deprived or abused would have a second chance by being exposed to compensatory sponsors and institutions exhibiting values and purposes around which social life could be focused and oriented. It is to these losses that we next turn.

## Decline of Consolidating Institutions

The impact of much of what has been described previously might be substantially lessened if concurrent or subsequent personal encounters and social customs were compensatory or restitutive, that is, if they repaired the intrapsychically destabilizing and destructive effects of problematic experiences.

Unfortunately, the converse appears to be the case. Whereas the cultural institutions of most societies have retained practices that furnish reparative stabilizing and cohering experiences, thereby remedying disturbed parent-child relationships, it is the thesis of this paper that the changes of the past two to three decades have not only fostered an increase in intrapsychic diffusion and splintering, but have also resulted in the discontinuation of psychically restorative institutions and customs, contributing thereby to both the incidence and exacerbation of features that typify borderline pathology. Without the corrective effects of undergirding and focusing social mentors and practices, the diffusing or divisive consequences of unfavorable earlier experience take firm root and unyielding form, displaying their structural weaknesses in clinical signs under the press of even modestly stressful events.

To illustrate: One of the by-products of the rapid expansion of knowledge and education is that many of the traditional institutions of our society—such as religion, which formerly served as a refuge to many, offering "love" for virtuous behavior and caring and thoughtful role models—have lost much of their historic power as a source of nurturance and control in our contemporary world.

Similarly, and in a more general way, the frequency with which families in our society relocate has caused a wide range of psychically diffusing problems. We not only leave behind stability, but with each move jettison a network of partially internalized role models and community institutions such as furnished in church, school, and friendships. What is undone, thereby, is the psychic structure and cohesion that could have been solidified to give direction and meaning to what are otherwise disparate elements of existence. Not only do children who move to distant settings feel isolated and lonely in these unfamiliar surrounds, and not only are they deprived of the opportunities to develop a consistent foundation of social customs and a coherent sense of self, but what faith they may have had in the merits of holding to a stable set of values and behaviors can only have been discredited.

### Disappearance of Nurturing Surrogates

The scattering of the extended family, as well as the rise of single-parent homes and shrinkage in sibling number, adds further to the isolation of families as they migrate in and out of transient communities. Each of these undermines the once powerful reparative effects of kinship support and caring relationships. Contemporary forms of disaffection and alienation between parent and child may differ in their particulars from those of the past. But rejection and estrangement have been and are ubiquitous, as commonplace as rivalry among sibs. In former times when children were subjected to negligence or abuse, they often found familial or neighborly parental surrogates—grandmothers, older sibs, aunts or uncles, even the kind or childless couple down the street who would, by

virtue of their own needs or identifications, nurture or even rear them. Frequently more suitable to parental roles, typically more affectionate and giving, as well as less disciplinary and punitive, these healing surrogates have historically served not only to repair the psychic damage of destructive parent-child relationships, but have "filled in" the requisite modeling of social customs and personal values that youngsters, so treated, are receptive to imitate and internalize.

In the past several decades, estranged and denigrated children have no longer found nurturing older sibs, aunts, or grandparents; nor are there the once accessible and nurturing neighbors. With increased mobility, kinship separation, single-parenting, and reduced sibling numbers, our society has few surrogate parents to pick up the pieces of what real parents may have fragmented and discarded, no less restore the developmental losses engendered thereby.

### Reemergence of Social Anomie

For some the question is not which of the changing social values they should pursue, but whether there are any social values that are worthy of pursuit. Youngsters exposed to poverty and destitution, provided with inadequate schools, living in poor housing set within decaying communities, raised in chaotic and broken homes, deprived of parental models of "success and attainment," and immersed in a pervasive atmosphere of hopelessness, futility, and apathy, cannot help but question the validity of the "good society." Reared in these settings one quickly learns that there are few worthy standards to which one can aspire successfully. Whatever efforts are made to raise oneself from these bleak surroundings run hard against the painful restrictions of poverty, the sense of a meaningless and empty existence and an indifferent, if not hostile, world. Moreover, and in contrast to earlier generations whose worlds rarely extended beyond the shared confines of ghetto poverty, the disparity between everyday realities and what is seen as so evidently available to others in enticing TV commercials and bounteous shopping malls is not only frustrating, but painfully disillusioning and immobilizing. Why make a pretense of accepting patently "false" values or seeking the unattainable goals of the larger society, when reality undermines every hope, and social existence is so pervasively hypocritical and harsh?

Nihilistic resolutions such as these leave youngsters bereft of a core of inner standards and customs to stabilize and guide their future actions, exposing them to the capricious power of momentary impulse and passing temptation. Beyond being merely "anomic" in Durkheim's sense of lacking socially sanctioned means for achieving culturally encouraged goals, these youngsters have incorporated neither the approved customs and practices nor the institutional aspirations and values of our society. In effect, they are both behaviorally normless and existentially purposeless, features seen in manifest clinical form among prototypal borderlines.

## Loss of Compelling Causes

As with the good fortunes that were anticipated upon the arrival of the Indian village's solar-powered water pump, so too have the "blessings" consequent to our modern-day standard of living produced their share of troublesome sequence. Until a generation or two ago children had productive, even necessary, economic roles to fill within the family. More recently, when the hard work of cultivating the soil or caring for the home were no longer requisites of daily life, youngsters were encouraged to advance their family's fortunes and status via higher education and professional vocation. Such needed functions and lofty ambitions were not only internalized, but gave a focus and a direction to one's life, creating a clear priority to one's values and aspirations, and bringing disparate potentials into a coherent schema and life philosophy.

Coherent aspirations are no longer commonplace today, especially among the children of the middle classes. In contrast to disadvantaged, yet anomic, youngsters, they are no longer "needed" to contribute to the family's economic survival: on the other hand, neither can upwardly mobile educational and economic ambitions lead them to readily surpass the achievements of already successful parents. In fact, children are seen in many quarters today as economic burdens, not as vehicles to a more secure future or to a more esteemed social status. Parents absorbed in their own lives and careers frequently view children as impediments to their autonomy and narcissistic indulgences.

But even among children who are not overtly alienated or rejected, the psychically cohering and energizing effects of "being needed" or of "fulfilling a worthy" family aspiration have been lost in our times. Without genuine obligations and real purposes to create intent and urgency in their psychosocial worlds, such youngsters often remain diffused and undirected. At best, they are encouraged to "find their own thing," to follow their own desires and create their own aims. Unfortunately, freedoms such as these translate for many as freedom to remain in flux, to be drawn to each passing fancy, to act out each passing mood, to view every conviction or ethic of equal merit, and, ultimately, to feel evermore adrift, lost, and empty.

Satisfying each momentary wish, consuming pleasures once shrouded in mystery, today's youngsters have, nonetheless, been deeply deprived—not of material wants, but of opportunities to fulfill both the minor daily chores now routinely managed by modern technology and the more distant goals that kept the minds of yesterday's children centered around a value hierarchy and oriented toward ultimate achievements.

While many of this generation have their bearings in good order, some have submerged themselves in aimless materialism. Others remain adrift in disenchantment and meaninglessness—a state of disaffected malaise. Some have attached themselves to naive causes or cults that ostensibly provide the passion and purpose they crave to give life meaning, but even these solutions too often prove empty, if not fraudulent. In earlier times, the disenchanted and disenfranchised, often dislocated from burdened homes or cast out as unwelcome troublemakers, joined together in active protest and rebellion. Problematic economic, social, and political conditions were shared by many of the profoundly dissatisfied, who formed philosophic movements such as the German Sturm and Drang of the late 18th century or the *Wandervogels* of the late 19th. In this century, as well, we have witnessed similar though more benign movements whose origins stemmed from an antipathy to parental ideals and cultural norms, such as the "Beat" and "Hippie" generations of the past quarter century.

Children today, however, are "rebels without a cause." Whereas earlier generations of disaffected youth were bound together by their resentments, their opposition to economic or political oppression, motivated by discernible and worthy common causes that provided both group camaraderie and a path to action, today's middle-class youngsters have no shared causes to bring them together. Materially well nourished and clothed, unconstrained in an open society to follow their talents and aspirations freely, the purposelessness and emptiness they experience is essentially an internal matter, a private rather than a collective affair, with no external agents against whom they can join with others to take to the streets. It is these rebels without a cause, unable to forego the material comforts of home and ineffective in externalizing their inner discontents upon the larger scene, yet empty and directionless, who comprise a goodly share of today's borderlines. Were it not for the general political, economic, and social well-being of our times, many would band together, finding some inspiration or justification to act out in concert.

With advances in modern education we have seen a marked growth in our populace's psychological-mindedness, sufficient to encourage the parents of youngsters such as have been described to turn to our profession for guidance in solving the perplexing character of their children's emotional and social behaviors: for example, "I don't understand him; he has everything a young person could want." What in other times might have taken root as a social movement of disaffected young radicals has taken the form of an epidemic of materially prosperous youth who possess the freedom to pursue abundance and contentment, but who feel isolated, aimless, and empty, and whom we "treat" for a deeply troubling psychological disorder.

## CONCLUDING COMMENT

The preceding pages describe a number of the contributory elements that comprise the broad mosaic of BPD-disposing influences of our times. Although bypassed in their specifics, there are salient ingredients of a biogenic nature in this multifactorial mix of determinants. Similarly, and prior critiques notwithstanding, this mosaic should be seen as encompassing the psychogenic role of adverse early nurturing and rearing.

What is troubling to those who seek an "ecumenical" synthesis among rival etiologic models is not the observation that some biogenic and analytic authors hold the view that this constitutional proclivity or that ordeal of early life is crucial to the development of a particular personality disorder. Rather, it is when claimants couple empirically unproven or philosophically untenable assumptions with the assertion that it is they alone who possess the sole means by which such etiologic origins can be revealed. Perhaps it is too harsh to draw parallels, but presumptions such as these are not unlike biblical inerrantists who claim their construals of the Bible to be "divine" interpretations, or conservative legalists who assert their unenlightened views to correspond to the "original intent" of the Constitution's framers. So, too, do many of our more self-righteous interpreters practice blindly what some have judged our "hopelessly flawed craft" (Grunbaum, 1984), one in which we demonstrably can neither agree among ourselves, nor discover either the data or methods by which a coherent synthesis may be fashioned among our myriad conjectures (Gunderson, 1984; Meissner, 1984; Stone, 1980).

Accordingly, it is hoped that the reader will recognize that the social learning thesis presented here assumes that future BPDs are likely either to possess troublesome constitutional proclivities and/or to have been subjected to early and repetitive experiences of a psychically diffusing or divisive nature: by contrast, youngsters endowed with an emotionally sturdy disposition and/or reared in a uniform, dependable, and stable manner are not likely candidates for a BPD, whatever their encounters may have been with the social forces described herein.

The present thesis is conceived best, then, as an addendum, one that seeks to affix the final ingredient of that trio of biopsychosocial influences that coalesce to form the borderline personality disorder.

# REFERENCES

Eagle, M. (1984). *Recent developments in psychoanalysis: A critical evaluation.* New York: McGraw-Hill.

Easterlin, R. A., & Crimmins, E. M. (1985). *The fertility revolution.* Chicago: University of Chicago Press.

Grunbaum, A. (1984). *The foundations of psychoanalysis: A philosophical critique.* Berkeley: University of California Press.

Gunderson, J. G. (1984). *Borderline personality disorder.* Washington, DC: American Psychiatric Association Press.

Klerman, G. L. (1987, January). *The current age of youthful melancholia. Agent blue.* Lecture presented to the Royal College of Psychiatrists, London, England.

Meehl, P. E. (1972). Specific genetic etiology, psychodynamics, and therapeutic nihilism. *International Journal on Mental Health, 1,* 10–27.

Meehl, P. E. (1977). Specific etiology and other forms of strong influence: Some quantitative meanings. *Journal of Medicine and Philosophy, 2,* 33–53.

Meissner, W. W. (1984). *The borderline spectrum.* New York: Aranson.

Millon, T. (1969). *Modern Psychopathology.* Philadelphia: Saunders (Reprinted 1985, Prospect Heights, IL: Waveland Press).

Millon, T. (1981). *Disorders of personality.* New York: Wiley-Interscience.

Millon, T. (1987a). Social learning models. In R. Michels (Ed.), *Psychiatry: Personality disorders and the neuroses.* New York: Basic Books.

Simonsen, E., & Mellergard, M. (in press). Changes in the borderline diagnosis in Denmark from 1975–1985. *Journal of Personality Disorders.*

Stone, M. H. (1980). *The borderline syndromes.* New York: McGraw-Hill.

Wicker, T. (1987, September 24). The pump on the well. *New York Times,* p. 23.

# The Relationship of Depression to Disorders of Personality

A considerable amount of research and theory has been directed toward identifying individuals prone to develop clinical depressive illness. Examination of the relevant literature makes it clear that no consensus has been reached regarding the characteristics of the so-called depressive personality. Discrepant findings may, in large part, be attributed to the complexities and methodological difficulties in carrying out research of this sort (Chodoff, 1972). The accurate assessment and classification of both depression or personality are difficult enough themselves without having also to tease out the effects of depression on personality functions, or the impact of premorbid personality on the symptomatic expression of depression (Metcalf, 1968; Paykel & Weissman, 1973).

Of the numerous explanations offered to account for the relationship of depression and personality, the most widely held possibility is that personality is etiological; that is, that personality patterns precede the onset of depression and therefore, determine the vulnerability to symptom formation (Klerman, 1973). This viewpoint, most heavily supported by psychoanalytic theorists, emphasizes the developmental history and early family environment as factors that shape individuals and predispose them to the depressogenic feelings of helplessness, worthlessness, and dejection (McCranie, 1971). A related concept is that certain personalities may repeatedly elicit interpersonal conflict and create stressful life circumstances that favor the development of depressive episodes (Akiskal, Khani, & Scott-Strauss, 1979). Illustrative

of this are borderline personalities with their erratic lifestyle and propensity toward tumultuous relationships and self-destructive behaviors. In a similar fashion, characterologic features may render an individual vulnerable to certain psychosocial stressors. The growing body of research on stress events and depression reflects the mounting interest in this theory. Studies have shown that depressions are frequently preceded by stressful events associated with separation or loss (Paykel, Myers, & Dienelt, 1970). Since not all people who experience stress become depressed, it is felt that either a genetic predisposition and/or life history factors (e.g., personality style, effectiveness of coping mechanisms, or available supports) may predispose certain individuals toward a depressive response (Becker, 1977). The passive-dependent individual, for example, tends to be quite susceptible to feelings of depression under the conditions of interpersonal loss, abandonment, or rejection. An alternate viewpoint is that some "personality disorders" may actually represent subclinical or subaffective manifestations of major affective illness (Akiskal et al., 1979; Akiskal, Hirschfield, & Yerevanian, 1983). From this perspective, lifelong affective traits or "affective personalities" (e.g., the cyclothymic personality) may represent gradual stages of transition to full syndromic affective episodes (e.g., manic-depressive illness).

It might be argued further that rather than increasing vulnerability to depression, personality may exert a pathoplastic effect upon depression, in that it colors and molds the particular expression of the depressive symptoms (Paykel, Klerman, & Prusoff, 1976). Depending on the premorbid personality, depressive symptoms, such as hopelessness, helplessness, and self-deprecation, may serve a variety of goals. Among the secondary gains of depression are the eliciting of nurturance from others, an excuse for avoiding unwanted responsibilities, a rationalization for poor performance, or a method for safely (albeit indirectly) expressing anger toward others. Partly determined by the gains received, depressive symptoms may take the form of dramatic gestures, irritable negativism, passive loneliness, or philosophical intellectualizations. Finally, there is evidence to suggest that personality characteristics may influence a depressed individual's response both to psychopharmacological and psychotherapeutic treatment (Akiskal, Rosenthal, Paykal, Lemmi, Rosenthal, & Scott-Strauss, 1980; Charney, Nelson, & Quinlan, 1981).

Recently, several depressive subtypes (based upon symptomatic presentations) with corresponding typologies of depression-prone personalities have been proposed (Arieti & Bemporad, 1980; Beck, 1981; Blatt, 1974). While these theoretical endeavors represent an improvement over previous attempts to identify a single personality stereotype for depressive illness, they are still restrictive in that they deal with only a limited number of personality configurations.

It will be the task of this chapter to provide a more extensive review of the interaction between depression and personality characteristics drawing upon theoretical deduction, as well as the recent clinical and empirical literature. A "continuum" conception of depression will be employed in this evaluation rather than a clearly demarcated typology.

Depression will be viewed as a multifaceted syndrome that manifests affective, cognitive, and vegetative symptoms. The most prominent feature, of course, is a disturbance of mood, in which the individual feels sad, blue, apathetic, or hopeless. Expressions of discouragement, self-deprecation, and guilt frequently are present, along with somatic disturbances, such as loss of energy, social interest, and sexual desire, as well as disruptions in sleeping, eating, and ability to concentrate. In severe cases, preoccupation with suicidal ideation is often present.

Personality, like depression, may best be conceived as falling on a continuum of severity. The concept of personality refers to deeply etched characteristics which pervade all aspects of the individual's functioning. Derived from the complex and progressive interactions of constitutional and experiential factors, these patterns (including perceptions, attitudes, and behaviors) tend to persist with little change throughout the individual's lifetime, regardless of the adaptive level of the individual's functioning. Pathological personality patterns or personality disorders are distinguished from normal/healthy patterns by their adaptive inflexibility, their tendency to foster vicious circles of inefficient and self-defeating behaviors, and their tenuous stability under conditions of stress (Millon, 1969, 1981).

While the interpretations offered here may be extended to include the more adaptive and "healthy" personality traits and patterns, the focus of this chapter will be on the relationships between depression and the 11 disorders of personality depicted on Axis II of the DSM-III (American Psychiatric Association, 1980).

# THE DEPENDENT PERSONALITY

Distinguished by their marked need for social approval and affection, and by their willingness to live in accord with the desires of others, dependent personalities are among the most likely individuals to become depressed. Characteristically, these individuals are docile, noncompetitive, and passive. Apart from requiring signs of belonging and acceptance, dependents make few demands on others. Their own needs are subordinated and their individuality denied, as these individuals assume a submissive, self-sacrificing, and placating role in relation to others. Social tension and interpersonal conflicts are carefully avoided, while troubling events are smoothed over or naively denied. Beneath their warm and affable presentation, however, may lie a plaintive and pessimistic quality. Dependents perceive themselves as weak, fragile, and ineffective. The recognition of their helplessness and utter reliance upon others may result in self-effacement and denigration. In addition, they may become excessively conciliatory in relationships to the point of submitting themselves to intimidation and abuse (Millon, 1981).

Given their pronounced susceptibility to separation anxiety, dependent personalities are quite likely to experience any number of affective disorders. Frequently, the underlying characterological pessimism of these individuals lends itself to a chronic, but mild depression or dysthymia. When faced with possible abandonment or the actual loss of a significant other, a major depression may ensue. Initially, these individuals may react with clinging helplessness and pleas for reassurance and support. Expressions of self-condemnation and guilt are also likely, as such verbalizations serve to deflect criticisms and evoke sympathetic reactions. Feelings of guilt can also act as a defensive maneuver to check outbursts of resentment or hostility. Fearful that their underlying feelings of anger might cause further alienation or retribution, dependents typically turn their aggressive impulses inward, discharging them through a despondency colored by self-derisive comments and contrition. On occasion, dependent personalities may make a desperate attempt to counter or deny emerging feelings of hopelessness and depression, through a temporary reversal of their typical passive, subdued style to that of hypomanic activity, excitement, and optimism. Such dramatic shifts in affective expression may resemble a bipolar disorder.

The dependent personality corresponds to the psychoanalytic "oral character" type, and more specifically, to what has been termed the *oral sucking* or *oral receptive* character.

For both Abraham (1911/1968) and Freud (1917/1968), the orally fixated depressive or melancholic has great oral needs, manifested by sucking, eating, and insatiable demands for oral expressions of affection. Emphasis is also placed on affectional frustrations occurring during the pre-Oedipal period. In essence, the melancholic has experienced a pathological introjection, or identification with the ambivalently regarded love object through the process of oral incorporation. Thus, an interpersonal conflict is transformed to an intrapsychic conflict, with the angry desire to devour the frustrating love object being turned inward and experienced as depression.

As psychoanalytic theory developed, the concept of orality was extended to include the general feelings of warmth, nourishment, and security. The dependent personality's reliance on external approval and support for maintenance of self-esteem made it particularly vulnerable to depression resulting from the loss of a significant other. Rado (1968) described melancholia as a "despairing cry for love," while Fenichel (1968) describes the orally dependent depressive as a "love addict."

A theory of depressive subtypes, based on attained level of object representation has been developed by Blatt (1974). Of the two depressive subtypes offered, "anaclitic" and "introjective," the anaclitic depressive would correspond most closely to the dependent depressive. Individuals with this form of depression have histories of impaired object relations at the primitive, oral level of development. Anaclitic depression is associated with intense dependency on others for support and gratification, vulnerability to feelings of deprivation, and considerable difficulties in managing anger expression for fear of alienating the love object. Blatt, D'Afflitti, and Quinlan (1976) provide empirical support for the division of depression into anaclitic and introjective subtypes. A Depressive Experiences Questionnaire was constructed to tap phenomenological experiences (rather than observed symptoms) of depression. Three stable factors emerging from this questionnaire included dependency, self-criticism, and efficacy. Corresponding with anaclitic depression is the dependency factor, which consists of items reflecting feelings of loneliness and helplessness, reliance on others, needs for closeness, fears of rejection and abandonment, and uneasiness about anger expression. Further empirical support was provided for Blatt's depressive subtypes in the study by Blatt, Quinlan, Chevon, McDonald, and Zuroff (1982). Here clinical judges successfully predicted type of depression based on the case records of psychiatric patients. In the high-dependency patients, clinical records contained evidence of oral excesses (i.e., alcohol, food, and drug abuse), a history of early object loss or deprivation, and issues of abandonment and loneliness.

A depressive typology similar to that of Blatt (1974) is offered by Arieti and Bemporad (1980). Depression is characterized as resulting from a "limitation of alternate ways of thinking and is self-inhibition from new experiences" (p. 1360). On the basis of clinical experience (i.e., long-term psychoanalytic therapy with 40 depressed patients), the three following premorbid types of depressive personality are proposed: (1) "dominant-other" type, (2) "dominant-goal" type, and (3) "chronic character structure, (4) or personality disorder. Akin to the dependent or anaclitic depressive, the dominant-other depressive personality is characterized by "clingingness, passivity, manipulativeness, and avoidance of anger" (p. 1361). Depression in these individuals may be precipitated by the loss of an esteemed other.

While agreeing that depressives are typically orally dependent personality types, Bibring (1953) offers a slightly different emphasis from the traditional psychodynamic focus on orality in depression. He argues that depression is a basic ego state reflecting feelings of helplessness about fulfilling needs critical to the maintenance of self-esteem. According to Bibring, the infant's recurrent experiences of frustrated helplessness and ensuing depression result in the formation of a prototypical reaction pattern that is reactivated by similar events in the future. Thus, with the loss of a significant object, or the perceived inability to control an aversive event, a reactivation of the helpless ego state (rather than a regression due to oral fixation) results in passivity, inhibition, and the belief that striving is meaningless.

Bibring's emphasis on feelings of helplessness in depressives is quite similar to Seligman's (1974) behavioral theory of depression. Seligman hypothesizes that reactive depression is essentially a state of learned helplessness, characterized by the perception of noncontrol. A reformulation of Seligman's theory (Abramson, Seligman, & Teasdale, 1978) proposes that the severity and chronicity of depression is related to the attributions made to account for the perceived lack of control. If an individual assumes personal responsibility for his/her inability to control events, and further assumes that inner deficiencies are likely to continue to result in feelings of helplessness in future situations, then a rather chronic state of depression, associated with lowered self-esteem is likely to occur. An individual is then more likely to behave more helplessly, initiating fewer responses to control reinforcement, and having more difficulty in recognizing the successful responses that result in reinforcement. A related behavioral theory of depression is offered by Lewinsohn (1974) who proposes that a low rate of response-contingent positive reinforcement causes depression. Insufficient reinforcement can result from at least three causes: few events are reinforcing to the individual; few potentially reinforcing events are available in the environment, and/or the instrumental behaviors emitted by the individual infrequently elicit reinforcement (Blaney, 1977; Lewinsohn, 1974).

Both Seligman's (1974) and Lewinsohn's (1974) models of depression are relevant to the experience of depression in dependent personalities. Such individuals with their self-perceptions of inadequacy and ineffectiveness perpetuate behavioral helplessness by relying almost totally upon others for their support and reinforcement. By passively clinging to one or two individuals for nurturance, the dependents restrict their interpersonal and activity range, which in turn limits exposure to alternate sources of reinforcement and diminishes the probability of learning more appropriate coping skills. Lewinsohn's (1974) observation that "some depressed individuals are clearly over involved with one significant person to the exclusion of most other potential relationships" (p. 180), is reminiscent of Arieti and Bemporad's (1980) "dominant-other" depressive personality and their characterization of depressives as inhibiting themselves from new experiences and limiting alternate ways of thinking.

Critical in the dependent personalities propensity toward depression are their beliefs that they are ineffective, inferior, and unworthy of regard. This negative cognitive set of the depressive, that is, poor self-concept, disparaging view of the world, and the projection of continued hardships and frustrations in the future, is central to Beck's (1974) cognitive theory of depression. Recently (1981), Beck has extended his cognitive formulation to include other predisposing and precipitating factors, including personality attributes that may lead to depression. He proposes two basic personality modes, the "autonomous"; and the "socially dependent," and describes the respective depressive symptom patterns of each. Individuals within the socially dependent cluster depend on others for safety, help, and gratification and are characterized by passive receiving. Such individuals require stability, predictability, and constant reassurance in relationships. As rejection is considered worse than aloneness to the socially dependent, no risks are taken that might lead to alienation from sources of nurturance (e.g., asserting oneself with others). Similarly, socially dependents avoid making changes and exposing themselves to novel situations, as they feel ill-equipped to cope with

the unexpected. Depression in these individuals is usually precipitated by the experience of interpersonal rejection or loss, and is accompanied by a diminishment in confidence and self-esteem. The socially dependent depressive is more likely than the depressed autonomous personality to cry, complain of sadness and loneliness, and make demands for help. Such individuals evidence greater emotional lability and are more likely to experience an "anxious depression." They are also more optimistic about the benefits of help and respond better (at least temporarily) to support and reassurance.

Considerable overlap can be seen among the anaclitic depressive, the dominant-other depressive, and the socially dependent depressive, The emphasis on premorbid dependency in depressives is also apparent in the constructive-developmental model of depression, offered by Kegan, Rogers, and Quinlan (1981). Based on Kohlberg's (1976) sociomoral developmental stages, Kegan et al. (1981) have generated three subtypes of depression, relating to (1) egocentricity and control issues, (2) issues of interpersonal dependency, and (3) issues of self-definition and evaluation. Kegan's interpersonal dependency subtype correlates closely with depression in the dependent personality, in that feelings of dysphoria are directly related to the establishment and breaking of social bonds. Individuals with this form of depression often feel abandoned, unloved, betrayed, alienated, and unworthy of attention and regard. Again, problems with the expression of anger are common, as anger might threaten the stability of an established dependent relationship.

There also appears to he at least one dependent personality counterpart among the depressive typologies generated through factor analytic studies. In one of the earliest attempts to empirically classify subgroups of depression, Grinker and associates (Grinker, Miller, Sabshin, Nunn, & Nunnally, 1961) assessed feelings and concerns, as well as behavior of 96 depressed hospitalized patients and 10 nondepressed psychiatric controls. While many valid criticisms have been leveled at Grinker's study (Wittenborn, 1965), the five depressive patterns yielded by factor analysis in this landmark investigation still warrant consideration. "Factor Pattern B" seems particularly relevant to the current discussion on the dependent depressive. It depicts a depressed individual who is characterized by dismal, hopeless attitudes, low self-esteem, anxiety, and clinging demands for attention. It is speculated that some external event resulted in the release of repressed aggression in such an individual, which is, in turn, reacted to with guilt and self-punishment. Such patients are helped by support and kindness and typically do well in psychotherapy.

A number of correlational studies lend support to the role of dependency in depression. For example, Wittenborn and Maurer (1977) found that family informants, in describing the premorbid personalities of depressed patients, referred to low self-confidence, dependence on the opinions of others, and the tendency to deny anger and avoid confrontation. Paykel et al. (1976) found that depressives with a neurotic symptom pattern more frequently showed evidence of oral dependent personalities (according to both relatives' interviews and self-report personality inventories). Similarly, in a longitudinal, follow-up study of 40 depressed women, Paykel and Weissman (1973) found submissive dependency and family attachment to be closely related to symptomatology.

Altman and Wittenborn (1980) employing a self-descriptive inventory developed for their study, found that the following five factors discriminated formerly depressed women from a matched group of women with no psychiatric history: low self-esteem, unhappy outlook, narcissistic vulnerability, helplessness, and lack of self-confidence. In a follow-up and extension of Altman and Wittenborn's (1980) work, Cofer and Wittenborn again successfully discriminated depressed women in remission from a matched nonpsychiatric control group on the basis of a modified version of Altman and Wittenborn's (1980) self-descriptive inventory. Factor analysis identified three of the factors reported in the initial study (i.e., unhappy outlook, narcissistic vulnerability, and low self-esteem), as well as the additional factors of critical mother and dependency fostering father. The authors suggest that their findings lend corroboration to other studies and theories (e.g., Blatt et al., 1976; Bibring, 1953; Seligman, 1974) that emphasize the role of low self-esteem and the perception of helplessness in the development of depression. More recently, Matussek and Feil (1983) found that on the basis of numerous self-report inventories, as well as psychiatric interviews, endogenous unipolar patients were characterized by a lack of autonomy and assertiveness, conformism, passive-submissiveness, dependency on others, and avoidance of responsibility.

## THE HISTRIONIC PERSONALITY

Histrionic personalities, like dependent personalities, are characterized by intense needs for attention and affection. Unlike the passive receptive stance of the dependent, however, the histrionic actively solicits the interest of others through seductive, immaturely exhibitionistic, or self-dramatizing behaviors. Toward assuring a constant receipt of the admiration and esteem that they require, histrionics develop an exquisite sensitivity to the desires and moods of those they wish to please. While others may perceive them as being rather ingenuine or shallow, they are nonetheless typically viewed as gregarious, entertaining, and superficially charming. The histrionics extreme other-directedness and approval-seeking results in a capricious and fickle pattern of personal relationships. Unlike the dependent's blind loyalty and attachment to one significant other, the histrionic is lacking in fidelity and dissatisfied with single attachments. Their interpersonal relationships tend to be characterized by demandingness, manipulation, and at times, childish dependency and helplessness. These behaviors are particularly pronounced in heterosexual relationships where the histrionic demonstrates a marked appetite for fleeting romantic encounters (Millon, 1981).

Histrionics tend to be emotionally overreactive and labile. Frustration tolerance is quite low and there is a proneness toward immature stimulation seeking and impulsive responsiveness. Such individuals crave excitement, pleasure and change, and become easily bored with normal routines. A well developed sense of inner identity is typically lacking in histrionics. Their perception of themselves is conceptualized in terms of their relationships and their effect upon others. In contrast to their hypersensitivity to the thoughts and moods of others, such individuals are lacking insight into their own feelings. Their orientation is toward external stimuli and only fleeting, impressionistic attention is paid to details. Their cognitive style is marked with difficulties in concentration and logical thinking. Experiences are poorly integrated and learned, and consequently, judgment is often lacking. In part, their cognitive flightiness results from their attempts to avoid potentially disrupting ideas and urges; for example, a recognition of their ravenous dependency needs and their resultant vulnerability to loss or rejection. Consequently, histrionic personalities will simply seal off, repress, or dissociate large segments of their memories and feelings.

The histrionics virtually insatiable needs for attention and approval make them quite prone to feelings of dejection and anxiety, should they fail to evoke the recognition they desire. Signs of indifference or neutrality on the part of others are frequently interpreted as rejection and result in feelings of emptiness and unworthiness. Unlike the dependent's flat and somber symptom picture, dysthymic disorder in histrionic personalities is characteristically overplayed in dramatic and eye-catching gestures, characteristic of the histrionics exhibitionistic display of mood. Episodes of the milder forms of depression are usually prompted less by fear of abandonment than by a sense of emptiness and inactivity. Such dysphoria is likely to occur when histrionics find themselves stranded between one fleeting attachment and another, or between one transitory excitement and the next. At such times of noninvolvement, histrionics sense their lack of inner substance and direction, and begin to experience fears of an empty life and aloneness.

Depressive complaints in histrionic personalities tend to be expressed in current, fashionable, or intellectualized terms (e.g., *"existential anxiety"* or *"estrangement from the mass society"*). Expressing this distress through such popular jargon enables histrionics to rationalize their personal emptiness and confusion and, perhaps more importantly, provides them with a bridge to others, at a time when they feel most isolated from the social life they so desperately seek. Such pseudosophisticated expressions of disenchantment entertain and interest others and identifies the histrionic as being part of an "in" subgroup. Histrionics are also among the personality styles that may "mask" an underlying depression through psychosomatic disorders, hypochondriacal syndromes, or through acting-out behaviors, such as drug abuse, overeating, or sexual promiscuity (Akiskal, 1983; Lesse, 1974).

Major depressions in histrionics are primarily precipitated by anticipated losses in dependency security and are more likely to be evidenced in an agitated rather than a retarded form (Millon, 1981). In the hope of soliciting support and nurturance, histrionics may wail aloud and make well known their feelings of helplessness and abandonment. Suicidal threats or gestures are not uncommon at such times. Major depressions may also be colored with irritability and anger, although reproving reactions, especially from significant others, will cause histrionics to withdraw and substitute their anger with dramatic declarations of guilt and contrition.

Histrionic personalities may be particularly susceptible to bipolar and cyclothymic disorders, as these syndromes are consistent with their characteristic socially gregarious and exuberant style. Severe separation anxieties or the fear of losing social approval may intensify the histrionic's habitual behavior pattern until it reaches the forced and frantic congeniality of hypomania. To stave off the growing feeling of depressive hopelessness, tension may be released through hyperactivity and a frenetic search for attention.

Many of the psychoanalytic writings of the depressed oral dependent's pronounced affectional needs are equally applicable to depression in the histrionic personality. Freud (1932) wrote that a "dread of loss of love" governed the behavior of hysterics, while Rado (1951) referred to the predepressive's strong cravings for narcissistic gratification and low tolerance of affectional frustration. In addition, the active manipulative qualities of the histrionic are stressed. Bemporad (1971) describes a manipulative depressive who engages in "bargaining relationships" to ensure fulfillment of dependency needs and who decompensates if sufficient gratifications from others cannot be obtained. Chodoff (1972) describes the low frustration tolerance of the oral depression-prone individual and the various techniques, for example, "submissive, manipulative, coercive, piteous, demanding, and placating" (p. 670) that are employed to satisfy their narcissistic needs, Finally, while Blatt (1974) characterizes anaclitic depressives as typically being more passive and helpless than oral dependents, case history studies of these patients also revealed evidence of histrionic features, such as impulsive behavior, suicidal gestures, and acting-out through oral excessives of drug and alcohol abuse (Blatt et al., 1982).

Considerable attention has been paid to the clinical presentation of depression in histrionic personalities. While it has been argued that the dramatic behavioral styles of histrionics may obscure a clear view of an underlying depression (Akiskal et al., 1983), others believe that the histrionic's "high spirits" and gregariousness protect against or mitigate the emergence of depressive feelings. Lazare and Klerman (1968) studied a small group of hospitalized depressed women who also carried the diagnosis of "hysterical personality." Assessment during the time of their illness revealed that hysterical patients, as compared to depressed patients without hysterical features, showed less intense feelings of depression, hopelessness and worthlessness, less retardation, fewer paranoid and obsessional symptoms, but more somatic complaints. Hysterical depressed patients also differed in their behavioral presentation while hospitalized, in that they were described as irritable, demanding, manipulative, and more hostile than patients without hysterical features. Follow-up studies (Paykel & Prusoff, 1973; Paykel et al., 1976) utilizing clinical interviews, self-report inventories, and ratings by relatives, supported the initial findings. Neurotic depressives showed more oral dependent traits, while depressed patients with hysterical personalities tended to be less severely ill, showing patterns of depression mixed with hostility and irritability, but little evidence of anxiety.

Such studies suggest that a key component in the histrionic personalities' apparent resistance to severe depression is their ability to express hostility. Classical psychodynamic formulations emphasize the depressive's turning of aggression against the self in punishment of the internalized, frustrating love object. Recent studies (Gershon, Cromer, & Klerman, 1968; Schless, Mendels, Kipperman, & Cochran, 1974) have challenged the universality of aggression turned inward as the depressive mechanism, arguing that depression is seen in those who overtly express hostility, as well as in individuals where hostility remains covert. There does appear to be at least some evidence, however, to suggest that hostility expressed outward may be associated with less severe depression, as well as hysterical features. In a rather extensive study of a very small group of hospitalized depressives, Gershon et al. (1968) found that while "hostility-in" was positively correlated with depressive symptoms, "hostility-out" appeared to be associated with depression only in the few subjects described as having hysterical personalities. For these patients, significantly fewer verbalizations of depression were noted, while the degree of hostility expressed appeared to be closely and positively related to the severity of depression.

Schless et al. (1974) found in their study group of 37 depressed patients, an approximately equal distribution of patients turning hostility inward and outward. Several indicators of outward hostility in this study were related to the presence of hysterical features and resentment. While the degree of turning hostility inward appeared to be related to the severity of depression, the most severely depressed patients had an increase in both inwardly and outwardly directed hostility. In addition, the more depressed patients felt their angry feelings to be relatively impotent, while anger in others was perceived as quite threatening. The authors proposed that depression, hostility, and anxiety are all signal emotions in reaction to certain stimuli. In their formulation, all of these "signals" have a parallel relationship and can occur together in different degrees and combinations. Hostility may thus serve as a secondary defense to depression. When this defense begins to fail in the highly depressed patients, they perceive their anger to be ineffective. The portrayal of hostility as a secondary defense in depression gains some support from Lazare and Klerman's (1968) study where hostility was quite pronounced in hysterical personalities during the time of their clinical depression, but diminished as the patients' depressive symptoms abated.

Consistent with the position that the histrionic personality structure confers protection against severe depression, is the association of histrionic features with neurotic rather than endogenous depression (Charney et al., 1981; Paykel & Prusoff, 1973). A growing body of theory and research also suggests that the histrionic personality may be more prone toward chronic mild depression and characterological depressions (Akiskal et al., 1980).

Paykel (1971) conducted a cluster analysis on 35 rating variables derived from 165 depressed patients from varied treatment settings. Two major groups akin to the endogenous and reactive dimensions were further divided into four depressive subtypes, two of which seem particularly relevant to depression in the histrionic. *Hostile depressives* were characterized by moderately young patients who evidenced moderately severe depression, flavored with hostility and self-pity. *Young depressives with personality disorders* were the youngest group (typically in their 20s) and evidenced relatively mild depression with situationally reactive mood fluctuations. Patients in this group (which overlaps somewhat with the hostile depressives) were high on neuroticism but also evidenced disturbed social relations suggestive of personality disorder. Support for the validity of Paykel's four depressive subtypes was derived from a second study (Paykel, 1972) where patient's self-reports and ratings by relatives revealed differences in symptomatology among the depressive subtypes. Hostile depressives and young depressives with personality disorders showed more evidence of hysterical personality features than the other two subgroups.

Grinker and associates' (1961) earlier factor analytic work also generated a depressive subtype with features that conform to the histrionic depressive. Patient's corresponding to "Factor Pattern C" evidenced less than average depressed affect, guilt, or anxiety. Their behavior is marked by agitated, demanding, hypochondriacal complaints, associated with psychosomatic symptoms. In contrast to the irrational, complaining attitudes noted in these patients is the very low loading on dismal and hopeless affect.

Charney et al. (1981) found histrionic, hostile, and borderline personality traits more frequently in the nonmelancholic forms of depression. Significantly more nonmelancholic as opposed to melancholic depressives also showed evidence of personality disorders. The subgroup of nonmelancholic depressives with personality disorder had an earlier onset of depressive illness and showed a poorer treatment response. Akiskal and colleagues (Akiskal, 1983; Akiskal et al., 1980) describe a similar type of depressive patient which they portray as predominantly neurotic, younger, mildly depressed, and possessing features consistent with personality disorder. Akiskal (1983) addresses the dysthymic disorder, and its associated conditions of chronic minor depression, characterologic depression, and hysteroid dysphoria. He divides chronic depressives into the following three groups: (1) primary depressives with residual chronicity, (2) chronic secondary dysphoria, and (3) characterologic depressions. The early onset, characterologic depressions are further divided into (a) character-spectrum disorders, and (b) subaffective dysthymic disorders. In discussing the poor response to treatment among characterologic depressives, Akiskal et al. (1980) refers to this subtly "oral hysterical" features, but also emphasizes the anti social, unstable, and even schizoid qualities that may be seen (e.g., immature and manipulative behaviors, impulsivity, interpersonal instability, and a high incidence of drug and alcohol abuse). Characterologic depressives typically have early histories of unstable object relations and evidence of a hypersensitivity to romantic disappointment, and other forms of separation events.

The characterologic depression described by the Akiskal group (Akiskal et al., 1980; Akiskal, 1983) shows considerable overlap with Liebowitz and Klein's (1981) "hysteroid dysphoria." Described as chronic, repetitive, nonpsychotic depressed moods, this disturbance is more frequent in women with pronounced needs for attention, approval, and praise, especially within a romantic relationship. Extreme intolerance of personal rejection is the hallmark of this disorder. Depression in these individuals is usually of short duration and manifested symptomatically in overeating or craving for sweets, oversleeping or extreme fatigue. Alcohol or drug abuse during episodes of depression may also be common. Described as "attention junkies" with "addictions" to approval, hysteroid dysphorics, on the surface, would seem to possess many of the features characteristic of the histrionic personality. As with Paykel's (1971) and Charney et al.'s (1981) young depressives, however, the hysteroid dysphorics also evidence considerably more "unstable" features (e.g., being prone toward angry outbursts, impulsive acting-out and physically self-damaging acts), which are suggestive of a more severe level of personality disorganization, such as the borderline personality.

## THE SCHIZOID PERSONALITY

The essential features of the schizoid personality are a profound defect in the ability to form social relationships and an underresponsiveness to all forms of stimulation. Such individuals exhibit an intrinsic emotional blandness; an imperviousness to joy, anger, or sadness. Seemingly unmoved by emotional stimuli, the schizoid appears to possess a generalized inability to be aroused and activated; a lack of initiative and vitality. Their interpersonal passivity then, is not by intention or for self-protective reasons, but due to a fundamental imperceptiveness to the moods and needs of others (Millon, 1981).

Schizoid personalities typically prefer limited interpersonal contact and only a peripheral role in social and family relationships. They tend to choose interests and vocations that will allow them to maintain their social detachment. Colorless and lacking in spontaneity, they are usually perceived as unresponsive, boring, or dull in relationships. Their speech tends to be characterized by emotional flatness, vagueness, and obscurities, and there is a seeming inability to grasp the emotional components of human interactions and communications. They seem indifferent to both praise and criticism. Consistent with their interpersonal style, schizoids possess little awareness of themselves and employ only minimal introspection. Lacking in insight and relatively untroubled by intense emotions or interpersonal conflicts, the schizoid possesses limited and uncomplicated intrapsychic defenses.

Schizoid personalities' pervasive imperviousness to emotions puts them among the personality styles least susceptible to depression or other affective distress. Having failed to develop an "appetite" for social stimulation (including affection and attachment), these individuals are not vulnerable to dejection resulting from "object loss." In addition, since schizoids derive only limited pleasure from themselves, they are not particularly susceptible to loss of self-esteem or self-deprecation. Emotional distress may develop, however, when faced with unusual social demands or responsibilities, or when stimulation levels become either excessive or drastically curtailed. In addition, their inner barrenness and interpersonal isolation may occasionally throw them into a fear of nonbeing or petrification.

On rare occasions, schizoids may exhibit brief, frenzied episodes of manic-like excitement in an attempt to counter the anxieties of depersonalization. A fleeting and erratic course of frantic and rather bizarre conviviality may then temporarily replace the schizoid's characteristic impassive, unsociable pattern. More frequently, however, the schizoid reacts to disequilibrium with increased withdrawal and dissociation. Lacking an investment and interest in self, as well as external events, the, schizoid fails to acquire a coherent and well-integrated inner identity. Disruption is to the consistency of the schizoid's lifestyle, as might result from unwanted social overstimulation or prolonged periods of social isolation, may consequently result in a kind of splitting or disintegration. During such periods of self-estrangement, schizoids may experience irrational thinking and compounding of their typical emotional poverty. Behaviorally, this might be manifested in profound lethargy, lifeless facial expressions, and inaudible speech, simulating but not reflecting a depressive mood.

Should depression be seen in the schizoid, certain aspects of behavioral theory may account for it. Lewinsohn's (1974) theory of depression stresses the role of low rates of response-contingent positive reinforcement. In the schizoid's case, few events (either within or without) are reinforcing. Schizoid personalities evidence a general state of unresponsiveness to innumerable sources of stimulus events, which for other individuals might cause pleasure, joy, or anger. In addition, few reinforcing events are available in the environment, because the schizoid lacks the perceptual capacities to perceive them, as well as the social skills to elicit them. Their infrequent social activities decrease opportunities for growth stimulation, and their insensitivity, impassivity, and disjointed thought and communicative skills make it unlikely that others will respond positively to them. Since this low rate of response contingent positive reinforcement is characteristic or constant for the schizoid, it may not, by itself, explain the development of depression. However, should those few reinforcements suddenly drop, or a fear of nonbeing develop, the schizoid's inability to detect or elicit new reinforcement may contribute to depression.

While empirical data on affective disorders in schizoid personalities is lacking, at least two of the factor analysis generated subtypes would seem to fit the experience of depression in these individuals, "Factor Pattern A" generated in the 1961 study by Grinker et al. is described as a depressive who is not particularly anxious, clinging or attention-seeking, but rather isolated, withdrawn, and apathetic. A slowing in thought and speech, with some evidence of cognitive disturbance is also seen. The absence of large amounts of "gloomy affect," complaining, or attempts at restitution give this depressive subtype the appearance of an "empty person." While much of this description would fit the theoretical picture of depression in the schizoid, Grinker et al. (1961) give other features of this depressive factor pattern which might be more characteristic of a compulsive premorbid personality.

The "retarded depression" generated by Overall and Hollister (1980) might also be consistent with the symptomatic presentation of depression in the schizoid. Such depression is characterized by retardation in speech, gross motor behavior, and social interaction. A diminishment in affective responsiveness may frequently accompany the "generalized behavioral inhibition" (p. 376) that is present in this form of depression.

## THE AVOIDANT PERSONALITY

While the schizoid and avoidant personalities may appear superficially rather similar, they differ in several important ways, including their susceptibility to depression. Both personalities may appear withdrawn, emotionally flat, and lacking in communicative and social skills. The affective flatness of the avoidant, however, is typically a defensive maneuver against underlying emotional tension and disharmony.

Similarly, the apparent detachment and interpersonal withdrawal of avoidants develop in response to a fear of intimacy and a hypersensitivity to rejection and ridicule. Strong desires for affection and acceptance exist in these individuals, but are denied or restrained out of apprehension and fearful mistrust of others. Not infrequently, avoidants have had experiences of painful social derogation, which resulted in an acute sensitivity and alertness to signs of ridicule and humiliation. This hypersensitivity and vigilance often results in the misperceiving of innocuous social comments or events as critical rejection (Millon, 1981).

For the most part, avoidants engage in self-imposed isolation and social withdrawal. They will, however, enter into relationships with a limited number of people, if provided with strong guarantees of uncritical acceptance. Avoidants may become quite dependent on the one or two people they do allow into their lives. However, they are likely to remain rather cautious in relationships, engaging in frequent, subtle testing of their partner's sincerity.

While the avoidant may view people in general as critical, betraying and humiliating,

they are usually very dissatisfied with the peripheral social role they feel forced to play and experience painful feelings of loneliness and alienation. Avoidants tend to be excessively self-critical, blaming themselves for their social undesirability. Consequently, they may become estranged from themselves as well as from others. They tend to resort to extreme defensive coping strategies to deal with the chronic feelings of interpersonal ambivalence and affective distress that they experience. In addition to active avoidance and withdrawal from threatening social situations, they may attempt to block and interfere with their own troubling cognitions, resulting in a fragmentation of their thoughts and disjointed verbal communications, as well as the appearance of being emotionally confused or socially irrelevant.

Avoidant types are among the most vulnerable of the personality patterns to psychiatric symptom disorders. Perhaps most frequently, the avoidant will suffer from feelings of anxiety and ruminative worry. Also, like the schizoid, prolonged estrangement from self and others can result in varied forms of dissociative disorders. Avoidants are also quite prone to feelings of deep sadness, emptiness, and loneliness. Frustrated yearnings for affection and approval, coupled with the self-deprecation they experience for their unlovability and ineffectuality may result in a chronic melancholic tone to these personalities. Depression may nonetheless be difficult to detect in the avoidant, given their characteristic affective flattening, and their typical presentation of slowness of speech and movement. Furthermore, avoidants will attempt to hide and contain their feelings of inner despair for fear that overt expressions of such weakness and suffering might render them even more vulnerable to social ridicule, humiliation, and rejection. While major depressive episodes in these individuals may be similar to the symptomatic presentation of depressed schizoids (i.e., psychomotor retardation, extreme social withdrawal, and apathy), avoidants may also experience anxiety or obsessive ruminations with their depression.

The avoidant's susceptibility to depression can be readily explained from a cognitive/behavioral framework. First is the avoidant's tendency to view things pessimistically; that is, contempt directed at the self, fear and suspicion of others, and a sense of future despair. Next is the limited possibility the avoidant has for experiencing reinforcing events. Characteristically, these individuals tend to be inflexible, confining themselves to a small range of potentially reinforcing experiences. Although possessing the innate capacity to experience pleasure, the interpersonal anxiety felt by avoidants may cause them to deny themselves the satisfaction they could derive from others, and to discount praise, compliments, and other social reinforcers. Similarly, the distorted view of self as ineffectual and unlovable, precludes the possibility of pleasure coming from within.

Although the avoidant personality is a relatively new concept to psychiatric nosology (Millon, 1969), the characteristics of this pattern have frequently been cited in the literature on depression. Arieti and Bemporad (1980), in their proposal of three premorbid types of depressive personality, describe a depressive personality structure that is characterized by constant feelings of depression lurking in the background, and an inhibition of nearly any form of gratification. Further, features of this form of chronic character structure are:

"A chronic, mild sense of futility and hopelessness which results from a lack of involvement in everyday activities. . . . emptiness because they do not develop deep relationships for fear of being exploited or rejected. . . . harsh, critical attitude towards themselves and others" (Arieti & Bemporad, 1980, p. 1362).

According to the authors, such depressive subtypes experience episodes of clinical depression when they are forced by some event to reevaluate their mode of existence, and confronted with the barrenness and meaninglessness of their lives.

Metcalfe (1968) described a group of recovered, depressed women as being characterized by ruminative worrying, a denial of fantasy, and a rigid, limited, habit-bound lifestyle. He suggests that the depressive is not necessarily an individual who is prone to develop depression, but one who lacks the "resistance" necessary to recover from such illness. Hirschfeld and Klerman (1979) also described the depressed patients in their study to be more worrisome, insecure and sensitive, less socially adroit, and more likely to break down under stress. These individuals were further characterized as being more needy and obsessional than normal controls.

A similar personality subtype is proposed by Akiskal (1983) in his discussion of the two characterologic depressive subtypes, the "character-spectrum disorders," and the "subaffective dysthymic disorders." In the latter subgroup, the depressive personality characteristics are considered as milder, but lifelong (subaffective) expressions of a primary depressive disorder. Individuals prone to subaffective dysthymic disorders exhibit anhedonic, "guilt-ridden," and retarded depressions. Akiskal views such patients as conforming to Schneider's (1958) depressive typology in that they are:

". . . (1) quiet, passive, and nonassertive, (2) gloomy, pessimistic, and incapable of fun, (3) self-critical, self-reproaching, and self-derogatory, (4) skeptical, hypercritical, and complaining, (5) conscientious and self-disciplining, (6) brooding and given to worry, and (7) preoccupied with inadequacy failure and negative events to the point of a morbid enjoyment of one's failures" (Akiskal, 1983, p. 17).

The characteristics described thus far are obviously not exclusive to the avoidant personality. However, a great many of them are prominent features in the avoidant style. In a recent critical review of research on personality on factors in affective disorders,

Akiskal et al. (1983) suggest that introversion and low sociability have emerged as consistent and relatively robust premorbid features of nonbipolar depressive disorders. Among the studies cited in their review was that of Hirschfeld, Klerman, Clayton, and Keller (1983) where personality data from recovered, depressed women was compared to similar data from formerly depressed female relatives as well as female relatives with no prior psychiatric history. The recovered depressives in this study were described as very introverted, "shy, withdrawn, reserved, restrained, serious, deliberate, and controlled" (p. 997). While these individuals showed an extreme dependence on one significant other, they tended not to be very sociable or enjoying of company. The authors conclude social introversion to be "the most powerful" personality characteristic associated with primary nonbipolar depression, while heightened interpersonal dependency is viewed as "modest second factor" (p. 997). Clearly the premorbid depressive features of introversion and low sociability have applicability to the avoidant personality.

## THE SCHIZOTYPAL PERSONALITY

The hallmark of this disorder is a variety of peculiarities of behavior, speech, thought, and perception that are not severe enough to warrant the diagnosis of schizophrenia. There is considerable variability in the presentation of this syndrome (e.g., magical thinking, ideas of reference or suspiciousness, illusions, depersonalization, and hypersensitivity with undue social anxiety), and no single feature is invariably present. It is our contention that the schizotypal syndrome should be viewed as an advanced dysfunctional personality (akin in severity to the borderline or paranoid types), and that it is best understood as a more pathological version of the schizoid and avoidant patterns. Such a framework allows a greater appreciation of the schizotypal characteristics of social impoverishment, and the tendency toward distant rather than close

interpersonal relationships. In fact, the observed oddities in behavior and thought, such as paranoid ideation, magical thinking, and circumstantial speech stem in part from the schizotypal's withdrawn and isolated existence. Without the stabilizing influences and repetitive corrective experiences that come with frequent human contact and social interactions, individuals may lose their sense of behavioral judgment and gradually begin the process of acting, thinking, and perceiving in peculiar and eccentric ways. In the advanced stages of such a dysfunctional progression, schizotypals may merely drift aimlessly from one activity to another, leading meaningless and ineffectual existences, and remaining on the periphery of societal life.

Depending on which of the detached patterns (i.e., schizoid or avoidant) that schizotypals resemble, they may be emotionally flat, sluggish and apathetic, or hypersensitive, anxious and socially apprehensive. In a similar fashion, schizotypal personalities vulnerability to depression or other symptom disorders, is in part, dependent upon whether they have evolved from the sensitive and suffering avoidants or the innately bland, unfeeling schizoids. Empirical and theoretical literature on the relationship of affective disorder to the schizotypal personality is virtually nonexistent. To gain some appreciation of this phenomenon, the reader is referred to the preceding sections on the depressive experience in schizoid and avoidant personalities.

## THE ANTISOCIAL PERSONALITY

The DSM-III provides a rather detailed listing of the delinquent, criminal, and socially undesirable behaviors that may be found among antisocial personalities, but fails, in our opinion, to deal with the personality characteristics from which such antisocial behaviors stem. In adopting a focus on the "criminal personality," insufficient attention is paid to individuals with similar propensities and basic traits who have managed to avoid criminal involvement (Millon, 1981). It is our contention that antisocial personalities are best characterized by: hostile affectivity, excessive self-reliance, interpersonal assertiveness, callousness, and a lack of humanistic concern or sentimentality. Such individuals exhibit rebelliousness and social "vindictiveness," with particular contempt being directed toward authority figures. Irascible and pugnacious, antisocials exhibit frequent, verbally abusive, and at times even physically cruel behaviors. Other notable features in the antisocial personality include a low tolerance for frustration, impulsivity, and an inability to delay gratification. Consistent with this is a tendency to become easily bored and restless with day-to-day responsibilities and social demands. Not only are such individuals seemingly undaunted by danger and punishment, they appear attracted to it, and may actually seek it out or provoke it. Our portrayal of the antisocial personality is more consistent with the concept of the sociopathic or psychopathic personalities as depicted in the incisive writings of Cleckley (1941). These individuals are most notable for their guiltlessness, incapacity for object love, impulsivity, emotional shallowness, superficial social charm, and an inability to profit from experience.

An argument may also be made for a "nonantisocial" variant of the sociopathic personality. Such individuals may view themselves as assertive, energetic, self-reliant, and hard-boiled, but realistic, strong, and honest. In competitive society, these traits tend to be commended and reinforced. Consequently, such individuals may achieve positions of authority and power, which provide socially sanctioned avenues for expressing their underlying aggressiveness.

Antisocials tend to be finely attuned to the feelings, moods, and vulnerabilities of others, taking advantage of this sensitivity to manipulate and control. However, they typically evidence a marked deficit in self-insight and rarely exhibit foresight. While inner tensions, frustrations, and dysphoria inevitably occur, such discomforts are not tolerated for very long, being discharged through acting-out, rather than intrapsychic mechanisms. Frequent references are made to the antisocials active avoidance of, and inability to tolerate awareness of depression (Reid, 1978). From this framework, conscious feelings of depression are viewed as a failure of the defensive mechanisms which permitted the previous involvement in antisocial behaviors (Cornier, 1966; Reid, 1978).

An appreciation of the antisocial's resistance to depression can be drawn from the psychoanalytic conceptualization of depression as a turning of hostility inward (Gershon, Cromer, & Klerman, 1968; Paykel & Prusoff, 1973; Schless et al., 1974), wherein, the inherent hostile affectivity, resistance to social dependency and interpersonal forcefulness of the antisocial all serve as safeguards against depression. This position is also consistent with cognitive-behavioral formulations.

Seligman (1974), for example, proposed that the individuals most resistant to depression (and helplessness) are those whose lives (especially childhood) have been filled with mastery and extensive experience controlling and manipulating sources of reinforcement, while Beck (1974) writes:

The satisfactory expression of hostility seems to be a very powerful means of increasing a person's subjective feeling of effectiveness, thus increasing his self-esteem and combating the negative cognitions which I hold to be so important in the generation of depression." (1974, p. 21)

While the antisocial's active independence, internal locus of control, and appetite for stimulating change may militate against the impact of life stressors, these same characteristics can also make the antisocial vulnerable to occasional major depressive episodes. Precipitants for depression might include situations of forced interpersonal submissiveness or curtailed personal freedom (e.g., incarceration or required military service), as well as internal conditions (e.g., medical illness or age-related physical decline) that result in incapacitation, passivity, or immobility. It has also been suggested (Reid, 1978) that depression may ensue when antisocials are forced to confront their inner emptiness, emotional void, and tenuous object relations. Again, this forced recognition is most likely to occur when antisocials are made to feel inadequate or weakened in a way which strips from them their "resilient shell of narcissism" (Reid, 1978, p. 499).

Although rather meager in comparison to the attention paid to the dependent, introversive, and obsessive characteristics of depressives, a growing body of literature argues for a depressive subtype whose salient features are autonomy, self-control, and aggressiveness. In addition to his "socially dependent" mode of depression, Beck (1981) proposes an "autonomous mode" characterized by a great investment in "preserving and increasing his independence, mobility and personal rights" (p. 272). For such action-oriented individuals, their well-being is dependent on their ability to maintain their autonomy and direct their own activities without external constraint or interference. There is little sensitivity to the needs of others with a corresponding lack of responsiveness to external feedback and corrective influences. It should be noted that the autonomous individuals described by Beck are also characterized by excessively high-internalized standards and criteria for achievement, features which may be more indicative of the compulsive character structure, or the noncriminal variant of the antisocial personality. Such individuals tend to experience a hostile depression, characterized by social withdrawal, rejection of help, self-criticism, resistance to change, and "active" violent forms of suicide attempts.

More recently, Matussek and Feil (1983) compared etidogenous unipolar, endogenous bipolar, and nonendogeneous depressive patients with normal controls on numerous self-report personality inventories (completed during symptom-free periods), as well as on data derived from several hours of psychiatric interviewing. They reported nonendogenous depressives to have disproportionately high scores on measures of autonomy, describing them as obstinate, nonadaptive, high-handed, independent, and egocentric" (p. 788). These patients were further characterized as demonstrating aggressive self-assertiveness, with a dissatisfied, negative attitude toward life. Unlike the antisocial characterization, however, the nonendogeneous depressives also showed "auto-destructive tendencies," including self-reproach, guilt, and fears of losing significant others.

Of particular relevance to the experience of depression in the antisocial personality is the "self-sacrificing depressive" included among the three subtypes in Kegan et al.'s (1981) sociomoral developmental formulation of depression. Characterized by egocentricity and control issues, these depressives experience dysphoria and discontent when unable to satisfy their desires due to external sources that constrain their freedoms or deprive them of the opportunity to act as they choose. For such individuals, issues of control, power, and influence are central. In a sense, a victim of their own impulses and desires, other people are viewed as either being instrumental, or as a source of opposition and threat toward achieving their needs.

The fear is that to relinquish living in the flux of each moment and satisfying each want is to relinquish the self, to compromise away the core experiences of self. Where "guilt" is expressed or experienced, it is not a matter of self-punishment but of anxious anticipation that other parties will punish or curtail. (Kegan et al., 1981, p. 4)

When depression does occur in the antisocial personality, and if not "masked" through an exaggeration of acting-out behaviors, it is likely to be colored by bitterness, angry complaints, and accusations. Periods of self-loathing may occur at the perception of inner weakness and ineffectualness, and the sympathy of others would he actively shunned. Such features might be consistent with the

"Factor Pattern D" depressive subtype described by Grinker et al., (1961). Demonstrating the traits of gloom, hopelessness and anxiety with some guilt feelings, these patients do not cling or demand attention, nor do they evidence hypochondriacal symptoms. Described as the "angry depressives," these patients typically exhibit demanding, provocative behavior, and are most likely to have had narcissistic and overaggressive premorbid personalities. Having traditionally assumed the role of authority and power at home and in business, depression may be precipitated by frustration or the inability to continue this pattern due to external factors. Such patients are difficult to treat as they resist psychotherapy in their constant struggle to remain "on top," and may express their rage eruptions through serious suicide attempts. A similar, empirically derived, depressive subtype is offered by Overall and Hollister (1980). The hostile depressive is characterized by anxiety, irritable complaining, and anger with suspiciousness sometimes accompanying feelings of hostility.

## THE NARCISSISTIC PERSONALITY

The essential feature of this personality style is an overvaluation of self-worth and a grandiose sense of self-importance and uniqueness. In seeming contradiction to the inflated self-concept is an inordinate need to be loved and admired by others. Unlike the ravenous affectional needs of histrionic and dependent personalities, however, narcissists believe that they are entitled to tribute and praise by virtue of their "specialness." These personalities also share the antisocial features of egocentricity, interpersonal exploitation, and exaggerated needs for power and success. Unlike the anger and vindictiveness of antisocials, however, narcissists are characterized by a benign arrogance and a sense that they are "above" the conventions and reciprocity of societal living. There is little real empathy for others but rather, a tendency

to use people for self-enhancement and for indulging their desires. Those who satisfy their needs are idealized, while others who can serve no immediate purpose are devalued and even treated contemptuously. This shifting of overvaluation and denigration may occur frequently within the same relationship. There is an expectation of preferential treatment and special favors, without assuming reciprocal responsibilities.

Narcissistic personalities are cognitively expansive, enjoying fantasies of unrealistic goals, with a tendency to overestimate their abilities and achievements. However, these exaggerated feelings of personal importance can leave the narcissist quite vulnerable to injuries of self-esteem and pronounced feelings of unworthiness, should their grandiose self-expectations not be met. Although characteristically imperturbable and insouciant, repeated failure and social humiliations may result in uncertainty and a loss of self-confidence. Over time, with the growing recognition of inconsistencies between their self-perception and their actual performance, comes self-disillusionment, feelings of fraudulence, and in some cases, a chronic state of dysthymia. In other instances, a psychic blow generated from a single event (e.g., a humiliating defeat or a public criticism) may be precipitate a brief, but severe, major depressive episode. Such states rarely endure for extended periods, as depression is not experienced as consonant with the narcissist's self-image. The symptomatology of the narcissistic depression may be quite variable, shifting between dramatic expressions of worthlessness and self-deprecation to irritable demandingness and criticism of others. These feelings of helplessness may accompany their depression; such perceptions tend to be attributed to external, "universal" causes rather than to personal, inner inadequacies (Abramson et al., 1978). Consistent with this formulation, a narcissist may subtly accuse others of not supporting or caring for them enough. At other times, hostility may be directly expressed, as the narcissist becomes enraged at others being witness to his/her shame and humiliation.

Owing to the infrequency of enduring major depression in these individuals, little mention has been made of premorbid narcissistic characteristics in depressed patients. There appears to be some overlap, however, between the "oral" depressive's pronounced affectional needs, and the "narcissistic" depressive's craving for admiration. Rado (1928) characterized the depressive personality as having a low tolerance for narcissistic frustrations, with even trivial disappointments precipitating a marked loss of self-esteem. According to Rado, after actively courting and securing the affection and devotion of a love object, the predepressive may then proceed to treat this individual with a sublime "nonchalance" or tyrannical domination. Characteristically, unaware of this mistreatment of the love object, the predepressive may react with embittered "vehemence," should the love object withdraw or retaliate (1928, p. 422).

Klerman (1974) described depression as a response to fallen self-esteem, a signal of discrepancies within the self-system between "ideal expectations and practical reality" (p. 139). In a similar fashion, Salzman (1970, 1972) described the predepressive as an individual characterized by exceptionally high standards and an unwillingness to accept compromises. Depression in such individuals follows the inability to maintain the unreasonable expectations set for oneself and others. A premorbidly independent depressive is described by Salzman (1970) which shares features of Beck's (1981) "autonomous mode," depressive, Kegan and associates' (Kegan et al., 1981) "self-sacrificing" depressive, and the "angry depressive" reported by Grinker et al. (1961). The independent depressive's overvaluation of autonomy and personal abilities is also reminiscent of the depressive experience in narcissistic personalities.

While he feels helpless and dependent, he is loath to accept any help, since his standards require total independence and omnipotence. He frequently rejects or distorts any sympathetic reassurance or aid, even while he needs and asks for it, insisting that it is insufficient or patronizing. (Salzman, 1970, p. 115)

It is Kernberg (1975) who provides perhaps the most relevant and eloquent description of the process of self-disillusionment and depression in the narcissistic.

For them, to accept the breakdown of the illusion of grandiosity, means to accept the dangerous, lingering awareness of the depreciated self—the hungry, empty, and lonely primitive self surrounded by a world of dangerous sadistically frustrating and revengeful objects. (1975, p. 311)

## THE PARANOID PERSONALITY

The paranoid personality may be viewed as a more dysfunctional variant of the antisocial and narcissistic patterns, with each sharing an independent orientation, and preoccupation with matters of adequacy, power, and prestige. Among the more prominent features of paranoid personalities are a pervasive and unwarranted mistrust of others, hypersensitivity to signs of deception or malevolence, and restricted affectivity. These individuals are fearful of external sources of influence, and may be resistant to forming intimate relationships for fear of being stripped of their power of self-determination. In spite of their air of self-importance, invincibility and pride, paranoid personalities tend to experience extreme jealousy and envy at the "good fortune" of others. To justify these feelings of resentment, they constantly search for signs of deception and actively construct situations to "test" the sincerity of others. Inevitably, their provocative and abrasive behaviors elicit the very signs of malice that they project upon others. Even the slightest, most trivial cues are seized upon and magnified to justify their preconceptions. Data that contradicts their perceptions are ignored, with the paranoid accepting no responsibility or blame for his role. This distortion of events, while personally logical, is irrational, and at times verging on delusional.

In their attempts to remain constantly on guard and mobilized, the paranoid may exhibit an edgy tension, irritability, and rigid defensive posture. To protect themselves from the sadistic treatment and betrayal that they anticipate, these individuals maintain an interpersonal distance and attempt to desensitize themselves from tender and affectionate feelings toward others. They become hard and insensitive to the suffering of others, as well as alienated from their own emotions and inner conflicts.

Although dysfunctionally rigid this stance of social withdrawal, callousness, and projection of personal malevolence and shortcomings onto others provides the paranoid with a glorified self-image and relative freedom from intrapsychic distress. Under circumstances of real or imagined threats to their autonomy or challenges of their competency, however, the paranoid's tenuous sense of self-determination and superiority can be badly shaken. Initially, these individuals may construct new "proofs" to fortify their persecutory fantasies, while vigorously struggling to reestablish their former autonomy and esteem.

During the course of their self-assertion, considerable hostility may be unleashed upon others. In paranoids with prominent narcissistic features, threats to their illusion of omnipotence and superiority may elicit a self-exalted and pompous variant of manic disorder, with an exaggerated cheerfulness, excitement, and buoyancy, reminiscent of their former state of complacency, these individuals are frantically driven to recover their lost exalted status. In some instances, their previous sense of self-determination and confidence cannot be easily reconstructed. Time and again, the paranoid's competencies have been shown to be defective, and they have been made to look foolish. Defeated and humiliated, their past arrogance and self-assurance now submerged, a deep sense of helplessness and major depression may ensue. As with the other independently oriented personalities (i.e., the narcissist and antisocial), the weakness and dependency associated with depression is perceived as unacceptable and humiliating. Consequently, their depression may be colored with anger, agitation, and a suspicious mistrust, that precludes the acceptance of outside help. Many of these behavioral features would correspond to Grinker et al.'s (1961) Factor Pattern D, "angry depressive" pattern, as well as with Overall and Hollister's (1980) "hostile depression," which is described as:

anxiety combined with depressive mood, but in this type irritable complaining, or angry feelings are also significantly present. Suspiciousness may accompany hostility in the hostile depression type which would suggest a mild paranoid-like syndrome. (1980, p. 376)

As the disorder is relatively infrequent in paranoid patterns, little has been written on the depressive experience in these personalities. Several components of the cognitive-behavioral models of depression, however, may be employed in understanding how and why depression may arise in such individuals. Beck's formulation (1974) for example, would emphasize the paranoid's proneness to distorted thought processes, such as arbitrary inference, selective abstraction, overgeneralization, personalization, and magnification. While paranoids do not characteristically hold negative self-perceptions, instead attributing any existing feelings of helplessness to external, unavoidable causes (Abramson et al., 1978), they do view others as malevolent and threatening. In Beck's (1974) terms, these individuals seem to possess a "template" or cognitive structure which predisposes them to distort perceptions and increase their sensitivity to certain events (e.g., social slights).

The Lewinsohnian model (Lewinsohn, 1974) which links low rates of reinforcement to depression, could also be applied to the paranoid. Sources of reinforcement from the environment are very limited for these individuals, due to their adaptive inflexibility, defensive rigidity, and the fears they harbor of interpersonal intimacy or unknown situations. As previously noted, once becoming depressed, these maladaptive characteristics make it very difficult for paranoids to seek or respond to potentially corrective experiences.

## THE PASSIVE-AGGRESSIVE PERSONALITY

The DSM-III characterization and diagnostic criteria for the passive-aggressive syndrome is narrowly focused upon one essential trait: resistance to external demands. We propose a more comprehensive concept of a "negativistic personality" to reflect this general contrariness and disinclination to doing as others wish. Beyond the passive-resistance of these individuals is a capricious impulsiveness, an irritable moodiness, an unaccommondating, fault-finding pessimism that characterizes their behavior (Millon, 1981). The broader formulation of the passive-aggressive or negativistic personality taken here is consistent with the "oral sadistic melancholic" described in the writings of early psychoanalysts. Characterized by deep-seated and pervasive ambivalence, consequent to difficulties arising in the "oral biting" stage, these individuals have been described as spiteful, petulant, and overdemanding with a pessimistic mistrust of the world (Menninger, 1940). More recently, Small, Small, Alig, & Moore (1970) in a study of 100 patients diagnosed as passive-aggressive personalities suggested that these individuals were characterized by:

interpersonal strife, verbal (not physical) aggressiveness, emotional storms, impulsivity and manipulative behavior. Suicidal gestures and lack of attention to everyday responsibilities commonly accompanied this intensive style of relating. (p. 978)

Based on the characteristics most frequently reported in both the theoretical and research literature, we propose the following to be among the most essential features of the passive-aggressive or negativistic personality:

1. Irritable affectivity (e.g., quick-tempered and moody).
2. Behavioral contrariness (e.g., passive-aggressive, obstructive, and sulking behaviors).
3. Discontented self-image (e.g., feels misunderstood, unappreciated, and disillusioned about life).
4. Deficient regulatory controls (e.g., capricious and poorly modulated emotional expression).
5. Interpersonal ambivalence (e.g., conflicts concerning dependency and self-assertion, unpredictable, and exasperating social behaviors).

The characteristic vacillation, discontentment, and socially maladaptive behaviors of passive-aggressive personalities almost inevitably result in varying states of interpersonal conflict and frustration as well as emotional confusion and distress. Consequently, such individuals are highly susceptible to psychiatric symptomatology, including anxiety, somatoform disorders, and especially depression. While major depressive episodes are not uncommon, passive-aggressive personalities are probably most likely to experience chronic forms of dysthymic disorder. Typically, these individuals display an agitated form of dysphoria, shifting between states of anxious futility, self-deprecation and despair to demanding irritability and bitter discontent. They may struggle between their desire to act out defiantly and their social sense that they must curtail their resentments. Although passive-aggressive personalities are accustomed to directly venting their feelings, anger will be restrained and turned inward should they sense that such expression might result in rejection or humiliation. Their grumbling, moody complaints, and sour pessimism, however, serve as a vehicle of tension discharge, relieving them periodically of mounting inner and outer directed anger. A secondary, but important function of these behaviors is to intimidate others and induce guilt, which provides the passive-aggressive with some sense of retribution for the miseries others have caused them in the past. After a time, however, the sullen moodiness and complaining of the passive-aggressive may tend to annoy and alienate others. Although the piteous distress of these depressed individuals may inhibit others from directly expressing their frustration and annoyance, their exasperation is readily perceived by the hypersensitive passive-aggressive and taken as further evidence of the low esteem others hold for him/her.

The dynamics of the passive-aggressive's depressive cycle is well formulated in Salzman's (1972) interpersonal theory of depression, as well as Coyne's (1976) interactional description of depression. Both theorists describe a process of a downward depressive spiral which starts with the depressive's initial expression of helplessness and hopelessness successfully engaging others and eliciting support. Questioning the sincerity of the attention received or dissatisfied with the extent of it, the depressive may then proceed to test others or complain of their lack of caring. Although irritated, the increasingly guilt-ridden and inhibited members of the social environment may continue, initially, to provide gestures of reassurance and support. The continuing abnegating tendencies and bemoaning of the depressive may ultimately, however, cause others to replace their sympathy with annoyance and their compassion with contempt. As noted earlier, the downward depressive spiral is especially likely to occur in the negativistic, passive-aggressive personality, who, in Lewinsohn's (1974) terms, lacks the social skills necessary to elicit and sustain consistent positive response from others.

Much of the theoretical and research literature on the young, hostile, unstable, and characterological depressives (Akiskal, 1983; Charney et al., 1981; Overall & Hollister, 1980; Paykel, 1972) is pertinent to the depressive experience in passive-aggressive personalities. In a study of characterological traits among a large group of depressed women, Wittenborn and Maurer (1977) noted the following features to persist before and after depressive episodes: a tendency to blame others, a demanding and complaining attitude, and low self-confidence. Two additional traits, obsessionalism and a tendency to dysphoria, manifested by worry and moodiness appeared as persisting traits among a subgroup of the depressed patients. In other patients, these latter traits, in addition to sulky-angry withdrawal, appeared in the prodromal phase of the depression. The authors speculate that the features appearing primarily at the onset of the depressive episode, might serve a defensive function against feelings of being overwhelmed and fears of losing control. An "atypical" or "hysteric" depressive subtype is described in the pharmacologic studies of British investigators, West and Daily (1959) and Sargant (1961). Patients within this category are described as being prone to both neurotic depression and anxiety hysteria. In contrast to the somatic symptoms of the endogenous depressives, atypical depressives manifested emotional overreactivity, anxiety, lethargy, irritability, and bitter complaining with a tendency to blame others. According to these investigators, such patients appear to have histories of good premorbid functioning, but were left depressed and feeling unable to cope by some precipitating stress event. Their emotional lability, hysterical exaggeration of their symptoms and fearfulness which appeared during their illness was not necessarily characteristic of their prior functioning.

In a factor analytic study of depressed women, Rosenthal and Gudeman (1967) reported two clinically meaningful factors. The first formed an endogenous symptom pattern, while the second was associated with self-pity, hypochondriasis, complaining and demanding behavior, irritability hostility, and anxiety. This second factor bears a resemblance to two of Paykel's (1972) depressive subtypes: the hostile depressives, characterized by verbal belligerence, and self-pity and the young personality disordered depressives who evidenced negativism and persisting disturbances in social and interpersonal relationships. Two additional empirically derived depressive subtypes appear to be descriptive of the depressive experience in passive-aggressive personalities. The first is the "agitated depression," as reported by Overall and Hollister (1980). This profile is characterized as an anxious depression, accompanied by tension, excitement, and psychomotor agitation. The second subtype which shares some of the features of the passive-aggressive depressive is the "Factor Pattern C," generated by Grinker et al. (1961), which is characterized by agitation, demandingness, complaining, and hypochondriasis.

Finally, similarities can be drawn between characteristics of the passive-aggressive and the "autodestructive-neurotic" factor of depression recently reported by Matussek and Feil (1983). As described by the authors, this factor is associated with withdrawal tendencies and contact disturbances, but is characterized primarily by:

mistrust (suspicion), dissatisfaction, a negative attitude toward life, anger, reproaches towards self and others, vulnerability and being easily hurt by petty matters. (p. 787)

It will be recalled that the authors of this study reported unipolar nonendogenous depressives to share many of the features previously reported to be associated with neurotic depressions, including chronic pessimism, loneliness, dissatisfaction, hostility, guilt feelings, and low-frustration tolerance.

## THE BORDERLINE PERSONALITY

The term borderline rightfully has been criticized for its overinclusiveness and failure to convey a behavioral pattern with distinctive stylistic features (Akiskal, 1981; Millon, 1981; Perry & Klerman, 1978). Depending upon the theoretical orientation taken, the label has been used to connote:

1. A character organization existing at a level of personality cohesion midway between neurotic and psychotic (Kernberg, 1970; Knight, 1953).

2. An incipient precursor of schizophrenia.

3. A set of personality variants within the affective disorders spectrum (Akiskal, Khani, & Scott-Strauss, 1979; Stone, 1979).

4. A relatively stable and moderately severe level of functioning that encompasses a variety of different personality subtypes (Grinker, Werble, & Drye, 1968; Millon, 1969).

The borderline label is employed by the DSM-III to reflect a discrete syndromal entity. As described by Akiskal (1981), the borderline personality features an unstable sense of self, stemming from disturbances in the individuation-separation phase of development.

The disorder is conceptualized in characterologic terms and defined by impulsivity, drug-seeking behavior, polymorphous sexuality, affective lability (i.e., display of unmodulated affects such as rage and panic), boredom, anhedonia, bizarre attempts at self-harm and "micropsychotic episodes." (Akiskal, 1981, p. 25)

From our perspective, the borderline concept is best used to represent a moderately severe level of functioning that may occur in virtually any of the personality disorders (perhaps with the exception of the schizoid and antisocial styles). Most frequently, however, the borderline personality appears as an advanced dysfunctional variant of the dependent, histrionic, antisocial or most commonly, the passive-aggressive personality. Regardless of the background personality history, borderlines are characterized by intense, variable moods and irregular energy levels, both of which frequently appear to be unrelated to external events. The affective state characteristically may be either depressed or excited, or noted by recurring periods of dejection and apathy, interspersed with episodes of anger, anxiety, or euphoria. There is a notable fear of separation and loss with considerable dependency reassurance required to maintain psychic equilibrium. Dependence upon others is colored with strong ambivalent feelings, such as love, anger, and guilt. Chronic feelings of anxiety may be present as borderlines struggle between feelings of anger and shame at being so dependent, and fears that self-assertion will endanger the security and protection that they so desperately seek. In an attempt to secure their anger and constrain their resentment, borderlines often turn against themselves in self-critical, condemnatory manner, which at times may lead to self-mutilating and suicidal thoughts as well as self-damaging behaviors.

As a result of their instability of both affect and behavior, borderlines are prone to rather checkered histories in their personal relationships and in school and work performance. Most exhibit repeated setbacks, a lack of judgment and foresight, tendencies to digress from earlier aspirations and failures to utilize their natural aptitudes and talents. For the most part, despite their setbacks, borderlines manage to recoup and regain their equilibrium before slipping into a more pernicious and serious decompensation. At times, however, when overwhelmed with mounting internal pressures, the borderline's tenuous controls may break down, resulting in an eruption of bizarre behaviors, irrational impulses, and delusional thoughts. These minipsychotic episodes tend to be brief and reversible and seem to assist borderlines in regaining their psychic balance. Afterward such episodes are usually recognized by the individual as being peculiar or deviant.

As noted earlier, overt and direct expressions of hostility in borderlines tend to be exhibited only impulsively, for fear that such actions might result in abandonment or rejection. A characteristic form of anger control in these individuals is to turn feelings of resentment inward into hypochondriacal disorders and mild depressive episodes. Borderlines tend to overplay their helplessness and anguish, employing their depression as a means of avoiding responsibilities and placing added burdens upon others. Their exaggerated plight causes guilt and discomfort among family and friends, as they try to meet the borderline's "justified" need for attention and care. As with passive-aggressive personalities, the dour moods and excessive complaints of the borderline may evoke exasperation and rebuke from others. In this event, borderlines may turn their anger upon themselves even more intensely, voicing a flood of self-deprecatory comments about their worthlessness, evilness, and their inordinate demands upon others. This self-derision may be accompanied by thinly veiled suicidal threats, gambling, drug abuse, or other impulsively self-damaging acts that serve not only to discharge anger, but often succeed in eliciting forgiveness and reassurance, if not compassion from others.

As evident from the preceding, borderlines succumb frequently to major depressive episodes. While the symptomatic features of their affective disorder tend to be rather mixed or erratic, varying in quality and focus according to the individual's specific vulnerabilities, it is typically some composite of depression and hostility.

Agitated depressions are most common, with the borderline exhibiting an apprehensive and tense despondency, that is accompanied by a querulous irritability and hostile depressive complaints. Some borderlines may demonstrate a more intropunitive, self-deprecatory depression, manifest by expressions of self-doubt, feelings of unworthiness, delusions of shame and sin, and suicidal thoughts. In other borderlines, a retarded form of depression is expressed, where guilt and self-disparagement is accompanied by lethargy, feelings of emptiness, boredom, and "deadness."

Borderline personalities may also display periods of bipolar disorder, similar to schizoaffective states, displaying a scattering of ideas and emotions, and a jumble of disconnected thoughts and aimless behaviors. As the borderline's moods are quite changeable and inconsistent with their thoughts and actions, it is virtually impossible for others to comprehend or empathize with their experiences. In their more euphoric moments, the borderline's zestful energy and joviality may temporarily engage and entertain others. The irrational, self-expansive quality of the borderlines' forced sociability, along with their lapses into irritability, eventually exasperate and drain others, however, destroying any patience or goodwill that was previously evoked.

The literature on depression contains many references to atypical treatment-resistant variants of depressive illness (e.g., character-spectrum disorder, hysterical dysphoria) that appear to be strongly associated with unstable, hostile, and "borderline" personality features (Akiskal, 1981; Charney et al., 1981; Winokur, 1979). In Grinker et al.'s (1968) landmark study of the borderline syndrome, depression is mentioned in each of the four borderline sub types: the Group I patients characterized by inappropriate and negative behaviors as well as hostile, angry depression; the Group II or "core" borderlines exhibiting a vacillating involvement with others and acting out of expressions of anger, alternating with a lonely, hopeless depression; the Group III patients, similar to DSM-III's schizoid personality, with a withdrawn, affectless depression; and the Group IV borderlines characterized by gross defects in self-esteem and confidence and a depressive quality not associated with anger or guilt feelings.

More recently, a drift has occurred in theoretical and research literature toward conceptualizing the borderline syndrome as a personality variant that falls within the spectrum of affective disorders. On the basis of differential responsiveness to pharmacologic agents, Klein and colleagues (Klein, 1975; Liebowitz & Klein, 1981) have asserted that the borderline designation subsumes several heterogeneous subtypes that all share a vulnerability toward affective dysfunction. Of the three borderline personality subtypes that he proposes, the phobic-anxious, the emotionally unstable, and the hysterical dysphorics, it is the hysteroid dysphoric syndrome which has generated the most attention and controversy (Spitzer & Williams, 1982; Stone, 1979). It will be recalled that the disorder is defined as a chronic, nonpsychotic disturbance involving repeated episodes of abruptly depressed mood in response to feeling rejected. The predisposing characteristics of the disorder include an inordinate need for affection and approval with an extreme intolerance of personal (especially romantic) rejection. According to Liebowitz and Klein (1981):

These vulnerabilities often give rise to a lifelong pattern of affective instability, difficulty being alone, and feelings of chronic emptiness, as well as to unstable or chaotic interpersonal and vocational functioning and a proneness toward angry outbursts, impulsive behavior, and physically self-damaging acts. In essence, the vulnerabilities that we posit as the core of hysteroid dysphoria may be sufficient to produce many of the features of borderline personality disorder. (p. 73)

Stone (1979) concurs with the authors, reporting that in his own experience, hysteroid dysphorics almost invariably met the traditional borderline criteria, and in many cases, had at least one first-degree relative with a serious affective disorder.

Another group of contemporary biological researchers, led by Akiskal (1983, 1981), has also argued strongly for the inclusion of the borderline syndrome within the subaffective spectrum. On the basis of affective family history, positive dexamethasone suppression test findings, major affective episodes, and high risk of suicide during prospective follow-up, Akiskal (1983) has suggested that approximately 50 percent of patients with severe characterologic disturbances, subsumed under the "borderline" rubric seem to suffer from lifelong affective disorders. He suggests that while about one fifth of borderline patients do suffer severe, primary characterological pathology in the form of somatization disorder and sociopathy, the largest group of borderlines exhibit "atypical, chronic and complicated forms of affective disorder with second a personality dysfunction" (Akiskal, 1981, p. 31). Akiskal argues that while such patients may superficially present the picture of a personality disorder, an underlying biological affective illness may be "masked" by characterologic disturbances. He proposes a variety of subaffective disorders that may fall within the borderline realm. According to Akiskal, subaffective disorder, as opposed to major affective disorders, manifest only subsyndromal and intermittent (often lifelong) affective psychopathology, which only infrequently crystallizes into discrete syndromal episodes. The mood changes associated with such disorders may be quite subtle, with behavioral and interpersonal disturbances (in part having resulted from the affective instability) dominating the clinical picture.

Akiskal et al. (1979) have argued perhaps most strongly for the conceptualization of "cyclothymia" as a subclinical, borderline, affective disorder. They suggest that the bipolar spectrum may merge at one end with psychotic, schizoaffective states and overlap at the other extreme with certain characterological and temperamental disorders. The authors point out the difficulty in diagnostically differentiating the borderline personality disorder from the cyclothymic disorder, a position reflecting Millon's (1969) earlier formulation of the "borderline cycloid" personality. Akiskal notes that the two syndromes may share such features as irritable and angry outbursts, repeated conjugal or romantic failures, uneven work on academic records, geographic instability, and alcohol or drug abuse. A similar state of diagnostic confusion is suggested when the clinician is faced with differentiating the so-called bipolar II disorders from borderline characterologic psychopathology.

Both Akiskal and the authors of this chapter proposed that the unstable sense of self which is characteristic of the borderline may be less of an ego development problem and more a consequence of a constitutional affective disorder with associated unpredictable, uncontrollable mood swings. It is further suggested that the borderline's relatively poor response to psychotherapy may result in many

cases, from a failure to provide pharmacologic treatment of the underlying, affective disorder. Stone (1979) also cites the similarities of the two disorders, observing that a large number of cyclothymic patients, in addition to having depressive and hypomanic bouts, favorably respond to lithium, and that relatives with bipolar or unipolar illness also exhibit characteristics that meet the criteria for borderline personality disorder.

The overlap between the borderline and dysthymic concepts has also been addressed (Akiskal, 1983; Snyder, Sajadi, Pitts, & Goodpaster, 1982). Similar to cyclothymia, dysthymic disorders arc defined as chronic, intermittent, subaffective manifestations of unipolar depressive disorders. Akiskal offers a typology of chronic, low-grade dysphoric states, including "characterologic depression," which he considers to be closest to the DSM-III dysthymic syndrome. In this form of dysthymic disorder, onset typically occurs prior to adulthood and affective states are tightly interwoven with personality traits. On the basis of response to thymoleptic drugs, characterologic depressions are further divided into "subaffective dysthymic disorders," where personality features appear secondary to frequent low-grade endogenous depression, and "character-spectrum disorders," which are primarily characterologic pathology. This latter subtype reportedly occurs more frequently in female patients with "unstable" personality traits including substance abuse. Individuals falling within the character-spectrum group exhibit normal REM latency, typically poor response to somatic therapies, and an irritable dysphoria that is seldom complicated by discrete depressive episodes. Family history tends to be positive for alcoholism and sociopathy, but not for affective illness. Akiskal (1983) disagrees with Winokur (1979) speculation that there is a genetic basis to this disorder. Instead, he emphasizes that the developmental histories of such individuals (e.g., parental loss and broken homes) lend themselves to characterologic disturbance and an exquisite sensitivity to separation, loss, or romantic disappointment during adult life. From this perspective, Akiskal (1981), argues that what Liebowitz and Klein (1981) have described as "hysteroid dysphoria," is best placed in the character-spectrum category, rather than with primary affective disorders.

Relevant to the issue of dysthymic disorder in borderline personalities is the work of Snyder et al. (1982). Using standardized observer- and subject-rated scales for depression, the authors compared patients satisfying the DSM-III criteria for both syndromes. While the scales as a whole failed to differentiate between the depressions of the borderline disorder and the dysthymic disorder, certain features, extracted from the rating scales (e.g., anger, affective instability, impulsiveness, and suspiciousness) were "strikingly" more common in the borderline patients.

## THE COMPULSIVE PERSONALITY

The most prominent features of the compulsive personality include excessive emotional control and interpersonal reserve, preoccupation with matters of order, organization and efficiency, indecisiveness, and a tendency toward being overly conscientious, moralistic, and judgmental. It is our belief that much of the personality organization of the compulsive individual arises in reaction to marked underlying feelings of interpersonal ambivalence. Like passive-aggressive personalities, compulsive personalities are torn between their leanings toward submissive dependence on the one hand and defiant autonomy on the other (Millon, 1981). Unlike the overt emotional lability and chronic vacillation of passive-aggressives, however, compulsive personalities bind and submerge their rebellious and oppositional urges through a rigid stance of overcompliance, conformity, and propriety. By clinging grimly to rules of society and insisting upon regularity and uniformity in relationships and life events, these individuals help restrain and protect themselves against their own aggressive impulses

and independent strivings. Although this behavioral and cognitive rigidity may effectively shield the individual from intrapsychic conflict as well as social criticism, it may also preclude growth and change, cause alienation from inner feelings and interfere with the formation of intimate and warm relationships.

To others, compulsives appear to be industrious and efficient, but lacking in flexibility, imagination, and spontaneity. They may also be viewed as stubborn or stingy and picayune, with a tendency to get lost in the minutiae, rather than appreciate the substance of everyday life. Compulsives are easily upset by the unfamiliar or by deviations from their accustomed routines. Their perfectionistic standards and need for certainty may result in a tendency toward indecisiveness and procrastination. While the social behavior of compulsives is typically polite and formal, there is a definite tendency to relate to others on the basis of their rank or status. Compulsives require considerable reassurance and approval from their superiors and consequently may relate to them in a deferential, ingratiating, and even obsequious manner. In contrast, compulsives may be quite autocratic and condemnatory with subordinates using their authority and the rules they represent to justify the venting of considerable hostility and criticalness.

Compulsives devalue self-exploration and exhibit little or no insight into their motives and feelings. Beset with deep ambivalence and contrary feelings, extensive defensive maneuvers must be employed to transmute or seal off frightening urges from conscious awareness. While rigid moralism and behavioral conformity bind much of their hidden feelings of defiance and anger, these individuals also find it necessary to compartmentalize or isolate their emotional responses to situations. They may particularly attempt to block or otherwise neutralize reactions to stressful events, for fear that signs of emotional weakness may become apparent and lead to embarrassment or disapproval.

Despite their elaborate defensive strategies, compulsives tend to be among the personality styles that are most troubled by psychiatric symptoms. Their cognitive and behavioral organization make them particularly susceptible to affective disorders of virtually every type. Plagued by their own exacting standards, as well as the high expectations that they perceive others to hold for them, compulsives frequently feel as though they have fallen short of their criteria for acceptable performance. Although angry at themselves for being imperfect and resentful toward others for their unyielding demands, compulsives dare not expose either their own shortcomings or their hostility toward others. Rather than voicing their defiance or venting their resentment and thereby being subject to social rebuke, they turn their feelings inward, discharging their anger toward themselves.

In this regard, the compulsives propensity toward experiencing guilt, expressing self-reproval, and acting contrite serves as a form of expiation for hidden, unacceptable feelings while preventing humiliation or condemnation from others. The anger-guilt, self-degradation sequence may occur quite frequently in compulsives, resulting in a chronic, mild depression, or dysthymic disorder. Major depressive states may be quite common among compulsives in later life, usually following a period of reflection and self-evaluation. At such times, compulsives are confronted with the realization that their lofty life goals and long-held standards of excellence have not been attained and further, that rigid conformity to external values has yielded a rather barren existence with the denial of a multitude of potentially satisfying experiences. Severe depression in compulsives tends to have an agitated and apprehensive quality, marked by feelings of guilt and a tendency to complain about personal sin and unworthiness. The tense and anxious coloring of their depression may be a reflection of their struggle to contain their hostility and resentments, as well as their fear that contrition and despondency will prompt derision and condemnation from others.

On occasion, in an exaggerated portrayal of their premorbid drive and achievement strivings, compulsives will attempt to counter a melancholic depression with brief periods of accelerated activity directed toward some unrealistic goal. Such manic-like episodes of grandiosity and self-assertion tend to be short lived, however, as they may generate considerable anxiety.

The compulsive personality (also known as the anankastic obsessive, or conforming personality) is undoubtedly the most frequently cited personality in depression literature. Its psychoanalytic counterpart, the anal character, has often been described in association with neurotic depression, manic-depression and involutional melancholia. Abraham (1924/1966), noting marked similarities between obsessive-compulsives and melancholics, suggested that both syndromes arose from fixations in the anal stage of psychosexual development, with obsessives emerging from the more advanced anal retentive phase and melancholics arising from complications in the more primitive anal-expulsive phase. Abraham cites a number of shared anal character traits between the obsessive-compulsive and the melancholic, including excessive punctuality, orderliness, obstinacy, parsimony, and marked feelings of ambivalence in interpersonal relationships.

A number of other theorists with analytic leanings have offered depressive subtypes akin to the anal-obsessive. A "subvalid" personality has been proposed by Swedish psychiatrist Sjobring (1973) in his multidimensional theory of personality. The subvalid individual is described as cautious, reserved, precise, industrious, and scrupulous. Numerous researchers (Coppen, 1966; Perris, 1966) employing the Nyman-Marke Temperament Scale (NMTS), which objectives Sjobring's concepts, found depressed individuals (especially of the unipolar endogenous type) to exhibit a significant tendency toward subvalidity. As used on the NMTS, the subvalid concept has a somewhat broader meaning, referring to individuals who are bound to routine, easy to fatigue, cautious, tense, neurasthenic, and meticulous (Akiskal et al., 1983). Chodoff (1970) focused upon the interpersonal ambivalence and unexpressed hostility of premorbid depressives. He offered two behavioral paths that might be taken in response to such dependency conflicts: utilization of "extractive techniques" and the active manipulation of others, or the denial of such needs and the internalization of unrealistic self-standards. Chodoff (1970) suggested that the latter approach may lead to the development of a "perfectionistic, neurotically, prideful obsessive" (p. 58).

In Blatt's (1974) depressive typology, which is based on the level of object representation achieved, he describes a depression subtype associated with issues of "superego formation and the relatively advanced and complex phenomenon of guilt." The "introjective depression" is characterized by intense feelings of inferiority, guilt, and worthlessness. On the basis of a factor analytic study employing the Depressive Experiences Questionnaires, Blatt et al. (1976) identified a "self-criticism" factor that relates closely to the concept of introjective depression. According to the authors, the self-criticism factor in comparison with the other two factors identified, had the highest correlation with traditional psychometric measures of depression. This factor consisted of items relating to:

concerns about feeling guilty, empty, hopeless, unsatisfied, and insecure, having failed to meet expectations and standards, and being unable to assume responsibility, threatened by change, feeling ambivalent about self and others, and tending to assume blame and feel critical toward self. (Blatt et al., 1976, p. 385)

A later study (Blatt et al., 1982) involving the identification of depressive subtypes on the basis of psychiatric case histories showed clinical records of the self-criticism group to be characterized by:

social isolation, intense and self-critical involvement in work, professional and/or academic strivings, feelings of worthlessness and failure, a history of a very critical or idealized parent, obsessive and paranoid features, anxiety and agitation. (Blatt et al., 1982, p. 120)

In a similar fashion, Arieti and Bemporad (1980) propose a "dominant goal" predepressive among their three premorbid types of depressive personality. Described as "usually seclusive, arrogant, and often obsessive," this form of personality organization is reported to be more common in men. According to Arieti and Bemporad (1980) dominant-goal individuals have learned from their parents that achievement is rewarded with support and acceptance. Consequently, these individuals come to derive their sense of meaningfulness, satisfaction, and self-esteem from fantasies about obtaining some lofty objective. In pursuing their goals, other activities may be shunned as a diversion from their quest. For such individuals, the realization that a selected goal is unobtainable may threaten not only their sense of self-esteem, but the very structure upon which their life's meaning is based.

The two basic depressive personality modes of Beck (1981) have already been discussed. The "autonomous mode" shares several features of the compulsive including: internalized standards, goals, and criteria for achievement that tend to be higher than the conventionally accepted norms; an emphasis on independence, control and action, and a tendency to be direct, dogmatic, and authoritarian. Individuals operating within the autonomous mode are vulnerable to depression when they feel they have failed in their attempts to reach a crucial goal. Beck (1981) describes the "autonomous depression" as being permeated with the theme of defeat or failure, as the individual "blames himself continually for falling below his standard (self-attribution), and excoriates himself for his incompetence (self-punishment)" (Beck, 1981, p. 276). Beck also notes that such individuals experience a striking behavioral shift when depressed, from having been "self-sufficient, inner-directed, and active" to appearing "powerless, devoid of initiative and self-control" (Beck, 1981, p. 276).

From a slightly different theoretical perspective (i.e., sociomoral development), Kegan et al. (1981) proposed a "self-evaluative depression" in which "dysphoria and discontent are described in terms of the failure to live up to one's own hopes for oneself, falling short of one's standards" and "negative self-evaluation" (Kegan et al., 1981, p. 6). In this form of depression, there may also be a sense of not being whole, as "the price of self-determination and control has been the exclusion of important parts of oneself," and "self-imposed isolation, and the inability to experience true intimacy" (Kegan et al., 1981, pp. 6–7).

As mentioned earlier, the compulsive personality has been frequently cited in association with involutional melancholia. While the syndrome of involutional depression has been the subject of considerable debate (Chodoff, 1972), the concept of an endogenous unipolar or psychotic depression, occurring for the first time in middle age, has received widespread clinical recognition. In association with this syndrome, a melancholic personality has been proposed that is characterized by some "oral," but predominantly "anankastic" features. Von Zerssen (1977) in his review of the international literature, found the clearest association between affective disorders and personality traits to be that between unipolar depressive psychosis (including involutional melancholia) and the melancholic personality. His description of the "melancholic type" includes the features of "orderliness, conscientiousness, meticulousness, high value achievement, conventional thinking and dependency on close personal relationships" (Von Zerssen, 1977, pp. 97–98). The association of the late onset endogenous depression with anankastic, obsessional traits has been reported by a number of other researchers.

Paykel et al. (1976) found older depressed patients in their study group to be significantly less neurotic, hysterical, and oral, but more obsessive. On symptomatic measures, these patients also evidenced a more severe endogenous pattern of depression, accompanied by a greater level of anxiety than seen in younger patients. Cadoret, Baker, Dorzab, and Winokur (1971), employing Cattell's personality inventory, found that scores on the factor denoting "superego strength" were highest in depressive patients having the onset of their illness after the age of 40. Scores on this factor were also higher in their healthy, first degree relatives, as compared to early-onset depressive patients. On the basis of such studies, Yerevanian and Akiskal (1979) concluded that:

there appears little reason to dispute the classic notion that portrays the late-onset (usually psychotic) depressive as a self-critical, conscientious, hardworking, and well-integrated (into the dominant culture) individual who has responded to losses and life reverses with self-punitive and self-denigrating cognitions. (p. 603)

In recognition of studies that have failed to confirm the age association between obsessionalism and unipolar depression (e.g., Snaith, McGuire, & Fox, 1971; Kendell & Discipio, 1970), Chodoff (1972) drew a more conservative conclusion:

among individuals suffering depressive breakdowns for the first time in middle life, there exists a certain well-defined subgroup, among men as well as women, who display premorbid obsessional personality characteristics. (1972, p. 667)

Interpretation of the apparent age effect upon personality and depressive features is not straightforward. As mentioned earlier, mid-life reflection and self-evaluation may confront conforming, "obsessive" individuals with the realization that: (a) idealized internal standards have rarely been met; (b) productivity and the capacity to achieve are likely to decline sharply with advanced age,

(c) the choice for an industrious, conforming lifestyle has been at the expense of interpersonal intimacy and emotional fulfillment. An alternate explanation for these age-associated features is that personality traits may actually be altered with age, leading to the development of "more obsessive, less hysterical, less dependent and less emotionally labile patterns" (Paykel et al., 1976, p. 332).

As with involutional melancholia, anankastic, compulsive personality traits have held a prominent place in the psychoanalytic literature on manic-depressive illness. Kolb, in his 1973 revision of Noyes' original text, provides the following description of the premorbid personality of a depressed-type manic-depressive:

Many have been scrupulous persons of rigid ethical and moral standards, meticulous, self-demanding, perfectionistic, self-depreciatory, prudish, given to self-reproach, and sensitive to criticism. Their obsessive-compulsive tendency have doubtless been defensive mechanisms for handling hostility, which characteristically they cannot express externally. (Kolb, 1973, pp. 372–373)

A number of empirically based studies have suggested that bipolar disorders are not necessarily associated with cyclothymic, hyperthymic, or unstable characterologic features. Rather, there is evidence to suggest that the illness may occur most frequently among individuals who, except for "obsessive" features, are otherwise unremarkable (Donnelly, Murphy, & Goodwin, 1976; Hirschfeld & Klerman, 1979; Perris, 1971). Consistent with this is the recent factor analytic study of Matussek and Feil (1983) which identified a "hypomanic success and achievement" factor that differentiated endogenous bipolar patients from "normals," as well as from other types of depressed patients. The authors report that this factor reflects a personality substructure that is characterized by:

hypomanic drive for success, high aspiration level, anankastic features, pectantry, subordi-

nate to authority, perseverance in difficult tasks, and detachment for achievement. (Matussek & Feil, 1983, p. 787)

The authors note that the strong achievement orientation, exaggerated aspiration level, pronounced sense of duty, and scrupulousness of the endogenous bipolar patients all serve to make the individual exquisitely vulnerable to feelings of inadequacy and failure, while reaching a lofty goal may trigger a mania if it subjectively represents a great success after hard work.

Akiskal and his colleagues (Akiskal et al., 1983; Akiskal et al., 1979) have commented on the difficulty in differentiating the ambitious, driven, hyperthymic individual with an inordinate capacity for work, from the dutybound and work-addicted compulsive individual. Similarities are also drawn between the premorbid adjustment of bipolar patients and the "Type A" coronary-prone behavior pattern, which is characterized by extremes of competitiveness, achievement striving, time urgency, and aggressiveness. It is suggested that future research might well be directed at detecting the incidence of frank manic-depressive illness in the families of people displaying the Type A pattern. Akiskal et al. (1979) also suggest similarities between compulsive personalities and manic-depressive patients in terms of pharmacological treatment response. They note the ample number of anecdotal reports winch have suggested favorable and sometimes dramatic effects of lithium carbonate upon both the compulsive drivenness of manic-depressives during intermorbid periods, as well as the driveness, indecisiveness, and anxious worry seen in several compulsive personality disorders.

Finally, this same group of researchers (Akiskal, 1983; Akiskal et al., 1983) have described a subaffective dysthymic disorder that is associated with: higher rates of familial bipolar illness, anhedonic, guilt-ridden, hypersomnic retarded depressions, occasional hypomanic responses to tricyclic antidepressant therapy, and favorable responses to lithium. Akiskal (1983) suggests that the depressive personality characteristics exhibited by such patients; that is, introversion with brief periods of hypomanic extroversion, are best considered lifelong, subaffective expressions of a primary depressive disorder. It will be recalled that this syndrome has been associated with numerous Schneiderian depressive features (e.g., nonassertiveness, pessimism, self-criticism, conscientiousness, and worried preoccupations about inadequacy and failure) that are also consistent with the compulsive personality organization.

At this point in the literature review, an important distinction must be made between compulsive personality traits and obsessive-compulsive symptoms as they occur in depression. While there is some evidence that obsessions, ruminative worry, and compulsive behaviors are more likely to occur in individuals with "obsessive" or compulsive premorbid personalities (Vaughan, 1976; Videbech, 1975), these same symptoms are frequent accompaniments of depressive episodes in a variety of other personality types. Studies that have attempted to carefully tease apart depressive symptomatology from enduring characterologic traits, however, have revealed considerable differences with respect to the intensity and duration of obsessive-compulsive symptoms in depression.

Wittenborn and Maurer's (1977) investigation of characterologic traits among depressives (reviewed earlier in this chapter) found two traits, worried moodiness and obsessionalism to be persistent features among only a subgroup of the depressed patients. In other patients, these features appeared as prodromal intensification of the episode, remitting with the development of the depression. Kendell and Discipio (1970) found that on measures of obsessionalism, recovered unipolar depressives had scores intermediate between those of obsessional neurotics and two "normal" groups. Comparisons between neurotic and psychotic depressives found neurotic depressives to be more obsessional premorbidly while psychotic depressives developed more new obsessional symptomatology during their depressive illness. Contrary to other reports (Gittelson, 1966; Videbech, 1975), obsessional traits did not appear to intensify during the depressive episode among premorbidly obsessional individuals. Vaughan (1976) found obsessive symptoms to occur more frequently in depression among a group of patients with obsessional personalities. He further reported that premorbidly obsessive patients evidenced less anxiety during their illness, while the presence of obsessive symptoms in other depressed patients tended to be associated with an agitated and anxious form of depression.

Of particular interest is the suggestion among some of these studies that obsessional symptoms and traits serve as a defense against depression. Wittenborn and Maurer (1977) hypothesize that intensification of obsessionalism and denial of anger at the onset of the depressive episode may serve a defensive function among individuals feeling overwhelmed by environmental stressors and sensing an impending loss of control. Kendell and Discipio (1970) suggested that marked premorbid obsessionalism seemed to offer protection against the development of manic episodes. Von Zerssen (1977), in his review of the literature, postulated that many of the traits of the "melancholic-type" resulted from the tendency to build defenses against the negative emotions involved in depression. He cites as an example, the melancholic's strivings toward self-confirmation in performance, as a strategy to avoid a lack of self-esteem. Consistent with this line of thought and in summary, Yerevaniati and Akiskal (1979) have noted that:

the psychoanalytical literature has suggested that the anankastic traits of orderliness, guilt and concern for others are a defense against the depressive's tendency for disorganization, hostility and self-preoccupation. (1979, p. 604)

## CONCLUSIONS

A sizable body of literature has been reviewed in this chapter in an attempt to better elucidate the relationship between personality and depressive disorders. For the most part, our discussion has been restricted to the role that personality may play in the etiology and pathogenesis of affective disorders. While research in this area has been rather speculative, unsystematic, and for some personality disorders, quite sparse, it is our contention that a sufficient amount of both clinical and empirical evidence argues for the inclusion of a wide variety of characterologic features among the predisposing factors to depression. Furthermore once a depressive illness has emerged, it may be argued that disorders of personality, as well as specific personality traits may exert a pathoplastic effect, coloring the depressive symptom picture and influencing treatment compliance, responsivity and ultimately, outcome.

This chapter has paid only modest attention to the viewpoint that both personality and depressive disorders are expressions of shared genetic or constitutional endowments, whereby personality features may be conceptualized as a milder or alternative expression of affective illness. Similarly, we have not addressed the possibility that personality features may arise as complications or sequelae or effective illness. In this regard, Akiskal et al. (1983) have suggested the following possibilities as to how personality may be altered by affective illness: (1) personality presentation (i.e., behaviors, judgment, motivation, and emotional expression) may be changed during an affective episode, (2) interpersonal maladjustments and familial conflicts may immediately follow the resolution of a depressive or manic episode, and (3) long-term alterations in personality organization as well as social deterioration may result from chronic affective illness or frequently recurring affective episodes.

To date, methodologic limitations have clouded our understanding of some of issues raised here. It remains the formidable task of future research to identify the range of genetic-constitutional, developmental, sociocultural, and experiential factors from which both personality and depression emerge. Only then can an appreciation of the complex interrelationship of the two be obtained.

## REFERENCES

Abraham, K. (1966). A short study of the development of the libido, viewed in the light of mental disorders. In B. D. Lewin (Ed.), *On character and development.* New York: Norton. (Original work published 1924)

Abraham, K. (1968). Notes on the psychoanalytical investigation and treatment of manic-depressive insanity and allied conditions. In W. Gaylin (Ed.), *The meaning of despair* (pp. 26–50). New York: Science House. (Original work published 1911)

Abramson, L. Y., Seligman M. E., & Teasdale, R. (1978). Learned helplessness in humans: Critique and reformulation. *Journal of Abnormal Psychology, 87,* 49–74.

Akiskal, H. S. (1981). Subaffective disorders: Dysthymic, cyclothymic and bipolar II disorders in the "borderline" realm. *Psychiatric Clinics of North America, 4*(1), 25–46.

Akiskal, H. S. (1983). Dysthymic disorder: Psychopathology of proposed chronic depressive subtypes. *American Journal of Psychiatry, 140*(1), 11–20.

Akiskal, H. S., Hirschfield, R., & Yerevanian, B. (1983). The relationship of personality to affective disorders. *Archives of General Psychiatry, 40,* 801–810.

Akiskal, H. S., Khani, M. K., & Scott-Strauss, A. (1979). Cyclothymic temperamental disorders. *Psychiatric Clinics of North America, 2*(3), 527–554.

Akiskal, H. S., Rosenthal, T. L., Paykal, R. F., Lemmi, H., Rosenthal, R. H., & Scott-Strauss, A. (1980). Characterological depressions: Clinical and sleep EEG findings separating "subaffective dysthymias" from "character-spectrum disorders." *Archives of General Psychiatry, 37,* 777–783.

Altman, J. H., & Wittenborn, J. R. (1980). Depression-prone personality in women. *Journal of Abnormal Psychology, 89,* 303–308.

American Psychiatric Association. (1980). *Diagnostic and statistical manual of mental disorders (DSM-III)*. Washington, DC: Author.

Arieti, S., & Bemporad, J. R. (1980). The psychological organization of depression. *American Journal of Psychiatry, 137,* 1360–1365.

Beck, A. T. (1974). The development of depression: A cognitive model. In R. J. Friedman & M. M. Katz (Eds.), *The psychology of depression: Contemporary theory and research (pp. 3–19)*. Washington, DC: Winston.

Beck, A. T. (1981). Cognitive therapy of depression: New perspectives. In P. Clayton & J. Barrett (Eds.), *Treatment of depression: Old controversies and new approaches*. New York: Raven Press.

Becker, J. (1977). *Affective disorders*. New York: General Learning Press.

Bemporad, J. (1971). New views on the psychodynamics of the depressive character. In S. Arieti (Ed.), *World biennial of psychiatry and psychotherapy* (Vol. 1, pp. 219–243). New York: Basic Books.

Bibring, E. (1953). The mechanism of depression. In P. Greenacre (Ed.), *Affective disorders*. New York: International Universities Press.

Blaney, P. H. (1977). Contemporary theories of depression: Critique and comparison. *Journal of Abnormal Psychology, 86,* 203–223.

Blatt, S. J. (1974). Levels of object representation in anaclinitic and introjective depression. *Psychoanalytic Study of the Child, 29,* 426–427.

Blatt, S. J., D'Afflitti, P., & Quinlan, D. M. (1976). Experiences of depression in normal young adults. *Journal of Abnormal Psychology, 85,* 383–389.

Blatt, S. J., Quinlan, D. M., Chevon, E. S., McDonald, C., & Zuroff, D. (1982). Dependency and self-criticism: Psychological dimensions of depression. *Journal of Consulting and Clinical Psychology, 50,* 113–124.

Cadoret, R., Baker, M., Dorzab, J., & Winokur, G. (1971). Depressive disease: Personality factors in patients and their relatives. *Biological Psychiatry, 3,* 85–93.

Charney, D. S., Nelson, J. C., & Quinlan, D. M. (1981). Personality traits and disorder in depression. *American Journal of Psychiatry, 138,* 1601–1604.

Chodoff, P. (1970). The core problem in depression: Interpersonal aspects. In J. Masserman (Ed.), *Depressions: Theories and therapies, science and psychoanalysis* (Vol. 17, pp. 56–65). New York: Grune & Stratton.

Chodoff, P. (1972). The depressive personality: A critical review. *Archives of General Psychiatry, 27,* 666–673.

Cleckley, H. (1941). *The mask of sanity*. St. Louis, MO: C. V. Mosby.

Coppen, A. (1966). The Marke-Nyman temperament scale: An English translation. *British Journal of Medical Psychology, 39,* 55–59.

Cornier, B. M. (1966). Depression and persistent criminality. *Canadian Psychiatric Association Journal, 11,* 208–220.

Coyne, J. C. (1976). Toward an interactional description of depression. *Psychiatry, 39,* 28–40.

Donnelly, E., Murphy, D., & Goodwin, F. (1976). Cross-sectional and longitudinal comparisons of bipolar and unipolar depressed groups on the MMPI. *Journal of Consulting and Clinical Psychology, 44,* 233–237.

Fenichel, O. (1968). Depression and mania. In W. Gaylin (Ed.), *The meaning of despair* (pp. 108–154). New York: Science House.

Freud, S. (1932). Libidinal types. In *Collected Papers* (English translation, Vol. 5, 1950). London: Hogarth.

Freud, S. (1968) Mourning and melancholia. In W. Gaylin (Ed.), *The meaning of despair* (pp. 50–70). New York: Science House. (Original work published 1917)

Gershon, E., Cromer, M., & Klerman, G. (1968). Hostility and depression. *Psychiatry, 31,* 224–235.

Gittelson, N. L. (1966). The effect of obsessions on depressive psychosis. *British Journal of Psychiatry, 112,* 253–259.

Grinker, R. R., Miller, J., Sabshin, M., Nunn, R., & Nunnally, J. (1961). *The phenomenon of depressions*. New York: Hoeber.

Grinker, R. R., Werble, B., & Drye, R. C. (1968). *Borderline syndrome*. New York: Basic Books.

Hirschfield, R., & Klerman, G. (1979). Personality attributes and affective disorders. *American Journal of Psychiatry, 136,* 67–70.

Hirschfield, R., Klerman, G., Clayton, P., & Keller, M. (1983). Personality and depression. *Archives of General Psychiatry, 40,* 993–998.

Kegan, R., Rogers, L., & Quinlan, D. (1981). *Constructive-developmental organizations of depression.* Invited paper presented to a symposium on New Approaches to Depression, American Psychological Association annual meeting, Los Angeles.

Kendell, R. E., & Discipio, W. J. (1970). Obsessional symptoms and obsessional personality traits in patients with depressive illness. *Psychological Medicine, 1,* 65–72.

Kernberg, O. F. (1970). A psychoanalytic classification of character pathology. *Journal of the American Psychoanalytic Association, 18,* 800–822.

Kernberg, O. F. (1975). *Borderline condition and pathological narcissism.* New York: Jason Aronson.

Klein, D. F. (1975). Psychopharmacology and the borderline patient. In J. E. Mack (Ed.), *Borderline states in psychiatry.* New York: Grune & Stratton.

Klerman, G. L. (1973). The relationship between personality and clinical depressions: Overcoming the obstacles to verifying psychodynamic theories. *International Journal of Psychiatry, 11,* 227–233.

Klerman, G. L. (1974). Depression and adaptation. In R. J. Friedman & M. M. Katz (Eds.), *The psychology of depression: Contemporary theory and research* (pp. 129–145). Washington, DC: V. H. Winston & Sons.

Knight, R. P. (1953). Borderline states. *Bulletin of the Menninger Clinic, 17,* 1–12.

Kohlberg, L. (1976). Moral stages and moralization: The cognitive developmental approach. In T. Lickona (Ed.), *Moral development and behavior.* New York: Holt, Rinehart & Winston.

Kolb, L. C. (1973). *Modern clinical psychiatry* (8th ed.). Philadelphia: W. B. Saunders.

Lazare, A., & Klerman, G. L. (1968). Hysteria and depression: The frequency and significance of hysterical personality features in hospitalized depressed women. *American Journal of Psychiatry, 11,* 48–58.

Lesse, S. (1974). Depression masked by acting-out behavior patterns. *American Journal of Psychotherapy, 28,* 352–361.

Lewinsohn, P. M. (1974). A behavioral approach to depression. In R. J. Friedman & M. M. Katz (Eds.), *The psychology of depression: Contemporary theory and research* (pp. 156–185). Washington, DC: V. H. Winston & Sons.

Liebowitz, M. R., & Klein, D. F. (1981). Interrelationship of hysteroid dysphoria and borderline personality disorder. *Psychiatric Clinics of North America, 4*(1), 67–87.

Matussek P., & Feil, W. (1983). Personality attributes of depressive patients. *Archives of General Psychiatry, 40,* 783–790.

McCranie, E. J. (1971). Depression, anxiety and hostility. *Psychiatric Quarterly, 45,* 117–133.

Menninger, K. (1940). Character disorders. In J. F. Brown (Ed.), *The psychodynamics of abnormal behavior.* New York: McGraw-Hill.

Metcalfe, M. (1968). The personality of depressive patients. In A. Coppen & A. Walk (Eds.), *Recent developments in affective disorders.* London: Royal Medico-Psychological Association.

Millon, T. (1969). *Modern psychopathology.* Philadelphia: W. B. Saunders.

Millon, T. (1981). *Disorders of personality.* New York: Wiley-Interscience.

Overall, J., & Hollister, L. (1980). Phenomenological classification of depressive disorders. *Journal of Clinical Psychology, 36*(2), 372–377.

Paykel, E. S. (1971). Classification of depressed patients: A cluster analysis derived grouping. *British Journal of Psychiatry, 118,* 275–288.

Paykel, E. S. (1972). Correlates of a depressive typology. *Archives of General Psychiatry, 27,* 203–210.

Paykel, E. S., Klerman, G. L., & Prusoff, B. A. (1976). Personality and symptom pattern in depression. *British Journal of Psychiatry, 129,* 327–334.

Paykel, E. S., Myers, J. K., & Dienelt, M. N. (1970). Life events and depression. *Archives of General Psychiatry, 21,* 753–760.

Paykel, E. S., & Prusoff, B. A. (1973). Relationships between personality dimensions: Neuroticism and extroversion against obsessive, hysterical and oral personality. *British Journal of Social and Clinical Psychology, 12,* 309–318.

Paykel, E. S., & Weissman, M. M. (1973). Social adjustment and depression. *Archives of General Psychiatry, 24,* 659–663.

Perris, C. (1966). A study of bipolar (manic-depressive) and unipolar recurrent depressive

Psychosis. *Acta Psychiatrica Scandinavica, 42* (Suppl.) 194.

Perris, C. (1971). Personality patterns in patients with affective disorders. *Acta Psychiatrica Scandinavica, 221* (Suppl.) 43.

Perry, J. C., & Klerman, G. L. (1978). The borderline patient. *Archives of General Psychiatry, 35,* 141–150.

Rado, S. (1928). The problem of melancholia. *International Journal of Psychoanalysis, 9,* 420–438.

Rado, S. (1951). Psychodynamics of depression from the etiologic point of view. *Psychosomatic Medicine, 13,* 51–55.

Rado, S. (1968). Psychodynamics of the depressive from the etiologic point of view. In W. Gaylin (Ed.), *The meaning of despair* (pp. 96–108). New York: Science House.

Reid, W. H. (1978). The sadness of the psychopath. *American Journal of Psychotherapy, 32,* 496–509.

Rosenthal, S., & Gudeman, J. (1967). The self-pitying constellation in depression. *British Journal of Psychiatry, 113,* 485–489.

Salzman, L. (1970). Depression: A clinical review. In J. Masserman (Ed.), *Depression and therapies science and psychoanalysis* (Vol. 17). New York: Grune & Stratton.

Salzman, L. (1972). Interpersonal factors in depression. In F. Flach & S. Draghi (Eds.), *The nature and treatment of depression.* New York: John Wiley & Sons.

Sargant, W. (1961). Drugs in the treatment of depressions. *British Medical Journal, 1,* 225–227.

Schless, A., Mendels, J., Kipperman, A., & Cochran, C. (1974). Depression and hostility. *The Journal of Nervous and Mental Disease, 159,* 91–100.

Schneider, K. (1958). *Psychopathic personalities.* Trans. by M. W. Hamilton. London: Cassell.

Seligman, M. E. (1974). Depression and learned helplessness. In R. J. Friedman & M. M. Katz (Eds.), *The psychology of depression: Contemporary theory and research* (pp. 83–109). Washington: Winston.

Sjobring, H. (1973). Personality structure and development: A model and its applications. *Acta Psychiatrica Scandinavica Supplement 244,* 1.

Small, I., Small, J., Alig, V., & Moore, D. (1970). Passive-aggressive personality disorder: A search for a syndrome. *American Journal of Psychiatry, 126,* 973–983.

Snaith, R. P., McGuire, R. J., & Fox, K. (1971). Aspects of personality and depression. *Psychological Medicine, 1,* 239–246.

Snyder, S., Sajadi, C., Pitts, W. M., & Goodpaster, W. A. (1982). Identifying the depressive border of the borderline personality. *American Journal of Psychiatry, 139,* 814–817.

Spitzer, R. L., & Williams, J. B. W. (1982). Hysteroid dysphoria: An unsuccessful attempt to demonstrate its syndromal validity. *American Journal of Psychiatry, 139,* 1286–1291.

Stone, M. H. (1979). Contemporary shift of the borderline concept from a subschizophrenic disorder to a subaffective disorder. *Psychiatric Clinics of North America, 2*(3), 577–593.

Vaughn, M. (1976). The relationships between obsessional personality, obsessions in depression and symptoms of depression. *British Journal of Psychiatry, 129,* 36–39.

Videbech, T. (1975). A study of genetic factors, childhood bereavement, and premorbid personality traits in patients with anancastic endogenous depression. *Acta Psychiatrica Scandinavica, 52,* 178–222.

Von Zerssen, D. (1977). Premorbid personality and affective psychoses. In G. D. Burrows (Ed.), *Handbook of studies on depression* (pp. 79–103). Amsterdam, The Netherlands: Excerpta Medica.

West, E. D., & Daily, P. J. (1959). Effects of iproniazid in depressive syndromes. *British Medical Journal, 1,* 1491–1494.

Winokur, G. (1979). Unipolar depression: Is it divisible into autonomous subtypes. *Archives of General Psychiatry, 36,* 47–52.

Wittenborn, R. R. (1965). Depression. In B. Wolman (Ed.), *Handbook of clinical psychology.* New York: McGraw-Hill.

Wittenborn, J. R., & Maurer, H. A. (1977). Persisting personalities among depressed women. *Archives of General Psychiatry, 34,* 968–971.

Yerevanian, B. I., & Akiskal, H. S. (1979). Neurotic, characterologic and dysthymic depressions. *Psychiatric Clinics of North America, 2,* 595–617.

**PART IV**

# *INSTRUMENTATION*

# On the Renaissance of Personality Assessment and Personality Theory

The long drought is over and a revival of the rich heritage of the Forties and Fifties is under way. For some 25 to 30 years now, the enthusiasm that once characterized our adherence to one or another personality theory, as well as our faith in this or that personality instrument, has been buffeted by trivial, as well as just criticisms. Additionally, the passage of time and the aging of once preeminent ideas and techniques has led not only to a creeping ennui, but also to the value schisms that inevitably separate generations. Hence, the marvelous theories (e.g., Lewin, Murray, Murphy, Sullivan, Horney, Fromm) and incisive methods (e.g., Rorschach, TAT, Bender-Gestalt, Sentence completion, Figure drawing) of yesteryear have faded inexorably, or so it appears, to a status more befitting quaint historic notions and intriguing, albeit ancient, tools.

Were the powers that once enabled comprehensive and valid personality assessments a fantasy of the past, impertinent, if not grandiose, acts by a then immature and arrogant young science? Were the personality theories then espoused equally ill-considered, presumptuous aspirations of ill-informed and naive, if not cavalier, speculators who asserted knowledge to themselves far greater than "the facts" would warrant? On both scores, I think not! Defense, however, is not my purpose here. Rather, I prefer to take a more constructive road, first, by reviewing historic trends that led to the respective declines of both assessment and theory; second, by drawing attention to several encouraging events of the recent past which signify their mutual renaissance; and third, by elaborating one of these promising signs, that pertaining to the reemergence and maturity of the so-called personality disorders.

## THE DOWNTREND IN ASSESSMENT

As Holt (1967, 1968) and Korchin and Schuldberg (1981) have ably enumerated, there are obvious and constructive reasons why assessment has diminished since its apogee in the Forties and Fifties. Testing was then virtually the only professional activity available to the clinical psychologist. Gradually and fortuitously, new roles opened up in teaching, research, administration, consultation and, most significantly, in psychotherapy, especially as carried out in independent and shared office practice. With more choices of interest from which to select, assessment was bound to decrease, as would any activity that previously had been the only alternative. Other changes of a similar professional character also imposed time and economic constraints on assessment. Personality appraisals depended on a complex test battery composed of time-consuming administrations and interpretations. Perhaps these were justified when therapies were expected to endure a year or more, but the rationale for extensive and expensive assessments could no longer be sustained when brevity typified treatment and a much sought-after goal in federally supported community centers was cost containment.

Other professional developments contributed their share to the decline as well, not the least of which were a series of manifest anti-test attitudes that were expressed in several significant, if disparate, quarters. Humanistic psychologists attacked the ethical grounding of assessment, declaring that professional evaluations were not only irrelevant, given that it is the person's phenomenological state and not an abstract external judgment that matters, but further that assessments were an intrusion that deprived "the client" of both his individuality and dignity. Along similar lines, socially minded psychologists viewed the diagnostic task as synonymous with labeling, a process they judged both dehumanizing and counter-therapeutic. From those more psychometrically oriented, it was concluded that clinically based predictions were distinctly inferior to statistically derived ones. Whether the data favoring this conclusion were tangential or not to the primary aims of clinical assessment, this well-reasoned, if misguided assertion served as both impetus and justification for other, quasi-scientific segments of the profession to launch their long-awaited assault upon the empirical foundations of assessment, especially those related to the projective techniques. Inclined to view the very notion of personality and its dispositions as suspect, behaviorally oriented psychologists set out to find clinical meaning, not in traits but in situations.

Most assuredly, the psychodiagnostic enterprise contained more than its share of mystique. Not only were assessments undertaken as an exercise in oracular craft and intuitive artistry, but they were often obscured by dazzling insights, clothed in esoteric jargon and stated in a manner that invited either divergent or unfalsifiable conclusions. Whether the early wizards of assessment were merely clever beguilers or genuine masters of art and substance is no longer an issue. For good or bad, their talents are only rarely found in our graduate schools today; unusual is the program that assigns its most senior and clinically adept faculty to the teaching of assessment. That task is typically assigned junior staff members whose self-doubt and skepticism often supersede their assessment competencies and their commitment to serve as role models. Hence, the unraveling process expanded and the decline speeded up. From all quarters, assessment came to be viewed as the activity of second-class citizens. "Unscientific," and thereby shunned or demeaned by the academic, judged unexalted by votaries of psychotherapy who claimed treatment with proper province of mature clinicians, diagnostics was relegated progressively to a lesser and lesser status, Although "objective" assessment techniques satisfied the standards of psychometric purists and devotees of scientific rigor, these instruments removed the intrigue and challenge of clinical deduction from the diagnostic process and served to diminish the status of clinician as interpretive diviner, if not infallible seer. Moreover, structured inventories seemed terribly pedestrian and barren, designed intentionally to resist subjective logic and reasoning, and manifestly insensitive to clinical subtleties and dynamics.

Where then might the deeply committed and richly talented psychodiagnostician turn? Most held on for dear life, isolated from everyday peers and meeting biannually in ever-shrinking associations, waiting for the day when their contributions would again be recognized and appreciated.

## ON THE DECLINE OF THEORY

Matters were no more heartening in personality theory. What were once the splendidly astute and discriminating clinical portrayals of Freud, Horney, Fromm, and Sullivan, each of whom stirred our curiosities and inspired us to further our desire to know, were now outdated curiosities, grandiose speculations to be replaced by tightly focused and empirically anchored constructs. The conceptual models and cogent insights of Lewin, Murray, and Murphy resonated with our early, personally more prosaic efforts to penetrate and give order to the mysteries of our patients' psychic worlds, but they too were out of vogue, skillfully rent by what I term the anticoherency and anticonsistency movements.

No longer was personality to be seen as an integrated gestalt, a dynamic system comprising more than the mere sum of its parts. The pendulum swung toward empiricism and positivism; only observable facts were in the ascendance. The personality configuration was segmented into its ostensive constituents, construed as S-R bonds by some, statistical factors by others, dimensional traits elsewhere, and so on. This loose, anticoherency amalgam, however divergent its members may have been on other scores and they were quite vociferous about *their* disagreements, did agree on one matter—that personality was best disassembled, arranged in one set of component parts or another. Given that most were nomothetically, rather than idiographically inclined, this new breed of quasi-empiricist made a shambles of the inspired "personalities-a-coherent-whole" theories which nurtured those of us who entered the clinical field in the post-World War II era.

Adding insult to the segmenting injuries of the anticoherency movement was the clever, if not cynical, assault of the anticonsistency group. This egregious attack was based on a facile and highly selective reading of the research literature, a reading so biased in its choices and interpretations that it justifies the very denunciations its promulgators employed themselves in condemning personality concepts such as disposition, stability, and generality. Widely read, printed and reprinted in every text, as well as blandly (blindly?) accepted by journal editors as factually grounded, these critiques (e.g., Mischel, 1969) challenged the very foundations of the personality construct no less its assessment. Comparable in several respects to Eysenck's (1952)

earlier, adroit "decimation" of the efficacy of psychotherapy, those comprising the anticonsistency movement boldly confronted believers in any and all personality theories with an ostensively impeccable evidential base for the insubstantiality of these sentiments. And, with the empirical grounding of personality in question, with the very logic of intrapsychic coherence and behavioral consistency under attack, adherents and proponents of an integrative or holistic view of personality not only withdrew from open display, tails property tucked, but were driven both from texts and journals, losing their once vaunted academic respectability and shamed should they publicly exhibit their archaic and "unscientific" beliefs.

The Sixties and Seventies were difficult times indeed. Of all the favored tools and ideas of an earlier epoch, it was the projective techniques and psychoanalytic theory which were hit hardest. Perhaps most serious of all, however, was the slow but inexorable loss of the intellectually curious, abstractly philosophical and ambiguity-tolerant student, the kind that had been turned on by the very intangibles of "mind," those intuitively sensed, yet ever obscure and difficult-to-fathom processes which sustained and gave coherence to the observable world. Both psychiatry and psychology suffered this loss, and for similar reasons. Emotionally attuned medical students were attracted in the Forties and Fifties to the psychoanalytic orientation then characterizing psychiatry. Similarly, graduate students drawn to the dynamics of a recondite intrapsychic world were intrigued by opportunities to study it via the new and fascinating projective methods. Over the decades, however, analytic theory and projective assessment came under the attacks to which we earlier referred, being judged either or both unscientific and socially irrelevant. The community mental health movement soon took hold in the Sixties and early Seventies, followed closely and concurrently by clinical behaviorism in psychology and clinical biochemistry in psychiatry. And with these movements the character of incoming students began to change. "Intellectual types" who were attracted by the inscrutable and intangible, stirred by abstruse unknowns and the enigmatic, no longer found the field quite as intriguing as in earlier days. Consonant with the character of the decade, the Sixties solicited the socially committed, the student who saw psychology and psychiatry as vehicles to change an unjust society. Worthy though such aspirations may have been, they drew a different breed of students than theretofore. Although different in outlook, these new recruits were among the most able students seeking careers in line with idealistic social goals. Quality remained high, but of a different character as mental health expanded its frontiers beyond the inner recesses of the patient's private world. The student body took its next and sharpest turn when the seductions of "scientism" (Koch, 1971) were preferred in the guise of clinical behaviorism and psychiatric biochemistry. No longer were the two primary professions of mental health oriented to attract the intellectually reflective or the socially idealistic, they set out to entice anew those seeking ennoblement via scientific rigor and empiricism, the tangible and the "objectively real." Good fortune still draws many a first rate student to the field, but there has been a significant decline in both their numbers and quality.

Although the reasons for this recession are several, I contend the loss of the intellectually reflective and socially idealistic student is attributable to the primacy given of late to what I judge to be our second-rate psychological science and second-rate psychiatric medicine. Let me elaborate, albeit briefly, Ph.D. oriented students of the first rank who are enamored by "science" will rarely be enticed by the "softer" psychologies. They find the demanding and challenging "hard" sciences, such as molecular biology and particle physics to be more suitable to their aspiration and aptitudes. Similarly, medical students of

similar talents will find the current biochemistry's of psychiatry to be awesomely simple-minded, especially as compared to those of a host of genuinely inspiring medical specialties. The upshot is that neither clinical behaviorism, even as embellished in its recent cognitive garb, nor psychopharmacologic psychiatry, can draw the student these professions attracted in former days.

All in all, by the late 1970s we had devolved into a most sorry state.

## THE REBIRTH OF PERSONALITY ASSESSMENT AND THEORY

A change in the fortunes of personality theory and assessment was brewing through the Seventies. Slow though this reawakening may have been, there were signs of emerging new ideas and challenges that gave promise of regaining the luster of the Forties and Fifties. By virtue of time, reflection and, not the least, of a growing disenchantment with available alternatives, evident notably in significant position reversals among its most fevered critics, the place of personality as a construct began to regain its formerly solid footing.

On the assessment side, even "mechanical" tools such as the MMPI were being interpreted almost exclusively in terms of configural profiles. No longer approached as a set of separate scales, formerly segmented instruments were now being analyzed as holistic integrations that possessed clinical significance and meaning only as gestalt composites. The former insistence that interpretation be anchored precisely to empirical correlates gave way to "free-form" clinical syntheses, including even the dynamics of the much maligned projectives. Although part-function instruments, oriented to one single pathology or another (e.g., anxiety or depression) still abound, the newest of tools moved increasingly toward the analysis of composite structures, that is, "whole" personalities, such as the borderline or the schizotypal. These personality formulations were not conceived as random sets of discrete attributes (i.e., scales) that must be individually deduced and then pieced together, but as holistic or integrated configurations from the very start. Hence, we have seen the development of various tools explicitly designed to diagnose, for example, "the borderline" personality. My own set of instruments, particularly the MCMI, represent the latest trend in "holistic" personality scales, going one step beyond most of the newer techniques by including all of the DSM-III personality disorders in a single inventory (Millon, 1982). Holism is not limited to inventories alone. New structured interview schedules and clinical rating scales have been developed recently to provide a rich source of data for psychodiagnostic assessment (Baron, Asnis, & Gruen, 1981; Gunderson, Kolb, & Austin, 1981; Reich, 1983, Soloff, 1981; Strack, 1983).

Not to be overlooked in reviewing these newer tools is the sound psychometric manner in which most have been constructed, thereby wedding the empirical and quantitative features that were the major strength of the structured objective inventories with the clinically dynamic and integrative qualities that characterized the more intuitive projective techniques.

Especially promising also is the observation that the essential element that gives substance to "personality" as a construct—the fact that people exhibit distinctive and abiding characteristics—has reemerged (Block, 1977; Epstein, 1977) despite the early attacks of anticonsistency and anticoherency critics. This durability attests, at the very least, to its intuitive consonance with authentic observation, a viability all the more noteworthy when one considers the spirited, if misguided, academic efforts to undo it. This renaissance is particularly impressive when one considers the vast number of recently popular constructs that have faded to a status consonant with their trivial character, or have succumbed, under the weight of their scientific inefficacy, to scholarly boredom.

Personality theory also appears to have weathered its mettlesome assaults. Witness the position reversals of its most ardent critic (Mischel, 1984), moreover, it seems to be undergoing a wide-ranging resurgence. Notable here are the widely acclaimed formulations of contemporary analytic theorists, particularly Kernberg (1975) and Kohut (1971). No less significant in this realm are theoretical ideas posited by a re-activated interpersonal school, led by such post-Sullivan and post-Leary theorists as Benjamin (1986), Wiggins (1979), and Kiesler (1986). Of perhaps even greater note, though not necessarily in the substantive merit of their proposals, but rather in the striking shift their ideas have taken from their former anticonsistency and anticoherency position, are the recent "ecumenical" formulations of social learning theorists such as Bandura (1977) and Mischel (1984). Shedding an earlier behavioristic dogmatism and no longer assigning primacy to situational determinants, these theorists have "reconnected" behaviorism to cognitivism, asserting not only an intrinsic coherence between them, but proclaiming that generalities do exist among psychic functions as a consequence of the coordinating effects of cognitive processes. As the inherent unity of personality regains its former standing and becomes increasingly fashionable. I anticipate its erstwhile adversaries will soon "discover" the merits of a psychoanalytic-cognitive-behavioral synthesis of psychological functions, as well as promulgate the efficacy of parallel "multidimensional" approaches to treatment. How interesting it is that those who led the anticonsistency and anticoherency effort in the Sixties to bury personality as a concept are now moving subtly to the forefront in its resuscitation.

The revival of personality as central to the clinical enterprise arises from other, more mundane and practical considerations. For example, most mental health practitioners employ their professional skills today in outpatient rather than inpatient settings. Their "clients" are no longer the severely disturbed "State Hospital" psychotic, but ambulatory individuals seen in office settings or community clinics, beset with personal stressors, social inadequacies, or interpersonal conflicts, typically reported in symptoms such as anxiety, depression, or alcoholism, but which signify the outcroppings of longstanding and deeply ingrained patterns of maladaptive behaving, feeling, thinking, and relating: in other words, their "personality style."

It is not only the changing patient population of clinical practice, or the emergence of attractively new theories of personality from refurbished analytic, interpersonal or social learning perspectives, or even advances in the realm of quantitative assessment and psychometrics that signify the growing prominence of the construct. The very special status assigned the personality syndromes in the DSM-III (American Psychiatric Association, 1980) is both a reflection of these changes and instrumental in their further promotion. With the advent of this official classification, personality disorders not only gained a place of consequence among syndromal categories, but became central to its multiaxial schema. The logic for assigning personality its own axis is more than a matter of differentiating syndromes of a more acute and dramatic form from those of a longstanding and prosaic character. More relevant to this partitioning decision was the assertion that personality can serve usefully as a dynamic substrate from which clinicians can better grasp the significance and meaning of their patients' transient and florid disorders. In the DSM-III, then, personality disorders not only attained a nosological status of prominence in their own right, but were assigned a contextual role that made them fundamental to the understanding and interpretation of other psychopathologies.

## TOWARD THE FUTURE OF PERSONALITY DIAGNOSIS

As I have commented elsewhere (Millon, 1983, 1986a), many of the advances in the

DSM-III offer a promise and not an achievement. They represent a conceptual step in the right direction, but are, as yet, an unfulfilled aspiration. Let me illustrate.

Although the introduction of multiple "diagnostic criteria" to characterize each syndrome must be viewed as a singular achievement that will enhance communication clarity, assessment precision, and research reliability, the specific criteria themselves are but crude approximations, speculative proposals that lack diagnostic comparability, syndromal comprehensiveness, and empirical foundations. Those of us working to upgrade this auspicious beginning in the DSM-III have recommended numerous proposals for criteria modification and elaboration (see Millon, 1986b).

Concluding, as did Weiner (1983) in his recent "distinguished contribution" address, I too am quite pleased with the future of "psychodiagnosis." To complement his observations, I see not only bright prospects ahead in personality assessment but, perhaps more fundamentally, in its scientific foundations. The psychometric developments among holistic and psychodynamic inventories, the revival and refinements in personality theory, the specification of parallel explicit criteria for the personality disorders, and the recognition that personality serves both as core and context for understanding other psychopathologies, all bode extremely well for us as professionals and, more importantly, for the patients we serve.

## REFERENCES

American Psychiatric Association. (1980). *Diagnostic and statistical manual of mental disorders (DSM-III)*. Washington, DC: American Psychiatric Association.

Bandura, A. (1977). Self-efficacy: Toward a unifying theory of behavior change. *Psychological Review, 84*, 191–215.

Baron, M., Asnis, L., & Gruen, R. (1981). The schedule for schizotypal personalities (SSP):

A diagnostic interview for schizotypal features. *Psychiatry Research, 4,* 213–228.

Benjamin, L. S. (1986). Adding social and intrapsychic descriptors to Axis I of DSM-III. In T. Millon & G. L. Klerman (Eds.), *Contemporary directions in psychopathology.* New York: Guilford.

Block, J. (1977). Advancing the psychology of personality: Paradigmatic shift or improving the quality of research. In D. Magnusson & N. S. Endler (Eds.), *Personality at the crossroads: Current issues in interactional psychology.* Hillsdale, NJ: Erlbaum.

Epstein, S. (1977). Traits are alive and well. In D. Magnusson & N. S. Endler (Eds.), *Personality at the crossroads: Current issues in interactional psychology.* Hillsdale, NJ: Erlbaum.

Eysenck, H. J. (1952). The effects of psychotherapy: An evaluation. *Journal of Consulting Psychology, 16,* 319–324.

Gunderson, J. G., Kolb, J. E., & Austin, V. (1981). The diagnostic interview for borderline patients. *American Journal of Psychiatry, 138,* 896–903.

Holt, R. R. (1967). Diagnostic testing: Present situation and future prospects. *Journal of Nervous and Mental Disease, 144,* 444–465.

Holt, R. R. (1968). Foreword. In R. R. Holt (Ed.). D. Rappaport, M. M. Gill, & R. Schafer, *Diagnostic psychological testing* (rev. ed.). New York: International Universities Press.

Kernberg, O. (1975). *Borderline conditions and pathological narcissism.* New York: Jason Aronson.

Kiesier, D. J. (1986). The 1982 interpersonal circle: An analysis of DSM-III personality disorders. In T. Millon & G. L. Klerman (Eds.), *Contemporary directions in psychopathology.* New York: Guilford.

Koch, S. (1971). Reflections on the state of psychology. *Social Research, 30,* 669–709.

Kohut, H. (1971). *The analysis of self.* New York: International Universities Press.

Korchin, S. J., & Schuldberg, D. (1981). The future of clinical assessment. *American Psychologist, 36,* 1147–1158.

Millon, T. (1982). *Millon Clinical Multiaxial Inventory manual* (3rd ed.). Minneapolis: National Computer Systems.

Millon, T. (1983). The DSM-III: An insider's perspective. *American Psychologist, 38,* 804–814.

Millon, T. (1986a). A theoretical derivation of pathological personalities. In T. Millon & G. L. Klerman (Eds.), *Contemporary directives in psychopathology.* New York: Guilford.

Millon, T. (1986b). Personality prototypes and their diagnostic criteria. In T. Millon & G. L. Klerman (Eds.), *Contemporary directives in psychopathology.* New York: Guilford.

Mischel, W. (1969). Continuity and change in personality. *American Psychologist, 24,* 1012–1018.

Mischel, W. (1984). Convergences and challenges in the search for consistency. *American Psychologist, 39,* 351–364.

Reich, J. (1983, May). *Instruments measuring DSM-III Axis II personality disorders.* Paper presented at the annual meeting of the APA, Washington, DC.

Soloff, P. H. (1981). A comparison of the borderline with depressed and schizophrenic patients on a new diagnostic interview. *Comprehensive Psychiatry, 22,* 291–300.

Strack, S. N. (1983). *Development of the personality adjective checklist (PACL).* Unpublished doctoral dissertation, University of Miami.

Weiner, I. B. (1983). The future of psychology revisited. *Journal of Personality Assessment, 47,* 451–461.

Wiggins, J. (1979). A psychological taxonomy of trait-descriptive terms: The interpersonal domain. *Journal of Personality and Social Psychology, 37,* 395–412.

# Intrapsychic and Phenomenological Research Methods

The wisdom of tackling a research problem depends, in large part, on the availability and character of the instruments by which its data will be gathered. Theoretically important and beautifully designed studies may prove impossible to execute because there may be no technique available to tap the variables comprising the research hypothesis; thus, many a well-reasoned and well-formulated notion has had to be set aside until adequate devices were invented to elicit, discern, and quantify the concepts under inquiry. Our goal in this chapter is to acquaint the student with some of the more commonly used techniques in psychopathology.

Data collection techniques provide "operational measures," those concrete procedures that elicit, highlight, and quantify the actions of research subjects. They deal, in effect, only with the response and organismic variables of a study, not with the stimulus variables.

We shall comment only sparingly on the adequacy of the methods to be described; in general, few satisfy the stringent set of criteria we have set forth. Through these examples, we hope to indicate the special strengths of certain measures, to note the weaknesses and limitations of several frequently used but inefficient instruments, and to provide a background for the proper selection of relevant test data collection techniques.

## INTRAPSYCHIC METHODS

Intrapsychic concepts rarely are operationally defined. At best, they take the form of intervening variables, although they tend to be anchored rather loosely to the empirical events that signify their existence. Most are hypothetical constructs, metaphors, and analogies that are of undoubted heuristic value as clinical and theoretical tools, but are extremely elusive for purposes of systematic research.

Overt behaviors and phenomenological reports often serve as the basis for intrapsychic deductions; in fact, most of what clinicians infer about a patient's intrapsychic world is pieced together from data gathered through nonintrapsychic methods. In this section however, our focus will center on those techniques that uniquely gather intrapsychic phenomena, that is, those designed specifically to elicit and maximize their expression. Four such methods are currently employed: free association, dream analysis, hypnosis, and projective techniques.

## FREE ASSOCIATION

This classical psychoanalytic technique was developed by Freud to overcome obstacles to exposing the workings of the "unconscious mind." Since the unconscious is hidden, unusual procedures had to be devised to evoke and lay bare its processes and contents. In addition to the then-established method of hypnosis, which Freud employed with inconstant success, he improvised two new techniques: free association and dream analysis. We shall present the first of these in this section; the second will be discussed later.

Let us quote from Erich Fromm, who succinctly described the logic of the free-association process and distinguished it from other features of the psychoanalytic interview (1955):

What Freud discovered was that a person, even if he is not asleep and dreaming, even if he is not insane, nevertheless, can hear the voice of his unconscious, provided that he does something which seems very simple: namely, that he leave the realm of conventional, rational thought, and permit himself to voice ideas which are not determined by the rules of normal, conventional thinking. If he does this, ideas emerge, not from his head but, as the Chinese would say, from his belly; ideas which are not part of his official personality, but which are the language of this dissociated, hidden personality. Furthermore, Freud discovered the fact that if I permit myself to associate freely, then these very thoughts which come from this dissociated realm attract other relevant and germane thoughts from the realm of the unconscious.

In short, the free-association method seeks to unmask and unfold the linkages of the intrapsychic world by reducing to a minimum the processes of conscious selection and exclusion, or any other interference with the spontaneous expression of feelings and thought.

Useful though free association has been in furnishing clinical insights, Generates, like most interview procedures, extremely unwieldy data that is often entirely refractory to research management. Not only are these bound by the usual limitations of human observation and judgment, but as Kubie (1960) has pointed out:

. . . psychoanalysis has had to struggle with unique difficulties which are consequences of the fact that it has been dependent largely upon auditory data, with only minor visual additions. Because of the dominant importance and speed of the spoken work as an instrument of communication, because of the slower pace of writing, and because of the limited range of variations and the consequent relative stereotype of gesture and expression as methods of communication,

the ear has been the major source of psychoanalytic data. To an even greater extent than visual data, auditory data are vulnerable to distortion both in the moment of perception and in recall.

It is impossible to listen to ordinary speech without distorting our perceptual records of it. It is even less possible to take in and record and recall a string of free associations. They are distorted first at the time of perception, and again to an even greater degree in retrospect: this is true no matter how phonographic the mind of the listener.

Fortunately, it is now possible to surmount man's fallible memory and distorted recollections by the use of video, motion picture, and sound recording techniques (Shakow, 1960; Gottschalk & Auerbach, 1966). Extremely promising and long overdue approaches to the systematic study of free association data have been initiated by Colby (1960) and Bordin (1966). For example, Bordin, using advanced students in clinical psychology obtained impressively high interjudge agreement on a series of rating scales that categorize both the flow and the content of tape-recorded free-association productions. Although not limited to free-association data, Dollard and Auld (1959) have devised a coding schema that focuses on intrapsychic content of psychoanalytic interviews. With such procedures, a shift from exploratory single case studies as the major design to surveys and other designs will be possible.

## Dream Analysis

Seventy years have passed since Freud published his classical interpretation of dreams. To him, this body of strange and seemingly nonsensical data represented, in part at least, memories and feelings that the dreamer dared not express in waking life; by decoding the disguises and distortions of this unconscious state, Freud's understanding of the intrapsychic mechanisms employed in the formation of neurotic and psychotic disorders was ostensibly enlightened. Little systematic research was done on the process of dreaming in the ensuing 50 years, and the interpretations that clinicians offered about the meaning of dream content-remained entirely a matter of plausible speculation.

In recent years, there has been a burgeoning of interest and research concerning the neurophysiological correlates of dreaming. This began with the accidental discovery by Aserinsky and Kleitman (1953) of a direct relationship between nocturnal dreaming and bursts of rapid eye movement (REM). The outcome of this discovery has made the evanescent process of dreaming more accessible to study, and has led to an impressive series of investigations (Dement, 1964, 1965; Tart, 1965; Witkin & Lewis, 1967).

Although the ease of recognizing the REM state has greatly facilitated the monitoring of dreams, this clue has led, not to advances in the understanding of the content and psychological meaning of the dream, but to a marked increase in knowledge about the neurophysiology of the sleep state. Thus, this new and fresh avenue for unearthing intrapsychic data has resulted in substantive progress that goes little beyond that formulated by Freud 70 years ago.

There are two sources of "dream data" in addition to that produced during nocturnal sleep. The *hypnogogic reverie state* is a brief period of drowsiness shortly preceding the time of falling asleep; here, the subject is asked to keep on talking until he dozes off completely, recounting aloud his thoughts, feelings, and images, usually in a more disjointed and undirected manner than that generated in free association (Rapaport, 1951). The second data source is that of *daydreaming, the monologue interieur* which persons fantasize and conjure up events that transcend the realities of past and present, or the probabilities of the future (Singer, 1966).

The intrapsychic analyses of dream content is fraught with even more complications than that encountered in the interpretation of free-association materials. Despite the impregnable faith that psychoanalytic writers have in dream analysis, there are no studies

and few procedures by which the "meaning" they attribute to these data can be empirically confirmed or disconfirmed. As matters now stand, analysts provide only circumstantial evidence for the plausibility of their interpretations. The only conclusive evidence for the validity of these analyses would be through predictions and postdictions of behavior made independently of other sources of information.

Before such studies could be undertaken, however, considerable work must be done to operationally define, scrutinize, and categorize the data of dream reports, and to develop reliable criteria for rating and ascribing meaning to them; an important first step in this regard has recently been provided by Hauri et al. (1967). Two recent books (Witkin & Lewis, 1967; Singer, 1966) have summarized a number of experimental approaches employed to decipher the psychological process and content of nocturnal dreams and daydreams. Together with newer scales for rating dream reports, the techniques described in these works may serve to establish the necessary formal procedures for objectifying, quantifying, and ultimately validating the intrapsychic analysis of dreams.

## Hypnosis

Brief note should be made of the principal forerunner of modern tools of intrapsychic exploration, that of hypnosis. Although it is of lesser significance today than before (e.g., the topic of hypnosis was not even listed in the subject index of the monumental 1965 *Handbook of Clinical Psychology),* this technique served a seminal role in pointing up the presence of unconscious ideas and emotions. It has had a spasmodic history since Freud's decision to forego its use at the turn of the century; although it continues to crop up in the research literature, questions still remain as to how it occurs and what elements constitute the hypnotic trance (Wolberg, 1959). Its status as an ancillary therapeutic technique seems well established, but it has borne little fruit as a device for explicating the content and processes of the intrapsychic world.

As with the techniques of free association and dream analysis, hypnosis provides the investigator with data that are shorn of the constraints of conscious selection and control. During the trance period, the patient withdraws his attention from the outside world, and is able to focus on aspects of his inner life that elude him in the wakeful state. With proper prodding, memory residuals of past experiences can be activated and brought to light; moreover, under proper conditions, the patient may display a vivid array of symbolic images and emotions that ostensibly reflect the primitive processes of the unconscious. Unfortunately, with the exception of a few exploratory forays (reviewed in Hilgard, 1961; Weitzenhoffer, 1953; Gordon, 1966), there are no truly systematic methods for organizing this wealthy fund of intrapsychic data.

In general, hypnosis has been employed in research merely to demonstrate the existence of unconscious phenomena; the well-known techniques of hypnotic memory recall and posthypnotic suggestion illustrate this approach. Experimental hypnotic studies of clinical processes have also been done. Some years ago, for example, Farber and Fisher (1943) showed that the form and content of dreams could be partially controlled by hypnotic suggestions; more recently, experiences implanted in the unconscious via hypnosis were systematically "treated" via two therapeutic approaches, as a means of comparing the efficacy of these techniques in relieving intrapsychic disturbances (Gordon, 1957).

## PROJECTIVE TECHNIQUES

Unquestionably, the most popular tools for eliciting, categorizing, and analyzing intrapsychic data are the methods labeled by Lawrence Frank in 1939 as projective techniques. In use for some time prior to World War II, they only began to flourish during the great surge of psychological testing in the late 1940's and 1950's. Although their underlying premises and rationales are not in question, subsequent validation research has shown that many of the diagnostic powers attributed to these techniques cannot be supported. Despite their sparse record in systematic evaluative research and their questionable superiority over other diagnostic instruments, there is still reason to believe that their promise as tools for exposing the realm of the unconscious will materialize. The inherent weaknesses of scoring, quantifying, and interpreting the more established of the older techniques are gradually being overcome (Holtzman et al., 1961; Zubin et al., 1965).

The value of the projective approach derives, at least in part, from the unusual character of the task presented to the subject. By providing an unstructured set of materials to which he is asked to respond, the subject is forced, so to speak, to draw upon his inner imaginative resources; moreover, he is likely to be unable to fathom the meaning or significance of his responses. Thus, unguided by the character of the task, and incapable of disguising what he may prefer to mask, he is apt to "project from within" perceptions and interpretations that disclose his emotional preoccupations, styles of thinking, ways of coping, etc., in short, data that expose and illuminate his intrapsychic world.

Projective techniques have been classified in numerous ways as a means of highlighting their commonalities and differences (Frank, 1939; Sargent, 1945; Campbell, 1950, 1957; Cattell, 1951; Lindzey, 1960). Our discussion will be guided by the schema proposed by Lindzey, which stresses the type of response produced by the subject; by organizing our presentation in this way, the student may be led to consider projective techniques as instruments providing response variables, rather than as clinical tests. We have sought, in narrowing the list of techniques discussed, to mention the two or three methods in each category that are most commonly employed by researchers.

Detailed presentations, critiques, and research reports using these techniques may be found in Buros (1965, 1969), Murstein (1965), and Zubin et al. (1965).

## ASSOCIATIVE TECHNIQUES

According to Lindzey's classification, associative techniques are those in which the subject is set to respond to a stimulus with the first word, thought, or image that occurs to him; the intent is to evoke an immediate reaction, that is, one without reflection and reasoning.

The oldest of these techniques, embodying in a standardized form certain features of Freud's then newly devised free-association method, was formulated by his erstwhile disciple Jung. This procedure, known as the word-association test, consists of a list of words, presented one at a time to a subject with the request that he respond to them with the first word that comes to mind. Although the word-association method still has its adherents, it has given way to other, more complicated methods. The idea of employing association as a projective procedure has been most extensively developed with the use of inkblots as the evocative stimulus.

### Rorschach Inkblots

Not only is the Rorschach the most widely used clinical diagnostic instrument but it has also been the subject of over 3000 articles and books since its construction in 1921. Named after its originator, Swiss psychiatrist Hermann Rorschach, this instrument consists of ten symmetrical inkblots printed on separate cards; five are in shades of black and gray, and five are multicolored. In the standard administration, the subject is presented with one card at a time and asked to associate aloud the various impressions it suggests to him. The subject's responses are transcribed verbatim, and the timing and position in which the cards are held are likewise recorded. Following this initial associative phase of administration, the cards are again presented, one at a time, in a procedure termed the "inquiry"; here, the subject is asked to distinguish the various areas of each blot that contain the percepts he saw (the location score), and to describe the elements of the blot that suggested these perceptions (the determinant scores, such as form, movement, color, shading). In a frequently employed final step of administration, termed "testing the limits," the examiner probes more directly, seeking to elicit percepts and determinants that the subject failed to give in the associative and inquiry stages.

Several systems for scoring and interpreting the data of the Rorschach have attained a measure of popular recognition and use; among them are those of Rorschach himself (1942), Klopfer et al. (1954, 1956), Beck (1945, 1952, 1961), Piotrowski (1957), and Schafer (1954). In addition to scoring response locations and determinants, most of these systems evaluate the timing, content, popularity, and degree of correspondence between responses and the stimulus features of the cards. In addition to these data, inferences on intrapsychic characteristics are frequently drawn from the ratios among various scoring categories and the sequential pattern of responses as they unfold between and within each card. The interpretive process is largely dependent on the experience and "intuitive" skills of the clinician.

As noted earlier, serious questions have arisen concerning the discriminability, reliability, and validity of the Rorschach. Nevertheless, the technique has gained immense popularity, and has been used extensively as an instrument in psychopathological research. For illuminating discussions of these issues, as well as a survey of studies relevant to psychopathology, see Zubin et al. (1965).

### Holtzman Inkblots

Many derivatives of the Rorschach inkblot method have been devised. Among those of special, but limited, utility are the Levy Movement Blots and the Color-Cut-Out Test; the literature of both of these instruments, which attempt to highlight only one of the major "determinants" of inkblot perception, is discussed fully in Zubin et al. (1965).

The most promising of the newer Rorschach variants is the Holtzman Inkblot Technique (1961, 1966). This instrument consists of two sets of inkblots, comprising 45 cards each, and provides a system of administration, scoring, and interpretation that is better standardized and more "objective" than that of the traditional Rorschach technique. Holtzman has extracted 6 "factors" in an analysis of 22 scoring variables; these data were gathered with 15 different populations, ranging from normal children to adult psychotics. Recent studies of the discriminatory powers and validity of the instrument are impressive. Although its utility for clinical diagnostic purposes has not been adequately documented, its format is better suited for purposes of research than the Rorschach.

## CONSTRUCTION TESTS

Construction techniques, according to Lindzey's schema, call upon the subject to create a more or less elaborate imaginative story, usually in response to a picture stimulus. No demand is made for immediacy in response; instead, the subject is asked to organize the suggestive features of the stimulus into a sequential plot or story theme.

### Thematic Apperception Test (TAT)

This instrument, devised by Morgan and Murray (1935), ranks second in popularity only to the Rorschach as a diagnostic test. Parts or variants of it have been extensively used in research.

The basic instrument consists of 31 cards (30 with pictures and 1 entirely blank), although only 10 or so are usually administered. In contrast to the totally amorphous character of inkblots, the figures and objects portrayed on these cards are entirely identifiable; the events, and the thoughts and feelings of the characters, are sufficiently ambiguous,

however, to allow the subject to "read in" what may be taking place. One card at a time is presented in the standard administration; the subject is requested to formulate a theme or story that includes "what is happening, what the people involved are thinking and feeling, what led up to the events portrayed in the picture, and what the outcome will be."

In contrast to the Rorschach, with its three or four popular scoring and interpretive systems, the TAT has spawned numerous such procedures, none of which has caught on as "the standard" method. The rationale, and technique of several of these systems are well presented and discussed in Schneidman et al. (1951), Murstein (1963), and Zubin et al. (1965); the latter two references also provide thorough and up-to-date reviews of evidence concerning the validity and reliability of the technique, as well as summaries of its use in psychopathologic research. Particularly notable for purposes of quantitative research are the standardized and objective administration and scoring procedures devised by Zubin and his associates (Zubin et al., 1965).

### TAT Derivatives

Several notable variants of the construction picture technique have been developed since the TAT was first introduced.

The *Make-a-Picture-Story Test (MAPS),* designed by Schneidman (1948, 1952), consists of 22 cardboard background scenes presented one at a time along with 67 cut out, movable human and animal figures. In contrast to the TAT, the respondent is free to compose his own scenes by selecting and placing the figures as he desires; he then constructs a story depicting his arrangement. Presumably, the subject will become more engrossed and display more of his intrapsychic world in stimulus situations that he himself has created than in those that are uniform and less malleable; moreover, according to Schneidman, the examiner is able to discern qualities of performance (e.g., choice of figures, planning logic, etc.) that illuminate features of personality not observable in the standard TAT. Although it is of value as a diagnostic tool, the difficulties involved in standardizing and developing normative data make the MAPS of limited research utility.

Three TAT derivatives have been developed for adolescent and child populations. The *Children's Apperception Test (CAT)* is perhaps the best known and most frequently used of these clinical tools (Bellak, 1954); similar in construction and use is the *Blacky Pictures,* devised by Blum (1949, 1962). Both tests consist of cartoon drawings of animals about which the child creates a story; both were based on Freudian psychosexual theory and were designed specifically to elicit responses indicative of the child's experiences and manner of coping with the events ascribed to the Freudian stages of development. Research bearing on their reliability and validity is scanty or equivocal, and they have been infrequently used as instruments for investigational purposes.

The *Michigan Picture Test (MPT),* developed under the auspices of the Michigan Department of Mental Health (1953) for use with adolescents, illustrates many of the features of a well-constructed instrument, and is frequently commended for its careful design, adequacy of norms, and repeated attempts at cross-validation (Freeman, 1962; Zubin et al., 1965). Despite efforts to construct quantitative interpretive scales, the test is not measurably superior for research purposes to other projective techniques.

## COMPLETION INSTRUMENTS

Completion techniques, to follow Lindzey's format again, usually consist of a series of suggestive but abbreviated stimuli which the subject is asked to fill out in any manner he wishes, consistent with the instructions provided him.

Among the methods grouped in this category are the *Picture-Frustration Test* (Rosenzweig, 1945) and the *Insight Test* (Sargent, 1955). The Picture-Frustration Test, providing a series of cartoon situations in which the subject is asked to supply a response to a frustrating experience, gained a measure of clinical and research use in the late 1940's and 1950's (Lindzey & Goldwyn, 1954), but has gradually lost its initial favor. The Insight Test, in which the subject is asked to furnish answers to problem situations, provides useful intrapsychic information, but has generated little research to date.

The most popular and simplest of the completion techniques are those in which the subject supplies a word or phrase to fill out an incomplete or truncated sentence. Several variants of the sentence completion method have been devised, the best known and most frequently researched of which is Rotter's *Incomplete Sentences Blank* (Rotter & Willerman, 1947; Rotter & Rafferty, 1952). Illustrative of the typical sentence "stems" completed by subjects are: "My mother always . . ." "A voice . . ." "When I was a . . ." "My greatest worry is . . ."

In routine clinical work, the data provided through the sentence completion procedure are usually gleaned in a subjective fashion. Formal scoring methods have been devised by their test constructors, but apparently are rarely used. Goldberg (1965) has published a thorough and largely favorable review of the validity and research usefulness of these techniques.

## EXPRESSIVE PROCEDURES

In these techniques there is as much emphasis placed on the manner or style with which the subject performs the task as on the end product of his efforts. Thus, in the two major expressive methods, drawing and play techniques, the subject allegedly reveals as much of himself in the process of carrying out what he does as in the character of his final creation.

Play techniques are employed almost exclusively with children. Formal scoring procedures are used rarely since the activity process is extremely fluid and difficult to capture with anything less than film or video recordings. The work of Levy (1933), Sears et al., (1953), Murphy (1956), and Bandura and Walters (1963) illustrate the range of variables (e.g., aggression, dependency) these techniques can evoke. More often than not, however, the data they furnish are used to represent behavioral rather than intrapsychic concepts.

Among the better known drawing techniques, with well-formulated scoring and interpretive guidelines, are those developed by Machover (1948) and Buck (1949). In Machover's *Draw-a-Person* procedure, the subject simply sketches a figure, and then, upon completion, is asked to produce a second "of the opposite sex." Buck's *House-Tree-Person (HTP)* technique requires the subject to produce free-hand drawings of a house, tree, and person, in that order, followed by an inquiry phase in which he is asked to describe or develop a story in conjunction with his productions. Despite the undoubted and steadfast clinical popularity of these two graphic techniques, their use as research instruments is infrequent, and evidence bearing on their reliability and validity has been largely negative (Swenson, 1957, 1968; Roback, 1968).

## EVALUATIVE COMMENTS

The rich vein of information tapped by intrapsychic methods has been a boon to clinicians, but a source of perplexity and despair to researchers. More than any other group of techniques, intrapsychic methods generate data fraught with complexities that bewilder the most sophisticated of investigators. There are formidable, perhaps even insurmountable, problems inherent in the use of these techniques since intrapsychic processes are, by definition, unobservable; thus, their presence cannot be confirmed, logically speaking, and they cannot be exposed to objective and quantitative measurement.

Although hard-nosed scientists tend to be overly strict in their standards, they do have a point in claiming that one must "get hold of some thing tangible" with which to do the business of research. Moreover, intrapsychic concepts not only refer to intactile phenomena but they are also viewed to be intrinsically amorphous and pliant; thus, to complicate matters further, intrapsychic processes are considered unstable and fleeting, expressing themselves first this way and then that, meaning different things in one context than in another, or from one moment to the next.

The fact that the unconscious comprises a world of obscure and evanescent processes is not in question. What is troublesome are the serious problems these concepts create for research since they are difficult to tie down to empirical coordinates and cannot be investigated with precise and reliable measures.

In light of these difficulties, some researchers contend that it is futile, even meaningless, to study intrapsychic phenomena, and that to expend one's efforts on theories with so feeble a data base can only be futile. They assert, with reasonable justification, that more substantial progress can be made in explicating the genesis, structure, and therapy of psychopathology by excluding such data from the scientific enterprise (Skinner, 1954).

Although it may be that more fruitful research alternatives are available, the "reality" of intrapsychic events cannot be dismissed. The inevitable difficulties, and the marked paucity of reliable and valid instruments, should serve as a challenge, giving the scientist all the more reason to devote his energies to articulating the amorphous stream of intrapsychic events, and to developing methods by which this rich body of data can be transformed into researchable variables.

Even if one grants the difficulties posed by these concepts, intrapsychic measures must be gauged by the same criteria employed to judge other research instruments. Certainly, intrapsychic researchers cannot dismiss these criteria cavalierly and then expect sensible scientists to take their data seriously. Primitive instruments must be recognized as such, and the data they generate must be viewed with a healthy degree of skepticism, no matter how illuminating and promising they appear. Although this is not the place to labor the limitations and faults of these techniques, a few comments are in order.

1. Much of the difficulty of intrapsychic techniques stems from their dependence on clinical inference. Since the data in question cannot be directly observed and are often claimed to signify different intrapsychic processes in different contexts, it is impossible to assign them a standard or unequivocal meaning. To resolve these ambiguities, investigators typically interpret intrapsychic data in accord with the principles of certain "well established" theoretical schemas. Facile and plausible though these interpretations may be, we know only too well the pitfalls of subjective appraisals; most intrapsychic theories are so malleable as to "explain" any set of findings, even those that patently contradict the theory. In short, intrapsychic methods lack a standardized and objective basis for data interpretation, leading all too frequently to controversial conclusions.

2. Intrapsychic methods are notoriously coarse; many provide only the crudest of guidelines concerning data interpretation. Inferences drawn from a global analysis of a dream or a free-association stream may prove "correct," but there is need to specify the particular elements of these complex responses that "cue" the inferences drawn. Where distinct scoring categories are established, it is possible to order the data into a series of quantitatively discriminable scales; at the very least, such intrapsychic methods meet the minimal criteria of researchable instruments.

3. The relative absence of normative information looms as a further limitation to the use of several of the intrapsychic techniques, for example, free association and dream analysis. Until data obtained

with known ·and relevant population groups are available, the significance and comparability of findings gathered with these methods will be sharply curtailed.

4. The critical comments noted above would carry little import if intrapsychic methods were demonstrably valid in their present forms. Empirical validity, that is, evidence of an instrument's predictive accuracy and its capacity to differentiate among relevant criterion groups, is a pervasive issue with these methods since their interpretation is characterized, not by "proven" evidence of accuracy, but by speculative inferential "leaps." With the exception of projective techniques, practically no systematic evidence has been gathered to test the validity of intrapsychic methods. Numerous efforts have been made to evaluate the predictive and differential validity of several projective instruments; for the most part, these studies have yielded negative results, although some, rather meager, positive findings are scattered in the literature (Zubin et al., 1965). Although less discouraging, reliability data are far from satisfactory.

In conclusion, the general status of intrapsychic methods as research instruments leaves much to be desired. All of the techniques described are shot through with measurement and validation problems. Nevertheless, they do yield data that are obtainable in no other way. Until more objective and quantitative intrapsychic instruments are developed, their unique powers to tap this data level justify their continued use. Needless to say, they must be employed with circumspection and care, and efforts must be made to reduce the risks involved to a minimum.

# PHENOMENOLOGICAL METHODS

The problems that beset research using intrapsychic data are not unique; similar complications arise in investigating all varieties of data, but most notably the phenomenological. Phenomenology represents the study of conscious experience, events as seen from the subjective frame of reference. As with intrapsychic data, the substantive content of phenomenological research deals with the unseen "private world"; such data are elusive, difficult to pin down or infer from observables, and therefore fraught with operational obscurities and methodological complexities.

Despite the inevitable hazards they involve, psychopathologists cannot afford the luxury of bypassing either intrapsychic or phenomenological data. The events they portray are "real"; they represent elements of experience that are no less significant than concrete observables and, therefore, must be tapped to fill out the entirety of our knowledge of the psychopathologic process.

Troublesome though these data may be to methodologically "pure" researchers, phenomenal events have been studied systematically since the "method of introspection" had its heyday in the first two decades of this century. Although this method fell into disrepute following the rise of behaviorism, the study of subjective conscious experience continued unabated, though "under various aliases," as Boring once put it (1953). In this section we shall review some of the many procedures employed to investigate this rich source of data. Although none fully resolve the problems inherent in researching subjective processes, most institute correctives to minimize their effects.

Two methods for gathering phenomenological data will be described. The first, *interview procedures,* consists of two major techniques: one seeks to deduce the patient's phenomenological state through a post-interview analysis of the content of his verbalizations; the other gathers specific types of information during the interview proper through a series of focused questions. In *self-report inventories,* the second of the methods discussed, the patient characterizes his attitudes toward self and others in response to a series of printed "test" questions. . . .

## INTERVIEW PROCEDURES

The interview has been the backbone of clinical psychopathology, but it is only in the past 10 to 15 years that its components have been systematically analyzed, and its use as a source of "private" events has been exploited for purposes of research. Although many other techniques have been devised to uncover important phenomenological data, such as attitudes, memories, feelings, and self-evaluations, this chief tool of clinical information and detection has lagged far behind in scientific scrutiny and development. Fortunately, with the recent growth of interest in the therapeutic "process," increasing numbers of investigators have turned to an analysis of the elements and mechanisms of interview content and interaction.

We shall focus on the phenomenological significance of what is said in the interview. Two kinds of techniques have been employed to gather these data systematically: *post-interview content analysis* and *prearranged interview schedules.* The first categorizes the content of communication *after* it has been collected; the second organizes the interview in advance, thereby maximizing the probability that relevant data will initially be collected.

### Post-Interview Content Analysis

These techniques attempt to categorize and quantify the attitudes and feelings of a patient by reviewing and coding transcribed verbal communications. Although the "latent" qualities of these communications may be analyzed for their intrapsychic significance, content analysis generally focuses on the "manifest" or overt content of what is said; it takes communication data at its face value, accepting it as an indication of conscious experience and intent, rather than of unconscious distortion or symbolism. For this reason, we have included content analysis as a technique for deciphering phenomenological data; when content analysis contains interpretation of symbolism, it represents an intrapsychic method.

Many aspects of what is said in the interview can be categorized; the character of the categories selected will depend, of course, on the researcher's interest. These categories may code fairly simple and straightforward dimensions of content or rather subtle ones. Whatever the coding system developed, the researcher examines samples of interview transcripts and classifies specified units of the patient's verbalizations in accord with predetermined criteria. As he progresses in his transcript analysis, the relative frequencies of the various content categories begin to cumulate, providing him with a quantitative distribution of what was said. Through this procedure, he extracts a series of empirically anchored scores that transform the elusive free flow of communication into statistically manageable units; if the coding criteria are relevant and unambiguous, he should be assured of an accurate characterization of the attitudes and feelings conveyed by the interviewee. Excellent discussions of the steps and complications involved in devising a content analysis system may be found in Cartwright (1953), Berelson (1954), and Sellitiz et al. (1959).

Many features of the interview interaction, aside from content, can be subjected to systematic analysis. Each of the components of interview processes can be neatly separated now that we have at our disposal recording devices such as sound tapes, films, and videotape; for example, in an excellent early study, Giedt (1955) sought to compare the relative quality of information provided in interviews by presenting four types of data to clinical judges: (1) visual cues (silent film), (2) verbal content (verbatim written transcripts), (3) content plus auditory cues (sound alone), and (4) content plus auditory plus visual cues (complete sound film). In recent years, a number of investigators have begun to study not only nonverbal aspects of

interview behavior, such as facial movements and gestures, etc. (Haggard & Isaacs, 1966; Ekman & Friesen, 1968; Mahl, 1968) but so a variety of noncontent facets of verbal behaviors such as total speaking time, ratio of adjectives to verbs, frequency of pauses, etc. (Matarazzo, 1961; Matarazzo et al., 1968). These latter techniques of analysis do not deal directly with the phenomenological content of the interview but with the subject's observable behavior; they will be discussed in a later section dealing with behavior research methods.

Attention in this section will be directed to procedures that focus primarily on verbal content. It should be noted before we proceed that the methodology of content analysis has been fruitfully employed to decode communications other than those contained in interviews, for example, suicide notes (Osgood & Walker, 1959); our discussion here, however, will be limited only to interview data.

The methods to be described have been divided into two groups: (1) those designed to elicit only one dimension of feeling or attitude, and (2) those that seek to analyze several phenomenological dimensions simultaneously. Thorough reviews of research employing these systems have been published by Auld and Murray (1955) and Marsden (1965).

### Single Dimension Systems

Each of the two measures described in this section attempt to extract only one variable from the complex stream of ideas and feelings that unfold in the interview.

The *Discomfort Relief Quotient (DRQ)* was originally devised by Dollard and Mowrer (1947) as a method for measuring tension as expressed in written documents; its value in analyzing therapy transcripts was recognized shortly thereafter. The technique requires segmenting the protocol into "clause or thought units" according to definite rules, and then classifying each unit as an expression of discomfort (suffering, pain, unhappiness), or relief (comfort, pleasure, enjoyment), or neither. The DRQ is obtained by dividing the number of discomfort units by the total number of discomfort *and* relief units. In a typical research study, a sequence of quotients are calculated at various intervals both before, during, and after treatment, thereby providing a quantitative index of change in phenomenological discomfort.

The *Positive-Negative-Ambivalent Quotient (PNAvQ),* devised by Raimy (1948), categorized statements reflecting feelings toward self. The unit here is all words spoken by the interviewee between two responses of the interviewer. Six categories are coded: P—positive self-reference; N—negative self-reference; Av—ambivalent self-reference; A—ambiguous self-reference; O—no self-reference; and Q—nonrhetorical questions. The PNAvQ is obtained by dividing the number of N and Av units by the number of N, Av, and P units. The final quotient may range between zero and one, with quotients closer to zero signifying greater self-approval.

### Multidimensional Systems

In contrast to the content coding schemas presented above, the systems included here attempt to simultaneously categorize the same interview data on several dimensions. They are simply more encompassing and complex than the methods discussed earlier, and do not differ intrinsically in their technique or analysis.

The *Leary-Gill Omnibus System* (1959) illustrates how complex the analyses of content can be. The format employed is undoubtedly the most comprehensive and richly varied system yet formulated but, as with many such detailed and complicated devices, it has failed to enlist the interest of interview researchers. Although it consists of only five basic categories, there is a profusion of subcategories and modifiers that make the system extremely unwieldy. Essentially, Leary and Gill set out to devise not only a method of coding the final content of communication (the constituent category) but also interplay of both therapist and patient, and whether the

subject matter under discussion was "discharged," "admitted to awareness," "admitted into speech," or elaborated "insightfully." These coding scales have not been used in published studies of interview material; the model upon which they were based, however, has been used for simpler content analysis schemas.

The *Holzman-Forman Five-Dimensional System* (1966) is a somewhat less cumbersome, but nonetheless comprehensive, set of content categories. The basic unit for coding (the meaning unit) is the sentence or logical segments thereof; statements of both therapist and patient are categorized. Five separate dimensions of each unit are coded where possible: (1) its grammatical structure, (2) its manifest content, (3) persons or objects relevant to the patient, (4) manifest expressions of approval or disapproval of the "other" in therapy, and (5) references to the "locus" of the patient's difficulty.

Gottschalk and his associates (Gottschalk & Gleser, 1964; Gottschalk et al., 1966) have devised a number of interview coding scales for cognitive disorganization and expressions of hostility and anxiety. Termed the *Affect and Cognitive Functioning Scales,* and operating from an intrapsychic frame of reference, the majority of categories included represent consciously voiced feelings and thoughts. Gottschalk's system depends on verbal content alone and classifies the patient's communications in terms of variables such as: (1) their frequency of occurrence per standard units of time, (2) the intensity of the affect expressed, and (3) the degree of personal involvement of the speaker with the event discussed. The relative case of scoring, and the fact that the coding reliabilities and scale validities have been well documented, augurs well for the continued use of this system in psychopathology research.

### Prearranged Interview Schedules

Whereas content analysis extracts relevant data *after* it has been gathered in a relatively unstandardized and free-flowing interview, the use of a fixed schedule of questions in a structured interview ensures that data relevant to research are obtained *during* the interview itself. Moreover, by organizing the interviewer's attention in advance to a uniform set of topical subject's the prospects for gathering comparable data from all subjects is greatly enhanced. Although the casual air and flexibility of approach that characterizes unstructured interviews are lost when a standardized schedule is followed, more important to most research is the availability of specified classes of data collected under relatively uniform conditions.

Interview schedules and questionnaires are employed to gather a wide range of data relevant to psychopathology, for example, epidemiologic surveys, sociometric preferences, family case histories, etc. Space does not permit a discussion of these manifold uses, nor the problems and procedures involved in constructing and conducting either open-ended or prearranged interviews. The reader will find excellent presentations of these matters in Maccoby and Maccoby (1954), Kahn and Cannell (1957), Kornhauser and Sheatsley (1959), and Richardson et al. (1965).

We shall limit our attention in this section to interview schedules that focus on the patient's "mental status," that is, those that pose questions designed to detect such items as cognitive clarity and insight, emotional preoccupations, complaints, self-attitudes, moods, etc. By selecting a representative sample of patient verbalizations that can be reliably· elicited and quantified, the resultant scores can be compared to appropriate norm groups or be used for purposes such as gauging changes consequent to therapy. The two interview schedules to be presented are notable for the care given their construction, the publication of normative data, and impressive evidence favoring their reliabilities and validities.

The *Psychiatric Status Schedule (PSS)* was devised by several research associates at the New York State Psychiatric Institute (Spitzer et al., 1964; Spitzer, 1966); it consists of a standardized interview schedule and a matching inventory of 492 precoded, dichotomous items of both pathological behavior and social adaption. The interviewer follows the prescribed order of the schedule to elicit a wide range of comments concerning the patient's symptoms and functioning during the past week. Most of the questions are open ended, enabling the patient to reveal not only the content but also the character of this thoughts and feelings. Juxtaposed opposite each question, or series of questions, are items comprising the inventory; these items characterize typical responses of subjects, and are rated as the interview proceeds by marking statements as true or false. Although questions are posed in a casual manner, the fixed schedule and order of presentation ensures that data obtained with different interviewers will be comparable.

A few items call for relatively complex judgments, but most are brief, nontechnical descriptions of phenomenological attitudes or feelings, and recollections of recent behaviors or habits; in general, unconscious processes are not evaluated. Where necessary, optional follow-up questions are suggested to smooth the flow of the interview and for purposes of elaboration or clarification.

Numerous clinical and social subscales have been, and are being, developed via factor analysis; these will provide quantifiable indices not only of psychopathological symptom clusters (depressive mood, paranoid ideation) but also of role functioning, work adjustment, level of aspiration, etc.

Somewhat similar in format and procedure to the PSS is the *Structured Clinical Interview (SCI),* devised also by investigators associated with the New York State Psychiatric Institute (Burdock & Hardesty, 1964, 1966, 1968). It is briefer than the PSS and is designed to *evoke* immediate and salient pathology, rather than surveying a wide range of events and feelings associated with the patient's recent life. The interview consists of a schedule of open-ended questions, juxtaposed with an inventory of 179 items; as the interview progresses, these items are judged by the interviewer as *True* or *Not true* on the basis of the subject's responses and behaviors.

Since the focus of questioning is on current phenomenological attitudes and feelings, rather than on historical information or intrapsychic material, the instrument lends itself readily to repeated use, such as would be necessary in evaluating the extent of changes consequent to therapy. The data gathered are grouped into ten subscales: (a) anger-hostility, (b) conceptual dysfunctioning, (c) fear and worry, (d) incongruous behavior, (e) incongruous ideation, (f) lethargy-dejection, (g) perceptual dysfunctioning, (h) physical complaints, (i) self-depreciation, and (j) sexual deviance.

## SELF-REPORT INVENTORIES

Robert Woodworth, a well-known American psychologist, was called upon in the First World War to devise a "psychological test" that would be more efficient and economical than the time-consuming psychiatric interview as an instrument for military inductees. The "test" he developed, known as the *Personal Data Sheet,* was essentially a self-administered interview in which the respondent replied to a standard series of printed questions dealing with his past and present habits, feelings, and attitudes. The inventory of items covered the same ground as that of the interview, but saved considerable professional time. In this paper-and-pencil form, the interview was transformed into a well-standardized, highly efficient, and easily quantified measurement tool; these tools were labeled "self-report inventories." The fact that the "personal touch" and flexibility of the psychiatric interview was lost, and that answers had to be limited to fixed response categories such as "yes," "no," or "cannot say," was well compensated by the large number of subjects that could be assessed simultaneously and the simplicity and uniformity of both test administration and scoring. The inventory rapidly became a popular tool.

Authors of early self-report inventories selected their items on the basis of their *face validity,* that is, they "looked right" in that their content dealt with topics that had an *obvious* relationship to personality traits and psychopathology. Questions were raised, however, as to whether such items had relevance to any systematic theory of psychopathology, whether the sheer obviousness of the items invited deliberate misrepresentation on the part of the respondent, and whether such tests "really" discriminated among different pathological states. Several approaches to test validation were formulated to deal with these questions (Loevinger, 1957): *external* (empirical-criterion), *structural* (factorial-trait), and *substantive* (theoretical-rational).

The first approach, *external,* initiated with the development of the Humm-Wadsworth Temperament Scale (1935), and brought to its fullest refinement in the MMPI (Hathaway and McKinley, 1942), involves choosing items that have an empirically demonstrated correspondence with relevant external criteria, such as clinically diagnosed pathological types. Although the pool of self-descriptive items used in these empirically validated instruments were usually selected on face-valid grounds, the final items retained for the tests consisted only of those that held up when checked against real-life criteria (i.e., had predictive and/or concurrent validity).

The second procedure of validation, termed *structural,* is based on statistical and factor analytic procedures; its goal is to produce several homogeneous scales representing relevant traits of personality functioning with as small a number of items is necessary. In contrast to the external approach, which retains items on the basis of their empirically demonstrated correlations with significant clinical criteria, structurally validated tests select items that will ensure trait representativeness and internal consistency within scales.

The third method of validating self-report inventories, *substantive,* draws its items from a clearly formulated theoretical framework.

The theory established a series of clinically relevant categories and provides a fund of diverse behaviors characteristic of patients in each category. Items within scales that represent the typical behaviors of each clinical category are generated and then grouped, in accordance with the theory, to form the separate clinical scales of the inventory. In contrast to the two previous approaches to test validation, which may be viewed as empirical and statistical, the substantive method derives its items rationally in terms of a theoretical scheme. Since there are few theories of psychopathology from which self-report items can be rationally derived, the number of inventories constructed on this basis are few indeed. Ideally, inventories should be developed employing all three methods of item validation. No such clinical instrument is in current use, but several that follow this three-stage format are being constructed; one inventory of this type will be discussed briefly in later paragraphs.

For the present, we shall divide inventories into two groups, those which focus on a single clinical characteristic and those that encompass and distinguish among several such characteristics.

## Single Dimension Instruments

These self-report inventories select and highlight one class of variables from the total personality matrix for analysis and measurement. Several personality dimensions have been isolated, but we shall limit our discussion to three of the more important and extensively researched variables: *anxiety, affect-mood,* and *self-acceptance.*

### Anxiety Scales

Because of its central role in psychopathology, anxiety has been a favorite concept for test constructors. Levitt (1967) provides an excellent review of the concept, describes more than ten recent "anxiety" inventories, and discusses, albeit briefly, the special attributes and limitations of each.

The most frequently used and researched of these inventories is *Taylor's Manifest Anxiety Scale* (1951, 1953), one of a number of instruments constructed from the 566 item pool of the Minnesota Multiphasic Personality Inventory (to be discussed later). The scale includes 225 of the MMPI items, of which only 50 contribute to the anxiety score; the remainder serve as "filters" to disguise the intent of the measure. Although devised originally for use as a measure of an organismic variable in experimental studies of learning, the scale's success in distinguishing between normal and psychiatric populations has led to its wide use as an instrument in general psychopathological research.

There are other, less extensively researched, anxiety inventories that are worthy of note; among them are the *S-R Inventory of Anxiousness* (Endler et al., 1962), and the *State-Trait Anxiety Inventory* (Spielberger & Gorsuch, 1966).

### Affect-Mood Scales

Despite the obvious importance of mood as an element of the personal experience of emotionally disturbed persons, it is only recently that systematic attempts have been made to devise quantifiable self-report instruments. Only a few of these inventories provide reasonably satisfactory evidence of reliability and validity; among them are the *Mood Adjective Checklist,* the *Multiple Affect Adjective Checklist,* and the *Personal Feeling Scales.* A brief description of each will suffice for our purposes.

The *Mood Adjective Checklist* (Nowlis, 1956; Nowlis & Nowlis, 1965) attempts to capture moment-to-moment states of conscious mood. The list consists of 130 mood-related adjectives, for example, uncertain, apprehensive, carefree, down-hearted, which the subject is asked to read through rapidly and rate on a four-point intensity scale reflecting his feelings while taking the test. Factor analysis of intercorrelations among responses from several populations have resulted in eight mood factors, for example, aggression, anxiety, depression, social affection. The sensitivity of this instrument to experimentally induced drug states, sleep deprivation, boredom, emotionally charged films, etc., has been well documented by Nowlis and his associates.

Similar to the above, but even simpler to administer, is the *Multiple Affect Adjective Checklist* (Zuckerman & Lubin, 1966), which consists of some 60 items that are merely checked by the subject if he believes they characterize either his current or his general feelings, depending on the instructions provided. The instrument covers three areas with rationally derived scales: anxiety, depression, and hostility.

The *Personal Feeling Scales* (Wessman & Ricks, 1966) are completed daily for several days and summarize the intensity of several different feelings experienced during each day. There are 16 separate bipolar feeling categories, for example, elation-depression, harmony-anger, tranquillity-anxiety, each graded on a 10-point scale; the subject is asked to record in the evening which of the 16 categories he rated as the "highest," "lowest," and "average," using the 10-point scale. Although this instrument has not been subjected to factorial analyses and has not yet been validated with psychopathologic populations, it is more richly differentiated and refined in structure than previous comparable tools, and promises to be a useful inventory for appraising complex mood variations over a number of days.

## Self-Acceptance Scales

Central to most phenomenological theories is the notion that unfavorable self-evaluations comprise the essence of psychopathology, and that changes toward higher self-esteem are the sine qua non of successful therapy. To measure the self-concept variable, researchers have devised inventories in which the subject characterizes both his actual self, as phenomenologically perceived, and his ideal self, that is, what he would like to be.

Discrepancies between actual and ideal ratings comprise a self-acceptance measure.

The most common format for these self-report evaluations are sorting procedures in which the subject distributes a series of descriptive statements, printed on individual cards, into a graded series of categories depicting the degree to which the items are "like" or "unlike" himself. In a typical study, Rogers and Dymond (1954) had patients perform a "self-sort" and an "ideal-sort" both prior to and after client-centered therapy; they gauged the effectiveness of treatment by the extent to which the discrepancy between the initial self-ideal sorts decreased on resorting after therapy.

Comparisons between actual and ideal ratings are employed in the *Self-Ideal-Other-Q-sort* (Rogers & Dymond, 1954), the *Interpersonal Checklist* (LaForge & Suczek, 1955), and the *Adjective Checklist* (Gough & Heilbrun, 1964). Other instruments probe self-evaluations directly; among these measures are the *Self-Acceptance Scale* (Berger, 1952), the *Self-Rating Inventory* (Brownfain, 1952), and the *Self-Evaluation Questionnaire* (Farnham-Diggory, 1964). Several of these instruments have been carefully developed, but there is little empirical data bearing on their validity with distinct psychopathologic syndromes.

## MULTIDIMENSIONAL INSTRUMENTS

It is often useful for research purposes to employ an inventory that encompasses a more extensive range of personality characteristics than tapped by the single dimension instruments described above. Several such inventories have been devised; we shall concentrate on three instruments that typify the external, structural, and substantive approaches to test construction and validation.

### Minnesota Multiphasic Personality Inventory (MMPI)

There is little question but that the MMPI, developed by Hathaway and McKinley

(1942), is currently the most popular self-report inventory, ranking along with the Rorschach and TAT, not only as "standard" instruments of psychopathologic analysis, but as the three most extensively researched clinical tools. More than 2000 articles and books have been written about it, and more than 200 tests have been devised using the question items of which it is composed.

The construction of the MMPI was thoroughly empirical. An original pool of over 1000 items, to which subjects responded "true," "false," or "cannot say," was reduced to 566 items on the basis of their demonstrated success in discriminating between psychiatric patients and "normal" adults. More specifically, patients were divided into subdiagnostic groups, and items that discriminated a particular psychiatric group from normals were categorized together to form a scale; each of these psychiatric scales was keyed so that the greater the number of items on a scale endorsed by a subject, the more similar he was assumed to be to the particular diagnostic group with which the scale was first constructed. Nine different clinical scales were developed in this fashion, as well as four validity scales to check against errors, evasiveness, and deception. . . .

In scoring the inventory, the number of responses keyed to each scale is totaled; this total is converted into standard scores, known as T-scores, and plotted on a profile sheet. A T-score of 50 corresponds to the average number of items on a scale responded to in the keyed direction by "normal" persons; T-scores of 70 or higher are considered to indicate the presence of pathological signs that characterize the clinical population with which the scale was developed. . . .

Although there is some question as to whether a valid picture of a patient's status can be gauged by examining his scores on a scale-by-scale analysis, the overall profile pattern has been shown in recent research to be a reasonably useful basis for diagnostic interpretation. Profile configurations, based on relative magnitudes of several T-scores, have themselves been empirically correlated with

a variety of other diagnostic, as well as prognostic and therapeutic, variables. Thus, interpretation is guided by results obtained with known external correlates, and is not left to the speculative deductions of the clinician; in fact, these data have recently been programmed into a computer, providing automated interpretive suggestions (Pearson and Swenson, 1967; Fowler, 1969). Useful empirically based guides to MMPI profile interpretation are furnished in Dahlstrom and Welsh (1960), Marks and Seeman (1963), and Gilberstadt and Duker (1965); the *MMPI Manual* (Hathaway & McKinley), revised last in 1951, has been outdated and will soon be replaced.

## Sixteen Personality Factor Questionnaire (16 P-F)

Whereas the MMPI exemplifies an inventory constructed by external or empirical-criterion methods, the 16 *P-F Questionnaire* (Cattell, 1949–1963) is a prime example of an instrument devised on the basis of structural- or factorial-trait procedures. In developing this instrument, Cattell amassed an impressive number of personality trait descriptions ultimately reducing them to 171 items, which he then intercorrelated to produce 12 factors. On the basis of these results, plus 4 additional factors identified in subsequent studies, Cattell prepared his 16 factor questionnaire, now available in three forms of 187, 187, and 106 items respectively.

Considerable use has been made in personality research with the 16 *P-F Questionnaire,* but there is a paucity of data on clinical populations. Moreover, although the construction of the instrument may have been impeccable, it suffers many of the problems inherent in factor-based scales. Some have questioned whether the 16 separate dimensions are reasonably homogeneous and internally consistent, the sine qua non of the structural approach; and there is insufficient evidence that the scales are adequately reliable or relate empirically to significant external criteria. Cattell and his associates recognize these shortcomings, and are continuing, with skill and imagination, to further refine and validate their instrument.

## Millon-Illinois Self Report Inventory (MI-SRI)

The initial item pool for this instrument (Millon, 1972), consisting of over 3000 self-descriptive statements, was derived on a rational basis from a systematic theory of psychopathology (Millon, 1969); hence, it illustrates the substantive approach to test validation in its initial stages of construction. Item lists for 19 theoretically based clinical scales . . . were reduced so as to furnish two equivalent Provisional Forms of 566 statements each. Empirical studies with relevant and diverse clinical populations provided data for item analyses and refinements in scale homogeneity and reliability. Provisional Form items were eliminated on the basis of these studies, resulting in a single structurally validated Research Form of 566 statements. Current work investigating the correlation of scale scores and profiles with various criterion measures, such as clinical ratings, biographical data, and several perceptual and cognitive tasks, should furnish a basis for further item reductions and scale refinements. As these steps provide data for external validation, the final or Clinical Form of the instrument will be published for general diagnostic use. In the interim, the Research Form, derived from a systematic theory and displaying evidence of internal consistency and reliability, lends itself well as an instrument for a wide range of experimental studies (note that the MISRI served as the basis of the MCMI, to be discussed in the next paper).

## EVALUATIVE COMMENTS

Phenomenological data are more tangible and more readily evoked than those of the intrapsychic level, but both derive from highly subjective "inner" sources and are subject, therefore, to numerous distorting influences.

What has contributed to the greater adequacy of phenomenological data is not so much their greater tangibility and ease of evocation, but the care with which potential sources of distortion have been avoided by those who have constructed phenomenological instruments. To illustrate, great pains were taken in the *Structured Clinical Interview* to standardize the data-gathering process and to ensure that idiosyncrasies in interviewer questioning and interpretation were kept to a minimum. Similarly, in the MMPI, efforts were made to construct scales that would detect respondent evasiveness and "faking."

1. The data of post-interview content analysis are often gathered in highly dissimilar settings; moreover, interviewers may have conducted their sessions in idiosyncratic fashions. Both of these factors decrease markedly the comparability of data, and it may not be possible to compensate for this lack of uniformity, even with clearly articulated systems of content analysis. Among other shortcomings of these systems is the lack of adequate normative data gathered on relevant psychopathologic groups; evidence for their validity in the psychiatric field is also almost nonexistent.

   Data uniformity is not a problem with prearranged interview schedules; in fact, standardization at the input end is among their prime virtues. However, since most of these instruments are of recent vintage, there is little evidence that they provide a balanced cross section of factorially "pure" phenomenological data; moreover, minimal information is available of a normative nature, or of their validity as instruments of clinical discrimination or prediction. Such data are being accumulated.

2. Despite the highly structured character of self-report inventories, they are subject to distortions that may invalidate the data they furnish. For example, researchers

cannot assume that all subjects interpret the items similarly, or that they have sufficient self-knowledge to reply informatively, or that they may not be dissembling or faking their replies. Few of the "single dimension" instruments described earlier were designed to obviate these problems, nor did their authors take adequate precautions to minimize their effects.

It is to the credit and distinction of the constructors of the MMPI that they established adequate "control" scales to avoid or detect these complications. Moreover, by validating their test items against relevant external criteria, they circumvented a variety of problems inherent in phenomenological data, such as respondent self-knowledge and test-taking attitudes; thus, it does not really matter "why" a subject responds as he does since the response, whatever its basis, correlates empirically with a known and significant external criterion. Unfortunately, evidence of the validity of the separate MMPI scales as instruments for discriminating among clinical syndromes has fallen far short of its developers' original expectations, although its validity in distinguishing broad categories such as psychoses, neurosis, and normality has stood up well.

Perhaps the factorial impurity of the MMPI scales accounts, in part, for their failure to correlate with clinically derived diagnostic distinctions. Cattell's 16 P-F questionnaire is composed of reasonably independent factors, but its scales have not been sufficiently validated empirically against external criteria of psychopathology. In fact, there is little normative data available on clinical populations, thereby decreasing its utility for comparative research studies.

# REFERENCES

Aserinsky, E., & Kleitman, N. Regularly occurring periods of eye mobility, and concurrent phenomena, during sleep. *Science*, 1953, *118*, 273–274.

Auld, F., & Murray, E. J. Content-analysis studies of psychotherapy. *Psychol. Bull.*, 1955, *5*, 377–395.

Bandura, A., & Walters, R. *Social learning and personality development.* New York: Holt, Rinehart & Winston, 1963.

Beck, S. J. *Rorschach's test: II. A variety of personality pictures.* New York: Grune & Stratton, 1945.

Beck, S. J. *Rorschach's test: III. Advances in interpretation.* New York: Grune & Stratton, 1952.

Beck, S. J. *Rorschach's test: I. Basic processes.* New York: Grune & Stratton, 1961.

Bellak, L. *The Thematic Apperception Test and the Children's Apperception Test in clinical use.* New York: Grune & Stratton, 1954.

Berelson, B. Content analysis. In G. Lindzey (Ed.), *Handbook of social psychology.* Reading, MA: Addison-Wesley, 1954.

Berger, E. M. The relation between expressed acceptance of self and expressed acceptance of others. *J. Abnorm. Soc. Psychol.*, 1952, *47*, 778–782.

Blum, G. S. A study of the psychoanalytic theory of psychosexual development. *Genet. Psychol. Monogr.*, 1949, *39*, 3–99.

Blum, G. S. A guide for the research use of the Blacky Pictures. *J. Proj. Tech.*, 1962, *26*, 3–29.

Bordin, E. S. Free association: An experimental analogue of the psychoanalytic situation. In L. Gottschalk and A. Auerbach (Eds.), *Methods of research in psychotherapy.* New York: Appleton-Century-Crofts, 1966.

Boring, E. A history of introspection. *Psychol. Bull.*, 1953, *50*, 169–189.

Brownfain, J. J. Stability of the self-concept as a dimension of personality. *J. Abnorm. Soc. Psychol.*, 1952, *47*, 597–606.

Buck, J. N. The HTP technique: A qualitative and quantitative scoring manual. *J. Clin. Psychol.*, 1949, *5*, 37–76.

Burdock, E. I., & Hardesty, A. S. Quantitative techniques for the evaluation of psychiatric treatment. In P. Hoch and J. Zubin (Eds.), *The evaluation of psychiatric treatment.* New York: Grune & Stratton, 1964.

Burdock, E. I., & Hardesty, A. S. Behavior patterns of chronic schizophrenics. In P. Hoch and J. Zubin (Eds.), *Psychopathology of schizophrenia.* New York: Grune & Stratton, 1966.

Burdock, E. I., & Hardesty, A. S. Psychological test for psychopathology. *J. Abnorm. Psychol.,* 1968, *73,* 62–69.

Buros, O. K. (Ed.) *The sixth mental measurements yearbook.* Highland Park, NJ: Gryphon Press, 1965.

Buros, O. K. (Ed.) *Personality: Tests and measures.* Highland Park, NJ: Gryphon Press, 1969.

Campbell, D. T. The indirect assessment of social attitudes. *Psychol. Bull.,* 1950, *479,* 15–38.

Campbell, D. T. A typology of tests, projective and otherwise. *J. Consult. Psychol.,* 1957, *21,* 207–210.

Cartwright, D. P. Analysis of qualitative material. In L. Festinger and D. Katz (Eds.), *Research methods in the behavioral sciences.* New York: Dryden, 1953.

Cattell, R. B. *Manual for Forms A and B. Sixteen Personality Factor Questionnaire.* Champaign, IL: IPAT, 1949–1963.

Cattell, R. B. Principles of design in projective or misperception tests of personality. In H. Anderson and G. Anderson (Eds.), *An introduction to projective techniques.* Englewood Cliffs, NJ: Prentice-Hall, 1951.

Colby, K. M. Experiment on the effects of an observer's presence on the image system during psychoanalytic free-association. *Behavioral Sci.,* 1960, *5,* 197–210.

Dahlstrom, W. G., & Welsh, G. S. *An MMPI handbook: A guide for use in clinical practice and research.* Minneapolis: University of Minnesota Press, 1960.

Dement, W. C. Experimental dream studies. In J. Masserman (Ed.), *Science and psychoanalysis.* Vol. 7. *Development and research.* New York: Grune & Stratton, 1964.

Dement, W. C. An essay on dreams: The role of physiology in understanding their nature. In *New directions in psychology II.* New York: Holt, Rinehart & Winston, 1965.

Dollard, J., & Auld, F. *Scoring human motives: A manual.* New Haven: Yale University Press, 1959.

Dollard, J., & Mowrer, O. H. A method of measuring tension in written documents. *J. Abnorm. Soc. Psychol.,* 1947, *42,* 3–32.

Ekman, P., & Friesen, W. V. Nonverbal behavior in psychotherapy research. In J. Shlien et al. (Eds.), *Research in Psychotherapy.* Vol. III. Washington, DC: American Psychological Association, 1968.

Endler, N. S., Hunt, J. M., & Rosenstein, A. J. An S-R inventory of anxiousness. *Psychol. Monogr.,* 1962, *76,* No. 537.

Farber, L. H., & Fisher, C. An experimental approach to dream psychology through the use of hypnosis. *Psychoanal. Quart.,* 1943, *12,* 202–216.

Farnham-Diggory, S. Self-evaluation and subjective life expectancy among suicidal and nonsuicidal psychotic males. *J. Abnorm. Soc. Psychol.,* 1964, *69,* 628–634.

Fowler, R. D. The current status of computer interpretation of psychological tests. *Amer. J. Psychiat.,* 1969, *125,* 21–27.

Frank, L. K. Projective methods for the study of personality. *J. Psychol.,* 1939, *8,* 389–413.

Freeman, F. S. *Theory and practice of psychological testing.* (3rd. ed.). New York: Holt, Rinehart & Winston, 1962.

Fromm, E. Remarks on the problem of free association. *Psychiat. Res. Rpts.,* 1955, *29,* 1–6.

Giedt, F. H. Comparison of visual, content, and auditory cues in interviewing. *J. Consult. Psychol.,* 1955, *19,* 407–416.

Giberstadt, H., & Duker, J. *A handbook for clinical and actuarial MMPI interpretation.* Philadelphia: Saunders, 1965.

Goldberg, P. A. A review of sentence completion methods in personality assessment. In B. I. Murstein (Ed.), *Handbook of projective techniques.* New York: Basic Books, 1965.

Gordon, J. E. Leading and following psychotherapeutic techniques with hypnotically induced repression and hostility. *J. Abnorm. Soc. Psychol.,* 1957, *54,* 405–410.

Gordon, J. E. (Ed.). *Handbook of clinical and experimental hypnosis.* New York: Macmillan, 1966.

Gottschalk, L. A., & Auerbach, A. H. (Eds.). *Methods of research in psychotherapy.* New York: Appleton-Century-Crofts, 1966.

Gottschalk, L. A. The measurement of emotional changes during a psychiatric interview: A working model toward quantifying the psychoanalytic concept of affect. In L. Gottschalk and A. Auerbach (Eds.), *Methods of research in psychotherapy.* New York: Appleton-Century-Crofts, 1966.

Gottschalk, L. A., & Gleser, G. C. Distinguishing characteristics of the verbal behavior of schizophrenic patients. In *Disorders of communication.* Baltimore: Williams and Wilkins, 1964.

Gough, H. G., & Heilbrun, A. B. *Manual for the Adjective Check List.* Palo Alto, CA: Consulting Psychologists Press, 1964.

Haggard, E. A., & Isaacs, K. S. Micromomentary facial expressions as indicators of ego mechanisms in psychotherapy. In L. Gottschalk and A. Auerbach (Eds.), *Methods of research in psychotherapy.* New York: Appleton-Century-Crofts, 1966.

Hathaway, S. R., & McKinley, J. C. *Minnesota Multiphasic Personality Inventory.* Minneapolis: University of Minnesota Press, 1942.

Hathaway, S. R., & McKinley, J. C. *The Minnesota Multiphasic Personality Inventory Manual (Revised).* New York: Psychological Corporation, 1951.

Hauri, P., Sawyer, J., & Rechtschaffen, A. Dimensions of dreaming: A factored scale for rating dream reports. *J. Abnorm. Psychol.,* 1967, *729,* 16–22.

Hilgard, E. R. Hypnosis and experimental psychodynamics. In H. W. Brosin (Ed.), *Lectures on experimental psychiatry.* Pittsburgh: University of Pittsburgh Press, 1961.

Holtzman, W. H. *Inkblot perception and personality: Holtzman Inkblot Technique.* Austin: University of Texas Press, 1961.

Holzman, M. S., & Forman, V. P. A multidimensional content analysis system: Applied to the analysis of therapeutic technique in psychotherapy with schizophrenic patients. *Psychol. Bull.,* 1966, *66,* 263–281.

Humm, D. G., & Wadsworth, G. W. The Humm-Wadsworth Temperament Scale. *Amer. J. Psychiat.,* 1935, *929,* 163–200.

Kahn, R. L., & Cannell, C. F. *The dynamics of interviewing.* New York: Wiley, 1957.

Klopfer, B. *Developments in the Rorschach Technique. Vol. 1. Technique and theory.* Yonkers-on-Hudson, NY: World Book, 1954.

Klopfer, B. *Developments in the Rorschach Technique. Vol. 11. Fields of application.* Yonkers-on-Hudson, NY: World Book, 1956.

Kornhauser, A., & Sheatsley, P. B. Questionnaire construction and interview procedure. In C. Selitiz et al. (Eds.). *Research methods in social relations.* New York: Holt, 1959.

Kubie, L. S. Psychoanalysis and scientific method. *J. Nerv. Ment. Dis.,* 1960, *131,* 495–512.

LaForge, R., & Suczek, R. F. The interpersonal dimension of personality: III. An interpersonal check list. *J. Pers.,* 1955, *24,* 94–112.

Leary, T., & Gill, M. The dimensions and a measure of the process of psychotherapy. In E. Rubinstein and M. Parloff (Eds.), *Research in psychotherapy.* Washington, DC: American Psychological Association, 1959.

Levitt, E. E. *The psychology of anxiety.* Indianapolis: Bobbs-Merrill, 1966.

Levy, D. M. Use of play technique as experimental procedure. *Amer. J. Orthopsychiat.,* 1933, *3,* 266–277.

Lindzey, G., & Goldwyn, R. M. Validity of the Rosenzweig picture-frustration study. *J. Pers.,* 1954, *229,* 519–547.

Lindzey, G., Lykken, D. T., & Winston, H. P. Infantile trauma, genetic factors, and adult temperament. *J. Abnorm. Soc. Psychol.,* 1960, *61,* 7–14.

Loevinger, J. Objective tests as instruments of psychological theory. *Psychol. Rpts.,* 1957, *3,* 635–694.

Maccoby, E. E., & Maccoby, N. The interview: A tool of social science. In G. Lindzey (Ed.), *Handbook of social psychology.* Reading, MA: Addison-Wesley, 1954.

Machover, K. *Personality projection in the drawing of the human figure.* Springfield, IL: Thomas, 1948.

Mahl, G. F. Gestures and body movements in interviews. In J. Shlien et al. (Eds.), *Research in psychotherapy. Vol. III.* Washington, DC: American Psychological Association, 1968.

Marks, P. A., & Seeman, W. *The actuarial description of abnormal personality: An atlas for use with the MMPI.* Baltimore: Williams and Wilkins, 1963.

Marsden, G. Content-analysis studies of therapeutic interviews: 1954 to 1964. *Psychol. Bull.,* 1965, *63,* 298–321.

Matarazzo, J. D. Prescribed behavior therapy: Suggestions from interview research. In A. Bachrach (Ed.), *Experimental founda-*

*tions of clinical psychology.* New York: Basic Books, 1961.

Matarazzo, J. D. Speech and silence behavior in clinical psychotherapy and its laboratory correlates. In J. Shlien et al. (Eds.), *Research in psychotherapy. Vol. III.* Washington, DC: American Psychological Association, 1968.

Michigan Department of Mental Health. *Michigan Picture Test Manual.* Chicago: Science Research Associates, 1953.

Millon, T. *Theories of psychopathology.* Philadelphia: Saunders, 1967.

Millon, T. *Modern psychopathology.* Philadelphia: Saunders, 1969.

Millon, T. *Millon-Illinois Self-Report Inventory Manual: Provisional and Research Forms.* (Limited to research investigators), 1972.

Morgan, C. D., & Murray, H. A. A method for investigating fantasies: The Thematic Apperception Test. *AMA Arch. Neurol. Psychiat.,* 1935, *34,* 289–306.

Murphy, L. B. *Personality in young children.* New York: Basic Books, 1956.

Murstein, B. I. *Theory and research in projective techniques (emphasizing the TA 7).* New York: Wiley, 1963.

Murstein, B. I. *Handbook of projective techniques.* New York: Basic Books, 1965.

Nowlis, V. Research with the Mood Adjective Checklist. In S. S. Tomkins and C. Izard (Eds.), *Affect, cognition and personality.* New York: Springer, 1965.

Nowlis, V., & Nowlis, H. H. The description and analysis of mood. *Ann. N. Y. Acad. Sci.,* 1956, *65,* 345–355.

Osgood, C. E., & Walker, E. G. Motivation and language behavior: A content analysis of suicide notes. *J. Abnorm. Soc. Psychol.,* 1959, *59,* 58–67.

Pearson, J. S., & Swenson, W. M. *A user's guide to the Mayo Clinic automated MMPI program.* New York: Psychological Corporation, 1967.

Piotrowski, Z. A. *Perceptanalysis.* New York: Macmillan, 1957.

Raimy, V. C. Self reference in counseling interviews. *J. Consult. Psychol.,* 1948, *12,* 153–163.

Rapaport, D. *Organization and pathology of thought.* New York: Columbia University Press, 1951.

Richardson, S. A., Dohrenwald, B. S., & Klein, D. *Interviewing: Its forms and functions.* New York: Basic Books, 1965.

Roback, H. B. Human figure drawings: Their utility in the clinical psychologist's armamentarium for personality assessment. *Psychol. Bull.,* 1968, *70,* 20–44.

Rogers, C. R., & Dymond, R. F. (Eds.). *Psychotherapy and personality change.* Chicago: University of Chicago Press, 1954.

Rorschach, H. *Psychodiagnostics.* Berne: Hans Huber, 1942.

Rosenzweig, S. The picture-association method and its application in a study of reactions to frustration. *J. Pers.,* 1945, *14,* 3–23.

Rotter, J. B., & Rafferty, J. E. *The Rotter Incomplete Sentences Blank Manual.* New York: Psychological Corporation, 1952.

Rotter, J. B., & Willerman, B. The incomplete sentence test. *J. Consult. Psychol.* 1947, *11,* 43–48.

Sargent, H. D. Projective methods; Their origin, theory and application in personality research. *Psychol. Bull,* 1945, *42,* 257–293.

Sargent, H. D. *The Insight Test.* New York: Grune & Stratton, 1955.

Schafer, R. *Psychoanalytic interpretation in Rorschach testing.* New York: Grune & Stratton, 1954.

Schneidman, E. S. Schizophrenia and the MAPS test. *Genet. Psychol. Monogr.,* 1948, *38,* 145–224.

Schneidman, E. S. (Ed.). *Thematic test analysis.* New York: Grune & Stratton, 1951.

Schneidman, E. S. Manual for the MAPS test. *Proj. Tech. Monogr.,* 1952, *1,* No. 2, 1–92.

Sears, R. R. et al. Some child-rearing antecedents of aggression and dependence in young children. *Genet. Psychol. Monogr.,* 1953, *47,* 135–236.

Selltiz, C., Jahoda, M., Deutch, M., & Cook, S. (Eds.) *Research methods in social relations.* (Rev. ed.) New York: Holt, 1959.

Shakow, D. The recorded psychoanalytic interview as an objective approach to research in psychoanalysis. *Psychoanal. Quart.,* 1960, *299,* 82–97.

Singer, J. L. *Daydreaming. An Introduction to the experimental study of inner experience.* New York: Random House, 1966.

Skinner, B. F. Critique of psychoanalytic concepts and theories. *Scientific Monthly,* 1954, *799,* 300–305.

Spitzer, R. L. The Mental Status Schedule: Rationale, reliability, validity. *Comprehen. Psychiat.,* 1964, *5,* 384–395.

Spitzer, R. L. The Mental Status Schedule: Potential use as a criterion measure of change in psychotherapy research. *Amer. J. Psychother.,* 1966, *20,* 156–167.

Swenson, C. H. Empirical evaluation of human figure drawings. *Psychol. Bull.,* 1957, *549,* 431–466.

Swenson, C. H. Empirical evaluations of human figure drawings.: 1957–1966. *Psychol. Bull.,* 1968, *709,* 20–44.

Tart, C. T. Toward the experimental control of dreaming: A review of the literature. *Psychol. Bull.,* 1965, *64,* 81–90.

Taylor, J. A. The relationship of anxiety to the conditioned eyelid response. *J. Exp. Psychol.,* 1951, *41,* 81–92.

Taylor, J. A. A personality scale of manifest anxiety. *J. Abnorm. Soc. Psychol.,* 1953, *489,* 285–290.

Weitzenhoffer, A. *General techniques of hypnotism.* New York: Grune & Stratton, 1953.

Wessman, A. E., & Ricks, D. F. *Mood and personality.* New York: Holt, Rinehart & Winston, 1966.

Witkin, H. A., & Lewis, H. B. (Eds.). *Experimental studies of dreaming.* New York: Random House, 1967.

Wolberg, L. R. Hypnotherapy. In S. Arieti (Ed.), *American handbook of psychiatry.* New York: Basic Books, 1959.

Zubin, J., Eton, L. D., & Schumer, F. *An experimental approach to projective techniques.* New York: Wiley, 1965.

Zuckerman, M., & Lubin, B. *Manual for the Multiple Affect Adjective Check List.* San Diego: Educational and Industrial Testing Service, 1966.

# MCMI: Substantive, Structural, and Criterion Validation

This chapter presents the rationale and strategy that guided the development of the MCMI-I and the MCMI-II. An outline of the steps that were followed in constructing a series of preliminary forms for the inventory is provided. The intent was to successively refine earlier forms so that the final instrument satisfied ideal construction criteria and would be maximally efficient in assessing patients on a number of significant personality and clinical characteristics. . . .

## RATIONALE

According to Loevinger (1957) and Jackson (1970), validation should be an ongoing process involved in all phases of test construction, rather than a procedure for corroborating the instrument's effectiveness following its completion. With this principle in mind, validation of the MCMI-I and MCMI-II became an integral element at each step of development rather than an afterthought.

Once a commitment was made to this strategy, the question remained as to what validation procedures should be used to make the final product as efficient as possible in achieving the goals of differential diagnostic and clinical interpretive utility. In her highly illuminating monograph, Loevinger (1957) proposes that development validation possesses three sequential components: substantive, structural, and external. Each of these is a necessary component in construction, but not a sufficient one.

Where feasible, steps should be taken to progress from the first stage through the third. A validation sequence such as this departs from procedures employed in the construction of past clinical inventories. A brief introduction to the rationale and methods of each of these three components may be a useful précis of the procedures followed in developing both the MCMI-I and the MCMI-II.

The first validation stage, relabeled "theoretical-substantive," and more recently termed the "deductive approach" by Burisch (1984), examines the extent to which the items comprising the instrument derive their content from an explicit theoretical framework. Such a theory has been developed (Millon, 1969, 1981, 1986a). In both MCMIs, it provides a series of clinically relevant constructs for personality trait and syndrome definition to be used as a guide in writing relevant scale items. Moreover, since both clear boundaries and anticipated relationships between syndromes can be established on rational grounds, the test can be constructed with either distinct or interrelated scales at the initial stage of development.

The second stage, "internal-structural," refers to the model (that is, the purity of the separate scales or the character of their expected relationships) to which the instruments items are expected to conform. For example, each scale may be constructed as a measure of an independent trait in accord with a factorial model. In another model, each scale may be designed to possess a high degree of internal consistency, yet may be expected to display considerable overlap with other, specific scales. In the structural phase, items that have already been substantively validated are administered to appropriate populations. For the MCMI-I and the MCMI-II, the items that survived this second stage were those which maximized scale homogeneity, displayed a measure of overlap with other theoretically congruent scales, and demonstrated satisfactory levels of endorsement frequency and temporal stability.

The third stage, noted here as "external-criterion validation," includes only those items and scales which have met the requirements of both the substantive and the structural phases of development. It pertains to the empirical correspondence between each test scale and a variety of nonscale measures of the trait or syndrome under study. This third stage entails correlating results obtained on preliminary forms of the inventory with relevant clinical behaviors. When performed in conjunction with other assessment methods and employing diverse external criteria, this procedure may also establish each scale's convergent and discriminant validity (Campbell & Fiske, 1959).

In a set of classic papers, Hase and Goldberg (1967) and Goldberg (1972) compared alternative construction strategies and found that each displayed equivalent levels of validity across a set of diverse criteria. After reviewing several subsequent parallel studies, Burisch (1984) concluded that these findings of method equivalence continued to be supported. It would seem, nevertheless, that a sequential validation strategy that employed all three of these approaches would, at the very least, prove equal to any single method alone and perhaps enjoy a measure of superiority. With this untested assumption in mind, developmental validation studies were begun on the MCMI-I. It was hoped that each stage would produce increasingly more refined and accurate forms of the inventory.

# THEORETICAL-SUBSTANTIVE VALIDATION

Some of the major principles and aims that guided the development of the MCMI-I and the MCMI-II are presented in this section. The steps taken to generate the preliminary items of the MCMI-I are also presented.

## THE USE OF THEORY

Reflecting on her years of experience in test construction and evaluation, Loevinger (1972) concludes:

If I were to draw a single conclusion from my own studies of personality measurement, it would be this: I consider it exceedingly unlikely that either by accident or by automation one will discover a measure of a major personality variable. There is no substitute for having a psychologist in charge who has at least a first-approximation conception of the trait he wishes to measure, always open to revision, of course, as data demand. Theory has always been the mark of a mature science. The time is overdue for psychology, in general, and personality measurement, in particular, to come of age. (p. 56)

Commenting on the development of the MMPI, Norman (1972) notes that criterion keying was the only recourse possible, since no adequate theory or body of established empirical data was available as an alternative. Meehl (1945), the most persuasive exponent of the criterion keying approach has shifted from an earlier anti-theoretical position to one in which a guiding theory is seen as a valuable test development tool (Meehl, 1972). In his usual insightful fashion, Meehl states:

One reason for the difficulties of psychometric personology, a reason I did not appreciate in my "dustbowl empiricist" paper of 1945, is the sad state of psychological theory . . .

I now think that at all stages in personality test development, from initial phase of item pool construction to a late-stage optimized clinical interpretive procedure for the fully developed and "validated" instrument, theory and by this I mean all sorts of theory, including trait theory, developmental theory, learning theory, psychodynamics, and behavior genetics—should play an important role . . .

I believe that psychology can no longer afford to adopt psychometric procedures whose methodology proceeds with almost zero reference to what bets it is reasonable to lay upon substantive personological horses. The "44 theory" . . . may be only weakly corroborated but I think we have to make do with it anyway. (pp. 149–151)

. . . the preliminary item pool should be constructed in reliance upon all of the facts and theories bearing upon the test. Even one who advocates a relatively atheoretical "blind empirical criterion keying". . . need not deprive himself of whatever theoretical insight is available at the item construction stage . . . I now believe (as I did not formerly) that an item ought to make theoretical sense. . . . (p. 155)

Although Meehl maintains his strong commitment to the critical role played by external validation, his recognition of the guiding value of a theoretical model served significantly to reinforce the strategy undertaken in developing both the MCMI-I and the MCMI-II. Together with Loevinger, Meehl's growing appreciation of the use of theory, strengthened the belief that such a course would prove both wise and fruitful.

## THE GUIDING THEORETICAL SYSTEM

Some thoughts on the nature of clinical syndromes will be noted before describing the theoretical system that underlies the MCMI-I and the MCMI-II scales.

### The Nature and Value of Clinical Prototypes

A clinical effort to develop an instrument that attempts to unravel all of the elements of a patient's past and present would be an exhausting task indeed. To make the job less onerous, the instrument must limit its focus to certain salient aspects of behavior. This reduction process requires a series of decisions regarding which data are likely to prove most productive in achieving the goals of the instrument. That is, a nucleus of factors must be selected which will capture the most relevant and essential characteristics of patients. This nucleus of attributes that focuses on the core of distinguishing features of a syndrome or disorder may be spoken of as a clinical prototype (Cantor, Smith, French, & Mezzich, 1980; Millon, 1986a, 1986b; Rosch, 1978).

Several assumptions are made when the diagnostic focus is narrowed to a limited range of clinical behaviors. Most basically, it is assumed that specific clinical behaviors will be shared by a distinctive group of patients. Further, it is assumed that prior knowledge concerning the characteristics of these distinctive patient groups will facilitate a variety of diagnostic and treatment goals.

If diagnosis assumes that prototypal groups display distinctive and common clinical behaviors, the question still remains about whether identifying a patient as a member of such a prototype serves functions other than that of "labeling." The aim of prototypal diagnosis is to clue the clinician to aspects of a patient's history and behavior that may not have been previously identified. A further hope is that clinicians will use prior knowledge about other patients displaying the disorder and generalize that knowledge in a useful and valid manner for all new patients diagnosed as having that disorder.

The notion that patients can be classified into clinical prototypes is not undermined by the fact that all patients evidence unique traits and individual differences (Millon, 1987). No classification can or should be expected to be entirely homogeneous. The pragmatic question is whether placement in a category impedes or facilitates clinically significant goals. If diagnostic placement simplifies clinical tasks such as alerting the diagnostician to features of the patient's history and present functioning that have not yet been observed, enabling clinicians to communicate effectively about their patients, guiding the selection of beneficial therapeutic plans, or assisting researchers in designing better studies, then the process of diagnostic identification will have served many useful purposes.

## Desirable Features of a Classification System

In their excellent review of classification problems in psychopathology—no less applicable today than it was more than 25 years ago—Zigler and Phillips (1961) draw the following conclusions:

The authors are impressed by the amount of energy that has been expended in both attacking and defending various systems of classifications. We believe that a classification system should include any behavior or phenomenon that appears promising in terms of its significant correlates. At this stage of our investigations, the system should be an open and expanding one . . . Systems of classification must be treated as tools for further discovery, not bases for polemic disputation. (p. 616)

Given this perspective, as well as a comparable conclusion drawn by the author in an extensive examination of psychiatric taxonomies (Millon, 1987), one might ask: What features should be considered essential to a good classification system? Three of those which guided the development of the theory underlying both MCMIs are briefly summarized below.

1. Categories should be differentiated according to severity. Most diagnostic instruments gauge severity in terms of scale elevation alone; clear demarcations of type and degree of pathology are difficult to determine with this approach. To facilitate these distinctions, the MCMI-II differentiates ten basic "personality disorder" (Axis II) scales, which tap mild severity, from three more severe personality pathology scales, which reflect moderate or marked levels of impairment. Similarly, six "clinical syndrome" (Axis I) scales identify disorders of moderate severity, and three other scales gauge disorders of marked severity. Along with the addition of two new basic personality disorder scales, the MCMI-II represents a revision of the personality and clinical scales found on the MCMI-I. Despite these distinctions, it is important to provide for the commonalities and continuities that exist between similar disorders that differ in their degree of severity. To achieve this, the MCMI-I and the MCMI-II were constructed so that the more serious impairments are appraised as distinctive, but integrally related, variants of their less severe correlates.

2. Categories should be arranged to reflect the fact that the presenting clinical picture is composed of several covarying traits and symptoms. Diagnostic scales that focus on one, usually dramatic, behavioral sign fail to recognize this inherent complexity. When each MCMI-I and MCMI-II scale was constructed, a number of different clinical features were included to tap the intricacy and diversity of both personality styles and symptom syndromes.

3. Each diagnostic category should be shown, where appropriate, to be a precursor, an extension or a modification of other clinical categories, rather than stand on its own as a discrete entity. This is in accord with the polythetic structure that guides the nature of categories formulated in MCMI-I and MCMI-II theory. For example, in both the MCMI-I and MCMI-II theory and inventories, all clinical syndromes of Axis I are viewed as disruptions in a patient's basic personality pattern (Axis II) that emerge under stress. In this formulation, clinical syndromes are not conceived as discrete diagnoses, but as integral elements of a larger complex of clinical features within which they are embedded.

## THEORY-BASED
## DIAGNOSTIC CATEGORIES

As noted earlier, a consistent theoretical system upon which to base a coherent classification of syndromes and a framework for developing a parallel set of inventory scales is extremely useful. The guiding texts for the MCMI-I and the MCMI-II, *Modern Psychopathology* (Millon, 1969), *Disorders of Personality* (Millon, 1981), and *Contemporary Directions in Psychopathology* (Millon & Klerman, 1986a, 1986b) describe such a theoretical system. Despite its wide range of clinical applicability, the theory is based on derivations from a simple combination of a few variables or constructs. Essentially, it posits 10 basic styles of personality functioning that can be formed logically from a 5 x 2 matrix consisting of two basic dimensions. Previously, 8 basic styles were posited from a 4 x 2 matrix and served as the basis for the MCMI-I basic personality disorder scales.

The first dimension pertains to the primary source from which patients gain comfort and satisfaction (positive reinforcements) or attempt to avoid emotional pain and distress (negative reinforcements). Patients who experience few rewards or satisfactions in life, be it from self or others, are referred to as detached types; circumstances which lead patients to reverse positive or negative reinforcement, or to substitute pain for pleasure are termed discordant personalities; those who measure their satisfactions or discomforts by how others react to or feel about them are described as dependent; where gratification is gauged primarily in terms of one's own values and desires, the patient is said to exhibit an independent personality style; finally, those who experience considerable conflict over whether to be guided by what others say and wish or to follow their own opposing desires and needs are referred to as ambivalent personalities.

The second dimension of the theoretical matrix reflects the basic pattern of instrumental or coping behavior that the patient characteristically employs to maximize rewards and to minimize pain. Those patients who seem aroused and attentive, intervening and manipulating life events to achieve gratification and avoid discomfort display what is termed an active pattern; in contrast, those who seem apathetic, restrained, yielding, resigned, or seemingly content to allow events to take their own course without personal regulation or control, possess what is termed a passive pattern.

## PERSONALITY STYLES
## AND PATHOLOGIES

Combining the five sources of primary reinforcement together with the two instrumental or coping patterns results in 10 basic personalities: active and passive detached; active and passive discordant; active and passive dependent; active and passive independent; and active and passive ambivalent.

Personality styles reflect deeply etched and pervasive characteristics of patient functioning. These characteristics tend to perpetuate themselves and aggravate everyday difficulties, but they are so embedded and automatic a way of life that the patient often is unaware of their nature and their self-destructive consequences. Under conditions of persistent adversity, the patient's maladaptive style of functioning may begin to decompensate, acquiring features that justify the designation of moderate or marked severity. These advanced stages of personality pathology reflect an insidious and slow deterioration of the personality structure, and usually accentuate the patient's lifelong style of functioning. Despite evident changes in psychic cohesion, social competence and emotional control, the patient continues to display the major personality characteristics that were previously evident.

## PROCEDURAL STEPS

The theoretical substantive validation phase in the development of the MCMI-I (the first edition of the MCMI) consisted of three sequential steps: (a) creating a theoretically based initial item pool, (b) reducing the item pool on rational grounds, and (c) selecting items to establish two equivalent provisional forms of the instrument.

## Creating a Theoretically Based Initial Item Pool

The construction of the MCMI-I went one step beyond the traditional procedure of content or in "face valid" item selection, since item pools were prepared for each syndrome scale on the basis of theoretically derived definitions (Gynther, Burkhart, & Hovanitz, 1979; Holden & Jackson, 1979; Wrobel & Lachar, 1982). Detailed characteristics of each syndrome, published in earlier work, provided a fund of typical response behaviors for different syndromes expressed in various situational contexts. Writing and initially selecting items from this broad spectrum of characteristics ensured that the content of the initial pool was both comprehensive and representative. In addition to *Modern Psychopathology* (Millon, 1969)—the major theory-based text at that time—a total of more than 80 sources, including textbooks in psychiatry and psychology, rating scales, and published personality tests, were exhaustively combed to produce more than 3,500 self-descriptive, content-oriented item statements. Then a set of 20 theory-based clinical scales was arranged for the initial classification of items; three of the original scales were dropped from later research and replaced with scales of potentially greater clinical use. The subset of basic personality scales varied in number from 177 items for the Schizoid pattern category to 432 for the Antisocial group; the severe personality disorder scales ranged from 179 items in the Schizotypal category to 200 in the Borderline group; the clinical syndrome scales varied in number from 70 items in the Somatoform category to a high of 94 in the

Anxiety group. All items at this stage of development were phrased so that the response "True" would signify the presence of the scale syndrome. Although there was some initial concern regarding "acquiescent" bias (Jackson & Messick, 1961), subsequent research indicated that its role was likely to be minor (Rorer, 1965). Moreover, preliminary trials suggested that negatively worded items would lack sufficient differential specificity to be useful; that is, numerous patient syndrome types are likely to conclude that a particular behavioral item is not true of them, whereas only a few syndrome types are likely to say that the behavior is true of them. This expectation has been supported in subsequent studies by others when negatively worded items proved to be of considerably less differential diagnostic use (Holden, Fekken, & Jackson, 1985).

## Reducing the Item Pool on Rational Grounds

The process of rational item reduction included several stages of editing against criteria such as grammar, clarity, simplicity, content validity, and scale relevance. As a first step, readers eliminated items that were inexplicit, excessive complex, possibly objectionable, contained desirability bias, were likely to be unreliable, and probably would be of extreme endorsement frequency. Most significantly, items were selected because they exemplified traits that characterized the specific scale for which they were written. Several efforts were made to select items to achieve convergent and discriminant validity, that is to judge items not only in terms of their relevance for a specific scale, but their "lack of fit" with other selected syndrome scales (Campbell & Fiske, 1959). Another important criterion was that of covering the full domain of traits and behaviors characterizing each syndrome. Rather than concentrating on one or two features that might be most distinctive of a personality pattern or clinical syndrome, efforts were made to provide a balanced and representative sample of all of the characteristics of the scale (Wiggins, 1973).

In addition to the above preliminary reduction steps, four additional empirical procedures for winnowing the set further were employed at this stage.

First, a small sample of patients was asked to read the remaining items and judge them for clarity and ease of self-rating.

Second, when the list was reduced by patient judgments, eight mental health professionals well versed in the theory and nosology were asked to sort all items on a blind basis into their theoretically most appropriate categories; items were retained only if six or more of these clinicians placed them correctly, that is, according to the theoretical model.

Third, items that survived these initial "best-fit" clinical sortings were re-sorted for second- and third-best fits, first within their own subsection (except in the pathological personality subsection of three scales where only a second-best fit sorted) and second, within the other subsections. These data were stored for later decisions concerning the multiple scoring of items.

Fourth, items surviving the first series of sortings were sorted once again for first and second "negative fit," that is, for those unlikely to be endorsed by certain personality styles or disorders. For example, an item signifying a strong interest in social activities would be negatively sorted in the Schizoid personality scale. These data were also kept as background information for the plan to key False responses at a later stage of test development.

### Establishing Substantively Valid Provisional Forms

Using the criteria and steps noted above, the initial pool was reduced to the 1,100 best-fit items, which were then divided into various scale categories (second- and third-best fit

and negative-fit selections were not used as data for this stage of research). In addition, they included 36 items as a check against random, denial, and complaint distortion tendencies; protocols displaying high scores on these distortion scales were discarded. Because of the time-consuming and statistically unwieldy nature of an inventory of 1,100-plus items, the reduced pool was divided following item matching for representativeness into two provisional forms, each consisting of 566 items. The specific figure of 566 for each form was determined by the availability of appropriately designed answer sheets of that figure. Since the items of both forms were selected for consistency with the theoretically derived sets of syndromes, the scales were viewed as having met the criteria of a substantially valid instrument.

## INTERNAL-STRUCTURAL VALIDATION

As described and elaborated by Loevinger (1957), the structural component of validity refers to an instrument's fidelity to its underlying model. Thus, relationships found among the tests items and scales should correspond to the structural pattern of the instruments theory. For example, assume that a theory posits the existence of personality characteristics formulated as independent or "pure" traits. In this case, the instrument should be designed with a factorial structure; that is, the items comprising each scale should intercorrelate positively with one another and correlate negatively with all other scales of the instrument. The test would then exhibit fidelity to its guiding theory.

Despite its popularity with many distinguished psychometricians (e.g., The Eysenck Personality Inventory and Cattell's Sixteen Personality Factor Questionnaire), a factorial model is not universally applicable, since many personality theories do not accept the notion of trait independence (Allport, 1937, 1950).

## MCMI-II Polythetic Structural Model

Like the MCMI-I, the MCMI-II was constructed in accord with a "polythetic" structural model that stresses internal scale consistency but does not require the scale independence that characterizes factorial approaches. To accord with the underlying "prototypal" model of its guiding theory and its polythetic syndromal structure (Cantor et al., 1980; Horowitz, Wright, Lowenstein, & Parad, 1981; Millon, 1986a, 1987; Rosch, 1978), the scales of the MCMI should possess a high level of internal consistency, yet, at the same time, should display selective overlap and a high degree of correlation with other theoretically related scales. For example, according to the theory, the basic personality scale, Avoidant, is viewed as a less severe precursor of the pathological personality disorder scale, Schizotypal. Because they represent relatively coherent clinical syndromes, each scale should exhibit reasonably strong evidence of internal consistency. At the same time, because of their polythetic structure and, hence, the inherent commonalities between these two syndromes, many items should overlap both scales, resulting in substantial interscale correlations. When high interscale correlations of this sort occur, it is often suggested that one scale could be readily substituted for the other. For a variety of reasons beyond their polythetic nature, not the least of which are the different prevalence base rates for these scale syndromes, this contention is neither logical in terms of clinical theory, nor pragmatic.

## Merits of Item Redundancy and Scale Overlap

In contrast to the MMPI, in which scale overlap through joint item keying evolved strictly as a result of empirically derived commonalities in diagnostic efficiency (Wakefield, Bradley, Doughtie, & Kraft, 1975), item and scale overlap with the MCMI-I and MCMI-II both anticipated and guided by the polythetic structural model and the dynamic features of its underlying theory. In addition, as stated by Dahlstrom, Welsh, and Dahlstrom (1972, p. 23): "If the syndrome used in developing a given scale is relatively complex and is characterized by a wide variety of symptoms, then the scale, reflecting this behavioral heterogeneity, is likely to show important relationships with some other scales in the profile."

It is Dahlstrom (1969), a distinguished and active MMPI researcher, who has provided an articulate rationale for scale redundancy. Reflecting on whether two scales showing a high level of intercorrelation are really two measures or one, Dahlstrom recounts the experience of McKinley and Hathaway (1944), who found a substantial overlap between the Hysteria and the Hypochondriasis scales:

These investigators indicated that their initial temptation was to drop one or the other of these scales on general psychiatric cases because the two scales correlated .71. Yet careful examination of the clinical contributions of each of these scales led McKinley and Hathaway to retain both scales. . . . Several kinds of evidence were used (such as the fact that 32% of the cases of conversion hysteria had scores beyond the arbitrary cutting score on Hysteria, while being missed by the Hypochondriasis scale), but the most compelling reasons for retaining both scales lay in their configural relationships. The way these scales related to each other and the third scale in the neurotic triad, the Depression scale, provided useful data in psychodiagnostic evaluations of anxiety, depression, and somatic reactions. Information provided by such indices as hit rates or summarized in nonlinear combinations of test scales is not adequately represented in tables of intercorrelations nor accurately preserved in factor solutions . . . (which do) serious injustice to clinical assessment formulations that operate outside a narrow, geometrical view of human personality. (pp. 23–24)

In essence, Dahlstrom argues that the foundation for important clinical decisions can be significantly strengthened, not in spite of, but because of, substantial scale overlapping—a position compellingly argued by Broughton (1984) in proposing a "prototype strategy" for the construction of personality scales. Increased valid-to false-positive ratios (hit rate), accuracy in applying base rate normative data, and the availability of illuminating diagnostic information from configural patterns, may all be lost by eliminating highly correlated but subtly different clinical scales. This argument, persuasive for the MMPI, is all the more relevant to the MCMI-I and the MCMI-II, in which both prototypal theory and polythetic structure call for the use of scales with redundant item content.

Accepting the view that intercorrelated scales have potential clinical use does not resolve a question concerning the manner in which these interrelationships should be structured. A major criticism of the MMPI is its failure to specify an a priori logic for the relationships that evolved strictly by empirical correspondence. Norman (1972) notes: "Whatever one thinks of the desirability of the original construction of the basic clinical scales. . . . it is abundantly clear that they are about as inappropriate and maladapted a set as one could imagine for their current uses in profile analyses and interpretation and typal class definition" (p. 64).

What systematic grouping for the MMPI would have been more logical and fruitful? Again, it is Dahlstrom (1972), in his article, "Whither the MMPI," who provides the most persuasive answer, one that is entirely consistent with the structural theory that guided the development of the MCMI-I and the MCMI-II and has served as a rationale for the distinction between Axis I and Axis II in the DSM-III (Millon, 1981). Examining different ways in which the MMPI could be "rehabilitated," Dahlstrom writes:

. . . there are two general kinds of assessment evaluations intermixed in these current applications of the MMPI: personality structure and current emotional status. That is, many of the descriptors pertain to the question: What kind of person is this? Whereas other items seem to deal more with the question: What, if anything is wrong with him? In the first kind of appraisal, the configural correlates bear upon enduring attributes of the person: his character, his personality style, and his stability or lack of it. In contrast to these general characteristics, there are also many descriptors that refer to the person's mood and feelings, his contact with reality, or his present level of control. (p. 86)

Dahlstrom's suggestion for revising the MMPI consists largely of devising separate scales for personological predispositions (personality pattern scales) and for psychopathological states (clinical syndrome scales), precisely the distinction developed in constructing both MCMIs. And, in accord with these instruments' underlying theory, Dahlstrom comments that a separation of scales along these lines would enable researchers to test the thesis that specific ties exist between particular personality types and the clinical disorders each will exhibit under stress, as well as the specific kinds of disorders to which each type is most susceptible. The underlying theory of the MCMI-I and the MCMI-II can contribute most usefully in formulating these hypothesized relationships.

## LOGIC OF NONFACTORIAL INTERNAL CONSISTENCY

Dahlstrom (1972) alerts future test developers to a major difficulty that may arise in attempting to distinguish enduring personality style scales from current or transient symptom scales:

Are the effects of momentary emotional status so pervasive in the records obtained from acutely disturbed patients that it is meaningless to search for measures of more enduring characterological or personality features in their self-descriptions at those times? It seems well worth the effort to try to work out some means of accomplishing both kinds of assessment. It may, however, turn out to be an impossible task for the inventory approach. (p. 96)

Dahlstrom's caveat is well worth noting, since the task of successfully overcoming the pervasive and blurring effects of an acute or intense emotional state is a difficult one indeed as recent research has shown (Hirschfeld et al., 1983; Reich, Noyes, Coryell, & O'Gorman, 1986; Reich, Noyes, Hirschfield, et al., 1987). Yet, as Dahlstrom notes, it is well worth the effort. The question is how to go about doing it.

At the internal-structural state of validation, a first approximation both to the expected polythetic structure of scales, as well as to moderating the blurring of "state" and "trait," can be achieved by insisting that each item of a scale demonstrates a higher level of correlation with that scale than with any other. For example, although an item designed to tap an acute depressive disorder may correlate with nondepression scales, its highest point-biserial correlation should be with the Depression scale.

Whether it differentiates acute symptom states from personological traits or makes any other set of comparisons, the ideal solution for maximizing discriminations among scales would be to produce factorially pure scales. This goal would be difficult to achieve, since, as Dahlstrom notes, there are powerful blurring effects produced by pervasive emotional states. More important, however, is the fact that a factorial model runs counter to the natural covariations and interrelationships that exist among clinical syndromes, an observation convincingly explicated with regard to its application to personality structure (Lykken, 1971). According to the MCMI theory, no personality type or psychopathological state consists of entirely homogeneous and discrete psychological properties. Rather, as Broughton (1984) has presented in his argument favoring a prototypal model, they are comprised of diffuse and complex characteristics, which share many traits as well as contain certain more distinctive features.

To ensure an optimum level of scale homogeneity, that is, to accept the inevitability of clinical overlap and achieve theoretically desirable levels of redundancy that accord with a polythetic conception of syndromes, items comprising each designated scale should exhibit their strongest association with that scale, but not a unique one. Further, there should be theoretical justification for retaining items that correlate secondarily with scales other than the one for which they were intended. For example, an item selected substantively for the Avoidant scale may, in studies of internal consistency, correlate .50 with its own scale and .35 with the Schizotypal scale; redundancy in this case would be theoretically congruent. However, if a substantive Avoidant item were to correlate .50 with its own scale and .50 with the theoretically incongruent Histrionic scale, there should be serious reservations about including the item on either scale.

Statistical and theoretical considerations, however, are not the ultimate test of an item's or a scale's efficiency. That is determined by their discriminatory or predictive power as empirically demonstrated in studies with significant external criteria, a topic to be discussed at length in a later section. For the present, it will suffice to say that factorial purity is a goal that is neither clinically feasible nor theoretically preferred. Further, procedures that enhance high item-scale homogeneity through studies of internal consistence are the best methods currently available for optimizing, rather than maximizing, discriminations between scales in accord with a polythetic model of clinical syndromes.

## PROCEDURAL STEPS

Let us turn from the abstract issues of structural rationale to the concrete, and empirical steps employed to select items that conform to the guiding polythetic MCMI-I and MCMI-II model. The following procedures were used to reduce the 566 items of each

MCMI-I provisional form, which had been constructed on the basis of theoretical-substantive validation data.

## Administering the Provisional Forms

Each of the two forms was administered to a diverse clinical sample. Considerable planning was done to assure that participating clinicians gathered a predetermined ratio of patients with regard to age, sex, and race. To ensure representation of the major diagnostic groups for whom the MCMI-I was designed, several subsamples were included from a variety of short-term and long-term psychiatric hospitals, private practice settings, outpatient community mental health centers, and family service agencies. A total of 130 patients completed provisional Form A only; 123 took provisional Form B only; and 52 patients completed both forms with test administrations separated by a period of two or three days. Equivalent form scale reliabilities were gauged with this latter group, which ranged from a low of .69 for the Depression clinical syndrome scale to a high of .86 for the Histrionic basic personality scale; the median reliability was .81 for all 20 clinical scales.

## Calculating Item-Scale Intercorrelations and Item Endorsement Frequencies

Although there are numerous procedures for item analysis, only a few seemed relevant to the goals of this stage of test development. Several steps were followed after the substantively validated provisional forms had been administered to the patient samples. First, individual responses were punched on computer cards; six test inventories were dropped because of invalid responding. The second step consisted of evaluating item-scale homogeneities through measures of internal consistency. The third was a simple computation of the True and False endorsement frequencies

obtained with each of the 1,100-plus provisional form items.

Point-biserial correlations (corrected for overlap) were calculated between each item and each of the original provisional form clinical scales. A similar procedure was followed for substantively selected items comprising the three scales that subsequently replaced those included in the original group of 20 scales.

To maximize scale homogeneity, only those items which show their highest correlation with the scale to which they were originally assigned were retained for additional study. With few exceptions, items evidencing less than a .30 correlation were eliminated from further consideration because of their low level of internal consistency; the median biserial correlation for all selected items prior to scale refinement was .47; following scale refinement, through item reduction, the median correlation reached .58.

A next major step was that of developing multiple-scale keying, that is, arranging a scoring system in which individual items could be keyed on several scales, a step that accords fully with the instrument's polythetic structure. The plan was to select items that would achieve a pattern of item-scale overlapping that optimized the fidelity of the MCMI-I to its underlying theoretical model. Only those items which had already met the criterion of exhibiting its highest correlation with its substantively selected scale were included. All high-positive or high-negative biserial correlations (greater than .30 or −.30) with scales other than an item's original assigned scale were evaluated. These correlations were coordinated with matching "second-best-fit" and "negative-fit" data obtained during the clinical scoring, substantive-validation phase.

As a final step, items which showed extreme endorsement frequencies, that is, less than .15 or over .85, were judged of low priority and were screened out in most cases. Items beyond those endorsement-frequency boundaries usually possess minimal discriminating power and may reflect extremes in desirability.

## Establishing a Structurally Valid Research Form

Of the original 1,132 items in the two provisional forms, 440 met the initial criteria of exhibiting their highest correlation with their substantively designated scale and achieving an endorsement frequency within the acceptable range. These 440 remaining items were screened further according to two additional criteria. First, an effort was made to maintain adequate representation of each scale's trait diversity or syndrome complexity. Second, items were eliminated if their correlation pattern of overlapping scales was inconsistent with the theory's structural model; for example, an item that exhibited a high biserial correlation with both Avoidant and Histrionic scales would probably be dropped. Items comprising the three scales that were added at a later development state were not included in these analyses because they would confound previously established statistics and base rate data. These various screening procedures reduced the substantively valid 1,100-plus provisional items to 271 "clinical" and 18 "correction" items, a total of 289 that would comprise the revised Research Form of the MCMI-I. Despite this marked reduction in items, the number of scorable units per scale changed only minimally, because the scoring format was expanded to allow for the multiple keying of individual items and the inclusion of both False and True responses as scale discriminants. Decisions concerning these additional item-scale keying were based, in part, on the data of earlier, substantive sortings on second-and third-best and negative fits. To optimize the instrument's theoretical fidelity and polythetic structure, these were combined with matching data on positive and negative biserial correlations between items on scales in the item consistency study.

All of the validation steps taken to this point were considered refining and narrowing, but essentially tentative, process. Data obtained through external-criterion studies would be the final basis for the selection and keying of items. However, because items at this stage of development had been chosen and keyed following evidence of endorsement acceptability, scale homogeneity, theory congruence, and syndrome or trait representatives, the MCMI-I Research Form had met the basic criteria of a structurally valid instrument.

# EXTERNAL-CRITERION VALIDATION

The central idea behind using external-criterion validation is quite straightforward. Items comprising a test scale should be selected on the basis of their empirically verified association with a significant and relevant criterion measure. The procedure by which this association is gauged is also direct. Preliminary items should be administered to two groups of subjects which differ on the criterion measure. The "criterion" group exhibits the trait with which the item is to be associated; the "Comparison" group does not. After the test is administered, the True and False endorsement frequencies for both groups on every item are calculated. Items that statistically differentiate the criterion group from the comparison group are judged "externally valid." To ensure that these item discriminations are not spurious or do not occur merely by chance, they should be reassessed through additional studies with new, cross-validation samples.

The prime virtue of the external-criterion method is that it verifies, in fact, what is only intuitively, structurally, or theoretically assumed to be an item-criterion relationship. Moreover, the method may uncover associations which are neither obvious nor readily deduced on consistency or theoretical grounds. Among the incidental advantages that may accrue from the criterion method is the identification of subtle or indirect items which subjects would have difficulty falsifying or dissembling.

There are several disadvantages to test development procedures that depend exclusively on external validation methods. These are especially problematic when diverse cross-validation follow-up studies have not been done. The items this method produces may stem from chance relationships that characterize the particular population sample used for item selections. Significant item discriminations that emerge with the construction sample, particularly those that are surprising in terms of clinical "logic," often fail to hold up when reevaluated with an apparently similar, but new, cross-validation sample.

One of the merits of both the MCMI-I and MCMI-II construction procedure is that all items survived the criteria of theoretical-substantive and internal-structural validity, before being subjected to external validation. Hence, those which survive this final stage are not likely to be judged either "surprising" or logically "inconsistent."

Accepting the rationale of external-criterion validation still leaves two additional problems. First, there is the question of the nature of the criteria to be chosen for external reference. Second, a decision must be made about which comparison groups would be most relevant for contrast with the criterion groups.

## USE OF PRAGMATIC CRITERIA

The use of practical or pragmatic criteria for external validation reference has been a subject of much debate for many years. (Cattell, 1946; Lord, 1955; Loevinger, 1957; Gough, 1965). The issue is whether the criteria chosen should be composed of real clinical functions and decisions for which the test will be a substitute gauge or whether the criteria should be less specific and reflect more generalized functions, traits, and purposes.

Lord (1955) writes that the goal of generalized, nonpragmatic validity is neither feasible nor relevant. Rather, the true measure of validation is the instrument's discriminating power for specific decision problems. Similarly, Gough (1965) argues that the ultimate standard for validation should be the setting within which the test will be used; that is, the instrument should be evaluated by its predictive or descriptive use in a real-world, functional setting. This pragmatic philosophy for external criteria, successfully applied in validating the Strong Vocational Blank, the Minnesota Multiphasic Personality Inventory (MMPI), and the California Personality Inventory (CPI), achieves its greatest value by ensuring that an instrument is directly relevant to the operational services it is intended to perform.

Applying the pragmatic model to both MCMI's suggests that its use would be best gauged by its ability to predict what clinicians are likely to say in describing their patient's personality characteristics and symptom disorders. Because the items of both MCMI's had already been screened in accord with theoretical-substantive and internal-structural validation procedures, the instrument fulfilled the goals of those who espouse less pragmatic and more generalizable criteria. Enhancing both MCMI's practical use seemed to be fully justified for the ensuing external state of validation. A careful selection of pragmatic criteria would not only refine the instrument by providing additional validation data, but would also help make both MCMI's maximally useful to clinicians who employ it primarily for differential diagnostic and interpretive purposes.

There are numerous methods by which useful data can be gathered about patients. The most direct and clinically relevant approach would be to obtain assessments by mental health professionals who are well acquainted with the specific psychological traits and disorders of particular patients. Diagnostic appraisals by experienced psychologists, psychiatrists, and psychiatric social workers, in contrast to those of non-professional relatives and acquaintances, would discriminate psychologically subtle, as well as gross, differences among patients. Thus, an operational criteria composed of professional clinical assessments would not only be pertinent and practical but would also furnish those more precise discriminations necessary to make the instrument an efficient differential diagnostic tool.

## NEED FOR RELEVANT COMPARISON GROUPS

Earlier literature points out the importance of selecting items by comparing the responses of target diagnostic groups with other psychologically disturbed patients, rather than comparing them to so-called normals. Meehl and Rosen (1955) state this idea well: "If a test is to be used in differential diagnosis among psychiatric patients, evidence of its efficiency for this function cannot be established solely on the basis of discrimination of diagnostic groups from normals" (p. 197).

In a classic paper, Campbell and Fiske (1959) note that it is not only necessary to provide evidence which shows that a test correlates appropriately with relevant external criteria (convergent validity), but also that it exhibits independence from, or is negatively correlated with, distinctive unrelated criteria (discriminant validity). However, the difficulty of establishing discriminant validity when comparing overtly similar, but fundamentally different, clinical groups has not been stressed. For example, the scales of the MMPI were not devised to differentiate clinical syndromes from one another, but rather to distinguish them from a population of normal respondents. Norman (1972) states the discriminant problem of the MMPI in a persuasive manner.

. . . one can achieve substantial increases in resolution or differentiate diagnostic subgroups over that which has typically been attained by the very simple expedient of conducting one's search for discriminating items within an appropriate frame

of reference. Once we have concluded that we are confronted with a patient who has either a neurosis or a character disorder, it is hardly relevant to examine scores on variables whose main claim to fame is that they distinguish normals from one or the other of these two kinds of patients. But that is just the sort of thing we have been doing by limiting ourselves to information yielded by the current MMPI clinical scales, virtually all of which were built to discriminate various diagnostic classes from a "distal" group of normals. (p. 69)

It was Rosen (1962) who first contrasted MMPI responses of a large clinical syndrome with those of a general psychiatric population. Following his lead, the decision was made to compare the True and False endorsement frequencies for every MCMI-I and MCMI-II item of every target diagnostic group to that of every other diagnostic group. As in Rosen's study, the comparison would not be between specific diagnostic populations and normals, but among all clinical criterion groups. Comparing response data among clinical syndromes makes it possible to minimize the common and blurring effects of what may be called "general psychopathology" variance. Since inventory items may be contaminated by this general factor, they are likely to intercorrelate spuriously and thus lose their power for discriminating specific diagnostic entities. For example, if the scales for Anxiety and Hypomania correlate .80 because each reflects a common dimension of general psychopathology, the efficient of both scales to differentiate their separate syndromes will be substantially attenuated. Reduced discriminability of this kind is precisely what may occur if item selections are based on comparisons between clinical syndromes and normals, rather than on discriminations within a population composed entirely of clinical groups.

## REFERENCES

Allport, G. W. (1937). *Personality: A psychological interpretation.* New York: Holt.

Allport, G. W. (1950). *The nature of personality. Selected papers*. Cambridge, MA: Addison-Wesley.

Broughton, R. (1984). A prototype strategy for construction of personality scales. *Journal of Personality and Social Psychology, 47*, 1334–1346.

Burisch, M. (1984). Approaches to personality inventory construction: A comparison of merits. *American Psychologist, 39*, 214–227.

Campbell, D. T., & Fiske, D. W. (1959). Convergent and discriminant validation by the multitrait-multimethod matrix. *Psychological Bulletin, 56*, 81–105.

Cantor, N., Smith, E. E., French, R., & Mezzich, J. (1980). Psychiatric diagnosis as prototype categorization. *Journal of Abnormal Psychology, 89*, 181–193.

Cattell, R. B. (1946). *Description and measurement of personality*. Yonkers-on-Hudson: World Book.

Dahlstrom, W. G. (1969). Recurrent issues in the development of the MMPI. In J. N. Butcher (Ed.), MMPI. *Research developments and clinical applications* (pp. 1–40). New York: Mc-Graw-Hill.

Dahlstrom, W. G. (1972). Whither the MMPI? In J. N. Butcher (Ed.), *Objective Personality Assessment* (pp. 85–116). New York: Academic Press.

Dahlstrom, W. G., Welsh, G. S., & Dahlstrom, L. E. (1972). *An MMPI handbook, Vol. I*. Minneapolis, MN: University of Minnesota Press.

Goldberg, L. R. (1972). Parameters of personality inventory construction and utilization: A comparison of prediction strategies and tactics. *Multivariate Behavioral Research Monographs*, No. 72-2.

Gough, H. G. (1965). *Some thoughts on test usage and test development*. Paper presented at the annual meeting of the American Personnel and Guidance Association, Los Angeles, CA.

Gynther, M. D., Burkhart, B. R., & Hovanitz, C. (1979). Do face-valid items have more predictive validity than subtle items? The case of the MMPI Pd scale. *Journal of Consulting and Clinical Psychology, 47*, 295–300.

Hase, H. D., & Goldberg, L. R. (1967). Comparative validity of different strategies of constructing personality inventory scales. *Psychological Bulletin, 67*, 231–248.

Hirschfeld, R. M. A., Klerman, G. L., Clayton, P. J., Keller, M. B., MacDonald Scott, M. A., & Larkin, B. H. (1983). Assessing personality: Effects of the depressive state on trait measurement. *American Journal of Psychiatry, 140*, 695, 699.

Holden, R. R., Fekken, G. C., & Jackson, D. N. (1985). Structured personality test item characteristics and validity. *Journal of Research in Personality, 19*, 386–394.

Holden, R. R., & Jackson, D. N. (1979). Item subtlety and face validity in personality assessment. *Journal of Consulting and Clinical Psychology, 47*, 459–468.

Horowitz, L. M., Wright, J. C., Lowenstein, E., & Parad, H. W. (1981). The prototype as a construct in abnormal psychology: A method for deriving prototypes. *Journal of Abnormal Psychology, 90*, 568–574.

Jackson, D. N. (1970). A sequential system for personality scale development. In C. D. Spielberger (Ed.), *Current topics in clinical and community psychology* (Vol. 2) (pp. 61–92). New York: Academic Press.

Jackson, D. N., & Messick, S. (1961). Acquiescence and desirability as response determinants on the MMPI. *Educational and Psychological Measurement, 21*, 771–790.

Loevinger J. (1957). Objective tests as instruments of psychological theory. *Psychological Reports, 3*, 635–694.

Loevinger, J. (1972). Some limitations of objective personality tests. In J. N. Butcher (Ed.), *Objective personality assessment* (pp. 45–58). New York: Academic Press.

Lord, F. M. (1955). Some perspectives on "the alternation paradox in test theory." *Psychological Bulletin, 52*, 505–510.

Lykken, D. T. (1971). Multiple factor analysis and personality research. *Journal of Experimental Research in Personality, 5*, 161–170.

McKinley, J. C., & Hathaway, S. R. (1944). The Minnesota Multiphasic Personality Inventory: V. Hysteria, hypomania, and psychopathic deviate. *Journal of Applied Psychology, 28*, 153–174.

Meehl, P. E. (1945). The dynamics of "structured" personality tests. *Journal of Clinical Psychology, 1*, 296–303.

Meehl, P. E. (1972). Reactions, reflections, projections. In J. N. Butcher (Ed.), *Objective personality assessment.* (pp. 131–189). New York: Academic Press.

Meehl, P. E., & Rosen, A. (1955). Antecedent probability and the efficiency of psychometric signs, patterns, or cutting scores. *Psychological Bulletin, 52,* 194–216.

Millon, T. (1969). *Modern psychopathology.* Philadelphia: Saunders. (reprinted; Prospect Heights, IL: Waveland Press).

Millon, T. (1981). *Disorders of personality: DSM-III, Axis II.* New York: Wiley.

Millon, T. (1986a). A theoretical derivation of pathological personalities. In T. Millon & G. L. Klerman (Eds.), *Contemporary directions in psychopathology: Toward the DSM-IV* (pp. 639–670). New York: Guilford.

Millon, T. (1986b). Personality prototypes and their diagnostic criteria. In T. Millon & G. L. Klerman (Eds.), *Contemporary directions in psychopathology: Toward the DSM-IV* (pp. 671–672). New York: Guilford.

Millon, T. (1987). On the nature of taxonomy in psychopathology (pp. 3–85). In C. Last & M. Hersen (Eds.), *Issues in diagnostic research.* New York: Plenum Press.

Norman, W. T. (1972). Psychometric considerations for a revision of the MMPI. In J. N. Butcher (Ed.), *Objective personality assessment* (pp. 59–84). New York: Academic Press.

Reich, J., Noyes, R., Coryell, W., & O'Gorman, T. W. (1986). The effect of state anxiety on personality measurement. *American Journal of Psychiatry, 143,* 760–763.

Reich, I., Noyes, R., Hirschfeld, R., Coryell, W., & O'Gorman, T. W. (1987). State and personality in depressed and panic patients. *American Journal of Psychiatry, 144,* 1160–1162.

Rorer, L. G. (1965). The great response-style myth. *Psychological Bulletin, 63,* 129–156.

Rosch, E. H. (1978). Principles of categorization. In E. H. Rosch & B. B. Lloyd (Eds.), *Cognition and categorization.* Hillsdale, NJ: Erlbaum.

Rosen, A. (1962). Development of the MMPI scales based on a reference group of psychiatric patients. *Psychological Monographs, 76,* 8, 527.

Wakefield, J. A., Bradley, P. E., Doughtie, E. B., & Kraft, I. A. (1975). Influence of overlapping and nonoverlapping items on the theoretical interrelationships of MMPI scales. *Journal of Consulting and Clinical Psychology, 43,* 851–857.

Wiggins, J. (1973). *Personality and prediction: Principles of personality assessment.* Reading, MA: Addison-Wesley

Wrobel, T. A., & Lachar, D. (1982). Validity of the Weiner subtle and obvious scales for the MMPI: Another example of the importance of inventory-item content. *Journal of Consulting and Clinical Psychology, 50,* 469–470.

Zigler, E., & Phillips, L. (1961). Psychiatric diagnosis: A critique. *Journal of Abnormal and Social Psychology, 63,* 607–618.

# Foundations of the MIPS Scales

## INTRODUCTION

This chapter is intended for readers who wish to explore the theoretical models undergirding the MIPS scales. While the logic and rationale presented here may be more abstract than in other sections of the manual, the discussion will furnish a perspective regarding how the constructs were derived and why we believe them to be consonant with recent developments in the field of personology.

As written previously (see Paper 1 in this volume), this is a time that seems optimal for ventures designed to generate new ideas and syntheses. The territory where "personality," "psychopathology," and "normality" intersect is one of the areas of significant academic activity and clinical responsibility. Providing theoretical formulations that bridge these intersections would alone represent a major intellectual step, but we want to do more. To limit our focus to contemporary research models that address these junctions directly might lead us to overlook the solid footings provided by our field's historic thinkers (such as Freud and Jung), as well as our more mature sciences (such as physics and evolutionary biology). If we fail to coordinate propositions and constructs with principles and laws established by these intellectual giants and advanced disciplines, the different domains comprising our subject will continue to float on their own, so to speak, unconnected to other realms, and, hence, will require that we return to the important task of synthesis another day.

Therefore, as stated earlier, we go beyond current conceptual and research boundaries in personology and incorporate the contributions of past theorists as well as those of our more firmly grounded "adjacent" sciences. Not only may such steps bear new conceptual fruits, but they also may provide a foundation to guide our own discipline's explorations.

Much of psychology as a whole remains adrift, divorced from broader spheres of scientific knowledge, isolated from deeper and more fundamental, if not universal, principles. As illustrated and argued in prior papers, the propositions of our science are not in themselves sufficient to orient its development in a consistent and focused fashion. Consequently, psychology has built a patchwork quilt of dissonant concepts and diverse data domains. Preoccupied with but a small part of the larger pie, or fearing accusations of reductionism, we have failed to draw on the rich possibilities that may be found in both historical and adjacent realms of scholarly pursuit. With few exceptions, cohering concepts that would connect current topics to those of the past have not been developed. We seem repeatedly trapped in (obsessed with?) contemporary fads and horizontal refinements.

A search for integrative schemas and constructs that will link us to relevant observations and laws in other fields of contemporary "science" is also needed. The goal, admittedly, a rather "grandiose" one—is to refashion our patchwork quilt into a well-tailored and cohesive tapestry that interweaves the diverse forms in which nature expresses itself.

There is no better sphere within the psychological sciences to undertake such a synthesis than the subject matter of personology—the study of persons. The individual person is the only organically integrated system in the psychological domain, evolved through the millennia and basically created from birth as a natural entity. The individual person is not simply a culture-bound and experience-derived gestalt. The intrinsic cohesion of the person is not a rhetorical construction but an authentic substantive unity. Personological features may be differentiated into normal or pathological, and may be partitioned conceptually for pragmatic or scientific purposes, but they are segments of an inseparable biopsychosocial entity.

## THEORY PROVIDES A STRONG FOUNDATION FOR PERSONALITY CONSTRUCTS

Some 50 years ago, Kurt Lewin wrote that "there is nothing so practical as a good theory" (1936, p. 5). Theory, when properly fashioned, ultimately provides more simplicity and clarity than unintegrated and scattered information. Moreover, as Hempel (1965) and Quine (1977) have pointed out, it is theory that provides the glue that holds a subject domain together and gives it its scientific relevance.

Doubts have arisen when introducing theory into the study of personology. Given our intuitive ability to "sense" the correctness of a psychological insight or speculation, theoretical efforts that impose structure or formalize these insights into a scientific system are likely to be perceived not only as cumbersome and intrusive but also as alien. This discomfiture and resistance does not arise in fields such as particle physics, where everyday observations are not readily available and where innovative insights are few and far between. In such subject domains, scientists are not only quite comfortable with but turn readily to deductive theory as a means of helping them explicate and coordinate knowledge. It is paradoxical but true and unfortunate that

psychologists learn their subject quite well merely by observing the ordinary events of life. As a consequence of this ease, they may shy away from the seemingly obscure and complicating, yet often fertile and systematizing, powers inherent in formal theory, especially theories other than those learned in their student days.

Despite the shortcomings of historical and contemporary theoretical schemas, systematizing principles and abstract concepts can "facilitate a deeper seeing, a more penetrating vision that goes beyond superficial appearances to the order underlying them" (Bowers, 1977, p. 130). For example, pre-Darwinian taxonomists, such as Linnaeus and others, limited themselves to apparent similarities and differences among animals as a means of constructing their categories. Darwin was not "seduced" by appearances. Rather, he sought to understand the principles by which overt features came about. His classifications were based not only on keenly observed descriptive qualities but also on those that were genuinely explanatory.

## ORIENTATION

One goal of this chapter is to connect the conceptual structure of personality to its foundations in the natural world, which also was an aim of both Freud and Jung. The formulation that will be presented here is akin to Freud's abandoned "Project for a Scientific Psychology" (1895/1966). Freud was endeavoring to advance our understanding of human nature by exploring interconnections among disciplines that evolved from ostensibly unrelated bodies of research and that used manifestly dissimilar languages. The approach here is also akin to Jung's effort to explicate personality functions with reference to the balancing of deeply rooted bipolarities, a theory most clearly formulated in his book Psychological Types (1921/1971).

In recent times, we have seen the emergence of sociobiology, a new "science" that explores the interface between human social functioning and evolutionary biology

(Wilson, 1975, 1978). Contemporary formulations by psychologists likewise have set forth the potential and analyzed the problems involved in combining evolutionary notions with theories of individual differences and personality traits (for example, D. Buss, 1990). The common goal among these proposals is not only to apply analogous principles across diverse scientific realms but also to reduce the enormous range of psychological concepts that have proliferated throughout history; this might be achieved by exploring the power of evolutionary theory to simplify and order previously disparate personality features.

For example, all organisms seek to avoid injury, find nourishment, and reproduce their kind if they are to survive and maintain their populations. Each species is marked by commonalities in its adaptive or survival style. Within each species, however, there are differences in style and in the success with which various members adapt to the diverse and changing environments they face. On this basic level, "personality" would be employed as a term to represent the more or less distinctive style of adaptive functioning that a particular member of a species exhibits as it relates to its typical range of habitats, or environments.

"Normal personality," so conceived, would reflect a species member's specific modes of adaptation that are effective in "average" or "expectable" environments. "Disorders of personality," in this context, would represent different styles of maladaptive functioning that can be traced to deficiencies, imbalances, or conflicts in a member's capacity to relate to the environments it faces.

A few more words should be said concerning comparisons made between evolution and ecology, on the one hand, and normal and abnormal personality, on the other.

During its life history, an organism develops an assemblage of traits that contributes to its individual survival and reproductive success—the two essential components of fitness formulated by Darwin. Such assemblages, termed "complex adaptations and strategies" in the literature of evolutionary ecology, may be conceptualized as the biological equivalents to personality styles in the mental health literature. Biological explanations of an organism's lifetime strategy of adaptations refer primarily to variations among constituent biogenetic traits, their overall covariance structure, and the nature and ratio of favorable to unfavorable ecological resources that have been available for purposes of extending longevity and optimizing reproduction. Such explanations are not appreciably different from those used to account for the development of normal and pathological personality styles.

A relevant and intriguing parallel may be drawn between the phylogenetic evolution of a species' genetic composition and the ontogenetic development of an individual organism's adaptive strategies (that is, its "personality style"). At any point in time, a species will possess a limited set of genes that serve as trait potentials. Over succeeding generations, the frequency distribution of these genes will likely change in their relative proportions, depending on how well the traits they undergird contribute to the species' "fittedness" within its varying ecological habitats.

In a similar fashion, individual organisms begin life with a limited subset of their species' genes and the trait potentials they subserve. Over time, the salience of these trait potentials—not the proportion of the genes themselves—will become differentially prominent as the organism interacts with its environments. It "learns" from these experiences which of its traits "fit" best—that is, are optimally suited to its ecosystem. In phylogenesis, then, actual gene frequencies change during the generation-to-generation adaptive process, whereas in ontogenesis, it is the salience or prominence of gene-based traits that change as adaptive learning takes place. Parallel evolutionary processes occur, both within the life of a species and within the life of a member organism, respectively.

What is seen in the individual organism is a shaping of latent potentialities into adaptive and manifest styles of perceiving, feeling, thinking, and acting. It is the author's view that these distinctive modes of adaptation, engendered by the interaction of biological endowment and social experience, comprise the elements of what are termed personality styles, whether normal or abnormal. There is a formative process over the course of a single individual's lifetime that parallels gene redistributions within a whole species during its entire evolutionary history.

## THE THREE MOTIVATING-AIMS BIPOLARITIES

### EXISTENCE, ADAPTATION, AND REPLICATION

Recent developments bridging ecological and evolutionary theory are well underway, offering some justification for extending their principles to both normal and abnormal styles of human functioning. A conceptual background from these sciences is part of the theoretical foundations for the three MIPS Motivating Aims, through the three previously noted formulations termed "existence," "adaptation," and "replication" (Millon, 1990).

*Existence* relates to the serendipitous transformation of physical states that are more or less ephemeral and unorganized into those possessing greater stability and/or organization. It pertains to the formation and sustenance of discernible phenomena, to the processes of evolution that enhance and preserve life, and to the psychological bipolarity of pleasure and pain.

*Adaptation* refers to homeostatic processes employed to foster survival in open ecosystems. It relates to the manner in which organisms adapt to their surrounding ecosystems, to the mechanisms employed in modifying or accommodating these environments, and to the psychological bipolarity of activity and passivity.

*Replication* pertains to reproductive styles that maximize the diversification and selection of ecologically effective attributes. It refers to the strategies utilized to replicate ephemeral organisms, to the methods of maximizing individuation (of self) and nurturance (of progeny), and to the psychological bipolarity of self and other.

## FREUD'S CONTRIBUTIONS AND THEIR CURRENT PARALLELS

### Three Early Polarities

The three major bipolarities articulated in this section have theoretical forerunners that may be traced as far back as the early 1900s. Although some parallel schemas were proposed earlier, these MIPS conceptions may be referenced to ideas presented by Sigmund Freud. In 1915, Freud (1915/1925) wrote his seminal papers on metapsychology—of particular interest here, the section entitled, "The Instincts and their Vicissitudes." Speculations that foreshadowed several concepts developed more fully later, both by Freud and by his disciples, were presented in preliminary form in these papers. Notable is a framework of interlocking polarities that Freud advanced as central to understanding the "mind" (unfortunately, he never developed this preliminary work as a formal system for conceptualizing psychological patterns of normality and abnormality). Oppositions framed by him at that time are as follows:

Our mental life as a whole is governed by three polarities, namely the following antitheses:
Subject (ego)-Object (external world)
Pleasure-Pain
Active-Passive
The three polarities within the mind are connected with one another in various highly significant ways. (Freud, 1915/1925, pp. 76–77)

We may sum up by saying that the essential feature in the vicissitudes undergone by instincts is their subjection to the influences of the three great polarities that govern mental life. Of these three polarities we might describe that of activity-passivity as the biological, that of the ego-external world as the real, and finally that of pleasure-pain as the economic, respectively. (Freud, 1915/1925, p. 83)

Although Freud failed to pursue the potential of his tripartite schema of polarities, his followers continued to draw upon its elements for many decades to come, as seen prominently in the development from Freud's own instinct or "drive theory," where pleasure and pain were the major forces, to "ego psychology," where "activity" and "passivity" were central constructs, and, most recently, to "self psychology" and "object-relations" theory, where the self/other polarity is the key issue (Millon, 1990).

### Toward the MIPS Approach

The scaffolding comprising the above three polarities was fashioned anew by this author in the late 1960s (Millon, 1969). Because the author was unacquainted with Freud's proposals at the time and was employing a biosocial learning model, a framework was constructed similar to Freud's "great polarities that govern all of mental life," but phrased in the terminology of learning concepts. The model comprised three bipolar dimensions: positive versus negative reinforcement (pleasure/pain); self versus other as the source of reinforcement; and the instrumental styles of active versus passive. The author stated:

By framing our thinking in terms of what reinforcements the individual is seeking, whether he is looking to find them and how he performs, we may see more simply and more clearly the essential strategies which guide his coping behaviors.

These reinforcements [relate to] whether he seeks primarily to achieve positive reinforcements (pleasure) or to avoid negative reinforcements (pain).

Some patients turn to others as their source of reinforcement, whereas some turn primarily to themselves. The distinction (is) between others and self as the primary reinforcement source.

On what basis can a useful distinction be made among instrumental behaviors? A review of the literature suggests that the behavioral dimension

of activity-passivity may prove useful. Active patients (are) busily intent on controlling the circumstances of their environment. Passive patients wait for the circumstances of their environment to take their course, reacting to them only after they occur. (Millon, 1969, pp. 193–195)

### Other Parallels

There is a growing group of contemporary scholars whose work relates to the bipolar dimensions of pleasure/pain, activity/passivity, and self/other, albeit indirectly and partially. For example, a modern conception anchored to biological foundations has been developed by the distinguished British psychologist Jeffrey Gray (1964, 1973). A three-part model of temperament, matching the three-part Motivating-Aims model in most regards, has been formulated by the American psychologist Arnold Buss and his associates (Buss & Plomin, 1975, 1984).

Circumplex formats based on factor-analytic studies of mood and arousal that align well with the polarity schema have been published by Russell (1980) and Tellegen (1985). Deriving inspiration from a sophisticated analysis of neuroanatomical substrates, the highly resourceful American psychiatrist Robert Cloninger (1986, 1987) has deduced a threefold schema that is coextensive with major elements of the Millon model's three motivation bipolarities. Less oriented to biological foundations, recent advances in both interpersonal and psychoanalytic theory likewise have exhibited strong parallels to one or more of the three bipolar dimensions. (For a detailed review of these and other parallels, see Millon, 1990.)

The following pages summarize the rationale and characteristics of the three-part model of MIPS Motivating Aims. . . .

### THE MIPS ENHANCING AND PRESERVING AIMS

The most basic of all motivations, that of existence, is twofold. One aspect pertains to the enhancement or enrichment of life—that is, creating or strengthening ecologically viable organisms. The second is concerned with the preservation of life—that is, creating survivability and security by avoiding events that might terminate life. Although we disagree with Freud's concept of a death instinct (Thanatos), we believe he was essentially correct in recognizing that a balanced, yet fundamental, biological opposition exists in nature and has its parallel in the physical world. As he wrote in one of his last works, "The analogy of our two basic instincts extends from the sphere of living things to the pair of opposing forces—attraction and repulsion—which rule the inorganic world," (Freud, 1940/1949, p. 72).

Among humans, the first aspect of existence may be seen in life-enhancing acts that are experientially recorded as "pleasurable" events (positive reinforcers); the latter aspect may be seen in life-preserving behaviors oriented toward repelling or avoiding events that are experientially characterized as "painful" (negative reinforcers). More will be said of these fundamental, if not universal, mechanisms for countering entropic disintegration in the next section.

Existence is literally a to-be or not-to-be issue. In the inorganic world, "to be" is essentially a matter of possessing qualities that distinguish a phenomenon from its surrounding field—that is, existence is a matter of not being in a state of entropy. Among organic beings, "to be" is a matter of possessing the properties of life, as well as being located in ecosystems that facilitate processes that enhance and preserve life by maintaining the integrity of the organism within its surrounding field. In the phenomenological, or experiential, world of sentient organisms, events that extend life, on the one hand, and preserve it, on the other, correspond to metaphorical terms such as pleasure and pain; that is, recognizing and pursuing life-enriching rewards is related to pleasure, and recognizing and eschewing life-threatening emotions and sensations is related to pain.

This pleasure/pain-oriented bipolarity not only places sensations, motivations, feelings, emotions, moods, and affects on two contrasting dimensions but also recognizes that each possesses separate and independent quantitative gradations: Events that are attractive, gratifying, rewarding, or positively reinforcing can be experienced on a continuum from weak to strong, as can those that are aversive, distressful, sad, or negatively reinforcing. What distinguishes a bipolarity from a simple polarity is that both positive and negative emotions may display the full quantitative range independent of the other. In this case, low levels of pleasure are not the same as pain, and vice versa; further, high and low levels of positive emotionality may coexist with varying levels of negative emotionality. Several theorists associate levels of intensity of pleasure and pain with the dimension of arousal/activation. In our judgment, however, the constructs of activity and passivity belong to a separate evolution-based bipolarity, to be described more fully shortly.

Over the years, numerous theories of motivation/emotion have proposed models that refer essentially to affective expressions of this pleasure/pain bipolarity. Most closely akin to the MIPS approach in the recent literature are the factor-analytic dimensions of positive and negative emotionality described by Tellegen (1985) and his students (Clark & Watson, 1988; Watson & Clark, 1984; Watson & Tellegen, 1985).

Although there are many philosophical and metapsychological issues associated with the "nature" of pain and pleasure as constructs, it is not our intent to inquire into them in detail here. That they recur as a polar phenomenon time and again in diverse psychological domains (for example, learned behaviors, unconscious processes, emotion and motivation, as well as their biological substrates) has been elaborated in another publication (Millon, 1990).

### Enhancing

Descriptively, those who score high on this scale possess attitudes and behaviors designed to foster and enrich life, to generate joy, pleasure, contentment, fulfillment, and thereby strengthen their capacity to remain competent physically and mentally. These individuals are likely to assert that human existence calls for more than life preservation and pain avoidance alone. Moreover, very high scorers are driven by the desire to enrich their lives, to seek invigorating experiences and challenges, to venture and explore, all to the end of magnifying if not escalating their vitality and viability.

### Preserving

Among these persons, we see a significant tendency to focus attention on potential threats to one's emotional and physical security, an expectation of and heightened alertness to the signs of potential negative feedback that can lead them to disengage from everyday relationships and pleasurable experiences. Most are successful in avoiding unnecessary risks and dangers, although often at the price of narrowing the range of their positive emotions and joyful experiences. As a consequence, they tend to be inhibited and restrained, worrisome and pessimistic, overly concerned with the difficulties of life.

## THE MIPS MODIFYING AND ACCOMMODATING AIMS

### An Ecological Perspective

The second polar dimension relates to what we have termed the modes of adaptation; it is also framed as a two-part bipolarity. One of the two major modes of adaptation is seen in the lifestyle of the animal kingdom where, a basic inclination toward ecological modification is observed. There is an active tendency to change or rearrange the elements comprising the larger milieu—to intrude upon otherwise quiescent settings. A versatility is exhibited in shifting from one niche to another as unpredicted events arise. This is a mobile and interventionist mode that actively stirs, maneuvers, causes to yield, and, at the human level, substantially transforms the environment to meet its own survival aims.

At the other pole of adaptation is the mode of ecological accommodation, signifying inclinations to passively "fit in." There is desire to locate a niche and remain securely anchored there, subject to the vagaries and unpredictabilities of the environment—with one crucial proviso: that the surrounding environment will furnish both the nourishment and the protection needed to sustain existence. Although based on a somewhat simplistic bifurcation among adaptive strategies, this mode (of passive accommodation) is one of the two fundamental methods that living organisms have evolved as a means of survival. It represents the core process employed in the evolution of the plant kingdom—a stationary, rooted, yet essentially pliant and dependent survival mode.

Both modes—active and passive—have proved impressively capable of nourishing and preserving life. Whether the bipolarity sketched above is phrased in terms of modification versus accommodation, activity versus passivity, or animal versus plant, it represents, at the most basic level, the two fundamental modes that organisms have developed to sustain their existence. This second, Modifying/Accommodating bipolarity differs from the first, Enhancing/Preserving (concerned with what may be called existential "becoming"), in that it characterizes modes of "being"—how what has become endures.

### A Philosophical Perspective

Broadening the activity/passivity bipolarity model to encompass human experience, we find that the vast range of behaviors humans engage in may be grouped according to whether they take initiative in altering and shaping life's events or whether their behaviors are reactive to and accommodate those events.

The distinction between modifying and accommodating (or active and passive) may be traced back to early notions of Thomas Hobbes (1650), who spoke of behavior as a response to the "vital spirits." Hobbes perceived humans as passive, helpless animals, reacting either to the "appetites" (pursuit of pleasure) or to the "aversions" (avoidance of pain). More or less traditional and mechanistic theories, like that of Hobbes, assert that humans are subject to and have minimal control over forces that compel them to behave as they do, whether these forces come from without (environmental pressures) or from within (biological drives or unconscious determinants).

By contrast, organismic theories, reflecting the views of more contemporary thinkers and cultures, dismiss the attitude that humans are essentially passive robots who merely react to external and largely unknown promptings. Rather, modern theorists assert that humans actively determine their own behaviors—that they confront life's opportunities and dilemmas, choose what courses of action they will take, and even initiate actions that alter the very character of their environments. In our judgment, both views are correct; humans sometimes are actors and other times reactors.

"Normal," or optimal, functioning, at least among humans, appears to call for a flexible balance that interweaves both extremes of each bipolarity. In the first bipolarity, behaviors encouraging both life enhancement (seeking pleasure) and life preservation (avoiding pain) are likely to be more successful in achieving survival than actions confined to one or the other motivation alone. Similarly, regarding adaptation, modes of functioning that exhibit both ecological accommodation and ecological modification are likely to be more successful than either by itself.

It is our contention, however, that significant individual differences of personological significance are to be found along this activity/passivity dimension. No individual is wholly at one or the other pole, but employs both modes in varying proportions; this difference in individuals is relevant to the assessment of personality styles, and we again put forth two scales to represent the degrees to which persons balance these two adaptive modes.

## Modifying

Descriptively, those who are at the active end of the bipolarity are best characterized by their alertness, vigilance, liveliness, vigor, forcefulness, stimulus-seeking energy, and drive. Some individuals plan strategies and scan alternatives to circumvent obstacles or avoid the distress of punishment, rejection, and anxiety. Others are impulsive, excitable, rash, and hasty, seeking to elicit pleasures and rewards. Although their specific goals vary and change from time to time, actively modifying individuals seek to alter their lives and to intrude on passing events by energetically and busily shaping their circumstances.

## Accommodating

Those who are passively oriented are often reflective and deliberate. They employ few overt strategies to gain their ends. They display a seeming inertness, a phlegmatic quality, a tendency toward acquiescence, and a restrained attitude in which they initiate little to modify events, instead waiting for circumstances to take their course before making accommodations. Some may be temperamentally ill-equipped to rouse or assert themselves; perhaps past experience has deprived them of opportunities to acquire a range of competencies or confidence in their ability to master the events of their environments. Equally possible is that they possess a naive confidence that things will come their way with little or no effort on their part. From a variety of diverse sources, then, people at the passive end of the bipolarity appear merely to sustain their existence, engaging in few direct activities to intercede in life events or to generate change. They seem suspended, quiescent, placid, immobile, restrained, and listless, waiting for things to happen and reacting only after events occur.

## The MIPS Individuating and Nurturing Aims

The first Motivating-Aims bipolarity represented the promotion of order (existence/life/pleasure) and the prevention of disorder (nonexistence/death/pain); the second bipolarity differentiated the adaptive modes, modification (animal/activity) versus accommodation (plant/passivity). Although less profound than these two, the third bipolarity, based on distinctions in reproductive strategies (gene replication), is no less fundamental; it contrasts the maximization of reproductive propagation (self) with the maximization of reproductive rearing (other).

### Patterns in Population Biology

Evolutionary biologists (Cole, 1954; Trivers, 1974; Wilson, 1975) have recorded marked differences among species in both the cycle and pattern of their reproductive behaviors. Of special interest is the extreme diversity among and within species in the number of offspring spawned and the consequent nurturing and protective investment the parents make in the survival of their progeny. In population biology, the r-strategy represents a pattern of propagating a vast number of offspring but giving minimal attention to their survival; the K-strategy is typified by the production of few progeny and giving considerable attention to ensuring their survival. The r-strategy is employed by oysters, for example, which generate some 500 million eggs annually; the K-strategy is found among the great apes, which produce a single offspring every five to six years.

Jung had the foresight to anticipate this contrast in replication styles and its fundamental adaptive significance:

There are in nature two fundamentally different modes of adaptation which ensure the continued existence of the living organism. The one consists in a high rate of fertility, with low powers of defense and short duration of life for the single individual; the other consists in equipping the individual with numerous means of self-preservation plus a low fertility rate. This biological difference, it seems to me, is not merely analogous to, but the actual foundation of, our two psychological modes of adaptation. Blake's intuition did not err when he described the two classes of men as "prolific" and "devouring." Just as, biologically, the two modes of adaptation work equally well and are successful in their own way, so too with the typical attitudes. The one achieves its end by a multiplicity of relationships, the other by monopoly. (Jung, 1921/1971, pp. 331–332)

Species do not differ only in where they fall on the r-strategy to K-strategy continuum; within most animal species an important distinction also may be drawn between male and female genders. This latter difference undergirds what has been termed the Individuating (self-oriented) versus Nurturing (other-oriented) bipolarity, implications of which will be elaborated.

A human female typically produces about 400 eggs in a lifetime, of which no more than 20 to 25 can possibly mature into healthy infants. The energy investment expended in gestation, nurturing, and caring for each child is extraordinary. Not only is the female required to devote much of her energies to bringing the fetus to full term, but during this period she also cannot be fertilized again; in contrast, the male is biologically free to mate with numerous females, although this practice is strongly discouraged in most societies.

Should her child fail to survive, the waste in physical and emotional exertion not only takes an enormous personal toll, but amounts to a substantial loss of the mother's lifetime reproductive potential. There appears to be a good evolutionary reason, therefore, for females to have protective and caring inclinations, as is evidenced in their sensitivity to cues of distress in their offspring and a willingness to persist in attending to the children's needs and nurturing.

Although the male discharges tens of millions of sperm on mating, this is but a small investment, given the physical capacity for frequent reproductive acts. After fertilization, his physical and emotional commitment can end, with minimal consequences for the survivability of the offspring. Although the protective and food-gathering efforts of the male may be lost by his early abandonment of a female and an offspring, much more may be gained in terms of the survivability of the species by his investment of energy in achieving the wide reproductive spread of his genes. Compared with the female of the species, whose best strategy appears to be assuming responsibility for the care and comfort of child and kin— that is, using the K-strategy—the male is likely to be more effective by maximizing self-propagation, or adopting the r-strategy. By striving first to realize his own intrinsic potential—that is, by individuating—the male focuses primarily on self-replication and actualization, and only secondarily on nurturance.

In modern societies, of course, mating with multiple females and abandoning the offspring has important social, emotional, and financial consequences that cannot be ignored; yet, the biological fact remains that the offspring are likely to survive without the male progenitor.

In sum, males tend to be self-oriented, owing to the fact that such behavior maximizes the replicatory advantages of their genes. Conversely, females tend to be other-oriented, owing to the fact that their competence in nurturing their limited progeny maximizes the replicatory advantages of their genes.

The male's r-strategy can be translated into what we are calling Individuating behaviors, characterized as acting more from self-interest than interest in others. Male relationships often exhibit a "vertical," or hierarchical, quality, characterized by seeking dominance of self over others. By contrast, the female's K-strategy translates into what we are calling a Nurturing orientation. Females are more disposed to be other-promoting, affiliative, intimate, empathic, and protective (Gilligan, 1982; Wilson, 1978). Female relationships demonstrate a horizontal or even reverse hierarchical quality, founded either on egalitarian transactions or on giving priority to others.

Lest there be misunderstanding, no sharp line separates the genders; rather, these inclinations lie on a continuum with "soft" group discriminations and substantial overlapping. Our intent is not to draw attention to gender differences per se, but, rather, to identify the existence of a deep, biologically grounded spectrum of dispositions, in which the enhancement or propagation of self represents one polar extreme (the r-strategy), and the enhancement or nurturance of others represents the second (the K-strategy).

## Personological Translation

In the preceding paragraphs, we have presented a theoretical rationale based on concepts derived from evolutionary thinking as a way to account for a frequently studied dimension that contrasts striving, self-indulgent, enterprising, courageous, competitive, ambitious, dominating, self-assured and independent traits, at the one extreme, with love-oriented, altruistic, nurturant, intimate, harmony-seeking, warm, trusting, and cooperative behaviors, at the other. We believe these two broad orientations reflect a fundamental bipolarity that exists in nature and expresses itself in two contrasting aims of human motivation/emotion. The former aim, that of individuation, derives from and is most closely allied with the reproductive strategies available to the male gender; the latter aim, that of nurturing, stems from and is connected centrally to the reproductive options available to the female gender.

### Individuating

Self-focused, these persons tend to make up their own minds and reach their own decisions, without perceiving the need to seek input or gain approval from others. At their best, they are self-starting, self-actualizing, and strive to overcome obstacles that could be serious checks to fulfilling their potential, as they perceive it. These persons appear to others to have a strong sense of self-identity in which they seem to be in control of their lives, regulating their experiences and future with little external prompting or interference. In addition to being self-assured, striving, enterprising, and independent, those who score high on the individuation scale seek to become what they believe they were intended to be. When their behavior is not appropriately channeled, however, they may become self-centered and self-absorbed, caring little about the needs and priorities of others, and focusing largely on their own interests.

### Nurturing

Those high in this Motivating Aim seek to satisfy belonging and social needs. They establish intimate and caring relationships with significant others in which it is just as important to give love as it is to receive it. There is a warm relating with others and a capability of easily displaying intimacy and love for a parent, child, spouse, or close friend. Here they manifest a sense of oneness with the other and a deep concern for his or her welfare. They often attend to the needs of significant others before considering their own needs. Beyond their intimate family and friends, there is often an extension of warmth toward humankind at large, an understanding of the human condition and a feeling of kinship with most peoples.

Whether individual human males and females, in fact, give evidence of a balance between dispositions toward self and other is gauged by the third pair of Motivating Aims

of the MIPS, Individuating versus Nurturing, which completes its first section.

## THE FOUR COGNITIVE-MODES BIPOLARITIES

### AN EVOLUTIONARY PERSPECTIVE

Cognitive differences among individuals and the manner in which they are expressed have been much overlooked in generating and appraising personality traits. With an occasional, notable exception or two, little of the recent "revolution" in cognitive science that has profoundly affected contemporary psychology has impacted on the study of personology. Historically, the realms of intellect, aptitude, and ability have not been considered to be personality-related spheres of study.

Now, the focus of personology has been broadened to encompass the "whole person," an organically unified and unsegmented totality. Consequently, there is a growing recognition that cognitive dimensions and their various "styles" not only should be included but also may have significance equal to motivational and behavioral styles as a source of personality traits and differences (Millon, 1986b, 1988).

The various features and styles of cognition have not been included as central elements in most personality instruments. Nonetheless, in the author's judgment, they comprise what may be viewed as the fourth and most recent phase of evolution. The capacity to think abstractly—to transcend the immediate and concrete, to interrelate and synthesize diversity, to represent events and processes symbolically, to weigh, reason, and anticipate—these signify a quantum leap in the evolutionary potential of organisms for change and adaptation.

With the mind emancipated from the real and present, unanticipated possibilities and novel constructions may be created by particular styles of cognitive processing. The capacity to sort and recompose, to coordinate and arrange the symbolic representations of experience into new configurations, is, in certain ways, analogous to the biological processes of random recombinant replication, although more focused and intentional. To take more liberty with the analogy, genetic replication represents the recombinant mechanism underlying the adaptive progression of phylogeny, whereas abstract reasoning represents the recombinant mechanism underlying the cognitive progression of ontogeny.

The uses of physical replication are limited, constrained by the finite potential inherent in parental genes. In contrast, experiences, internalized and recombined through cognitive processes, are infinite. Over one lifetime, innumerable events of a random, logical, or irrational character transpire and are construed and reformulated time and again, some ideas and behaviors proving more, and others less, adaptive than the ideas and behaviors their originating circumstances may have called forth. Whereas the actions of most subhuman species derive from successfully evolved genetic programs, prompting behaviors of a relatively fixed nature that are suitable for a modest range of environmental settings, cognitive processing, both implicit and intentional, gives rise to adaptive competencies that are suited to radically divergent ecological circumstances, which themselves may be the result of far-reaching acts of symbolic and technological creativity.

The human mind may mirror outer realities, but it also reconstructs them, reflectively transforming perceptions into subjective modes of phenomenological reality and rendering external events subject to individualistic designs. Every act of apprehension is transformed by elements of projection. Not only are images of self and others emancipated from direct sensory realities, allowing them to become mental entities, but time also loses its immediacy and impact, becoming as much a construction as a tangible reality. Cognitive abstractions bring the past effectively into the present, and their power of

anticipation brings the future into the present, as well. With past and future embedded in the here and now, humans can encompass, at once, not only the totality of the cosmos but also its origins, nature, and evolution. Most impressive of all are the many visions humans have of life's indeterminate future, where no reality exists as yet.

As noted previously, we view cognitive functions to be the most recent stage of evolution's progression and, hence, as consonant with our biosocial formulations concerning the fundamental architecture that undergirds human functioning. We also judge cognitive processes to be the second step in our tripartite sequence that represents how organisms approach their environments. Rather than giving primacy either to the "driving" motivational and emotional roots of personality style (as in the author's formulation of the personality disorders), or to the overt behavioral expressions of personality (as explicated, for example, in a lexical approach that generates the Big-Five factor model; Goldberg, 1993), the MIPS approach seeks to conjoin these components of style by linking them to cognitive functions, thereby integrating all three expressions of personality into a single coherent whole.

## JUNG'S CONTRIBUTIONS AND THEIR CURRENT PARALLELS

### The Cognitive Orientation of Jung's Typology

Through the years, several bipolar dimensions have been proposed as the basis for a schema of cognitive styles. Contrasting terms such as "leveling versus sharpening," "narrow versus broad," "analytic versus synthetic," "constricted versus flexible," "inductive versus deductive," "abstract versus concrete," and "convergent versus divergent," have been used to illustrate the stylistic differences among cognitive functions. Although each of these pairs contributes to distinctions of importance in describing general cognitive processes, few were conceptualized with personality differences in mind, although they still could prove productive in that regard.

By contrast, one well-known bipolar schema intentionally formulated to serve as a basis for generating personality types was composed essentially of cognitive concepts. Although Jung did not speak explicitly of cognitive processes, it would not be unjustified to view his three bipolarities of Extraversion/Introversion, Thinking/Feeling, and Sensing/Intuiting as being anchored more firmly in a cognitive than in a motivational or behavioral domain.

To illustrate this thesis, we may ask, What did Jung mean by "Extraversion" and "Introversion"? The view commonly held by Jung's interpreters is that these terms refer to behavioral aspects of sociability, with Extraversion signifying social outgoingness, and Introversion signifying social reservation. It is the author's view that Jung intended something appreciably different: His was essentially a cognitive orientation, so that Extraversion and Introversion signified not a person's social style but the direction of his or her attentions and interests. Extraversion indicated that these attentions were extraceptive—oriented more toward the outer than the inner world; the person was inclined to trust "objective" events and to seek external sources of inspiration. Introversion denoted intraceptiveness—an internally oriented direction of attention and interest, involving a subordination of external sources of knowledge to those emanating from one's inner life and an attentiveness to inner promptings and "subjective" inspirations. In sum, Extraversion and Introversion, Jung's most accepted and durable personality concepts, do not pertain to types of motivation or to interpersonal behaviors but, rather, to cognitive styles.

It is even clearer that the other two bipolarities formulated by Jung—Sensing versus Intuiting, and Thinking versus Feeling—are distinctly cognitive in both their character and grounding. They represent not so much the reasons people act or their actions, but

the "attitudes" individuals take in attending to their environments and the "functions" they employ to interpret and transform their perceptions.

## Toward the MIPS Approach

As noted, numerous researchers and theorists have proposed useful dimensions and polarity schemas to represent cognitive styles, several of which remain as potentially important grounds for establishing personality traits. The author's earliest writings on the topic (Millon, 1969) focused essentially on styles of cognition characterizing and differentiating the personality disorders that eventually comprised Axis II of DSM-III (American Psychiatric Association, 1980). For example, the histrionic type was noted for cognitive dissociation, the narcissistic type for cognitive expansiveness, the antisocial/aggressive type for cognitive projection, the obsessive-compulsive type for cognitive constriction, and so on. Aspects of these cognitive styles were arranged in a circumplex model, along with aspects of self-image; in both domains of cognitive activity, therefore, a rough framework was provided for a bipolar schema.

A similar, but more developed, format of cognitive styles was proposed a decade and a half later (Millon, 1984, 1986b). Once again, the disorders were organized with reference not to basic personality styles but to the distinctive cognitive characteristics of each clinical type—e.g., the schizoid was characterized as cognitively impoverished, the avoidant as cognitively distracted, the dependent as cognitively naive, the histrionic as cognitively flighty, and so on.

Descriptively useful as these cognitive conceptualizations might have been, they were targeted to explicate pathological rather than "normal" styles; they expressed cognitive differences among core clinical types but did not express latent dimensions or fundamental polarities. Also problematic was the fact that pathologically oriented descriptions included cognitive content along with cognitive style, confounding further the desire to devise a schema of "pure" stylistic features.

Finally, a model was formulated by the author that separated cognitive activities into two superordinate functions. The first pertained to the contrasting origins from which cognitive data were gathered, or what have been termed "information sources"; the second pertained to the methods by which these data were reconstructed by the individual, or what have been labeled "transformational processes."

These two functions—the initial gathering and subsequent reconstruction of information—were further subdivided into two bipolarities each. As will be elaborated shortly, the "sources of information" were separated into (1) external versus internal, and (2) tangible versus intangible. "Transformational processes" were divided into (1) intellective versus affective, and (2) assimilative versus imaginative. The resulting four cognitive bipolarities of the MIPS are by no means exhaustive. Rather surprisingly and pleasantly, however, they turned out to be highly consonant with the model formulated in 1921 by Jung (1921/1971).

## The MIPS Extraversing and Introversing Modes

### An Evolution-Based Information-Processing Model

The first two contrasting functions considered significant to personality styles in the cognitive domain relate to the sources used by individuals in gathering knowledge about their world. Given our view that the two central elements that comprise the environmental field of an organism are itself and others, it should not be surprising that these very same components serve as the two primary sources from which an organism gathers information. Hence, turning attention to matters either internal or external to self is a key distinction in cognitive activity.

Although related materially to the Individuating versus Nurturing distinction drawn in the previous section on Motivating Aims, the correspondence is neither simple nor clear-cut, nor are individual score correlations between these bipolarities necessarily high. Because the two sets of constructs interrelate in more ways than one, and belong to broader configurations composed of different intensity levels, correspondences may be much more variable than their common point of origin would suggest. Thus, Individuating, for some people, may be best achieved by attending to external sources, whereas Nurturing may be enhanced by drawing inspiration primarily from internal sources.

It should be noted that useful parallels may be drawn between evolutionary processes and cognitive functions; the evolutionary model that undergirds our formulation is no less apt in this realm than it was in the sphere of motivation.

Information is seen by many as the opposite of entropy. Further, what energy or nutrients are to physical systems, information is to cognitive systems. A physical system sustains itself by "sucking order" from its environs, taking in energy or nutrients and transforming them to meet tissue needs; a cognitive system does something similar by "sucking information" from its environs—that is, taking in data and transforming it to meet its cognitive needs.

In much the same way as any other open system, a cognitive structure needs to maintain itself as an integrated and cohesive entity. In the physical world, the integrity of a system is achieved by making adaptations that preserve and enhance the physical structure, thereby precluding the entropic dissipation of its ordered elements. Similarly, a cognitive system achieves its integrity through a variety of preserving and enhancing adaptations that reduce the likelihood of events that may diminish the order and coherence of its knowledge base.

Moreover, an open cognitive system is purposefully focused, as is a physical system. Just as a physical system must be selective about its nutrition sources in order to find those suitable to meet its tissue needs, so, too, must a cognitive system be selective about information sources, choosing and processing particular raw inputs according to specific cognitive goals. A cognitive system can no more process random input than a physical system can ingest random material. Hence, information (negative entropy) must be acquired selectively rather than randomly or diffusely; some sources of information will be heeded and others ignored or suppressed.

Coherence may be optimized by adopting and maintaining a preferred and regular information source, thereby ensuring a consistent confirmatory bias in favor of a cognitive structure's "world view" and organizational architecture. Conversely, a cognitive structure that is exposed to dissonant or contradictory sources, or that heeds diverse or multitudinous sources, ultimately may be challenged successfully or may be exhausted beyond its ability to maintain coherence. In other words, burdensome processing and discordant sources are likely to result in increasing cognitive entropy. A more structured and coherent focus that strengthens and confirms prior sources of information becomes useful in ensuring optimal cognitive survivability.

## PERSONOLOGICAL TRANSLATION

In light of the preceding argument, in sum, we see two primary sources of information, that which originates external to the self and that which originates internally. Whether this polar cognitive orientation is termed external versus internal, extraceptive versus intraceptive, or extraversing versus introversing, each bipolarity provides a replicable reservoir for cognitive information—a selectively narrowed wellspring of knowledge to which the person will continue to be exposed.

### Extraversing

A few lines from Jung may be of value in highlighting core features of his conception of the externally oriented attitude:

Extraversion is characterized by interest in the external object, responsiveness, and a ready acceptance of external happenings, a desire to influence and be influenced by events, a need to join in and get "with it," the capacity to endure bustle and noise of every kind, and actually find them enjoyable. (Jung, 1936/1971, p. 550)

### Introversing

Similarly, the following brief excerpt from Jung's writings clearly states his view of the internally oriented attitude:

The introvert is not forthcoming, he is as though in continual retreat before the object. He holds aloof from external happenings, does not join in. For him self-communings are a pleasure. His own world is a safe harbour, a carefully tended and walked-in garden, closed to the public and hidden from prying eyes. His own company is the best. He feels at home in his world, where the only changes are made by himself. His best work is done with his own resources, on his own initiative and in his own way. (Jung, 1936/1971, pp. 550–551)

## THE MIPS SENSING AND INTUITING MODES

Information, whether its source is internal or external to the self, can be classified in numerous ways. A core distinction can be drawn between information that is tangible versus that which is intangible. By "tangible" is meant identifiable by the human sensory capacities, well-defined, distinctive, recognizable, and knowable—referring to phenomena that are concrete, factual, material, realistic, or self-evident. In contrast, information that is termed "intangible" takes in phenomena that lack an intrinsically distinctive order and structural clarity; they are inherently ambiguous, abstract, insubstantial, vague, mysterious, and obscure. Such phenomena usually can be fathomed only by means that are unknown, unconscious, and percipient, or by glimmerings into their diffuse and elusive nature that are materially tenuous or psychical in form.

The readiness of some individuals to be receptive to information that is well-structured and tangible, and of others to receive information that is obscure and intangible, constitutes, in our view, a fundamental difference in cognitive style that is of appreciable personological significance. Although Jung's language is only partially formulated in cognitive terms, close parallels again can be seen between the bipolarity presented here and that offered by Jung in his distinction between Sensing and Intuiting:

Here we should speak of sensation when sense impressions are involved, and of intuition if we are dealing with a kind of perception which cannot be traced back directly to conscious sensory experience. Hence, I define sensation as perception via conscious sensory functions, and intuition as perception via the unconscious.

Sensation and intuition make us aware of what is happening, but do not interpret or evaluate it. They do not proceed selectively, according to principles, but are simply receptive to what happens. (Jung, 1931/1933, pp. 538–539)

### Sensing

Favoring tangible, structured, and well-defined sources of information that call upon one's five senses will, no doubt, correlate with a wide range of associated behaviors, such as choosing actions of a pragmatic and realistic nature, preferring events in the here and now, and attending to matters calling for facts and quantitative precision. As Jung conceived it:

There are people for whom the . . . accent falls on sensation, on the perception of actualities, and elevates it into the sole determining and all-overriding principle. These are the fact-minded men, in whom intellectual judgment, feeling, and intuition are driven into the background by the paramount importance of actual facts. (Jung, 1936/1971, p. 554)

### Intuiting

In contrast, preferring the intangible, unstructured, and ambiguous is likely to be associated with actions inspired by possibilities, challenges, potentials, and thoughts of an abstract, complex, connotative, and symbolic character, as well as by matters that depend on novelty, mystery, and speculation. To quote Jung:

On intuition actual reality counts only in so far as it seems to harbour possibilities which then become the supreme motivating force, regardless of the way things actually are in the present. (Jung, 1936/1971, p. 554)

## The MIPS Thinking and Feeling Modes

The first two pairs of cognitive functions were grouped according to sources and styles of gathering information. The next two pairs of bipolarities represent transformational processes, referring to what is done to information once it has been received. Cognitive science has articulated a number of concepts related to registering, encoding, and organizing life experiences. These concepts pertain to various questions, such as: Through what cognitive mode will information be received—intellective or affective? How shall information be organized; will it be assimilated into preformed memory systems or will it be recast through imagination into novel schemas? Although individuals may be positioned on several other continuums or bipolarities—e.g., convergent versus divergent, serial versus hierarchical, primary versus secondary, verbal versus visual—it is the author's view that the most fruitful cognitive transformational distinctions relevant to personality are the pairs selected in this and the following section.

Simplifying matters, there are essentially two pathways through which experiences pass once recorded by our senses, if they are of sufficient magnitude to activate an encoded response. The first pathway evaluates whether information is objective and reasoned, eliciting a thought-based judgment that signifies in an articulate and organized way that the registered experience "makes sense"—that is, it is intellectually logical and coherent. The second pathway elicits a subjective, emotional response, a feeling reaction, signaling, in a less organized and often diffuse and global way, that the registered experience was recorded as affectively neutral, positive, or negative.

### Thinking

The intellective pole, what Jung meant by "thinking," indicates a preference for interpreting experience in light of reason and logic. Although life events may derive from internal or external sources, and may be of a tangible or intangible nature, the interpretive and evaluative process is inclined toward the objective and impersonal, as events are analyzed by means of critical reason and the application of rational and judicious thought. By increasing affective detachment—reducing the unruly emotional input of others and the upsetting effects of one's own emotional state—it may be possible to sustain a high degree of cognitive cohesion and continuity. Objective analysis and affective detachment protect against unwanted incursions upon cognitive stability, but often at the price of promoting behavior that is rigid, overcontrolled, and unyielding.

### Feeling

In contrast, experiences processed affectively will activate subjective states such as liking versus disliking, feeling good versus feeling bad, comfort versus discomfort, attracted versus repelled, valuing versus devaluing, and so on. Through empathic resonance, the route of affectivity inclines the individual to record not so much what other people think but, rather, how he or she feels about matters. The individual who inclines toward the Feeling pole uses "psychic vibrations" to learn more from the emotional tone words convey than from their content or logic. The usual modality for those who exhibit an affective style is that of subjective reality, a more or less "gut" reaction composed of either global or differentiated positive or negative moods. There are, of course, individuals who are notably introspective, inclined to pursue inner affective states with an intellective cognitive style. These individuals are not merely psychological-minded; they may exhibit an obsessive search for self-insight. For the most part, however, the affective transformational style indicates individuals who evince modest introspective analysis, combined with an open and direct empathic response to others, and a subconscious susceptibility to the emotional facets of experience in as pure a manner as possible.

## THE MIPS SYSTEMATIZING AND INNOVATING MODES

The final cognitive transformational bipolarity addresses the question whether new information is shaped to fit preformed memory schemas (assimilated within preexisting cognitive systems), or is organized through the imagination and cast into more novel forms. Evolutionary theory suggests that the best course may be to reinforce (cognitive) systems that have proved stable and useful. On the other hand, progress will not be made unless promising new possibilities are explored. A beneficial tension in evolution clearly exists between conservation and change, between adhering to the habitual and unleashing the creative. These two contrasting cognitive styles demonstrate the two options—assimilating experiences into already established systems versus exploring innovative ways to structure them.

### Systematizing

In the MIPS schema, systematizers are akin in certain features to those who exhibit the "Judgment preference," which Katherine Briggs and Isabel Briggs Myers abstracted from Jung's notions (Myers, 1962). Both Systematizing and having a Judgment preference indicate persons with well-structured memory systems, to which they routinely attach new cognitive experiences. Disposed to operate within established perspectives, systematizers assimilate new information to previous points of view, exhibiting thereby a high degree of dependability and consistency, if not rigidity, in their functioning. Typically, such people are predictable, conventional, orderly, planful, decisive, methodical, exacting, formal, disciplined, conscientious, faithful, loyal, and devoted. Hence, in evolutionary terms, the assimilative polarity leads to continuity and tradition, or to the maintenance of existing levels of cognitive entropy; this cognitive style promotes an architectural cohesion that remains unchallenged by risky variations that could potentially diminish established levels of order.

### Innovating

In contrast, those at the Innovating pole are characterized by an openness to forming new and imaginative cognitive constructions of an impromptu character. They are inclined to search for creative ideas and solutions, to find novel ways to order information, and to accumulate negative entropy, so to speak, by stepping outside of what is known and given so as to establish a new or higher level of cognitive organization. Innovators stretch beyond confirmed perspectives, seeking to broaden interpretations of experience, and are not concerned with demonstrating their reliability. The imaginative mode is typically associated with being open-minded, spontaneous, extemporaneous, informal, adaptable, flexible, resilient, impressionable, creative, inventive, and resourceful.

## THE FIVE INTERPERSONAL-BEHAVIORS BIPOLARITIES

Numerous authors have suggested that the interpersonal-behavior dimension provides particularly useful information for clinical and normal personality assessments. Along the same line, some authors suggest that since the way people relate is crucial to everyday experiences, interpersonal variables should take primacy over other personological domains. This thesis applies especially to nonclinical personality patterns. A style of relating will determine the future course of much of a person's work, family, and social experiences. The strategies an individual uses to achieve his or her goals with others elicits reactions that influence whether life progresses in a satisfactory or unsatisfactory way.

In one form or another, interest in interpersonal behaviors can be found in the ideas of the earliest contributors to psychiatric and personological thought. No single, giant figure of the historic stature of Freud and Jung stands out in this realm of study, but several writers are worthy of note, especially in the past half-century. In addition, a number of researchers in the past two decades have focused all their efforts on interpersonal matters, albeit with several divergent models.

## THE CONTRIBUTIONS OF SULLIVAN AND LEARY AND THEIR CURRENT PARALLELS

### Meyer and Sullivan

Although both Adolph Meyer (1951) and his student, Harry Stack Sullivan (1953), overlapped with Freud and Jung, their writings were rather sparse. However, both focused on the psychosocial worlds of their patients and gave particular attention to the role of interpersonal relationships. Like Freud and Jung, Meyer and Sullivan recognized that psychiatric disturbances reflected the impact of early life experiences. However, they brought to the foreground the importance of ongoing social roles and relationships. It fell to Sullivan to assert that the primary task of psychiatric inquiry did not center on the biological basis of psychopathology or the revealing of past unconscious processes; rather, it required the disentangling of communication distortions that take place between interacting persons—that is, the decoding of their everyday interpersonal transactions.

To Sullivan, problematic behavior stemmed from disordered interrelating, both verbal and nonverbal. His delineations of personality traits and types were presented primarily through informal lectures and seminar discussions in the 1930s and 1940s. Notable among the several personality types he proposed were the "self-absorbed" person, who engages in a series of intimacies that end in profound disillusionment; the "incorrigible" person, who is identified by a pattern of unfriendly and morose behaviors, and by a tendency to complain bitterly about those in authority; the "negativistic" person, who refuses to subscribe to the views of others; and the "ambition-ridden" person, who is characterized by his or her exploitiveness, competitiveness, and unscrupulousness.

Little of the formal structure that characterizes the theoretical writings of Freud and Jung is found in Sullivan. Nevertheless, his emphasis on the central role of interpersonal behavior in personality and psychopathology was adopted by numerous followers. These include Gregory Bateson and his associates (1956), who helped develop studies of family interaction; Eric Berne, who developed a schema for transactional analysis (1961); plus several researchers who developed interpersonal circumplex models of personality (Benjamin, 1974; Kiesler, 1979; Wiggins, 1979). It is the latter developments to which we will attend briefly, along with making a brief excursion into the Big-Five factor model (Costa & McCrae, 1985; Goldberg, 1993; Tupes & Christal, 1992).

## Leary's Typology

Drawing inspiration from the work of Sullivan and Karen Horney (1937, 1950), another early and central figure of the interpersonal school, Timothy Leary (1957), along with his associates, constructed an interpersonal typology based on two dimensions: dominance/submission and hate/love. Utilizing gradations and a visual circumplex model to represent the bipolar nature of his personality typology, Leary established 16 behavioral segments, which he then grouped into eight distinct interpersonal types. Each was identified by two variants, a mild and an extreme form; hence, two labels were used to designate each of the eight types—the first signifying the mild, or more adaptive, variant; the second indicating the more extreme, or pathological, variant.

One pattern, the "cooperative-overconventional" personality, describes the person who strives to be liked and accepted by others, and who displays an extraverted friendliness and sociability. In a more extreme form, this personality displays an effusiveness, a shallow optimism, an immature naiveté, a histrionic or dramatic expressiveness, and a hyperdistractability. Another of Leary's types, the "docile-dependent" personality, is characterized by overt displays of both friendliness and affiliation. A central feature is voicing unusual trust and admiration of others; in the extreme form, we might observe an ingratiating and clinging dependency, and a constant beseeching for help and advice.

The "responsible-hypernormal" personality is noted for efforts to maintain the appearance of personal integrity, for excessive striving to achieve an inner ideal of proper and conventional behavior, and for being orderly and perfectionistic. In the extreme form, this personality may feel isolated by his or her propriety and correctness, and removed from both the external realities of life and his or her inner feelings. In the "self-effacing-masochistic" personality, there is modesty and an unpretentious reserve, along with a tendency to downplay his or her abilities and to avoid appearing capable and confident; in the extreme form, the person tries to evoke deprecation and humiliation from others, with consequent neurotic feelings of anxiety, depression, and uncertainty. Arranged in a circumplex, each of the preceding four types is matched by an opposite personality—that is, a personality with characteristics that are at the other end of a bipolar dimension.

## From Leary to the Big-Five Model

Two points should be made with regard to Leary's interpersonal formulations: First, many investigators have elaborated his work; second, the eight types (four bipolarities) he conceived correspond closely to the first four factors comprising the Big-Five model.

Soon after Leary published his group's impressive interpersonal model of personality, a number of researchers expanded its intriguing themes, while others sought to develop instruments to operationalize its dimensions. Early writers such as Heider (1958), Schutz (1958), and Lorr and McNair (1963), were soon followed by Carson (1969) and Swensen (1973), each of whom provided thoughtful analyses that reinforced the logic and strength of interpersonal dimensions. The most recent contributions and methodologies have been formulated by Benjamin (1974, 1986), Kiesler (1979, 1986), and Wiggins (1979), each generating highly creative schemes for their interpersonal models.

Approaching the subject of personality from a completely different vantage point, a number of psychometricians, starting with Thurstone (1934), began using factor-analytic procedures as a means of extracting commonalities from the popular lexicon of descriptive psychological traits. Thurstone was followed in this quest by Cattell (1943); more recently, Costa and Widiger (1993), Goldberg (1993), and others have pursued this trail. A high degree of correspondence also exists between the first four factors of the Big-Five model, which pertain to behavioral characteristics (as contrasted with cognitive or motivational ones), and the four extremes comprising Leary's bipolar circumplex. A side-by-side examination of the "big-four" and Leary's four pairs of behavioral types should prove illuminating. The Big-Five factors are usually numbered and labeled as follows: Factor I is Extraversion (surgency); Factor II, Agreeableness; Factor III, Conscientiousness; Factor IV, Neuroticism (versus Emotional Stability); and Factor V, Openness to Experience (Intellect, Culture), which will be discussed in a later paragraph.

Factor I, Extraversion, appears closely related to Leary's "cooperative-overconventional" type (characterized by Leary as exhibiting an extraverted friendliness and sociability). Factor II, Agreeableness, corresponds to Leary's "docile-dependent" type (portrayed by Leary as demonstrating an affiliativeness, an unusual degree of trust and admiration for others, as well as submissiveness, accommodation, cooperativeness, and amicability). Factor III, Conscientiousness, is similar to Leary's "responsible-hypernormal" type (characterized by Leary as a desire to achieve an ideal of proper and conventional behavior, as well as behaving in an orderly and perfectionistic manner). Factor IV, Neuroticism, exhibits features of Leary's "self-effacing-masochistic" type (identified by its tendency to evoke deprecation and humiliation from others, resulting in feelings of anxiety, depression, and uncertainty).

## Toward the MIPS Approach

Both Leary's extension of Sullivan's interpersonal focus and the Big-Five's foundation in common descriptors of human transaction address behavioral traits—that is, features that characterize the actions of people, what they do rather than what motivates them or how they function cognitively. The "universal" lexicon of descriptive terms pertains primarily to what can be seen by others—the overt, tangible behaviors of people. Our common speech does not record with clarity or distinctiveness "inner characteristics," which must be inferred or deduced; in its common usage, our inferential language falters both in scope and precision. Moreover, psychological-mindedness and sophistication in personologic matters are recent developments; hence, they are not strongly encoded in our lexicon (here we must exclude the exceptional insights of authors such as Shakespeare). The ambiguities of cognition and motivation only recently have become part of both our everyday and professional vocabulary. It is striking, to this author at least, that personality instruments have failed to characterize cognitive and motivational traits, centering attention almost exclusively on behavior, and only recently focusing on behavioral traits of an interpersonal character.

In a related matter, puzzlement within the field of personology regarding Factor V of the Big-Five model can be understood in part by noting that it is the only factor of the basic five that relates to cognitive processes as opposed to behavioral features. Perhaps the confusion over its "proper" name (e.g., Openness, Intellect, Culture) resides in the fact that it pertains to an inferred rather than an observable process. In fact, we find that the MIPS Intuiting scale is the highest correlate of Costa and McCrae's (1985) "Openness to Experience." Whether the difficulty with Factor V can be attributed to the fuzziness in our lexicon of inferred personality constructs, or the problem is that humans are less capable of drawing personality distinctions in cognitive and motivational domains, will have to be decided by future research. Toward that end of clarification, we believe it will be helpful that all three personality domains are encompassed in the MIPS.

Turning back to the interpersonal behavioral domain, it has been argued earlier in this chapter, as well as in earlier publications (Millon, 1967, 1969, 1986b, 1987c, 1990, 1991), that the foundation for a scientific conception of personality dimensions or disorders cannot rest solely on empirical data or clinical grounds. These data provide valuable confirmations and inspirations, but the "meaning" of a scientific schema requires an explicit and systematic theoretical rationale. Theory provides a coherent set of principles that should explain how and why empirical and clinical findings take the form they do.

The following paragraphs will outline a rationale for the five sets of bipolar interpersonal dimensions covered by the MIPS. Thereafter we will seek to demonstrate, albeit briefly, how this format corresponds both to Leary's interpersonal types and to the Big-Five (or four+) factor model.

Regarding the five pairs, earlier publications (Millon, 1969, 1986a, 1986b) outlined a biosocial/learning theory based on the nature and source of reinforcers, and passive and active instrumental strategies. A 5 x 2 format served as a foundation for generating 10 of the DSM, Axis II personality disorders. Although this arrangement was supplanted by an evolutionary model (Millon, 1990), the basic architecture of the original theory remains as a useful framework for conceptualizing interpersonal dimensions of normal personalities (Millon, 1991).

## THE MIPS RETIRING AND OUTGOING BEHAVIORS

As the first behavioral bipolarity, what might be called a "gregarious/aloof" dimension contrasts two interpersonal styles of relating that represent extremes in degree of friendliness and communicativeness. This feature of sociability (or the lack thereof) is present in almost all systems of personality traits, and is most commonly referred to as Extraversion/Introversion. As noted previously, however, we have adopted Jung's notion of Extraversion/Introversion as originally intended—that is, to signify a cognitive "attitude" or expectation in relation to the object, and not a behavior. Factor I of the standard Big-Five schema, in contrast, encompasses both cognitive and behavioral facets of extraversion and introversion.

In the author's view, the "gregarious/aloof" dimension is best narrowed to a "pure" behavioral bipolarity that characterizes people who relate to others with differing degrees of sociability and companionability. This description can be qualified by saying that although most persons are occasionally "retiring" and occasionally "outgoing," they are likely to behave one way more often than the other.

### Retiring

Those persons scoring higher on the Retiring scale—that is, displaying more features tapped by the "aloof" than by the "gregarious" pole—evince few social or group interests. They exhibit (albeit in nonclinical form) certain of the attributes seen in the DSM schizoid personality. Their needs to give and receive affection and to show feelings tend to be minimal. They are inclined to have few relationships and interpersonal involvements, and do not develop strong ties to other people. They may be seen by others as calm, placid, untroubled, easygoing, and possibly indifferent. Rarely expressing their inner feelings or thoughts to others, they seem most comfortable when left alone. They tend to work in a slow, quiet, and methodical manner, almost always remaining in the background in an undemanding and unobtrusive way. Comfortable working by themselves, they are not easily distracted or bothered by what goes on around them. Being somewhat deficient in the ability to recognize the needs and feelings of others, they may be seen as socially awkward, if not insensitive, as well as lacking in spontaneity and vitality.

### Outgoing

At the "gregarious" pole, gauged by high scores on the Outgoing scale, we find attributes opposite from the above constellation. At the most extreme levels of the Outgoing pole are persons characterized by features similar to the DSM's histrionic personality. At less extreme levels, gregarious persons go out of their way to be popular with others, have confidence in their social abilities, feel they can readily influence and charm others, and possess a personal style that makes people like them. Most enjoy engaging in social activities, and like meeting new people and learning about their lives. Talkative, lively, socially clever, they are often dramatic attention-getters who thrive on being the center of

social events. Many become easily bored, especially when faced with repetitive and mundane tasks. Often characterized by intense and shifting moods, gregarious types are sometimes viewed as fickle and excitable. On the other hand, their enthusiasms often prove effective in energizing and motivating others. Inclined to be facile and enterprising, outgoing people may be highly skilled in manipulating others to meet their needs.

## THE MIPS HESITATING AND ASSERTING BEHAVIORS

The Hesitating/Asserting bipolarity, which also might be termed "insecure" versus "confident," taps differences in social composure, or poise, self-possession, equanimity, and stability. These attributes convey either self-assurance and self-control or their antitheses, as seen in behaviors signifying unsureness, timidity, uncertainty, constraint, and wariness. Parallels might be expected between those scoring at the highest end of the Hesitating scale and the DSM's avoidant personality, while those at the high extreme of the Asserting scale are likely to evince traits not unlike the DSM's narcissistic personality.

### Hesitating

The Hesitating scale represents attributes of social inhibition and withdrawal. This "insecure" (as opposed to "confident") pole has some common ground with the self-effacing segment of Leary's self-effacing-masochistic pattern, notable for its tendency to downplay personal abilities, to be shy and sensitive, and to experience feelings of anxiety and uncertainty. Similarly, this pole is akin to Factor IV of the Big-Five, usually termed Neuroticism (as opposed to Emotional Stability). Those scoring high on the Hesitating scale have a tendency to be sensitive to social indifference or rejection, to feel unsure of themselves, and to be wary in new situations, especially those of a social or interpersonal character. Somewhat ill at ease and self-conscious, these individuals anticipate running into difficulties in inter-relating and fear being embarrassed. They may feel tense when they have to deal with persons they do not know, expecting that others will not think well of them. Most prefer to work alone or in small groups where they know that people accept them. Once they feel accepted, they can open up, be friendly, be cooperative, and participate with others productively.

### Asserting

An interpersonal boldness, stemming from a belief in themselves and their talents, characterize those high on the opposite, Asserting scale. Competitive, ambitious, and self-assured, they naturally assume positions of leadership, act in a decisive and unwavering manner, and expect others to recognize their special qualities and cater to them. Beyond being self-confident, those with an Asserting profile often are audacious, clever, and persuasive, having sufficient charm to win others over to their own causes and purposes. Problematic in this regard may be their lack of social reciprocity and their sense of entitlement—their assumption that what they wish for is their due. On the other hand, their ambitions often succeed, and they typically prove to be effective leaders.

## THE MIPS DISSENTING AND CONFORMING BEHAVIORS

The degree to which persons flout tradition or are tradition-oriented undergirds the third bipolarity. The Dissenting versus Conforming dimension recognizes that some individuals act in a notably autonomous fashion, are not social-minded, and are not inclined to adhere to conventional standards, cultural mores, and organizational regulations; at the other pole, individuals are highly compliant and responsible, as well as conscientious and diligent about fulfilling their duties. In the clinical realm of the DSM, those at the very high end of the "unconventional" bipolarity, as gauged by the MIPS Dissenting scale, would exhibit

some similarity to the antisocial personality. In contrast, those at the upper extreme of the "dutiful" polarity, as measured by the MIPS Conforming Scale, would tend to show obsessive-compulsive personality traits.

### Dissenting

High scorers on the Dissenting scale include unconventional persons who seek to do things their own way and are willing to take the consequences of doing so. They act as they see fit regardless of how others judge them. Inclined at times to elaborate on or shade the truth, as well as to ride close to the edge of the law, they are not conscientious—that is, they do not assume customary responsibilities. Rather, they frequently assert that too many rules stand in the way of people who wish to be free and inventive, and that they prefer to think and act in an independent and often creative way. Many believe that persons in authority are too hard on people who don't conform. Dissenters dislike following the same routine day after day and, at times, act impulsively and irresponsibly. They will do what they want or believe to be best without much concern for the effects of their actions on others. Being skeptical about the motives of most people, and refusing to be fettered or coerced, they exhibit a strong need for autonomy and self-determination.

### Conforming

At the other extreme of the unconventional/dutiful bipolarity are those who score high on the Conforming scale. This pole represents traits not unlike Leary's responsible-hypernormal personality, with its ideal of proper, conventional, orderly, and perfectionistic behavior, as well as bearing a similarity to Factor III of the Big-Five, termed Conscientiousness. Conformers are notably respectful of tradition and authority, and act in a responsible, proper, and conscientious way. They do their best to uphold conventional rules and standards, following given regulations closely, and tend to be judgmental of those who do not. Well-organized and reliable, prudent and restrained, they may appear to be overly self-controlled, formal and inflexible in their relationships, intolerant of deviance, and unbending in their adherence to social proprieties. Diligent about their responsibilities, they dislike having their work pile up, worry about finishing things, and come across to others as highly dependable and industrious.

## THE MIPS YIELDING AND CONTROLLING BEHAVIORS

There is a clear and marked contrast between persons who are docile, obedient, subservient, and self-demeaning and those who are dominating, willful, forceful, and power-oriented. Well-established in the literature as a major dimension of interpersonal style (e.g., Wiggins, 1982), one polarity corresponds to the masochistic segment of Leary's self-effacing-masochistic diagnosis, with this personality's tendency to evoke deprecation and humiliation from others through "weak and spineless actions." The other extreme of the polarity parallels Leary's managerial-autocratic personality, which commands obedience and respect from others, and makes domineering attempts to control and manipulate their lives. The MIPS "submissive," or Yielding, type also exhibits nonclinical qualities not unlike those of the recently deleted DSM self-defeating personality. Similarly, what we term the "dominant," or Controlling, polar extreme evinces nonclinical interpersonal qualities akin in some ways to those of the DSM's recently expunged sadistic personality.

### Yielding

Although similar to Factor II of the Big-Five, labeled Agreeableness, the Yielding bipolarity conveys more than cooperativeness and amicability; it involves a disposition to act in a subservient and self-abasing manner. Placing themselves in an inferior light or abject position, those high on the Yielding scale allow, even encourage, others to take advantage of them. They are unassertive and deferential, if not servile. Often viewing themselves as their own worst enemies, they behave in an unpresuming, self-effacing, even self-derogating manner, and tend to avoid displaying their talents and aptitudes. Obsequious and self-sacrificing in their interactions with others, they can be depended on to adhere to the expectations of those they follow. Most people in this category possess abilities far in excess of those they lay claim to.

### Controlling

Those scoring high on the Controlling scale of the dominance bipolarity enjoy the power to direct and intimidate others, and to evoke obedience and respect from them. They tend to be tough and unsentimental, as well as gain satisfaction in actions that dictate and manipulate the lives of others. Although many sublimate their power-oriented tendencies in publicly approved roles and vocations, these inclinations become evident in occasional intransigence, stubbornness, and coercive behaviors. Despite these periodic negative expressions, controlling types typically make effective leaders, being talented in supervising and persuading others to work for the achievement of common goals.

## THE MIPS COMPLAINING AND AGREEING BEHAVIORS

This fifth and final interpersonal dimension takes up social negativism, or "discontent"—a Complaining style—versus social amenability or "congeniality," which is named an Agreeing style. The former bipolar extreme signifies a general displeasure both with oneself and others, combined with a tendency to act in a petulant, resentful, irritable, and oppositional manner. The latter pole represents a general inclination to be pleasant in relationships, and to act in a consenting, affable, and peaceable way (without the self-demeaning and self-abasing tendencies seen in the submissive/yielding pattern described previously).

It was noted above that the Yielding polar type exhibits similarities to the DSM's erstwhile self-defeating pattern, while the Controlling type shows a partial correspondence to the DSM's former sadistic personality. In contrast, the Agreeing bipolarity corresponds more closely to the DSM dependent personality, and the Complaining type shows a similarity to the DSM negativistic (passive-aggressive) personality type.

### Complaining

Those scoring high on the Complaining scale often assert that they have been treated unfairly, that little of what they have done has been appreciated, and that they have been blamed for things they did not do. Opportunities seem not to have worked out well for them, and they "know" that good things do not last. Often resentful of what they see as unfair demands placed on them, they may be disinclined to carry out responsibilities as well as they could. Ambivalent about their lives and relationships, they may get into problematic wrangles and disappointments as they vacillate between acceptance one time and resistance the next. When matters go well, they can be productive and constructively independent-minded, willing to speak out to remedy troublesome issues.

### Agreeing

Quite another picture is seen among those who score high on the Agreeing scale. This bipolar extreme is akin to the normal "cooperative" segment of Leary's cooperative-overconventional interpersonal style, representing an accommodating, participatory, compromising, and agreeing pattern of behavior. As noted previously, Agreeing also corresponds more closely to the Big-Five's Factor II, Agreeableness, than does the Yielding scale, in conveying a self-respecting concordance with others; a congenial obligingness is voluntary rather than being coerced or being a product of self-derogation. Those who fit the congenial/Agreeing pattern are notably cooperative and amicable. Disinclined to upset others, they are willing to adapt their preferences to be compatible with those of others. Trusting others to be kind and thoughtful, they are also willing to reconcile differences and to achieve peaceable solutions, as well as to be considerate and to concede when necessary. Cordiality and compromise characterize their interpersonal relationships.

## CONCLUSION

The framework developed for this instrument was motivated by a desire to operationalize a theoretical conception of personality, and by a belief that there exists an intelligible model that faithfully portrays the core dimensions in a coherent and unified way. As many other theorists have proposed, hidden beneath the surface complexity of motivations, cognitions, and behaviors there is likely to be a simple and elegant order of deep and interlocking linkages from which the diverse expressions of personality derive.

What should be seen in the theoretical model is not a handful of immutable traits, but sets of dynamically interacting dispositions that blend into the diverse configurations we term personality styles. Further, there are both "positive" and "negative" aspects to all personality styles. Each style represents adaptive patterns that fit certain environments and situations quite well, and others less well. No personality trait is uniformly good or bad.

## REFERENCES

American Psychiatric Association. (1980). *Diagnostic and statistical manual of mental disorders.* 3rd ed. Washington, DC: Author.

Bateson, G., Jackson, D., Haley, J., & Weakland, J. (1956). Toward a theory of schizophrenia. *Behavioral Science, 1,* 251–264.

Benjamin, L. S. (1974). Structural analysis of social behavior. *Psychological Review, 81,* 392–425.

Benjamin, L. S. (1986). Adding social and intrapsychic descriptors to Axis I of DSM-III. In T. Millon & G. Klerman (Eds.). *Contemporary directions in psychopathology*. New York: Guilford.

Bowers, K. S. (1977). There's more to Iago than meets the eye: A clinical account of personality consistency. In D. Magnusson & N. S. Ender (Eds.), *Personality at the crossroads*. Hillsdale, NJ: Erlbaum.

Buss, A., & Plomin, R. (1975). *A temperament theory of personality development*. New York: Wiley.

Buss, A., & Plomin, R. (1984). *Temperament: Early developing personality traits*. Hillsdale, NJ: Erlbaum.

Buss, D. (Ed.). (1990). Biological foundations of personality. *Journal of Personality, 58*, 1–345.

Carson, R. C. (1969). *Interaction concepts of personality*. Chicago: Aldine.

Cattell, R. B. (1943). The description of personality: Basic traits resolved into clusters. *Journal of Abnormal and Social Psychology, 38*, 476–506.

Clark, L. & Watson, D. (1988). Mood and the mundane: Relations between daily life events and self-reported mood. *Journal of Personality and Social Psychology, 54*, 296–308.

Cloninger, C. R. (1986). A unified biosocial theory of personality and its role in the development of anxiety states. *Psychiatric Developments, 3*, 167–226.

Cloninger, C. R. (1987). A systematic method for clinical description and classification of personality variants. *Archives of General Psychiatry, 44*, 573–588.

Cole, L. C. (1954). The population consequences of life history phenomena. *Quarterly Review of Biology, 29*, 103–137.

Costa, P. T., & McCrae, R. R. (1985). *The NEO Personality Inventory Manual*. Odessa, FL: Psychological Assessment Resources.

Costa, P. T., & Widiger, T. (Eds.). (1993). *Personality disorders and the five-factor model of personality*. Washington, DC: American Psychological Association.

Freud, S. (1895/1966). Project for a scientific psychology. In *Standard Edition* (English Translation, vol. 1). London: Hogarth.

Freud, S. (1915/1925). The instincts and their vicissitudes. In *Collected Papers* (vol. 4). London: Hogarth.

Freud, S. (1940/1949). *An outline of psychoanalysis*. New York: Liveright.

Gilligan, C. (1982). *In a different voice*. Cambridge, MA: Harvard University Press.

Goldberg, L. R. (1993). The structure of phenotypic personality traits. *American Psychologist, 48*, 26–34.

Gray, J. A. (Ed.). (1964). *Pavlov's typology*. New York: Pergamon.

Gray, J. A. (1973). Causal theories of personality and how to test them. In J. R. Royce (Ed.). *Multivariate analysis and psychological theory*. New York: Academic Press.

Heider, F. (1958). *The psychology of interpersonal relations*. New York: Wiley.

Hempel, C. G. (1965). *Aspects of scientific explanation*. New York: Free Press.

Hobbes, T. (1650). *Human nature*. London: Bowman.

Horney, K. (1937). *The neurotic personality of our time*. New York: Norton.

Horney, K. (1950). *Neurosis and human growth*. New York: Norton.

Jung, C. (1921/1971). *Psychological types*. Zurich: Rasher Verlag

Jung, C. J. (1931). A psychological theory of types. In *Modern man in search of soul*. London: Kegan Paul.

Jung, C. J. (1936/1971). Psychology typology. In *Psychological types*. Princeton, NJ: Princeton University Press.

Kiesler, D. J. (1979). A psychological taxonomy of trait-descriptive terms: The interpersonal domain. *Journal of Personality and Social Psychology, 37*, 395–412.

Kiesler, D. J. (1986). The 1982 interpersonal circle: An analysis of DSM-III personality disorders. In T. Millon & G. Klerman (Eds.). *Contemporary directions in psychopathology*. New York: Guilford.

Leary, T. (1957). *Interpersonal diagnosis of personality*. New York: Ronald.

Lewin, K. (1936). *Principles of topographical psychology*. New York: McGraw-Hill.

Lorr, M., & McNair, D. (1963). An interpersonal behavior circle. *Journal of Abnormal and Social Psychology, 67,* 68–75.

Meyer, A. (1951). *The collected papers of Adolf Meyer.* Baltimore: The John Hopkins Press.

Millon, T. (Ed.). (1967). *Theories of psychopathology.* Philadelphia: Saunders.

Millon, T. (1969). *Modern psychopathology: A biosocial approach to maladaptive learning and functioning.* Philadelphia: Saunders.

Millon, T. (1984). On the renaissance of personality assessment and personality theory. *Journal of Personality Assessment, 48,* 450–466.

Millon, T. (1986a). Theoretical derivation of pathological personalities. In T. Millon & G. Klerman (Eds.), *Contemporary directions in psychopathology.* New York: Guilford.

Millon, T. (1986b). Personality prototypes and their diagnostic criteria. In T. Millon & G. Klerman (Eds.), *Contemporary directions in psychopathology.* New York: Guilford.

Millon, T. (1987a). On the genesis and prevalence of the borderline personality disorder: A social learning thesis. *Journal of Personality Disorders, 1,* 354–372.

Millon, T. (1987b). On the nature of taxonomy in psychopathology. In C. Last & M. Herson (Eds.), *Issues in diagnostic research.* New York: Plenum.

Millon, T. (1988). Personologic psychotherapy: Ten commandments for a post eclectic approach to integrative treatment. *Psychotherapy, 25,* 209–219.

Millon, T. (1990). *Toward a new personology: An evolutionary model.* New York: Wiley-Interscience.

Millon, T. (1991). Normality: What may we learn from evolutionary theory? In D. Offer & M. Sabshin (Eds.), *The diversity of normal behavior.* New York: Basic Books.

Myers, I. B. (1962). *The Myers-Briggs Type Indicator.* Palo Alto, CA: Consulting Psychologists Press.

Quine, W. V. O. (1977). Natural kinds. In S. P. Schwartz (Ed.), *Naming, necessity, and natural kinds.* Ithaca: Cornell University Press.

Russell, J. A., (1980). A circumplex model of affect. *Journal of Personality and Social Psychology, 39,* 1161–1178.

Schutz, W. C. (1958). *FIRO: A three-dimensional theory of interpersonal behavior.* New York: Holt, Rinehart & Winston.

Sullivan, H. S. (1953). *Conceptions of modern psychiatry.* New York: Norton.

Swenson, C. H. (1973). *An introduction to interpersonal relations.* Glenview, IL: Scott Foresman.

Tellegen, A. (1985). Structures of mood and personality and relevance to assessing anxiety, with an emphasis on self-report. In A. H. Tuma & J. Maser (Eds.), *Anxiety and the anxiety disorders.* Hillsdale, NJ: Erlbaum.

Thurstone, L. L. (1934). *The vectors of mind.* Psychological Review, 41, 1–32.

Trivers, R. L., (1974). Parental investment and sexual selection. In B. Campbell (Ed.), *Sexual selection and the descent of man 1871–1971.* Chicago: Aldine.

Tupes, E., & Christal, R. (1992). Recurrent personality factors based on trait ratings. *Journal of Personality, 60,* 225–251.

Watson, D., & Clark, L. (1984). Negative affectivity: The disposition to experience aversive emotional states. *Psychological Bulletin, 96,* 465–490.

Watson, D., & Tellegen, A. (1985). Toward a consensual structure of mood. *Psychological Bulletin, 98,* 219–235.

Wiggins, J. S. (1982). Circumplex models of interpersonal behavior in clinical psychology. In P. Kendall & J. Butcher (Eds.), *Handbook of research methods in clinical psychology.* New York: Wiley-Interscience.

Wiggins, J. S. (1979). An interpersonal communication analysis of relationship in psychotherapy. *Psychiatry, 42,* 299–311.

Wilson, E. O. (1975). *Sociobiology: The new synthesis.* Cambridge: Harvard University Press.

Wilson, E. O. (1978). *On human nature.* Cambridge: Harvard University Press.

**PART V**

# *INTERVENTION*

## PAPER 15

# Issues and Methods of Psychological Treatment

No book on "mental illness" would be complete without surveying in some depth the therapeutic techniques which practitioners employ to alter psychopathology . . .

As noted, man has always been intrigued by the bizarre actions and emotions displayed by his fellow man. Along with this curiosity, man sought to devise remedies that might alleviate the anguish of these unfortunate beings. For the greater part of history, techniques were based on superstition and magic. In preliterate times and in the early Egyptian civilizations the shaman or priest served as the therapist; his tools were those of ritualistic incantation, "medicinal" herbs and spiritually healing objects such as amulets and charms. The early Greeks, led by Hippocrates and Aristotle, turned from these fruitless rituals and instituted what proved to be a sound although short-lived approach of "rational" therapy. Although retaining the view that mental illness stemmed from spiritual forces, the Greeks and Romans employed such therapeutic practices as rest, dietetics and the sympathetic counsel of physician-priests. This humanistic approach came to an end during the latter phases of the Roman period. Throughout the centuries of the Middle Ages, "scientific" and compassionate methods gave way to cruel measures based on fear, witchcraft and a punitive Christian theology. Not until the late eighteenth century, commencing with Pinel's "open door" and "fresh air" policies, was a more benign era again ushered in. For roughly the next century advances were limited, however, to programs of custodial care.

Treatment as we know it today did not begin until the discovery of hypnosis and its relation to hysteria. The early work of Charcot and Bernheim was instrumental in leading Freud to the thesis that mental illness was essentially a psychological process traceable to the persistence of unconscious memories and conflicts. Psychoanalysis, the first of the systematic and rationally grounded treatment techniques, was designed by Freud to release these intrapsychic forces and reconstruct the self-defeating defenses that patients employed to deal with them. For many years, well into the midpart of this century, psychotherapy was viewed as synonymous with Freud's psychoanalytic procedure. Although new techniques were conceived, they were for the most part modifications of the Freudian approach.

It was not until the 1930s, with the resurgence of "medical" therapy, that alternatives to "intrapsychic" treatment came to the fore. This new movement began with the development of convulsive and surgical procedures; these early biophysical techniques were followed in the 1950s by the discovery of psychopharmacological methods.

Newer psychological methods were also devised in the 1940s and 1950s; they differed substantially in both rationale and technique from psychoanalysis. Among them are the several procedures that we shall group under the labels of phenomenological reorientation and behavior modification.

Thus, as man begins the latter third of the twentieth century, he has at his disposal for the first time a variety of alternative treatment techniques. Although their efficacy has not been fully validated, these methods provide the clinician with a real choice as to which tools he can use to achieve the goals of therapy.

## GOALS OF THERAPY

It was Hippocrates, the *first* of the great "scientific" physicians, who outlined the basic goals of medical treatment: to do no harm or wrong to the patient, relieve his suffering and assist "nature's" healing processes. Phrased in more contemporary terms, the therapist first must be sure that his techniques will not make matters worse than they already are; *second,* he must alleviate the patient's present discomfort; and *third,* he must facilitate the development of a healthier and more resilient state. In these three guidelines, Hippocrates set down treatment goals that are applicable to all health professions and to all varieties of illness. How can we translate them in terms more relevant to psychopathology?

To achieve this translation we must recognize first that psychopathology encompasses a wide range of problems. What is best for one type of difficulty may be damaging to another. Treatment goals and techniques must be geared, then, to the specific nature of the problem. To illustrate from general medicine, one case may require antibiotics, another call for surgery and a third require simple rest in a changed climate. In a similar manner, therapy in psychopathology must be selected in terms of the patient's specific problem. Psychopathology is no less varied than physiopathology; each subvariety of illness may call for different treatment goals and techniques.

Let us turn now to Hippocrates' first goal, that of doing no harm or wrong to the patient. Therapists may do their patients a disservice if they employ treatment techniques that are inapplicable and inefficient, thereby worsening the situation or postponing the employment of more effective procedures. This occurs all too frequently since many therapists apply the same treatment methods regardless of the specific nature of the patient's presenting problem. Psychotherapeutic inflexibility is no different than the often condemned chiropractic practice of utilizing bone manipulation for such diverse cases as asthma, urinary infections and myopia.

The achievement of Hippocrates' second goal, relief from suffering, is shared both by therapist and patient. Although the particular methods selected to achieve this objective differ among therapeutic "schools," all desire to reduce discomforting symptoms. Some accomplish this by dislodging the "unconscious roots" of the symptom, others by modifying its biophysical substrate, others by changing attitudes which give rise to it and still others through direct behavior extinction procedures.

Hippocrates' third goal, to facilitate the development of a healthier and more resilient state than before, presents a number of ethical as well as practical problems. Many patients, having achieved the immediate goal of symptom relief, do not foresee the possibility that further therapy may assist them in attaining a degree of "positive" mental health substantially greater than that which they achieved previously. Therapists who seek to fulfill this goal are faced with the ethical question of whether or not to guide their patients, either through open discussion or implicit therapeutic procedures, into pursuing the aim of "deeper" insight and "self-actualization." Therapists differ as to the emphasis they give to these more sweeping goals. Some consider "personality growth" to be the primary objective of psychotherapy; others, although they value positive mental health no less, orient their methods to more circumscribed objectives. As matters now stand, there is no evidence that techniques explicitly designed to effect growth and self-actualization are appreciably more successful in achieving these objectives than methods with more modest aims (Frank, 1961).

## LEVELS OF THERAPEUTIC FOCUS

One would think from the disparate techniques employed by the various schools of therapy that they would have substantially different goals. This is not the case. Psychoanalysts, existentialists, pharmacologists and behaviorists, despite conceptual and procedural differences, seek to "do no harm," "to relieve suffering" and "to promote growth and durable health." How then do they differ?

Numerous scholars have sought to classify alternative therapies in the hope of discerning basic commonalities and divergencies (McNair & Lorr, 1965; London, 1964; Patterson, 1966). No simple and agreed upon classification has emerged as a consequence of these efforts since each of the so-called schools are far from "pure" or consistent within themselves. For example, within the same "school," therapists may be distinguished in terms of their underlying philosophy of man, e.g., some view him to be no more than a composite of habit systems; others conceive man as a responsible choicemaking agent. Another distinction relates to the therapist's conceptions of psychopathology and its development, e.g., some place importance on early childhood experiences, others do not. A major division among therapists lies in the sphere of treatment process, e.g., some believe that therapeutic techniques should be based on experimentally derived principles whereas others give primacy to clinical theory; some believe that the therapist should take the lead in directing the course and goals of treatment, others allow the patient to assume this role; in some approaches the therapist is impersonal, acting in accord with certain strict and unvarying procedures, in others he acts in a warm, personal or spontaneous manner.

It is our contention that the techniques employed by therapists are determined first and foremost by the kind of data they focus upon in therapy. As noted, alternative approaches to psychopathology and its treatment are shaped primarily by the "level" of data that the scientist has chosen to emphasize. Once a particular class of data has been selected, the types of concepts and theories he will formulate and the therapeutic techniques and procedures he utilizes follow logically and inevitably. If he chooses to stress overt behavior, his theoretical schema and treatment approach will perforce be different than if he focuses on the biophysical substrate, phenomenological experience or intrapsychic mechanisms.

We shall organize later presentations in accord with these four levels. Let us briefly note here their principal characteristics.

*Biophysical* therapists consider the biological substrate to be the most fruitful level for therapeutic modification. These men, trained usually in the tradition of psychiatric medicine, often contend that the primary source of pathology lies in the anatomical or neurophysiological make-up of the individual. It follows logically, then, that the biological defect should be treated directly. Thus, these therapists employ pharmacological agents as a means of altering biochemistry and physiological thresholds, surgical management as a way of destroying pathological tissue or electrical stimulation to modify patterns of neural organization.

*Intrapsychic* therapists focus on the data of unconscious processes. These men, trained in the tradition of psychodynamic psychiatry, often assert that the primary source of difficulty stems from the persistence of repressed childhood anxieties and defensive maneuvers. The task of therapy, then, is to bring these residues of the past into consciousness where they can be reevaluated and reworked in a constructive fashion. To accomplish these goals, these therapists assume a passive role and attempt to revive early memories and conflicts through methods such as free association and dream interpretation.

*Phenomenological* therapists turn their attention to the data of conscious experience, that is, to the patient's subjective perception of events. These men, most of whom follow in the tradition of clinical personology, believe that the root of psychic disturbances lies in the individual's cognitive distortions of himself and others. The primary role of therapy, then, is not to explore the unconscious or to remove overt symptoms, but to "free" the patient so that he may develop an enhanced image of his self-worth and a constructive outlook on life. To accomplish this task, phenomenological therapists engage in "freewheeling" discussions in which the patient is guided or encouraged to find more wholesome attitudes.

*Behavioral* therapists concern themselves with the data of overt action and performance. Their focus in treatment is the patient's socially maladaptive or deficient behaviors, not internal states such as phenomenological experience, unconscious conflicts or constitutional dispositions. These men, trained in the tradition of academic experimental psychology, conceive their techniques in terms like stimulation and reinforcement. They assert that differences between adaptive and maladaptive behaviors reflect differences in the reinforcement experiences to which individuals were exposed. Therapy consists of the direct application of experimentally derived principles of learning and unlearning. The therapist seeks neither to remove "underlying causes" nor to give the patient free rein to explore his attitudes and feelings; rather, he arranges a program in which the behaviors he wishes to eliminate are unlearned, and those he wishes to enhance are strengthened through reinforcement or imitation. (Parenthetically, we must note that although behavior therapists utilize techniques devised initially in experimental learning research and concepts derived from learning theories, there is no justification for the common practice of exclusively restricting the term "learning therapies" to their methods. Phenomenological and intrapsychic approaches are also "learning therapies" since they, too, proceed in accord with principles that deal with how patients "learn" psychopathology and how these pathologies may be "unlearned" in therapy. Learning concepts and principles, then, are not the exclusive province of behavior therapy; therapists who focus on phenomenological and intrapsychic data levels utilize their own "brand" of learning theory, and do so with equal justification, if not with equal consistency or explicitness.)

# EVALUATION OF THERAPY

The ultimate test of a treatment program is not its rationale, theory or philosophy, but whether or not it works. Facile, even ingenious, explanations as to why and how beneficial changes *should* occur cannot replace the simple empirical fact that a treatment is or is not successful.

Every advocate of a therapeutic method claims a significant measure of success for his cherished technique, including those who espouse faith healing, warm baths, a diet of soy beans or the manipulation of bones. The question of successful treatment is not whether one achieves success, but whether the degree of success is significantly greater than that attained by patently "unscientific" methods, or through the mere passage of time alone. Moreover, the results of therapy should be gauged, at least in part, by objective as well as subjective criteria, and should be judged repeatedly through long-term follow-up evaluations to assure that changes are more than transitory.

Until the last decade or two, most therapists paid little attention to questions of effectiveness; either they took success for granted or they themselves served as judges of therapeutic effectiveness. Heavily involved in direct clinical service, few therapists had time for evaluative studies, and fewer still were trained to undertake objective, controlled, and systematic research.

This sorry state of affairs has begun to be remedied. In the last ten years, increasing numbers of investigators have brought their methodological talents to bear on the problem of therapeutic evaluation. This rapidly proliferating body of research has focused on two interrelated problems: the *efficacy* of therapy, that is, whether or not beneficial changes do take place in conjunction with treatment (often referred to as "outcome" studies); and the therapeutic *mode of action,* that is, the features or ingredients of the treatment procedure that are centrally involved in effecting beneficial changes (often referred to as "process" studies).

Much of the research done in the past has suffered from weak experimental design, inadequate sampling, ill-defined criteria, poor measuring instruments and unjustified generalizations. Thus, before we discuss the two principal issues of evaluative research, outcome and process, we will briefly discuss two subsidiary problems, the selection of relevant *evaluative criteria* for assessing therapeutic change, and the nature of the *patient sample* selected for research.

## EVALUATIVE CRITERIA

How does one determine if beneficial changes have taken place? Who makes the judgment, what measures are used, and at what point in the treatment program are they applied?

Establishing criteria for evaluating change is not a simple matter, nor is there consensus as to what criteria should be employed. Few would take issue with amorphous generalities such as "relief from suffering" and a "healthier, more resilient state than before." But how are these generalities to be spelled out and given the form of explicit and judicable criteria, gauged in accord with precise and objective measures? It is at the point of detailed criteria specification that consensus among researchers breaks down, and the need for reasonable agreement is so much needed.

Numerous and varied criteria of therapeutic change have been employed. These range from self-reports, therapist ratings, symptom checklists, intratherapy verbalizations, psychological test data and physiological indices, but many problems exist with regard to the reliability and validity of these criteria.

In addition to utilizing valid criteria and establishing a measure of consensus and uniformity in their application, it is important that several different criteria be used in evaluating the efficacy of therapy. Most forms of psychopathology are highly complex and manifest their features in varied ways. Different aspects of pathology may exhibit different degrees of change, even producing contrasting results. For example, the patient's subjective appraisal of change may fail to correspond with judgments made by others; thus, he may claim to be feeling better, having begun to express his formerly restrained hostile attitudes, but, as a consequence, may be judged by his family to be increasingly destructive socially. In short, single criterion measures may provide a misleading picture of improvement.

Multiple criteria are particularly important in studies designed to compare different therapeutic approaches. For example, after 15 or 20 sessions, behavior therapy may be judged quite successful if gauged by a symptom check list whereas intrapsychic therapy, oriented to the goal of "basic personality reconstruction," will in all likelihood be evaluated as unsuccessful at this point in treatment and according to this criterion. In short, since different forms of therapy focus on different levels of personality functioning and seek to achieve their aims after different lengths of treatment, it is important to utilize a comprehensive and repeated set of criteria so as to specify the precise nature of their impact and to delineate the timing and sequence of these beneficial effects.

Despite the value of combining criteria such as therapist ratings, test scores and intratherapy communications, the most significant criterion, *manifest changes in real-life situations,* is often neglected or bypassed because of difficulties involved in obtaining relevant data. Signs of improvement exhibited in institutional settings or changes noted within the therapeutic office, may or may not be "transferred" to everyday family, vocational and community relationships. The crucial test of therapeutic effectiveness, then, is *not* what can be reported, measured or seen in the therapeutic setting, but what is generalized to and carried out in extratherapeutic life.

## PATIENT SAMPLE

The effect of therapy, whether it be biological or psychological, varies as a function of who is treated; what works with one patient may not work with another. Despite the obvious character of this observation, many investigators have pursued their research on the unwarranted assumption that their clinical sample was homogeneous, with each patient equally disposed to respond favorably or unfavorably to the treatment to which he was subjected. In short, patients were not differentiated either in terms of their prognoses or other significant variables such as types of problems, target symptoms or chronicity. Those who have attempted to differentiate their patients have done so in accord with the traditional system of diagnostic categories. As was noted in earlier chapters, the official nosological schema is notoriously unreliable, and groups together patients who differ in significant if not crucial variables. As a result, most studies have produced data that confuse rather than clarify judgments of efficacy, and provide no information concerning which forms of pathology are most receptive to the therapy being investigated. Keisler comments on this point as follows (1966):

Because of these initial patient differences, no matter what the effect of psychotherapy in a particular study (be it phenomenally successful or a dismal failure), one can conclude very little if anything. At best, one can say something such as: for a sample of patients coming to this particular clinic over this particular period, psychotherapy performed by the clinic staff during that period on the average was either successful or unsuccessful. No meaningful conclusions regarding the types of patients for whom therapy was effective or ineffective are possible. This is inevitably the case since no patient variables crucially relevant for subsequent reactivity to psychotherapy have been isolated and controlled.

Meaningful evaluations of therapy require, then, that research patients be distinguished so that those who respond favorably can readily be identified. With this information in hand, it may be possible to learn which patients and problems are benefited most by which treatment techniques.

Once a comprehensive set of objective and reliable criteria has been selected and relevant distinctions drawn within the patient sample, the investigator has met two of the central requirements needed to determine whether or not certain treatment approaches are associated with beneficial changes, and which ingredients of the therapeutic procedure are instrumental in achieving them. These two sides of the same evaluative coin were referred to previously as "efficacy" and "mode of action." Let us turn to some of the issues and problems involved in each.

## EFFICACY (OUTCOME STUDIES)

Investigations that seek an answer to the question of whether or not therapy is effective have been termed "outcome studies." What must be achieved in the design of these studies is some assurance that observed changes in patients can be attributed to therapy rather than to nontherapeutic factors. Confounding factors can affect the results of these studies in two opposite ways; they may obscure what otherwise might have been valid positive findings or give a false impression of positive results when, in fact, there were none. Proper design requires that all extraneous and obscuring effects that might distort the results should be placed under careful control; with confounding variables removed or accounted for, the precise consequences of the therapeutic intervention itself can be properly gauged.

Biased results will be obtained if the patient sample possesses either a notably good or poor prognosis at the start of therapy, e.g., were the patients relatively healthy college students faced with pressing although minor and transitory problems of a social or vocational nature, or were they hard-core, back ward hospital patients with ingrained personality patterns of long duration? The first group is likely to resolve current problems with or without therapy in a relatively short period; the problems of the second group, however, are pervasive, long-standing, deeply entrenched and therefore highly resistant to solution, even with the "best" and most concerted of therapeutic programs.

Another set of factors confounding research data are incidental environmental events that take place concurrently with therapy, e.g., the death of a close relative, finding a boyfriend, flunking out of college, receiving a long sought for job promotion and so on. There is need to control or account for extratherapeutic events which are *not* a direct consequence of therapy, but which often influence the course of therapeutic progress.

How can these inevitable and invariably confounding variables be prevented from distorting the assessment of therapeutic efficacy?

This crucial aspect of research design is accomplished by employing a "control-group," that is, a group of *comparably ill* patients who do not receive therapy, but are likely to be subject to the same random collection of incidental experiences as those who are involved in therapy. The progress or lack of progress of the control group serves as a base line of improvement against which the therapeutic group can be compared.

Other potential difficulties which should be resolved in the planning of efficacy studies relate to the frequency and time intervals between evaluations. Long-term assessments should be scheduled to appraise the durability of therapeutically induced change. Short-term evaluations cannot be overlooked, however, since immediate albeit temporary relief has its values as well, e.g., preventing suicide. It is wise, then, to obtain repeated measurements of efficacy rather than a single "end point" evaluation, especially since end point evaluations often reflect entirely random fluctuations in pathology and lead the investigator to mistake a transient episode for a "final" state. Moreover, repeated measurements may be useful since different patients may respond to treatment at varying and uneven rates.

In summary, evaluations of therapeutic efficacy require "matched" control groups that serve as base lines for comparison. Furthermore, both therapeutic and control groups should be subjected to repeated evaluations; this will provide a picture of the course as well as the "outcome" of treatment and will eliminate the misleading effects of transitory or unreliable findings.

## MODE OF ACTION (PROCESS STUDIES)

If therapy is unrelated to outcome, that is, if it fails to be associated with beneficial change, then there is little reason to explore in detail the ingredients of the therapeutic regimen. On the other hand, if treatment is beneficial, there is good reason to distinguish those elements of the therapeutic "process" which contributed to the beneficial outcome from those which are entirely specious; certainly, not all the events that occur in the treatment setting can be assumed to be of therapeutic value. To achieve this goal, the total matrix of intratherapeutic variables must first be disentangled. Once this is accomplished, the investigator can set out to observe or manipulate each of these variables until he can determine which ones are crucial to therapeutic change.

Before we proceed, let us note that the distinction between process and outcome research is often misleading in that it creates the illusion that the process of therapy is independent of its outcome. Many investigators have become engrossed in "process" for its own sake, in methodological refinements and technology, and lose sight of the primary goal of evaluative research. The purpose of process studies, insofar as it refers to therapeutic evaluation, is not to record how frequently a patient makes remarks that indicate anxiety and hostility or to measure the relationship between these remarks and a host of physiological indices such as heart rate and respiration, but to isolate the ingredients of a therapeutic technique and correlate them with outcome criteria. Although events that take place in therapy provide an excellent research laboratory for investigating the interplay and correlates of human interaction, the primary goal of process studies is to delineate therapeutic variables that are crucial to favorable change in psychopathology.

The job of unraveling the complex and interwoven elements which comprise even the simplest of therapeutic procedures is enormously difficult. Determining what exactly is going on in therapy, and isolating, weighing and evaluating the components involved, e.g., separating the therapist's attitude and "personality" from the content of what he says, is a much more challenging task than that of verifying the "overall" outcome itself. However, if meaningful discriminations are to be made between alternative therapeutic approaches, and if maximally efficient techniques are ever to be devised, it is mandatory that this challenge be faced and surmounted. We know that many contemporary treatment methods, despite differences in theory and despite acrid controversies about their respective merits, are substantially alike with regard to certain basic ingredients, e.g., the therapist's sympathetic and seemingly "all-knowing" attitude; the process of implicit if not explicit reinforcement of "healthy" behaviors; and the therapist as a model of "reason" and emotional and cognitive control. On the other hand, alternative therapies do entail distinctive procedural features; these must be isolated and studied if we are to construct techniques in the future that are more efficacious than those of the present.

Numerous methodologies have been utilized to disentangle the flow of process variables. "Real" therapy as it unfolds in its natural setting is extremely complex, comprising several simultaneously operating variables that are often inextricably interwoven. The task of analyzing and separating these components calls for highly refined methods of observation and assessment.

In recent years, experimental procedures have been designed to decrease the complexity of "real" therapy and to isolate, in relatively uncomplicated form, what are believed to be its essential ingredients. In what is termed "analogue research," a simulated therapeutic interaction is arranged so that researchers can systematically explore specified variables of the natural treatment complex without the interference of extraneous factors. This is done most

often in a laboratory mock-up with experimental subjects rather than with real patients, although the latter practice is becoming commoner. Questions have been raised concerning the generalizability to real therapy of findings obtained in these simulated analogue studies. Whatever its limitations, it does provide a useful technique for delineating with precision several of the crucial variables that operate in natural therapy. Moreover, it allows investigators to experiment with entirely new therapeutic procedures based on a growing body of research dealing with the processes of behavior change.

# A PROPOSED ECLECTIC ORIENTATION

Before we proceed to the details of the principal forms of therapy, it will be useful, as a précis, to propose that they be viewed from a multitherapeutic perspective.

The "science" of therapy is in its infancy, despite popular illusions and professional pretensions to the contrary. For the most part, the efficacy of the principal techniques employed today is yet to be proved. Much more research is needed. Newer techniques must continue to be explored and older ones subjected to systematic evaluation. Such research and the rewards it promises will occur only if practitioners are willing to reexamine their traditional methods and bring the same refreshing objectivity to them as they hope their patients will bring to the solution of their habitual behaviors. The disinclination of clinical practitioners to submit their cherished techniques to detailed study or to revise them in accord with critical empirical findings is most lamentable. Therapeutic advances, so vital to the welfare of hundreds of thousands of patients, cannot take place unless practicing therapists give up their inertia and resistance to outside scrutiny.

Despite the fact that the theories underlying most therapeutic approaches are burdened with irrelevant conceptualizations and that most research leaves much to be desired in the way of proper controls, sampling and evaluative criteria, there is one overriding fact about therapy that comes through clearly: therapeutic techniques must be suited to the patient's problem. Simple and obvious although this statement is, it is repeatedly neglected by therapists who persist in utilizing and argue heatedly in favor of a single approach to *all* forms of psychopathology. No "school" of therapy is exempt from this notorious attitude.

It should be elementary, given the history of medicine, that no single treatment method works for all problems. Would it not be ludicrous and shocking if a physician prescribed his favorite remedy for all patients, regardless of the disease or difficulty they suffered? Should it not be equally distressing if a psychotherapist did likewise? Obviously, the diversity of psychopathological problems calls for a variety of different therapies, singly or in combination, geared to deal with the specific problem at hand.

The primary reason most approaches to therapy appear to be equally "good or bad" is that they succeed with only a small proportion of the many varieties of psychopathology they set out to treat. The probability of success in a mixed or varied patient population will be increased, it seems to us, if several approaches, rather than one approach, are employed.

As we review the specific techniques described in the next two chapters, let us keep in mind that no single approach is sufficient to deal with all the types and multidimensional complexities that comprise the body of psychopathology. Each therapeutic approach carves out a small slice of this vast complex for its special province. Let us remember that conceptual systems . . . are "inventions" created by man to aid him in understanding nature, and are not realities themselves. Theories and the therapies they generate must fit reality, not the other way around.

Given the paucity of current knowledge, there can be no justification for employing one therapeutic technique to the exclusion of others; multiplicity and flexibility in approaches are mandatory. Until unequivocal data exist to enable us to exclude as ineffective certain therapeutic methods and to specify the optimal matching of treatment to problem, we must assume an eclectic approach, employing the best for each case and continuing to experiment with alternative methods. . . .

## SOME HISTORICAL NOTES

Until that day in the distant future when practitioners can specify exactly which "pill" will dissolve the discomforts of psychopathology, patients will continue to be treated with drugs whose mode of action is only partially understood and whose effectiveness is highly limited. Unfortunately, this state of confusion and minimal efficacy is paralleled among the equally perplexing and inefficacious psychological therapies.

Beset with troublesome "mental" difficulties, patients are given a bewildering "choice" of psychotherapeutic alternatives that might prove emotionally upsetting in itself, even to the well balanced individual. Thus, patients may not only be advised to purchase this tranquilizer rather than that one or told to take vacations or leave their jobs or go to church more often, but if they explore the possibilities of formal psychological therapy, they must choose among myriad "schools" of treatment, each of which is claimed by its adherents to be the most efficacious and by its detractors to be both ineffective and unscientific.

Should a patient or his family evidence a rare degree of "scientific sophistication," they will inquire into the efficacy of alternative therapeutic approaches. What they will learn, assuming they chance upon an objective informant, is that the "outcome" of different treatment approaches is strikingly similar, and that there is little data available to indicate which method is "best" for the particular difficulty they face. Moreover, they will learn the startling fact that most patients improve without benefit of psychotherapy almost as frequently as those who are subjected to prolonged psychological treatment. This state of affairs is most discouraging. However, the "science" as opposed to the "art" of psychotherapy is relatively new, perhaps no older than one or two decades. Discontent concerning the shoddy empirical foundations of therapeutic practices was registered in the literature as early as 1910 ( Patrick & Bassoe), but systematic research did not begin in earnest until the early 1950s, and has become a primary interest of able investigators only in the last five or ten years ( Rubinstein & Parloff, 1959; Strupp & Luborsky, 1962; Hoch & Zubin, 1961; Goldstein & Dean, 1966; Gottschalk & Auerbach, 1966; Stollak, Guerney, & Rothberg, 1966; Shlien et al., 1968).

Given the confusing picture that prevails among psychological treatment methods, it may appear that a logical ordering of techniques at this time would be both unwise and premature. Nevertheless, it is necessary that we set forth as clearly as possible the basic rationales that differentiate the alternative therapies in practice today. To accomplish this in a reasonably useful pedagogical fashion requires first, that we review briefly the historical development of psychological procedures and second, that we outline the major dimensions by which they can be analyzed. With this as a foundation, we will have a perspective from which the principal types of psychological treatment can be described and evaluated.

Psychotherapy has a long history, although the concept of treatment by psychological methods was first formally proposed in 1803 by Johannes Reil. In this section we will briefly review some of the relevant points. . . . arranging the history of psychotherapy into six phases or periods, several of which overlap and extend into the present.

1. "Psychological" treatment was first recorded in the temple practices of early Greeks and Egyptians in the eighth century B.C. In Egyptian "hospices," physician-priests interpreted dreams and suggested solutions both to earthly and heavenly problems. In the Grecian Asclepiad temples, located in regions remote from sources of stress, the sick were provided with rest, given various nourishing herbs, massaged and surrounded with soothing music. During the fifth century B.C., Hippocrates suggested that exercise and physical tranquillity should be employed to supplant the more prevalent practices of exorcism and punishment. Asclepiades, a Roman in the first century B.C., devised a variety of measures to relax patients, and openly condemned harsh "therapeutic" methods such as bloodletting and mechanical restraints. The influential practitioner Soranus (120 A.D.) suggested methods to "exercise" the mind by having the patient participate in discussions with philosophers who could aid him in banishing his fears and sorrows. Although doubting the value of "love" and "sympathy" as a therapeutic vehicle, Soranus denounced the common practices of keeping patients in fetters and darkness and depleting their strength by bleeding and fasting. The value of philosophical discussions espoused by Soranus may be viewed as a forerunner of many contemporary psychological therapies.

Humane approaches to the treatment of the mentally ill were totally abandoned during medieval times when witchcraft and other cruel and regressive acts were employed as "therapy." In the early years of the Renaissance, medical scientists were preoccupied with the study of the body and its workings and paid little attention to matters of the mind or the care of the mentally ill. Institutions for the insane were prevalent throughout the continent, but they continued to serve as places to incarcerate and isolate the deranged rather than as settings for medical or humane care.

2. The second phase of psychological treatment, what may be termed the period of

"hospital reformation" and "moral treatment," began with the pioneering efforts of Philippe Pinel following the French Revolution. Guided by the belief that institutionalized patients could be brought from their state of degradation and depravity by exposure to a physically attractive environment and by contact with socially kind and moralistically proper hospital personnel, Pinel initiated an approach to mental hospital care that took hold, albeit gradually and fitfully. Moral treatment as practiced by responsible and considerate hospital personnel failed to take root for many years. This occurred for several reasons: there was a decline in the nineteenth century of psychiatric "idealism"; innumerable practical difficulties prevented the staffing of institutions with adequately motivated workers; and there was a resurgence from the mid-nineteenth to the early twentieth century of the medical disease model, turning the attention of psychiatrists to methods of physical rather than psychological treatment.

3. The practice of office psychiatry, characterized by treatment techniques that focus on one patient at a time and attempt to uncover the unconscious basis of his problems, may be said to have begun with Mesmer's investigations of "animal magnetism," i.e., hypnotism. Although the concept of magnetic forces was soon dispelled, Mesmer's occult procedures set the stage for a more scientific study of unconscious processes and strengthened the view that "suggestion" can be a potent factor in influencing mental symptoms. Moreover, Mesmer's enormous success with well-to-do "neurotics" in his private salon may be viewed as a precursor of modern day office practice.

Charcot explored the use of hypnotism in his studies of hysteria. Exposed to the ideas of Charcot and Bernheim and to the discovery by Breuer of emotional "abreaction," Freud elaborated an intricate theory of psychic development and a highly original system of therapeutic practice, both of which he termed "psychoanalysis." Subjected soon thereafter to dissenting views, even among its early adherents, the practice of psychoanalysis splintered into numerous subvarieties. Despite these deviations, the focus on unconscious processes and the office practice model with individual patients remained well entrenched as a treatment prototype still in vogue today.

4. The fourth stage of psychological treatment may be said to have begun with the opening of mental health clinics for the young. This movement led to a new therapeutic goal, "freeing" the patient to develop his full potentials without the constraints of misguided and inhibiting social forces.

"Clinics" were common in medicine for many centuries. But it was not until Lightner Witmer opened the first psychoeducational clinic in 1896 at the University of Pennsylvania that the problems of the young became a major focus of psychological treatment. Therapy until then had been practiced almost exclusively with institutionalized psychotics. Together with psychoanalysis, which concentrated on the "strange" physical maladies of adults, the emergence of school guidance and college counseling centers extended psychological treatment to the full range of psychopathological difficulties.

The character and problems of children and adolescents led inevitably to a therapeutic philosophy that differed from those formulated in the service of hospital psychotics and adult neurotics. The clientele of school and college clinics was composed of moderately well-compensated young people who appeared to be suffering from parental, social, and educational forces that interfered with and blocked their efforts to develop natural "growth" potentials. To remedy these difficulties, clinical therapists began to devise techniques which would "free" the patient to be himself, to "actualize" his capacities and to develop a sense of "personal self-regard."

Thus, by the early 1940s, the ideas of Rank on "will therapy," and those of Rogers on "client-centered" therapy, gradually came to the fore as the primary psychological methods employed in outpatient clinics and school counseling services. In time, their views took root as a worthy philosophy not only in clinic centers, but in office practice and hospital settings as well.

5. Concurrent with the development of "office psychoanalysis" and "clinic self-actualizing therapy," laboratory scientists were gathering a body of empirical data on the basic processes of learning and behavior change. It was many years, however, before the early work of Pavlov, Thorndike, and Watson and the later concepts of Hull and Skinner began to be translated into principles applicable to therapy. By the mid 1950s, a variety of "behavior modification" techniques, employing procedures such as reinforcement and extinction and eschewing notions such as "unconscious forces" or "actualizing needs," were devised and promulgated by men such as Mowrer, Wolpe, Eysenck, and Ferster. The emergence of these treatment methods, in contrast to other psychological techniques, grew not out of clinical need and observation, but out of systematic laboratory research. Although less than two decades old, behavior techniques quickly rose to the status of one of the major alternatives of psychological therapy.

6. The most recent stage in this historical progression has not been the development of new therapeutic procedures, but the application of research methodology in the evaluation of the "efficacy" and "process" of established procedures.

Until the 1950s, the efficacy of alternative therapies was, for the most part, an article of faith rather than proof. At best, the merits of these techniques were "demonstrated" in crudely designed and easily faulted clinical studies. "Success" was gauged subjectively by the therapist himself according to ambiguous criteria rather than through objective measures undertaken by independent judges. Rarely were controls employed, and improvement rates were presented without reference to such relevant variables as chronicity, symptomatology, and so on. In short, what little had been done was done poorly.

Despite questions concerning effectiveness, proponents of each technique were not only convinced of the utility of their cherished procedures, but prospered and confidently inculcated each new generation of fledgling clinicians. Disputes among "schools" of therapy were evident, of course, but they were handled by verbal polemics rather than empirical research.

As long ago as 1910, Hoche noted that therapists were not scientists but cultists, willing promulgators of dubious measures that rested on the most unreasonable of assumptions (Patrick & Bassoe, 1910). Despite these early warnings, it was not until the late 1940s that clinicians such as Carl Rogers and J. McV. Hunt, trained both in scientific method and therapeutic practice, pioneered the first controlled studies of psychological therapy (Rogers & Dymond, 1954; Hunt, 1952). Spurred further by the critical reviews of Eysenck (1952), Zubin (1953), and Levitt (1957), increasing numbers of investigators began to reexamine the empirical underpinnings of psychotherapy and set out to design efficacy and process studies that employed proper controls, criteria and measurement techniques. The fruits of this newest phase in history of psychotherapy have not yet materialized, but the seeds of the "scientific" era of psychotherapy have finally been well-planted.

# MAJOR DIMENSIONS OF PSYCHOLOGICAL TREATMENT

As was pointed out earlier in the text, we can approach any complex subject from a variety of vantage points, focusing first on one feature or characteristic and then on another. Thus, no single organizational format can do justice to the diverse attributes that comprise each variant of psychotherapy. In the following paragraphs, we will outline four of the many dimensions by which alternative therapies can be differentiated—setting, goals, process, and data focus. Each of the principal techniques can be analyzed in accord with these factors. For example, "client-centered" therapy is practiced in an individual treatment *setting;* its goals are determined by the patient and are oriented toward the objective of "growth"; the therapeutic *process* consists of techniques which foster self-insight and the ventilation of emotions; and the therapist *focuses* his attention on phenomenological *data.*

## SETTING

Although by no means mutually exclusive, therapy is usually practiced in one of three settings: *individual patient-therapist relationships, small group interactions,* and *institutional milieus.*

The first of these settings, the treatment by a therapist of one patient at a time, is the most common arrangement in which psychotherapy is carried out. All systems and schools of therapy have employed this arrangement (e.g., behavior modification and psychoanalysis), and every type of psychopathology has been treated within it.

Small group interactions, generally referred to as group treatment methods, usually have one therapist working simultaneously with several patients. Central to this setting is the interplay among patients and the unfolding of social attitudes and interpersonal styles of behavior. Several variants of group treatment have been devised (e.g., analytical groups, family therapy, and psychodrama) and employed with numerous types of pathological conditions. Group procedures are often carried out in conjunction with individual therapy.

In contrast to the two arrangements just noted, in which patients are seen several

hours a week at most, the institutional milieu setting encompasses the management and therapeutic planning of every aspect of the patient's life. Each day, from waking to sleeping, activities are coordinated to provide a "total push" toward rehabilitation; this includes ward schedules, occupational therapy, educational programs, and physical and recreational games, as well as more formal individual and group therapy sessions.

## GOALS

Two elements comprise the character of therapeutic goals. The first deals with *who* selects the goals, the second refers to *what* these goals are.

1. The problem of who determines the goals of treatment distinguishes what have been termed "directive" and "nondirective" therapies.

   In directive approaches, the therapist, by virtue of his professional knowledge and the patient's emotional state, assumes responsibility for choosing the objectives and procedures of treatment; the "doctor" diagnoses what is wrong and guides the patient through what he decides is the best course of action.

   In nondirective approaches, the patient decides more or less the steps and aims of the therapeutic process; in fact, it is the patient's increasing capacity to choose his life goals that is considered central to the therapeutic experience. Nondirective therapists intrude minimally into the patient's commentaries and reminiscences; at most, he helps the patient clarify his discursive thoughts and inchoate feelings.

2. Therapists may be distinguished by the goals they emphasize.

   Some therapists focus on extinguishing maladaptive behaviors or relieving pathological emotions; the aim of treatment is to bring the patient back to a nonpathological state rather than to spur him to a "better" way of life. If growth should occur, it is expected to follow of its own accord, once the troublesome symptomatology has been eliminated.

Other therapists exert their primary efforts in the direction of developing new, more effective behaviors, considering the reduction of symptomatology to be of less significance than the acquisition of "better" ways of life. As they view it, current symptoms should fade of their own accord once the patient has gained alternative and more adaptive ways of resolving difficulties and achieving fulfillments.

Few therapists are committed firmly to one or another of these divergent goals; however, predilections toward "symptom extinction" versus "constructive response alternatives" may be noted among different therapies.

## PROCESS

Of the several dimensions in which therapies are differentiated, none is more crucial to our understanding than the process by which they seek to produce beneficial changes. The major distinction here is between *insight-expressive* and *action-suppressive* processes.

Those inclined to the *insight-expressive* end of the continuum maintain that improvement is facilitated by new self-understandings and by the ventilation of highly charged but previously unexpressed emotions. To them, overt behaviors are merely surface phenomena that represent deeply rooted attitudes and feelings which must be understood and discharged. The process of therapy, then, consists of methods to uncover and release these attitudes and feelings. With insight and emotional ventilation achieved, it is expected that the patient will be able to confront life's tasks with equanimity, new powers of rational thinking and rapid personality growth.

Therapists inclined to the *action-suppressive* end of this dimension devalue the significance of self-understanding and emotional ventilation. They do not believe that insight is the sine qua non of therapy or that emotional ventilation leads to adaptive changes.

Self-understanding and emotional catharsis are viewed at best as adjuncts to the ultimate goal of treatment, that is, producing demonstrable alterations in *real life behaviors.* The principal task of therapy, then, is to effect adaptive *actions* or *responses.* If necessary, the therapist will intervene in the patient's social environment, advising as many significant persons as needed to facilitate the patient's opportunity to alter his pathological behaviors.

## DATA FOCUS

The four-fold breakdown in data that has been followed throughout the text may be employed to increase our understanding of the various forms and techniques of psychotherapy. . . . The varied settings, goals, processes, and data levels which differentiate psychological treatment methods may lead one to conclude that the field of psychotherapy comprises a motley assemblage of techniques. However, despite substantive differences in verbalized rationales and technical procedures, psychotherapies "sound" more dissimilar than they are in practice. Close inspection reveals that their aims are fundamentally alike and that their methods, although focusing on different facets or levels of psychological functioning deal essentially with the same pathological processes.

It may be appropriate at this point to comment on the student's inevitable desire to find a single "definition" of psychological treatment. It should be evident from the foregoing, as was the case in defining psychopathology, that no single descriptive phrase will do. Wolberg (1967), for example, lists 6 different definitions in the recent literature. Obviously, psychotherapy means different things to different people. Definitions of psychotherapy cannot be formulated by reference to an abstract set of principles; rather, therapy is more or less whatever data, goals, setting, and process a therapist employs in his practice. Thus, a behaviorally oriented therapist, who adheres to an action-suppressive process, will define psychotherapy differently than an intrapsychically oriented therapist, who is inclined to follow an insight-expressive procedure. Definitions *follow,* then, rather than precede the orientation adopted by the therapist. No single definition can fully convey the variety of philosophies and techniques with which psychotherapy is executed.

Since there is no simple way to define therapeutic techniques, it may be argued that it would be best simply to catalogue the myriad approaches currently in use, leaving their classification to some later date when a clear-cut organizational logic may have evolved. However, as was noted in earlier discussions concerning the classification of pathological syndromes, no format will ever be fully satisfactory since it is impossible to encompass all of the many dimensions and features by which a complex set of phenomena can be grouped.

Despite the inevitable limitations of classification, there are certain logical relationships among therapies which enable us to coordinate techniques in a reasonably systematic fashion. Unless we employ some rational format, advances in therapeutic science will become lost in a sea of incidental and scattered observations. Some frame of reference must be employed, then, to ensure that alternative techniques will be differentiated: in this way, we may accumulate a body of evaluative data that will enable therapists to determine the methods that are "best" for different types of psychopathology.

# REFERENCES

Eysenck, H. J. (1952). The effects of psychotherapy: An evaluation. *J. Consult. Psychol., 16,* 319–324.

Frank, J. (1961). *Persuasion and healing.* Baltimore: Johns Hopkins University Press.

Goldstein, A. P., & Dean, S. I. (Eds.). (1966). *The investigation of psychotherapy.* New York: Wiley.

Gottschalk, L. A., & Auerbach, A. H. (Eds.). (1966). *Methods of research in psychotherapy.* New York: Appleton-Century-Crofts.

Hoch, A. (1910). Constitutional factors in the dementia praecox group. *Review of Neurology and Psychiatry, 8,* 463-475.

Hoch, P. H., & Zubin, J. (Eds.). (1964). *The evaluation of psychiatric treatment.* New York: Grune and Stratton.

Hunt, J. McV. (1952). Toward an integrated program of research on psychotherapy. *J. Consult. Psychol., 16,* 237–246.

Keisler, D. J. (1966). Some myths of psychotherapy research and the search for a paradigm. *Psychol. Bull., 65,* 100–136.

Levitt, E. E. (1957). The results of psychotherapy with children: An evaluation. *J. Consult. Psychol., 21,* 189–196.

London, P. (1964). *The modes and morals of psychotherapy.* New York: Holt, Rinehart & Winston.

McNair, D. M., & Lorr, M. (1965). Differential typing of psychiatric outpatients. *Psychol. Rec., 15,* 33–41.

Patrick, H. T., & Bassoe, P. (1910). *Nervous and mental diseases.* Chicago: Year Book Publishers.

Patterson, C. H. (1966). *Theories of counseling and psychotherapy.* New York: Harper & Row.

Rogers, C. R., & Dymond, R. F. (Eds.). (1954). *Psychotherapy and personality change.* Chicago: U. of Chicago Press.

Rubenstein, E. A., & Parloff, M. B. (Eds.). (1959). *Research in psychotherapy.* Washington, DC: American Psychological Association.

Shlien, J. M. (Ed.). (1968). *Research in psychotherapy.* Vol. III. Washington, DC: American Psychological Association.

Stollak, G. E., Guerney, B. G., & Rothberg, M. (Eds.). (1966). *Psychotherapy research.* Chicago: Rand McNally.

Strupp, H. H., & Luborsky, L. (Eds.). (1962). *Research in psychotherapy.* Vol. II. Washington, DC: American Psychological Association.

Wolberg, L. R. (1967). *The technique of psychotherapy.* 2nd ed. New York: Grune and Stratton.

Zubin, J. (1953). Evaluation of therapeutic outcome in mental disorders. *J. Nerv. Ment. Dis., 117,* 95–111.

# Personologic Psychotherapy: Ten Commandments for a Post-Eclectic Approach to Integrative Treatment

The ancient Hebrews come to mind when contemplating the status of contemporary integrative therapists. Both wandered over 40 years with a similar idea (Goldfried, 1982); on the one hand, that there be one integrated God; on the other, that there be one integrated therapy. The ancient Hebrews did find a home finally, but only after Moses brought the Ten Commandments down from the Mount.

Permit me to indulge in what is merely a nonclinical grandiose analogy, by assuming the mantle of Moses for this article and presenting for consideration ten commandments for integrative psychotherapy. As with Moses, who was born a Hebrew but was raised an Egyptian, so too—to extend this pedagogic grandiosity—I have been raised not as a therapist, but as a personality theorist and diagnostician. I should like to think, however, that the circuitous route traveled may contribute, not to the foundations of a religion—as with the ancient Hebrews—but to our science of psychopathology and its methods of intervention.

Before turning to substantive psychological matters, I would like to comment briefly on philosophical issues. They bear on a rationale for developing theory-based treatment techniques and methods, that is, methods that transcend the merely empirical (e.g., electroconvulsive therapy for depressives).

I have hesitated to write on psychotherapy in the past owing to my conviction that other aspects of our science must be further advanced if we are to succeed in constructing a genuine theory of psychotherapy. There are several features, I believe, that signify and characterize mature clinical sciences: 1) They embody conceptual theories from which propositional deductions can be derived, as well as; 2) coherent taxonomies that characterize the central features of their subject domain (in our case, that of personality and psychopathology, the substantive realm within which psychotherapeutic techniques are applied); 3) These sciences possess a variety of empirically oriented instruments with which they can identify and quantify the concepts that comprise their theories (in our subject, methods that uncover developmental history and furnish cross-sectional assessments); 4) In addition to theory and diagnostic tools, these sciences possess change-oriented intervention techniques that are therapeutically optimal in modifying the pathological elements of their domain.

A comment must also be made, albeit briefly, on what I judge to be an epistemologically spurious issue (Millon, 1983a). It is found in its most obtuse form in debates concerning which treatment orientation (cognitive, behavioral, biologic, intrapsychic) is "closer to the truth," or which therapeutic method is intrinsically the more efficacious. What differentiates these orientations and treatment methods has little to do, I submit, with their theoretical underpinnings or their empirical support, but to the fact that they attend to different levels of data in the natural world; their differences would be akin to physicists, chemists, and biologists arguing over which of their fields was a truer representation of nature. It is to the credit of those of an eclectic persuasion that they have recognized (Marmor & Woods, 1980; Ryle, 1978), albeit in a "fuzzy way" (Messer & Winokur, 1980; Murray, 1986), the arbitrary if not illogical character of such contentions, as well as the need to bridge schisms that have been constructed less by philosophical considerations or pragmatic goals than by the accidents of history and professional rivalries (Meehl, 1978).

There are numerous other knotty and essentially philosophical issues with which integrative therapy must contend (e.g., differing "worldviews" concerning the essential nature of psychological experience; Pepper, 1942). There is no problem, as I see it, in encouraging active dialectics among these contenders—although I personally hold to an "organismic" or "synthetic" view of nature's phenomena.

Let us turn to issues more substantively relevant to the concerns of this article—not that I wish to obviate philosophical matters; they are often closer to the heart of the problems we face than matters of ostensibly more direct or palpable psychological significance.

Although the approach that has come to be called integrative therapy has its applications to a variety of diverse clinical conditions (Feldman, 1979; Wachtel, 1977)—a view I wholeheartedly endorse—I will seek in this article to outline some reasons why personality disorders may be that segment of psychopathology for which integrative psychotherapy is ideally and distinctively suited—in the same sense as behavioral techniques appear most efficacious in the modification of problematic actions, cognitive methods optimal for reframing phenomenological distortions, and intrapsychic techniques especially apt in resolving unconscious processes.

The cohesion (or lack thereof) of complexly interwoven psychic structures and functions is what distinguishes the disorders of personality from other clinical syndromes; likewise, the orchestration of diverse, yet synthesized techniques of intervention is what differentiates integrative from other variants of psychotherapy. These two, parallel constructs, emerging from different traditions and conceived in different venues, reflect shared philosophical perspectives, one oriented toward the understanding of psychopathology, the other toward effecting its remediation.

It is not that integrative psychotherapies are inapplicable to more focal pathologies, but rather that these therapies are *required* for the personality disorders (whereas depression may successfully be treated either cognitively or pharmacologically); it is the very interwoven nature of the components that comprise personality disorders that makes a multifaceted approach a necessity.

Crafting ten commandments for integrative psychotherapy is merely a pedagogic device but nevertheless one that may prove helpful in highlighting the points I wish to make.

Let us turn to the first and essentially philosophical commandment.

## 1. Thou Shall Not Take the Name "Integrative" in Vain

Much of what travels under the "eclectic" or "integrative" banner sounds like the talk of a "goody goody"—a desire to be nice to all sides, and to say that everybody is right. These labels have become platitudinous "buzzwords," philosophies with which open-minded people certainly would wish to ally themselves. But, "integrative psychotherapy" must signify more than that.

First, it is *not* eclecticism. Perhaps it might be considered *post-eclecticism,* if we may borrow a notion used to characterize modern art just a century ago. Eclecticism is not a matter of choice. We all must be eclectics, engaging in differential (Frances et al., 1984) and multimodal (Lazarus, 1981) therapeutics, selecting the techniques that are empirically the most efficacious for the problems at hand.

Moreover, integration is more than the coexistence of two or three previously discordant orientations or techniques. We cannot simply piece together the odds and ends of several theoretical schemas, each internally consistent and oriented to different data domains. Such a hodgepodge will lead only to illusory syntheses that cannot long hold together. Efforts such as these, meritorious as they may be in some regards, represent the work of peacemakers, not innovators and not integrationists.

Integration insists on the primacy of an overarching gestalt that gives coherence, provides an interactive framework, and creates an organic order among otherwise discrete units or elements. It is eclectic, of course, but more. It is a synthesized and substantive system whose distinctive meaning derives from that old chestnut: The whole is greater than the sum of its parts.

The personality problems our patients bring to us are an inextricably linked nexus of behaviors, cognitions, intrapsychic processes, and so on. They flow through a tangle of feedback loops and serially unfolding concatenations that emerge at different times in dynamic and changing configurations. And each component of these configurations has its role and significance altered by virtue of its place in these continually evolving constellations.

In parallel form, so should integrative psychotherapy be conceived as a configuration of strategies and tactics in which each intervention technique is selected not only for its efficacy in resolving particular pathological features but also for its contribution to the overall constellation of treatment procedures of which it is but one.

Let us turn next from philosophy to the syndromes for which our interventions are designed to remedy; I record three commandments here.

## 2. Thou Shall Recognize the Disorders of Personality to Be Integrative Constructs

At the center of all therapies, whether we work with "part functions" that focus on behaviors, or cognitions, or unconscious processes, or biological defects, and the like, *or* whether we address contextual systems which focus on the larger environment, the family, or the group, or the socioeconomic and political conditions of life, the crossover point, the place that links parts to contexts is the person, the individual, the intersecting medium that brings them together.

But persons are more than just crossover mediums. They are the only organically integrated system in the psychological domain, inherently created from birth as natural entities, rather than experience-derived gestalts constructed via cognitive attribution. Moreover, it is persons who lie at the heart of the psychotherapeutic experience, the substantive beings that give meaning and coherence to symptoms and traits—be they behaviors, affects, or mechanisms—as well as those beings, those singular entities, that give life and expression to family interactions and social processes.

It is my contention that integrative therapists should take cognizance of the person from the start, for the parts and the contexts take on different meanings, and call for different interventions in terms of the person to whom they are anchored. To focus on one social structure or one psychic form of expression, without understanding its undergirding or reference base is, as I see it, to engage in potentially misguided, if not random, therapeutic techniques.

Regarding Commandment 2, let me record a major shift in medical thinking that parallels what I have been saying. It highlights the fact that modern-day health providers no longer focus on symptoms—as they did a century ago—nor do they focus on intruding infectious agents—as they did a decade or two ago—but have turned their attentions to the structure and mechanisms of the immune system. . . .

The parallel to Axis I in physical disorders characterizes where medicine was 100 and more years ago; in the early and mid nineteenth century physicians defined their patients' ailments in terms of manifest symptomatology—their sneezes and coughs and boils and fevers, labeling "diseases" with terms such as consumption and smallpox. Shifting to Axis IV of DSM-III, the related medical focus, uncovered approximately 100 years ago, was that illness no longer be conceived only in terms of overt symptomatology, but with reference to minute microbes which intruded upon and disrupted the body's normal functions; in time, medicine began to assign diagnostic names that reflected ostensive etiologies—such as infectious sources, for example, relabeling dementia paralytica to neurosyphilis.

Psychopathology has progressed in making this shift from symptom to cause all too slowly. We still focus on what can be done about "dysthymia" or "anxiety," giving our prime attention to the surface symptoms that comprise the syndromes of Axis I. Among those who consider themselves to be "sophisticated" about such matters, there is recognition that dysthymia and anxiety are merely a psychic response to life's early or current stressors, such as those which comprise DSM-III's Axis IV—marital problems, child abuse, and the like—psychic intruders, if you will, that parallel the infectious microbes of a century ago.

But medicine has progressed in the past decade or two beyond its turn-of-the-century "intrusion disease" model, an advance most striking these last 5 or 6 years owing to the tragedy of the AIDS epidemic. This progression reflects a growing awareness of the key role of the immune system, the body's intrinsic capacity to contend with the omnipresent multitude of potentially destructive infectious and carcinogenic agents that pervade our physical environment. What medicine has learned is that it is not the symptoms—the sneezes and coughs—and not the intruding infections—the viruses and bacteria—that are the key to health or illness. Rather, the ultimate determinant is the competence of the immune system. So too, in psychopathology, it is not anxiety or dysthymia, nor the stressors of early childhood or contemporary life that are the key to psychic well-being. Rather, it

is the mind's equivalent of the body's immune system—that structure and style of psychic processes that represents our overall capacity to perceive and to cope with our psychosocial world—in other words, the psychological construct we term "personality." Fortunately we have begun to catch up with medicine this past decade, to turn our attentions from symptoms and stressors toward "persons," and the psychic structures and styles that signify their disordered character.

## 3. Thou Shall Conceptualize All Personality Disorders from an Integrative Theory

It is not enough to make a platitudinous announcement that personality disorders comprise an integrative construct or that it is the natural parallel and setting for integrative therapies. So too might it be merely sententious to speak of an "integrative theory." . . .

Theory, when properly fashioned, ultimately provides more simplicity and clarity than unintegrated and scattered information. Unrelated knowledge and techniques, especially those based on surface similarities, are a sign of a primitive science, as has been effectively argued by contemporary philosophers of science (Hempel, 1961; Quine, 1961).

All natural sciences have organizing principles that not only create order but also provide the basis for generating hypotheses and stimulating new knowledge. A good theory not only summarizes and incorporates extant knowledge, but is heuristic, that is, has "systematic import," as Hempel has phrased it, in that it originates and develops new observations and new methods. As we have seen over the past century, both learning and analytic theories have spawned new therapeutic techniques of considerable power and utility, for example, the behavior methods of desensitization and skill acquisition, as well as the psychodynamic methods of free association and dream analysis.

Unfortunately, a unifying theory for all human behavior, including psychotherapy, must await our next Newton or Einstein. In the interim, however, we can generate fruitful microtheories which may encompass and give coherence to many of the facets that comprise our subject domain. It is toward that end that I have sought to develop an integrative or unified microtheory of the personality disorders (Millon, 1969, 1981, 1986a), disorders which are themselves exemplar integrative constructs in the larger domain of psychopathology.

Theories in psychopathology should be able to generate answers to a number of key questions. For example, how do its essential constructs interrelate and combine to form specific personality disorders? And, if it is to meet the criteria of an integrative or unifying schema, can it derive all of the personality disorders with the same set of constructs; that is, not employ one set of explanatory concepts for borderline personalities, another for schizoids, a third for compulsives, and so on. If we may recall one of the great appeals of early analytic theory, it was its ability to explain several "character types" from a single developmental model of psychosexual stages. Can the same be said for other, more encompassing theories?

The theoretical model presented all too briefly in the following paragraphs is but one of several schemas for conceptualizing personality processes; hence, it is a selective perspective on the ways in which psychotherapy and personality may be integrated. The model is distinctive in several respects. First, it attempts to coordinate the three elements referred to previously that comprise a clinical science, namely, the theoretical constructs it employs, the assessment procedures it formulates, and the therapeutic strategies it recommends. Notable also is its focus on the more molar level of personality disorders, rather than on traits or symptoms, preferring to use these all-encompassing constructs as the initiating and guiding focus for therapeutic action. Perhaps most controversially, the theory seeks to derive the full range of personality disorders comprising Axis II of DSM-III-R from a set of three "metabiologic polarities"

(Millon, 1988) which, to use Freud's words in formulating a parallel model, "govern all of mental life" (Freud, 1915).

Extending Freud's original conception, these polarities draw upon basic evolutionary principles and survival strategies to provide explanatory hypotheses concerning normal and clinical forms of personality (Millon, in press b). Condensing matters, the three polarities may be framed as follows: regarding the *aims of survival,* there are two balanced opposites—seeking life-enhancing or "pleasurable" experiences versus eschewing life-threatening or "painful" incidents; the second concerns *the focus of survival,* and likewise contains two polar choices—promoting and extending one's "self" versus nurturing "others" and seeking their protection; the third relates to the primary *mode of survival,* similarly represented in paired opposites— assuming a "passive," inert, reactive, and static style versus being "active," alert, initiating, and mobile. What the theory states is that from knowledge of defects or imbalances in these three polarities it is possible to deductively derive all of the disorders that comprise our current personality taxonomy (Millon, 1969, 1981, 1986a, 1986b). . . .

There are therapeutic implications to this theoretical model in that the various polar combinations point to central aspects of what is conceived to be each personality disorder's core survival problem (e.g., to increase life-enhancing pleasure or to minimize life-threatening pain; to optimize survival by drawing upon more self or more other-focused sources; to take a more active than passive stance in maximizing one's survival; to resolve ambivalences between the foci of survival, and so on).

## 4. Thou Shall Consider Personality Disorders to Be Theory-Derived Hypothetical Constructs, Not Reified Entities

Syndromes, and even the symptoms and signs of which they are composed, are essentially prototypal statements, that is, conceptual constructs that highlight certain clinical features and transcend the raw observational data from which they were formulated. Even such tangible and homogeneous categories as "depression" are often imbued with characteristics that go beyond their concrete observational referents, for example, reactive, endogenous. Inductive methods of concept construction based on observed covariations among diverse signs have usefully been employed to develop even complex syndromes such as personality disorders (Horowitz et al., 1981; Livesley, 1987), but I am persuaded that the diverse configurations comprising these disorders are given their greatest clarity when derived from a theory-based deductive framework (Millon, 1986a; 1987a). Once having their most prominent and distinctive features generated in this deductive manner, personality constructs can be evaluated for their clinical validity and utility via more inductive-empirical procedures.

The essential point to be recognized is that the personality disorder categories that comprise Axis II of DSM-R are not composed of so-called objective "disease entities," for example, measles, smallpox, but are, regardless of their method of derivation, hypothetical constructs that correspond, however loosely, to well-recognized and recurrent clinical observations. However, given their lack of sharp boundaries and multiple overlappings, they are best conceived in polythetic rather than monothetic form (Frances & Widiger, 1986; Millon, 1987a), that is, possessing central features in common, but exhibiting marginally different forms of expressions, all of which leads to our next commandment, the first in a trinity of *assessment* commandments.

## 5. THOU SHALL NOT VIEW ALL PATIENTS WITH THE SAME DIAGNOSIS AS POSSESSING THE SAME PROBLEM

Assuredly platitudinous though this commandment may be, care must be taken not to force patients into the procrustean beds of our diagnostic entities. Our taxonomic

categories must be conceived as flexible and dimensionally quantitative, permitting the distinctive characteristics of patients to be displayed in their full complexity (Millon, 1987a). The multiaxial schema of DSM-III is a step in the right direction in that it encourages multidimensional considerations (Axis I, II, IV), as well as multidiagnoses that approximate the natural heterogeneity of patients, such as portrayed in personality profiles. In line with this orientation, we should become comfortable diagnosing personality mixtures such as borderline-avoidants, borderline-histrionics, borderline-antisocials, or any other combination of two or more prototypes.

Although I am hardly enamored of all aspects of our current taxonomy (Millon, 1983b), I am even more troubled by the novel and rather idiosyncratic constructs formulated by many eclectic therapists. Their efforts will likely fall on deaf ears. If we are to relate our therapies to our diagnoses (Hayes et al., 1987), a most worthy goal, we must translate our conceptual language into common, and preferably "official" diagnostic terms—troublesome as they may be in many regards.

## 6. THOU SHALL EMPLOY AN INTEGRATED SET OF COMPARABLE CLINICAL ATTRIBUTES WHEN EVALUATING PATIENTS

Although Lazarus (1981) and I approach the assessment task from appreciably different perspectives, I from personality theory and diagnosis, he from an atheoretical eclectic therapy, our methods and attributes intersect in many ways, as do their implications point to similar concerns regarding therapy interventions. Let me illustrate some recent work with which my associates and I have been engaged these past 3–4 years. These do not employ the *patient self-report* modality, as in the various inventories with which my name is associated (e.g., Millon et al., 1982, 1983; Millon 1987b). Nor do they derive directly from my theory either. Rather, they seek to advance the development of *clinician judgments* as a mode of personality assessment (Millon, 1986a, 1986b).

Specifically, they comprise sets of clinical attributes through which personality pathologies are expressed and with which all of the personality disorders may be systematically compared.

Several criteria were used to select and develop the clinical attributes that comprise these new assessment tools: a) that they be varied in the features they embody; that is, not be limited just to behaviors or cognitions, but to encompass a full range of clinically relevant characteristics; b) that they parallel, if not correspond, to many of our profession's current therapeutic modalities (e.g., *self*-oriented analytic techniques; methods for altering dysfunctional *cognitions,* procedures for modifying *interpersonal* conduct); and c) that they not only be coordinated to the official schema of personality disorder prototypes but also that each disorder be able to be characterized by a distinctive feature on each clinical attribute. As stated previously, both the outlined theory and the criteria formulated here comprise one alternative among several which may be employed to illustrate the integrative approach (Goldfried, 1982).

Eight clinical domains were selected for differentiation among the 13 personality disorders of DSM-III-R. They have been divided into what are termed functional and structural attributes, the former defined as "expressive modes of regulatory action," the latter as "deeply embedded dispositions of a quasi-permanent nature" (Millon, 1986b, 1988). Among the *functional* processes are: expressive acts, cognitive styles, interpersonal conduct, and regulatory mechanisms; the *structural* components include: object representations, self-image, morphologic organization, and mood/temperament. It is to counter the pathological consequences of these attributes that we employ our therapeutic techniques, be they behavioral, cognitive, interpersonal, intrapsychic, or whatever. Although core defects lie in deficiencies or imbalances in one or another of the three survival polarities, it is through these functional

and structural realms of expression that the pathologies of personality are revealed and to which we ply our change-oriented psychotherapies. . . .

A major treatment implication recorded in prior paragraphs noted that clinical domains can serve as useful points of focus for corresponding modalities of therapy. It would be ideal, of course, if patients were "pure" prototypes, and all attributes prototypal and invariably present; were it so, we could line up each diagnosis and automatically know its matching attribute feature and corresponding therapeutic mode. Unfortunately, "real" patients rarely are pure textbook prototypes; most, by far, are complex mixtures, exhibiting, for example, the behavioral features of the schizoid prototype, the interpersonal conduct and cognitive style features of the avoidant prototype, the self-image feature of the schizotypal, and so on. Further, these attributes are not likely to be of equal clinical relevance or prominence in a particular case; thus, the interpersonal characteristic may be especially troublesome, whereas cognitive processes, though problematic, may be of lesser significance. Which attributes should be selected for therapeutic intervention is not, therefore, merely a matter of making "a diagnosis," but requires a comprehensive assessment, one that appraises not only the overall configuration of attributes, but differentiates their degrees of salience.

# 7. Thou Shall Keep in Mind That Presenting Symptoms (Axis I) Are Best Understood in Their Personologic (Axis II) and Situational (Axis IV) Contexts

Whether one addresses the clinical "syndromes" of Axis I, or the personality "disorders" of Axis II, or the psychosocial "stressors" of Axis IV, they are best seen as an interactive mix in which the role of each requires an awareness of the role of the others. To illustrate, the emergence of a depressive "syndrome" should be understood to be a product of the interaction of a particular personality type enmeshed in a specific situational context for which that personality is vulnerable; change either the personality type involved or the situational stressors, and depression might not result.

We turn next to the three commandments that relate directly to *Integrative Therapy.*

## 8. Thou Shall Not Employ the Same Therapeutic Approach with All Patients

Self-evident? Yet the approach used by most therapists accords more with where they were trained than with the nature of their patients' pathologies. To paraphrase what I wrote 20 years ago (Millon, 1969), there continues to be a disinclination among clinical practitioners to submit their cherished techniques to detailed study or to revise them in accord with critical empirical findings. As has been stated by many a more knowledgeable therapeutic researcher than I, advances in the quality of our techniques, so vital to the welfare of hundreds of thousands of patients, cannot take place unless practicing therapists give up their inertia and resistance to outside scrutiny.

Despite the fact that most of our research efforts leaves much to be desired in the way of proper controls, sampling, and evaluative criteria, there is one overriding fact about therapy that has come through repeatedly: therapeutic techniques must be suited to the patient's problem. Simple and obvious although this statement is, it is repeatedly neglected by therapists who persist in utilizing and argue heatedly in favor of a particular approach to *all* variants of psychopathology. No "school" of therapy is exempt from this notorious attitude.

## 9. Thou Shall Formulate an Integrated Therapeutic Strategy

What is meant here is perhaps best grasped if we think of personality attributes as analo-

gous to that of the sections of an orchestra, and the clinical attributes of a patient as a clustering of discordant instruments. To extend this analogy, therapists may be seen as conductors whose task is to bring forth a harmonious balance among *all* the instruments, muting some here, accentuating others there, all to the end of fulfilling their knowledge of how "the composition" can best be made consonant. The task is not that of altering one instrument, but of all, *in concert.* What is sought in music, then, is a balanced score, one composed of harmonic counterpoints, rhythmic patterns, and melodic combinations. What is needed in therapy is a likewise balanced program, a coordinated strategy of counterpoised techniques designed to optimize sequential and combinatorial treatment effects.

Let me be more concrete. Specifically, what makes therapy integrated, rather than eclectic?

In the latter, there is a separateness among techniques, just a wise selectivity of what works best. In integrative therapy there are psychologically designed composites and progressions among diverse techniques. As I have begun to formulate them in my current writings (Millon, in press a), terms such as "catalytic sequences" and "potentiating pairings" are employed to represent the nature and intent of these treatment plans. In essence, they comprise therapeutic arrangements and timing series which promote and effect changes that would otherwise not occur by the use of one technique alone.

In a "catalytic sequence," for example, one might seek first to alter a patient's stuttering by direct behavior modification procedures which, if achieved, may facilitate the use of cognitive methods in producing self-image changes in confidence which may, in its turn, foster the utility of interpersonal techniques in effecting improvements in social relationships. In "potentiated pairing" one may simultaneously combine, as is commonly done these days, both behavioral and cognitive methods so as to overcome problematic interactions that might be refractory to either technique alone.

A key feature of personality disorders is that they are themselves pathogenic; I have described this process as "self-perpetuation" (Millon, 1969); Horney (1937) has spoken of it in her use of the concept of "vicious circles"; Wachtel (1977) has recently suggested the term "cyclical psychodynamics." It is these ceaseless and entangled sequences of repetitive cognitions, interpersonal behaviors, and unconscious mechanisms that call for the use of simultaneous or alternately focused methods. The synergism and enhancement produced by such catalytic and potentiating processes is what comprise, as I see it, genuine integrative strategies.

## 10. Thou Shall Select Treatment Techniques Only as Tactics to Achieve Integrative Goals

Depending on the pathological style and structure to be modified, and the overall treatment strategy one has in mind, the goals of therapy should be oriented toward the improvement of imbalanced or deficient polarities by the use of techniques that are optimally suited to modify their expression in problematic clinical attributes. It is here where much work remains to be done.

From the broadest perspective, there are four major spheres of action in which the efforts of integrative psychosocial therapists can be directed . . . For the purposes of this article, we will bypass discussing the syndromal, family dynamic, and social system spheres, important though each of these may be in the large scheme of therapeutic work. We highlight our focus on the clinical domains most relevant to the personality disorders. Each lends itself to a variety of therapeutic techniques, the efficacy of which must be gauged through experience and systematic research. For the present, our repertoire is a rich one. Thus, in addressing dysfunctions in the realm of "interpersonal conduct" we may employ any number of family (Gurman & Kniskern, 1981) or group (Yalom, 1986) therapeutic methods, as well as a series of recently evolved and explicitly formulated interpersonal techniques (Anchin & Kiesler, 1982). Methods of classical analysis or its more contemporary schools may be especially suited to the realm of "object representations," as would the methods of Beck (1976), Ellis (1970), and Meichenbaum (1977) be well chosen to modify difficulties of "cognitive style" and "self-image." In what I and my former students have termed personologic psychotherapy (Everly, 1987; Hyer, 1987; Millon, in press a), the goals, as well as the strategies and modes of action for when and how one might practice integrative therapy with the personality disorders, have begun to be specified.

## REFERENCES

Anchin, J. C., & Kiesler, D. J. (Eds.). (1982). *Handbook of interpersonal psychotherapy.* New York: Pergamon.

Beck, A. T. (1976). *Cognitive therapy and the emotional disorders.* New York: International Universities Press.

Ellis, A. (1970). *The essence of rational psychotherapy: A comprehensive approach to treatment.* New York: Institute for Rational Living.

Everly, G. S. (1987). The principle of personologic primacy and personologic psychotherapy. In C. Green (Ed.), *Proceedings of the First Conference on the Millon Clinical Inventories.* Minneapolis: National Computer Systems.

Feldman, L. B. ( 1979). Marital conflict and marital intimacy: An integrative psychodynamic-behavioral-systemic model. *Family Process, 18,* 69–70.

Frances, A., Clarkin, J., & Perry, S. (1984). *Differential therapeutics in psychiatry.* New York: Brunner/Mazel.

Frances, A., & Widiger, T. A. (1986). Methodological issues in personality disorder diagnoses. In T. Millon & G. L. Klerman (Eds.), *Contemporary directions in psychopathology: Toward the DSM-IV.* New York: Guilford Press.

Freud, S. (1915). The instincts and their vicissitudes. In *Collected papers* (English translation, vol. 4, 1925). London: Hogarth.

Goldfried, M. R. (1982). On the history of therapeutic integration. *Behavior Therapy, 13,* 572–593.

Gurman, A. S., & Kniskern, D. (Eds.). (1981). *The handbook of family therapy.* New York: Brunner/Mazel.

Hayes, S. C., Nelson, R. O., & Jarrett, R. B. (1987). The treatment utility of assessment. *American Psychologist, 42,* 963–974.

Hempel, C. G. (1961). Introduction to problems of taxonomy. In J. Zubin (Ed.), *Field studies in the mental disorders.* New York: Grune & Stratton.

Horney, K. (1937). *The neurotic personality of our time.* New York: W. W. Norton.

Horowitz, L., Post, D., French, R., Wallis, K., & Siegelman, E. (1981). The prototype as a construct in abnormal psychology: 2—Clarifying disagreement in psychiatric judgments. *Journal of Abnormal Psychology, 90,* 575–585.

Hyer, L. (1987). Personologic primacy of later life patients. In C. Green (Ed.), *Proceedings of the First Conference on the Millon Clinical Inventories.* Minneapolis: National Computer Systems.

Lazarus, A. A. (1981). *The practice of multimodal therapy.* New York: McGraw-Hill.

Livesley, W. J. (1987). Theoretical and empirical issues in the selection of criteria to diagnose personality disorders. *Journal of Personality Disorders, I,* 88–94.

Marmor, J., & Woods, S. M. (Eds.). (1980). *The interface between psychodynamic and behavioral therapies.* New York: Plenum.

Meehl, P. E. (1978). Theoretical risks and tabular asterisks: Sir Karl, Sir Ronald, and the slow progress of soft psychology. *Journal of Consulting and Clinical Psychology, 46,* 806–834.

Meichenbaum, D. (1977). *Cognitive-behavioral modification.* New York: Plenum.

Messer, S. B., & Winokur, M. (1980). Some limits to the integration of psychoanalytic and behavior therapy. *American Psychologist, 35,* 818–827.

Millon, T. (1969). *Modern psychopathology: A biosocial approach to maladaptive learning and functioning.* Philadelphia: Saunders.

Millon, T. (1981). *Disorders of personality: DSM-III, Axis II.* New York: John Wiley.

Millon, T. (Ed.). (1983a). *Theories of personality and psychopathology.* New York: Holt, Rinehart & Winston.

Millon, T. (1983b). The DSM-III: An outsider's perspective. *American Psychologist, 38,* 804–814.

Millon, T. (1986a). A theoretical derivation of pathological personalities. In T. Millon & G. L. Klerman (Eds.), *Contemporary directions in psychopathology: Toward the DSM-IV.* New York: Guilford Press.

Millon, T. (1986b). Personality prototypes and their diagnostic criteria. In T. Millon and G. L. Klerman (Eds.), *Contemporary directions in psychopathology: Toward the DSM-IV.* New York: Guilford Press.

Millon, T. (1987a). On the nature of taxonomy in psychopathology. In C. Last & M. Hersen (Eds.), *Issues in diagnostic research.* New York: Plenum.

Millon, T. (1987b). *Millon Clinical Multiaxial Inventory II, Manual.* Minneapolis: National Computer Systems.

Millon, T. (1988). *Toward a clinical personology: Integrating personality theory, assessment and therapy.* Henry A. Murray Lecture, Michigan State University.

Millon, T. (In press a). *Disorders of personality: DSM-IV: Axis II* (2nd ed.). New York: John Wiley.

Millon, T. (In press b). Normality: What can we learn from evolutionary theory. In D. Offer and M. Sabshin (Eds.), *The diversity of normality.* New York: Basic Books.

Millon, T., Green, C. J., & Meagher, R. (1982). *Millon Behavior Health Inventory, Manual.* Minneapolis: National Computer Systems.

Millon, T., Green, C. J., & Meagher, R. (1983). *Millon Adolescent Personality Inventory, Manual.* Minneapolis: National Computer Systems.

Murray, E. J. (1986). Possibilities and promises of eclecticism. In J. C. Norcross (Ed.), *Handbook of eclectic psychotherapy.* New York: Brunner/Mazel.

Pepper, S. P. (1942). *World hypotheses: A study in evidence.* Berkeley: University of California.

Quine, W. V. O. (1961). *From a logical point of view* (2nd ed.). New York: Harper & Row.

Ryle, A. (1978). A common language for the psychotherapies? *British Journal of Psychiatry,* *132,* 585–594.

Wachtel, P. (1977). *Psychoanalysis and behavior therapy: Toward an interpretation.* New York: Basic Books.

Yalom, I. D. (1986). *The theory and practice of group psychotherapy* (3rd ed.). New York: Basic Books.

# How Can Knowledge of Psychopathology Facilitate Psychotherapy Integration? A View from the Personality Disorders

## INTRODUCTION

An historic and still frequently voiced complaint about diagnosis, be it based or not on the official classification system, is its inutility for therapeutic purposes. Most therapists, whatever their orientation or mode of treatment, pay minimal attention to the possibility that diagnosis can inform the philosophy and technique they employ. It matters little what the syndrome or disorder may be, a family therapist is likely to select and employ a variant of family therapy, a cognitively-oriented therapist will find that a cognitive approach will probably "work best," and so on, including integrative therapists who are beginning to become a "school" and join this unfortunate trend of asserting truth that our approach is the most efficacious.

Do we think that there is some truth to the integrative faith, that is, that there is a class of disorders for whom the deepest logic of the integrative mindset is the optimal, if not invariably the most therapeutic choice?

Although the approach that has come to be called integrative therapy has its applications to a variety of diverse clinical conditions (e.g., Norcross & Goldfried, 1992)—a view I wholeheartedly endorse—we will seek in this article to outline some reasons why personality disorders may be that segment of psychopathology for which integrative psychotherapy is ideally and distinctively suited—in the same sense that

behavioral techniques appear most efficacious in the modification of problematic actions, cognitive methods optimal for reframing phenomenological distortions, and intrapsychic techniques especially apt in resolving unconscious processes.

The cohesion (or lack thereof) of complexly interwoven psychic structures and functions is what distinguishes the disorders of personality from other clinical syndromes; likewise, the orchestration of diverse, yet synthesized techniques of intervention is what differentiates integrative from other variants of psychotherapy. These two, parallel constructs, emerging from different traditions and conceived in different venues, reflect shared philosophical perspectives, one oriented toward the understanding of psychopathology, the other toward effecting its remediation.

It is not that integrative psychotherapies are inapplicable to more focal pathologies, but rather that these therapies are *required* for the personality disorders (whereas depression may successfully be treated either cognitively or pharmacologically); it is the very interwoven nature of the components that comprise personality disorders that makes a multifaceted and synthesized approach a necessity.

In the following pages we will present a few ideas in sequence. First, that integrative therapies require a foundation in a coordinated theory, that is, they must be more than a schema of eclectic techniques, a hodge-podge of diverse alternatives assembled de novo with each case. Second, although the diagnostic criteria that comprise DSM syndromes are a decent first step, they must be comprehensive and comparable, that is, be systematically revised so as to be genuinely useful for treatment planning. Third, a logical rationale can be formulated as to how one can and should integrate diversely focused therapies when treating the personality disorders.

Before turning to these themes, we would like to comment briefly on some philosophical issues. They bear on a rationale for developing theory-based treatment techniques, that is, methods that transcend the merely empirical (e.g., electroconvulsive therapy for depressives). It is our conviction that the theoretical foundations of our science must be further advanced if we are to succeed in constructing an integrative approach to psychotherapy. We believe that four features signify and characterize mature clinical sciences: 1) They embody conceptual theories from which propositional deductions can be derived; 2) These theories should lead to the development of coherent taxonomies that characterize the central features of their subject domain (in our case, that of personality and its disorders, the substantive realm within which scientific and psychotherapeutic techniques are applied); 3) These sciences possess a variety of empirically oriented instruments with which they can identify and quantify the concepts that comprise their theories (in the personality disorders, methods that uncover developmental history and furnish cross-sectional assessments); 4) In addition to theory, nosology, and diagnostic tools, mature clinically-oriented sciences possess change-oriented intervention techniques that are therapeutically optimal in modifying the pathological elements of their domain.

Most current therapeutic schools share a common failure to coordinate these four components of an applied science. What differentiates them has more to do with the fact that they attend to different levels of data in the natural world; their differences are akin to physicists, chemists, and biologists arguing over which of their fields was a truer representation of nature. It is to the credit of those of an eclectic persuasion that they have recognized, albeit in a "fuzzy way," the arbitrary if not illogical character of such contentions, as well as the need to bridge schisms that have been constructed less by philosophical considerations or pragmatic goals than by the accidents of history and professional rivalries. . . .

## ON THE IMPORTANCE OF AN INTEGRATIVE THEORY

What exactly do we mean when we say that therapy must be integrated and must be grounded in a logical and coordinated theory (Arkowitz, 1992)? . . .

As written previously, integration is more than the coexistence of two or three previously discordant orientations or techniques. We cannot simply piece together the odds and ends of several theoretical schemas, each internally consistent and oriented to different data domains. Such a hodgepodge will lead only to illusory syntheses that cannot long hold together. Efforts such as these, meritorious as they may be in some regards, represent the work of peacemakers, not innovators and not integrationists.

Integration . . . is eclectic, of course, but more. It is a synthesized and substantive system . . . The personality problems that our patients bring to us are an inextricably linked nexus of behaviors, cognitions, intrapsychic processes, and so on. They flow through a tangle of feedback loops and serially unfolding concatenations that emerge at different times in dynamic and changing configurations. Each component of these configurations has its role and significance altered by virtue of its place in these continually evolving constellations.

In parallel form, so should integrative psychotherapy be conceived as a configuration of strategies and tactics in which each intervention technique is selected not only for its efficacy in resolving particular pathological features but also for its contribution to the overall constellation of treatment procedures of which it is but one. . . .

As noted in prior papers, it is necessary . . . to go beyond current conceptual boundaries, more specifically to explore carefully reasoned, as well as "intuitive" hypotheses that draw their principles, if not their substance, from more established, "adjacent" sciences. Not only may such steps bear new conceptual fruits, but they may provide a foundation that can undergird and guide our own discipline's explorations. Much of personology, no less psychology as a whole, remains adrift, divorced from broader spheres of scientific knowledge, isolated from firmly grounded, if not universal principles, leading us to continue building the patchwork quilt of concepts and data domains that characterize the field. Preoccupied with but a small part of the larger puzzle, or fearing accusations of reductionism, many fail thereby to draw on the rich possibilities to be found in other realms of scholarly pursuit. With few exceptions, cohering concepts that would connect personology to those of its sister sciences have not been developed.

We seem preoccupied by horizontal refinements. A search for integrative schemas and cohesive constructs that link its seekers closely to relevant observations and laws developed in more advanced fields is needed. The goal—albeit perhaps a rather "grandiose" one—is to refashion the patchwork quilt into a well-tailored and aesthetic tapestry that interweaves the diverse forms in which nature expresses itself.

And what better sphere is there within the psychological sciences to undertake such syntheses than with the subject matter of personology. As noted, persons are the only integrated system in the psychological domain, evolved through the millennia as natural entities. The intrinsic cohesion of persons is not merely a rhetorical construction, but an authentic substantive unity. While personologic features may often be dissonant, and may be partitioned concep-

tually for pragmatic or scientific purposes, they are nonetheless segments of an inseparable biopsychosocial entity.

To take this view is not to argue that different spheres of scientific inquiry should be equated, nor is it to seek a single, overarching conceptual system encompassing biology, psychology, and sociology (Millon, 1983, 1990). Arguing in favor of establishing explicit links between these domains calls neither for a reductionistic philosophy, a belief in substantive identicality, or efforts to so fashion them by formal logic. Rather, one should aspire to their substantive concordance, empirical consistency, conceptual interfacing, convergent dialogues, and mutual enlightenment.

Integrative consonance is not an aspiration limited to ostensibly diverse sciences, but is a worthy goal within the domains of each science. Particularly relevant in this regard are efforts that seek to coordinate the often separate realms that comprise a clinical science, namely: its theories, the classification system it has formulated, the diagnostic tools it employs, and the therapeutic techniques it implements. Rather than developing independently and being left to stand as autonomous and largely unconnected functions, a truly mature clinical science should embody explanatory and heuristic conceptual schemas that are consistent with established knowledge in both its own and related sciences. From these, reasonably accurate propositions concerning pathological conditions can be both deduced and understood, enabling thereby the development of a formal taxonomic classification of disorders derived logically *from the theory*. In turn, this formal organization will permit the development of coordinated assessment instruments, that is, tools that are empirically grounded and sufficiently sensitive quantitatively to enable the theory's propositions and hypotheses to be adequately investigated and evaluated. Given such framework, the categories comprising the nosology should be readily identifiable and measurable, thus making target areas for treatment interventions apparent.

When translated into psychological terms, a theory of psychopathology should be able to generate answers to a number of key questions. For example, how do its essential constructs interrelate and combine to form specific personality disorders? And, if it is to meet the criteria of an integrative or unifying schema, can it derive all of the personality disorders with the same set of constructs; that is, not employ one set of explanatory concepts for borderline personalities, another for schizoids, a third for compulsives, and so on. If we may recall one of the great appeals of early analytic theory, it was its ability to explain several "character types" from a single developmental model of psychosexual stages. Can the same be said for other, more encompassing theories? . . .

## THEORETICALLY-BASED PERSONOLOGIC THERAPY

One aspect of a theoretical model worthy of commentary and especially relevant to our topic is its generativity. A good theory allows for the derivation of numerous hypotheses. There are therapeutic implications to the theoretical model summarized above in that the various polar combinations point to central aspects of what is conceived to be each personality disorder's core survival problem (e.g., to increase life-enhancing pleasure or to minimize death-threatening pain; to optimize survival by drawing upon more self or more other-focused sources; to take a more active than passive stance in maximizing one's survival; to resolve ambivalences between the foci of survival, and so on).

[It may be useful to provide] a synopsis of what may be considered the theoretically-derived goals of integrated therapy for the personality disorders according to the polarity model. Therapeutic efforts responsive to problems in the pain-pleasure polarity would, for example, have as their essential aim the enhancement of pleasure among schizoid and avoidant personalities (+pleasure). Given the probability of intrinsic deficits in this area,

schizoids might require the use of pharmacologic agents designed to activate their "flat" mood/temperament. Increments in pleasure for avoidants, however, are likely to depend more on cognitive techniques designed to alter their "alienated" self-image, and behavioral methods oriented to counter their "aversive" interpersonal inclinations. Equally important for avoidants is reducing their hypersensitivities especially to social rejection (−pain). This may be achieved by coordinating the use of medications for their characteristic "anguished" mood/temperament with cognitive methods geared to desensitization. In the passive-active polarity, increments in the capacity and skills to take a less reactive and more proactive role in dealing with the affairs of their lives (−passive; +active) would be a major goal of treatment for schizoids, dependents, narcissists, masochists, and compulsives. Turning to the other-self polarity, imbalances found among narcissists and antisocials, for example, suggest that a major aim of their treatment would be a reduction in their predominant self-focus, and a corresponding augmentation of their sensitivity to the needs of others (+other; −self).

## ON THE ROLE OF DIAGNOSTIC CRITERIA AND CLINICAL DOMAINS

To make unbalanced or deficient polarities the primary aim of therapy is a new, theoretically-derived focus and a goal as yet untested. In contrast, the clinical domains in which problems are expressed lend themselves to a wide variety of therapeutic techniques, the efficacy of which must, of course, continue to be gauged by ongoing experience and future systematic research.

One major effort to specify and elaborate the clinical domains of psychopathology was made in the DSM-III with the introduction of "diagnostic criteria." Each disorder was thereby composed of several major attributes that, in effect, served to define it. This step was of potential great utility in therapeutic planning. With the diagnostic criteria spelled out, the therapist had before him/her the specific characteristics that call for remedial action. No longer were the features of a diagnosis "fuzzy" and discursively described, but they were clearly articulated in a series of clinical attributes that could serve as the explicit goals of therapeutic change.

The spelling out of diagnostic criteria is also beneficial to the practitioner in that it serves to highlight the specific inclusion and exclusion components that comprise the elements of a diagnostic decision. It is this very precision in articulating specific and uniform rules of definition, originally and significantly termed "operational" criteria, that makes the DSM-III so serviceable and potentially fruitful also as a therapeutic tool (Millon, 1991a). Not only do the criteria delineate the components that will enable reasonably homogeneous group assignments, but its application as a standard national (and, hopefully, international) gauge will ensure at least a modicum of reliability and comparability among therapeutic studies undertaken at diverse settings. To illustrate, the "borderline" pattern will no longer be characterized one way at Massachusetts General Hospital, another at the Menninger Clinic, a third at Michael Reese Hospital, and a fourth at Langley Porter Institute. Although the painfully slow progress of verifiable therapeutic knowledge cannot be attributed solely to the paucity of replicable research, the joint use of uniform DSM criteria should help stem the tide of insubstantial, unreliable, or, at best, minimally generalizable data that have come to characterize therapeutic publications.

While it is reasonable to assume that increased reliability will flow from the use of diagnostic criteria, there is no assurance of increased validity, and these criteria offer *no more than a promise* at this time. Some interjudge reliability data have been obtained in DSM-IV studies and field trials, and these are encouraging, especially when compared to prior studies utilizing earlier classifications. However, and despite diligent efforts

by the various DSM-IV Work Groups, most of the criteria lack adequate empirical support. Moreover, some are inadequately explicit, while others are overly concrete in their operational referents. Many are redundant both within and across other diagnostic classes. Others are insufficiently comprehensive in syndromal scope or display a lack of parallelism and symmetry among corresponding categories.

At best, then, the diagnostic criteria of the DSM represent a significant *conceptual* step toward a future goal when clinical characteristics of appropriate specificity and breadth will provide both reliable and valid indices for identifying the major syndromal prototypes. Although beyond the scope of this article, the categorical syndromes of the DSM are conceptual and not tangible entities (Millon, 1991a). Given that these syndromes are, in the main, only theoretical constructs, it will more than suffice for both clinical and research purposes to employ what has been devised—a standardized, reliable, and internally coherent mosaic of criterion descriptors. To the extent that the DSM has provided this foundation of clinical prototypes, it can fairly be judged to have made an advance worthy of commendation.

Despite the inherent limitations that are built into syndromic and prototypic categories, several shortcomings among the DSM diagnostic criteria should and can be remedied. These difficulties arise in part from a lack of comparability among diagnostic criteria: for example some categories require all defining features to be present (e.g., dependent personality), whereas others allow choice among the criteria (e.g., borderline personality). Axis II is inconsistent in the extent to which the members of each category are assumed to be homogeneous. This heterogeneity in diagnostic requirements will bear directly on the efficiency and utility of each definitional feature as well as possibly compromise the validity of the covariates that ostensibly comprise each syndrome.

Heterogeneous requirements are especially problematic in classically structured syndromes, that is, those requiring singly necessary or jointly sufficient diagnostic criteria. Prototypic categories, by contrast, are composed intentionally in a heterogeneous manner, that is, they accept the legitimacy of syndromic diversity and overlap. Nevertheless, there still is need to reduce the "fuzziness" between boundaries so as to eliminate excessive numbers of unclassifiable and borderline cases. One step toward the goal of sharpening diagnostic discriminations and, hence, therapeutic goals, is to spell out a distinctive criterion for every diagnostically relevant clinical attribute aligned with every prototypal category. For example, if the attribute "interpersonal conduct" is deemed of clinical value in assessing personality, then singular diagnostic criteria should be specified to represent *the* characteristic or distinctive manner in which *each* personality "conducts its interpersonal life."

By composing a taxonomic schema that includes all relevant clinical attributes (e.g., behavior, affect, cognition), and that specifies a defining feature on every attribute for each of the 14 DSM-IV personalities, the proposed prototypal model would both be fully comprehensive in its clinical scope and possess parallel and directly comparable criteria for therapeutic intervention among all Axis II categories. A format of this nature will not only furnish logic and symmetry to the DSM taxonomy, but will enable investigators to be systematic in determining the relative diagnostic efficacy of presumed prototypal covariates. Moreover, clinicians would be able to appraise both typical and unusual syndromal patterns as well as establish the coherence, if not the "validity" of both recently developed and classically established diagnostic entities. Most significantly, these criteria can then be appraised in terms of their utility in defining therapeutic goals and in gauging their role in effecting therapeutic change.

. . . We have replaced the DSM's somewhat noncomparable and noncomprehensive diagnostic criteria with a full set of clinical domains. No longer are criteria specified at different levels of generality within and across the personality disorders. Rather than being a hodge-podge, each is composed of attributes at approximately an equivalent level of generality across the domains in which personality pathologies are expressed, allowing all of the personality disorders to be systematically contrasted, and ensuring a content valid approach.

Several criteria were used to select and develop the clinical domains that comprise these new assessment tools: a) that they be varied in the features they embody; that is, not be limited just to behaviors or cognitions, but to encompass a full range of clinically relevant characteristics; b) that they parallel, if not correspond, to many of our profession's current therapeutic modalities (e.g., self-oriented analytic techniques; methods for altering dysfunctional cognitions; procedures for modifying interpersonal conduct); and c) that they not only be coordinated to the official schema of personality disorder prototypes, but also that each disorder be characterized by a distinctive attribute in each clinical domain. As stated previously, the criteria formulated here comprise one alternative among several which may be employed to illustrate the integrative approach (Goldfried, 1982).

Many signs, symptoms, and characteristics of patients can usefully be categorized and dimensionalized for purposes of clinical analysis. . . . One basis for organizing diagnostic features would be to distinguish them in accord with the *data levels* they represent, (e.g., biophysical, intrapsychic, phenomenological, and behavioral). This differentiation reflects the four historic approaches that characterize the study of psychopathology; namely, the biological, the psychoanalytic, the cognitive, and the behavioral (Millon, 1983). Another, and obviously useful, schema for evaluating personality characteristics is to group them in accord with whether the data obtained derive primarily from the patient as opposed to those observed or inferred by the clinician.

Eight clinical domains were selected for differentiation among the personality disorders of DSM. They have been divided in recent papers into what are termed functional and structural attributes, the former defined as "expressive modes of regulatory action," the latter as "deeply embedded dispositions of a quasi-permanent nature" (Millon, 1986b, 1988). Among the *functional* processes are: expressive acts, cognitive styles, interpersonal conduct, and regulatory mechanisms; the *structural* components include: object representations, self-image, morphologic organization, and mood/temperament. It is to counter the pathological consequences of these attributes that we employ our therapeutic techniques, be they behavioral, cognitive, interpersonal, intrapsychic, or whatever. Although core defects lie in deficiencies or imbalances in one or another of the three evolutionary polarities, described previously, it is through these functional and structural realms of expression that the pathologies of personality are revealed and to which we ply our change-oriented psychotherapies. . . .

Clinicians need not limit themselves to only one attribute (e.g., distraught, hostile, labile) of a domain (e.g., mood/temperament) to characterize a particular patient, but can record a measure of degree of severity to represent the prominence or pervasiveness of that domain's attribute. Moreover, clinicians are encouraged, where appropriate, to record and quantify more than one attribute per clinical domain (e.g., if suitable, to note both "distraught" mood and "labile" mood). A procedure for systematically making such discriminations will be available soon, in the Millon Personality Diagnostic Checklist, an instrument which is being refined in connection with the forthcoming Millon Clinical Multiaxial Inventory (MCMI-III).

The purpose of this procedure is to affirm the view that categorical (qualitative distinction) and dimensional (quantitative distinction) models of classification need not be framed in opposition, no less be considered mutually exclusive (Millon, 1991a). Assessments can be formulated, first, to recognize qualitative (categorical) distinctions in what

attribute best characterizes a patient, permitting the multiple listing of several such attributes, and, second, to differentiate these attributes quantitatively (dimensionally) so as to represent their relative degrees of clinical prominence or pervasiveness. For example, on the "interpersonal conduct" domain, patient A may be appraised as deserving quantitative ratings of 10 on the "aversive" attribute, 6 on the ambivalent attribute, and 4 on the secretive attribute. Patient B may be assigned a rating on 9 on the "ambivalent" attribute, 7 on the "aversive," and 2 on "paradoxical." Both patients are characterized by the "aversive" and "ambivalent" attributes, but to differing extents; they are not only distinguishable quantitatively (dimensionally) on two of the same qualitative grounds, but one has exhibited "secretive," and the other "paradoxical" interpersonal conduct attributes.

Cumulative "scores" across multiple clinical domains obtained via such assessment procedures will result in personality configurations composed of mixed diagnostic assignments. These diagnostic profiles are highly informative and can be especially useful, for example, in identifying which domain should serve as the initial focus of therapy, for example, deciding to address that attribute of interpersonal conduct that may benefit by "group or family techniques," or pinpointing a feature of mood expression that may be especially responsive to "psychopharmacologic treatment," or discerning the character and level of morphologic organization that may be conducive to "psychodynamically oriented therapy," and so on.

## ON INTEGRATING PERSONOLOGIC THERAPY

As described in the preceding paragraphs, "real" patients do not fit our categories in simple and predictable ways. Indeed, a major treatment implication of our earlier discussion is noted that clinical domains and attributes can serve as useful points of focus for corresponding modalities of therapy. It would be ideal, of course, if patients were "pure" prototypes, and all domain attributes prototypal and invariably present; were it so, we could line up each diagnosis and automatically know its matching domain attribute and corresponding therapeutic mode. As noted previously, "real" patients rarely are pure textbook prototypes; most, by far, are complex mixtures, exhibiting, for example, the behavioral attributes of the schizoid prototype, the interpersonal conduct and cognitive style attributes of the avoidant prototype, the self-image attribute of the schizotypal, and so on. Further, these attributes are not likely to be of equal clinical relevance or prominence in a particular case; thus, the interpersonal characteristic may be especially troublesome, whereas cognitive processes, though problematic, may be of lesser significance. Which domains and attributes should be selected for therapeutic intervention is not, therefore, merely a matter of making "a diagnosis," but requires a comprehensive assessment, one that appraises not only the overall configuration of attributes, but differentiates their degrees of salience.

What is meant here may be grasped if we think of personality attributes as analogous to that of the sections of an orchestra, and the clinical attributes of a patient as a clustering of discordant instruments. To extend this analogy, therapists may be seen as conductors whose task is to bring forth a harmonious balance among *all* the instruments, muting some here, accentuating others there, all to the end of fulfilling their knowledge of how "the composition" can best be made consonant. The task is not that of altering one instrument, but of all, *in concert.* What is sought in music, then, is a balanced score, one composed of harmonic counterpoints, rhythmic patterns, and melodic combinations. What is needed in therapy is a likewise balanced program, a coordinated strategy of counterpoised techniques designed to optimize sequential and combinatorial treatment effects.

Let us be more concrete. Specifically, what makes therapy integrated, rather than eclectic?

In the latter, there is a separateness among techniques, just a wise selectivity of what works best. In integrative therapy for personality disorders, where there are multiple clinical attributes across numerous domains, we must construct psychologically coordinated composites and progressions among diverse therapeutic techniques. As formulated in other writings (Millon, 1990), terms such as "catalytic sequences" and "potentiating pairings" are employed to represent the nature and intent of these coordinated treatment plans. In essence, they comprise therapeutic arrangements and timing series which promote and effect changes that would otherwise not occur by the use of one technique alone. . . .

As recorded in previous papers, each clinical domain lends itself to a variety of therapeutic techniques, the efficacy of which must be gauged through experience and systematic research. For the present, our repertoire is a rich one. Thus, in addressing dysfunctions in the realm of "interpersonal conduct" we may employ any number of family or group therapeutic methods, as well as a series of recently evolved and explicitly formulated interpersonal techniques. Methods of classical analysis or its more contemporary schools may be especially suited to the realm of "object representations," as would cognitive reframing methods be well chosen to modify difficulties of "cognitive style" and "self-image."

Depending on the personality style and domain to be modified, and the overall treatment strategy of catalytic sequences and potentiated pairings, the goals of therapy should be oriented toward the improvement of imbalanced or deficient polarities by the use of combinatorial techniques that are optimally suited to modify their expression in problematic clinical attributes.

The complexity of such a formulation sounds formidable, and indeed it is. Nevertheless it is the formulation most consistent with the root metaphor of the personality construct itself, with integration. In our treatment of personality disorders and the Axis I pathologies embedded in them, we must remember that personality disorders are themselves pathogenic. Their ceaseless and entangled sequences of repetitive cognitions, interpersonal behaviors, and unconscious mechanisms call for the use of simultaneous or alternately focused methods. The synergism and enhancement produced by such catalytic and potentiating processes is what comprise, as we see it, genuine integrative strategies, strategies which can be informed and guided by a systematic theory and its derived classification of clinical domains.

# REFERENCES

Arkowitz, H. (1992). Integrative theories of therapy. In D. Freedheim (Ed.), *The history of psychotherapy: A century of change.* Washington, DC: American Psychological Association.

Goldfried, M. R. (1982). On the history of therapeutic integration. *Behavior Therapy, 13,* 572–593.

Millon, T. (1983). The DSM-III: An insider's perspective. *American Psychologist, 38,* 804–814.

Millon, T. (1986b). Personality prototypes and their diagnostic criteria. In T. Millon & G. L. Klerman (Eds.), *Contemporary directions in psychopathology: Toward the DSM-IV.* New York: Guilford Press.

Millon, T. (1988). *Toward a clinical personology: Integrating personality theory, assessment and therapy.* Henry A. Murray Lecture, Michigan State University.

Millon, T. (1990). *Toward a new personology: An evolutionary model.* New York: Wiley-Interscience.

Millon, T. (1991a). Classification in psychopathology: Rationale, alternatives, and standards. *Journal of Abnormal Psychology, 100,* 245–261.

Norcross, J., & Goldfried, M. (1992). *Handbook of psychotherapy integration.* New York: Basic Books.

# Author Index

# Subject Index

Abstraction, defined, 9
Academy of Psychiatry and the Law, 141
Accommodating, MIPS scale, 271–272
Accommodation, ecological, 94–96
Action-suppressive process, 308
Active-ambivalent coping strategy, 66
Active-dependent coping strategy, 65
Active-detached coping strategy, 66
Active-independent coping strategy,
   65–66
Active-passive dimension, 63–65, 92
Active personality patterns, 64–65
Activity/passivity bipolarity, 272
Adaptation:
   complex, 7
   defined, 9
   MIPS scale, 267–268
   normality and, 93–97
   survival logic and, 7–8
Adaptive learning, 61
Adjective Checklist, 240
Adjustment disorder, 158
Adjustment reactions, 16–17
Adolescent disorders, 156
Advisory committees, DSM Task Force,
   140, 149
Affect, classification and, 110
Affect and Cognitive Functioning Scales,
   236
Affective disorders:
   borderline personality and, 202–203
   classification of, 157
   labeling, 148
Affective personalities, 18
Affect-mood scales, self-report inventories,
   239–240
Agent Blue, 171
Age of Science, 19

Aggression:
   depression and, 186
   development of, 61
   as personality characteristic, 14, 65–66
Agitated depression, 200
Agoraphobia, 157
Agreeableness, Big-Five factor model, 284,
   288
Agreeing, MIPS scale, 288–289
Alcohol abuse:
   depression and, 188
   family history of, 203
Altruism, 99
Ambivalence, 64
American Academy of Child Psychiatry,
   141, 155
American Academy of Psychoanalysis, 141,
   155
American Association of Chairmen of
   Departments of Psychiatry, 141
American Association of Marriage and
   Family Therapists, 155
American College Health Association, 141
American Group Therapy Association, 155
American Orthopsychiatric Association,
   141
American Psychiatric Association, 141–143
American Psychiatric Association
   Committee, 139
American Psychoanalytic Association, 141,
   155
American Psychological Association, 141,
   155, 161
Anaclitic depression, 181–182
Anankastic personality, *see* Compulsive
   personality
Anger, 66, 168. *See also specific personality
   disorders*